The Letters of Jack London

Volume One

Student at Oakland High School, 1895 (CSmH)

The Letters of
Jack London

Volume One: 1896-1905

Edited by Earle Labor, Robert C. Leitz, III,

and I. Milo Shepard

Stanford University Press, Stanford, California

1988

T23807

The preparation and publication of this work was made possible
in part by grants from the Division of Research Programs of the National
Endowment for the Humanities, an independent federal agency.

Stanford University Press, Stanford, California
© 1988 by the Board of Trustees of the Leland Stanford Junior University
Printed in the United States of America

CIP data appear at the end of Volume Three

With appreciation to our parents

Mildred K. and Robert C. Leitz, Jr.
Mildred and Irving Shepard
Sylvia and Phillips P. Steger

Acknowledgments

This edition, more than a decade in the making, could not have been completed without the encouragement and generous assistance of many people. Though such debts can scarcely be repaid in kind, we hope nonetheless to convey some measure of our gratitude to those who have enabled us to bring these three volumes of London's letters to fruition.

First of all, we wish to thank the directors and editors of the Stanford University Press who, from the initial signing of our contract in January of 1977, have been constant in their enthusiastic support, diligence, and patience: Leon Seltzer, Grant Barnes, J. G. Bell, Norris Pope, Helen Tartar, and Ellen F. Smith.

Of course, we could never have undertaken, much less have finished, a project of this scope without the assistance of those librarians and curators where London's letters are housed. Our indebtedness to the staff of the Henry E. Huntington Library is commensurate with the magnitude of their London collection. James Thorpe, Daniel H. Woodward, and Martin D. Ridge have furthered our work through Huntington research grants as well as through their personal encouragement. Carey S. Bliss, Alan Jutzi, Jean F. Preston, Mary Robertson, and Sara S. Hodson, curators of rare books and manuscripts, have been remarkably supportive, as have been Mary Isabel Fry, Virginia Renner, and our other friends on the Readers' Services staff at the Huntington: Gene Garcia, Susan Naulty, Fred Perez, Elsa Sink, Doris Smedes, Jon Stefansson, and Mary Wright. We also appreciate the help given us by Janet Hawkins, Barbara Quinn, and Robert Schlosser of the photographic services department. David Mike Hamilton, formerly a member of the Huntington staff, performed yeoman service in cataloging the enormous London Collection and helping us locate materials in that collection.

We are similarly indebted to the Special Collections staff of the Merrill Library at Utah State University, particularly to A. J. and Jeannie Simmonds, whose friendship and professional help over the years have been invaluable. We also appreciate the congenial assistance of Ann Buttars of the Special Collections Department.

Rangers Matt Atkinson and Gregory Hayes have been equally congenial in providing access to the letters in the Holman Collection at the Jack London State Historic Park.

We also wish to acknowledge with thanks our indebtedness to the following: Richard H. F. Lindemann, Public Services Assistant, and Gregory A. Johnson, Alderman Library, University of Virginia; Nancy Burkett, Assistant Curator of Manuscripts of the American Antiquarian Society; John Buechler, Head, Special Collections, Gus W. Baily Library, University of Vermont; James D. Hart, Director, and Estelle Rebec, Head of the Manuscripts Division, Bancroft Library, University of California, Berkeley; Donald Gallup, Curator, Collection of American Literature, Beinecke Rare Book and Manuscript Library, Yale University; Antoinette Ciolli, Chief, Special Collections Division, Brooklyn College Library; Robert Shatkin, Librarian, and Monte Olenick, Chief, at the Language, Literature and Fiction Division, Brooklyn Public Library; Gary Kurutz, California State Library, Sacramento; John C. Broderick, Chief, Manuscript Division, Library of Congress; Thomas E. Camden, Head, Special Collections Department, University of Georgia Libraries; Ruth M. Hauser, Special Collections Department Head, Honnold Library, Claremont College; Claire McCann, Manuscript Librarian, University of Kentucky Libraries; Kenneth W. Duckett, Curator, Special Collections, Southern Illinois University at Carbondale; Howard B. Gottlieb, Head of Special Collections, Mugar Memorial Library, Boston University; Anton C. Masin, Head, Department of Rare Books and Special Collections, University of Notre Dame Memorial Library; Daniel C. Williamson, Rare Book Bibliographer, Samuel Paley Library, Temple University; Gene DeGruson, Special Collections Librarian, Pittsburg (Kansas) State University; Heddy A. Richter, Curator, American Literature Collection, University of Southern California; Cathy Henderson, Director, Rare Books Department, and Ellen S. Dunlap, Research Librarian, Harry Ransom Humanities Research Center, University of Texas; Lyman W. Riley, Assistant Director for Special Collections, Charles Patterson Van Pelt Library, University of Pennsylvania; Diane Kaplan, Head of Processing, Manuscripts, and Archives, Yale University Library; and the special collections librarians at the Boston Public Library, the New York Public Library, the Oakland Public Library, and the Lilly Library at Indiana University.

For helping us locate and acquire copies of a number of important London letters, we are obliged to Edward Allatt, Stephen Ennis, Waring Jones, Maurice Neville, Paul C. Richards, and David Holmes and Clarence Wolf of the George S. MacManus Co.

We have received unflagging support from friends and colleagues at both our institutions and wish to express special thanks to the following. At Centenary College of Louisiana: Donald A. Webb and his fellow administrative officers Darrell M. Loyless, Dorothy Bird Gwin, Harold

Bond, and Jesse Outlaw; members of the Magale Library staff, James G. Volny, Ella Edwards, Nancy E. Middleton, Mary Rademacher, and Anna White; and Lee Morgan, Michael Hall, Jeff Hendricks, David H. Jackson, and Anne B. Rogers of the English Department. At Louisiana State University in Shreveport: E. Grady Bogue, Wilfred L. Guerin, Mary G. Mc-Bride, A. J. Howell, William L. Ferguson, and Patricia T. Bates; and the following members of the Noel Memorial Library staff: Malcolm Parker, Mary Bowman, Sue Brown, Richard Colquette, and Anne King.

For their services in preparing the manuscript for this edition, we wish to express our thanks to Ruby George, Carla Hall, Marion Harrison, Sue Johnson, Florence Martin, Wes Monzingo, Patty Roberts, and Juanel Votaw.

Without considerable financial aid, it would have been extremely difficult, if not impossible, to have managed the extensive and time-consuming work of this project. Both Centenary College and Louisiana State University in Shreveport (LSUS) have been generous in providing this kind of encouragement through faculty travel and research grants; for these we wish to thank the Centenary Alumni Association, the Centenary Faculty Personnel and Economic Policy Committee, the LSUS Faculty Research Committee, the LSUS Faculty Development Committee, and Mr. and Mrs. Edwin C. Harbuck, sponsors of the Harbuck Memorial Endowment for English Faculty Studies. We are also grateful to the American Philosophical Society, the Henry E. Huntington Library, and the LSUS American Studies Program for their financial support of the project. And we are indebted, most of all, to the National Endowment for the Humanities, which provided five substantial grants—two to the editors and three to Stanford University Press—to insure the publication of this work. We express specific thanks to Helen Aguera, Margot Backas, and Kathy Fuller, at the NEH Washington headquarters.

For the use of other letters and copyrighted materials in our annotations, we acknowledge with thanks the following: James D. Hart, Director, Bancroft Library, University of California at Berkeley, for permission to quote from the George Sterling papers; the Macmillan Publishing Company and the New York Public Library for permission to quote from the correspondence of George P. Brett; the estate of Sinclair Lewis and its executor, Paul Gitlin, of Ernst, Cane, Berner, & Gitlin, Counsellors at Law; the estate of Joseph Conrad. Also our thanks to the Trust of Irving Shepard for permission to use and quote from London materials at the Huntington Library.

For the use of photographs and other illustrative material, we wish to thank the Huntington Library, Utah State University, the State of California Department of Parks and Recreation, and the Department of Special Collections and University Archives of Stanford University.

Although it would be impossible within the brief compass of this section to cite all those persons who have lent their support for this project, we feel compelled to mention a select number to whom we feel particularly indebted: George Arms, Sam S. Baskett, Ellen Brown, Louis J. Budd, David Chesnutt, William Bedford Clark, Glenn O. Carey, William E. Carigan, Don L. Cook, Richard Etulain, Edward Huberman, Royce G. Labor, Howard L. Lachtman, Christoph K. Lohmann, Sal Noto, Clarice Stasz, David H. Stewart, Dale L. Walker, Charles N. Watson, Jr., Earl Wilcox, and Hensley C. Woodbridge.

Before his death in 1986, James E. Sisson read through all the letters and annotations of our manuscript, enhancing the accuracy of our text with his perceptive corrections. His rigorous dedication to London scholarship will be a lasting tribute to his memory.

Russ Kingman, Executive Director of the Jack London Foundation and of the Jack London Research Center, has been a steady source of information and editorial wisdom from the beginning of this project. The reliability of this edition is due in considerable measure to his sound judgment and extensive knowledge of London's life and letters. He and his wife Winnie have freely given their time and friendship with no other reward than the realization that this edition is substantially better for their having been its constant supporters and contributors. Their magnanimous service is a reflection of the best in the spirit of Jack London himself.

Finally, Betty G. Labor and Ann V. Leitz surely merit our devoted appreciation for their enduring good nature and loving support throughout this project and the many others we have shared.

E.L.
R.C.L., III
I.M.S.

Contents

Illustration sections follow pages 218 and 378.
Indexes appear at the end of Volume Three.

Introduction

"And remember one thing, old man," Jack London confessed to Sinclair Lewis, "I'm the rottenest letter-writer that ever came down the pike. I hate letter-writing."[1] Despite many such protestations, London was, in fact, a conscientious letter-writer. "I am a pretty good correspondent," he assured Arthur T. Vance, the editor of *Woman's Home Companion*. "I answer all letters and all telegrams."[2] Moreover, he was usually prompt, thoughtful, and straightforward. It is apparently true that he answered "all letters and all telegrams," often in painstaking detail, regardless of the obscurity of the correspondent or the triviality of the contents. During his short, busy life he wrote thousands of letters, the most significant of which constitute this edition.

Reviewing the major events of his life, we can readily appreciate why he so begrudged the hours spent in epistolary busywork. He was a man of action first, a man of letters afterwards. As Alfred Kazin has remarked, "the greatest story Jack London ever wrote was the story he lived";[3] and no literary figure has more effectively captivated the popular imagination through the spectacle of his personal life. Farmboy at the age of seven; city newsboy at ten; factory "work beast" at fourteen; "Prince of the Oyster Pirates" at fifteen; able-bodied seaman at seventeen; hobo and convict at eighteen; "Boy Socialist" of Oakland at nineteen; Klondike argonaut at twenty-one; the "American Kipling" at twenty-four; internationally renowned author, social crusader, journalist, and war correspondent at twenty-eight; world traveler and adventurer at thirty-one; prizewinning stockbreeder and scientific farmer at thirty-five; legendary self-made millionaire by the time of his death at forty.

Significantly, London's rags-to-riches career, a paradigm of the American myth of success, meshed with one of the most dramatic transitional

[1] JL to Sinclair Lewis, November 1, 1910.
[2] JL to Arthur T. Vance, March 14, 1907.
[3] *On Native Grounds: An Interpretation of Modern American Prose Literature* (New York, 1942), p. 111.

epochs in our history. With the possible exceptions of the years of its birth and those of the Great Depression and Second World War, there has been no more revolutionary period in American history than that separating the Civil War and the First World War. During these years the Jeffersonian dream of an agrarian republic gave way to the reality of a new America of massive immigration, industrialization, and the closing of the frontier. By the end of this generation, Henry Adams prophesied, the United States was to be part of "a new world which would not be a unity but a multiple." And the "new American" was no longer an offspring of ax and plow but would become, as Adams envisioned him, "the child of steam and the brother of the dynamo." [4] During his lifetime Jack London would witness the appearance of the light bulb, the electric streetcar, the telephone, the wireless telegraph and radio, the dictaphone and the Victrola, the skyscraper, the moving picture, the automobile, and the airplane. It was an era of technological miracles and of profound cultural and spiritual instability. If it was the luminous age of Edison, Burbank, and the Wright brothers, it was at the same time the ominous age of Marx, Darwin, and Freud; and London's life and letters mirror the dark as well as the light of this dynamic age.

It was also the Golden Age of the Magazine, and London's achievement was due in large measure to the radical changes that had taken place in this marketplace by the end of the nineteenth century. The "new magazine," as promoted by such aggressive editors as George Horace Lorimer, S. S. McClure, Frank Munsey, Roland Phillips, and John Brisben Walker, was no longer a genteel and relatively intellectual recreation for a well-educated, well-to-do, and largely female audience. It was big business, dedicated to the proposition that magazines should be a mass medium, making their profit by entertaining the public. Lorimer, for example, increased the circulation of the *Saturday Evening Post* from less than two thousand to more than one million. And as Munsey wrote of one of his periodicals, entertainment was—after profitability—their only mission: "Good easy reading for the people—no frills, no fine finishes, no hair splitting niceties, but action, action, always action." [5]

In temperament and training Jack London was well equipped for this mission, his success being predicated upon his mastery of both the psychology and the economics of the literary marketplace. "Every magazine has its clique of writers," he explained to Mabel Applegarth on December 8, 1898. "Well, a newcomer must excell them in their own fields before he is accepted, or else he must create a new field." The degree to which London not only excelled but also created is reflected in the frequency with which his works were published in the leading periodicals of his

[4] *The Education of Henry Adams*, Modern Library ed. (New York, 1931), pp. 457, 461.
[5] "The Publisher's Desk," *Munsey's*, April 1899.

time. During the first decade of the twentieth century, scarcely a month
passed without his contributions appearing in popular magazines like
Century, Cosmopolitan, and the *Saturday Evening Post.* In less than
twenty years he produced some five hundred nonfiction pieces, nearly two
hundred short stories, and twenty novels (over fifty books in all), on such
varied subjects as adventure, agronomy, alcoholism, animal training, ar-
chitecture, assassination, astral projection, big business, ecology, economics, folklore, gold hunting, greed, hoboing, love, mental retardation,
mythology, penal reform, political corruption, prizefighting, psychology
(both animal and human), racial exploitation, revolution, science, seafaring, slum dwelling, socialism, stockbreeding, war, wildlife, and the
writing game.

A corollary factor in his success was his skill in authorial self-
promotion. He pioneered in the art of using the media to project the
writer as public celebrity, managing to generate a superabundance of
news copy about himself. Always the available man, he was a favorite of
the press: approachable, controversial, and outspoken. His socialistic
tirades against the exploitations of the working class by government and
big business were regularly reported—and sometimes misreported (as
when the newspapers attributed General Sherman Bell's "To hell with the
Constitution" remarks to London in 1905). His efforts to reach the front
lines made him the leading—and the most notorious—correspondent in
the Russo-Japanese War. His separation and divorce from Bessie London,
his several alleged liaisons (such as that with the actress Blanche Bates),
and his seemingly overhasty marriage to Charmian Kittredge provided
copious material for the gossip columnists. His oft-delayed voyage of the
Snark became the nationwide butt of journalistic jokes, and the press was
likewise delighted when President Theodore Roosevelt publicly attacked
him as "a nature faker." He was headlined as leading a band of insurgents
during the Mexican Revolution, even as he protested that he was at home
on his ranch. In short, virtually everything he did was considered news-
worthy; and when he died on November 22, 1916, the press gave more
space to Jack London than to the Emperor Franz Josef of Austria, who
had passed away the night before.

London displayed his self-promotional skills from the outset in his correspondence with editors and publishers. In an early letter to the editor of
the *San Francisco Bulletin,* he explained, "I have sailed and traveled quite
extensively in other parts of the world and have learned to seize upon that
which is interesting, to grasp the true romance of things, and to understand the people I may be thrown amongst."[6] Although this self-
assessment of his talents was accurate (human interest, romantic imagination, and sympathetic understanding are, to be sure, primary ingredients

[6] JL to the Editor, *San Francisco Bulletin,* September 17, 1898.

in his best work), London was quite capable of modulating the facts, when necessary, to fit them to the persona he developed very early in his career. For example, when writing to his first publisher, he stretched the truth to project his image as the Horatio Alger hero who, descended from good, solid American pioneer stock, had won to success by means of hard work and self-education. "My father was Pennsylvania-born, a soldier, scout, backwoodsman, trapper, and wanderer," he attested. "However, from my ninth year, with the exception of the hours spent at school (and I earned them by hard labor), my life has been one of toil. . . . In the main I am self-educated; have had no mentor but myself," he wrote, contradicting himself in the same letter by references to his adventures as an oyster pirate, tramp, and Klondiker, as well as to his formal education as a high school and college student.[7]

It is clear from his letters that Jack London deliberately cultivated this mythic image of himself as the American Adam, a figure defined by R. W. B. Lewis as "an individual standing alone, self-reliant and self-propelling, ready to confront whatever awaited him with the aid of his own unique and inherent resources."[8] Aside from the promotional rewards inherent in such an image, London wholeheartedly subscribed to the American dream. "Whether success depended upon brawn or brains was a question about which London might change his mind," says Kenneth Lynn, "but throughout his entire career he retained the firm belief that life was very much the sink-or-swim, do-or-die proposition that Alger had proclaimed it to be."[9] On November 30, 1898, with his family and friends pressing him to get a steady, respectable job, while editors were rejecting his manuscripts faster than he could pawn his bike and typewriter for postage money, he wrote to Mabel Applegarth: "I don't care if the whole present, all I possess, were swept away from me—I will build a new present; If I am left naked and hungry to-morrow—before I give in I will go on naked and hungry; if I were a woman I would prostitute myself to all men but that I would succeed—in short, I will."

Subsequent correspondence reveals that as the acceptances began to come regularly, he worked hard to sharpen his image of writer as businessman. In his letters to editors, agents, and publishers, London the literary entrepreneur was an aggressive, no-nonsense salesman capable of bargaining for the top dollar and willing to dump even his worst hack work on an eager market. Virtually every story, he insisted, was a "crackerjack," and every novel was "altogether new and different" from anything he had written before. Editors, until proven innocent, were in

[7] JL to Houghton, Mifflin & Co., January 31, 1900.
[8] *The American Adam: Innocence, Tragedy, and Tradition in the Nineteenth Century* (Chicago, 1955), p. 5.
[9] *The Dream of Success: A Study of the Modern American Imagination* (Boston, 1955), p. 86.

his estimation unscrupulous and conniving; he gave them no quarter—
with the notable exception of his correspondence with George P. Brett,
president of the Macmillan Company. From the start to the finish of their
fifteen-year association, even during his brief apostasy from Macmillan in
1912–13, London was seldom less than cordially respectful. Furthermore, he was uninhibited, often enthusiastic, in discussing his personal
plans with Brett (for example, his boat-building and ranching projects)—
partly, of course, because he was asking for advances on royalties, but
also because he regarded Brett as a benevolent father figure, someone he
could trust. Brett never betrayed this trust; and, what is more remarkable, he seldom lost his patience with London's ambitious plans and persistent requests for advances to offset his habitual overspending.

Beyond the myth and the self-promotion, the portrait that emerges
from London's letters is that of a confident yet unassuming, often sensitive human being—an exceptionally open and energetic individual capable of great personal courage and generosity but also susceptible to
spells of self-pity and willful abrasiveness, and to moments of brutal frankness. While he put more of his heart into the early letters, this image remains fairly consistent throughout the twenty years of London's available
correspondence. Many of the earliest letters are missing because he made
no copies and discarded everything (including the manuscripts of his published work). Fortunately, a few friends like Mabel and Ted Applegarth,
Cloudesley Johns, Elwyn Hoffman, and Anna Strunsky saved his letters;
and Charmian Kittredge London, who began typing for him in 1904,
made carbons and saved everything.

London's love letters are, as might be expected, most revealing. His earliest letters to his first great love, Mabel Applegarth, are missing, and his
ardor had cooled before he left for the Klondike in 1897. But after his
return, during the dark fall of 1898 when friends as well as fortune
seemed to have deserted him, it was to her that he confided his frustration
and insecurity. "From the hunger of my childhood, cold eyes have looked
upon me, or questioned, or snickered and sneered. What hurt above all
was that they were some [of] my friends—not professed but real friends,"
he complained in his letter of November 30, 1898. "So be it. The end is
not yet. If I die I shall die hard, fighting to the last, and hell shall receive
no fitter inmate than myself. But for good or ill, it shall be as it has
been—alone." In a Christmas letter to Mabel a few weeks later, he ral-
lied, displaying the militant will that characterized his drive to succeed:
"Well, the FIRST BATTLE has been fought. While I have not conquered, I'll
not confess defeat. Instead, I have learned the enemy's strongholds and
weak places, and by the same I shall profit when the SECOND BATTLE
comes off; and by what I learn through that, I will be better fitted for the
THIRD BATTLE—and so on, ad infinitum."

His letters to Anna Strunsky, his second great love, show London at his best in several ways: sensitive, good-natured, honest. "Take me this way," he wrote her on December 21, 1899, "a stray guest, a bird of passage, splashing with salt-rimed wings through a brief moment of your life—a rude and blundering bird, used to large airs and great spaces, unaccustomed to the amenities of confined existence." Shortly after his death, Strunsky, long since married to the wealthy socialist William English Walling, wrote of London's special charm: "He was youth, adventure, romance. He was a poet and a social revolutionist. He had a genius for friendship. He loved greatly and was greatly beloved." [10] This "genius for friendship" may be seen throughout in his correspondence with her. In the beginning, his infatuation appears to have been altogether intellectual. He was fascinated by Strunsky's vivacity and intelligence, and by a philosophical sophistication that challenged his own—qualities he found wanting in Bessie Maddern, whom he impulsively married in April 1900 because he felt he needed a steady domestic hand to settle him down. The idea of a collaborative treatise on love was born; and, as *The Kempton-Wace Letters* took shape, London, who assumed the epistolary persona of Herbert Wace, the scientific realist, fell in love with Strunsky, whom he began addressing as "Dear You," signing his letters first "Jack," then as "The Sahib." In love with him though she surely was, Strunsky had no intention of playing the role of mistress and homebreaker. While he was in the East End of London during the summer of 1902, she wrote to him making her feelings clearly known: having discovered that Bessie London was pregnant, she firmly closed the door to any further romantic involvement. "And now it is all over and done with," he responded. "So be it. Henceforth I shall dream romances for other people and translate them into bread & butter." [11] Although this letter marks the end of his romantic attachment to Strunsky, it was not the end of their correspondence or of their friendship.

London was mistaken, however, when he asserted that he would henceforth confine his romantic impulses to fiction. During the following summer, disabused of the notion of marrying for practical, scientific reasons, he fell quite madly and illicitly in love with Charmian Kittredge. We need only read a few of his clandestine missives to her to see through the public mask of Jack London, tough guy: "Ask people who know me today, what I am," he wrote to her on June 18, 1903. "A rough, savage fellow, they will say, who likes prizefights and brutalities, who has a clever turn of pen, a charlatan's smattering of art, and the inevitable deficiencies of the untrained, unrefined, self-made man which he strives with a fair measure of success to hide beneath an attitude of roughness and unconventionality.

---

[10] "Memoirs of Jack London," *The Masses*, 9 (July 1917): 13.
[11] JL to Anna Strunsky, September 28–29, 1902.

Do I endeavor to unconvince them? It's so much easier to leave their convictions alone." But Jack London, sentimental lover, revealed himself in his concluding lines: "I reach out my hand to meet yours across the hills and hours, Love, and our hearts touch with our fingers, and you are real and beside me and all about me now." And in July he declared to her: "I am filled with a great pride. It seems to me somehow that all my values have been enormously enhanced. And do you know why? Because you love me. O God, that's the wonder of it, the wonder of it, that you should find me worthy of you!" Also noteworthy is the devotion revealed in his later love letters to her, written during the summer of 1910 while she was recovering from the shock of their newborn daughter Joy's death. "Dearest Mother-Woman," he addressed her on July 24, "Take good care of yourself, among other things that you may run more quickly to my arms. If you only knew how often these days I congratulate myself that I'm married to a *good* woman who knows most everything and is a dead game sport." And five days later he expanded his salutation to "Dearest Mother-Woman, Mate Woman, Wife-Woman, Kid-Woman, My-Woman"—adding "Dear Love-Woman" in the text of his letter. "There's nothing like you in the world for me," he proclaimed. "You *will* be God Almighty & the Resurrection. . . . If you knew how often, here, and in Oakland I have looked at the dear things possessed by you and loved them for your own sake! . . . Home! It takes you to make it."

Equally revealing are London's early letters to his fellow literary neophytes and intellectuals—notably Ted and Mabel Applegarth, Cloudesley Johns, and Elwyn Hoffman. In these letters he may be seen excitedly sharing new ideas, laboring to master the tools of his trade, and trying to keep his manuscripts in circulation among the magazines, which returned his unwanted contributions with clockwork regularity. On June 22, 1897, he wrote apologetically to Ted Applegarth, then in England, that he was sending the letter through Mabel because he could not afford overseas postage: "Stamps are ephemeral—last week I had half-a-dollar's worth. Next week I shall receive numerous letters all graced on the outside by that same half-dollar's worth of stamps—this is why I have Mabel forward this." In the same letter he also indicated the extent to which he had dedicated himself to his newly chosen profession: "I have isolated myself in almost claustral seclusion in my sanctum sanctorum, and am grinding out article after article." This letter, composed just five weeks before London departed for the Gold Rush, and one of the few pieces of correspondence extant from his pre-Klondike years, corroborates the seemingly exaggerated accounts of his literary rites of passage in *Martin Eden* and *John Barleycorn*.

His Klondike adventure in 1897–98 was the turning point in London's career. "It was in the Klondike I found myself," he recollected. "There you get your perspective. I got mine." [12] Although he was forced by an attack of scurvy to return home after less than a year in the Northland, and although he brought back very little actual gold, he did bring home a wealth of experiences—his own and also those of the argonauts and sourdoughs with whom he had spent the richest winter of his life, experiences he would now transmute into marketable fictions, the kind of authentic stuff the magazine editors and publishers were after. The apprentice writer—at first groping, uncertain, trying to master not only verse forms but spelling and grammatical forms as well—is still apparent in the post-Klondike letters, but he was approaching maturity very rapidly. Writing to Ted Applegarth on September 13, 1898, in one of his first letters after returning home, London revealed the intensity of his regimen: "I have been writing like a tiger all day, it is now past one in the morning & I must be up at five to go riding with Mabel." In this same letter he set forth a literary principle that would manifest itself in all his work: "Never sacrifice thought to sound, ryhme [*sic*] or meter," he counseled Ted in criticizing his poetry. "If you cannot clothe the thought without injuring it—throw it away." Later, writing to Elwyn Hoffman on January 6, 1901, he used the same metaphor: "After all, it is the substance that counts. What is form? What intrinsic value resides in it? None, none, none—unless it clothe pregnant substance, great substance."

In the year after his return from the Klondike, London the writer came of age, rising from obscurity to become one of California's most celebrated young authors—published not only in such popular magazines as the *Overland Monthly* and *Youth's Companion* but also in the prestigious *Atlantic Monthly*. At the end of 1898, he was still self-consciously engrossed in improving his literary skills. "The art of omission is the hardest of all to learn," he confessed to Mabel Applegarth, "and I am weak at it yet. I am too long-winded, and it is hard training to cut down." [13] Six months later, still not sure of himself, he told Cloudesley Johns, "You see, I am groping, groping, groping for my own particular style, for the style which should be mine but which I have not yet found." [14] But the next month he received a letter from the *Atlantic Monthly* accepting his "Odyssey of the North" if he would shorten the story by three thousand words. This acceptance gave him the confidence he had been wanting. He settled into the lifelong task of turning out one thousand words a day, with virtually no time spent on revisions. "Let me tell you how I write," he explained to Elwyn Hoffman: "I type as fast as I write, so that each day sees the work all upon the final MS. which goes for editorial submission. And *on* the day I finish the MS. I fold it up and send it off without once going back to see what all the previous pages were

[12] *Jack London by Himself*, undated promotional pamphlet published by Macmillan.
[13] JL to Mabel Applegarth, ? December 31, 1898.
[14] JL to Cloudesley Johns, June 12, 1899, first letter.

like. So, in fact, when a page is done, that is the last I see of it till it comes out in print." [15]

By this time he was also feeling secure enough to lecture his fellow writers on how to become successful like himself. On June 16, 1900, he explained to Cloudesley Johns that to write good fiction, he must eliminate himself as author in the work: "You are handling stirring life, romance, things of human life and death, humor and pathos, etc. But God, man, handle them as they should be. Don't you tell the reader the philosophy of the road (except where you are actually there as participant in the first person). Don't you tell the reader. Don't. Don't. Don't. But HAVE YOUR CHARACTERS TELL IT BY THEIR DEEDS, ACTIONS, TALK, ETC. Then, and not until then, are you writing fiction and not a sociological paper upon a certain sub-stratum of society." Furthermore, he continued, "[you must] get your good strong phrases, fresh, and vivid. And write intensively, not exhaustively or lengthily. Don't narrate—paint! draw! build!— CREATE!"

London's willingness to share the tricks of the trade, so rigorously mastered during his own apprenticeship, is apparent in letters throughout his career. Despite protests that he could not begin to read all the materials submitted by aspiring writers, he was prepared to offer one consistent note of advice: success can be won only through hard work—a young writer must pay his dues. "If a fellow harnesses himself to a star of $1000 a week, he has to work proportionately harder than if he harnesses himself to a little glowworm of $20.00 a week," he explained to Max Feckler. "The only reason there are more successful blacksmiths in the world than successful writers, is that it is much easier, and requires far less hard work, to become a successful blacksmith than does it to become a successful writer." [16] One attitude is equally consistent: unequivocal candor. "If you know my career, you know that I am a brass-tack man. And I have given you the brass tacks right here," was his characteristic answer to another young writer. "If you can beat all the rest of us, without serving your apprenticeship, go to it. Far be it from us to advise you." [17]

The same "brass-tack" attitude is evident in London's letters to editors and publishers. "Right here at the start, please know you are dealing with a man who is always hopelessly frank. It saves time," he wrote to William Ellsworth, president of the Century Company, on April 22, 1913, in ending his temporary defection from Macmillan. Earlier, when George Brett suggested that the subject matter of *The Road* might be offensive to some readers and might therefore jeopardize the sales of his other books, London was quick to respond: "In *The Road*, and in all my work, in all that I have said and written and done, I have been true. This is the character I

[15] JL to Elwyn Hoffman, June 17, 1900.
[16] JL to Max E. Feckler, October 26, 1914.
[17] JL to Jess Dorman, September 28, 1913.

have built up; it constitutes, I believe, my biggest asset. . . . I have always insisted that the cardinal literary virtue is sincerity, and I have striven to live up to this belief." [18]

While marketed as a profitable feature of his literary persona, sincerity was also a cardinal personal virtue for London, as may be seen throughout his correspondence. He was seldom one to mince words; and on occasion, especially when he felt cheated, betrayed, or directly challenged, his candor deteriorated into bullying meanness. Such instances, though exceptional, are nonetheless important in revealing his darker side. His outbursts were understandable—even justifiable—in his dealings with dishonest publishers and conniving promoters, but they seem gratuitously cruel in letters to his ex-wife Bessie, whom he never forgave for refusing to allow his two daughters to visit him and Charmian at the ranch, and to his daughter Joan, who was occasionally the victim of his resentment toward her mother. London may be seen at his worst in these letters and in the spiteful 1916 correspondence with his sometime admirer and ranch guest Spiro Orfans, who caught the full force of London's diatribes against "racial mongrelism."

These ugly moods occurred with greater frequency during the latter part of his career, for several reasons. He was harried by increasingly severe financial worries: adding to the acreage, the livestock, and the buildings of Beauty Ranch; struggling amidst a host of legal entanglements, including battles with the new film industry for his fair share of the profits; investing thousands of dollars in such fruitless business ventures as eucalyptus trees, the Jack London Grape Juice Company, and the Millergraph lithographing process; and pouring more thousands into the building of Wolf House, the magnificent home designed to stand for a thousand years. His dreams of the good life seemed to have turned to ashes by the end of 1913. The events of that one year were emotionally as well as financially devastating: the threatened loss of his copyrights by the lawsuit of the Balboa Amusement Company, the destruction of his fruit crops in a late frost, the damaging of his eucalyptus trees by locusts, the scorching of his cornfields by unseasonably hot winds, the accidental killing of one of his prize mares by a hunter, and the burning of Wolf House. During 1913 London also suffered an attack of appendicitis; and the operation, though successful, revealed that his kidneys were badly diseased. His declining health occasionally affected his later writings, as it did his personal relationships, contributing to the sudden changes of personality and fits of temper.

In most of his correspondence London kept these outbursts fairly well in check, however, maintaining to the end his public image as a robust adventurer, dynamic literary entrepreneur, scientific rancher, tough-

[18] JL to George P. Brett, March 7, 1907.

minded social realist, and gregarious host, at whose home the latchstring was always out. It was a demanding role for a healthy man in his prime; it was an incredible accomplishment for a man dying of uremia.[19]

What vision of this man ultimately emerges, then, from his letters? Beyond the images of the young man driven by the dream of success and of the mature writer in full possession of his talents, cannily marketing his goods for top dollar, we may discern London the avowed materialistic monist who is at heart a practicing humanist and an incorrigible optimist. "My one great weakness is the study of human nature," he had confessed to Cloudesley Johns on March 30, 1899. "Knowing no God, I have made of man my worship; and surely I have learned how vile he can be. But this only strengthens my regard, because it enhances the mighty heights he can bring himself to tread. How small he is, and how great he is!" Many years afterwards, scolding his friend Lorrin Thurston, editor of the *Honolulu Advertiser,* he wrote: "My idea . . . has been that of a cleaner, better, nobler world, more immediately accessible for all humanity than you could ever dream to hope for."[20] And, in a letter to Louise Bronson West written on December 21, 1914, he asserted: "If, just by wishing, I could change America and Americans in one way[,] I would change the economic organization of America so that true equality of opportunity would obtain; and service, instead of profits, would be the idea, the ideal, and the ambition animating every citizen."

Despite the disasters that plagued the last years of his life, London never lost his enthusiastic capacity for hope. Had his dream house burned? He would rebuild it: within months following the disaster he had already cut the redwood timbers needed for that work. Had he and Charmian lost their second child through miscarriage—and thereby any chance of children—and had Bessie refused to allow his own two daughters to set foot on his ranch? He would become father to all the children on the ranch by establishing a school for them: indeed, this was the subject of his final conversation with his stepsister Eliza on the night before his death. Had the theories of Karl Marx lost their cogency for him? He found the revolutionary insights of Carl Jung even more exciting: "I tell you," he announced to Charmian in the summer of 1916, "I am standing on the edge of a world so new, so terrible, so wonderful, that I am

---

[19] Despite strong evidence that London died from natural causes, the notion that he took his own life, either deliberately or accidentally, by means of an overdose of drugs, has persisted since the publication of Irving Stone's biographical novel *Sailor on Horseback* (Cambridge, Mass., 1938). For a cogent refutation of the suicide theory, see Alfred S. Shivers, "Jack London: Not a Suicide," *The Dalhousie Review,* 49 (Spring 1969): 43–57. Four attending physicians signed the news bulletin attributing London's death to "a gastrointestinal type of uremia." Russ Kingman, Director of the Jack London Research Center in Glen Ellen, California, has accumulated substantial evidence that the actual cause of London's death was stroke and heart failure.

[20] JL to Lorrin A. Thurston, June 11, 1910.

almost afraid to look over into it."[21] But he was not afraid to incorporate this new world into his fiction; and during the last six months of his life, he produced a half-dozen extraordinary stories in which he synthesized Hawaiian mythology with Jung's theory of archetypes and the collective unconscious. Had his Socialist Labor Party failed him, "because of its lack of fire and fight"?[22] He would dedicate his resources to improving "our one indestructible asset," the land on which we live: "I am that sort of farmer," he wrote to Geddes Smith on October 31, 1916, "who, after delving in all the books to satisfy his quest for economic wisdom, returns to the soil as the source and foundation of all economies."

If Jack London was, in the final analysis, a highly complex personality, we may nevertheless discern a two-stranded theme that informs the pattern of his life and works: an unfailing love of humanity bonded to an essential love of life itself. "Be not too quick to criticize others until God himself whispers in your ear that you are absolutely perfect and greater than Christ. Love, that you may be loved," he admonished one of his correspondents in 1915. "Two men who are kind each to the other, can shake the skies. A thousand men, criticizing one another, can produce nothing more than a madhouse, and an expense to the community that confines them."[23] Later that year, when another of his readers wrote to him, apparently worried by the morbid ending of *The Little Lady of the Big House*, London reassured her that "after having come through all of the game of life, and of youth, at my present age of thirty-nine years I am firmly and solemnly convinced that the game is worth the candle. I have had a very fortunate life, I have been luckier than many hundreds of millions of men in my generation have been lucky, and, while I have suffered much, I have lived much, seen much, and felt much that has been denied the average man. Yes, indeed, the game is worth the candle."[24]

This spirit of vital affirmation—his insistence upon the value of life, of love, and of optimism regardless of misfortune—is perhaps our best clue to Jack London's enduring appeal.

[21] Charmian Kittredge London, *The Book of Jack London* (New York, 1921), II, 323.
[22] JL to Members of Local Glen Ellen, Socialist Labor Party, March 7, 1916.
[23] JL to G. B. McLean, April 18, 1915.
[24] JL to Ethelda Hesser, September 21, 1915.

About This Edition

Until now, a significant number of London's letters have been available in only two books: Charmian Kittredge London's two-volume biography, *The Book of Jack London* (New York, 1921), and *Letters from Jack London*, edited by King Hendricks and Irving Shepard (New York, 1965). Charmian London's work is characteristic of the nineteenth-century "life in letters" approach. Her transcriptions are sometimes inaccurate; letters are often fragmentary (of the 434 letters she includes, only 209 are complete); her choices are highly partisan; and her editing is not only arbitrary but sometimes misleading. A notable example is the letter London wrote to Anna Strunsky from England on August 25, 1902, reacting to her "Dear John" letter. London's original letter, only recently acquired by the Merrill Library at Utah State University, clearly reveals Strunsky's reasons for breaking off their liaison, as well as his attempt to justify his own role in their affair. Yet there is no hint of any of this in the fragment published by Charmian London, which merely tells of his misery after spending the night walking the street with the homeless people of the East End.

The Hendricks and Shepard volume is a more reliable and scholarly work, containing some four hundred letters (402, to be precise); yet it entirely omits such important segments of London's correspondence as his letters to his close friend Ted Applegarth and his fellow aspiring writer Elwyn Hoffman, not to mention the early love letters to Charmian Kittredge and the increasingly mordant correspondence with Spiro Orfans, which reached its climax the year London died. Why the highly informative letters to Applegarth and Hoffman were not included is something of a mystery; possibly the editors were unaware of their existence. But there is little question about the others: Hendricks and Shepard probably excluded the letters written to Charmian Kittredge during the summer of 1903 in the hope of protecting the family's image of the Londons; similar motives may have prompted their omission of the letters to Orfans. Yet all these letters are important to our full understanding—and to our ultimate appreciation—of Jack London the man.

One other important source of London's published letters is Georgia

Loring Bamford, *The Mystery of Jack London* (Oakland, Calif., 1931). This book, withdrawn shortly after publication because Charmian London objected to its unauthorized printing of the 54 letters London had written to Frederick Irons Bamford, was virtually unavailable until it was reprinted in 1969 (soon thereafter, a number of copies of the original edition, which had evidently been in storage, were placed on sale by the Holmes Book Company in Oakland). None of these letters appears in either *The Book of Jack London* or *Letters from Jack London*; yet a number of them are significant, not only because Bamford (Christian socialist, reference librarian at the Oakland Public Library, and co-founder of the Ruskin Club) was an important friend, but also because the bulk of them were composed during 1905 and 1906, probably the happiest period of London's life, as he and Charmian discovered the pastoral delights of his "Valley of the Moon."

In selecting the 1,557 letters of this edition, the editors have examined more than four thousand letters written by Jack London and a comparable number written to him. The main repository for these letters (many of which are carbon copies) is the Henry E. Huntington Library in San Marino, California. The second largest collection is housed in the Merrill Library at Utah State University. Other libraries with significant collections of London's letters are the New York Public Library, the Bancroft Library of the University of California at Berkeley, and the University of Virginia Library. The original copies of London's letters to Bamford are housed in the vault at the Jack London State Park, Glen Ellen, California. Many other original copies are in the hands of private collectors; and more, of course, have been lost or destroyed.

The main principle of selection in the present edition has been informative relevance: that is, we have chosen letters that reflect significant facets of London's personality and provide important information about his life, his personal and professional relationships, and his various careers as writer, businessman, social reformer, traveler, and scientific farmer. We have excluded letters that are clearly routine and duplicative. Much of his business correspondence, for example, consists of such routine matters as writing to his publisher for advances, asking about the dispositions of manuscripts or for statements of his account, acknowledging receipt of checks or of extra copies of books he had ordered, and so forth; substantive information in such letters is provided as excerpts in notes to related letters. We should add that the majority of London's letters to literary agents and publishers are mundane and impersonal; from these we have attempted to select a representative sample. Duplications (sometimes routine as well) consisted mainly of follow-up inquiries to publishers and magazine editors, of telegrams and letters on the same subject, and of letters written to several different editors or to his American and English agents when he was promoting a new story or novel for serialization. Another example is the duplicate letter he wrote in 1913 to such major writers as Winston Churchill, George Bernard Shaw, and H. G. Wells, asking them to tell him (confidentially) what rates they received for their works from various magazines and publishers in England and America. And of course his 1916 letter of resignation from the Socialist Labor Party was sent out broadcast. In such cases, significant recipients are identified in the notes.

Our editorial objective in presenting these letters has been to preserve London's spontaneous epistolary style and to retain his syntax, spelling, punctuation, and paragraphing, but in a form that will not create irrelevant distractions for the reader. We supply complete extant texts of all letters included. The following editorial principles have been applied throughout the three volumes of this edition:

1. Letters are arranged chronologically. If two or more letters bear the same date, they appear alphabetically by correspondent unless there is evidence of the order in which London wrote them. Known dates for undated or incorrectly dated letters have been supplied in brackets. Conjectural dates for undated letters are also given in brackets, with a question mark.

2. Pertinent bibliographical information immediately follows the text of each letter. This usually consists of the owner or location of a letter, its length (number of pages), the form of the manuscript (e.g., typed letter or autograph letter, signed), and places of previous publication. Letters drawn from published sources are identified by conventional source citations; many of these are also contained in London's scrapbooks of clippings at the Huntington Library. Abbreviations may be found in the list on pp. xxx–xxxi.

3. The annotation following each letter is generally explanatory rather than interpretive and focuses primarily on the identification of people, places, literary works, and historical events.

4. Misspelled words and grammatical errors positively attributed to London in holograph letters have been retained insofar as they do not cause confusion. We have silently corrected typographical errors in letters known to have been typed by London's secretaries, and routine typos (e.g., "theie" for "their" or "teh" for "the") resulting from London's usual haste in writing or typing and his failure to reread his letters for accuracy. All contractions have been closed up, although London often typed them open (e.g., "could n't"; see his letter to the editor of *Cosmopolitan*, February 12, 1907). All other emendations are made in square brackets. Incomplete words, false starts, and random characters (e.g., "of a a," "the i best") have not been recorded. "[*Sic*]" has not been used at all in the text of letters.

5. London's often erratic punctuation has been retained, except in certain instances. In typed letters, London or his typist often redundantly punctuated sentences, adding a period after a semicolon in midsentence

or ending a sentence with two periods. We have silently corrected these errors. Some forms of redundant punctuation, however, seem to be idiosyncrasies of London's style, since they appear regularly in both autograph and typed letters: for example, he frequently used a short dash after a colon in the salutation and occasionally in the body of a letter or the postscript. Often he inserted a dash after a comma, period, or semicolon in midsentence, or after a period, question mark, or exclamation point at the end of a sentence in the middle of a paragraph. He also frequently placed commas before and after parenthetical comments. In these instances the redundant punctuation has been retained. In autograph letters, however, dashes between a period or other terminal punctuation and London's signature have been dropped. Dashes after a colon or "P.S." are represented by an en dash; all others have been normalized to em dash. Omitted periods have been provided under an apostrophe to complete an exclamation point or at the end of a sentence containing no other mark of punctuation. Where necessary, quotation marks and parentheses have been completed, ellipses have been normalized, and quotation marks have been moved outside final periods or commas. In telegrams, the only punctuation marks we include are periods at the end of sentences.

6. Proper names (except titles of works), the pronoun "I," and words at the beginning of sentences have been capitalized, regardless of London's inconsistencies. We have transcribed in italic capital and lowercase London's adjustable date stamp, which had only capitals; however, we have retained the all-capitals form of telegrams.

7. Without regard for London's eccentric placement, we have normalized paragraph indentation, letter headings, and the position of complimentary close, signature, and postscript. Lists and long quotes are set off only if they received distinctive treatment in the original. All letters in this edition, except fragments, appear as having been signed by London, although carbon copies, when not stamped with his autograph stamp, usually contain no signature. In some instances, notably letters to Charmian Kittredge London, Joan London, Cloudesley Johns, Blanche Partington, and George Sterling, London signed his letters with only his first name or with a name of endearment (e.g., "Mate-Man," "Daddy," "Wolf"). Since no name appears on carbon copies of some of the letters for which the original is unavailable, the conjectural signature is supplied in square brackets unless otherwise noted.

8. All above-line insertions have been brought down to the printed line. A blank line space replaces lines drawn between sections of a letter.

9. Three asterisks mark the missing part or parts of letter fragments, usually the beginning or end. In transcripts of fragmentary letters (e.g., those written from Korea in 1904), asterisks indicating indefinite omissions within the body of a letter have been normalized to ellipses.

10. To avoid confusion among titles, especially between short stories and collections of the same name, we have followed the editorial procedure of Hendricks and Shepard in *Letters from Jack London*, italicizing titles of books or independent publications and placing in quotes titles of short stories, essays, and so forth. London's own usage has been followed, however, in capitalization, in phrasing, and in the determination of what is included (e.g., whether or not a city name is treated as part of a newspaper's title).

11. Place names and dates in letter headings have been faithfully reproduced. When the place is not given, it has been supplied in brackets, often from Charmian London's diary. For London's many place stamps, only place names and street addresses, in italics, are recorded: for example, "Jack London / 56 Bayo Vista Avenue / Oakland, Calif."; "Jack London / Piedmont / Alameda Co., Calif."; and "Jack London / Glen Ellen / Sonoma Co., Cal. / U.S.A." appear in this edition, respectively, as "*56 Bayo Vista Avenue / Oakland, Calif.*"; "*Piedmont, Calif.*"; and "*Glen Ellen, Calif.*" London often used one of his home address stamps while traveling; in such cases we have given his actual location in brackets.

Two indexes—one of correspondents and one general—are located at the end of Volume Three.

Abbreviations

al.	autograph letter
als.	autograph letter, signed
apcs.	autograph postcard, signed
Batchelder	collection of Robert Batchelder
Bernatovech	collection of Carl Bernatovech
BJL	Charmian K. London, *The Book of Jack London*, 2 vols. (New York, 1921)
C	California State Library, Sacramento
CCamarSJ	St. John's Seminary, Camarillo, Calif.
CCC	Claremont College
cctl.	carbon copy of typed letter
CLSU	University of Southern California
CLU	University of California, Los Angeles
CO	Oakland (California) Public Library
Cresmer	collection of C. J. Cresmer
CSf	San Francisco Public Library
CSfU	University of San Francisco
CSmH	Henry E. Huntington Library
CSt	Stanford University
CtY	Yale University
CU	University of California, Berkeley
DLC	Library of Congress
drtel.	draft of telegram
GU	University of Georgia
IaU	University of Iowa
ICU	University of Chicago
InGD	DePauw University
InNd	University of Notre Dame
InU	Indiana University
IU	University of Illinois, Urbana
JLB	Richard O'Connor, *Jack London: A Biography* (New York, 1964)

JL Ranch	Jack London Ranch, Glen Ellen, Calif.
JL Reports	King Hendricks and Irving Shepard, eds., *Jack London Reports: War Correspondence, Sports Articles, and Miscellaneous Writings* (Garden City, N.Y., 1970)
JL State Park	Jack London State Park, Glen Ellen, Calif.
JL Times	Joan London, *Jack London and His Times* (New York, 1939; rpt., Seattle, 1968)
Jones	collection of Waring Jones
Kingman	collection of Russ Kingman
KPT	Pittsburg (Kansas) State University
L	King Hendricks and Irving Shepard, eds., *Letters from Jack London* (New York, 1965)
Labor	collection of Earle Labor
LNHT	Tulane University
MacManus	George S. MacManus Co., Philadelphia
MB	Boston Public Library
MBU	Boston University
Mentor	Dale Walker, ed., *No Mentor But Myself* (Port Washington, N.Y., 1979)
MoSW	Washington University
MWalB	Brandeis University
Mystery	Georgia Loring Bamford, *The Mystery of Jack London* (Oakland, Calif., 1931; rpt. 1969)
NB	Brooklyn Public Library
Neville	collection of Maurice Neville
NhD	Dartmouth College
NN	New York Public Library
NNWML	Wagner College, Staten Island, N.Y.
Noto	collection of Sal Noto
OrU	University of Oregon
pbd	published
PBL	Lehigh University
Pictorial Life	Russ Kingman, *A Pictorial Life of Jack London* (New York, 1979)
PU	University of Pennsylvania
Sinclair	Upton Sinclair, *My Lifetime in Letters* (Columbia, Mo., 1960)
tel.	telegram
tl.	typed letter
tls.	typed letter, signed
typs.	typescript
ULA	Utah State University
ViU	University of Virginia
VtU	University of Vermont

Chronology: 1876-1905

1876
January 12: JL born in San Francisco, California, the only child of Flora Wellman, who named as his father William Henry Chaney, with whom she had lived as common-law wife in 1874–75; the infant was named John Griffith Chaney.

September 7: Flora Wellman Chaney married John London, and the child was renamed John Griffith London.

1878
After JL and his stepsister Eliza suffered near-fatal attacks of diphtheria, the family moved across San Francisco Bay to Oakland, where John London sold produce to local markets and ran a grocery store.

1881
Family moved to a farm in Alameda.

1882
Started grade school in Alameda.

1886
March 27: Family bought a house in Oakland after living on farms in San Mateo County and Livermore.

1891
Graduated from Cole Grammar School (eighth grade) and took a job in Hickmott's Cannery. A few months later, with money borrowed from Virginia ("Mammy Jennie") Prentiss, purchased the *Razzle-Dazzle* and became an oyster pirate on San Francisco Bay.

1892
Worked as a deputy patrolman for the California Fish Patrol in Benicia.

1893
January–August: Served as an able-bodied seaman aboard the *Sophia Sutherland*, a sealing schooner on an eight-month voyage to Hawaii, the Bonin Islands, Japan, and the Bering Sea.
Late August: Took a job in a jute mill at ten cents an hour for ten-hour-plus workdays.
November 11: "Story of a Typhoon off the Coast of Japan" was published as the best descriptive article in a contest for young writers sponsored by the *San Francisco Morning Call*.

1894
Worked as a coal heaver in the power plant of the Oakland, San Leandro, and Haywards Electric Railway.
April 6: Left Oakland to join Kelly's Army, the western contingent of Coxey's Industrial Army of the Unemployed, in its march on Washington to protest economic conditions.
May 25: Left Kelly's Army at Hannibal, Missouri, to begin tramping on his own.
May 30: Visited World's Fair grounds in Chicago.
June 29–July 29: Arrested in Buffalo, New York, and served a thirty-day sentence for vagrancy in the Erie County Penitentiary.
Toured the East Coast and returned west by coalcar across Canada, earning passage from Vancouver as a coal stoker aboard the SS *Umatilla*.

1895
Attended Oakland High School; published short stories and articles in *The High School Ægis*. Participated in the Henry Clay Club. Fell in love with Mabel Applegarth.

1896
Joined the Socialist Labor Party in April. Left high school. Briefly attended the University Academy in Alameda to prepare for entrance examinations at the University of California, then studied independently for three months and, with tutoring from Mabel and Ted Applegarth, Fred Jacobs, and Bessie Maddern, was admitted to the University of California.

1897
February 4: Left the University after one semester and, after a brief period of writing and socialist work, took a job in the Belmont Academy laundry.
July 25: Sailed with his brother-in-law, Capt. James H. Shepard, aboard the SS *Umatilla* for Port Townsend, Washington, then aboard the *City of Topeka* for Juneau, Alaska, to join the Klondike Gold Rush.

Spent the winter in an old cabin on Split-Up Island, between the Stewart River and Henderson Creek, eighty miles from Dawson City, Yukon Territory.

1898
Suffering from scurvy, left the Klondike, rafting down the Yukon River from Dawson to St. Michael on the Bering Sea. Worked his way home as a coal stoker, arriving in Oakland in late July. Started an intensive regimen to become a professional writer.

1899
January: "To the Man on Trail" published in the *Overland Monthly*, which then requested a series of Northland stories.
July 29: "An Odyssey of the North" accepted for publication in the January 1900 issue of the *Atlantic Monthly*.
December: Met Anna Strunsky.
Published during the year a total of twenty-four items, including essays, jokes, poems, and stories.

1900
April 7: Married Bessie Mae Maddern.
Book published:
  The Son of the Wolf (Houghton Mifflin)

1901
January 15: Birth of daughter Joan.
July: First journalism assignment, covering the Third National Bundes Shooting Festival for Hearst.
Defeated as Socialist Democrats' candidate for mayor of Oakland (received 245 votes).
Book published:
  The God of His Fathers (McClure, Phillips)

1902
August–September: Lived in East End of London, collecting material for and writing *The People of the Abyss*; traveled in Europe for three weeks.
October 20: Birth of daughter Bess (Becky).
Books published:
  A Daughter of the Snows (Lippincott)
  Children of the Frost (Macmillan)
  The Cruise of the Dazzler (Century)

1903
Fell in love with Charmian Kittredge; separated from Bessie London.
  Bought the sloop *Spray* for sailing on San Francisco Bay.
Books published:
  The Kempton-Wace Letters, with Anna Strunsky (Macmillan)
  The Call of the Wild (Macmillan)
  The People of the Abyss (Macmillan)

1904
January–June: In Korea as a war correspondent for Hearst, covering the
  Russo-Japanese War.
June 28: Suit for divorce filed by Bessie, on grounds of desertion; Anna
  Strunsky named as cause of separation.
Books published:
  The Faith of Men (Macmillan)
  The Sea-Wolf (Macmillan)

1905
February–March: Took a sailing trip up the Sacramento River on *Spray*
  with Cloudesley Johns. Defeated as Social Democrats' candidate for
  mayor of Oakland (received 981 votes).
April–September: Spent summer at Wake-Robin Lodge in Glen Ellen,
  Sonoma County.
June 6: Purchased the 129-acre Hill Ranch, the beginning of his "Beauty
  Ranch."
October 18: Began socialist lecture tour of the East and Midwest.
November 19: Married Charmian Kittredge in Chicago the day after the
  divorce from Bessie London became final.
December 27: Interrupted lecture tour for a honeymoon in Jamaica
  and Cuba.
Books published:
  War of the Classes (Macmillan)
  The Game (Macmillan)
  Tales of the Fish Patrol (Macmillan)

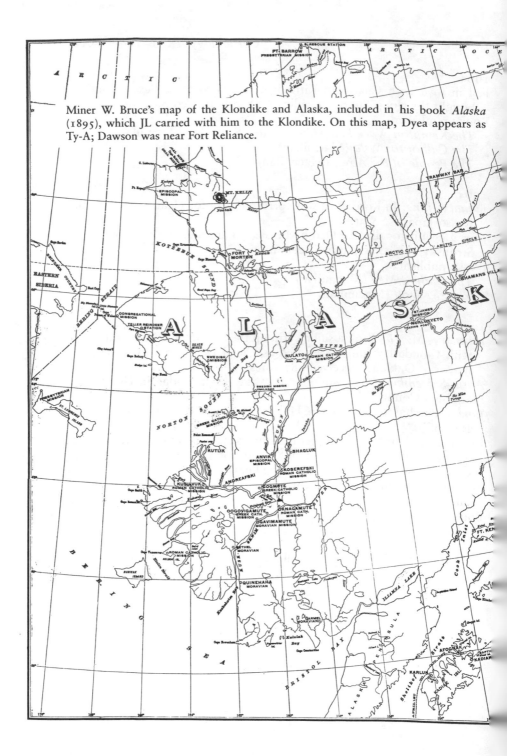

Miner W. Bruce's map of the Klondike and Alaska, included in his book *Alaska* (1895), which JL carried with him to the Klondike. On this map, Dyea appears as Ty-A; Dawson was near Fort Reliance.

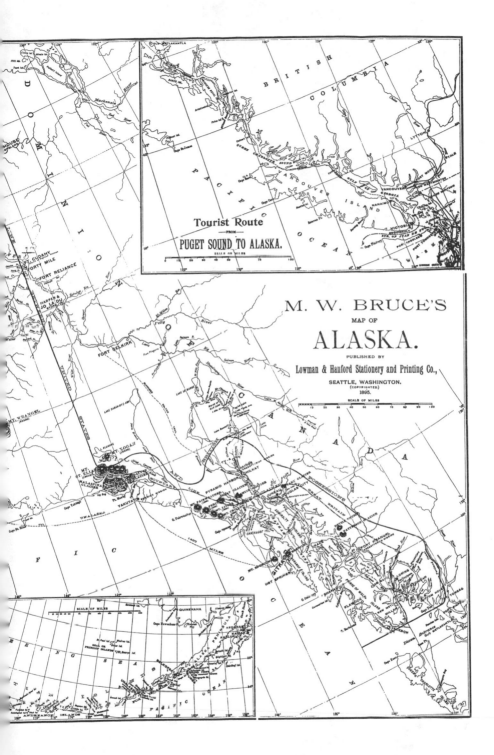

Tourist Route
—FROM—
PUGET SOUND TO ALASKA.

M. W. BRUCE'S
MAP OF
ALASKA.
PUBLISHED BY
Lowman & Hanford Stationery and Printing Co.,
SEATTLE, WASHINGTON.
(COPYRIGHTED)
1895.

1896-98

Sailor on the *Sophia Sutherland,* 1893 (CSmH)

To the Editor, *Oakland Times*

[Oakland]
[July 29, 1896]

Editor *Times*:

As an assiduous reader of the many communications published in your columns, I have failed to see the Socialist represented.[1] The Non-Partisan management of your paper would warrant the same, so I take advantage of it.

The Socialist labor party has been subjected to much contumely by the Populists, for its "keep in the middle of the road" policy. The Populists have told us, "We know that your doctrines are good; we know that they strike at the very root of the industrial and social evils; but we also know that it is too stupendous a step and that you cannot get it all at once, so come over to us. We have in our platform, many steps toward the goal you wish to attain. We have direct legislation, government ownership, and many planks which harmonize with your teachings. Come with us—half a loaf is better than none—and get what you can get, now!"

The Socialist labor party refused this offer and brought upon itself a flood of Populistic denunciation. But we have bided our time, and behold the result. The Democrats have said to the Populists, "You cannot get all your reforms at once—half a loaf is better than none—come with us, get what you can get, now, and be it free silver!"[2]

The Populists have fallen—in as much, that their fundamental reform principles have been forgotten, and silver, a minor consideration, a side issue, has been made the main issue of their campaign. As they would have swallowed the Socialists, so have they been swallowed by the Democrats, who have stolen their thunder.

The Socialist labor party, not of the United States but of the world, is cognizant of one important truth. This truth is, that for a "third party," fusion is synonymous with destruction. In the United States we have had many third parties. Where are they now? In every instance, fusion with one or the other of the old parties, has heralded their absorption and loss of individuality.

The Socialists of Germany, France, Italy, Spain, Belgium and other European countries, will not fuse—will not set aside their doctrines for mere palliatives. The main issue is public ownership of all the facilities of production and distribution, and they never drift away from it to measures, which are mere temporary alleviations and not permanent cures. As the years roll by their numbers increase faster and faster, while their steadfast policy disallows any possibility of absorption or corruption by mingling with other parties.

The adoption of the California State platforms of the Socialist labor party, was the source of further antagonism with the Populists. The financial plank declared openly against the free coinage and remonetization of silver.

And this is why they declare against it. Under the competitive system and the world's recognition of intrinsic value in money, it is impossible for one nation, by mere fiat, to raise the intrinsic value of silver 100 per cent—to say that 50 cents of silver is worth a dollar. The absurdity of the silver doctrine is apparent. If they are fiat money men, let them declare for fiat money; if they are intrinsic value money men, let them declare for a bi-metallic standard, in which silver is coined at the present market ratio existing between it and gold; as it is, they mingle the two theories and from the chaos conceive a third which partakes of both, and which, as a sailor would describe it, is an "herumfrodite" policy.

The silver men say that the "crime of '73," [3] by contracting the circulating medium, decreased the value of commodities, increased the purchasing power of money and doubled the burden of the debtor class. The debtor class now proposes to turn the tables by expanding the currency and thus increase the value of commodities, decrease the purchasing power of money and lighten their burden by half. Let us interrogate this proposition. The labor of the United States is not the debtor class. They owe nothing for the simple reason that no one will trust them. Who composes this debtor class? The men of small capital—the men, who, when a debtless laborer produces ten dollars' worth of wealth, pockets eight of it and gives him two as a wage. What, in reality, does this debtor class propose to the labor class? It is this: "We, the small fry capitalists, have been riding on the back of labor; but the large capitalist has shoved us off. We are liable to become laborers ourselves—save us from this dreadful doom! Vote for free silver and decrease our indebtedness so that we may again be boosted on the back of labor and ride a little farther."

Jack London.

SOURCE: *Oakland Times*, July 29, 1896; also pbd. *Oakland Item*, date unknown.

1. In 1896, the American socialist movement was on the eve of its transformation from a broad spectrum of small and unrelated groups, ranging from communitarians to Marxist ideologues, into a mass organ of protest. The Socialist Labor Party, founded in 1877, represented the most Marxist-oriented of these socialisms; in its early years, its chapters tended

to center on a core of German or Russian immigrants, or on a foreign-language newspaper. The founding of Eugene V. Debs's Social Democracy of America on June 18, 1897, was to give socialism a more broadly based popular appeal. JL came to socialism in his teens and almost immediately began a career as a socialist public speaker that was to last a good part of his life. He was a member of the Socialist Labor Party of Oakland, which had been founded in 1892 by a group of middle-class intellectuals and which sponsored both theoretical discussions and lectures for party members, and propagandizing speeches at street corners or in open-air meetings. See Philip S. Foner, *Jack London: American Rebel*, rev. ed. (New York, 1964), pp. 23–29; and *JL Times*, 106–38.

2. "Free silver," a bimetallic monetary standard allowing for the free and unlimited coinage of silver at a ratio to gold of sixteen to one, was the central issue in the 1896 presidential campaign. The Republican Party, which nominated William McKinley, advocated maintenance of the single gold standard, as well as a high protective tariff; the Democrats nominated William Jennings Bryan and came out in favor of free silver, with a tariff for revenue only. Both parties split over the issue, however. The Populist Party, along with the splinter National Silver Republicans, joined the Democrats in endorsing Bryan. In general, free silver was backed by Western, agricultural, and labor interests as an inflationary policy that, by increasing the volume of circulating money, could be a means of increasing farm prices and wages. JL voiced the general opinion that a bimetallic standard would benefit the working class in his essay "Direct Legislation Through the Initiative and Referendum," *Oakland Times*, May 9, 1896. In the present letter, he appears to be following the Socialist Labor Party line; rather than endorse the silver candidate, the party ran its own presidential nominee, Charles H. Matchett, in the election.

3. The Coinage Act of February 12, 1873, which had made gold the sole U.S. monetary standard.

To the Editor, *Oakland Times*

[Oakland]
[August 12, 1896]

Editor *Times*:

A word on competition, both local and national. Competition is the life of trade; it gives incentive to capital and labor and benefits the consumer. It stimulates business and is the index of a nation's prosperity. It quickens in to life the latent energies of a people; develops the resources of a country; and bequeaths to a nation, as a necessary heirloom, both individual and collective independence.

This, and very much more, is the result—or is said to be the result—of competition. The people, the great seething masses, believe it, hence it must be so. But the people have been, are, and can be deceived. As an illustration, take the shell game. It is simple—the pea, the shells, the manipulator are before one's very eyes. Yet how many men have come to grief on attempting the petty feat of pointing out under which shell the pea is? Still, they decide just as hastily on the merits and demerits of competition, which is a myriad fold more intricate. If every citizen would give it an honest, thoughtful analysis, how different would be his conclusion.

Let us analyze, taking for example the merely local affair presented to us by Oakland's rival water companies. The Contra Costa Water Company, but a short time ago supplied all Oakland with water. It was a monopoly, and hence distasteful to the citizens and damaging to their interests. They clamored for a change, and the great elixir, competition, was offered them. They took the dose and are happy—happy as the opium-eater under the sway of his subtle drug. But when its effects have passed away and the reaction comes, how miserable the opium eater is! So it is with the people of Oakland; they are now experiencing the action; the reaction is yet to come.

The Contra Costa Water Company had the necessary water supply, the necessary facilities for distributing it, and as a logical conclusion, the necessary capital to operate it with. It is obvious that further capital was not needed to furnish Oakland with water. The Oakland Water Company sprang into existence, and twice the capital was now required to give Oakland water. It paralleled the older company's pipes, tore up our streets anew, and dug, tunneled and dammed in our hills to obtain the precious commodity. Then the war began and rates were cut ruinously, while our citizens enjoyed the spectacle and saved their pockets at the same time. They forgot that tomorrow always comes. With such a competition duly inaugurated and a rate war in progress there can be three, and only three, results.[1]

In the first place, selling water at a loss, the company with the smallest capital, being less capacitated to stand the strain, will go under. The other company will now be a monopoly and its first move will be to retrench. It will make the Oaklanders who enjoyed the low rates sweat, by raising them.

In the second place, the fight may be so bitter and show such signs of long continuance, that the wealthier company will buy out the poorer one. What follows? It has been forced to double its invested capital and to obtain a dividend on the same, equivalent to its previous dividend, it will have to double the previous rates. Also, having lost money during the period of competition, it will further raise the rates in order to reimburse itself.

In the third place, if both companies have about equal strength, they may continue the war till both are in the verge of bankruptcy. Then they will awake to the dangers of the situation. They will confer with each other and come to the conclusion that if it is properly managed, both may reap good dividends on the investment. They will then pool interests and mutually raise the rates to any height agreed upon. Since double the capital is now invested, double the interest is required and that the old rates will be doubled to obtain it, is a foregone conclusion.

Outside of these three, there is no other way in which the competition of the Oakland water companies can be settled. The reaction will have come—the opium eater will have awakened!

The Valley railroad can be thus analyzed,[2] and so, in fact, can every similar scheme. If one company is ably fitted to perform its business, the eruption of a second can but end in one of the ways I have mentioned. If the company is too small to handle the business required of it and another small company appears on the scene, there can be very little competition for neither will be in the position to grasp the other's trade, while, if the new company is of sufficient magnitude, it will freeze the older one out.

If, in a community of 100 workers, all of them are at work legitimately producing the necessaries and luxuries of life, one would decide that it were more prosperous than a second community of 100 workers, in which twenty were engaged in the unremunerative task of pumping the ocean dry. Suppose Dingee[3] employed 500 men for one year of 300 working days, the day's labor being ten hours. Then 1,500,000 hours of labor have been uselessly, spuriously expended since the Contra Costa Water Company was well able to supply Oakland with water.

It seems apparent that such competition necessitates a waste of labor and capital, and always results in monopoly. Is there any path out of the wilderness? Can the reader suggest a remedy for Oakland's rival water companies? If he cannot, I would ask him if he has ever heard of municipal ownership?

Jack London.

SOURCE: *Oakland Times*, August 12, 1896; also pbd. *Oakland Item*, date unknown.

   1. In 1866 the Contra Costa Water Company was formed to furnish Oakland and its suburbs with fresh water, first from Temescal Creek and later, in 1875, from San Leandro Creek. Over the next two decades the company built a reservoir containing nearly six billion gallons of water and installed about two hundred and seventy-five miles of pipe to distribute the water. On December 15, 1893, the Oakland Water Company, with a capital stock of three million dollars, incorporated to compete with the Contra Costa Water Company. It supplied water from artesian wells near Alvarado and duplicated the existing supplier's distribution network. From the outset competition was intense and often violent: a series of rate wars, which caused prices to drop from four dollars a month to twenty-five cents a month for residential customers, and sabotage of facilities by the rival companies lasted for three years and threatened the existence of both. On May 15, 1899, the Contra Costa Water Company took over the Oakland Water Company.

   2. In 1896 the Valley Road was begun to compete with the Southern Pacific Railroad in the San Joaquin Valley. Originally intended to operate from Oakland to Bakersfield, the new line at first ran only between Stockton and Fresno. In 1897 it expanded to Bakersfield, but was taken over that same year by the Atcheson, Topeka and Santa Fe.

   3. William J. Dingee (*b.* 1853), president of the Oakland Water Company and a land developer in Alameda County.

To the Editor, *Oakland Times*

[Oakland]

[August 24, 1896]

Editor *Times*:—

   A correspondent has announced through your columns the not very recent discovery of a panacea guaranteed to cure all social ills. He holds that this elixir is single tax.[1] But there are some discrepancies in this proposition, worthy of mention.

It is asserted that single tax will force the large land-holders to give up their possessions and thus allow the landless to gain and work them for their own. One cannot deny this truth as regards land, the owners of which allow it to remain idle, waiting for a rise in value. But competition would still reign, and, while the single tax would not permit the worker of rich soil to undersell the worker of poor soil, it would not, could not interfere with the workers of equal soil.

Suppose A has fifty acres adjacent to 10,000 acres of B, and both are raising wheat. It is a truth that needs no interrogation, that B can produce wheat, ready for market, at a less cost than A. Hence—a logical conclusion—with competition active, B can undersell A (of course, not willingly, but he is forced to through the middleman handling his products). The land value is equal as regards productiveness, though B, having greater capital invested in land and machinery, produces not more in proportion but more cheaply. In fact, single tax, as it is preached by Henry George, cannot touch B. As a result, all the large B's will crowd the small A's to the wall. If an attempt is made to reduce this inequality by imposing a higher tax on B, single tax would have to be discarded, for this would be in direct contradiction.

In the first place, Henry George has elaborated a theory of land-values, a condensation of which is as follows: Land in the primeval prairie is valueless. A settler comes along and goes to farming, and while he may continue to improve it till doomsday, it will never be worth more than the value of the improvements, for on all sides is the same land to be obtained for nothing. But a second, a third and a fourth man settles around the first-comer. Now comes into play the land value, for soon there is no longer any land without an owner. Each successive settler has raised the price of land by the mere virtue of his reducing the quantity of unoccupied land. A and B, having their land equally productive and equally well situated, cannot either value his at more than the other. A tax levied otherwise would not be the orthodox single tax.

In the second place, if a heavier tax were placed on B than on A, because he could produce more cheaply, it would actually, though indirectly, be a tax upon his improvements in the way of machinery, etc. This would not be single tax, which does not apply to such.

Again, since the single tax is not levied, on improvements, capital will continue to run all the factories, and on a barren rock with but a nominal tax, an untaxable building can be reared and filled with untaxable machinery. What can single tax do to prevent the holders of their capital from enriching their coffers to the tune of several millions annually? Furthermore what is to prevent these holders from investing their gains in land, buying up the small A's crowded out by the large B's?

The three factors of wealth are land, labor and capital. Land is already created; labor is self-creative; and capital is but the unconsumed surplus of the wealth created by the application of labor to land. Hence labor produces all wealth. Taxes are paid in wealth; labor produces all wealth; therefore, labor pays all taxes. If single tax reduces all to material equality (which it cannot), then why not impose a tax on all of so much a head? It would be far simpler.

But, John McLees, you are on the right track: pursue it. Single tax has been the preparatory school for tens of thousands of socialists in England and the United States. You have become possessed of many truths. You say, "No man can justly reap where he has not sown." "The necessary thing yet to be provided is a system of equitable distribution of the products of labor." "Leaving to labor its products, will very soon cause all to become industrious and want presently will disappear." "The right of each to a share in the use of the soil can no more be taken away than the right to live, as the one involves the other." All this is socialism. Read Carl Marx's *Capital*; get a grasp of the economics of socialism; discover that equitable production is as of equal importance as equitable distribution; and you will have gained the path by which your goal is to be attained.[1]

As long as the single tax advocate allows money to breed money; as long as he allows one man to pocket the major portion of the wealth produced by another; as long as he allows middle-man B, to buy from producer A, and sell to consumer C; that long will the increasing distress of the masses, divorced from land, capital and machinery, continue.

Jack London.

SOURCE: *Oakland Times*, August 24, 1896.

1. JL was responding to John McLees, "The Single Tax Theory," *Oakland Times*, August 22, 1896. McLees argued: "Labor saving machinery is not an evil; the less labor we are forced to perform in supplying our wants the better we are suited. The necessary thing yet to be provided is a system of equitable distribution of the products of labor. No man can justly reap where he has not sown. Idle land can be made free to those who need its use by collecting [for] public uses the annual rent from those who hold it whether in use or not. Leaving to labor its product will very soon cause all to become industrious and want presently to disappear. The just application of the single tax is the thing needed to restore prosperity." McLees was summarizing the ideas of the American economist Henry George (1839–97), set forth in *Progress and Poverty* (1879), that land and natural resources are the source of all wealth and that, by appropriating economic rents as the sole, or single, tax, governments could eliminate poverty. George's theory had been taken up by a nationwide movement of single taxers, which was particularly strong in the San Francisco area, where *Progress and Poverty* had been written. In his letter, JL counters the single taxers' belief that exclusive ownership of land was the sole basis of economic exploitation with Marx's labor theory of value and a socialist concern with all the means of production. See *JL Times*, 114–15.

2. JL began his own reading of Marx, John Ruskin, William Morris, and other writers on politics and economics during his affiliation with the Henry Clay Club, a debating society that existed from 1891 to 1896 and was made up of boys from Oakland high schools. JL took *Das Kapital* with him to the Klondike.

To Edward Applegarth

1327–25th Ave.
East Oakland
June 22, 1897.

Dear Ted:–[1]

I hardly know what to write—stamps are ephemeral—last week I had half-a-dollar's worth. Next week I shall receive numerous letters all graced on the outside by that same half-dollar's worth of stamps[2]—this is why I have Mabel[3] forward this.

As for news, I am completely stagnated. I have none. I have isolated myself in almost claustral seclusion in my sanctum sanctorum, and am grinding out article after article.

Do you think there would be any chance for a market in London? I am turning out better work than ever before.

Positively, I do not know what to write. Don't tell me about the Jubilee[4]—the papers can do it much better.

If you do not read our papers, or rather, since you do not, let me give you one bit of news. Organized labor, headed by Debs & beginning with the American Railway Union, has commenced a change of front. The old method of strikes & boycotts to obtain shorter hours & better pay has been abandoned. They now strike for political power, their openly-avowed goal being the co-operative commonwealth.[5] That is, the Socialist propaganda in the United States is assuming greater proportions.

Jack London.

MS: CSt; 2 pp., als.

1. Edward (Ted) Applegarth (1876–1964), English-born friend whom JL had met in the Henry Clay Club. Like JL, Applegarth was a neophyte writer. His family lived in Oakland and later moved to San Jose.

2. JL refers to manuscripts sent to magazine editors with return postage. The spring and summer of 1897 was a period of intense creative activity.

3. Mabel Maude Applegarth (1873–1915), sister of Ted Applegarth. She was JL's first serious love and became the model for Ruth Morse in *Martin Eden* (New York: Macmillan, 1909). JL probably first met her in 1895, when she was a student at the University of California at Berkeley.

4. Probably Victoria's Diamond Jubilee, held on June 22, 1897, to celebrate the sixtieth anniversary of the Queen's accession to the crown. Applegarth may have been in London to cover this story for a newspaper.

5. Eugene V. Debs (1855–1926), labor organizer, socialist leader, and first president of the American Railway Union, organized in 1893. In 1894 the union successfully struck against the Great Northern Railroad and the Pullman Palace Car Company; for his part in the Pullman strike, Debs was arrested and served a six-month prison sentence. In 1897, after his conversion to socialism, the American Railway Union was dissolved, and in its place the Social Democracy of America was founded, with Debs as chairman. Among its programs, the new organization adopted the utopian-socialist colonizing scheme of the Brotherhood of the Co-operative Commonwealth, with which Debs had earlier been involved; this proposed setting up pilot industrial cooperatives in a sparsely populated West-

ern state, which socialist immigration would subsequently capture as a socialist political entity. See Bernard J. Brommel, *Eugene V. Debs: Spokesman for Labor and Socialism* (Chicago, 1978), pp. 46–64; and *JL Times*, 121–22.

To Mabel Applegarth

Dyea,[1]
August 8, 1897.

Dear Mabel: –

I am laying on the grass in sight of a score of glaciers, yet the slight exertion of writing causes me to sweat prodigously.

We lay several days in Juneau, then hired canoes & paddled 100 miles to our present quarters. The Indians with us brought along their Squaws, papooses & dogs. Had a pleasant time. The 100 miles lay between mountains which formed a Yosemite Valley the whole length, & in many places the heights were stupendous. Glaciers & waterfalls on every side. Yesterday a snow slide occurred & the rumble & roar extended for fully a minute.

I expect to carry 100 lbs. to the load on good trail & on the worst, 75 lbs. That is, for every mile to the Lakes,[2] I will have to travel from 20 to 30 miles. I have 1000 lbs. in my outfit. I have to divide it into from 10 to fifteen loads according to the trail. I take a load a mile & come back empty that makes two miles. 10 loads means 19 miles, for I do not have to come back after the 11th. load for there is none. If I have 15 loads it means 29 miles.

Am certain we will reach the lake in 30 days.

Including Indians there are about 2000 people here & half as many at Skagawa Bay, 5 miles from here.

Pleas forward to Teddy—have little time to write now—but next winter will be able to write good, long, & real letters. This is not a letter—but am to rushed for anything better.

Yours
Jack London

MS: CSt; 2 pp., als.

1. News of the discovery of gold in the Klondike had reached the United States in July 1897. JL left San Francisco for Juneau aboard the *Umatilla* on July 25, 1897; from there he traveled to Dyea, Dawson, and Henderson Creek. See the map on pp. xxxvi–xxxvii.

2. Lakes Lindeman, Bennett, Tagish, Marsh, and Laberge, northeast of Dyea, were en route from Dyea to Dawson.

To Edward Applegarth

962 East 16th st.
Oakland, Calif.,
Sept. 13th 1898.

Dear Ted:—

Yours of 31st. ult. at hand. A thousand pardons for not writing sooner but I have not really been home very long. Right after my arrival I was off to the mountains on a prospecting trip & have but recently returned, *sans* result. Very blundering of you, I am sure, addressing my letters "Dyea." But all's well that ends well.

As to my trip—I came down with scurvy in May, fought it off till June 7th. & then, in company of two others, pulled out from Dawson to St. Michaels in a small boat. We did those two thousand miles of river & sea in 21 days, including all delays & stopovers.[1] I did not bring anything out with me. My partners[2] are still on the inside and it all depends as to what they write me whether I go back in February or not. As to what I may make out of our claims I don't know—maybe nothing, maybe several thousand— *Quien Sabe?*

Mrs. Applegarth is still in the mountains but Mabel is back—she looks & seems about the same but I imagine that she does not weigh as much. Fred & Herbert are off to Manilla[3]—I assure you I don't envy them—not the danger or the hardship, for they are incomparable with an Alaskan trip, but what they must put up with from their superiors. A soldier's life is a dog's life at the best. As to the war, I was in favor of it, & social-istically too, strange as it may seem. While contractors & speculaters may have made money out of it, I feel sure that money was not the motive power. As all the institutions of men are but the transient guises or rather formulas of evolution, it is easily apparent that political democracy must come before industrial democracy. The Hispano-American, or as some call it the Yanko-Spanko, War was but a stroke against monarchy & for political democracy—the latter gradually grows into industrial democ-racy—and there it is, perfect political & industrial democracy combined are really what?—Socialism. Yet I see that we are being classed with the anarchists in reference to the recent assassination of the Empress of Aus-tria.[4] Still, while I unqualifiedly condemn such heroic measures as utterly wrong, my sympathy goes out to the poor devil who faces life imprison-ment for his act, and there are really two sides to the question. The gen-eral public calls it wrong to kill a harmless old woman. But in the first place there was no personal animus—she merely represented an institu-tion or rather was one of a group of individuals, whose existence as mem-bers of the group is pernicious & unwholesome for the rest of mankind. In the second place, nature, evoloution, call it what you will, or rather, come to think of it, Natural Selection does away with such organs of the individual that become useless or detrimental. Such a position the Empress occupied in relation to the social organism. When the drones can no longer subserve the general welfare of the hive they are removed by the worker-bees. That poor devil of an anarchist worked for his living—By God! What did the Empress do? She took a portion of the revenue wrung from the toilers & spent it on her self, whether in good eating or sleeping, dress, jewels or racehorses, she spent what the producer should have spent. In short, she was (though not commonly recognized as such) an anachronism. The place for her & hers in society, no longer practically exists. Durrant was considered a useless appendage to society & a menace;[5] the coyote likewise has suffered in California. It was not Durrant's fault that he was born Durrant, nor the coyote's fault that it was born a coyote—but their interests & actions clashed with those of society—in the eyes of social evoloution they were rudimentary & dangerous— society removed them. Poor woman it was not her fault for she was born so, she simply clashed with the unsentimental action of immutable law & perished. Survival of the Fittest raised her & hers to their lofty pinnacle. Survival of the Fittest will dash them down again, But enough of such things.

On the chance that nothing comes from the Clondyke & that I do not go back I purpose taking the Civil Service Exs. for the P.O. the first of October. My sister[6] seems unchanged though her lungs are not very strong. Jessie is going with a Fred Jergerwitz—six foot some odd in his stocking feet, weighing a couple of hundred pounds & a bicycle racer.[7] They expect to get married. God prosper them. If I were footloose I would be pulling out for London. I've got my jaw set however & I'll be there yet.

Is Will Brockmann's address London W.C.—or what are those two letters at the end & what do they stand for?

By the way, Ernestine[8] informs me that J. C. discovered we were corresponding & mentioned it in your household & that some way you got wind of the same thing—Who told you? I am a little curious. Don't mention it to Ernestine however, if you write her. She is in 'Frisco now, typewriting but I have as yet failed to visit her. What do you think of that? Can you conceive it to be the same old Jack?

In poetry, as everything else, results are judged, rather than legitimacy. Our best writers are full of technical errors. If you can bend the technique to the sense, the former not being glaring & the latter the real thought & utterance of poetry, I am sure it is pardonable. Scan the blank verse of some of the strongest of Shakspear & you will find that I am right. Poetry in the English language is bound to always be stilted, but the true aim of the artist should be, or the very essence of the art is to reduce the stilt to a minimum & still musically voice the poetic thought or fancy. Take Longfellows "Psalm of Life"[9] break up the stanzas & let line, or rather, verse follow verse, in prose style retaining same punctuation, and what do you find? That thought follows on thought, clause follows clause & sentence follows sentence so that if you for the moment could eliminate your consciousness of metre & rhyme, you would remark what a perfect prose style it was.

As against it array this verse from Browning:

> "So I said & did
> Simply. As simply followed, not at first
> But with the outbreak of misfortune, still
> One comment on the saying & doing—what?
> No blush at the avowal you dared buy
> A girl of age beseems your grand daughter,
> Like ox or ass?"
> —*The Ring & the Book*.[10]

I like your poems, and as I am replying at once, have not had time to choose my favorite. One thing you have got, and you have it good—it is the very essence & the fundament principle of poetry; it is real poetical thought & fancy. Without it, there can be no poetry, though miles & miles of perfect, musical metre & ryhme[11] be written. Turn to Chaucer's *Canterbury Tales*. Open at the poet's tale.[12] It is a bit against the French style existing at that time; which consisted of beautiful verse most remarkable for both its beauty & absence of thought. The poet goes on & on but what does he tell? Nothing, absolutely nothing. You will notice that the audience grows impatient & the poet is finally forced to tell his tale in prose, the only prose tale in the whole collection.

I like your preferred ending in "The Law of Actions," better.

Outside of that let me scan your double set of 2nd. & 3rd. stanzas on the following page showing imperfect & halting meter. (By the way, you call a stanza a verse—remember that a verse is a line.)[13]

With all force as ye could see	1. With all force as ye could see
(If ye fairly sought it),	2. . . . .
Thát ef/fécts must/fóllow/caúse	3. Caúse &/efféct/must év/er bé/
(But perhaps ye thought it)	4. . . . .
Fóllow/álways/thé same/wáy	5. Fóllow/ing ín/the sélf/same wáy/
For they cannot go astray.	6. For they cannot go astray.
With all mind, as ye shall know	7. With all mind as ye shall know
. . . .	. . . .
Mind effects must follow cause	9. Mínd ef/fects áf/ter caúse/must gó/
. . . .	. . . .
Follow as the night the day	. . . .
And they cannot go astray	. . . .
	(Don't mind pencil scanning)

Scan the two third lines: —∪/—∪/—∪/— and —∪/∪—/∪—/∪—/. Fifth lines &
ninth lines you will notice have similar error on scanning. All you have to
do is to repeat first one line & then the other to notice the tremendous
difference. You may have thought that you were writing this in Iambic but
it is really trochaic. I mistook it at first. The preferred stanza is the perfect
stanza. The 1, 3, 5 & 6 verses of preferred stanza are Trunctated Trochaic
Tetrameter.

Trunctated means that the final unaccented syllable is cut off, thus:

> Thát ef/fécts must/fóllow/caúse—/

The trouble in writing this is that in the middle of the verse you are
liable to jump the meter & go over to Iambic.

You will notice that the 2 & 4 verses are perfect Trochaic trimeter, thus

> Íf ye/fáirly/soúght it/

The combinations of trunctated Trochaic Tetrameter verses with perfect
Trochaic trimeter, make beautiful poetry.

You will also notice that in the third, fifth & ninth verses of unpreferred
Stanzas, that in scanning no elision is possible for making the meter ring
true.

Take the next to last verse in "Problem of Evil": On the rock of evoloution. There is no verse like it in the whole poem.

It breaks the unity of meter & is a positive discord, a discord coming
above all at the very last when the final taste is being left in our mouth,
and said taste must be good. You know the effect of anti-climax in style;
this has the same effect only more so.

I like the ring of your verse: "Above all, below all, & in all." Never
sacrifice thought to sound, ryhme or meter. If you cannot clothe the
thought without injuring it—throw it away.

In the first verse of "A Question" you have the word "blinking." To
make this ryhme you prostitute the thought & the sound. There is no real
poetical delicacy in the sound or the thought of "blinking."

Take for instance, "grinding"—in the description of a May morning or
a lover's song, it would have no poetic sound, it would be a discord. Yet
use it in describing a great disaster or battle & you will see at once, *by its
sound*,[14] describes the things & the feelings that they cause.

Take Tennyson's "Bugle Song" for an illustration of imitative sound.
Feel the *hush* that breathes forth from

> "The splendor falls on castle walls
> And snowy summits old in story."

And the *pure* tone, so *thin & clear*[15] of

> "O hark, O hear! how thin & clear,
> And thinner, clearer, farther going,

> O sweet & far, from cliff & scar,
> The horns of Elfland faintly blowing."

And the full, deep feeling from

> O love, they die in yon rich sky,
> They faint on hill or field or river;
> *Our* echoes *roll from soul* to *soul*,
> And *grow forever & forever*." [16]

> As the sea shell's song seems ever
> A sad echo of the sea." This is simply magnificent—
a delicate fancy, perfectly & most delicately clothed.

But in same poem your "sad sad" and "solemn solemn" constitutes one of the worst conditions of *pleonasm* or *Superfluity*, that of *repetition*. Now *repetition* is sometimes most necessary & most powerful, but you must exercise your discretion & *taste*. As you know, taste is a most important attribute to true *poesy*.

Look up the use of *alliteration* and *assonance*—great factors for putting music, over & above meter & ryhme, into poetry.

In your line "Above all, below all & in all" you will notice the full, round sound called the *orotund*, expressive of deep feeling, a sort of soul reaching sound. Compare with "Our echoes roll from soul to soul."

In "To the Children" capitalize "might have been" Might have been. It is proper, it diversifies the mere look of the verse, and is significant & impressive.

Your verse breathes a faint perfume as it seems to me of Swineburne, Tennyson & Browning—thought especially in relation to the latter. But I don't know as I have read no poetry for 14 months & am very rusty in all such things. But go ahead old man, you are doing dam well, send us some more.

I must close this letter as I have been writing like a tiger all day, it is now past one in the morning & I must be up at five to go riding with Mabel. Your letter just came & I reply at once.

Previous to my going to the Clondyke, I had just taken up the study of poetry individually. Will send you my every attempt. Since my return I have written just four verses—wrote them this morning as an introduction to the article I am now on—a sort of keynote you know:

> We worshipped at alien altars; we bowed our heads in the dust;
> Our law was might is the mightiest; our creed was unholy lust;
> Our law & our creed we followed—strange is the tale to tell—
> For our law & our creed we followed into the pit of hell.
> —*The Mammon Worshippers.*[17]

You will notice the *pleonasm*—I believe that it gives power here—too long to go into discussion however.

"Socialists Dream" was first attempt to merely think in meter—full of errors.

"Je Ris Espoir" "Hors de Saison" "Day break," were experiments in feminine endings.

"Gold," strange to say was just being written when I left [18]—It was my really first & only flight. You will see that I attempted an improvement on the "Spenserian Stanza" by adding a second Iambic hexameter verse.

Please return poetry as I have no duplicates.

Your affectionate chum

Jack London.

MS: CSt; 16 pp., als.

1. JL remained in the Northland until early July 1898, when he left St. Michael, Alaska, for Port Townsend, Washington, aboard the schooner *Bartlett*. From there he took a steamer to San Francisco. The best study of JL's Northland experience is Franklin Walker, *Jack London and the Klondike: The Genesis of an American Writer* (San Marino, Calif., 1966).

2. Capt. James H. Shepard, JL's brother-in-law and grubstake; Ira Merritt Sloper; Jim Goodman; and Fred C. Thompson. For a firsthand account of their trip, see David Mike Hamilton, ed., *To the Yukon with Jack London: The Klondike Diary of Fred Thompson* (Los Angeles, 1980).

3. Fred Jacobs (*d.* 1898), JL's schoolmate at Oakland High School and Anderson's University Academy in Alameda, a school that prepared students to pass the entrance examinations for the University of California; Jacobs had introduced JL to Ted Applegarth and also privately tutored JL in chemistry and physics. Herbert Shepard, son of Captain Shepard. The Spanish-American War was declared on April 20, 1898, and the U.S. occupation of the Philippines had been in effect since August 14. Jacobs, who had been employed at the Oakland Public Library, enlisted as a private in the hospital corps.

4. Elizabeth, Empress of Austria (1837–98), wife of Emperor Francis Joseph I, was assassinated in Geneva on September 10, 1898, by an Italian anarchist named Luigi Lucheni.

5. Theodore Durrant, "the demon in the belfry," executed at San Quentin on January 7, 1898, for the sensational murders of two young women in a San Francisco church where he served as assistant Sunday School superintendent.

6. Probably Ida London Miller (1870–1914), JL's stepsister, daughter of John London.

7. Jessie Shepard, daughter of Captain Shepard; Fred Jurgewitz, her future husband, who lived at 1017 East 16th St.

8. Possibly Ernestine Conghram, who later became a journalist and wrote under the pseudonym Nan Byxbie for the *San Francisco Morning Call* and the *Seattle Daily Star*. See also JL to Johns, December 5, 1899.

9. First published in Longfellow's *Voices of the Night* (1838).

10. Robert Browning, "Count Guido Franceschini," *The Ring and the Book* (1868–69), ll. 421–27.

11. Here JL crossed out "rhyme" for the spelling "ryhme," which he then used throughout the letter.

12. In *The Canterbury Tales*, Chaucer assigns two tales to himself. The first is the *Tale of Sir Thopas*, which ridicules the chivalric romances written by his contemporaries; when this tale is interrupted, Chaucer's persona begins the *Tale of Melibee*, a tedious prose translation of a French moral tale.

13. JL wrote the poem and the first five sentences of the following paragraph on a separate, interspersed sheet. The manuscript shows traces of his initial attempt to scan the verses as iambic; in the third and fifth lines, iambic divisions have been marked, then partially erased.

14. JL underlined "sound" three times.

15. JL underlined "hush," "thin," and "clear" twice.

16. Alfred Tennyson, "The splendour falls on castle walls," from *The Princess* (1847). JL quotes ll. 1–2, 7–10, and 13–16.

17. "The Mammon Worshippers" was written as an introduction to "The Devil's Dice Box." On September 23, 1898, this article was sent to *McClure's Magazine,* a popular illustrated monthly published in New York from 1893 to 1929 (when it was merged with *New Smart Set*). JL's manuscript was rejected and subsequently retired after several rejections from other magazines; it has been published in the *Saturday Evening Post,* December 1976.

18. "The Socialist's Dream," "Je Ris En Espoir" (I [live] in hope), "Hors de Saison" (out of season), "At Daybreak," and "Gold" were evidently written in July 1897 before JL departed for Alaska. On the typescript of his poem, as well as in this letter, JL wrote "Je Ris En Espoir"; however, he probably meant to write "Je Vis En Espoir," for the first line of each of the first four stanzas begins "I live in hope." Only "At Daybreak" was published: first submitted on July 8, 1897, to the *Wasp,* a literary weekly published in San Francisco from 1868 until 1928, it was then sent to several other magazines before being submitted on July 13, 1899, to the *National,* a general-interest illustrated monthly emphasizing national affairs and published in Boston from 1894 until 1933; JL's poem appeared in the *National,* August 1901, as "Daybreak."

To the Editor, *San Francisco Bulletin*

Oakland, Calif.
Sept. 17, 1898

Dear Sir:–

I have returned from a year's residence in the Clondyke, entering the country by way of Dyea and Chilcoot Pass. I left by way of St. Michaels, thus making altogether a journey of 2,500 miles on the Yukon in a small boat. I have sailed and traveled quite extensively in other parts of the world and have learned to seize upon that which is interesting, to grasp the true romance of things, and to understand the people I may be thrown amongst.

I have just completed an article of 4,000 words,[1] describing the trip from Dawson to St. Michaels in a rowboat. Kindly let me know if there would be any demand in your columns for it—of course, thoroughly understanding that the acceptance of the manuscript is to depend upon its literary and intrinsic value.

Yours very respectfully,
Jack London[2]

SOURCE: *L,* 3; also pbd. *Pictorial Life,* 83.

1. "From Dawson to the Sea," eventually published in the *Illustrated Buffalo Express,* June 4, 1899.

2. The editor answered in longhand on the bottom of JL's letter: "Interest in Alaska has subsided in an amazing degree. Then, again, so much has been written, that I do not think it would pay us to buy your story." Across the top, in CKL's hand, is written: "This is Jack's first letter to an editor" (*L,* 3, n. 1).

To Edward Applegarth

962 East 16th. st.,
Nov. 14, 1898.

Dear Ted:–

Yours of 13th. inst. at hand: am so sorry to hear that Mabel is ill. Don't procrastinate, but let me know quickly how she is getting along. Tell her that I have such a long letter for her, and that I have so much else on hand that I don't know how I am going to get at it.

Saw Bess[1] the other day. We will ride down if it don't rain; otherwise, the boat. Shall let you know beforehand. Authentic news has come of Fred's death, from an Oakland man who was with him when he died. He was buried at Manila with military honors. So be it. He has only solved the mystery a little quicker than the rest of us.

I think it was rather supererogatory to ask me to write what I thought of your poems to you and not to Mabel. When did I ever do anything like that?

Let x be accented, and a unaccented syllable. You give me this as a metre: x / a a x / a a x x / .

There is no such a foot as / a a x x / .

The last foot of your first verse is "of the twilight." Now you cannot pronounce twilight and accent both syllables; the first syllable is the proper accent. The same is true of "firelight." Here's your proper metre: x / a a x / a a x / a . You understand that the accents are not considered abstractly, but in relation to each other; for instance:

> When the bridegroom cometh
> x / a x / a x / a

In this case "groom" is unaccented; yet in this metre you'll find "groom" accented:

> I am the bride and the groom.
> x / a a x / a a x /

By the way, in the last line, "Soundless and silently say" notice the peculiar syntax—the conjunction connecting an adjective and an adverb; also the pleonasm.

God and life are one—you wouldn't say "Jack and Jill is married."

> "I heard that I
> Were doomed to die."

This is an exquisite little metre. But a question arises; is this the subjunctive mood. I don't think so. Still, strange to say, while it is an error in syntax, it does not offend the ear.

Perhaps your suggestion of an esoteric meaning has made me over-conscious, for to save my life I cannot catch any hidden significance. If it is an allegory, I fail to catch it; I can imagine it a dream.

Though not quite like, it reminds me of Herrick's "Headache"[2]

> My head doth ache,
> O Sappho, take
>   Thy fillet
> And bind the pain,
> Or bring some bane
>   To kill it.
>
> But less that part
> Than my poor heart
>   Now is sick:
> One kiss from thee
> Will counsel be
>   And physic.

Rhymes to song are: long—prong—strong—thong—throng—wrong—along—among—belong—ding-dong—prolong—bon-vivant—

"Any gladsome, joyous song" is pleonastic. "Rare refrain" has a nicer sound than "sweet refrain," besides being sweetly alliterative; but I can not judge between them. Use your own judgement and taste—"a rare refrain" and "a sweet refrain" both are good, both are nice, both are appropriate.

Why don't you try your hand at the ballade, the rondel, the rondeau, the roundel, the rondelay, the triolet, the sestina, or the villanelle? They are all pretty structures, and so severe as to give the best of training in versification.

Everybody well at 1068.[3] Stagnation of news up here.

Yours very sincerely,
Jack London.

MS: CSt; 2 pp., tls.

1. Bessie May Maddern (1876–1947), JL's first wife. Bessie Maddern was the daughter of an Oakland plumber and had been engaged to marry Fred Jacobs, who died aboard the troop transport *Scandia* in transit to Manila. Through Jacobs she had met JL in 1896 and had tutored him for his mathematics entrance examinations at the University of California. In 1898 she was coaching students in order to pay for her own college education.

2. Robert Herrick, "The Head-ake," in *Hesperides* (1648).

3. The address of JL's stepsister, Eliza London Shepard, was 1068 East 16th St., Oakland.

To Mabel Applegarth

962 East 16th. st.,
Nov. 16, 1898.

Dear Mabel:—

Mother[1] is sick and things are in confusion, so you must put up with a short letter. She has some stomach trouble—I never heard of an epidemic of stomach complaints, but this seems to be the matter. Mrs. Winkler and daughter were bothered with this. The other day I met Mammy Jennie,[2] and she told me that she had nearly died with it, citing numerous cases of similar sickness among her friends. Perhaps this is what the matter is with you. The doctors proclaim it to be an epidemic.

After Jessie[3] and everybody had gone, last night, I wrote the following before going to bed. It is my first attempt in the ballade line. The ballade structure is much stricter than that of the sonnet, and more closely confines one's thought. The rhymes must follow the initiative of the first stanza and occur in precisely the same order throughout. But you can work out the rules for yourself. Show it to Ted, as I recently mentioned a number of similar old French forms, and told him to try them as they would give the best of training in versification—the very severity and confinement forces one to be thorough.

I can only hope your illness is not serious, and that ere this, you have gained your feet again. Bess and I expect to ride down the day after Thanksgiving, if it don't rain; otherwise, the boat.

Very sincerely yours,
Jack.

MS: CSt; 1 p., tls.

1. Flora Wellman London (1843–1921), born in Massillon, Ohio. She moved to Seattle when she was a teenager. There she met William H. Chaney (1821–1902), an astrologer; they moved to San Francisco and lived for nearly a year as Mr. and Mrs. William H. Chaney. During that time JL was conceived. She married John London (1828–97) on September 7, 1876, eight months after JL's birth.

2. Virginia Prentiss, a former slave who married Alonzo T. Prentiss, a carpenter friend of John London. "Mammy Jennie" was JL's wet nurse when Flora London was unable to nurse her son. She and her husband lived at 15 Priest Street, San Francisco.

3. Jessie Shepard.

To Mabel Applegarth

962 East 16th. st.,
Nov. 27, 1898.

Dear Mabel:—

Forgive my not writing, for I have been miserable and half sick. So nervous this morning that I could hardly shave myself. I knew by Thanksgiving that you were expecting me; but I delayed, hoping to start every day and everyday. And now, I receive a letter from Frank Atherton,[1] telling me that he will arrive either Monday night or Tuesday morning. So if things should come my way, I would be unable to go to College Park till he finishes his visit.

Everything seems to have gone wrong—why, I have'nt received my twenty dollars for those essays yet.[2] Not a word as to how I stood in my Civil Service Exs.[3] Not a word from the *Youth's Companion*,[4] and it means to me what no one can possibly realize.

You seem to misunderstand. I thought I made it perfectly plain, that those squibs of poetry were merely diversions and experiments; yet you say—"But always the same theme." Theme had nothing to do with it; they were studies in structure and versification. Though it took me a long while, I have learned my lesson, and thanks to no one. I made ambitious efforts once. It makes me laugh to look back on them, though sometimes I am nearer to weeping. I was the greenest of tyros, dipping my brush into whitewash and coal-tar, and without the slightest knowledge of perspective, proportion or color, attempted masterpieces—without a soul to say "you are all wrong; herein you err; there is your mistake."[5]

Why, that poem on gold is one of the finest object-lessons in my possession—Ted has it now. I was ambitious in that. With no more comprehension of the aims and principles of poetry, than a crab, I proposed or rather, purposed to make something which would be something. I would strike out on new trails; I would improve upon the Spencerian Stanza; I would turn things upside down. So I tried what has been probably tried a thousand times and discarded because it was worthless; one Alexandrine at the end of the stanza was not enough; I added a second. I treated my theme as Dryden or Thompson[6] would have treated it. My elephantine diction was superb—I out-Johnsoned Johnson. I was a fool—and no one to tell me.

So you see, to-day, I am unlearning and learning anew, and as such things are merely principles, you can readily see why I don't care a snap for the theme. I have played Darius Green[7] once, and if my neck is broken a second time it will be my own fault. I shall not be ready for any flights till my flying machine is perfected, and to that perfection I am now applying myself. Until then, to the deuce with themes. I shall subordinate thought to technique till the latter is mastered; then I shall do vice a versa.

I do not know when I can be down—I may be digging sewers or shoveling coal next week. Am glad to hear you are better. Give my regards to every body.

Good bye,
Jack.

MS: CSmH; 2 pp., tls. Pbd: *L*, 3–4; *BJL*, I, 263–64; *Pictorial Life*, 85.

1. Frank Atherton, a classmate of JL at the Cole Grammar School in West Oakland and his closest boyhood friend. When Atherton married, JL was his best man. After JL had sepa-

rated from Bessie, the Athertons shared his apartment at 1216 Telegraph Avenue in Oakland. For an account of Atherton's reminiscences, see his "Jack London in Boyhood Adventures" (MS: CSmH).

2. JL won two prizes for essays, worth ten dollars each, in the Oakland Fifth Ward Republican Club contest for campaign songs, essays, cartoons, and poems. Evidently he was never paid. See JL to M. Applegarth, ? December 31, 1898.

3. JL had taken the Civil Service Examination for mail carrier on October 1, 1898, at the Oakland Post Office. See JL to M. Applegarth, January 28, 1899.

4. JL's 21,000-word, 7-chapter serial "Where Boys Are Men" was sent on October 29, 1898, to the *Youth's Companion*, a juvenile and family weekly published in Boston from 1827 until 1929. Subsequently rejected by this magazine, it was accepted by *Youth and Age* on May 2, 1899, but was never published.

5. Possibly Robert Browning, "My Last Duchess" (1842), ll. 37–39: "'Just this / Or that in you disgusts me; here you miss, / Or there exceed the mark.'"

6. James Thomson (1700–1748), Scottish poet, author of *The Seasons*.

7. In "Darius Green and His Flying Machine," a humorous poem by John Townsend Trowbridge collected in *The Vagabond and Other Poems* (1869), when Darius Green tests his contraption, instead of flying, he falls to earth, landing on his head.

To Mabel Applegarth

962 East 16th. st.,
Nov. 30, 1898.

Dear Mabel:—

Am replying at once. As to that medicine: since there is no certainty to my plans, I think it would be best to send up money to me and order to Owl Drug Co. Send at once, so Frank can take it back with him. He does not go before Saturday, and the chances are that he will stay even longer.

I do appreciate your interest in my affairs, but—we have no common ground. In a general, vaguely general, way, you know my aspirations; but of the real Jack, his thoughts, feelings, etc., you are positively ignorant. Yet, little as you do know, you know more about me than any body else. I have fought and am fighting my battle alone.

You speak of going to my sister: [1] I know how well she loves me; do you know how? or why? I spent years in Oakland and we saw nothing of each other—perhaps once a year looked on each others face. If I had followed what she would have advised, had I sought her I would to-day be a clerk at forty dollars a month, a railroad man, or something similar. I would have winter clothes, would go to the theatre, have a nice circle of acquaintances, belong to some horrible little society like the W.R.C.,[2] talk as they talk, think as they think, do as they do—in short, I would have a full stomack, a warm body, no qualms of conscience, no bitterness of heart, no worrying ambition, no aim but to buy furniture on the installment plan and marry. I would be satisfied to live a puppet and die a puppet. Yes, and she would not have liked me half as well as she does. Because I felt that I was or wanted to be something more than a laborer, a dummy; because I showed that my brain was a little bit better than it should have been, considering my disadvantages and lack of advantages; because I was different from most fellows in my station; because of all this she took a liking to me. But all this was secondary; primarily, she was lonely, had no children, a husband who was no husband,[3] etc., she wanted someone to love. A great deal of this same feeling has been lavished upon the W.R.C. for the same reason.

If the world was at my feet to-morrow, none would be happier than she, and she would say she knew it would be so all the time. But until that time—well, she would advise to not think of it, to sink myself in two score years of oblivion with a full belly and no worry, to die as I had lived, an animal. Why should I so study that I may extract joy from reading some poem? She does not and does not miss anything; Tom Dick and Harry do not, and they are happy. Why should I develop my mind? It is not necessary for happiness. A babble of voices, petty scandals, and foolish nothings, should satisfy me. It does Tom Dick and Harry, and they are happy.

As long as my mother lives, I would not do this; but with her gone to-morrow, if I knew that my life would be such, that I was destined to live in Oakland, labor in Oakland at some steady occupation, and die in Oakland—then to-morrow I would cut my throat and call quits with the whole cursed business. You may call this the foolish effervescence of youthful ambition, and say that it will all tone down in time; but I have had my share of toning down.

Why, as you have laid down my duty in your letter, if I had followed it what would I have been to-day? I would be a laborer, and by that I mean I would be fitted for nothing else than labor. Do you know my childhood? When I was seven years old, at the country school of San Pedro,[4] this happened. Meat, I was that hungry for it I once opened a girl's basket and stole a piece of meat—a little piece the size of my two fingers. I ate it but I never repeated it. In those days, like Esau, I would have literally sold my birthright for a mess of pottage, a piece of meat. Great God! when those youngsters threw chunks of meat on the ground because of surfeit, I could have dragged it from the dirt and eaten it; but I did not. Just imagine the development of my mind, my soul, under such material conditions.

This meat incident is an epitome of my whole life.

I was eight years old when I put on my first undershirt made at or bought at a store. Duty—at ten years I was on the street selling newspapers. Every cent was turned over to my people, and I went to school in constant shame of the hats, shoes, clothes I wore. Duty—from then on, I had no childhood. Up at three o'clock in the morning to carry papers. When that was finished I did not go home but continued on to school. School out, my evening papers. Saturday I worked on an ice wagon. Sunday I went to a bowling alley and set up pins for drunken Dutchmen. Duty—I turned over every cent and went dressed like a scarecrow.

Was there any duty owing to me?

Fred[5] worked in the cannery for a short summer vacation—aye the reward was to be a term at college. I worked in the same cannery,[6] not for a
vacation but for a year. For months at a time, during that year, I was up
and at work at six in the morning. I took half an hour for dinner. I took
half an hour for supper. I worked every night till ten, eleven and twelve
o'clock. My wages were small, but I worked such long hours that I sometimes made as high as fifty dollars a month. Duty—I turned every cent
over. Duty—I have worked in that hell hole for thirty-six straight hours,
at a machine, and I was only a child. I remember how I was trying to save
the money to buy a skiff—eight dollars. All that summer I saved and
scraped. In the fall I had five dollars as a result of absolutely doing without all pleasure. My mother came to the machine where I worked and
asked for it. I could have killed myself that night. After a year of hell to
have that pitiful—to be robbed of that petty joy.

Duty—had I followed your conception of duty, I should never have
gone to High School, never to the University,[7] never—I should have remained a laborer.

My body and soul were starved when I was a child, cannot they do
without a few little luxuries for me at this stage of the game?

Aye, I at last kicked over the traces; but [not] even then, did I wholly
run away from duty. Many a gold piece went into the family. When I returned from seven months at sea,[8] what did I do with my pay day? I
bought a second hand hat, some forty cent shirts, two fifty-cent suits of
underclothes, and a second hand coat and vest. I spent exactly seventy
cents for drinks among the crowd I had known before I went to sea. The
rest went to pay the debts of my father and to the family. When I was
working in the jute mills,[9] I received forty dollars pay and at the same
time twenty-five dollars from a prize in a literary contest.[10] I bought a ten
dollar suit of clothes and got my watch out of hock. That was all I spent.
Two days afterward, I had to soak my watch to get money for tobacco.

How often, as I swept the rooms at High School,[11] has my father come
to me at my work and got a half dollar, a dollar, or two dollars? And you
know I had a place to put every bit of it myself. Aye, I have had my father
come there, when I did not have a cent, and went to the *Ægis*[12] fellows
and borrowed it—mortgaged my next month's wages.

Do you know what I suffered during that High School and University
period? The imps of hell would have wept had they been with me. Does
any one know? Can any one know? O the hours I have eaten out my heart
in bitterness! Duty—I fought it off for two long years without cessation,
and I am glad. You knew me before those two years—did they do me any
good?

You say, "It is your duty, if you wish to hold the esteem of those whose
approval or companionship is worth having." If I had followed that,
would I have known you? If I had followed that, who would I now know
whose companionship I would esteem? If I had followed that from child-

hood, whose companionship would I now be fitted to enjoy?—Tennyson's? or a bunch of brute hoodlums on a street corner?

I cannot lay bare, cannot put my heart on paper, but I have merely stated a few material facts of my life. These may be cues to my feelings. But unless you know the instrument on which they play, you will not know the music. Me—how I have felt and thought through all this struggle; how I feel and think now—you do not know. Hungry! Hungry! Hungry! From the time I stole the meat and knew no call above my belly, to now when the call is higher, it has been hunger, nothing but hunger.

You cannot understand, nor never will.

Nor has anybody ever understood. The whole thing has been by itself. Duty said "do not go on; go to work." So said my sister, though she would not say it to my face. Every body looked askance; though they did not speak, I knew what they thought. Not a word of approval, but much of disapproval. If only some one had said, "I understand." From the hunger of my childhood, cold eyes have looked upon me, or questioned, or snickered and sneered. What hurt above all was that they were some my friends—not professed but real friends. I have calloused my exterior and receive the strokes as though they were not; as to how they hurt, no one knows but my own soul and me.

So be it. The end is not yet. If I die I shall die hard, fighting to the last, and hell shall receive no fitter inmate than myself. But for good or ill, it shall be as it has been—alone.

Mabel, remember this: the time is past when any John Halifax Gentleman ethics can go down with me.[13] I don't care if the whole present, all I possess, were swept away from me—I will build a new present; If I am left naked and hungry to-morrow—before I give in I will go on naked and hungry; if I were a woman I would prostitute myself to all men but that I would succeed—in short, I will.

Am sorry that I have devoted so much to myself, and glad that you are better. How I would like to come down, and I shall if things come my way.

Frank has been playing the violin and Johnny[14] the devil in the room while I have been writing this, so you will forgive its disconnectedness.

Tell Ted I shall write in a couple of days, and ask him to explain more fully what he meant about that hymn which was enclosed.

> Yours,
> Jack.

MS: CSmH; 7 pp., tls. Pbd: *L*, 4–8; *BJL*, I, 264–67.

1. Eliza London Shepard (1867–1939), JL's stepsister and the wife of Capt. James H. Shepard.

2. The Woman's Relief Corps, an auxiliary to the Grand Army of the Republic. Eliza Shepard was later president of this organization.

3. Capt. James H. Shepard (1843–1917) was a middle-aged widower with three children when he met Eliza, who was sixteen. They married in 1884 and moved to Oakland.

4. JL's family had moved to the northwestern coastal area of San Mateo County, south of San Francisco, when he was seven. John London owned a potato farm there.

5. Fred Jacobs.

6. In 1891 JL worked at a machine filling, closing, and soldering cans of fruits and vegetables for the R. Hickmott Canning Company, 625 Myrtle Street, Oakland.

7. JL entered the University of California in Berkeley in August 1896 but withdrew on February 4, 1897, because of his financial condition.

8. On January 20, 1893, JL signed on a three-masted sealing schooner, the *Sophia Sutherland*, bound for Japan. He returned home on August 26, 1893.

9. Probably the Pacific Jute Manufacturing Company, east of Lake Merritt, where JL worked at a machine winding the jute-twine from a bobbin in the fall of 1893.

10. "Story of a Typhoon off the Coast of Japan" won first prize in a descriptive-writing contest for writers under 22 sponsored by the *San Francisco Morning Call*. It was published in the *Morning Call*, November 12, 1893, and later included in *Dutch Courage and Other Stories* (New York: Macmillan, 1922).

11. JL entered Oakland High School in the winter of 1895 and also worked as a janitor at the school. For another description of his growing up, see JL to Houghton, Mifflin & Co., January 31, 1900.

12. The *Ægis*, a high school student publication in which JL published a number of articles and stories.

13. In Dinah Mulock's novel *John Halifax, Gentleman* (1857), a poor orphan boy achieves success through hard work, honesty, and an innate nobility of character.

14. Johnny Miller (1892–1966), son of Ida London Miller. His father, Frank H. Miller, had deserted the family shortly after Johnny was born. While JL was in the Klondike, Johnny had moved in permanently with Flora London and became part of the extended household JL supported.

To Edward Applegarth

962 East 16th. st.,
Dec. 6, 1898.

Dear Ted:–

Pardon my delay in acknowledging receipt of P.O. order. It came Sunday morning. I spoke to Frank about taking down your stove-shelf as well as medicine; but he seemed rather loath, so I did not mention it again. It only weighed a couple of pounds and was not at all awkward to carry— he could carry away a couple of my big Indian arrows without complaint, however.

Shall bring it down myself if I can ever come. I broke wheel in getting it off—will explain when I see you. I mean that pair of iron wheels.

I can't understand how you mean me to finish your "In the twilight." There are only four lines to it, and they are introductory, preparing one for what the shadows say. I have no cue to what you intended them to say. A thousand men would write a thousand different messages from that foundation. I see what you mean by the hymn style—if you can remember what you wrote in order to illustrate, you will notice a strong echo of phrases from Kipling, Buchanen,[1] etc., and those are the very phrases which you used to accentuate the hymn style, and that's why I avoided them.

Shall look up that bicycle commission business for you.

Don't know when I shall be able to come down.

I have at last seen *Cyrano de Bergerac*. If you get a chance, go to it. It's worth walking forty miles to see it. I went in a spirit of duty, because of the attention it has claimed. I had read portions of it, but never dreamed that the play, as a whole could amount to much. I wouldn't have missed it for a ten dollar gold piece at this moment, badly as I need it. The Tivoli staged it well; even Du pont Syle says Stevens rendering of Cyrano compared favorably with Mansfield's.[2] I can't say anything about it, except go when you get a chance.

Frank is gone, and I am writing a few letters and cleaning up. He celebrated his visit by getting sick. This latter disgusted me. I have seen both strong and weak men in agony, and have and can sympathize with them; but an exhibition of babyishness, such as Frank gave, makes me sick. If you get this before he brings the medicine, don't mention anything save that I wrote you he had been sick.

Have received a letter from Bess, but have not the clothes to pay her a call.

I'd give anything to see my way clear to come down. I am stifling here.

Yours,

Jack London.

MS: CSt; 2 pp., tls.

1. Possibly Robert W. Buchanan (1841–1901), Scottish poet, playwright, and novelist.

2. *Cyrano de Bergerac* played at the Tivoli Theatre in San Francisco, starring Edwin Stevens in the title role. Louis du Pont Syle (1857–1903), assistant professor of English at the University of California from 1892 to 1902 and drama critic for the *San Francisco Examiner* from 1898 to 1900, reviewed the play in "Remarkable Length of 'Cyrano de Bergerac' and Why It Lacks Dramatic Situation," *San Francisco Sunday Examiner Magazine*, December 4, 1898. Richard Mansfield (1854–1907), prominent German-born American actor in the romantic "grand style" and producer of the first plays of George Bernard Shaw to be staged in America, had opened his version of *Cyrano* at the Garden, New York, in October 1898. See JL to Brett, July 8, 1904, for Mansfield's later interest in staging *The Sea-Wolf*.

To Mabel Applegarth

962 East 16th. st.,

Dec. 6, 1898.

Dear Mabel:—

Frank is at last gone and I can do a little writing. Why did you not send me what you had written? Were you afraid of hurting my feelings—it seems your previous frankness, extending through several years, had precluded any such possibility.

Ere this you will have received your medicine, for I asked Frank to take it out at once as you needed it. I only hope you are so much better that you don't. It seems too bad; but then, it is better to be sick in winter than in summer.

Sent out in this mail, "trailers" after articles I mailed last September, and which have vanished utterly. Received a letter from the *Overland Monthly*.[1] This is the substance of it:— We have read your MS. Are so greatly pleased with it, that, though we have an enormous quantity of accepted and paid-for material on hand, we will at once publish it in the January number, if—aye, if you can content yourself with five dollars.

There are between three and four thousand words in it. Worth far more than five dollars, at the ordinary reportorial rate of so much per column. What do you think of that for a first class magazine like the *Overland*?[2] Every magazine has its clique of writers, on whom it depends, and whom it patronizes in preference to all other writers. True, they had to work into that position of preference. Well, a newcomer must excell them in their own fields before he is accepted, or else he must create a new field. Perhaps it was the latter that impressed the editors in favor of my article; but be it what it may, if worthy of publication, it were worthy of proper pay.

You wanted a sample of a villanelle—I wrote the enclosed in fifteen minutes, without even the refrains when I began. It's fine drill, forcing one to be trite, to sum his thought in small compass, to condense. No room for Johnsonian periods there—no verbosity, etc. You can figure out the rhyme and refrain structure.

We are getting ready to sue the Republican Club for our prizes. No word from *Youth's Companion*.

If I could only come down.

Hope this will find you in better health—I hate to think of you lying sick—if you get a chance, read the American translation of *Cyrano de Bergerac*;[3] but read slowly or not at all. Several portions of it were my own thoughts, my own moods.

Give regards to all, and believe me,

Good night,
Jack London

MS: CSmH; 2 pp., tls. Pbd: *L*, 8–9; *BJL*, I, 267.

1. JL submitted "To the Man on Trail" on November 10, 1898, to the *Overland Monthly*, a San Francisco–based monthly that focused primarily on California subjects and California authors and was published from 1868 to 1875 and from 1883 to 1935. JL's story was published as "To the Man on the Trail" in the *Overland*, January 1899, and later included in JL's first book, *The Son of the Wolf: Tales of the Far North* (Boston: Houghton Mifflin, 1900).

2. In fact, after its revival in 1883, the *Overland Monthly* failed to recapture the prestige it had enjoyed under the earlier editorship of Charles Warren Stoddard, Ina Coolbrith, and Bret Harte. Ambrose Bierce referred to the later magazine as the "warmed-*Overland Monthly*."

3. Howard Thayer Kingsbury's translation, published in 1898.

To Mabel Applegarth

962 East 16th. st.,
Dec. 22, 1898.

Dear Mabel:—

Have been very busy, so couldn't write. All this week and part of last I have spent in the superior court of San Francisco. One of my partners, Sloper,[1] has returned, and because he had not struck it rich, his wife, to whom he had deeded over four thousand dollars worth of property before he left, has sued him for a divorce, alleging desertion. (How's that for a loose sentence?) I had to serve as witness on various points.

No news from Republican Club. *Overland* has not paid five dollars yet. *Youth's Companion* yarn[2] came back—prime cause of rejection they state to be unusual length of each chapter, which length is never allowed, they say, "except in very special instances." In the beginning, in response to my queries, I was told that 3000 words made an average chapter, and in the end, none of my chapters exceeded that amount. I take it to be merely an alleged cause, or else a mistake on the part of the one who first advised me.

Enclosed, you will find the successful *Examiner* story.[3] Please keep it, remembering that strength of narrative and originality of plot were demanded by those in charge of contest. Some day, when the MSS. I submitted are published, I shall forward to you so that you may compare (I mean published elsewhere). Also, in the successful story I send you, please endeavor to find what plot there is, if any, or if it is a study, or pseudo-study.

Enclosed poem is for children, as you will see at a glance. I wrote it during the course of the trial. It is fanciful ballad thought, couched in a structure which I deem a pleasant change from the ballad structure. "Ulysses" came back like a shot, all the way from New York; I sent it there at the same time I sent the duplicate to you.[4] Needless to say, this Greek wanderer is abroad again. I see in the Christmas numbers, similar farces with greater claims to mediocrity—how the Dickens do they get there? Have sent a 2000 word

*   *   *

MS: CSmH; 1 p., fragment of tl.

1. Ira Merritt Sloper (1855–1942), a fellow passenger on the *Umatilla* from San Francisco to Juneau, who became one of JL's partners in the Klondike.

2. "Where Boys Are Men."

3. Anna Catherine Markham, "Christmas at Seven Devils," *San Francisco Examiner Christmas Magazine*, December 18, 1898. Markham's brief story, set in a California mining town on Christmas Eve, combines a regional color with such popular motifs as frontier justice, female virtue, and a love triangle.

4. "The Return of Ulysses—A Modern Version" (MS: CSmH), a one-act play in verse. On December 8, 1898, JL submitted this skit to *Collier's Weekly*, an illustrated magazine published in New York from 1888 until 1957 and noted for its excellent fiction, poetry, and

articles, as well as its use of the new photojournalism. He subsequently retired the manu-script after it had been rejected by five other magazines.

To Mabel Applegarth

962 East 16th. st.,
Xmas Morning [1898].

Dear Mabel:–

About the loneliest Christmas I ever faced—guess I'll write to you. Nothing to speak of, though—everything quiet. How I wish I were down at College Park, if for no more than a couple of hours. No body to talk to, no friend to visit—nay, if there were, and if I so desired, I would not be in position to. Hereafter and for some time to come, you'll have to content yourself with my beastly scrawl, for this is, most probably, the last machine-made letter I shall send you.

Well, the FIRST BATTLE has been fought. While I have not conquered, I'll not confess defeat. Instead, I have learned the enemy's strongholds and weak places, and by the same I shall profit when the SECOND BATTLE comes off; and by what I learn through that, I will be beatter fitted for the THIRD BATTLE—and so on, ad infinitum.

The typewriter goes back on the thirty-first of December. Till then I expect to be busy cleaning up my desk, writing business letters of various nature, and finishing the article I am at present on. Then the New Year, and an entire change of front.

I have profited greatly, have learned much during the last three months. How much I cannot even approximate—I feel its worth and greatness, but it is too impalpable to put down in black and white. I have studied, read, and thought a great deal, and believe I am at last beginning to grasp the situation—the general situation, my situation, and the correlative situation between the two. But I am modest, as I say, I am only beginning to grasp—I realize, that with all I have learned, I know less about it than I thought I did a couple of years ago.

Are you aware of the paradox entailed by progress? It makes me both jubilant and sad. You cannot help feeling sad when looking over back work and realizing its weak places, its errors, its inanities; and again, you cannot but rejoice at having so improved that you are aware of it, and feel capable of better things. I have learned more in the past three months than in all my High School and College; yet, of course, they were necessary from a preparatory standpoint.

And to-day is Christmas—it is at such periods that the vagabondage of my nature succumbs to a latent taste for domesticity. Away with the many corners of this round world! I am deaf to the call of the East and West, the North and South—a picture such as Fred used to draw is before me. A comfortable little cottage, a couple of servants, a select coterie of friends, and above all, a neat little wife and a couple of dimunitive models of us twain—a hanging of stockings last evening, a merry surprise this morning, the genial interchange of Christmas greeting; a cosy grate fire, the sleepy children cuddling on the floor ready for bed, a sort of dreamy communion between the fire, my wife, and myself; an assured, though quiet and monotonous, future in prospect; a satisfied knowledge of the many little amenities of civilized life which are mine and shall be mine; a genial, optimistical contemplation—

Ever feel that way? Fred dreamed of it, but never tasted; I suppose I am destined likewise. So be it. The ways of the gods are inscrutable—and do they make and break us just for fun? What a great old world! What a jolly good world! It contains so much which is worth striving for; and natheless, so much to avoid. But it's like a great Chinese puzzle—in every little community are to be found the Islands of the Blest, and yet we know not where to look for them. And if we do, our ticket in Life's Lottery bears the wrong number. An auspicious mingling of all the elements which go to make up the totality of human happiness—the capital prize—there are various ways of winning it, and still more various ways of losing it. You may be born into it, you may tumble into it; you may be dragged into it; but verily, you may not knowingly walk into it. The whole thing is a gamble, and those least fitted to understand the game win the most. The most unfortunate gamblers are those who have, or think they have systems to beat the game—they always go broke. The same with life. There are numerous paths to earthly happiness; but to find them, skill in geography or typography is worse than useless.

I shall forsake my old dogmas, and henceforth, worship the true god. "There is no God but Chance, and Luck shall be his prophet!" He who stops to think or beget a system is lost. As in other creeds, faith alone atones. Numerous hecatombs and many a fat firstling shall I sacrifice—you just watch my smoke (I beg pardon, I mean incense).

I started to write a letter; I became nonsensical; forgive me. I go to dine at my sister's. Happy New Year to all!

Jack.

MS: CSmH; 3 pp., tls. Pbd: *L*, 9–11; *BJL*, I, 268–70; *Pictorial Life*, 86.

To Edward Applegarth

962 East 16th. st.,
Dec. 31, 1898.

Dear Ted:—

A thousand apologies for not writing sooner, and as many thanks for your kindness in still writing me and for your criticism. I will answer your letters as they came to hand.

As regard pipes—Japanese pipes, I suppose: I don't know what's become of them. Everything I possessed, nearly, disappeared when I was at Klondike. Will try and look some up. I smoked "Plum" tobacco in them—ten cents per package of two ounces.

Will give you my version of "Twilight" in a few days. I think "soundlessly and silently" is unpardonable; of course, merely my individual opinion. I managed to take off one wheel, but on breaking the second, left it behind—they're not up to much, anyway.

I prefer "Lilith" with your first line, and see no objection to the double "you."

> Once in the days before the hour
>   That ever first man's memory knew,
> When, as an unknown secret power,
>   Lived but the thought of you;
> Then in the tracklessness of space
> God sent an ideal thought to trace
> Upon infinite a face
>   Which nature gave to you.[1]

I like the thought and the handling very much, and though the metre and rhyme scheme is unique, I cannot object to it. You will notice, if you did not so design it, that the two, and the only two trimeters, ending in "you," rhyme with the tetrameter ending with "knew." Reading it as a whole, it sounds as a perfectly rounded period should.

There is one *Health*, one advertising paper, two *Iconoclasts*, and a couple of *Waves* in my possession;[2] no letters or other circulars. I call as often as once a week at the P.O.

No reduction in G. and J. tires. They're ten dollars a pair up here, including inner tubes, four and a half are asked at my shop for one outer tire. I have them on my wheel.

As to the use of "aye," etc.: Aye is a common word with me and with most of the people I have known, especially in the Northland. "Yea" I used so to avoid a repetition of "aye," for it occurred in exactly similar sentence structure—since you have spoken I wish I had not. It does not sound right—not so with "aye." To show you its prevelance, I quote from your objection to it: "but it [is] hard, nay, impossible to avoid words seeming all right to you, that do not do so to others." Of course, you cannot permit "nay" without its companion "aye."

You made a mistake regarding "hath."—"'I know all which hath been, which is, and shall be, and no mortal hath ever lifted my veil.'" This is the way it was written; you will observe the double quotation marks. It is a popular—no, I have never seen it in print but once—quotation from the lines inscribed on the statue of Isis, in Egypt. Remember Malemute Kid was no artisan when he lived on the Outside. Also, Malemute Kid must be between thirty-five and forty years old. The sobriquet of "Kid" is no sign of being a fledgling. I have met men going on three score who possessed it. It is merely quoted in a joking manner—a transparent attempt at mysticism.

I agree with you regarding the past tense. I think a man liable to say "cleave unto to"; I think I would say it under similar circumstances; and I prefer it vastly to "stick to me." In moments of deep feeling, men often revert to their native accent or vernacular; and they often, sometimes consciously, revert to biblical forensic, or pulpit diction, with which they may be familiar. It is the dramatic instinct struggling for utterance. I have often noticed it with you—just like "nay," you may not be aware of it. If I could only talk to you I could make myself clear.

I appreciate my weakness in conversation, which you refer to as Lucille being Jack in bloomers.[3] Also agree with your distaste to musical terms, and greatly prefer the way you changed it.

"And everybody said he could play a violin better." You must consider this use of "a" with the context, and with the fact that it is the colloquial reflex of the Dawson judgement. Wish I could talk with you. Women are never the friends to their own sex that men are to theirs—consider this, it does not mean, nor can it be mistaken to mean that all women are not the friends to all women that all men are to all men. Then apply it to "men confide in men."[4] You just notice the summing of similar generalities you may run across.

The White Silence seems to strike you. Have another one of the series with that for a title.[5] Will send it to you some time. Please show this to Mabel, and what I write her in reference to the MS. I shall ask her to show you.

There are more words in this letter than the three I am answering of yours.

As to the clips—I asked Jessie's bethrothed,[6] and he said he would find out; but he has not. I am not on visiting terms with my shop just now, and Starrat's is just across the street. I don't think I would care to handle them—I never made a cent out of canvassing, etc, and any kind of percentage business—I haven't got it in me, unless I am far, far beyond the ken of even the most casual acquaintances. Come up any way; I don't see any need of my consulting anybody as to whom I shall entertain. Let me know beforehand, of course. Come in the evening. This is all qualified, however; you must be satisfied to put up with the crudest fare. I have never been so hard up in my life. Tell me what you think of "To the Man on Trail." The compositor or editorial censor had to change it to "To the Man on *the* Trail,"[7] and I do not thank them for it.

Very sincerely yours,
Jack.

MS: CSt; 4 pp., tls.

1. A copy of Applegarth's typescript is in CSt.

2. *Health* was a monthly magazine published in New York from 1881 until 1896 that was, according to its subtitle, "devoted to physical culture and out-door life"; the *Iconoclast* may have been back issues of the short-lived (1870–71) magazine of the National Liberal Reform League, published in Washington, D.C.; the *Wave* was a weekly journal that was published in San Francisco by the Southern Pacific Railroad from 1890 until 1900 and featured the poetry and fiction of local writers, book and drama reviews, and articles on local matters.

3. Lucille and Jack are characters in "The Test: A Klondike Wooing" (MS: ULA). The story was submitted to *Cosmopolitan* on September 25, 1898, rejected, then retired after being rejected by the *Overland Monthly* in January 1899.

4. The following sentence appears in the MS version of "The Test": "And he was, as everybody said, a jolly good fellow, who had greater luck and could play a violin better than any man in the country." The phrase "men confide in men" does not appear in the MS; JL may have sent Applegarth another version of the story that is no longer extant.

5. "The White Silence: Another Story of the 'Malemute Kid,'" *Overland Monthly*, February 1899; later included in *The Son of the Wolf*.

6. Fred Jurgewitz.

7. JL underlined "the" twice.

To Mabel Applegarth

[Oakland]
[? December 31, 1898]

*   *   *

the imagination"? And please don't spell it "imagionation."

About your wishing to know more about Lucille or Jack—room forbade. The art of omission is the hardest of all to learn, and I am weak at it yet. I am too long-winded, and it is hard training to cut down. As yet, it prevents me from writing perfect little gems, examples of which Ted sometimes sends me. In his "Lilith" he shows the right touch—comes naturally with him, while I, from a stylistic and constructive standpoint, have wandered afar after strange gods, and find it difficult to get back to the right trails.

My conversation is still learning to walk, as you will have observed. Apropos of the same, witness certain portions of Ted's letter. In "To the Man on Trail," I think I have picked up. There are a number of funny things in punctuation in it, not due to me. Who ever prepared it for the press, had an even greater regard for the semicolon than I. Don't criticise punctuation in my letters; I type them off as fast as I can think. Am going to try and get *Overland* to take the series, that is, if they will pay better.[1] I would have much published if I only had an illustrator—one of the difficulties I must struggle under.

"And the sleepy poppies dream," comes from "The Garden of Sleep." The only other reason of refusal by *Youth's Companion*, was loosely strung narrative, which I can't exactly see; at least the *Companion* is publishing much worsely strung, balder stuff every issue. So be it.[2]

I have reached a conclusion: there is no such thing as inspiration. I thought so once, and made an ass of my self accordingly. Dig is the arcana of literature, as it is of all things save being born with a silver spoon and going to Klondike. The only inspiration is that which comes to an orator when addressing a vast multitude, which is in sympathy with him.

Poor child! You took four guesses as to the fate of my wheel and missed it, every one—Soaked with my Hebrew uncle. Also other articles too numerous to mention. Lots of fun working under such conditions. You are in luck to obtain this *Overland*. It's the only one I possess, and I had to borrow the dime to buy it. Then I had no stamps, not one—only the wrapper which had not sufficient postage. But the unkindness of the Eastern Editors served your purpose. It is an old tale. I often receive my MSS. back, with their stamps on the envelope; mine being still in the fold of the MS. Yet it is no more than right for them to defray return, after refusing to read. Well, this morning I received four two cent stamps in this way, also two ones. Behold the letters and magazine.

Next Tuesday we meet to sue the Fifth Ward Republican Club. The *Black Cat* writes me concerning an MS. submitted to them. They want references, as I am unknown. Then they wish to know if I wrote it myself, if the idea is mine, if it has ever been in print in part or whole, if it has ever been submitted elsewhere, and if others have or will have a copy of it. I complied. Wonder what they'll pay? It is a pseudo-scientific tale, founded on hypothetical chemical, biological, and pathological laws, dealing with the diametric converse of chemical affinity and the mysteries of protoplasmic coagulation.[3] Very sorry, but can't forward definitions.

You construct portion of sentence thus: "an accent which never ceased to charm my ear; and long, long after, roused me from my sleep" etc. No noun after semicolon, and it must be a clause.

I sympathize with the man concealed in woman; many thanks for the thought—will work it up some day. I have *Cyrano de Bergerac*, but no stamps to forward; besides, I would vastly prefer reading it with you. It is a pirated edition, nothing to boast of, and I should be ashamed for having bought it.

Would like to talk Ella Wheeler Wilcox[4] over with you. You seem to misunderstand her.

You ask about the "Elder World": don't you remember reading about primeval man?—fur-clad savages, living in caves, smashing each others heads with huge clubs, and scratching sketches of the same on reindeer bone.

"Magnificent." No word bears exactly the same significance to any two persons. Barbaric splendor is magnificence to the barbaric mind. Two such specimens as Jack and Lucille, fur-dressed, be-moccasined, etc., may strike you as bizarre—it strikes me as possessing a crude magnificence.

Yes, some of the qualities of Jensen[6] go into Malemute Kid. But Malemute Kid is still something more. I shall tell more about Lucille, some day. In "The White Silence," I mention in Ted's

          *   *   *

MS: ULA; photocopy of 3 pp., fragment of tl. Pbd: *BJL*, I, 270–71.

1. The *Overland Monthly* agreed to accept seven of JL's Klondike stories at a rate of $7.50 each; all were published in 1899 and later included in *The Son of the Wolf*.

2. "The Garden of Sleep" has not been identified. JL is evidently discussing the rejection of "Where Boys Are Men."

3. "A Thousand Deaths," published in the *Black Cat*, May 1899. The *Black Cat* was a monthly short-story magazine published in Boston from 1895 until 1923.

4. Ella Wheeler Wilcox (1850–1919), a sentimental poet whose best-known book of verse is *Poems of Passion* (1883). In addition to poems, Wilcox wrote popular books and periodical articles; these often gave advice about personal relations, including sexual attraction.

5. The passage to which JL refers appears as follows in the MS of "The Test": "Cold, the morning; dreary, the scene; crude, the environment: but withal, magnificent, the picture. Filled with scintillating frost particles, the air is a sparkling, silvery sheen, a fairy gossamer. The mighty Yukon, the towering peaks, the far-reaching forest; monotonously white and sphinx-like in their brooding calm, sleep on the bosom of the awful Arctic silence. In garments of leather and fur, toil-worn and hardy, their eyes slumbering with latent action and power, the gold-seekers group like heroes of the Elder World. And there, in their midst, a veritable King of the Northland—'Lucky' Jack Harrington. From his wolverine cap to his Innuit *muclucs*, he stood a MAN amongst MEN. And she [Lucille], in buckskin and furs and beaded mocassins [*sic*], with her rosy cheeks and laughing eyes, was truly a dainty, Arctic princess."

6. Emil Jensen, a resident of San Francisco who met JL along the Stewart River in the Yukon Territory. For Jensen's recollections of his Klondike experiences with JL, see his "Jack London at Stewart River" (MS: CSmH).

1899

The young author, ca. 1899 (Trust of Irving Shepard)

To the Corresponding Editor,
Youth's Companion

962 East 16th. st.,
Oakland, Calif.,
Jan. 7, 1899.

Dear Sir:—

Your kind letter of December 29th. at hand. I have been quite sick, but am better now. I have vague recollections of what I wrote you, but they are so confused with what passed through my head in the several succeeding days and nights, that I cannot tell of how much I unburdened myself. I was on the verge of breaking down, so I suppose my letter had a strong tinge of hysteria. I had no friend to go to and had to break out on somebody. This working out one's soul is not a pleasant task.

I must thank you for your kindness in replying as you did. But first, a word in explanation, or rather, extenuation. You say: "The chapters should not exceed thirty-five hundred words in length, should be at least five and not more than seven in number. . . ." One objection to my MS.[1] was the excessive length of the chapters, a length never permissible save in "very special instances." Five of my seven chapters were within fifty of three thousand words; one exceeded that number by one hundred and fifty words; and another sank to about twenty-six hundred. Surely the double-spacing could not have led to a mistaken estimate of length.

I understand and appreciate your urging me to not make writing my means of livelihood. Enclosed ad. is the one I am at present running in the local papers.[2] Have been trying for work constantly. In the midst of *Youth's Companion* MS., broke off to take Civil Service Examinations for the Post Office. They are very slow at Washington, however, for I have yet to receive my standing in the same. I think I did very well.

Yet to me all work will be but a means to an end. I may labor till I am old and decrepid; but periods of idleness and sickness eating into the savings of labor and frugality, will have placed me in the proper position for the poor house. No, no; I have seen too much labor and too many laborers, not to understand the game. Some day I shall hit upon my *mag-*

nus opus. And then, if my struggling expression at last finds tongue, I will not have to go to the poor house because my muscles can no longer work. And if not—well, so be it.

Again thanking you, I promise some day, if the gods are propitious, to drop into Boston-town and shake hands with you.

Very truly yours,
Jack London.

MS: ULA; photocopy of 2 pp., tls. Pbd: *L*, 11–12; *Pictorial Life*, 87–88.
  1. "Where Boys Are Men."
  2. In the "Situations Wanted—Male" section of the classified advertisements in the *Oakland Tribune*, January 4–11, 1899, JL placed the following notice: "WANTED—Any kind of work; will typewrite reasonably, receive and deliver same. 962 East Sixteenth st."

To Mabel Applegarth

962 East 16th. st.,
Jan. 13, [1899].[1]

Dear Mabel:–

I doubt if you can understand how disappointed I have been—thirteen days since I wrote you, and no sign. At last I thought, "Perhaps she remembers my birthday and is waiting so her letter may arrive on that day."

Yesterday morning I thought surely It would arrive. When it did not the afternoon became invested with an infallible certainty. Alas! The postman brought a dun!

Well, yesterday was my birthday. I did not look for "many happy returns of the day"; nor did I receive many. My sister was the only one who wished me that, or anything else. Thought I would break the tediousness of my endless prose writing and take a little holiday (such an auspicious event, after such faithful application to the machine, surely deserved it). So I read the morning papers; answered a couple of pressing letters from people who are greatly concerned about certain matters; stood off the butcher and baker to satisfy the absurd cravings of life; wooed the Muse; and sat down to write poetry. The funniest part of the whole thing is that I did it from a sense of duty. For many weeks I have had four lines of a poem from Ted—you wrote me, once, telling me what he wanted me to do with it. I started in, and not liking its exact form started to mutilate it. Behold!

For in the hush of the twilight,
When at the close of the day,
Shadows thrown out by the firelight,
Soundlessly, silently say:[2]

This is as it was, and this is my amendation:

> When, in the hush of the twilight,
> Night draws the hem of the day,
> Shadows thrown out by the firelight—

and then I was in despair. To save my life I couldn't fix the fourth verse.
(Ted

             *   *   *

MS: CSmH; 1 p., fragment of tl. Pbd: *BJL*, I, 271–72.

   1. Originally typed "Jan. 13, 1898," the date has been corrected, apparently in CKL's hand.

   2. On the original "Wisper as softly & say" has been written below in another hand, possibly Mabel Applegarth's.

To Mabel Applegarth

962 East 16th. st.,
Jan. 28, 1899.

My dear Mabel:–

Right in the neck—don't mention it. 'Tisn't exactly right to ask for criticism, and then criticize—I understand that, but, well, I wanted to show the point of view by which I worked. I was wrong in doing it, and besides, did it rather rudely. Still, I believe you're none the worse for it. I wish I could talk with you; I might explain better.

One other thing. I don't know whether you share this belief with Ted, but think you do—that I do not take time enough; do not let a thing cool; do not write and write and rewrite; do not, in short, exhibit the peculiar, or rather, exercise the peculiar methods of the lapidary. To this, I believe, you attribute the weakness of the characters I have drawn. Two other possibilities arise. First, as I stated before, the lack of effect may be laid to your egregious ignorance of such types. Secondly, the fault may lie with me, but not in the trick of the hand or phrase. The latter may do their work very thoroughly, admirably, and through no weakness on their part, produce a puerile result. This then, is due to insincerity of vision on my part; and all the polishing of the MS. will never succeeding in bettering it. You see what I am driving at. I am sure what I have written reflects almost perfectly the thought the image in my mind. I know, if I draw the complete character of Malemute Kid in one short story, all raison de etra of a Malemute Kid series ceases.

Am very sorry to hear you are worse; and you had been so hopeful, too. Hope my last letter had no bad effect—if it stirred you up, as it evidently did Ted, it was really criminal on my part. Forgive me. Though I guess you know already what a rough-shod barbarian I am, even at my best. At least you cannot say I am anything but candid. Unless Ted mentions it, don't let him know you know I was lectured—it's only Jack, anyway.

By the way, forgot to tell you in last letter, that I stand first on the eligible list for carriers. My percent was 85.38. My postman tells me I stand a good show for appointment. At first one goes on as extraman, making about forty-five dollars per month. After about six months of that he becomes regular with sixty-five dollars. But the whole year may elapse before I get anything at all.[1]

Ted is getting along all right—nothing to be feared.

You are unusually prejudiced against Ella Wheeler Wilcox; Ted shares it with you; I am sure your mother does too; and hence, with no further search, you fan each other's distaste. Tell me what you think of the following—style and thought:

"The effect of the sweetly good woman upon man is like the perfume of a flower that grew in his childhood's garden, or a strain of music heard in his youth. He is ashamed of his grosser appetites when he is in her presence. He would not like her to know of his errors and vices. He feels like another man when near her and realizes that he has a spiritual nature. Yet as the effect of the strain of music or the perfume of the flower is necessary, so often her influence ceases when he is absent from her, unless she be the woman who rules his life."[2]

"Now!" cried the reviewers, "here is a pedestal for you—up you go!"

"Gentlemen," blubbered Patient Merit, "you are too kind—but, help me up!"

And they helped him up.

And when he was well posed they proceeded to throw potsherds at him.

Speaking of magnificent, glance at the use of the following adjective by Frederic Harrison, one of the famous English literatti: "Mr. Ruskin once hazarded the GLORIOUS paradox that Cary's *Dante* was better reading than Milton's *Paradise Lost*."[3]

Speaking of marriage—the following is what Zangwill calls Spinoza's "aphorism on marriage":[4] "It is plain that Marriage is in accordance with Reason, if the desire is engendered not merely by external form, but by a love of begetting children and wisely educating them; and if, in addition, the love both of husband and wife has for its cause not external form merely, but chiefly liberty of mind."

John Keats wrote to Miss Jeffry: "One of the reasons that the English have produced the finest writers in the world is that the English world has ill treated them during their lives and fostered them after their deaths."[5]

What do you think of it? Don't harbor the idea for a minute that I deem myself in that category. I consider myself a clumsy apprentice, learning from the master craftsmen and striving to get my hand in.

It's midnight, and I'm going to mail this before I turn in, so you must put up with a very dry letter. Ted is over in 'Frisco, gone to the theatre I believe. I shall read in bed till his return. If the *Overland, Black Cat,* and

Republicans pay me next week, within a couple of days of each other, I may be able to come down. Goodnight Mabel,

Jack.

MS: CSmH; 3 pp., tls. Pbd: *L*, 12–14; *BJL*, I, 272–73.
    1. JL's score was the highest in his group, but he rejected an appointment when it was offered to him, early in 1899.
    2. Ella Wheeler Wilcox, "Women's Influence on Man," in *Men, Women, and Emotions* (1894), p. 115. Wilcox is distinguishing between the sweetly good woman, who does good because she cannot help it, and the passionately good woman, who can sympathize with the full range of human emotions. The following passage has not been identified but also appears in JL to Johns, March 15, 1899.
    3. Frederic Harrison (1831–1923), English critic, historian, and essayist, discussing the verse translation of the *Divine Comedy* by Henry Francis Cary (1772–1844), published in 1805 (*Inferno*) and 1812 (*Purgatorio* and *Paradiso*). JL cites Harrison's "The Choice of Books," in *The Choice of Books and Other Literary Pieces* (London, 1886), p. 49.
    4. Israel Zangwill (1864–1926), English novelist and short story writer, author of *Children of the Ghetto* (1892), *Ghetto Tragedies* (1893), and other books dealing with life in Jewish ghettos. Zangwill's reference to Spinoza has not been identified.
    5. Keats to Sarah Jeffrey, June 9, 1819.

To Cloudesley Johns [1]

962 East 16th St.,
Oakland, Calif.,
Feb. 10, 1899.

Dear sir:—

What an encouragement your short note was! From the same I judge you can appreciate one's groping in the dark on strange trails. It's the first word of cheer I have received (a cheer, far more potent than publisher's checks).

If a strong chin and a perhaps deceptive consciousness of growing strength, will aid in the fulfilment of your prophecy, it may to a certain extent be realized.[2] Yes, my name is Jack London[3]—rather an un-American heritage from a Yankee ancestry, dating beyond the French and Indian Wars.

Thanking you for your kindness,

I am,
Very truly yours,
Jack London.

MS: CSmH; 1 p.; tls. Pbd: *L*, 14; *BJL*, I, 277.
    1. Cloudesley Johns (1874–1948), neophyte writer, socialist, and the son of Tremenhare L. Johns and Geniz (Jeanie) Spring MacKaye (later Peet), a poet, short-story writer, and sculptor. Born in San Francisco, Johns became a newspaperman in Los Angeles and then was successively reporter, city editor, and music, drama, and literary critic for the *San Francisco Post*. For more on Johns, see his autobiography, "Who the Hell *Is* Cloudesley Johns?" (MS: CSmH).

2. Johns noted in the margin of this letter: "I prophesied greatness, and told him not to disappoint me."

3. JL's full name was John Griffith London, but he took offense at being called "John" or "Johnny." He was listed in the city directories as John London, Jr., until he started publishing.

To Cloudesley Johns

962 East 16th. st.,
Feb. 22, 1899.[1]

Dear sir:—

Pardon my not sending postal acknowledging receipt of MS. You see, the same did not arrive till the last mail, and I am replying at once. "Charge it to the Company" or "Buzzard & Co.," would make fair titles to your story. I would prefer the first; yet I think you could cudgel your brains a little and find still better. But at the outset, it were well I explained the utter impossibility of my rendering a fair judgement on the style of anything, except it be printed or type-written. One standard I can apply to written MS.—that of ear by reading aloud. But my own stuff stands or falls by the eye, by the look of it. Hence, it must be printed or typed. But, in turn, you must understand what I mean when I say judging by the eye. You know, when one first begins to scan or write verse, he unavoidably has recourse to counting on his fingers; but, as he becomes proficient, he gradually and unconsciously gets out of the habit—in the same way, sight gives me the swing and the structure.

But to return: your story is virile, has the smack of rough life and real life about it. Here's what I would recommend: cut out all direct reference to the Norton-Drake Co., and spend another thousand words in making real men out of your Mexicans, who are puppets, and in amplifying the characters of M'Carthy and O'Connel. The last two are real, but make them moreso, go into the psychology of it, into the racial delineation a little more. In short, give us a little more of their mental attitudes, temperaments, etc.

It's hard to explain what I mean. Thus, for the Mexicans— Statistics are not emotional, when stated in statistical manner. Don't say the Co. treated the men this way, or cheated them that way. Let the reader learn these facts through the minds of the men themselves, let the reader look at the question through their eyes. There are a variety of ways by which to do this—the most common would be to have them talk with each other. Let them carambo' and speak out the bitterness of their hearts, the injustice they suffer or think they suffer from the Co., the hatred they bear their bosses etc. etc. You see what I mean.

Again, put us more in sympathy with M'Carthy. Show us more clearly his sterling qualities which I know you had in your mind at the time. Remember, the reader does not know him; you do. To you, every action of M'Carthy is the action of the M'Carthy you know; to the reader, only of the M'Carthy you have described, etc.

As to Norton-Drake Co. Though half the world declaims against them, there are many novels written with a purpose—try and recollect the short stories you have seen written with a purpose. It is not the legitimate field of such literary productions. A journalistic article (3000 words), expositional and sensational, and not in the form of a story, would be the proper method in attacking and exposing such a company—and it should be done through the columns of the press. You know there is an eternal fitness of things.

Don't mention your Co. or R.R. by name—give them fictitious names, or better still, be wholly abstract. Any fool will be able to read between the lines.

Keep yourself wholly out of the story—I noticed a number of "I"'s.— they jar. Let it be all third person.

Don't permit repetition (it is sometimes allowable, but rarely). P—I—3 Par.—in four words, "waves" appears twice—change to billows, anything else.

(Individual taste) following sentence—I should change "and the railroad ran through."

Next sen.—strike out "and" following "out." You have another in the same period and can afford it.

"Got" is a good solid standby, but you use it too frequently—substitute "been," etc. once in a while.

3 par. P. 3, see if you can duplicate the sentence with any of other modern writers? Too much colon and semicolon (my op.).

P. 4,—would you consider Norton-Drake Co., a singular noun?—if so, shouldn't "have" be "has"?

P. 5—Let the Mexicans speak of the killing of two bosses, as also of facts laid down on previous page. If not colloquially, introduce the reader to the same, still using the attitude, or way of the men's looking at it, for a medium.

P. 6—"But that"—hurts the tongue and ear—possible change: "but a buzzard will return . . .; this is a fact . . ."

P 6—Strike out "of which we can have no conception"—while you cannot elucidate the why or how, you, in same sentence, you clearly do conceive the possibility of such a thing.

P. 7—3 line—strike out second "that."

Use the relative pronoun "which" for "that," once in a while. There is great latitude allowed in the use of "that," but it may be overstepped.

Your style occasionally reminds me of Bierce.[2]

P. 10—"he knew that he had"—strike out "that."

P. 11—I would not be so ghastly with that intestine, strike out "and hung down" (my taste only, yet I appreciate such things for I have seen much of them).

I like O'Connel's turning, dying, and his last words to M'Carthy,—a true stroke and a strong stroke.

P 12—how many ribs can a knife pass between?

Some vivid, realistic work in "the living half of the ghastly thing squirmed, etc." The fact of limbs being dead through broken back.

In conclusion: you have powerful material in this tale, strong types, racial contrasts, primal instincts, etc. I would advise rewriting entirely. Try and sway the readers more with sympathy for the actors in the tragedy, etc. Now the tale, as it is, isn't bad; but I advocate this because there are such possibilities in it. I know I have botched the whole thing, that you will mistake what I mean, and swear at me a dozen times for being such an ass, etc. But what would you? I never did any criticising, anyway; so I just say what I think—hence, you gain sincerity of me, if nothing else. If I could talk with you for a few minutes It would all be so much clearer.

Will send this off this mail. "Zebro" goes to-morrow's mail. Oh! one thing—I would advise you to soften your terseness a little, at least to remove an occasional jerky place.

Tender my thanks to your mother[3] for her short note, and tell her I can thoroughly appreciate rush. Agree with you as to "Old Don's Honor,"—I mean "Lucky Find." The former was a good subject, poorly treated—illustrations redeemed it however, in its effect on reader. Thanks for tip to *Western Press*;[4] I have some of my earlier, immature work with them now. Suppose I'll some day call my present work just as immature. I look forward to that day anyway.

Will take advantage of tip to *Vanity Fair.*[5] Yes; I have noticed certain phenomena of pessimism about you. As to foto of myself. You shall be one of a number of friends who wait and wait in vain for a likeness of yours truly. My last posed foto was taken in sailor costume with a Joro girl in Yokahama. Have but one. But I'll do this: tell you all about me. 23 years of age last January. Stand five foot seven or eight in stocking feet—sailor life shortened me. At present time weigh 168 lbs; but readily jump same pretty close to 180 when I take up outdoor life and go to roughing it. Am clean shaven—when I let 'em come, blonde moustache and black whiskers—but they don't come long. Clean face makes my age enigmatical, and equally competent judges variously estimate my age from twenty to thirty. Greenish-grey eyes, heavy brows which meet; brown hair, which, by the way, was black when I was born, then came out during an infantile sickness and returned positively white—so white that my negress nurse called me "Cotton Ball." Face bronzed through many long-continued liasons with the sun, though just now, owing to bleaching process of sedentary life, it is positively yellow. Several scars—hiatus of eight front upper

teeth, usually disguised with false plate. There I am in toto. Now reciprocate—your age has puzzled me most of all. Sometimes I would feel like
placing you at twenty, and other times at forty.

Tell me what you think of enclosed verse, and kindly return—was written a long time ago, but have had no outside criticism. Get your mother's
criticism too, that is, if she is not too busy. I just dabble in verse occasionally, sort of vacation. Must shut down if I catch this mail.

> Believe me,
> Sincerely yours,
> Jack London.

MS: CSmH; 5 pp., tls. Pbd: *L*, 14–17; *BJL*, I, 278–79.

    1. The date, unclear on the original, has been corrected, apparently in CKL's hand.

    2. Ambrose Bierce (1842–?1914), San Francisco journalist and author, renowned for
his biting wit. He wrote for the *Argonaut*, the *Overland Monthly*, the *Wasp*, and the *San
Francisco Examiner*.

    3. Jeanie Peet.

    4. For another reference to Johns's connection with the Western Press syndicate, see JL
to Johns, March 30, 1899.

    5. *Vanity Fair* was a weekly magazine published in London from 1868 until 1928; it
dealt primarily with literary, political, and financial topics.

To Cloudesley Johns

> 962 East 16th. st.,
> Oakland, Calif.,
> Feb. 27, 1899.

Dear Sir:—

Since you have taken an interest in my work, I hope you will not be
disappointed with my non-appearance in the March number of *The Overland*. The editor[1] has but recently returned from New York, and I had
been waiting to see him personally. He has been pleased with my work,
and if I can keep up the standard, will handle more.

I cannot express the effect of hearing that what I have written has
pleased others, for you know, of all people in the world, the author is the
least competent to judge what he produces. At least, such is my opinion.
When I have finished a thing I cannot, as a rule, tell whether it is good or
trash. When I first looked over the printed "White Silence," I was sick at
heart, felt that it was a most miserable performance, and was heartily
ashamed that it had escaped the waste-paper basket. Yet it seems its effect
on others was different.

My life has been such a wandering one that there are great gaps in my
reading and education, and I am so conscious of them that I am afraid of
myself—besides, in the course of a sketch, I become saturated with the
theme till at last it palls upon me.

I appreciate, in a way, the high praise of being likened to Tourgenieff.

Though aware of the high place he occupies in literature, we are as strangers. I think it was in Japan I read his *House of Gentlefolk*;[2] but that is the only book of his I have ever seen—I do not even know if the title is correct. There is so much good stuff to read and so little time to do it in. It sometimes makes me sad to think of the many hours I have wasted over mediocre works, simply for want of better.

I can only thank you for your kindness: it has put new life into me and at the same time placed a few landmarks on the uncharted path the beginner must travel. Would you tell me of the error you mentioned? The compositors made some bad mistakes, the worst being a willful change in the title, and a most jarring one. It was plainly typewritten "To the Man On Trail"; This they printed "To the Man on the Trail." What trail? The thing was abstract.

Yours sincerely,
Jack London.

MS: CSmH; 2 pp., tls. Pbd; *L*, 17–18; *BJL*, I, 279–80.
    1. James Howard Bridge (1856–1939), editor of the *Overland Monthly* from 1896 to 1900, editor of *Commerce and Industry* from 1902 to 1903, and curator of the Frick Art Collection from 1914 to 1928. For his comments on JL, see his *Millionaires and Grub Street* (New York, 1931), pp. 200–202.
    2. Ivan Turgenev, *A Nest of Gentlefolk* (1859).

To Mabel Applegarth

962 East 16th. st.,
Feb. 28, 1899.

Dear Mabel:—

Yours came to hand not half an hour ago. Am very sorry to hear of Ted's illness, and I can appreciate just about how well worn out every one is. Now as to my coming down. If absolutely necessary, telegraph, and I will be there. Yet much as I would like to, my hands are so full and there is so much to be done, that I could not be just to my family and myself did I come when it was not absolutely necessary. You know how we are living from hand to mouth, nothing coming in except what is earned, even yet much of my stuff is in pawn and bills running galore.

And I wish to turn out some good work in this coming month, for I expect a call from the Post Office in April if not sooner. As to the good work—I will explain. James Howard Bridge, Editor of the *Overland* has at last returned. He at once sent for me. I went last Saturday. This is the essence of our conversation:

While advising the majority of candidates for the magazine field to seek other pursuits, he would not do so in my case. I showed the proper touch, only needing bringing out. Different people had been asking about me, Sunday Editors of the *Examiner*, etc. He had bought the Feb. *Overland* on the train West, and was quite taken with my "White Silence." Said it was the most powerful thing which had appeared in the magazine for a year; but he was afraid it was a fluke and perhaps it would be impossible for me to repeat it. etc. Now to his proposition. The *Overland* prints forty pages of advertisements at thirty dollars per page, while *McClure's* prints one hundred pages at three hundred dollars per page; yet printing, plates paper, mail service, etc. cost just as much for the *Overland*. The only thing the *Overland* could scale down was the writers, and these it had to. While not in position to pay me well, he thought he could give me most valuable returns for my work. If I sustained the promise I had given, he would give me a prominent place in the pages of his magazine, see that the newspapers, reviews, etc. puffed me, and inaugurate a boom to put my name before the public. You can readily see how valuable this would be—putting future employment into my hands from publications which could afford to pay well. Yet the best he could do would be $7.50 per sketch. It would take too long to go over all we said. I may be called over again any day.[1]

You understand my position, I hope; yet frankly, should it be necessary you know you can call upon me. As I expect it to rain this week, the roads will be impassible and I will have to have recourse to Ferry to Alviso.

Had to laugh on hearing that you had not seen my letter to Ted, and that your mother had read it to him. I wonder if she read it verbatim. There were some rather stiff things in it, not personal, but stiff for a woman to read to a man as coming from a third party.

From what I have told you above, you may see that things are brightening, only as yet in the future. I may not fulfill expectations, break down, and have to still further develop before I come out; and if I do not, even present success is a matter of much waiting. Enclosed letter from Cloudesley Johns, return with what you think of it. Don't think I've got the swellhead. I was sick at heart when I read printed "White Silence," and I yet fail to see anything in it. Give my regards to all, not excepting a good share to yourself, and believe me ready to come if you cannot get along without me.

Jack.

MS: CSmH; 2 pp., tls. Pbd: *L*, 18–19; *BJL*, I, 274–76.

1. For JL's later comments on his dealings with the *Overland Monthly*, see JL to Johns, November 11, 1899.

To Cloudesley Johns

962 East 16th. st.,
Oakland, Calif.,
Mar. 7, 1899.

My dear sir:—

How I appreciate your complaining of your friends when they say of your work, "Splendid," "Excellent," etc. That was my one great trouble.

The farther I wandered from the beaten track, (I mean the proper trend of modern style and literary art), the more encomiums were heaped upon me—by my friends. And believe me, the darkness I strayed into was heartbreaking. Surely, I have since thought, they must have seen where I was blind. So I grew to distrust them, and one day, between four and five months ago, awoke to the fact that I was all wrong. Everything crumbled away, and I started, from the beginning, to learn all over again. At first I was completely lost—had no conception even of the relative values of the comma, colon, and semicolon. Since then have been digging.

Just previous to your letter I ran across "The Voice of the Juice" in a heap of old magazines. Was struck with it at the time. Did not see the "Celestial Crime," but the "Glen Echo Mystery" was a most miserable affair.[1] Have never read any of Morrow's work.[2] But I do join with you, and heartily, in admiration of Robert Louis Stevenson. What an example he was of application and self development! As a storyteller there isn't his equal; the same might almost be said of his essays. While the fascination of his other works is simply irresistible, to me, the most powerful of all is his *Ebb Tide*.[3] There is no comparison possible between him and that other wonderful countryman of his; there is no common norm by which we may judge them. And I see I do not share with you in my admiration of Kipling. He touches the soul of things. "He draws the Thing as he sees it for the God of Things as they Are."[4] It were useless for me to mention all my favorites of his; let one example suffice. "The Song of the Banjo," and just one line from it. Away in the wilderness where younger sons are striving for hearth and saddle of their own, the banjo is singing, reminding them of the world from which they are exiled.

> "—— confess;
> I am torture, I am town, I am all that ever went
> with evening dress."[5]

How often, a thousand miles beyond the bounds of civilization, thirsting for a woman's face, a daily paper, a good book, or better music,—sick for the charms of the old life—have I had that line recalled by the tumpy tum of a banjo, epitomizing the whole mood.

> "I am torture, I am town, I am all that ever went
> with evening dress!"

How prosaic and lame my explanation of it seems; it's a feeling, only to be understood by one who has undergone.

No; I appreciate how educating my roving has been. At the same time I am sorry that my years could not have been condensed in some magic way, so as to have introduced an equal amount of the scholar's life. That's the trouble of having one's nature dominated by conflicting impulses.

O yes; I have children constantly footing it to the "silent sullen peoples"[6] who run the magazines! The *Overland* has taken a fancy to my North-land tales. My experience with them has been prompt publication; but their pay is small—especially at first. "The Son of the Wolf" was sent to them a week ago; they will have it out in the April number, if possible, illustrated by Dixon.[7] I have seen some of his Indian work and think he's just the man for my types; but I do not know him.

Speaking of the *Black Cat*; sometime since, they accepted a pseudo-scientific tale from me. I want to warn you, in case it comes out in the next year or so, that it was written several years ago—so you will forgive it. I hardly remember what it is like. The title is enough—"By a Thousand Deaths."

Another friend made the same criticism of "sole speck of life."[8] I was saturated with my thought—on the relation of the soul to infinity, etc.—was dealing with the soul of Malemute Kid and did not at the time recognize the dogs. Such slips are liable, since, like you, I can't revise manuscript. My favorite method of composition is to write from fifty to three hundred words, then type it in the Ms. to be submitted. Whatever emendations are made, are put in in the course of typing or inserted with ink in the Ms. I may learn the lapidary's art some day. Have at last learned to compose first, to the very conclusion, before touching pen to paper. I find I can thus do better work.

I have not seen any of your work, nor your mother's either—have done very little reading in the last several years. But I would like to see some. Could you send me some: I can easily return should you have no duplicates. And I warn you, I am as harsh on others as I expect them to be on me. This primrose dalliance among friends never leads anywhere. I once had a friend[9]—we went to college and did much of our studying together—with whom we could candidly discuss each other, holding back nothing. But he lies dead in Manila now. Yet once in a while even he got angry when I expressed my opinion too plainly.

Happened to have the December *Land of Sunshine*. Looked at Mary Hallock Foote's story and saw the mistake you mentioned.[10] Do they pay well? Kind of hard the way they hold a fellow's work back!

How are you off for humor? To save my life, while I can appreciate extremely well, I cannot develop a creative faculty for the same. Am starting out in a few minutes for a run to San Jose on my wheel; expect to stay over two or three days. So pardon abrupt close,

Sincerely yours,
Jack London.

MS: CSmH; 3 pp., tls. Pbd: *L*, 19–21; *BJL*, I, 280–82.

1. Charles Stuart Pratt, "A Celestial Crime," *Black Cat*, December 1897; Walter Wellman, "The Glen Echo Mystery," *Black Cat*, December 1898. Both were winners of the thousand-dollar first prize in the *Black Cat* story competitions ending on March 31 of those years, and both were mystery stories resolved by a scientific or pseudoscientific twist. "The

Voice of the Juice" may have been a *Black Cat* prizewinner in 1896. Virtually every year the *Black Cat* promoted itself by story competitions that handed out an impressive sum in prize money.

2. William C. Morrow (1854–1923), author of *The Ape, the Idiot and Other People* (1897) and other works of fiction and nonfiction. Morrow also wrote for the Southern Pacific and for San Francisco and San Jose newspapers in the 1890's.

3. *The Ebb Tide: A Trio and a Quartette* (1894), written with Lloyd Osbourne.

4. Rudyard Kipling, "When Earth's Last Picture Is Painted" (1892), l. 12.

5. "Hear me babble what the weakest won't confess— / I am Memory and Torment—I am Town! / I am all that ever went with evening dress!" ("The Song of the Banjo," ll. 30–32.)

6. Rudyard Kipling, "The White Man's Burden" (1898), l. 47.

7. "The Son of the Wolf: Third of the 'Malemute Kid' Stories," *Overland Monthly*, April 1899; later included in *The Son of the Wolf*. L. Maynard Dixon (1875–1946), Oregon-born artist whose work, which employed Western motifs, appeared frequently in the *Overland Monthly* and in the *Land of Sunshine*, an illustrated monthly promoting Southern California that was published in Los Angeles from 1894 until 1935 (in January 1902, the name was changed to *Out West*).

8. "Sole speck of life journeying across the ghostly wastes of a dead world, he trembles at his audacity, realizes that his is a maggot's life, nothing more. Strange thoughts arise unsummoned, and the mystery of all things strives for utterance" ("The White Silence.")

9. Fred Jacobs.

10. Mary Hallock Foote (1847–1938), novelist and illustrator. JL's reference is unclear, since she did not have a story in the December 1898 issue of the *Land of Sunshine*.

To Edward Applegarth

962 East 16th. st.,
Mar. 15, 1899.

Dear Ted:—

Pardon my not writing sooner, but have been quite busy. Went down to 11th. ave., Sunday, to carry Miss Sally Applegarths message. No one at home; so left card. Went yesterday, again, and saw Bert. His mother is away somewhere, but they expect her back shortly. I would advise your Aunt to write up before she comes and find out concerning that return— that is, if she should happen to start soon.

Found Johnny[1] sick abed with measles. That was what my mother was fearing would turn into mumps when I left for your place. His mother had just been sick with accidental poisoning, so my maternal parent was all alone. Have not been feeling well myself. Chilled badly several times Saturday night (an unusual thing for me) Sunday night found me with much fever, sweating, flushing, etc. Ditto Monday, and to-night have a headache, sneezes, and a very sick stomach.

Well, how are you people getting along? J. C. should be convalescent by this time. How is Mabel? And your mother? It will be a wonder if she don't come down after all the strain she has undergone. And Nana? Give her my express regards, and apologize for me for my not coming up to say goodbye. Tell her it was so early in the morning, or she was asleep— anything like that.

"Father Roubeau's Confession" came back. I have revised it, and changed the title to "The Priestly Prerogative."[2] Also prefaced it with a quotation from "Proverbs." Also, added to that particular proverb. Am out of paper, so have not typed it yet. Sent off ten Mss., and have nine more ready to go, as soon as I get stamps. Revised three more, yesterday and to-day, and expect to revise another five thousand word one to-night.

It seems as though I am forgetting something, but to save my life I can't remember what it is. With regards to all, and hoping that you are nearly your old self by this time, I am,

Yours very truly,
Jack London.

MS: CSt; 1 p., tls.
1. Johnny Miller.
2. JL had submitted the story to *Munsey's* on January 29, 1899; he subsequently sent it to *Frank Leslie's* on March 20 and the *Pall Mall Gazette* on April 25. After it had been rejected by these magazines, he sent it to the *Overland Monthly* on May 15, where it was published in July 1899 as "The Priestly Prerogative: Sixth of the 'Malemute Kid' Stories." The story was later included in *The Son of the Wolf*.

To Cloudesley Johns

962 East 16th. st.,
Oakland, Calif.,
Mar. 15, 1899.

Dear Sir:—

I see I have mistaken your name—an illustration of my habitual carelessness. Shall not occur again. I agree with you that R.L.S. never turned out a foot of polished trash, and that Kipling has; but—well, Stevenson never had to worry about ways or means, while Kipling, a mere journalist, hurt himself by having to seek present sales rather than posthumous fame. Stevenson received from his people 93 pounds, I believe, per year. Think of it! forty dollars a month, with no one to care for but himself, and in a country where that forty dollars was equal in purchasing power to nearly eighty here.

How those lines, prefacing one of K's tales, have haunted me!

O Thou who hast builded the world!
O Thou who hast lighted the sun!
O Thou who has darkened the Tarn!
  Judge Thou
The sin of the Stone that was hurled
By the Goat from the light of the Sun,
As She sinks in the mire of the Tarn,
  Even now—even now—even now![1]

Kipling has his hand upon the "fatted soul of things."[2]

Speaking of humor—find enclosed triolets, the first, and also the last, I ever attempted. Perhaps there's no market for such things. *Judge* and *Life* refused them, and I quit.[3]

So you have completed a novel? Lucky dog! How I envy you! I have only got from ten to twenty mapped out, but God knows when I'll ever get a chance to begin one, much less finish it. I have figured that it is easier to make one of from thirty-five to sixty thousand words and well written, than one three or four times as long and poorly written. What do you think about it? Tell me about yours, how long it is, theme, etc.

Last November I spent a couple of hours over the last ten or twelve numbers of *Short Stories*. Of all I went through, there is only one I can remember anything about. I skimmed through most, skipped many, and only read those which attracted. The one I recollect, I think must be that of your mother's.[4] I don't know, now, what drew me to it, but anyway I read it. Doesn't it deal with a great wood-chopping peasant with an airy fairy creature of a wife, and situated in France somewhere at the close of the Hundred Year's War? Do not remember the divisions you mention as having been mangled by the editor, so I may be mistaken. The contrast of the man and wife and their love was well done, and the touch about the children which might have come was most pathetic—gave me the shivery sensation at the base of the spine, which is always mine when deeply touched or stirred. If that was not your mother's, and you have read it, you will surely remember it.

As you say, " 'Zebro' is not bad of its kind." The one trouble is that the literature of the times demand so much of that kind. It has unity, and the part of Zebro is well simulated. Interest is sustained, and I doubt if very many would anticipate. Am afraid I am hypercritical on this last point. Have worried so about being anticipated myself, that I always, self-consciously, set myself down to discover a writer's point in advance. I'll wager you can handle the same thing far better to-day. Still, you threw in a few hints of atmosphere, and how many things do we read which are totally devoid of that essential?

By the way, should you happen to have no duplicate you will wish it returned. Let me know. I like to be in possession of everything of my own—a sort of crystalization of one's labor, very pleasant to contemplate. Now that you speak of it, I remember *The Ape, the Idiot and Other People*—had forgotten author.[5] No; I shall not go into *Century* Competition.[6] Am not a grad. Left in my Sophomore year for Klondike,[7] and don't think I shall ever return. Struck the following some time ago:

"Now!" cried the reviewers, "here is a pedestal for you—up you go!"

"Gentlemen," blubbered Patient Merit, "you are too kind!—but help me up."

And they helped him up.

And when he was well posed they proceeded to throw potsherds at him.

> Very sincerely,
> Jack London.

MS: CSmH; 3 pp., tls. Pbd: *L*, 22–23; *BJL*, I, 282.
   1. Rudyard Kipling, "'By the Hoof of the Wild Goat,'" ll. 13–20. This poem appears as the epigraph to "To Be Filed for Reference" (1888).
   2. Rudyard Kipling, "The Song of the Banjo," l. 78.
   3. JL's triolets were "He Chortled with Glee," "When He Came In," "Just Over the Way," and "Trying to Miss His Trip to Hades." After rejection by three other magazines, all four triolets were sent to *Town Topics* on March 15, 1899. "He Chortled with Glee" was published in *Town Topics*, April 20, 1899 (JL received one dollar in payment on August 1); the other three triolets were rejected. JL's magazine sales record indicates that "When He Came In" was sent to *Town Topics* again on April 26, 1900, and accepted on May 10, 1900; but JL made no record of publication or payment. *Judge* (1881–1939) and *Life* (1883–1936) were weekly satire magazines published in New York.
   4. Jeanie Peet, "Big Maxime," *Short Stories*, August 1898. *Short Stories* is an all-fiction monthly published in New York; it was established in 1890.
   5. William C. Morrow.
   6. The *Century* Competition for College Graduates, which awarded prizes of $250 plus publication for the best essay, story, and poem submitted by college graduates of a given year. The *Century Illustrated Monthly Magazine* was published in New York from 1881 until 1929 and featured short stories, serial fiction, biography, and historical articles.
   7. JL actually left the University of California after the first term of his freshman year.

To Cloudesley Johns

> 962 East 16th. st.,
> Mar. 30, 1899.

My dear friend:—
   Three or four months on the edge of the desert, all alone—how I envy you; and again, how I thank heaven I am not in a similar position.[1] What a glorious place it must be in which to write! That's one of the drawbacks of my present quarters. Everybody comes dropping in, and I haven't the heart to turn them away. Every once in a while, some old shipmate turns up. With but one exception, this is their story: "Just returned from a long voyage; what a wonderful fellow Jack London is; what a good comrade he always was; never liked anybody in all the world so much; have a barrel of curios aboard which will bring over in a couple of days for a present; big payday coming; expect to get paid off to-morrow—" "Say, Jack old boy, can you lend us a couple of dollars till to-morrow?" That's the way they always wind up. And then I scale them down about half, give them the money and let them go. Some I never hear from again; others come back the third and fourth time.
   But I have the fatal gift of making friends without exertion. And they never forget me. Of course they are not of the above calibre; but I'd just

as soon give them the money and let them go, as to have them eat up my time as they always do. Among my feminine friends I am known as "only Jack." 'Nough said. Any trouble, tangles, etc., finds me called upon to straighten out. Since Saturday morning I have spent my whole time for one of them, and have accomplished what she and her friends failed to do in five years. This evening I shall finally settle the whole thing to her satisfaction;—but look at the time I have lost. Of course, remuneration is out of the question; but it will have so endeared me to her, that she'll call again the next time she gets into a scrape. And so it goes—time—time—time. How precious the hours are!

But I should not be unjust. The other afternoon I met an old friend on the car. Delighted to see me; must go back to the "society" again. I finally promised to go down the following night; but lo, he had spread the news among other friends who had not seen me for two long years. I really did not think they or people in general ever had cared so much for me, and I was ready to weep with sheer happiness at the sincerity of their delight on again seeing me. Couldn't escape; the whole night was lost among them; supper had been ordered, other forgotten friends invited; etc.

And to me, the strangest part is, that while considering myself blessed above all with the best of friends, I know that I have never done anything to deserve them or to hold them. Mind you the crowd I have reference to in previous paragraph, has never received a favor of me, nor is bound to me by the slightest social, racial, or perhaps intellectual tie. And so it goes.

But I have been isolated so much, that I can no longer bear to be torn away for long at a time from the city life. In this particular you will see my thankfulness at not filling your position. Yet you may keep in touch with the world with those trains ever passing.

I suppose you see many of the genus hobo, do you not? I, too, was a tramp once, and beat my way by the most approved methods from Ocean to Ocean, begging my meals from door to door.[2] I remember, one night, leaving a swell function in Michigan and crossing the Lake to Chicago. There, the following morning found me hustling at back doors for a breakfast. That night I made over two hundred miles into Ohio before they finally put me off the train. I wonder what the young lady whom I took into supper would have thought, had she seen me anywhere from twelve to twenty-four hours after.

How I chatter—all about self! I hope your sentiments about my criticism have not been disguised; I was prepared for most anything. The story is good; but I am so prone to see what might be done, that I cannot refrain from suggesting. I cannot re-write; but in turn, I write more slowly. I used to go at it like a hurricane, but found I failed to do myself justice, and gradually grew out of the bad habit. After sending criticism, and being reminded by the same of Bierce, I dug up *Soldiers and Civilians*.[3] I notice in his work the total absence of sympathy. They are wonderful in their way, yet owe nothing to grace of style; I might almost characterize them as having a metallic intellectual brilliancy. They appeal to the mind, but not the heart. Yes; they appeal to the nerves, too; but you well notice in a psychological and not emotional manner. I am a great admirer of him, by the way, and never tire of his Sunday work in the *Examiner*.[4]

Quite a encouraging letter, that of the Western Press. It is evident your work has struck them. Would like to read said article. Pity their pay is so small; but you may like another, realize more on the work when collected and presented to the public between covers. What field (I mean what papers) does that Syndicate cover?

It's very kind of you to surrender the western leadership to me; no more do I deserve it; our styles, methods, etc, are so utterly different, that such procedure would be absurd. But we shall do like Antony and Octavian—divide the world between us. What say you? I must confess your letters are refreshing, have a smack of personality, and a unique personality, about them. You at least would not be lost in the common herd. A strong will can accomplish anything—I believe you to be possessed of the same—why not form the habit of studying? There is no such thing as inspiration, and very little of genius. Dig, blooming under opportunity, results in what appears to be the former, and certainly makes possible the development of what original modicum of the latter which one may possess. Dig is a wonderful thing, and will move more mountains than faith ever dreamed of. In fact, dig should be the legitimate father of all self-faith.

Thanks for criticism of poem—merely an experiment, you know. However, I don't exactly agree with you about "absurd." I know the technical accent is on the second syllable, while the accent of either syllable is really indistinguishable as to importance. It was not till after I had completed it that I noticed the debt owing to Omar Kayam. And by the way, what do you think of Le Gallienne?[5] As a writer, I like him. As a man, I have no respect for him, dislike him; yet I know nothing about him as a man. Perhaps it's the ideas I got of the man, Le Gallienne, from reading his work. In his version of the *Rubaiyat*, I was especially struck by the following, describing his search for the secret of life:

"Up, up where Parrius' hoofs stamp heaven's floor,
My soul went knocking at each starry door,
   Till on the stilly top of heaven's stair,
Clear-eyed I looked—and laughed—and climbed no more."[6]

But I prefer Fitzgerald's.

It is well you appreciate the virtue in lack of wealth, and you seem to be all the better for it. Here's what wealth would have done for me: it would have turned me into a prince of good fellows, and, barring accidents, would have killed me of strong drink before I was thirty.

We are at one in many things. I, too, have worked like a horse, and eat like an ox; but as to the work—while no comrade can ever say Jack London shirked in the slightest, I hate the very thought of thus wasting my time. It's so deadening—I mean hard labor. We agree as to aversion to getting married; but not so as to women one might link oneself to for life. I am sure I have met a thousand such. As passionate as you, with probably less curb, I think I must have been created for some polygamous country. While I have a strong will, I deliberately withold it when it happens to clash with desire. I simply refuse to draw the curb. When I was just sixteen I broke loose and went off on my own hook. Took unto myself a mistress of the same age, lived a year of wildest risk in which I made more money in one week than I do in a year now, and then, to escape the inevitable downward drift, broke away from everything and went to sea.[7] My one great weakness is the study of human nature. Knowing no God, I have made of man my worship; and surely I have learned how vile he can be. But this only strengthens my regard, because it enhances the mighty heights he can bring himself to tread. How small he is, and how great he is! But this weakness, this desire to come in touch with every strange soul I meet, has caused me many a scrape.

I may go to Paris in 1900; but great things must occur first. I liked the story you sent. No sentimental gush, no hysteria, but the innate pathos of it! Who could not feel for Mrs. Anerton? Our magazines are so goody-goody, that I wonder they would print a thing as risque and as good as that. This undue care to not bring the blush to the virgin cheek of the American young girl, is disgusting. And yet she is permitted to read the daily papers! Ever read Paul Bourget's comparison of the American and French young women?[8]

Excuse poor typing, for I get seated and rattle it off. Don't take the care with correspondence as I do with regular composition.

Yours sincerely,
Jack London.

MS: CSmH; 5 pp., tls. Pbd: *L*, 24–27; *BJL*, I, 86, 282–85.

    1. Since 1895, Johns had been assistant postmaster (and general handyman) in Harold, California, a post he was to fill until April 1901. In 1894 his mother, Jeanie Peet, had purchased 160 acres of land near Harold, where she served as a postmaster. The "three or four months" to which JL refers have not been identified.

    2. JL tramped across the continent in 1894, an experience he later recounted in *The Road* (New York: Macmillan, 1907). See also Richard W. Etulain, ed., *Jack London on the Road: The Tramp Diary and Other Hobo Writings* (Logan, Utah, 1979). Cloudesley Johns had tramped around California in 1893, 1894, and 1897.

    3. Ambrose Bierce, *Tales of Soldiers and Civilians* (1891), his first collection of short stories.

    4. Bierce, writing under the pseudonym "Town Crier," wrote a satire column entitled "Prattle" for the *San Francisco Examiner*.

    5. Richard Le Gallienne (1866–1947), British journalist, essayist, poet, and novelist, and chief reader for the Bodley Head, prestigious London publisher of the 1890's avant-garde. His *The Rubáiyát of Omar Khayyám, a Paraphrase from Several Literal Translations*

was published in 1897. Le Gallienne's work occasionally appeared in the *San Francisco Examiner.*

6. Stanza 60. Le Gallienne has "Parwín's," not "Parrius'."

7. For an account of JL's life with the oyster pirates and the California Fish Patrol, see JL to the Corresponding Editor, *Youth's Companion,* March 9, 1903; JL to Houghton, Mifflin & Co., January 31, 1900; and chapters 7–12 of his autobiographical treatise *John Barleycorn* (New York: Century, 1913). JL used these experiences as the basis for *The Cruise of the Dazzler* (New York: Century, 1902) and *Tales of the Fish Patrol* (New York: Macmillan, 1905). In 1891, at the age of fifteen, he bought the boat *Razzle Dazzle,* became an oyster pirate, then joined the California Fish Patrol several months later, in 1892; in January of 1893 he began his seal-hunting voyage on the *Sophia Sutherland.* The "mistress" to whom he refers is identified as "Mamie . . . the Queen of the Oyster Pirates" and the niece of "Spider" Healey, "a black-whiskered wharf-rat of twenty" in *John Barleycorn* (p. 65); her true identity has not been determined (see *BJL,* I, 84).

8. Paul Bourget, *Outre-Mer: Impressions of America* (1895), pp. 71–109. Bourget described the independence and variety of American girls, saying that they became fully adult in character, freedom, and habits before marriage, whereas French girls expected to be molded after marriage by their husbands.

To Cloudesley Johns

962 East 16th. st.,
Oakland, Calif.,
April, 17, 1899.

My dear friend:–

Am afraid you will suffer offense every time I write to you. I never wrote a letter yet without forcing myself to it, and I never completed one without sighing a great sigh of relief. As a correspondent I shall never shine. But O how dearly I love to read the letters which come to me from those who little know how I dislike answering. And I never would answer, did I not know they would also cease. I like to write business letters of from one to six lines—can turn so many out in the course of half an hour, you know. Lassalle, the brilliant German Jew, friend to Bismarck and mainly responsible for the latter's State Socialism,—well, Lassalle made and maintained a rule that even his most favored correspondent must write him twice for his once. He broke with one of his best friends because that friend refused to yield to the imposition. And I don't blame the friend; at the same time I envy Lassalle the result of his nerve.[1]

You will notice "The City of the Dreadful Night." He wrote a later article under that title, discarding the first. It is very powerful, if I recollect correctly, for I read it a number of years ago. I have sought it often since, but always vainly.[2] I see you are opposed to Jingoism. Yet I dare not express my views, for to so do myself adequate justice, would require at least one hundred thousand words. An evoloutionist, believing in Natural Selection, half believing Malthus' "Law of Population,"[3] and a myriad of other factors thrown in, I cannot but hail as unavoidable, the Black and the Brown going down before the White.

I see, after stating that I would not express my views, I have done the contrary. Will shut up at once.

Have you ever done anything with the San Francisco *Argonaut*?[4] I see most of the stuff they print (usually an original short story each week), (2000 to 3500 words), is after your method, as exemplified in "Zebro" and "The Norton-Drake." Have never sent them any of my stuff, deeming it utterly different from what they required.

Town Topics has accepted a two eight-line stanza humorous fancy.[5] Have you ever dealt with them? What do they pay?

So you grow a-weary of the social whirl. Ditto here—only because it eats up so much time. To satisfy my various sides I should be possessed of at least a dozen astral selves, and even then my composite self would be well worked out. Temporary embarrassment led me into hypothecating my dress suit some months ago. You have no idea how easy it is to decline invitations after doing a thing like that. I think I shall allow it to remain, though I greatly fear it may be constantly rented out at so much per night. Most likely it was luckier than its master and shone with 'Frisco's swell-dom at the late seismic disturbance—commonly known as the grand opera. Well, if mine uncle does that, it at least will not suffer from moths.

What an acerbitous tongue, or rather, pen, you have in handling topics such as the Virginia Fair and Vanderbilt foregathering.[6] I greatly enjoy it, and have taken the liberty to read certain portions of the same to friends. I mean of your letters. The Fair-Vanderbilt, of course, in its entirety.[7]

What a delightful, fascinating woman, the mother of Ab must have been.[8] Find enclosed review of Gertrude Atherton's *Daughter of the Vine*.[9] I see the current *Argonaut* half intimates that its a sort of free version of some tale published in their columns some years ago. Enjoyed your "April" & "May"—nearly wore it out by carrying around in my pocket. You've a most virile swing to it.

And you are a man who writes jokes, who has written jokes—a real live man! Well, well. I used to think the joke writer a fictitious personage, a sort of solar myth. I once wrote a joke and sent it the rounds—it must have been a very poor joke. Now that the joke writer is a flesh and blood contemporary, I shall write another and start it off.[10] By the way, to satisfy a curious mortal, what was the "Four-in-hand" worth? "Sam Davis has Dropped the Pen for the Toga"—was it published in the *Examiner*? May I know what they paid for it? And may I retain it a week longer to send to a friend? I see the last is supererogatory—I shall have to retain it. From "The Trust Magnate," I imagine we come together somewhat on our political and economic views.

James Creelman has been branded for some time as an autotheist of the most pronounced type. Enclosed cable from him was published in the *Examiner*. A couple nights later it was parodied by a *Bulletin* reporter. I thought the latter neat.[11]

I concede that a natural proficiency is requisite, but add that not one in a hundred will develop without the requisite dig and plenty of it. I like those four lines from Chas. Holt, the infallible rover poet.[12] Too bad such men are not more plastic. I was once shipmates with a Holt. He was drowned with all hands the following year, and I just missed being with them by a miracle.[13]

I differ from you. I honestly can't think of an enemy I possess on either side of the grave. Yet I am very prone to read the law in unmistakable terms, and on occasion, have thrashed the very best of my friends. But in the latter case, only did it when they needed it very badly; and believe me, it always did them good, and made our friendship the better. But enemies—bah! There is no necessity. Lick a man, when it comes to the pinch, or be licked, but never hold a grudge. Settle it for once and all, and forgive.

All my life I have sought an ideal chum—such things as ideals are never attainable, anyway. I never found the man in whom the elements were so mixed that he could satisfy, or come any where near satisfying my ideal. A brilliant brain—good; and then the same united with physical cowardice—nit And vice a versa. So it goes and has gone. From what I have learned of you, you approach as nearly as any I have met. But, personality, as reflected by pen and paper, and personality face to face, are two very different things. But I imagine you to have the two main things I have sought.

We agree as to Le Gallienne—pray tell me how you reached your conclusions—I can't for the life of me see how I gained mine.

Next letter shall send you "A look into the gulf," by Markham, father of "Man With the Hoe." Bierce considers it genuine poetry, while he characterizes "Man with hoe" as sand-lot-ism.[14] Don't agree with him. The "look into the gulf" is excellent. It is away to a friend just now.

It's a great thing, this coming to believe "that the universe can continue to exist and operate in a satisfactory manner, without the perpetuation of one's own individuality." I am an agnostic, with one exception: I do believe in the soul. But in the latter case, I can only see with death, the disintegration of the spirit's individuality, similar to that of the flesh. If people could come to realize the utter absurdity, logically, of the finite contemplating the infinite!

I realize the truth in your criticism of ringing the changes on Malemute Kid; but I had started out with that intention, and made arrangements with the *Overland* accordingly. But you will notice in the "Son of the Wolf" that he appears only cursorily. In the June tale he will not appear at all, or even be mentioned.[15] You surprise me with the aptness of your warning, telling me I may learn to love him too well myself. I am afraid I am rather stuck on him—not on the one in print, but the one in my brain. I doubt if I ever shall get him in print. Your criticism is so true that I shall be delighted to not debate the question with you.

Several technical mistakes in "The Improved Exit." Which is neither here nor there, as Kipling would say. No; they did not go all the way to Klondike for salmon; but it was an important factor to existence to such as lived in the country—especially was it fed to the dogs through the long winters. The salmon run two and three thousand miles up the Yukon and its tributaries to spawn—finest salmon in the world. They are so exhausted by the long trip that they never get back to salt water again, dying in the fall as the river freezes up. They are so thick on some of the tributaries, and the bears come to feed upon them in such quantities that Indians shun such spots, as not being conducive to long life. In summertime, the dogs are worthless as far as sledding goes; so they turn them loose to shift for themselves. They make good livings and get fat, fishing for the salmon. They are very intelligent.

Don't agree with you regarding your criticism of face torn away by bear. Had forgotten Kipling's "Truce,"[16] but anyway it does not matter. Many men are killed yearly, up there, and many more fearfully mangled. If we should allow the successful men to copyright any topic they once happen to camp upon, what the devil would you and I and a very numerous tribe do? Thanks for yellow flag. Don't think I can turn away my friends so easily. Happened to mention in similar postals to yours that I was sick and busy, and at once received a couple of offers to come and take care of me, read to me, etc. Say! I answered very next mail, for fear they would not wait and come anyway.

How can I thank your mother for her criticism of my effusion. You see I am experimenting along those lines, and a blazed trail or a guide will save many mistakes. It was just what I needed. I shall certainly cut out last stanza, altogether, and remodel the penultimate one so that it will become the finish. Shall also, some day when the mood is on me, change the whole thing as per criticism. I can no more say how valuable your mother's advice was than can I thank her for it. It was very, very kind of her, to say the least.

I return hers to you—what a fascinating letter she writes!

Dead wall? Who doesn't strike dead walls? I have spent a day at a time, and then quit, with absolutely nothing to show. Don't believe in writing rapidly any more. Write a tenth as much and strive to make it ten times as good.

Run across these lines of Helen Hunt Jackson, have been haunting me ever since.

> "His thoughts were song, his life was singing,
>   Men's hearts like harps he held and smote,
> But ever in his heart went ringing,
>   Ringing the song he never wrote."[17]

Remember "Tragedy of the Muse"?[18] also letter with superscription of "dear you"? A very interesting woman who writes me regularly, began to use that phrase on me. And I was struck by it, and appropriated it. She also had read aforementioned tale and drawn it from that source.

O, if you only saw the pile of letters I must answer after this! They've been piling up for ten days.

I know I have forgotten something, but will have to let it slide.

Yours, as ever, sincerely,
Jack London.

MS: CSmH; 6 pp., tls. Pbd: *L*, 27–30; *BJL*, I, 285–86.

1. Ferdinand Lassalle (1825–64), Prussian revolutionist, disciple of Marx, and socialist propagandist; regarded as the founder of the German Social Democratic Party. He began his correspondence with the "Iron Chancellor," Otto von Bismarck, in 1863. The friend of Lassalle JL refers to in his anecdote has not been identified.

2. Rudyard Kipling, "'The City of Dreadful Night'" (1885), collected in *Life's Handicap: Being Stories of Mine Own People* (1891), centers on a description of the populace of Lahore, seen as corpses, asleep outside in the moonlight. Kipling did not discard his earlier sketch, but he used the same title for an extended account of Calcutta, published in 1891.

3. Malthus's *An Essay on the Principle of Population* (1798) claims that, if unchecked, population will increase geometrically, whereas the food supply will increase at best arithmetically.

4. The *Argonaut* was a San Francisco weekly magazine published from 1877 until 1958 that featured satirical commentary, social news, and articles on the arts.

5. "If I Were God One Hour," *Town Topics*, May 11, 1899. *Town Topics: The Journal of Society*, published in New York from 1879 until 1937, contained articles on society affairs, literature, poetry, and art. JL submitted the poem on March 15, 1899, and received $2.25 on August 1, 1899, after dunning the magazine. See JL to Johns, August 10, 1899.

6. On April 4, 1899, Virginia Fair married William K. Vanderbilt, Jr., in New York. In the hope of glimpsing the lavish gowns and decorations the newspapers had promised, throngs of women gathered before the wedding in the street outside; police had to restrain the crowd so that the guests could pass through.

7. The last two sentences of this paragraph were added as an afterthought, in JL's hand.

8. JL refers to Red-Spot, a character in Stanley Waterloo's *The Story of Ab: A Story of the Time of the Cave Men* (1897). Waterloo later accused JL of plagiarizing this novel in *Before Adam* (New York: Macmillan, 1907); see JL to B. W. Babcock, December 3, 1906, and JL to Waterloo, October 20, 1906, and February 15, 1908.

9. Gertrude Atherton (1857–1948), California novelist; *The Daughter of the Vine* (1899), a tale of a California heiress's losing battle with alcoholism, set in San Francisco in 1860. JL probably sent Johns "Gertrude Atherton's New California Novel Is Very Forceful," *San Francisco Sunday Examiner Magazine*, April 9, 1899.

10. JL sent six jokes to magazines, but only one was published: "Eggs Without Salt," *Town Topics*, August 11, 1899, for which he was paid fifty cents. JL's unpublished jokes were "Compound Fracture," "Poet's Corner," "Blinx and the Queen's English," "Tommy and the Filipino," and "Polly, Dolly and Secrets." JL's joke "Compound Fracture" (MS: ULA) is a sample of the jokes he submitted:

Mike.– An' what's the matter wid yer arm?
Pat.– Sure, an the Docther sez it's compound fracture, but it's meself belaves the bones
is broken.

JL submitted this joke seven times before retiring it.

11. James Creelman (1859–1915), Canadian-born journalist, then editorial-page editor for the *New York Journal*. JL refers to "*Lawton* with His Fighting Americans *Takes* the Rebel Stronghold of *Santa Cruz*," *San Francisco Examiner*, April 11, 1899, which reported

on a battle in the Filipino uprising; the parody of this article may have been "Rebels Chased to Their Lairs," *San Francisco Bulletin*, April 14, 1899.

12. Charles Holt, Southern California poet, who published in the *Land of Sunshine*.

13. Pete Holt, seal-hunter and JL's shipmate on the *Sophia Sutherland*. According to *John Barleycorn*, chap. 17, Holt was lost when the *Mary Thomas* went down in 1894 with all hands.

14. Charles Edwin Markham (1852–1940), Oregon-born poet and lecturer, who lived in California and is best known for *The Man with the Hoe and Other Poems* (1899) and *Lincoln and Other Poems* (1901). "A Look into the Gulf" and "The Man with the Hoe," which was subtitled "Written after Seeing Millet's World-Famous Painting," were published in the former. In addition to being a poet, Markham was an educator: in 1899 he was head-master of the Tompkins Observation School in Oakland, a facility affiliated with the University of California. Bierce's accusation of "sand-lotism"—a rhetoric reminiscent of the mass labor meetings held in the sand lots before San Francisco's City Hall in the 1870's—was directed at the poem's overt concern with the exploitation of labor. Perhaps Bierce was better pleased by the exoticism and metaphysical theme of "A Look into the Gulf," which seem more typical of 1890's verse. For Bierce's criticism of Markham's poetry, see "Edwin Markham's Poems," *Collected Works of Ambrose Bierce* (1909–12), vol. 10, pp. 137–48. JL reviewed *Lincoln and Other Poems* in the *San Francisco Sunday Examiner Magazine*, November 10, 1901.

15. "In a Far Country," *Overland Monthly*, June 1899; later included in *The Son of the Wolf*.

16. In Kipling's poem "The Truce of the Bear" (1898), collected in *The Five Nations* (1903), a blind beggar tells the story of how his face was completely torn away when, having cornered a bear, he hesitated when touched with pity for the bear's apparently human gesture of supplication and weakness as it reared upright for its final attack.

17. "The Song He Never Wrote," in *Sonnets and Lyrics* (1886), ll. 1–4. Helen Hunt Jackson (1830–85), poet, novelist, philanthropist, and lifelong friend of Emily Dickinson.

18. Edith Wharton (1862–1937), "The Muse's Tragedy," in *The Greater Inclination* (1899), her first collection of stories.

To Cloudesley Johns

962 East 16th. st.,
April 22, 1899.

My dear friend:–

Not to be thought of. When such time comes that I think I require two for one, I'll hire a secretary and let him write up alternate letters. I re-member "Thomas the Doubter," [1] now. A friend of mine quoted portions of it one night, but I was just dozing off and failed to follow him. It is very good, and how one can, in the face of it, stomach such things as the in-finite mercy of the most infinitely merciless of creators, is more than I can understand. Pardon the double superlative—"most infinite." By the way, is "infinite" capable of comparison? And again: your mother was wrong, at least I believe so, concerning "while." "Wile" means a trick, strategm, seduction, etc. "While" means to loiter, to cause time to pass away pleas-antly and without irksomeness.

"Master of His Fate" is something I have been trying to get hold of for a long while. Of course, philosophically, it is but part true; but it is often better to cast out such considerations when dealing with such subjects in any other save a philosophical way. I see, from present selections, that you enjoy tilting against the established theology.

Have you read *Cyrano De Bergerac*? I saw it ably staged last year, and have a pirated edition of it. I was greatly taken with it, and if you have not read it, and would care to, I'll send it down. What say? Shall retain selections till next I write you, as I wish to take off a couple of them.

I sometimes fear that, while I shall surely develop expression some day, I lack in origination. Perhaps this feeling is due to the fact that almost every field under the sun, and over it too, has been so thoroughly exploited by others. Sometimes I hit upon a catchy title, and just as sure as I do I find some one else has already used it. Which reminds me of a talented young fellow I met in the Klondike. Several of his librettos are running at the present time. He told me that his first opera was named *La Sonambula* and he speedily discovered that over a hundred others had been composed with similar titles. Then he composed one, *The Juke-Jukes*, only to be informed that several portions were direct infringements of portions of operas already staged. They offered to stage it at a cost of not less than twenty thousand, if he would make the requisite alterations, but he refused. I don't know what has happened to the same since. But so it goes. Look at the meters other men have rendered classic, and thus debarred the coming generations from for all time. What would happen to you or I, should we compose an epic in the measure of "Hiawatha"? And pray, where in the devil are we to originate new schools of fiction?

Did you ever notice that typewriting was not conducive to good letter-writing? "The Gila Monster"[2] smacks of just the flavor of most the stories I see in the *Argonaut*. And some of them are very clever. From the way you remark on *Town Topics* it is evident you have had an experience with them. Tell us about it. I forgot to say that they had also taken a triolet, "He chortled with glee." Guess I won't bother with any more of such work. Too much strain for such small returns. The only reason I ever venture such things is a desire to practice up thinking in meter. And the more rigid or more intricate structures are good training.

Ha! ha! You demand comfort in place of conventionality, eh? Ditto here. To-morrow I shall put on a white shirt, and I shall do it under protest. I wear a sweater most of the time, and pay calls, etc. in a bicycle suit. My friends have passed through the stage of being shocked, and no matter what I should do henceforth, would, I know, remark "It's only Jack." I once rode a saddle horse from Fresno to the Yosemite Valley, clad in almost tropical nudity, with a ball room fan and a silk parasol. It was amusing to witness the countryside turn out as I went along. Some of my party who lagged behind, heard guesses hazarded as to whether I was male or female. The women of the party were tenderly nurtured, and I hardly know if they have recovered yet, or if their proprieties rather have yet come down to normal. In fact, there was only one I failed to disturb, and he was the rugged old Chinese Cook—nothing shocked him except the Mariposa Big Trees.[3] Coming unexpectedly upon the first one, he could not conceal his astonishment, but blurted forth "Gee Klist! Chop'm up four foot ties, make'm one dam rail road!" After we arrived in the Valley he stayed in camp—he was rather set in his ideas, and considered the natural phenomena as innovations which should not be countenanced for a moment.

As to evening dress, I think many a man looks extremely well in it. Of course, not all by a large majority. I like that clean feeling of well fitting clothes, etc—which is strange for one who has passed through as many dirty periods as I have. But there are very few women I care to see in decollete (or however you spell it). As to the breeding of cripples—I shall try to get something uncompressed[4] before marrying, and then, if I have to take her off to a desert isle, I'll see that no compression goes on while she is carrying any flesh and bone of mine. Barrenness is a terrible thing for a woman; but the paternal instinct is so strong in me that It would almost kill me to be the father of a child not physically or mentally sound. Sometimes I think, because this is so very strong in me, that I am destined to die childless. I can understand a Napoleon divorcing a Josephine, even casting aside state reasons. At the same time, I could not do likewise under similar circumstances. I can condone in others what I haven't the heart, or have too much heart to do myself.

How one wanders on!

"Carvajal the Thorough" was good. If I am correct, Markham will never see forty-five again. He became a father about two weeks and a half ago.[5] I send his "Look Into the Gulf." To me it is a wonderful piece of work. Tell us what you think of it; keep it as long as you wish; but, don't fail to send it back in the end.

I also send you some of my schoolboy work.[6] Stuff written years ago. I found it accidentally, to-day, rummaging through an old trunk down in the basement. I had not seen it in years, and had forgotten its very existence. It is but a modicum of what I wrote during that period, but is fairly representative. Through reading it you may gain a comprehension of one of my many sides, though of course you must take into consideration my youth at the time of writing, if you should try to weigh my presentation of the subjects in hand. People thought I would outgrow that condition and fall back into the conservative ways of thinking. I am happy to say they were mistaken. But believe me, while a radical, I am not fanatical; nor am I anything but normal, and fallible, in all affairs of reason. Emotion is quite another matter. The trouble is so few understand Socialism or its advocates. But I shall cut this short, else I will be delivering a diatribe on the dismal science.

I see Edith Wharton, writer of the "Tragedy of the Muse," is just bringing out a volume of short stories in which that piece figures—Scribners, I think are the publishers. How the short story is growing in importance in modern literature! It almost seems the novel is destined to become extinct within a generation or two. I envy you your abnormal memory. I grasp easily, but memorize only in a fairly average sort of a way. I am sure there are thousands of books I have read, the very titles of which are forgotten.

There is only one kind of infallibility that I can tolerate, nay, I can enjoy it, and that is the infallibility of the goodnatured fool. As for cowardice in man: I can forgive the errors of a generation of women far more easily than one poltroon of the opposite gender.

> "In the fell clutch of circumstance
> I have not winced nor cried aloud,
> Under the bludgeoning of chance
> My head is bloody, but unbowed."[7]

Such, in all things, is what I admire in men. The "fine frenzy" of the poet can arouse no greater number of tingles along my spine than a Captain going down on the bridge with his ship; the leading of a forlorn hope; or even a criminal who puts up a plucky fight against overwhelming odds. Perhaps that is why I can have no regard for men of Richard Le Gallienne's ilk. Virility in a man, first and always. Say what you will, I love that magnificent scoundrel, Rupert of Hentzau.[8] And a man who can take a blow or insult unmoved, without retaliating—Paugh!—I care not if he can voice the sublimest sentiments, I sicken.

To me, the "Sea of Serenity" looks like a job. Markam received a somewhat similar boom about the time he brought out "The Man With the Hoe," but it happened in his case that he richly deserved it. Take for instance:

> "Slave of the wheel of labor, what to him
> Are Plato and the swing of Pleiades?
> What the long reaches of the peaks of song—
> . . . .
> Rebuild in it the music and the dream. etc."[9]

I send with this, Fawcett's "Anarchy,"[10] which same return. It is very powerful. *Summer in Arcady*: isn't it in that that the young college fellow who had returned to the farm, gets the best of the girl and immediately marries her? I read it a long while ago, and know it to be one of Allen's.[11] Have not read "Old King Solomon's Coronation."[12] Will look it up. As to "The thousand Lines" really, while appreciating your kindness, I cannot find it possible to tackle it. To tell you the truth, I don't feel able to; have often thought about trying such work, and as often said "Some day." And I am spending so much time, just now, reading up my history, that I couldn't sandwich the time in which to study up that, and in my case it would require an immense amount of reading, for I am awfully shaky on such things; besides, I am going through Shelley, just now, with a young lady who has an insatiable thirst for things English.[13] Have never thought of my favorite short story—think I would have to make up a list of my "hundred best." And now, in a most unsatisfactory, crowded way, good night, or rather, good morning.

Jack London.

MS: CSmH; 5 pp., tls. Pbd: *L*, 31–34; *BJL*, I, 287–89.
  1. This and a number of other works mentioned in this letter have not been identified.
  2. A story by Johns, which appeared in April 1900 in *Home Magazine*, the organ of the Commercial Travelers Home Association of America, published from 1893 to 1902.
  3. The Mariposa Grove, a famous stand of sequoias now included in Yosemite National Park.
  4. I.e., by a corset.
  5. Markham's only child, the future novelist Virgil Markham, was born in Oakland on April 2, 1899.
  6. See *Jack London's Articles and Short Stories in The Ægis* (Oakland, 1981), particularly JL's essay "Pessimism, Optimism, and Patriotism," pp. 17–20.
  7. W. E. Henley, "Invictus" (1875), first published in *A Book of Verses* (1888), ll. 5–8.
  8. Rupert of Hentzau is the handsome and unscrupulous villain in Anthony Hope Hawkins's novel *Rupert of Hentzau; from the Memoirs of Fritz von Tarlenheim* (1898), a sequel to *The Prisoner of Zenda* (1894).
  9. Edwin Markham, "The Man With the Hoe," ll. 23–25; l. 39.
  10. Edgar Fawcett (1847–1904), New York poet and writer of satirical novels and plays; "Anarchy" (in JL typescript: CSmH).
  11. James Lane Allen (1849–1925), Kentucky short-story writer and novelist; *Summer in Arcady: A Tale of Nature* (1896).
  12. James Lane Allen, "King Solomon of Kentucky" (1889), in *Flute and Violin, and Other Kentucky Tales and Romances* (1891), the story of a vagrant who reveals a latent heroism.
  13. Mabel Applegarth.

To Cloudesley Johns

962 East 16th. st.,
April [30], 1899.[1]

My dear friend:–

My turn to be charged with blunders. For one who uses Uncle Sam's mails as I do, such ignorance is inexcusable, but to tell the truth, I did not think more than one cent was demanded on the magazine which caused you so much trouble. For that matter, I suppose you have paid postage due on more than one letter of mine? Let us know if you have.

Your several poetical selections have been loaned to a lady friend, so I shall have to still further delay return. Yes; I like the form of refusal you sent me. Here you will find a couple I received the middle of this week. Disagree with both as a matter of course. Can't see any other ending, in the nature of things, to the *McClure* Ms.,[2] while *Frank Leslies*[3]—well, that poor young American girl who mustn't be shocked, nor receive anything less insipid than mare's milk—she seems to rule our destinies. Please return, also Kipling's "For to Admire." [4]

Another case of anticipation, Holt's "Quantum Mutatus." [5] I have been storing away ideas for some months now, for a reply to "O Why Should the Spirit of Mortal be Proud," [6] and only waiting a little better knowledge of poesy before attempting it.

Those Humors of the composing-room were great, many a hearty laugh have they caused since coming into my possession. Your idea concerning the plot of a story taking a minor place, may apply, in part, to *McClure's* criticism—that is, they wanted more action and a final event to what was really a spirited or very strong sketch. As for *Munsey* [7] and the rest of that ilk, they must really know how vicious their action is in calling for the stories they do.

I can't agree with you regarding *Cyrano*. Perhaps it is because I have seen it staged, but I think the ending is logical well done, and most fitting. That last scene, where he staggers to his feet, crying that he must meet Death still afoot and sword in hand, is to me superb, to the very wind-up, where he doffs his casque in Christ's fair halls with untarnished plume.

And what effective meters Kipling found! So you like the "Dipsy Chantey"? Ever compared it with his "First Chantey"? [8] I don't remember whether that's its name or not. Are you familiar with his "Lost Legion," beginning:

> "In the legion of the lost ones, in the cohort of the damned,
>   Of his brethren in their sorrows overseas,
>   Sings a gentleman of England, cleanly bred, machinely crammed,
>   And a trooper of the Empress if you please." [9]

So you, also, are a socialist? [10] How we are growing! I remember when you could almost count them on one's great toes in Oakland. Job Harriman is considered to be the best popular socialist speaker on the Coast; Austin Lewis the best historical, and Strawn-Hamilton the best philosophical. [11] The latter has just gone to his old home in Mississippi, where he remains till December. Then he will go to Washington to fill a private secretaryship under some legislative relative. He spent 48 straight hours with me a couple of days before he went. He has a marvelous brain, one, I think, which could [put] that of Macaulay's [12] to shame. He has served no less than twenty-nine sentences for vagrancy, to say nothing of the times turned up on trial, in the several years preceding his joining the socialists. As interesting a character in his way as your Holt, who, by the way, I would like to run across. The world is full of such, only the world does not generally know it. But I don't agree with you regarding the death stroke to individuality coming with the change of system. There will always be leaders, and no man can lead without fighting for his position—leaders in all branches. Sometimes I feel as you do about it, but not for long at a time.

I see we at least agree about courage. A man without courage is to me the most dispicable thing under the sun, a travesty on the whole scheme of creation. Have not read *Shrewsbury*[13]—is it good? And who wrote it?

You misunderstood me. It was the very strength of paternal desire, coupled with the perversity of things, which made me feel doubtful of ever realizing it. The things we wish the most for usually pass us by—at least that has been my experience. He who fears death usually dies, unless he is too contemptible, and then the gods suffer him to live on and damn his fellow creatures.

Yes; I would like to see that collection of magazine stories you spoke of. Is there any of the work of Lillian Corbett Barnes in it?[14] I have seen nothing of hers. Has she done much? See Frank Norris has been taken up by the McClures. Have you read his *Moran of the Lady Letty*?[15] It's well done.

My mother also wishes to be cremated. I think it is the cleanest and healthiest, and best;[16] but somehow, I don't care what becomes of my carcass when I have done with it. As for being buried alive—he's a lucky devil who can die twice, and no matter how sever the pang, it's only for a moment. I am sure the pain of dissolution can be no greater than the moment when the forceps are laid upon a jumping tooth. If it is greater, then it must be stunning in it's effect.

Do you remember Robert Louis Stevenson moralizing on death in his *Inland Voyage*?[17] It is a beautiful expansion of "Eat drink, and be merry, for to-morrow we die."

You asked about the age of Prof. Markham: I saw him down at the Section last Sunday night, when Jordan spoke on "The Man who Was Left."[18] He (Markham) is a noble looking man, snow white hair and beard, and very close to sixty. I send you a miserable reporter's account of the meeting, in which nobody or nothing is done justice.

You really must pardon this letter; my mind is dead for the time being. Have been reading a little too heavily. Just as a sample, I shall give you a list of what I am at present working on, to say nothing of three daily papers, and a stagger of an attempt at current literature.

Saint-Amand's *Revolution of 1848*.
Brewster's *Studies in Structure and Style*.
Jordan's *Footnotes to Evolution*.
Tyrell's *Sub-Arctics*.

and Bohm-Bawerk's *Capital and Interest*[19]—this latter is a refutation of Carl Marx's theory of values, as determined or measured by labor. He (Bohm-Barwerk) contends that "final-utility" is the only logical measure of value. Very interesting, I assure you.

Goodnight—by the way, I have forgotten to inform you that an un-welcome guest has annoyed me all evening, and is now getting ready to crawl into bed. This has bothered me not a little. He is such a fool.[20]

Jack London.

MS: CSmH; 9 pp., tls. Pbd: *L*, 34–37; *BJL*, I, 289–91.

1. Misdated "April 39, 1899."

2. The S. S. McClure Company wrote JL on April 20, 1899 (CSmH): "We read this story with very great interest; it seems to us to fail of its promise, and we feel disposed, if you will pardon the liberty to tell you, or rather try to tell you how; sometimes authors are pleased to hear these details of editorial opinion. It is very hard to convey subtle points of criticism in a hurried note, but we find this ending inadequate; differently treated the same events might be sufficient, but as it is the story is misleading—always a fatal error; the reader feels, not that he is reading a sketch, but that he is coming to an event,—so he is, but as treated it is not such a conclusive one as he is expecting. You will have to blend yourself to this crudely stated point of view to understand, but there is an important principle hinted at here."

3. *Frank Leslie's Popular Monthly* was an illustrated general-interest magazine pub-lished in New York from 1876 until 1904.

4. The poem "'For to Admire'" (1894).

5. Possibly a poem by Charles Holt.

6. William Knox, "O, Why Should the Spirit of Mortal Be Proud?" *The Songs of Israel* (1824). Knox's poem is a meditation on mortality; as an evolutionist, JL may have wanted to refute his assertation that "we are the same as our fathers have been; . . . And run the same course our fathers have run" (ll. 29, 32).

7. *Munsey's*, a general-interest monthly published in New York from 1891 until 1918, was, like *McClure's*, one of the first cheap newsstand magazines, aimed at a mass market. Frank Munsey's description of the *Quaker*, another of his mass-market magazines, indicates the tone of the stories such magazines sought ("The Publisher's Desk," *Munsey's*, April 1899): "Its mission is to entertain. It has no other mission. Good easy reading for the people—no frills, no fine finishes, no hair splitting niceties, but action, action, always ac-tion, characterizes its contents."

8. Kipling's "The Last Chantey" (1893) was reprinted by the Roycroft Shop in 1898–99 as "The Dipsy Chantey" in a limited-edition collection of that title; Johns may have seen this edition and referred to it in an earlier letter. What comparison JL intends is not clear: both this poem and "The First Chantey" (1893), the story of an elopement from a primitive tribe, concern the supernatural and the sea, but they are not otherwise similar in theme or treatment.

9. JL loosely quotes Kipling's "Gentlemen-Rankers" (1889), ll. 1–4.

10. Johns claimed to be a socialist, but he did not join the party until 1904.

11. Job Harriman (1861–1925), attorney and Socialist nominee for vice-president in 1900; Austin Lewis (1865–1944), California attorney and socialist, author of *The Church and Socialism* (1906), *The Militant Proletariat* (1911), and *The Rise of the American Pro-letariat* (1907); Frank Strawn-Hamilton, hobo socialist orator, model for the hobo hero Leith Clay-Randolph in *The Road*, and one of the four speakers at JL's memorial services in San Francisco on December 20, 1916.

12. Thomas Babington Macaulay.

13. Stanley J. Weyman, *Shrewsbury* (1898), a historical romance.

14. Lillian Corbett Barnes (*b*. ?1854), California short-story writer.

15. Benjamin Franklin Norris (1870–1902), journalist and novelist, best known for *McTeague* (1899) and *The Octopus* (1901). Frank Norris had joined the staff of *McClure's Magazine* in 1898; his novel *Moran of the Lady Letty*, a sea story reputedly based on a

personal account, was published the same year. JL wrote a highly favorable review of *The Octopus* in *Impressions*, June 1901.

16. JL retained these convictions. See JL to Erichsen, October 16, 1916.

17. Robert Louis Stevenson, *An Inland Voyage* (1878): "If a man knows he will sooner or later be robbed upon a journey, he will have a bottle of the best in every inn, and look upon all his extravagances as so much gained upon the thieves. And above all, where, instead of simply spending, he makes a profitable investment for some of his money, when it will be out of risk or loss. So every bit of brisk living, and above all when it is healthful, is just so much gained upon the wholesale filcher, death. We shall have the less in our pockets, the more in our stomachs, when he cries, Stand and deliver. A swift stream is a favorite artifice of his, and one that brings him in a comfortable thing per annum; but when he and I come to settle our accounts I shall whistle in his face for these hours upon the upper *Oise*."

18. David Starr Jordan (1851–1931), biologist, social and educational reformer, and from 1891 to 1913 the first president of Stanford University. JL met Jordan in 1892, when he took Jordan's university extension course in Oakland on evolution. On April 23 Jordan had delivered his address "The Man Who Was Left" at a meeting of the Oakland Section of the Socialist Party.

19. Arthur Leon Imbert de Saint Amand, *The Revolution of 1848*, trans. Elizabeth Gilbert Martin (1895); William T. Brewster, *Studies in Structure and Style* (1896); David Starr Jordan, *Footnotes to Evolution: A Series of Popular Lectures on the Evolution of Life* (1898); John Williams Tyrrell, *Across the Sub-Arctics of Canada, a Journey of 3,200 Miles by Canoe and Snowshoe Through the Barren Lands* (1897); Eugene R. Bohm von Bawerk, *Capital and Interest*, trans. William Smart (1890–91).

20. Commenting on this letter in *BJL* (I, 291), CKL explains, "This was one of the drawbacks of Jack's quarters—that he must share his bed with no matter what guest chose to remain, invited or otherwise. 'And I'd as soon sleep with a snake as with a man,' he complained to his sister."

To Cloudesley Johns

College Park
May 13/99.

Dear Friend:–

A friend has taken it into his head to die; so, in resultant tangle, am at present wasting time at present quarters. Must acknowledge receipt of *Splendid Spur*,[1] also of two letters, which same I shall answer on my return home. Yes; "Q" did good work when he completed *St. Ives*.[2]

Very truly yours,
Jack London.

I suppose you'll have to pay postage on this, for I've only two stamps left, and it now 1 A.M. and I'm going out with a cigarette to drop letter in box at the corner.

Jack London

How do you like my *scrawl*?[3]

MS: CSmH; 3 pp., als. Pbd: *L*, 22–23; *BJL*, I, 305.
1. Arthur T. Quiller-Couch, *The Splendid Spur: Being Memoirs of the Adventures of Mr. John Marvel, a Servant of His Late Majesty King Charles I., in the Years 1641–3* (1889).

2. Robert Louis Stevenson, *St. Ives; Being the Adventure of a French Prisoner in England* (1898). This novel was completed by Quiller-Couch.
   3. Written in the margin above the salutation; JL underlined "scrawl" twice.

To Cloudesley Johns

962 East 16th. st.,
May 18, 1899.

My dear friend:—

Back again at the machine. How one grows to miss it! And you did not mention my scrawl—said scrawl feels slighted. At last I return clippings of yours, which have traveled not a little. Find with this, two other selections from W. E. Henley.[1] Return me "Machine-made Fame" by Bailey Millard.[2] Keep the rest. Barry Pain's criticism of Kipling and Bierce is very good, coming, as it does, from an avowed lover of Bierce.[3]

I do most heartily agree with you as regards drowning.[4] My stock statement is that I should prefer hanging to drowning. From this you may infer that I, as a strong swimmer, have had some experience. One notable instance was similar to the one you mention as happening to you: that of being dragged down by another, who, perhaps, wasn't worth saving. It happened to me by the dock, with a crowd above but not a boat or boathook to be had, and the tide very low—twenty feet nearly from the water to the top of the wharf. I was about sixteen, and the lad I was trying to pull out, a wharf-rat of about twelve or thirteen. Really, I saw nothing of my past life, nor beautiful scenes, nor blissful sensations. My whole consciousness was concentrated upon the struggle, my sensation upon the awful feeling of suffocation. Another time, I fought a lonely battle in the ocean surf on a coral beach. Carelessly going in swimming from a sheltered nook, I had drifted too far out and along the shore, and not having the strength to stem my way back, was forced to a landing on the open beach. Not a soul in sight. The seas would swat me onto the beach and jerk me clear again. I'd dig hand and foot into the sand, but fail to hold. It was a miracle that I finally did pull out, nearly gone, in a fainting condition, and pounded into a jelly-like condition.

Another hard struggle was the result of a drunken attempt at suicide— rather, the chance came my way, and I drunkenly embraced it. I was not seventeen, yet, in the town of Benecia, midway on the Carquinez Straits, when it happened. Had been sowing wild; been on a straight drunk for three weeks, with but few intermittent spaces of partial sobriety. Fell overboard going aboard a yacht, with the "blues" heavy upon me, and decided to quit the whole thing. There is a terrific current in those Straights, and I went down with the ebb tide. Passing the Solano wharf, where there were lights and people, I cunningly kept silent so as to avoid rescue. It was past two in the morning. Clear of interruption, I lifted my voice to the

stars in my own dirge and quite enjoyed the thought of saying goodbye
to the whole works. As you know, it doesn't take much paddling to keep
afloat. But the cold water sobered me after a while, and I decided to rescue myself. Undressed and struck out. But went on down the line. As
daylight broke, I was in that nasty stretch of water where the Carquinez
Straits meet the Straits of Vallejo. And I was about gone, paddling as the
man in the *Black Cat* paddled,[5] with the land breeze sending each snappy
little wave into my mouth. Was still keeping afloat mechanically, when a
couple of fishermen from Vallejo picked me up, and can dimly recollect
being hauled over the side.

No, drowning is not a pleasant shuffle.

Have not read *Shrewsbury*. Have you read Townsend's *Jimmy Fadden
Explains?*[6] If you have not, will send it along when I finish it, which may
be quite a little while off. Miriam Michelson, whose "Zojas" I send you,
is a space-writer on the *San Francisco Bulletin*.[7] She is a young woman,
and is doing some magazine work, besides.

As with you, socialism was evolutionary, though I came to it quite a
while ago. You say, "that to retain a leadership one must possess, or acquire, all the virtues which society and politics demand of their favorites—hypocricy, insincerity, deceit, etc." Robt. Louis Stevenson was a
man looked up to, a leader of certain very large classes, in certain very
fine ways. I am sure he lacked those virtues. So it would be in all the arts,
sciences, professions, sports, etc. Of course, to-day this is already to a certain extent true; but accident of birth (through possibilities of development), and the necessary patronage of wealth, badly mar them. Of course,
I realize you mainly applied your statement to politics. But have you ever
figured how much of this fawning and low trickery, etc., is due to party
politics; and with the removal of party politics and the whole spoils system from the field, cannot you figure a better class of men coming to the
fore as political leaders—men, whose stirling qualities to-day prevent
them crawling through the muck necessary to attain party chieftainship?
It's an endless topic, and were better left alone, being only good when
tongues may war unceasingly.

I will give you an idea of the "Lost Legion," from memory, so pardon
gaps. The refrain tells the story of gentlemen rankers in India.

In the Legion of the Lost Ones, in the cohort of the damned,
    Of his brethren in their sorrow overseas,
Sings a gentleman of England, cleanly bred, machinely crammed,
    And a trooper of the Empress, if you please.
Yea, a trooper of the forces, who has run his own six horses,
    And faith he went the pace and went it blind;
For all the world was kin while he had the ready tin,
    But to-day the sergeant's something less than kind.
    Ba! Ba! Ba!

We're poor little lambs who've lost our way;
  Ba! Ba! Ba!
We're little black sheep who've gone astray—
  Gentlemen rankers out on the spree,
  Damned from here to eternity,
  God ha' mercy on such as we!

If the home we never write to, and the oaths we never keep,
  And all we hold most distant and most dear,
Across the snoring barrack-room return to break our sleep,
  Can you blame us if we soak ourselves in beer?
When the sleepy comrade mutters, and the great guard lantern gutters,
  And the horror of our fall is written plain,
Every secret self-revealing, on the aching white-washed ceiling,
  Do you wonder that we drug ourselves from pain?
                    (refrain)

We are done with love and honor, we are lost to hope and truth,
  We are slipping down the ladder rung by rung,
And the measure of our torment is the measure of our youth,
  God help us, for we knew the worst too young.
Our shame is clean repentance for the crime which brought the
    sentence,
  Our pride it is to know no spur of pride;
And the curse of Reuben holds us, till an Alien turf enfolds us,
  And we die, and none can tell them where we died.
                    (refrain) [8]

How do you like it? Have only given you the complete stanzas which I happened to recollect. There is no end to Kipling, simply no end.

As to the Post Office—I grant red tape, etc., galore; but say, what would it cost me to send a letter to Harold, were the P.O. in the hands of a private corporation?

Though bound to disagree on some points, I can hardly give you to understand how I value your criticism. You have a mind of your own, and you speak your mind. I suffer from a plethora of friends who say "Good," "very good" etc. At least know that I do appreciate. Let me explain my position toward the *Overland*. Last fall I wrote them concerning doing work for them. Was unacquainted with them. Reply was to the effect that they suffered from a press of matter. Sent them anyway, sometime later, a Klondike tale,[9] then a second ("White Silence"), with the proposition of a series. Editor was away. Skipped a month, till one day he sent for me, and arrangements for the series were made.[10] Have not been to the office since, nor seen any of them. So I have to go on with the tales. But, a couple of days prior to reception of yours in which you speak concerning this matter, I wrote the *Overland* people, telling them I thought a couple more would finish the series. In reply, they wished me to keep it up. I shall give several more, and then quit. I realize keenly the truth of all that you said, and heartily thank you for the same.

How concisely you analyzed the lack of Unity in the May tale!—a lack of Unity which you may see is recognized in the very title. "The Men of Forty Mile." [11] The sub-heading was not of my doing, as were none of the others. I wonder what you will think of "In a Far Country," which comes out in the June Number, and which contains no reference to Malemute Kid or any other character which has previously appeared. As I recollect my own judgement of it, it is either bosh, or good; either the worst or the best of the series I have turned out. I shall await your opinion of it with impatience.

I can sympathize with you in your isolation out there on the edge of the desert, deputies non-forthcoming, and teeth waxing clamorous.

Am happy I warned you in advance of the *Black Cat* tale. Yes, rather ponderous verbiage—suffer from that a little and not a very little little, in present work. Apropos of "Thousand Deaths," I enclose the following freak letter which speaks for itself.

Have you read *Prisoner of Zenda*?; and if so, have you read *Rupert of Hentzau*, its sequel? If not, I can send it to you.

We live and learn. With such letters as this, the stereotyped forms of ending have always tortured me. I now comprehend the beauty of yours and make haste to adopt it.

Jack London.

MS: CSmH; 7 pp., tls. Pbd: *L*, 37–39; *BJL*, I, 292–93.

    1. William Ernest Henley (1849–1903), English poet, critic, and dramatist, and a friend of Robert Louis Stevenson. Henley won poetic fame for his *Book of Verses* (1888); he edited the *New Review* from 1894 to 1898.
    2. Frank Bailey Millard (1859–1941), San Francisco newspaperman, poet, and novelist; editor of *Cosmopolitan* from 1906 to 1907. At this time, Millard was literary editor of the *San Francisco Examiner*; at various other times he also worked for the *Chronicle*, the *Call*, and the *Bulletin*. His "A Brief Discussion of the Article Known as Machine-Made Fame, with Modern Instances," *San Francisco Sunday Examiner Magazine*, April 30, 1899, reviews a reissue of James Lauren Ford, *The Literary Shop, and Other Tales* (1894), a book that satirizes publishing and reviewing practices.
    3. Barry Pain (1864–1928), author of *Eliza* (1900) and other humorous novels of domestic life. Pain published literary parodies in *Cornhill Magazine*, including a parody of Kipling's *Plain Tales* in "The Sincerest Form of Flattery," October 1890; these are collected in Pain's *Playthings and Parodies* (1892).
    4. Johns could not swim and nearly drowned on at least two occasions.
    5. In JL's "A Thousand Deaths," the protagonist nearly drowns at sea before he is rescued by his father's yacht.
    6. Edward W. Townsend, *Chimmie Fadden Explains; Major Max Expounds* (1895). The "Chimmie Fadden Stories," a series in dialect that originated with the *New York Sun*, were published in the *San Francisco Call*.
    7. Miriam Michelson (*b.* 1870); "The Awakening of Zojas," published in a short story collection of the same title in 1910.
    8. JL loosely quotes Kipling's "Gentlemen-Rankers" (1889), stanzas 1, 3, and 4.

9. "To the Man on Trail."
10. See JL to M. Applegarth, December 6, 1898, and February 20, 1899.
11. "The Men of Forty Mile: 'Malemute Kid' Deals with a Duel," *Overland Monthly*, May 1899; later included in *The Son of the Wolf*.

To Cloudesley Johns

962 East 16th. st.,
May 28, 1899.

My dear friend:–

One may be a leader without posing as one, and in this category—the best of all—may be placed R.L.S. I understood your application mainly to politics, and appreciate the truth of a great deal you say. And further, believe me, I do not look for the regeneration of mankind in a day; nor do I think man must be born again before socialism can attain its ends. The first motor principal of the movement is selfishness, pure, downright selfishness; the elevation merely an ultimate and imperative result of better environment.

But views like this cannot be elucidated on paper—at least in the course of correspondence. Your reference to building monuments to a man after he is dead, and after deriding him all the days of his life, reminds me of the following excerpt from a letter of John Keats to Miss Jeffrey: "One of the great reasons that the English have produced the finest writers in the world, is that the English world has ill-treated them during their lives and fostered them after their deaths."[1] How True!

I send you a poem by Kipling with the refrains, choruses, or whatever you wish to call them, cut out. By God! it smacks of life! The fellow believeing she has not been caught and is trying to work him. Her "So 'elp me Christ it's true!" or her anthitetical refrain "Ah, Gawd, I love you so."[2] Tell us what you think of it. Also a selection from Stephen Crane's *Black Riders*,[3] as strange a volume as has been put out in many a day—O, it's already old.

By Golly! If that's the case, I shall cut down your revenue on my letters. Two cents will carry. But don't let me make a mistake. Am I to understand that the face value of all stamps go to you, and that any overdue on a letter addressed to you, does not force you to replace them from your own pocket, but rather prevents them or their value going into your pocket?

Tell me what you think of enclosed perpetration. It's my first encounter with the Muse in many weary weeks, and also my first attempt at a sonnet. Have just finished it and send it off smoking hot.[4] And may I ask your opinion on the grammar of the first and last lines of the sestet: "if thou wert there," that is subjunctive mood, is it not? And "Thou wast not there," isn't that plain indicative? And are they not used properly? Nobody else has read them; the doubt has merely risen through contemplating them. There seems an awkwardness about them that jars on my ear, while they seem correct to my reason. Pray tell me how they strike you.

As you have lost your respect for Roosevelt,[5] so had I long ago mine for George Washington, because of the ill manner in which he, too, treated Paine—Paine, who in this case was a contemporary, and who had in his own way done probably as much for the American Revolution as had his immortal traducer.[6] However, I believe you to be less tolerant than I, at least concerning religion. Apropos of Dewey's[7] alleged remark that God superintended the fight in Manila Bay, and your conjecture as to whether he (Dewey) ever took the trouble to notice that God didn't prevent the blowing up of the *Maine*, brings to recollection a similar query from the *Social Contract* of Jean Jacques Rousseau: "All power comes from God, I acknowledge it; but all sickness comes from him too: does that mean that it is forbidden to call a physician?"[8]

Have been reading Schopenhauer's terrific arraignment of woman, or rather his phillipic against them. Let me quote a couple of extracts. Don't believe that I endorse them in toto.

"The more noble and perfect an animal, the later its maturity. The development of woman's reason ceases at eighteen, while that of man is imperfect before the age of twenty-eight. Woman's reason is accurate only as to objects which are quite near. In other regards she mistakes appearance for reality and trifles for truth." And again "It is only the man whose intellect is clouded by his impulses that would give the name of the *fair sex* to that under-sized, narrow-shouldered, broad-hipped, short-legged race, for the whole beauty of the sex is bound up in the sex-impulse. Instead of calling them beautiful, there would be more warrant for describing woman as the unaesthetic sex."[9]

Wow! wow! wow!

Pardon this letter of quotations. There is at least this consolation, should they happen to be new to you: they are far more valuable than what I would have written in their place.

Jack London.

MS: CSmH; 3 pp., tls. Pbd: *L*, 37–39; *BJL*, I, 294.

1. See JL to M. Applegarth, January 28, 1899.

2. In "'Mary, Pity Women!'" (1894), the poem's speaker, pregnant and unwed, addresses the cause of her misfortune. JL quotes l. 29 and the last line of stanzas 1, 3, 5, and 7; ll. 7–8 are typical of the "antithetical" refrain: "I 'ate you, grinnin' there. . . . / Ah, Gawd, I love you so!" JL has not sent Johns the even-numbered stanzas, which are a sort of chorus.

3. *The Black Riders and Other Lines* (1895), one of the first American collections of modernist verse.

4. On the same day, "Sonnet" was also sent to the *Century Magazine*. Rejected there, it appeared in February 1901 in the *Dilettante*, a monthly magazine of belles lettres published in Seattle.

5. Theodore Roosevelt (1858–1919), then governor of New York, a post he filled from 1898 to 1900. In his *Gouverneur Morris* (1888), Roosevelt referred to Paine as "the filthy little atheist" because of Paine's deistic beliefs.

6. In his *Letter to Washington* (1795), Paine criticized Washington for not interceding to obtain his release, as an American citizen, from a French prison.
7. Admiral George Dewey (1837–1917), hero of the Battle of Manila Bay.
8. Book I, chap. 3.
9. Arthur Schopenhauer, "On Women," in *Studies in Pessimism*, trans. T. Bailey Saunders (1890).

To Cloudesley Johns

962 East 16th. st.,
June 7, 1899.

Dear friend:—

"If a time came when you should know even the subject of what I should write, then my letters would cease to interest you."

Pray tell me, do you do that often?

I thoroughly appreciated and enjoyed your description of your youthful environment and your grandfather's mistaken altruistic efforts;[1] but— from what I read I was given to understand that all this was merely a discursion and that presently you would pick up the thread again. You even had the effrontery to insinuate at the close of said discursion that while I had most probably forgotten said thread, you certainly had not. And then you picked up the thread, threw in all the elements for a climax, and then wound up in above quoted manner. Don't do it again.

O I have been busy. Have been going out more than at any other time in the past eight months; have been studying harder than ever in my life before; and having been turning out more copy than hitherto. Finding that I must go out more and that I was becoming stale and dead, I have really ventured to be gay in divers interesting ways.

Yes; the time for Utopias and dreamers is past. Co-operative colonies, etc., are at the best impossible (I don't mean religious ones), and never was there less chance for their survival than to-day. From your attitude regarding the populace, I find I really must quote you some more, from Jordan's *Care and Culture of Men*:

"Some there are among us who wish we had a heaven-descended aristocracy, an aristocracy of brains at least, who could take these things out of the people's hands, out of your hands and mine, and make them and keep them right. I do not feel thus. It is better that the people should suffer, with the remedy in their own hands, than that they should be protected by some power not of themselves. Badly though the people may manage their own affairs, the growth of the race depends upon their doing it. We would rather the people would rule ill through choice than that they should be ruled well through force. The Reign of Terror gives more hope for the future than the reign of the good King Henry. The story of the decline and fall of empires is the story of the growth of man."

And again he says: "In these times it is well to remember that we come of hardy stock. The Anglo-Saxon race, with its strength and virtues, was born of hard times. It is not easily kept down; the victims of oppression must be of some other stock. We who live in America, and who constitute the heart of this republic, are the sons and daughters of him that over-cometh. Ours is a lineage untainted by luxury, uncoddled by charity, uncorroded by vice, uncrushed by oppression. If it were not so, we would not be here to-day. When this nation was born, the days of the government of royalty and aristocracy was fast drawing to a close. Heriditary idleness had steadily done its work, and the sceptre was already falling from nerveless hands. God said: 'I am tired of kings; I suffer them no more.' And when the kings had slipped from their tottering thrones, as there was no one else to rule, the sceptre fell into the hands of common men." [2]

While I am about it, I must give this from Carlyle: "For a man to have died who might have been wise and was not, this I call a tragedy." [3]

And this reply of Agassiz to a Boston publisher: "I have no time, sir, to make money." [4]

I think I have the very thing for you, "The Soul of Man under Socialism," by Oscar Wilde. I have not had a chance to read it myself, yet, but as soon as I do will forward it to you. Same volume contains in addition, "The Socialist Ideal—Art" by Wm. Morris, author of *Earthly Paradise*, etc., and "The Coming Solidarity," by W. C. Owen. [5]

Haven't got to *Chimmie Fadden* yet. Will send along *Book News* [6] in a couple of days. O how I am rushed for reading.

So I stuck it into you for a couple of stamps? Won't do it again, now that I know. But I fail to get it into my head yet. U.S. loses the postage due, who the devil gains it?

Apropos of leading essay mentioned above, the writer, I am told, goes on to contend that true individualism cannot, or rather, rarely flourishes under the present system; a contention which I have also always made.

By the way, have you a letter from some fellow of Asbury Park, to me relating to my *Black Cat* yarn? It's in a blue envelope, if I remember aright.

Your brother's [7] letter seems characteristic of your breed. He must be quite an interesting correspondent.

Of course you were correct about the wrong use of interrogation point in sonnet. I had never noticed it. Find enclosed a take-off on Stephen Crane's style, which, in turn, I deem to be a take-off on that of Walt Whitman's. Whiled away a few minutes on it, just for fun.

Francis S. Saltus [8] was a genius who did much, died young, but remained practically unknown because he could not tolerate the prevailing monotheism which happens to not be a monotheism. Don't judge his work to be similar to what I have sent you. He was very versatile, a profound scholar and linguist, wrote over five thousand poems in various languages, made innumerable translations, and did an infinite quantity of newspaper work under the pseudonym of Cupid Jones. In his "Moods of Madness,"—of which he has many—, have you never noticed the effect of words "sonorous, liquid, superb, immense"?

Jack London.

MS: CSmH; 4 pp., tls. Pbd: *L*, 40–41; *BJL*, I, 294.

1. Johns's grandfather, a millionaire named Marcus Spring, constructed on his estate at Eagleswood, New Jersey, an apartment building of one hundred units to house the families of artists, educators, actors, and writers. His colony, modeled after the communitarian experiment at Brook Farm, was called the Raritan Bay Union.

2. David Starr Jordan, "The Scholar in the Community" and "The Nation's Need of Men," in *The Care and Culture of Men* (1896), pp. 81–82, 58.

3. *Sartor Resartus* (1833–34), book III, chap. 4: "That there should one Man die ignorant who had capacity for Knowledge, this I call a tragedy."

4. Jean Louis Rodolphe Agassiz (1807–73), Swiss-born scientist and an acknowledged leader in American natural history. The quotation has not been identified.

5. The three works were published in a single volume, bearing all three titles, in 1892. Morris's *The Earthly Paradise* (1868–70) is a long poem based on Norse tales.

6. *Book News Monthly* was published in Philadelphia by the book department of John Wanamaker's department store from 1882 to 1918 and edited by Talcott Williams from 1889 to 1908. It featured book reviews and announcements, as well as reading lists for book clubs.

7. Possibly Herbert Heron Peet (1881–1968), Johns's half-brother, who in 1909 dropped the use of his last name.

8. Francis S. Saltus (1849–89), American poet, influenced by the Decadents. Saltus wrote poems in French, Italian, and Spanish as well as English; he published voluminous humorous verse under the pseudonym Cupid Jones. His poem "A Mood of Madness," in *Shadows and Ideals* (1890), celebrates, Salome-like, the debauched decapitation of the persona's pious wife; in this collection, several other poems with the same subtitle present similar satanist themes.

To Cloudesley Johns

962 East 16th. st.,
June 12, 1899.

My dear friend:—

Yes; I agree with you, "In a Far Country" should have been the best of the series, but was not. As to the clumsiness of structure, you have certainly hit it. I doubt if I shall ever be able to polish. I permit too short a period—One to fifteen minutes—to elapse between the long-hand and the final MS. You see, I am groping, groping, groping for my own particular style, for the style which should be mine but which I have not yet found.

As to plagiarism: you seem very hyper-sensitive on the subject. Know thou, that "In a Far Country" was written long after I had read your "Snorton-Drake Co." Yet I had no thought of the coincidence till you mentioned it. Great God! Neither you nor I have been the first to make use of a broken back, nor, because of this fact, should we be debarred from using it. How many broken legs, broken necks, broken hearts, etc., have been worked up, over and over again? Take, for instance, why I happened to make use of that incident. I had to kill the two men off, one had to kill the other; I did not wish the other to die at once, because of his dying it was my intention to make the conclusion. I cast about me, and a broken back suggested itself. Take "White Silence," how many have made use of a falling tree. For instance, Captain Kettle in June *Pearson's*,[1] the Doctor who helped him run away from the Congo Free State in the stolen steamer, has to be killed, and is killed by a falling tree.

I see no reason in the world why you should cut the broken back out of "Charge it to the Company."

The questionable moral! A la Munsey.[2] Say, I saw a clever turn to the chaste Young American girl idea, regarding reading—"books one would not like to see one's mother read." Did you ever try to read the *Argosy*?[3] I tried it the other day, but simply broke down and couldn't; my mind absolutely refused. Pardon brevity. I have been writing this and entertaining half a dozen friends at the same time. Really don't know what I have been saying.

Jack London.

MS: CSmH; 2 pp., tls. Pbd: *L*, 42; *BJL*, I, 294–95.

1. C. J. Cutcliffe Hyne, "The Fire and the Farm," *Pearson's Magazine*, June 1899. Capt. Owen Kettle, skipper of the *Flamingo*, was the central character in this popular series, which was published from June 1897 to June 1899 in *Pearson's*, a British monthly magazine published in London from 1896 to 1939. A U.S. edition was published from 1899 until 1925. For Johns's use of a broken back, see JL to Johns, February 22, 1899.

2. Frank A. Munsey (1854–1925), editor and publisher of *Argosy*, *Munsey's Magazine*, and other mass-market periodicals. Munsey had written "rags to riches" stories for *Argosy*, as well as moralizing stories about the business and social life of New York.

3. *Argosy*, originally a magazine for young people entitled the *Golden Argosy*, was a monthly pulp magazine for men and boys that featured adventure stories. It was initiated in New York in 1882.

To Cloudesley Johns

962 East 16th. st.,
June 12, 1899.

My dear friend:—

Have written and shipped you one letter to-day, but in a breathing spell between visitors, shall commence another, in reply to yours of last mail— but there's no telling when It will be posted. And I do not date my letters the time of mailing, either.

It seems I hit it right after all regarding the stamp question. Let me see if I have got it right. I mean, the time I sent a letter overweight I hit it right. If I did not send you anything, nobody would be the loser. If I send you a letter with six cents postage stamps on it, your revenue (individual revenue) is neither increased nor diminished. If I send six cents worth of letter with a two cent stamp, you balance the postage-due stamps with the amount awarded you by the U.S. on face value of stamps cancelled, and hence, lose nothing—it is just the same to you financially, as though I had put the whole six cents on before mailing. If all this is so, may I not then conclude that for me to send you, say, a *Cosmopolitan*[1] as second class and costing me six cents, would be a very foolish thing—very foolish, when I could send it you sealed as first class matter with but two cents upon it? Do you follow my reasoning? Am I right? In the one case I lose four cents, in the other, neither you nor any other individual loses anything, while I have saved four cents. Is this correct?

How I envy the thrill of life, such as must surely have been gained through your mix-up with the Greasers.[2] In this prosy city existence I have even failed to tangle up with a lone footpad. And one cannot really come to appreciate one's life, save by playing with it and hazarding it a little.

Thanks for *Criterion* suggestion;[3] I shall not fail to take advantage of it. And also thanks for *Cosmopolitan* prize offer announcement. I have already spotted it, and have quite a stack of notes already laid by, though I think I shall take a short vacation after I have finished a lot of stuff I have at present in mind, and before I write it (essay) up.[4]

Have also tried my hand at storyiettes for Munsey, but without success, then I ship same off to Tillitson & Son, 203 Broadway, N.Y.C. Figuring it up, it seems to me they pay somewhere around four dollars per thousand. They especially wish little ones of from 1300 to 1600 words, but they have taken one of mine which just exceeded the two thousand mark. They are a syndicate, as you most probably know; but their demand for such stuff seems unlimited. I don't like that kind of work, myself, as I can readily see you do not.

O say, I've tumbled to the error of my way. The P.M. at this end is supposed to affix the postage due stamps on my letters, and not you at your end. O what a lot of good paper has been spoiled!

Yes; going out more isn't a bad idea; but as to the less study, can't agree with you. My mind has at least reached partial maturity and I believe I know how far I may go without injury to it. And when I do go out, I assure you I go out with a vengeance, and throw utterly to the winds all thought and worry of my every-day life. And it has been my luck never to be without the one companion to share with me temporary oblivion. No; I don't mean dope, but a proper unadulterated good time with one who knows a good time when it is seen.

How rabid you are! I feel called upon, for that matter, to tell you that you are really narrow in some things. Remember, the infidel that positively asserts that there is no God, no first cause, is just as imbecile a creature as the deist that asserts positively that there is a God, a first cause. Have you ever read Herbert Spencer's *First Principles* of synthetic philosophy, and noted the line, the adamantine line of demarkation he draws between the knowable and the unknowable.[5] Pardon me, I should not have allowed myself this discursion, for I have never heard you make that rash negative assertion. But, as regards your Anglo-Saxon views. In one breath you say you are of pure Anglo-Saxon descent on both sides and that your descent (evidently on one side at least) can be traced to the Welsh Kings. Know thou, that the Welsh are farther away from the Anglo-Saxon, than are the French, Germans, Dutch, Belgians, Scandanavians, Switz, etc. etc. Know thou that the Welsh blood is really no nearer (save geographically) and no farther away from the Anglo-Saxon, than is the Hindoo blood of India or the Iranic of Persia. The Welsh, of which breed were the Welsh kings you mention, belongs to the Celtic branch of the Aryan Family, as the pure Russian does to the Slavonic, the Hindoo and Persian to the Indo-Iranic. All the same family, but distinctly different branches.

What is the Anglo-Saxon, as we understand it to-day. Let me make you miserable with a little history and ethnology. The Angles, Jutes, and Saxons, emigrating from Sleiswick during the earlier centuries of the present era, landed in England, which then contained Celtic blood with an admixture (small) of Roman. The name of the Jutes has subsequently fallen away. These peoples fought, they conquered, they mixed. (I am merely giving this without reference, so you will forgive slight chronology.) The Coasts of England were ravished and some of her fairest valleys settled by the Vikings, Norsemen, etc. The Danelagh, or the domination of the Danes brought an immense supply of other blood into England. So did the Normans. Because, from the many dialects spoken in England subsequent to the Norman Conquest, one dialect happened to be the medium chosen by the more gifted writers of that time, that dialect was elevated finally into the King's English, and elevated under the name of Anglo-Saxon. The Norman French spoken at Court finally disappeared.

They might have called it by other names derived from the other bloods which went to make it and the English population of that time up—with might have done this with equal justice. The Anglo-Saxon does not stand for the lineal descendants of the Angles and Jutes and Saxons, but for that whole commingling of bloods. As you know, the meaning of words, phrases, etc., constantly bows to evolution. To-day, Anglo-Saxon really conveys a meaning entirely at variance with its strict derivation.

But, one thing you will observe, that of all the bloods which go to make up the modern Anglo-Saxon, all are allied as shoots of the same branch of the Aryan family, namely, The Teutonic branch—with the exception of that Celtic element under which caption comes the Welsh, Highland

Scotch, and Irish. Substitute for Anglo-Saxon, all that portion of the Teutonic branch which speaks English. One is the same as the other.

Take all the bloods in the English to-day, and had they, with the exception of the Angles, Jutes, and Saxons, failed to migrate to England, they would be Danes, Norwegians, Swedes, French, Germans, Dutch, etc. etc. Why? Because these would be the various languages spoken by them. To-day, from the above mentioned peoples many individuals journey to the U.S. And speak, in time, modern Anglo-Saxon, and mix with the breed as some of their kinsmen did in previous centuries. In reality, the modern Anglo-Saxon stands for the English speaking portion of the Teutonic branch.

That the Teutonic is the dominant race of the world there is no question— The Slavs are a very young people, and have yet be heard from. They may never be heard from, and then again, they may.

Ah! You swear by that great cosmopolitan, Paine, and in the same letter thirst mightily for the chance to land with the most fiendish of hostile intentions on the shores of England. Come to recognize, as the world is recognizing, not only the interdependence of man, but the interdependence of nations, which latter is gradually but surely tearing down the geographical lines over which countless millions have fought and died. A man's a man, no matter what his blood, so long as that blood is good. The negro races, the mongrel races, the slavish races, the unprogressive races, are of bad blood—that is, of blood which is not qualified to permit them to successfully survive the selection by which the fittest survive, and which the next few centuries, in my opinion, will see terribly intensified.

But enough, this is not my hobby, as you may think, but only one portion of my philosophy or whatever you wish to call the entire edifice of my views. Some day we shall meet and I may be able to explain my self better.

I must now take up for the last time the stamp problem. Let me quote your final words on it: "Of course, if matter is addressed to a presidential office, the addressee loses; U.S. loses it only when matter is addressed to small fourth class office."

From that I conclude again, that I may send overweight first class matter to you and that the Government will pay or lose the difference. Tell me, for the love of heaven, am I right?

Ah! I see; you judge a nation by its past; pray do you judge the present generation by the past generations, and if so, do you not hate the present generation because of all the black deeds done by the past generations? Where are you at? Or am I waxing sophistical? Discover the fallacy, if there be one.

Jack London.

MS: CSmH; 6 pp., tls. Pbd: *BJL*, I, 295–96.

1. *Cosmopolitan* was an illustrated monthly begun in New York in 1886.

2. In the spring of 1899, Johns had confronted three Mexican men and one Mexican woman from Palmdale who owed him two dollars for an old stove bought by the woman. After the money changed hands, one of the men suggested that Johns return it and take the woman instead. Johns refused, and, rather than fight the armed Mexicans, he outran them. (Johns, "Who the Hell *Is* Cloudesley Johns?" pp. 206–7.)

3. *Criterion* was a sophisticated magazine of American arts and letters published in New York from 1896 until 1905.

4. *Cosmopolitan* was offering a prize of $200 for the best article entitled "What Communities Lose by the Competitive System." JL's essay was submitted to *Cosmopolitan* on August 5, 1899, won first prize, and was published in the November 1900 issue.

5. In *First Principles of a New System of Philosophy* (1860–62), Spencer maintains that a "known" and an "unknown," such as science and religion, "are the positive and negative poles of thought; of which neither can gain in intensity without increasing the intensity of the other" (p. 110).

To Cloudesley Johns

962 East 16th. st.,
June 23, 1899.

Dear friend:–

Have just got over having a house full of company, come to stop for several days; can not catch up with my correspondence. You have not learned the lesson of the white man's control of the tropics, very well. I agree with you that India, had not she exported, would have fed herself; agree that there have been many damnable negligiences on the part of England toward that colony; but—compare, contrast. What has England given to the millions who swarm there, in the way of education, system, government, justice? Not education, system, government, justice, such as we know to be the best, nor even the best possible under the circumstances, much less the best ideally. But compare and contrast all this with what they had before their countless millions fell prey to a handful of determined whites led by such men as Clive and Hastings.[1] What, both quantitatively and qualitatively, are the famines, plagues, injustices, they suffer under British rule, compared with what they did suffer under the heel of the petty princes?

Before I quit this subject, I wish you to answer me one question: WHERE ARE YOU GOING TO DRAW THE LINE? If no race has the moral right to survive to the destruction of lesser races, where, in the whole animal kingdom are you going to draw the line? If the bastard races of one of the richest continents of the world, the South Americans; if the niggers of Africa, the Indians, of America, the Blackies of Australia, should, for all their confessed inefficiency, continue to perpetuate themselves to the dwarfing, to the shutting-out of the stronger, better races, such as our own, where, I ask, are you to draw the line in the whole animal kingdom?

Do you know that the physiologists say that the difference between the highest forms of man and the lowest forms of man is greater than the difference between the lowest forms of man and the highest forms of the rest of the vertrebates? This being so (and it is so), where are you to draw the line? If the lowest forms of man are to be preserved, no matter what the moral logic involved, then, by that same logic, you must not exclude the higher forms of the rest of the vertrebates. This being so, by the same reasoning, you may not then draw the line in all the animal kingdom, down to the lowest protoplasmic cluster, down to where animal and vegetable commingle in the same organism. Why the codfish (only one in several millions of eggs reaches maturity)—the codfish, if let alone, would in a year (supposing they could be let alone and could gather sufficient nourishment), would choke our oceans from shore to shore in a year's time. Tell me, where are you to draw the line?

Remember, there is even a higher logic than moral or formal logic. Moral and formal logic demonstrate thoroughly that woman should vote; but the higher logic says she shall not. Why? Because she is woman; because she carries within her that which will prevent, that which will no more permit her economic and suffragal independence, than it will permit her to refrain from sacrificing herself to the uttermost to man. I speak of woman in general. So, with the race problem. The different families of man must yield to law—to LAW, inexorable, blind, unreasoning law, which has no knowledge of good or ill, right or wrong; which has no preference, grants no favors, whether to the atoms in a molecule of water or to any of the units in our whole sidereal system; which is unconscious, abstract, just as is Time, Space, matter, motion; of which it is impossible to postulate a beginning nor an end. This is the law, the higher logic, which the petty worms of men must bow to, whether they will or no.

Socialism is not an ideal system, devised by man for the happiness of all life; nor for the happiness of all man; but it is devised for the happiness of certain kindred races. It is devised so as to give more strength to these certain kindred favored races so that they may survive and inherit the earth to the extinction of the lesser, weaker races. The very men who advocate socialism, may tell you of the brotherhood of all men, and I know they are sincere; but that does not alter the law—they are simply instruments, working blindly for the betterment of these certain kindred races, and working detriment to the inferior races they would call brothers. It is the law; they do not know it, perhaps; but that does not change the logic of events.[2]

That paragraph of yours on the *Argosy* is rich. I shall send it to a friend of mine whose views coincide with yours regarding that magazine. "The Artist is known by what he omits." That is my chiefest obstacle, one that I am fully aware of, and one that I struggle ceaselessly to overcome. That is why I am trying my hand at storiettes. I do not like them, but I realize what excellent training they give. Also, the shekels they bring in are not exactly distasteful to me. To me, all my work is practice, experimentative, and I consider myself lucky to be able to sell the sheets of my copybook.

Forty-six stories—I have not written that many in all my life—why it's a book! Neither have I ever written a book. Nor shall I till I consider myself prepared, and time and place, and man are met.

Have you been following the political rows of France?[3] If you have, have you noted one thing? This thing, to me, is all important; it's significance is immeasurable. In the beginning of this generation (your mother may have been there at the time, at least Gilead Peet was)[4] a breed of socialists arose in Paris. They have since called it the Red Republic, they have since anathametized as one of the most horrible, atrocious perpetrations of man. It is also known as the Commune. The leaders were intelligent men, thinkers rather than men of executive abilities; besides, they did not have the advantages of the deductions we may now draw from evolution. They thought they could establish humanity and the rights of man by force. Well, that whole breed of socialists was wiped out. They stood alone, in Paris, against all the rest of France.

Now to the point. To-day, France in turmoil, with many of the cities, villiages, and surban districts under the political control of the socialists, with a very respectable minority in the Chamber of Deputies; with all that would seem to point toward a successful revolution—WHY DID NOT THE LEADERS GIVE THE WORD? Simply because they understand the law; they have profited by evolution. They know that it is ballots not bullets; that reaction is equal to action; that prematurity is an abortion which cannot live. They know these things, I say, and knowing them, they upheld the Republic.

Why, do you know that already the European leaders are adopting the Fabian process, that they are beginning to hold back.[5] We have not quite advanced to that stage in America, but soon, we, too, will have to apply the brake. We have almost topped the hill, and soon momentum will do its own work, and do it too well if unrestricted. This is evolution, this is law.

Ah! I have just opened your last letter, and I see you ask for the dropping of the race problem. Very good; but already I have gone and done it—well, you'll have to sweat over it if it excites you. I do sympathize with you living on the rim of hell with it one hundred and two in the refrigerator; and I hope you'll soon be able to get away. Am starting down country myself to-morrow. But write me at present address, as I do not know just yet what my future addresses will be. Your letters will be forwarded with no more delay than that involved in transhipment.

Yes; I agree with you, some mistake was made somewhere regarding "Cuba." I liked it very much. Tell me, how do you get such long type-paper? I have looked, but can find no sheets pasted.

Jack London.

Will return poem next time I write in a long envelope. I mean I will use a long envelope next time I write—

J. L.

MS: CSmH; 6 pp., tls. Pbd: *BJL*, I, 296–97.

1. Robert Clive (1725–74), Baron Clive, military founder of British India and governor of Bengal from 1765 to 1766; Francis Rawdon Hastings (1754–1826), first Marquis of Hastings, governor-general of Bengal from 1813 to 1822, who established British supremacy in central India.

2. For an instructive commentary on JL's blend of socialism and evolutionism, see Conway Zirkle, *Evolution, Marxian Biology, and the Social Scene* (Philadelphia, 1959), pp. 318–37. Zirkle points out that JL's concept of race is "in complete agreement both with the founders of communism and with modern Soviet secret doctrine, even if the agreement must now be denied publicly." Like Marx and Engels, both of whom were "frankly racists," says Zirkle, JL subscribed to Lamarck's theory that acquired characteristics could be inherited, which justified not only socialism but also a belief in superior races generated through good environments.

3. On June 15, 1899, Raymond Poincaré, a senator in the French government, attempted to form a cabinet; the following day he admitted failure. Senator Pierre Waldeck-Rousseau successfully formed the cabinet on June 22.

4. Dr. Gilead Peet, a surgeon and Johns's stepfather, organized the American Ambulance Corps in Paris to rescue and treat wounded soldiers during the Franco-Prussian War. The Paris Commune, formed near the end of the war, lasted from March to May 1871. Johns's mother was not in Europe at that time; while the fighting lasted, she and her brother Herbert did not make their annual winter pilgrimage to the south of France.

5. The Fabian Society, organized in England in 1884, advocated the gradual spread of socialism. In the 1890's, European socialist parties began to move away from revolutionary Marxism toward the position that capitalism could be gradually transformed from within by political means. Among the leaders of the movement was Jean Jaurès, socialist leader in the French Chamber of Deputies.

To Cloudesley Johns

962 East 16th. st.,
Oakland, Calif.,
July 5, 1899.

My dear friend:—

So, at last, you are getting your long-delayed vacation? Good! So you hiked part of the way? Do you ride underneath? or do they chase a fellow from the rods also. Must be pretty strict down that way. Ah! city life is the only life after all—there you meet people; as a rule you meet vegetables in the country. I really become heart-sick, if I mingle too long with our agrarian population. Of course, there are striking exceptions.

Have you been following the papers of late? Have you noticed the crisis in Belgium? By latest reports the King has capitulated, giving to the Socialists and Republicans a most welcome victory.[1] Have you noticed the troubles in Italy, where the parliament endeavored to pass a bill for a secret ballot on all labor questions. The Socialist members replied that it were far better to vote secretly on all other questions. They were a minority; what could they do when this damnable bill came up to be acted upon? They did the only possible thing—prevented the ballot by force, and this they will continue till the parliament is dissolved.[2] Consider the effect of all this on the people. Preventing the passing of the bill till the next election means the return of a far greater number of Socialist members, which means, in turn, a lessening of the chances of the bill's passage. O We're booming. Do you notice a socialist leader has taken his seat in President Loubet's new cabinet?[3] The two million socialist votes that this leader represented stands for an organized machine which prevented the rise of a New imperialism, and will forever more prevent such a rise.

It would be nice to see you; drop in on me when you come this way, and partake of my blanket, board, and hobbies. The last I give you fair warning against. Nor will I promise to introduce you in local society, for I have abandoned that with my dress suit. Takes too much time. Remember Omar Kayam's "O make haste"?[4] "Life's none so long," as Kipling says in his "Sestina of the Tramp Royal."[5]

Where am I to draw the line?—At the white. From the family unit, through the tribal dawning, to the race aggregation, you may trace the rise of an altruism, very similar for all its various manifestations. The line stops there. If a man would save an animal from pain, another kind of altruism is brought to bear; the same if he saves a nigger, or a red, a yellow, or a brown. But let Mr. White meet another white hemmed in by dangers from the other colors—these whites will not need to know each other—but they will hear the call of blood and stand back to back. Nor does it matter if one be a genius and the other a poor wretch cursed by congenital defectives, an hereditary inefficient—they will none the less hear the call, feel the bond, and answer. Better conditions (towards which we are constantly moving) from the cradle, will engender better antenatal conditions—these will act and react upon each other to the lifting of the race. Culture, training, eradication of acquired inefficiency (heriditary inefficiency kills itself off in short order when deprived of accessions from environment), all these factors will tend toward the weeding out, the clarifying of the race. Nursing the inferior whites, segregating the hopelessly vicious and idiotic so that they may not breed, and developing those that are not so, draws its own line. To-day, the very opposite prevails as regards the lower classes; that is no reason it should always be so. Mind you we must come to understand that nature has no sentiment, no charity, no mercy; we are blind puppets at the play of great, unreasoning forces; yet we may come to know the laws of some of the forces and see our trend in relation to them. These forces generated the altruistic in man; the race with the highest altruism will endure—the highest altruism considered from the standpoint of merciless natural law, which never concedes nor alters. The lesser breeds cannot endure. The Indian is an example, as is the black man of the Austrailian Bush, the South Sea Islander, the inhabitant of the Sub-Arctics, etc.

Apparently I am inconsistent. A man's duty is as his conscience dictates. We are, taken as a whole, blind factors in the action of natural selection among the races of men. England, as a whole, to-day does not consider the trend of her whole policy of generations to be inimical to the very existence of the lesser breeds. Yet her whole course is leading slowly up to that. She does not know it, hence, her duty lies in line with the dictates of her national conscience as reflected by her representative citizens. By that conscience she should have behaved better by her East Indian Empire; by conscienceless nature she has been permitted to do neither more nor less than evolution made possible and demanded. Remember, pain and pleasure, life and death, extinction and survival, all that concerns the individual, does not concern nature. She has no concerns; she does not reason; she does not feel; she is not to be swayed by a hair's breadth from her undeviating course.

Perhaps you will enjoy Rose-Soley's criticism of Frank Norris, and Frank Norris's rejoinder.[6]

Just got home this morning, and have been hard at it ever since. Have written fifteen hundred words of a new story,[7] transacted all my business, started a few more of my returned children on the turf (as you put it), and am now winding up the last letter of my correspondence. Go away again on Friday for a jaunt on wheels down country with a young lady[8] whom I have been promising for some time. She made me a call to-day and foreclosed. We stop with mutual friends along the way. By the way, is mutual used correctly in preceding sentence?

In "Priestly prerogative," I wish to call your attention to a case of editorial mutilation. I stated (type-written) that the advent of this woman meant a new hegira in their lives. Mr. Editor finds fault with the word and substitutes "era." Now the words are utterly different in their significance, and the substitute makes bosh. Hegira meaning a new period to date from, as, for instance, when I left Harold; "era" meaning the period lying between the the hegira and the present.[9] Damn Editors!

Keep us informed of your movements.

Jack London.

MS: CSmH; 4 pp., tls. Pbd: *L*, 42–44; *BJL*, I, 299.

1. In June 1899 a bill was introduced in the Belgian Chamber of Deputies that would have institutionalized the overrepresentation of the Clerical (Catholic) Party in the Chamber. A mass meeting of protest by the opposition parties (Liberals, Socialists, and Democrats) led to riots in Brussels on June 28 and 29. In response a motion was made in the Chamber to allow the expulsion of any deputy creating a disturbance. King Leopold II used his influence in the following days to have the original bill withdrawn and to allow peaceful demonstrations.

2. On June 30, 1899, the Socialists and extreme leftists in the Italian Chamber of Deputies battled with members of the conservative faction on the floor of the Chamber to prevent the use of the secret ballot on certain bills. In consequence, the Chamber was closed until November.

3. Emile Loubet (1838–1929), from 1899 to 1906 seventh president of the French Re-

public. In June 1899 Alexandre Millerand (1859–1943), a socialist, was appointed Minister of Commerce in Loubet's cabinet.

4. *The Rubáiyát of Omar Khayyám*, trans. Edward FitzGerald, 5th ed., stanza 48, l. 4.

5. "Sestina of the Tramp-Royal" (1896), l. 24. JL also quotes this in a prefatory note to *The Road*.

6. In "Miraculous Moran. What Frank Norris Does Not Know About the Sea," *San Francisco Sunday Examiner Magazine*, June 18, 1899, J. F. Rose-Soley criticized as ludicrous numerous incidents in *Moran of the Lady Letty*. Norris responded to Rose-Soley's comments in "A Miraculous Critic. What Mr. Rose-Soley Does Not Know About Literature, with Special Reference to 'Moran of the Lady Letty,'" *San Francisco Sunday Examiner Magazine*, June 25, 1900. For an account of this argument, see Robert C. Leitz, III, "The *Moran* Controversy: Norris's Defense of His 'Nautical Absurdities,'" *American Literary Realism 1870–1910*, 15 (1982): 119–24.

7. The "Wisdom of the Trail," sent to the *Argonaut* on July 7, 1899, and rejected; published in the *Overland Monthly*, December 1899.

8. Bessie Maddern.

9. "Hegira" was retained in the version of "The Priestly Prerogative" published in *The Son of the Wolf*: "Well, they could do without the husband; but a woman—why, they had not seen one all winter, and the presence of this one promised a new hegira in their lives."

To Macmillan & Company

> 962 East 16th. st.,
> Oakland, Calif.,
> July 10, 1899.

Gentlemen:—

Merely a letter of inquiry: Are your readers at work now? and if so, are you open to the consideration of a volume of short stories? And if you are open, and your readers are away, will you be kind enough to let me know when a submission of the MS. would suit you?

The volume in question consists of nine short stories, of which six have been recently published in magazine form, one is now awaiting publication, and the remaining two are hunting publication.[1] Each story is complete in itself, though the characters, places, conditions, etc., interlace. The scenes are laid in the Klondike Country. Needless to state, I have been there, and not as a summer tourist, either. The nine tales aggregate 49,000 words; there being one of 3,000; three of 3,500; one of 4,800; one of 5,800; one of 6,500; one of 6,800; and one of 12,250.

Please let me have an answer to my queries at early convenience.

> Very truly,
> Jack London.

MS: NN; 1 p., tls.

1. JL was seeking a publisher for *The Son of the Wolf*. The story awaiting publication was "The Wife of a King," *Overland Monthly*, August 1899; the two stories not yet committed for publication were "The Wisdom of the Trail" and "An Odyssey of the North." The latter appeared in the January 1900 *Atlantic Monthly*, which from 1880 to 1908 was published by Houghton Mifflin. *The Son of the Wolf* would be published by Houghton Mifflin in April 1900. For the beginning of JL's long association with Macmillan, see JL to Brett, January 4, 1902.

To Cloudesley Johns

962 East 16th. st.,
July 22, 1899.

My dear friend:—

There has been delay on both sides. While you have been taking your vacation, I have been taking quite a number of small ones, and I start out next Tuesday on another. A friend of mine and I start for a trip on our wheels around San Francisco Bay, including lay-overs and entertainment at Stanford University, San Jose, and Mount Hamilton where we shall tackle the big telescope.

But write never-the-less, for my mail will be forwarded to me.

Enclosed picture is an ametuer shot, taken by a friend on his lawn during the last trip. He worked hastily at the toning, etc, and spoiled all but a couple, and my mother, sister, and one friend got the good ones before I could say "Jack Robinson." This one is cut down from a cabinet because the rest of it was ruined. When some more are printed shall send you a good, complete one. Have you any of your own? Even if you have but one, which I may not keep, send it along and I will return it again.

So you did not go up Fresno way, but are sweltering in the desert heat, eh? How I pity you—which you will most probably assure me is a waste of good sentiment. I don't know why I used "needless to state." It's simply a stereotyped expression and of such common occurence that it just slipped in. Yet, there must be some raison d'etre for it, or it would not be so common. Analyzed as you have done it, it certainly does appear ridiculous. And your analysis certainly appears perfectly correct. When I get time I shall try and think out the philosophy of it.

The sum total of the story is that I played with a scene which was beyond me![1] It was written quite a good time ago. But, I disagree with you concerning the outcome—her going back to her husband—my point was to make it interest the reader till he or she longed mightily to see all social conventions contravened and the woman, baldly stated, commit adultery and go off with the other man. And after raising that longing, to disappoint the reader. This I am sure I succeeded in doing, and I doubt not that some few felt the injustice of observing, to the very letter, in all cases, our present marriage customs and laws. As for myself, I believe in these present marriage customs and laws, but that is no reason why I should sway my tale one way or the other for aught save the tale's sake. As for my judgement of the tale, I like it least of the series. Just about as much as I do the next[2] which is now in press and which is the last for the *Overland* series.

As to the hog-train—when a passenger goes by in the daylight, shunning six-wheelers, it has been my custom to swing under between the trucks and ride the rods—by this I do not mean the gunnels, brake-beams, or springs, or brake-rods. I have often gone along that way in the day time, with feet cocked up, reading a novel, peering out at the scenery, and enjoying a comfortable if sometimes dusty smoke.

Say, do you remember a certain—well, what's the good? I am sweating too freely as it is to wax sarcastic.

Have been reading Weisman's "Essay on Heredity." No, I have not; I mean Weisman's "Essay on the Duration of Life." [3] It is a wonderful piece of work, and gives food for immeasurable thought. I expect much good to accrue from this man's labors for the welfare of humanity. If you ever get a chance, read it up. He is good throughout.

You will probably notice the haste with which this has been typed. Pardon me, if you find it unintelligible, but I have been working like a Trojan, turning off all kinds of work. As soon as I get well enough ahead of the game—very problematical—I shall escape all my friends, and creditors alas! by engaging cabin passage on a big English ship for a Voyage round the horn to Europe. Shall go aboard with a box of books, a type-writer, and several boxes of paper, and say! I won't do a thing to things in general and particular. I'll write some sea yarns soaked in the atmosphere, besides other and what I would consider more important work, and do no end of reading up all that which the present and continuous flood of current literature will not permit me to enjoy. Ah! plans, plans! How many have I builded! and how few have I realized.

Jack London.

MS: CSmH; 3 pp., tls. Pbd: *BJL*, I, 300.

1. A reference to the love triangle involving Edwin Bentham, Grace Bentham, and Clyde Wharton in "The Priestly Prerogative."

2. "The Wisdom of the Trail."

3. August Weismann (1834–1914), German biologist. The two essays JL cites are from his *Essays upon Heredity and Kindred Biological Problems* (2 vols., 1891–92). Weismann effectively attacked Lamarck's theory of inherited acquired characteristics by setting forth his own theory of "germ plasm," which demonstrated that certain continuous lines of dividing cells persist from generation to generation. See Conway Zirkle, *Evolution, Marxian Biology, and the Social Scene*, pp. 117–25; and Hamilton Cravens and John C. Burnham, "Psychology and Evolutionary Naturalism in American Thought, 1890–1940," *American Quarterly*, 23 (1971): 635–57.

To Cloudesley Johns

962 East 16th. st.,
July 29, 1899.

My dear friend:—

Trip knocked out in the middle. Whole lot of company came to house—very small house. But shall make another try of it the latter part of this month. Well, we had some of our fun anyway.

Guests are at last gone, and am too flabbergasted to get to work. Have all kinds of work awaiting me, too. Did you ever write a yarn of, say, twelve thousand words, every word essential to atmosphere, and then get an order to cut out three thousand of those words, somewhere, somehow? That's what the *Atlantic* has just done to me.[1] Hardly know whether I shall do it or not. It's like the pound of flesh. Say, am hammering away at that *Cosmopolitan* Essay, at spare intervals, have two of the five thousand words finished.[2] Am thoroughly satisfied, as far as I have gone, which is saying a good deal for me— Am usually sick at this stage, and it's such dry dissertative stuff after all.

Many thanks for short story collection. All of Zangwill's I had read before—isn't he wonderful in his way? Kipling's I had read before, "King Solomon of Kentucky," also, and "A Matter of Interest"—what a clever style and treatment Chambers has!—"Survival of the Fittest"—just read this latter in a number of Morgan Robertson's tales collected under *Spun-Yarn*. Also read Cranes "Flannagin" and several others I do not just recollect. "Perfect" was among the new ones, but a few of which I have yet read.[3] I anticipate much delight in tackling them. For which my heartiest thanks. But to return to that "Perfect"—I was unusually struck with it— the woman who wrote it knew women, and say, she did know men— things she dealt in, and the methods with which she dealt, are among the many things I am deficient in and must develop.

What is the work you are so interested in, which may permit you to arrive here in a month, or will not for a year? It must be a Magnus Opus, which the month means desertion, the year achievment. Drop in on us when you do come.[4] Small house, but usually plenty of fair steak, chops, etc. in the larder. I am a heavy eater, but a plain one, fruit, vegetables and meat, and plenty of them, but with small regard for pastries, etc. If you're a sweet tooth you not receive accomodation here except in the fruit line and the candy stores.

O, by the way, just to show how this business of placing MSS. is a dispairing one. Long years ago—three, anyway, I wrote a synopsis of "The Road," under that title, describing tramps and their ways of living, etc. It has been everywhere—every syndicate and big Sunday edition refused it as a feature article; but I kept it going. And lo, to-day, came a note of acceptance of same from the *Arena*.[5] Think I'll resurrect some of my old retired third rate work and send it to *Harpers*,[6] *Century*, etc. That is, if there is any chance of their accepting what tenth class publications have refused. Ever had similar experiences—tell me of them.

And say, when a third rate magazine publishes something of yours, and you wait thirty days after publication for pay, and then dun them, and then they do not even answer your note, what do you do? Is there any way of proceeding against them? Or must one suffer dumbly? Tell me, tell me—I'd like to make it hot for some of those Eastern sharks.

And in these pay-on-acceptance fellows, did you ever get your check at the same time you were notified of acceptance? They always make me an offer, first, and then I needs must sit idly and grow weary and sick at heart waiting during the period between my closing with offer and the arrival of the all-needful. What has been your experience? There's a whole lot of these mysteries I'd like to solve.

Have shoved your picture up on the wall; now don't throw anything; but all my friends I have shown it too, have somewhere along the line of their considerations made the remark, "artistic." I myself likened it at once to such likenesses I have seen of Mark Twain. One other, a young lady, also independently remarked the same. I have but one fault to find with you, supposing your mother to have portrayed you correctly, and that is, your chin. Your chin, beginning from and including the lower lip I must confess I do not like. It belies the rest of the face which seems so strong. It almost has the touch of effemicacy about it which I so detest to see in men. And yet, from your letters I have always derived the opposite conclusion—that you were strongly masculine. It had seemed there was so much in you, of rudeness, roughness, wildness, hurrah-for-hell sort of stuff, such as I possess—a certain affinity you see. I can't reconcile the two. Perhaps your mother did not get that portion of it just right; and perhaps you give the lie inwardly to your exterior. Well, well, so be it. Gave you the nice stuff first, and then frankly gave you hell for what may not be yours.

As you say, I am firm. I may sometimes appear impatient at nothing at all, and all that; but this everybody who has had a chance to know me well have noticed: things come my way even though they take years; no one sways me, save in little things of the moment; I am not stubborn but I swing to my purpose as steadily as the needle to the pole; delay, evade, oppose secretly or openly, it's all immaterial, the thing comes my way. To-day I have met my first serious wall. For three long years the fight has been on; to-day it balances; is a deadlock; I may have met my master; I may not; the future will tell, and one or the other of us will break—and on top of it all I may say it concerns neither my interest nor theirs, nothing except the personal vanity and the clash of our wills. "I won't" and "I will" sums the whole thing up.

Firm? But I am firm in foolishness, as well as other things. Take things more seriously than you? Bosh! You don't know me. Ask my very intimate friends. Ask my creditors. Pshaw—let this illustrate: a very dear friend, a woman charming enough to be my wife and old enough to be my mother, discovered that my most precious possession, my wheel, was hocked. You know I only live for the day. She at once put up the all-needful so that I might regain it. She could well afford it, so that was all right; but mark you, she virtually had a lien upon it. Well, to top it—had been extravagant on the strength of receiving money which did not materialize. Creditors waxed clamorous; a few dollars judiciously scattered among them would have eased things; but credit exhausted; along comes a particularly nice person for a good time. A very nice person who wished to see things; wheel hypothecated and things seen for some forty odd hours. This is me all the time and all over—seriously take things of life—does it look like it? Pshaw. Ask those who know me.

And I am firm in my foolishness.

I am glad you took Jordan[7] in the right way. He is, to a certain extent, a hero of mine. He is so clean, and broad, and wholesome. Would to God he were duplicated a few thousand times in the U.S. Working for a sheepskin! That's what most fools do who go in for education, and most of the rest are geniuses and cranks, who get the kernel and then don't or won't use it.

Well, fiction is the strongest lever, eh? Take the French Revolution, alone—"that tragedy," as John Morley says, "the fifth act of which is yet dark."[8] Those are not his exact words, however. Here are three books, none fiction, not at all read to-day, and, for that matter, false and frail from start to finish when viewed through the cold glasses of to-day's knowledge. Pick me in any period three lovers of fiction which have accomplished a tithe of what they did. Here they are: Montesquieu's *Esprit de Loies*, Jean Jacques Rousseau's *Contract Social*, and Diderot and his *Encyclopedia*.[9]

As for my writing histories and works on economics—I may, some day—but I have little ambition to do so. The same may be said of any kind of writing under the sun. My only wish that way is the all-needful—it seems the easiest way. Had I an assured income, my ambition would be for music, music, music. As it is, impossible—I bend.

I have not read *Bab Ballads*, who are they by?[10] I shall look them up. Yes, I was laughing at some of the *Call's* absurdities concerning Ingersol.[11] I never cared for the man's work myself, while at the same time appreciating the enormous power he was for good among most men. He has done immense work for sanity, normality, sensibility, etc. among his fellows; but, to me, he was not deep enough. However, what I liked in him most of all was his life; they at least have not dared to attack that.

O that England which you do not understand! Let me quote lengthily from Jordan, I just ran across it a couple of days ago, and its effect is still strong. It is from his anti-expansion Essay "Lest we Forget," first in his latest book called *Imperial Democracy*.[12]

"Let us look for a moment at the policy of England. The United States is great through minding her own business; England through minding the business of the world. In the Norse Mythology the Mitgart Serpent appears in the guise of a cat, an animal small and feeble, but in reality the mightiest and the most enduring of all, for its tail goes around the earth, growing down its own throat, and by its giant force it holds the world together. England is the MitGart Serpent of the nations, shut in a petty island; as Benjamin Franklin said, 'an island which compared to America is but a stepping stone in a brook with scarce enough of it above water to keep one's shoes dry.' Yet, by the force of arms, the force of trade, and the force of law she has become the ruler of the earth. It is English brain and English muscle which hold the world together.

"NO OTHER AGENCY OF CIVILIZATION HAS BEEN SO POTENT AS ENGLAND'S ENLIGHTENED SELFISHNESS. Her colonies are of three orders.— friendly nations, subject nations, and military posts. The larger colonies are little united states. They are republics and rule their own affairs. The subject nations and the military posts England rules by a rod of iron, because no other rule is possible. Every year England seizes new posts, opens new ports, and widens the stretch of her empire. But of all this Greater Britain, England herself is but a little part, the ruling head of a world-wide organism. 'What does he know of England who only England knows?' No doubt as Kipling says, England

'thinks her empire still
'Twixt the Strand and Holborn Hill.'

But the Strand would be half empty were it not that it leads outward to Cathay. The huge business interests of Greater Britain are the guarantee of her solidarity. All her parts must hold together.

"In similar relation to the Mother Country, America must stand. GREATER ENGLAND HOLDS OVER US THE OBLIGATIONS OF BLOOD, AND THOUGHT, AND LANGUAGE, AND CHARACTER. ONLY THE SAXON UNDERSTANDS THE SAXON. ONLY THE SAXON AND THE GOTH KNOW THE MEANING OF FREEDOM. 'A sanction like that of religion,' says John Hay, 'enforces our partnership in all important affairs.' Not that we should enter into formal alliance with Great Britain. We can get along well side by side, but never tied together. When England suggests a union for attack and defense, let us ask what she expects to gain from us. Never yet did England offer us the hand in open friendliness, in pure good faith, not hoping to get the best of the bargain. THIS IS THE ENGLISH GOVERNMENT, WHICH NEVER ACTS WITHOUT INTERESTED MOTIVES. But the English people are friends in every real crisis, and that without caring over much whether we be right or not. War with England should be forever impossible. THE NEED OF THE COMMON RACE IS GREATER THAN THE NEED OF THE NATIONS. THE ANGLO-SAXON RACE MUST BE AT PEACE WITHIN ITSELF. NOTHING IS SO IMPORTANT TO CIVILIZATION AS THIS. A WAR BETWEEN ENGLAND AND AMERICA FOUGHT TO THE BITTER END MIGHT SUBMERGE CIVILIZATION. WHEN THE WAR SHOULD BE OVER AND THE SMOKE CLEARED AWAY THERE WOULD BE BUT ONE NATION LEFT, AND THAT, RUSSIA."

"The need of the common race is greater than the need of the nations."—Don't you see, understand how inevitable all this is? Do you appreciate, and if so, can you condemn "This is the English government, which never acts without interested motives." Great God! why shouldn't it! I needs must smile at the petty Joshuas who rise up to-day, confronting movements and evolutions born a thousand, aye, ten thousand centuries agone, and crying out with puny silliness "Stop! Worm that I am, I bid you stop!"[13] Pshaw!

The maggots!—small wonder they have the nerve to claim themselves gods! They would do anything in the face of that. Let me quote just one sentence from an essay of my own:

"Natural selection, undeviating, pitiless, careless alike of the individual or the species, destroyed or allowed to perpetuate, as the case might be, such breeds as were unfittest or fittest to survive."[14]

And, let me add, will continue to do so.

As the sheet is not used up, let me quote another sentence from same article.

"Drawing his strength and knowledge from the dugs of competition, he early learned the great lesson: THAT HIS STRENGTH LAY IN NUMBERS, IN UNITY OF INTERESTS, IN SOLIDARITY OF EFFORT—IN SHORT, IN COMBINATION AGAINST THE HOSTILE ELEMENTS OF HIS ENVIRONMENT."

Go ahead! Command the sun moon and stars to stand still you maggots, you gods! It were easier for a grasshopper to stop the lightening express.

> Good night,
> Jack London.

MS: CSmH; 9 pp., tls. Pbd: *L*, 46–49; *BJL*, I, 300–302.

1. JL had been asked to shorten "An Odyssey of the North."

2. See JL to Johns, June 12, 1899 (2d letter), n. 4.

3. The collection of short stories has not been identified. James Lane Allen, "King Solomon of Kentucky"; Robert W. Chambers, "A Matter of Interest" (1897); Morgan Robertson, "Survival of the Fittest," in *Spun-Yarn: Sea Stories by Morgan Robertson* (1898); Stephen Crane, "Flanagan and His Short Filibustering Adventure" (1897); "Perfect" has not been identified.

4. Johns did not meet JL for several months. He left Harold "in late December, 1899, for my first revisit to my native city of San Francisco" ("Who the Hell *Is* Cloudesley Johns?" p. 208). During his visit, he spent a week with JL. See JL to Johns, January 22, 1900.

5. The *Arena*, a monthly magazine published in Boston from 1889 until 1909 that championed literary realism as well as social and economic reform; edited by John Emery McLean. The *Arena* offered JL ten dollars in cash, ten dollars in subscriptions, and a dozen copies of the issue in which his story would appear. On March 10, 1900, however, "The Road" was returned to JL because of the editorial policies of the new owners who had taken over early in that year.

6. *Harper's New Monthly Magazine* was a general illustrated literary magazine begun in New York in 1850. It changed its name to *Harper's Monthly Magazine* in 1900.

7. David Starr Jordan.

8. John Morley (1838–1923), historian, biographer, and editor of the *Fortnightly Review* from 1867 to 1882 and of the *Pall Mall Gazette* from 1881 to 1883. The quotation has not been identified.

9. Montesquieu's *De l'esprit des lois* was published in 1748; Rousseau's *Le Contrat social*, in 1762; and Diderot's *L'Encyclopédie*, from 1751 to 1776.

10. William S. Gilbert, *The "Bab" Ballads: Much Sound and Little Sense* (1869), a collection of comic verse by the Gilbert later of Gilbert and Sullivan.

11. Robert Green Ingersoll (1833–99), lawyer and orator, known as "the great ag-

nostic" for his questioning of Christian orthodoxy in such lectures as "Some Mistakes of
Moses" and "About the Holy Bible." On July 25, 1899, four days after Ingersoll's death, the
San Francisco Call published an unflattering editorial entitled "Robert G. Ingersoll," term-
ing him neither "a great atheist nor a great agnostic" because of his inconsistency. "It was
idle for a man to deny the existence of God who confessed and proclaimed the principle of
fraternity. . . . The hard conception of annihilation had no place in sentences that were in-
fused with the glow and with the heat of immortality."

   12. *Imperial Democracy* (1899), pp. 17–19. Emphasis is JL's.

   13. JL refers to Joshua's (successful) command for the sun and moon to stand still
(Joshua 10:12–13).

   14. From "What Communities Lose by the Competitive System."

To Cloudesley Johns

962 East 16th. st.,
Aug. 10, 1899.

Dear Friend:—

   Same old tale. Wound off one visitor the first of last week, to receive at
once two more—they have just now gone home. I'll get even with them
yet, so that even their letters, much less themselves shall not reach me. I
see you have been suffering a similar affliction.

   Say! Remember telling me that if I got a check from *Town Topics* to
frame it? After acceptance I let them slip for several months, then wrote
them a nice little note of enquiry—five lines—and behold! They dug up a
dollar for that triolet—"he chortled with glee," and two twenty-five for
the poem "If I Were God One Hour." You mentioned the *Owl*[1] as a snare
and a delusion. Well, they haven't got the best of me yet, at least that's all I
can say. You know I wrote long ago a lot of stuff upon which I wasted
many stamps. Nor would I retire it if hope of getting my postage back still
lived. And I must say I have succeeded in disposing of quite a lot of rub-
bish that way by sending it to the way down publications. The *Owl* published a skit of mine a couple of months ago.[2] When they made the offer
for it, I almost fainted—One Dollar and Fifty cents for two thousand
words. But it more than paid for the stamps I had wasted on the thing,
and gave promise of release from at least one of my early night-mares, so I
closed with the offer. They have not yet paid me. Then the question
arises: why should they have made such a miserable offer if they intended
to take the whole works? And one answer suggests itself: that from very
shame at the smallness of the selling price, the author would refrain from
making any trouble on the event of non-payment. However, I am devoid
of that kind of shame.

   Yes, I cut the story for the *Atlantic*. There were 12,250 words; but
while they wanted it reduced three thousand, I only succeeded in getting
it down to an even ten thousand. So I don't know what they will do about
it. They seem very nice people from their letters, but that, however, re-

mains to be substantiated by something solid. Have also sent Houghton, Mifflin & Co., collection of tales.[3]

I closed with a cash offer of ten dollars, and five yearly subscriptions with the *Arena*, so probably it is alright with them. Say, it's great, learning the inner nature of some of these concerns!

O but I do take myself seriously. My self-estimation has been made in very sober moments. I early learned that there were two natures in me. This caused me a great deal of trouble, till I worked out a philosophy of life and struck a compromise between the flesh and the spirit. Too great an ascendancy of either was to be abnormal, and since normality is almost a fetish of mine, I finally succeeded in balancing both natures. Ordinarily they are at equilibrium; yet as frequently as one is permitted to run rampant, so is the other. I have small regard for an utter brute or for an utter saint.

A choice of ultimate happiness in preference to proximate happiness, when the element of chance is given due consideration, is, I believe, the wisest course for a man to follow under the sun. He that chooses proximate happiness is a brute; he that chooses immortal happiness is an ass; but he that chooses ultimate happiness knows his business.

So Cervantes overthrew Knight Errantry, eh? So we are told by the bellelettristic (or however it should be spelled) triflers of the past several generations. But I say not so. The specialization of industry, aided by the Overthrow of Constantinople and the spread of the "New Learning," gave time and space for the rise of the free cities, which, in turn, increased the kingly prerogative, softened the rigor of feudal dues, smashed the power of the feudal lords, broke down barriers, centralized power, increased trade, exploration, etc., spread civilization, destroyed the baronial power and increased that of the state, pitted a bourgeois aristocracy against a mediaeval one, etc. etc., and somewhere along and all along the line swept knight-errantry out of existence. The Knight of Mancha (or am I quoting from Irving?)[4] simply softened the blow to the nobility, or rather, reconciled them to the fact that knight-errantry was of little use in a work-a-day world. I have rattled this off too quick to do it justice.

Do you remember when Philip the Fair went up against the burghers of the Low Countries?[5] Why, those petty tradesmen could not fight, he said, regarding his steel-clad flowers of chivalry with proud eyes. And do you remember how Philip the Fair and his Knights came back? With their tails between their legs. The damned burghers could fight after all. Little things like that, illustrative of the changing order of things, go to show what really did overthrow Knight-errantry.

I doubt if even you would consider the novel avowedly with a purpose to be real literature. If you do, then let us abandon fiction altogether and give the newspaper its due, for the fixing or changing of public opinion especially on lesser things. But Spencer's *First Principles* alone, leaving out all the rest of his work, has done more for mankind, and through the ages will have done far more for mankind, than a thousand books like *Nicholas Nickleby*, *Hard Cash*, *Book of Snobs*, and *Uncle Toms Cabin*.[6] Why take the enormous power for human good contained in Darwins *Origin of Species* and *Descent of Man*.[7] Or in the work of Ruskin, Mill, Huxley, Carlyle, Ingersoll.

Those *Bab Ballads* are rich—I shall look them up. Received to-day your second installment of magazine stories. Many thanks; shall preserve them until you appear on the scene. Am not reading much fiction just now; but within several days shall get through much of the heavier stuff I am now on, and then I won't do a thing to those tales of yours.

As to "that retired stuff"—many thanks for your kind offer; but really, I shall never resurrect it again. When ever I get to thinking too much of myself I simply look some of it up, and am at once reduced to a more becoming modesty. No, it's put away for good. I have very little out, just now. And it's growing less all the time. It will soon catch me up, I'm afraid, If I don't get down and dig.

If you have not already seen it, I think you will appreciate Bierce's article on the *Call*'s editorial writer who wrote divers things concerning Ingersoll.[8]

Well, say, hold on a minute. Let me explain. But first let me say how glad I was that you liked "The Wife of a King." But I was candid, though I cannot for the life of me remember what a "shameful comparison" I made in letter to you concerning it. This is the way it happened. I had the most terrific dose of blues I ever was afflicted with in my life. I couldn't think of anything original, so I made a composite of three retired Mss. slapped them together, as I at the time considered, haphazard, with the crudest of dovetailing. Shipped the result off in disgust, and forgot all about it, save a most uncomfortable sense of general dissatisfaction. And for the first time, when I looked upon it printed, I was not wholly disgusted with myself—not because it was the best I had done, but because I had rated it so low that disappointment or disgust seemed impossible. Thanks for sending me "Three and a Extra."[9] I had read it a long while ago, but forgotten its existence. There is quite a similarity, and, as you stated, quite a dissimilarity.

Are there any phases of humanity, under any combinations which have not already been exploited? Yet I think I have for some time had an entirely original field in view, so why should I ask. But who knows. That "Theorist" of yours seems to cause lots of trouble. I should think the only way to write a novel would be to do it at a fair rate per day, and then ship off at once. If I can only get ahead of the game, I'm going to jump back to Jerusalem in the time of Christ, and write one giving an entirely new interpretation of many things which occurred at that time. I think I can do it, so that while it may rattle the slats of the Christians they will still be anxious to read it.[10]

Good night,
Jack London.

MS: CSmH; 5 pp., tls. Pbd: *L*, 50–52; *BJL*, I, 302–5.

1. The *Owl Magazine*, a five-cent monthly fiction magazine published in Boston from 1896 to 1899.

2. "The Handsome Cabin Boy," *Owl*, July 1899. JL dunned the *Owl* on August 9, 1899, and received payment on August 20.

3. *The Son of the Wolf*.

4. JL probably alludes to either Washington Irving's *A Chronicle of the Conquest of Granada* (1829) or his "Legends of the Conquest of Spain," in *The Crayon Miscellany* (1835).

5. Philip IV (1268–1314), King of France from 1285 until his death. On Philip's attempt to annex Flanders in 1301, the Flemish burghers rebelled, and in 1302 they defeated the French near Courtrai, Belgium, in the Battle of the Spurs, named for the spurs taken as trophies from the fallen French knights.

6. Charles Dickens, *Nicholas Nickleby* (1838–39); Charles Reade, *Hard Cash* (1863); William Makepeace Thackeray, *The Snobs of England. By One of Themselves* (1846–47); Harriet Beecher Stowe, *Uncle Tom's Cabin; or, Life among the Lowly* (1851).

7. JL had taken *On the Origin of Species* (1859) with him to the Klondike in 1897, *The Descent of Man* was published in 1871.

8. Ambrose Bierce, "Ingersoll, the Dead Lion," *San Francisco Examiner*, July 30, 1899. Bierce acknowledged Ingersoll's intellectual and stylistic limitations but claimed they "were a source of his power; at least they confined him to methods that are 'understanded of the people'; and to be understood by the greatest number should be the wish of him who tries to destroy what he thinks popular delusions."

9. Rudyard Kipling, "Three and—an Extra" (1886). Both this story and "The Wife of a King" concern a love triangle that is resolved when the wife flaunts her attractiveness at a public dance.

10. Notes for the proposed "Christ novel" are at CSmH. JL eventually used the material as chapter 17 of *The Star Rover* (New York: Macmillan, 1915).

To Cloudesley Johns

962 East 16th. st.,
Aug. 24, 1899.

My dear friend:—

'Frisco and Oakland has been roaring since last evening, when the *Sherman* was sighted.[1] Nor will things quiet down till the week is past. So no work for me—besides, have had another friend to stop with me.

Just been entertaining a queer sort of a fellow—does a free-lance sort of business for the 'Frisco papers in the way of newsgathering and Sunday feature articles, and thinks he will tackle short-story writing for a permanent thing. Poor devil, he hasn't it in him to commence with, is forty-five, and doesn't know a thing about the market, etc. etc. There's lots of disappointment in store for him, I fear. He heard I had just come back from

Klondike and had come to make a couple of columns out of me. Was disappointed on learning how long I had been back.

Was entertaining a Klondike chum last week[2]—just come out after two years of it—so hard up he had to shovel coal for his passage. But he was a sailor and used to rough life all his days.

So it goes. Am going down country the first of next month to pose as best man for a foolish friend of mine[3] who has abandoned the torturing of catgut for the harmony of matrimony. And I have to dig up a wedding present besides! Wow!

I saw "Girls" in current *Century*.[4] It was quite good. Funny, that "freak story," as you called it, by Grant Allen.[5] I had but recently finished reading some four hundred and odd pages of Weissmann's theory of the germplasm,[6] was deep in the study of those who had taken up the controversy of Weissmann, and had been evolving a tale on memory something similar to Grant Allen's. You will notice he had founded his idea on Weissman too. Anticipated again.

Have you read anything of Weissman's. He has struck a heavy blow to the accepted idea of acquired characters being inherited, and as yet his opponents have not proved conclusively one case in which such a character has been inherited. Another idea he advances well, is that death is not the indispensible correlative of life, as hitherto it has been supposed to be. In fact, his researches in the germ-plasm has proven quite to the contrary. Read him up, you will find him interesting. But it's heavy. If you have not studied evolution well, I would not advise you to tackle him. He takes a thorough grounding in the subject for granted.

Are you going in on that *Black Cat* Prize Competition?[7] It has just been announced, and the time is not up till the 31st. of March 1900. The style, etc., is worth imitating for the money—if one thinks he is able to do it. I intend having a go at it. I cut down to ten thousand instead of nine thousand, and to-day received confirmation of its acceptance from the *Atlantic*. But say, can you explain this to me?—I understand they pay well and also that they pay on acceptance. Well, to-day acceptance comes with assurance of publication in an early number, and that is all. No check, no nothing concerning rate of payment, when, or how. Now what am I to understand—that the check is liable to arrive anytime? or that I must wait till publication? What say you? And do you know anything of how much they pay?

I think "A Tragedy of Errors," is original; at least I know I have never seen a similar title. A number of friends I asked are also of the same opinion.[8] You have a story to come out soon in the *Land of Sunshine*—is it the September number?[9] Let us know. *Owl* dug up on being dunned in the proper spirit.

So you think it will be hard on the poor girl who will have to live with you, eh? I imagine the very opposite prevails concerning you and myself as regards disposition. I should think you would be more disagreeeeable on first acquaintance and grow better with association, and vice a versa I am a mild little lamb at first, etc. Those who come to know me, know my temper well. "Jack is irritable," all my old friends say. "But then," they usually conclude, "I don't mind it. You see it's Jack."

Was there ever a luckier fellow than I when it comes to friends? I doubt it. And between you and myself, I likewise greatly fear for the bit of femininity who takes me for little better and much worse.

I can thoroughly appreciate the condition you were in when you wrote me that last regular letter—writing late and heavy, and all that. Trouble with me, in a similar state, is that I have a terrific yearning after red, red wine.

But really, I shall have to ask you to accept this stuff as a letter. I have striven and striven and striven. It is warm; doors and windows are open. Three youngsters are playing on the porch before my window. Their elders are in the parlor. My guest and a temporary visitor are in the same room with me, waxing hotter and hotter over some mooted point in that much mooted question of telepathy, so I must call quits. Will do better by you next time.

Jack London.

MS: CSmH; 3 pp., tls. Pbd: *BJL*, I, 305–6.

1. The *Sherman*, a transport ship used to carry soldiers to and from Manila, arrived in San Francisco on August 23, 1899, bringing home from the Philippines the California Volunteers.

2. Probably John Thorson, who floated to the mouth of the Yukon River with JL.

3. Probably Frank Atherton.

4. Jeanie Peet, "Girls," *Century*, August 1899.

5. Grant Allen (1848–99), British novelist, short-story writer, and popular writer on science. By his own confession, Allen concentrated on stories concerning evolution and race. His "freak story" may have been "The Reverend John Creedy," collected in *Twelve Stories by Grant Allen* (1899). John Creedy, a Negro from Africa, had in his youth been taken to England for his education. After his study at Oxford he became an Anglican missionary, married a white woman, and returned to Africa. Gradually he forsook his English ways and returned to his native habits. His wife died of a fever, and after her death Creedy destroyed all remaining vestiges of European civilization in his possession.

6. August Weismann, *The Germ Plasm: A Theory of Heredity* (1893).

7. For *Black Cat* story competitions, see JL to Johns, March 7, 1899, n. 1.

8. Johns was probably thinking of using this title for one of his stories; it had in fact already been used by Frank A. Munsey for a book published in 1899.

9. Johns did not publish a story in *The Land of Sunshine* in 1899 or 1900.

To Cloudesley Johns

962 East 16th. st.,
Sept. 6, 1899.

My dear friend:–

Back again, but not yet settled down. Have blown myself for a new wheel ('99 Cleveland), and hence, between appearing at weddings in knickerbockers and rampaging over the country with bloomer-clad lassies, and celebrating the return of the California's,[1] I have been unable to chase ink. The way I happened to get said wheel is an illustration of how little rhyme or reason there is in placing Mss. Some time ago I wrote an avowedly hack article for an agriculture paper, expecting to receive five dollars for the same, and to receive it anywhere from sixty to ninety days after acceptance. But it was rejected and, being short at the time, I was correspondingly dejected. But straight away I shipped off the Ms. to *The Youth's Companion*, and lo and behold, without any warning, they forwarded me a check for thirty-five dollars—eleven dollars per thousand.[2] How's that for luck?

Yes; I received some time ago that *Scroll*[3] publishing scheme. Did you ever get something similar from a projected magazine which called itself *The Columbia Poeticia*? It agreed to publish *all* the poetry sent it by its subscribers. And if I remember rightly, to pay for it in some sort of way.

Don't weep over what the *National* did—they pay poorly. Sometime ago they accepted one of my ancient efforts, for which they gave five yearly-subscriptions, and five dollars cash, pay on publication.[4] I expect it to come out in the September Number. God bless the publishers. If the gods should smile upon me and some day put me on my feet, I won't do a thing to them—I mean some of these cheap-John publishers, not the gods.

I am awaiting the outcome of a little affair with *The Editor*, with great curiosity. James Knap—whatever the rest of his name is,[5] lists them in his *500 places to Sell MSS.* thus: "pay liberally." Feeling rather nervy one day, I sent them a skit of 1700 words of advice to young authors. But I did not tell them how to sell their wares, or to file material, or to dun gracefully, etc. The title will explain better: "On the Writer's Philosophy of Life."[6] They accepted Ms. with promise to pay on publication, said publication to be early. What I am curious about is to see what they consider liberal pay. Or will they expect me to take it out in trade? As I have never yet submitted Mss. anywhere for advice, I don't think I'll begin now. Well, we'll see what we'll see.

Oh! Chapple, Joe Chapple,[7] of the *National*, writes a fellow the most beautiful letters when buying things for a song. Did you ever receive one of his?

To save my life I cannot think of a title for those four lines of Jeanie Peet's. You see that hits me on origination, where I'm weak.

If I am not mistaken, I, in my last to you, or at some time when telling you of Weissman, I said: "do not mistake the meaning of *acquired characters*." You have muddled "acquired characters" with "fixed characters," it is these latter which are heriditary. Language is an acquired character; a Semetic nose a fixed character. The one is acquired in the life-time of the individual, the other inherited from an ancestor. No; I wouldn't write that refutation of Weissman if I were you.

I simply misunderstood you when you asked me if I had ever seen a similar title to "A Tragedy of Errors." I naturally thought on the instant of what had suggested it, but what I thought you were in quest of, was as to whether it had not already been suggested to and been used by some other writer.

Go it for the *Black Cat*! I cannot even think of a suitable plot—my damnable lack of origination you see. I think I had better become an interpreter of the things which are, rather than a creator of the things which might be. Many thanks for articles you sent. Did you take especial note of that article by Ray Stannard Baker on Dr. See's new law of temperature? I am afraid the old nebulae theory still holds notwithstanding.[8] Here is his law which you will probably recollect: Constant divided by radius equals temperature. Or, as he states it, "the temperature of a gaseous star varies inversely as the radius." But the compression of a gas is always accomplished under pressure—where is the pressure which compresses the sun? This question merely suggests itself, I have not taken the time to test its stability. Compression does not generate heat, as he conceives it; it merely radiates heat, forces it out, away from, much as one would squeeze the water out of a wet sock. One can not very well assert that the more water he squeezed out of the wet sock the wetter the wet sock became, surely not. Yet this seems to me an analogous assertion to that made by Dr. See. As the article is, it is a splendid bit of pseudo-science, but there is nothing substantial to it.

Trippler's liquid air has interested me not a little; but as yet I fail to see how he has got around the law of THE CONSERVATION OF ENERGY; yet he asserts that with three pounds of liquid air he can generate ten, a surplusage of seven pounds.[9] If this is so, then one may say that at last the lever and the fulcrum by which man may move the earth has at last been discovered. I guess not.

Well, time is flying; I've got a visitor, as usual, spending a few days with me, and as I hear the tinkle of his bicycle bell approaching, I must cut off. But just you watch my smoke some of these days—I intend shaking every mortal who knows me and going off all by myself. So there, now!

Jack London.

MS: CSmI I, 4 pp., tls. Pbd: *L*, 52 54; *BJL*, I, 306 7.

1. The California Volunteers.

2. "The King of Mazy May," initially submitted to the *American Agriculturist* on July 22, 1899, was sent to *Youth's Companion* on August 1, 1899. It was published November 30, 1899.

3. *Scroll* was a short-lived literary magazine published by the Authors' and Writers' Union of Chicago.

4. "A Lesson in Heraldry," *National*, March 1900. JL did not receive his five dollars until April 26, 1900.

5. James Knapp Reeve, founder of the *Editor* and compiler of *500 Places to Sell Manuscripts* (1899). The *Editor*, published from 1895 to 1942, identified itself in its subtitle as a monthly "journal of information for literary workers."

6. "On the Writer's Philosophy of Life," *Editor*, October 1899. For JL's payment for this essay, see JL to Johns, December 5, 1899.

7. Joseph M. Chapple (1867–1950), editor and publisher of the *National*.

8. Ray Stannard Baker (1870–1946), author and at this time a staff writer for *McClure's*. In "The Origin of the Sun and Planets," *McClure's*, May 1899, Baker explained the theory of the sun's heat put forth by Thomas J. J. See (1866–1962), an astronomer and professor of mathematics at the United States Naval Observatory. See argued against Laplace's "old nebulae theory" of the formation of the solar system, which stated that the planets were formed out of a rapidly revolving fiery mass by the pull of gravity. Dr. See's law, based on the principle that a gas, when compressed, gives out heat, states that by the attraction of gravitation, a gaseous star compresses itself and produces heat. Thus See believed that the sun was shrinking from its original size, which covered all of the space now occupied by the solar system; as it shrank, the gaseous and solid particles, unable to keep up with the sun's movement, detached and cooled to form the planets.

9. Charles E. Trippler, "Liquid Air—the Newest Wonder of Science," *Cosmopolitan*, June 1898. Trippler (*b.* 1847), a physicist and inventor, proved that 800 cubic feet of air could, under thousands of pounds of pressure, be compressed into one cubic foot of liquid. The law of the conservation of energy maintains that the amount of energy in a closed system is constant, even though its form (kinetic or potential) may change.

To Cloudesley Johns

962 East 16th. st.,
Sept. 12, 1899.

My dear friend:—

Between engagements, visitors, and friends, I have not yet succeeded in doing a tap. And to-morrow I start out on that postponed trip of mine to Stanford University and Mt. Hamilton, to say nothing of way points. And when I return from that I am going to lock myself up.

You say, in reference to the *McClure's* note, "Is there any editor, I wonder, who wants something besides merely stories?" Why my dear fellow, I am constantly on the lookout for editors who want stories, and I move to amend your query by striking out "something besides merely."

Now for a question: Suppose *McClure's* had accepted that study of yours. Would they have published it in the magazine, or would it have come out in some newspaper through the syndicate?[1] I am always afraid to send *McClures* anything that I consider good, for fear they will publish it through the syndicate, which syndicate I know nothing about. Can you enlighten me?

As to the *Black Cat* story: I am in such a state of anarchy, and have so much I wish to do, that I can not see my way to tackling your proposition. As it is, the period of the closing of the contest is so very far away that I am not figuring on it at all. I do not even know whether I shall go in for it. Perhaps I may try them with some of my unaccepted stuff.

So one's vocabulary is inherited. Well, well. Would you kindly amplify that statement a little, giving me the data you base it upon. If you can actually prove it you can turn the scientific world upside down. A certain monarch once isolated some babes upon a tower, where they were fed, etc., but allowed no vocal intercourse with the world. It was an experiment. When they had grown up it was found that they were simply idiots. Beyond a few inarticulate sounds by which they expressed the primary passions, they did not speak. Beyond the necessary actions corelated with mere existence they were idiots. Having received no vocabulary from their kind they were unable to think.

No man ever received one word from an ancestor by means of heredity.

I don't know where I'm at regarding the "Tragedy of Errors." I guess you're right, however. You misunderstood Trippler. The heat forced from the air does go somewhere. It is carried off by running water which is piped through the machine. This raised the question in my mind: how much energy would be required on shipboard to pump this running water for the liquid air engine. Of course, in a city, the energy which causes the water to run is supplied by the water company.

Does rotation cause compression? Figure it out.

How I envy you working away at your novel. I am most anxious to have a try at one myself. If I can only get far enough ahead of the game, I certainly shall. You see, I have a family to support, and that's hell when a man's young and single. Say, what do you know of The Western Press, down San Diego way? Sometime ago I sent them one of my failures. When the regulation thirty days was up, I sent a trailer. No answer. Sept. 1, I sent a second trailer, this time stamped and addressed envelope enclosed. Still no answer. As I had a "return" on the outside, I know they must have received it. Is this usual with them? Have they gone out of business, broken up, etc.?[2]

Shall do better by you regarding letter-writing, sometime. As it is, I'm not worth a rap for anything. The other day I chased a word several hours and failed to find it. And then, yesterday, lying out in the sand by the edge of the ocean, it came of its own free will, when my mind was many many leagues away. "Exotic" was the word. Such a simple word, but O the trouble it cost me!

Jack London.

Am going to try my luck at backhand from now on. How do you like it? Or do you think it possible for me to improve?[3]

J.G.L.

MS: CSmH; 3 pp., tls. Pbd: *L*, 54–56; *BJL*, I, 307.

1. The McClure Syndicate, the first newspaper syndicate in the United States, was founded by Samuel S. McClure in 1884.

2. JL sent "Their Alcove" to the Western Press on July 19, 1899. After five trailers he sent the story to several magazines; it was published in the *Woman's Home Companion*, September 1900.

3. The postscript is in longhand.

To Cloudesley Johns

962 East 16th. st.,
Sept. 20, 1899.

Dear Cloudesley:–

Back again. Had a glorious time. Stopped over at Stanford, where I met several students I knew, sat under the various profs., etc. And looked through the thirty-six inch reflector on top of Mt. Hamilton. There we saw the moon, Saturn and his rings, and quite a number of burgeois pigs. Yes, they were pigs, dressed like tourists. My companion and I, after seeing them, were exceeding proud of the fact that we were mere proletarians.

"The Quarry Foreman," is good, unqualifiedly good. And altogether different to "Zebro." It is strong, has unity, and the character is strong in conception and handled with bold, deft strokes. You haven't a bit of kick a-coming. Again I say it is good. Perhaps one or two touches may be slightly amateurish, but if so, they are very slightly so. Somehow, I have a vague feeling that the very last line or so might be bettered, bettered by some extremely slight change, perhaps only in the order of the words, perhaps in some simple modification. But beyond this, one can have nothing but praise for it. If that was done a year and a half ago I should like to see some of your later work.

The June *Black Cat* has a $350 prize yowl, and the September number a $500 one.[1] There are no others since May. Thanks for information about *Truth*.[2] They pay on acceptance I suppose? Is the announcement you sent something new? or is it of long standing?

Ah, therein you differ from me—it's money I want, or rather, the things money will buy; and I could never possibly have too much.[3] As to living on practically nothing—I propose to do as little of that as I possibly can. Remember, it's the feed not the breed which makes the man.

As to vocabulary—a person will write as they think. A small vocabulary will limit their thought. If they don't think they will not write; if they think slovenly, they will write slovenly. Let me illustrate by quoting from you. "I have met many people who have little memory, and who are sluggish thinkers, with more extensive vocabularies than mine. Mind you, I know all those words, but I do not, cannot, use them—they are not in my vocabulary."

Now what have you done? You have stated that you knew "all these words," that is to say, that they were in your vocabulary. If you know them, they certainly are in your vocabulary. Then in the next breath you say they are not in your vocabulary. You did not mean that, but you wrote it slovenly—why? Because you thought it slovenly. Had you stopped and thought carefully before you put it on paper, you would have clearly realized the distinction you wished to make, and you would have clearly wrote it thus: "I know all these words, but I do not, cannot, use them—they are not in my WORKING VOCABULARY."

Again, let me criticise you. You say "I don't know whether or not this sounds reasonable to you; but for myself, I am as sure of its truth as one can be sure of anything in this ridiculous world where every age contradicts the theories of that preceding it."

Now you did not stop to think that out before you wrote it. If you had you would not have voiced falsehoods which your sober judgement would not countenance. You know that the work of Euclid, a score of centuries old, has not once been contradicted; that Newton's Laws are still with us; that the teachings of Bruno,[4] Galileo and a host of others have not been contradicted. Of course they have been modified. But that is another story. The test of truth is: Will it work? Will you trust your life to it? Every day you behold working or trust your life to things which are directly the result of previous theorizing. Had you stopped to think this out, you would not have set your reason aside for a brilliant generalization.

In your writing I note many words, modern in their origin, which had little or no general use at the period you were conceived. Yet you use them. They were of course "acquired." Had you passed your whole life in solitude you would have had no vocabulary; had you been conceived just as you were and raised in the best Russian circles, you would have had a large Russian vocabulary, not one word of which you would have inherited from your lines of ancestors. Had you been raised in entirely different portions of the United States to those in which you were, you certainly would many idioms, etc., which were not entailed.

As an artisan cannot work without tools, so a man cannot think without a vocabulary, and the greater his vocabulary the better fitted he is to think. Of course, an ass may acquire the tools of an artisan and be unable to work with them, so with words. But that does not interfere with the broad statement I have laid down.

As to your illustration of J. E. Seeley's[5] spelling—In no court of justice, by no philosopher or scientist would such be permitted to pass as evidence. Do not make the mistake so common with women and lesser men, of taking a coincidence for a cause. To the Egyptian in his rainless land, the rising of the Nile was considered the greatest thing in the world, the most important. Now it happened that this rising of the Nile was marked by the rising in the heavens of the Dog-star Sirius. This was merely a coincidence, but the Egyptians mistook it for a cause, and worshipped the star because it caused the inundations. From this it was but a step to wander on into all the absurdities of astrology. If one star ruled terrestial affairs, all stars must have influence, and if with things, then certainly with men.

Of a surety, if a cerebral structure of an ancestor which renders him an idiot or a kleptomaniac is transmitted to you, you will resemble him in that, to a greater or less degree as excited or mollified by environment. So with color blindness, for instance, or a thousand and one other similar things. But a vocabulary does not come under this head at all, except that the cerebral formation inherited may be limited as regards memory or quantity of words. Yet this, however, will not effect what certain words go to make up that quantity. So many words may be acquired up to the limit, and then the acquirement of words will virtually cease.

Having done nothing but lecture, I shall now chop off.

Jack London.

MS: CSmH; 4 pp., tls. Pbd: *L*, 56–58; *BJL*, I, 307–8.

1. JL refers to second- and third-prize stories; *Black Cat* trickled its publication of prizewinners throughout an entire year.

2. *Truth* was an illustrated magazine published in New York from 1881 to 1902, featuring literature, art, and articles aimed at a feminine audience.

3. For JL's attitude on writing for financial rewards, see "First Aid to Rising Authors," *Junior Munsey Magazine*, December 9, 1900, later published as "The Material Side," *The Occident*, December 1916.

4. Giordano Bruno (?1548–1600), Italian philosopher, burned at the stake for heresy by the Inquisition. Bruno's pantheistic theories profoundly influenced later thinkers, especially Spinoza and Leibniz.

5. Edward J. Seeley, a friend of Johns's who worked in an artificial limb shop in Los Angeles and was a part-time inventor.

To Cloudesley Johns

962 East 16th. st.,
Sept. 26, 1899.

Dear Cloudesley:—

At last am at work; have completed my day's stint; am now clearing up my correspondence; and as soon as I finish this shall be off and away for a scorch on my wheel. Then to-night comes my studying as usual.

Did I ever mention a Ms. I received in response to a trailer, which same Ms. had been O.K'd and blue-pencilled?[1] Well, such happened to me sometime ago. Without removing marks or anything I shipped it off to *The Youth's Companion*. There were fifteen hundred words to it. Last week a check comes for twenty-five. Say I'm having lots of luck with the *Companion*, sending them my old, almost-ready-to-be-retired stuff. Have you ever tried them. They pay good and promptly. Though such work won't live it at least brings the ready cash.

Do you do any work for Tillotson & Sons? Either my work is deteriorating or else they have lowered their rates, for I find them paying less each time.

No; I did not like your "Quarry Foreman," through comparison with "Zebro"; but for itself. How I envy you when you say that you do not write for publication. There is certainly far greater chance for you to gain the goal you have picked out, than for me who am in pursuit of dollars, dollars, dollars. Yet I cannot see how I can do otherwise, for a fellow must live, and then there are also others depending upon him. However, once and awhile I shall make it a point to sit down and deliberately not write for publication.

"Because of your indifference to everything when compared with your work, and your habit of sacrificing everything which interferes with it"— ye Gods! that's the spirit to go at it with! You certainly should get there.

Have begun to isolate myself from my friends—a few at a time. But those I have managed to dispense with are the easy ones. I can't see my way clear to the others except by running away. But instead of the desert I'll take to sea. Many who know me, ask why I, with my knowledge of the sea, do not write some sea fiction. But you see I have been away from it so long that I have lost touch. I must first get back and saturate myself with its atmosphere. Then perhaps I may do some thing good.

I am afraid that brother of yours[2] has imbibed just a little of your confounded pessimism. That's bad. Viewing this world through the eyes of science I can see no reason at all why a person should be the slightest bit pessimistic. Why it's all good, considering man's relation to it.

Jack London.

P.S. Did I inform you that at last I am once more an uncle.[3] It was born nearly a month ago—a ten month's child—nails long enough to cut.

J.G.L.

MS: CSmH; 2 pp., tls. Pbd: *L*, 58–59; *BJL*, I, 308–9.
    1. "Pluck and Pertinacity," sent to *Success* on June 2, 1899, and returned after two trailers. It was sent to *Youth's Companion* on August 19, 1899, and was published in its January 4, 1900, issue.
    2. Herbert Heron Peet.
    3. Irving Shepard (1899–1975) was born on September 2 to Eliza and Capt. James Shepard.

To Cloudesley Johns

962 East 16th. st.,
Oct. 3, 1899.

Dear Cloudesley:–

That was good, that fable by Charles Battell Loomis. As you did not say return, I've sent it along the line. Is that the Loomis who edits the *Land of Sunshine?* or are there two Loomises?[1] Or does the other fellow spell his name Lumis? Or is it just some tangle of my own wits?

I think your explanation of your own particular pessimism (if pessimism it may be called), tallies very much with mine.

Therein we differ—dissipation is alluring to me. Last Sunday I went off with a very nice young lady[2] on a bicycle trip up to Mill Valley among the redwoods at the base of Mount Tamalpias. To do this we had to go to 'Frisco and take the ferry to Saucalito, and from thence to destination via pedals. Any number of lively young 'Frisco people take the same outing on Sundays, except that they do not ordinarily or even extraordinarily go on bikes. They patronize the railroad. Well, on the back trip to 'Frisco, a bunch of them took the deck and raised hell generally, to the shocking of many of the more sedate passengers. Am happy to state, however, that the girl I was with, while the kingdoms of the earth could not have lured her into getting up and doing likewise, at least highly enjoyed the performance. All of which is neither here nor there. But for myself, I was attacked by all kinds of feelings. Why my longing was intense to jump in and join them after the fashion of my wild young days, and go on after we arrived at 'Frisco and make the night of it which I knew they were going to make. Alluring? I guess yes.

And then again, I could feel how I had grown away from so much of that—lost touch. I knew if I should happen to join them, how strangely out of place it would seem to me—duck-out-of-water sort of feeling. This made me sad; for, while I cultivate new classes, I hate to be out of grip with the old. But say, it wouldn't take me long to get my hand in again. Just a case of lost practice.

By the way, my companion on that trip is somewhat of an amateur photographer, and the camera usually accompanies us on our trips. We have been waiting for a rainy day for developing and printing the shots we have taken—she's got some kind of a film or plate, or whatever it is, which does not require the sun for printing. Well, when we work them up, if there are any good ones of myself, I'll ship them along.

Have been going on chess drunks of late. Did you ever yield to the toils of the game?—toils in more ways than one. It's a most fascinating game, and one which has devoured well nigh as many of my hours as cards. However, I've done very little chess in the last year or so, and this is merely a temporary relapse.

Have also been feasting my soul with some of the new books: Kipling galore, Bullen's *Sea Idyls*, Grant Allen's *Adventures of Miss Gayly*, and among others, Beatrice Harraden's *Fowler*.[3] It's a strange sort of a work, but it dealt with or worked out a character which is the exact composite of two living models with whom I am acquainted. While no portion of the three hundred and odd pages may lay claim to special excellence, the thing as a whole is unusually well done. Read it when you get a chance. You have probably got an idea of it from the reviews. If you have not, I'll just say that it deals with a sort of creature who is not a man, and who at the same time is not a woman either—a sort of euneuch sort of thing, with a pair of pants on. Well, this creature is the fowler. He is a libertine—but not a physical but a metaphysical one. Women always feel safe with him—physically; and in this their intuition prompts them aright. But he assails their minds, which same he debauches thoroughly. It is a strange idea, but one which after all is not so uncommon in real life.

Am now doing a thousand words per day, six days per week. Last week I finished 1100 words ahead of the required amount. To-day (Tuesday), I am 172 ahead of my stint. I have made it a rule to make up next day what I fall behind; but when I run ahead, to not permit it to count on the following day. I am sure a man can turn out more, and much better in the long run, working this way, than if he works by fits and starts. How do you find it?

How time flies! Here is Christmas at hand, and Paris approaching—ah! I wonder if the gods will smile so that I may go![4]

Jack London.

MS: CSmH; 3 pp., tls. Pbd: *L*, 59–60; *BJL*, I, 309–10.

1. Charles Battell Loomis (1861–1911), humorist and author of *Just Rhymes* (1899); Charles Fletcher Lummis (1859–1928), writer, founder of the *Land of Sunshine* in 1894, and its editor until 1909; he later founded the Southwest Museum. Loomis's fable has not been identified.

2. Bessie Maddern.

3. Frank T. Bullen, *Idylls of the Sea* (1899); Grant Allen, *Miss Cayley's Adventures* (1899); Beatrice Harraden, *The Fowler* (1899). Harraden's novel portrays the psychological destruction of its self willed and independent heroine.

4. The Paris Exposition was to open on April 14, 1900.

To Cloudesley Johns

962 East 16th. st.,
Oakland, Calif.,
Oct. 24, 1899.

Dear Cloudesley:—

Everything in confusion, visitors still here. So you're a chess player. And it's the one form of dissipation which has any attraction for you. As I can hardly look upon it in that light concerning myself, I can but conclude that you are by far the better player. Why I have never met a good player—spent all my time teaching beginners, and you know nothing is worse for chess than that. And besides, I have never had the time to devote to it. For a year at a stretch I never see a board, and then, for a few short weeks I happen to mildly indulge. As I have not taken the time to learn properly, so I cannot play an intensive game; instead, I play viciously, not more than four moves ahead at the best, and endeavor to break up combinations as fast as my opponent forms them—that is, first, if they are threatening; and second, if the slightest and most insignificant gain will accrue to myself, such as the getting of another piece of mine in position by a trade, or by double-banking my opponent's pawns, or preventing his castling by forcing him to move his king in a trade. For the sake of this latter, when the gambit goes my way, I always trade queens. But a heavy player, once growing accustomed to my play, doesn't do a thing to me. So be it. I shall never learn chess.

Last article published by me, had, among other typographical errors, "something fresh for the jaded care of the world," instead of "something fresh for the jaded ear of the world."[1] On second thought it might have been worse.

Think you could train yourself into becoming a hermit? For me that would be far harder than to train myself to become a suicide. I like to rub against my kind, with a gregarious instinct far stronger than in most men. A hermitage—synonym for hell. I would also like to kill a few of my kind once in a while, which same I think I would do rather than to isolate myself.

O, speaking of the fotos—was initiated in the art of developing them last Sunday; expect to print and mount them next Sunday; and then expect one.

So we both suffer from a plethora of sketches. Dam plots; I don't think I could construct a decent one to save my life. And who, of the best short story writers, do write stories which are nearer stories than sketches. If a study is a sketch (and so the magazine editors seem to deem it), then under the generic term "story," few, very very few pen products of not more than six thousand words can be placed. What think you? Beyond the short detective story, did you ever see one first class short yarn which would answer the American magazine classification?

Lucrative mediocrity[?] I know, if I escape drink, that I shall be surely driven to it. By God! if I have to dedicate my life to it, I shall sell work to Frank A. Munsey. I'll buck up against them just as long as I can push a pen or they can retain a Ms. reader about the premises. Just on general principles, you know.

I remember Stevenson's reference in his letters to "The White Nigger," but I think it is an unpublished fragment.[2] I have never seen anybody who has read it, or who knew of any body else reading it. Am reading Stevenson's *Virginibus Puerisque* just now. Find in this mail his *Inland Voyage*. Return it when you have finished, as I wish to pass it along. It has just arrived. Have read it myself. Get such books for "Bull Durham" tobacco tags. Have sent for his *Silverado Squatters*—don't think much of it from previous reading, but it was a long time ago, and I did it too hurriedly, I'm afraid.[3] If you haven't read it I'll send it along later.

So you try experiments in letter writing. I never do nor never have. Haven't the slightest idea what I'm going to say when I sit down—just hammer it out as fast as I can. And right well am I pleased when I have finished the hateful task. I wouldn't do it at all, no more than I would work, were it not for the compensation. As for you, I get more originality in your letters than from all my rest put together—rather jerky and jagged but refreshing and interesting. Believe me, I'm not fishing for a loan.

O I don't blame them. I'd write rot myself—if somebody would only pay me for it. There's the rub. Have been reading Jacob's *More Cargoes*.[4]

You have surely seen some of his magazine work, haven't you? Also have been going through Kendrick Bangs' *The Dreamers* and *The Bicyclers and Other Farces.*[5] He's clever and humorous, in a mild sort of way.

Have been digging at Norman's *Eastern Question,*[6] preparatory to a certain economic dissertative article I intend writing—Asia touches one of the phases I wish to deal with. Besides, I have gone through Curzon's similar work, and wish to take up soon Beresford's *Break-up of China.*[7] Am going through Drummond on evolution, Hudson on psychology,[8] and reviewing Macaulay and De Quincey in the course of English in Minto which I am giving to a friend—the photographer.[9] She's well up in the higher math, etc. but not in general culture—coaches in the exact sciences for would-be university students, etc. Say, that reviewing does a fellow good. I had no idea how hazy I had gotten.

Society will never injure me—the world calls too loudly for that.

Good night,

Jack London.

MS: CSmH; 4 pp., tls. Pbd: *L*, 61–62; *BJL*, I, 310–12.

1. The error, in "On the Writer's Philosophy of Life," was corrected when the essay was reprinted in *The Occident: University of California Monthly*, December 1916.

2. Stevenson wrote to Sidney Colvin on April 10, 1888, describing a "tragic romance" about the Indian Mutiny, entitled "The White Nigger," which he was planning to write with Lloyd Osbourne (Sidney Colvin, ed., *The Letters of Robert Louis Stevenson*, 4 vols. [New York, 1911], 3: 65). The novel was never published.

3. *Virginibus Puerisque* (1881) is a collection of reminiscent essays; *An Inland Voyage* (1878) and *The Silverado Squatters* (1883) are travel narratives, the former describing a canoe trip down the Oise River from Belgium to France and the latter recording Stevenson's honeymoon in an abandoned silver mine in the Napa Valley.

4. William W. Jacobs, *More Cargoes* (1896), a collection of sea stories.

5. John Kendrick Bangs, *The Dreamers: A Club* (1899) and *Bicyclers and Other Farces* (1899). During his career Bangs (1862–1922), an editor and humorist, was on the staffs of *Life, Harper's Monthly, Harper's Weekly, Puck,* and other magazines. *The Dreamers* deals with a club whose members meet periodically to eat indigestible food and, after sleeping, recount their dreams, which are presented as parodies of Richard Harding Davis, Henry James, W. D. Howells, and other authors.

6. Henry Norman, *The Peoples and Politics of the Far East; Travels and Studies in the British, French, Spanish, and Portuguese Colonies, Siberia, China, Japan, Siam and Malaya* (1895).

7. Probably George N. Curzon, *Problems of the Far East* (1894), and Charles W. Beresford, *The Break-up of China, with an Account of Its Present Commerce, Currency, Waterways, Armies, Railways, Politics and Future Prospects* (1899).

8. Henry Drummond, *The Evolution of Man, Being the Lowell Lectures Delivered at Boston, Mass., Apr. 1893* (1893); Thomas J. Hudson, *The Divine Pedigree of Man, or The Testimony of Evolution and Psychology to the Fatherhood of God* (1899). Drummond reexamined evolutionary theory and found it incomplete. In addition to Darwin's "Principle of the Struggle for Life" is the "Struggle for the Life of Others," the ethical development of man through altruism. "These two functions run their parallel course—or spiral course, for they continuously intertwine—from the very dawn of life. They are involved in the fundamental nature of protoplasm itself" (p. 13).

9. Bessie Maddern.

To Cloudesley Johns

962 East 16th. st.,
Oct. 31, 1899.

Dear Cloudesley:—

Am ignorant of Eliza Otis, though I have a hazy recollection that the 'Frisco papers have laughed at her somewhere during the last several months.[1]

So it seems my immature judgement of *Silverado Squatters*, has been substantiated by another Stevenson lover. Guess I won't re-read it with so much else clamoring for my attention.

Say, by a still mate do you mean a smothered mate?

So you deem the world as fair a synonym for hell as I do hermitage. Can't see it. There are some redeeming features. As long as there is one good woman in it, or man either, it will not hold. Why I remember, once, when for several weeks I meditated profoundly on the policy of shuffling off. Seemed the clouds would never break. But at last they did, and I doubt if you could imagine the cause of my sweetened mood. A memory of a day, of an hour—nay, a few paltry minutes—came back to me, of a time almost lost in the dim past. I remembered—what? A woman's foot. We were by the sea; in a dare, we went in wading; had to stick our feet in the hot sand till they dried; and it was those few moments which came back to me, dripping with "sweetness and light." Hell. Nay, not so long as one woman's foot remains above ground.

Don't think I'm in love. Simply sentiment. Don't get that way often.

Well, I can't construct plots worth a dam, but I can everlastingly elaborate. Why, some time since, I started in to write a twenty-five hundred word article on "Housekeeping in the Klondike."[2] In choice of theme I had been forced to narrow, being aware of my miserable predeliction. And lo, before I had got into full swing, I found that the whole article could be comfortably taken up in a discussion of bread-making. And, still narrowing, it was soon apparent that this should be divided, one single sub-head to be discussed, viz. sour-dough bread-making. And so it goes. Never did a person need the gift of selection more than I.

Wow! How you love society! So that's the way to obtain lucrative imbecility. But, why should one wish to produce lucrative work? Because he needs the cash. And, how under the sun can one cultivate society (the necessary preliminary) when he hasn't the cash? Which reminds me of a point in the opera *Satanella*.[3] Having squandered his patrimony, the young fellow secludes himself in a ramshackle castle, his last remaining possession, reputed to have been last used several centuries previously by an alchemistic ancestor. He (the young fellow) discovers the wizard's book of formulas, incantations, etc. "Now," says he, "I will discover how to make gold and thus rehabilitate my fortunes." Turning to the index, "Ah! 'How to make gold,' page—." He turns to the page and reads, "'How to make gold. First, take some silver—'"

He breaks off abruptly and meditates. He has no silver. Then a bright idea strikes him. Returning to the index he looks up the receipt for the making of silver, and then turns to the proper page.

"'How to make silver: first, take some gold—'"

Have just completed Horace Vachell's *The Procession of Life.* Have you read it? Was quite interesting, but not of the first water. I believe he wrote *The Quicksands of Pactolus*, a serial, in the *Overland*, sometime ago.[4] And by the way, did you ever read that boyhood classic, *Phaeton Rogers*? Rossiter Johnston, who edits the "Whispering Gallery" of the *Overland*, is the author if it.[5] I must have read it twelve or fourteen years ago.

Many thanks for information concerning the *Press* prizes. I had not heard of them. And think, perhaps, that I shall try my hand at some of them. Let me know whether it's the N.Y. City *Press* or the Albany. Have you heard of the *National* prizes? They're not particularly enticing. Don't remember now, but think—yes one must be a subscriber—and they're not very large.

My *Atlantic* story[6] will come out, I believe, in the January Number. Received a check for one hundred and twenty dollars yesterday for it, with a year's subscription thrown in. They are very slow, but very painstaking. They even questioned the propriety of using my given name—*unconventional.* But they came around all right.

Have heard nothing more concerning my collection.[7] They do take their time about it. Nothing from the *Cosmopolitan* prize essay either.

How do you like my new machine. Haven't got used to it yet. Came to-day. When I get married, guess I'll have to marry a type-writer girl. I do most heartily hate the job.

So the poor little Boers have risen in their might.[8] God bless them! I can admire their pluck, while at the same time laughing at their absurdity. There be higher things than formal logic or formal ethics. When a detached, antiquated fragment of a race attempts to buck that race, a spectacle is presented at once pitiful and impotent. Fools, to think that man is the object of his own volition, inasmuch that a few of him may oppose the many in a movement which does not spring from the individual but from the race, and which received its inception before even they had differentiated from the parent branch! As well might a grasshopper buck the flying express—mean lightning express.

Find enclosed a story by Jacobs.[9] Also an opportunity for such budding genius which requires naught but a "name,"—which article the stony-hearted publishers will not permit it to possess.

Jack London.

MS: CSmH; 4 pp., tls. Pbd: *L*, 63–64; *BJL*, I, 312–13.

1. Eliza A. Otis (1833–1904), poet, journalist, and the author of *Echoes from Elf-Land* (1890), a book of children's verse. She regularly contributed to the *Los Angeles Times*.

2. "Housekeeping in the Klondike," *Harper's Bazaar*, September 15, 1900.

3. *Santanella, or, The Power of Love*, composed by Michael William Balfe, with a libretto by Edmund Falconer and Augustus G. Harris.

4. *The Procession of Life* (1899), a humorous, romantic novel set in Southern California, concerned the married lives of two couples; *The Quicksands of Pactolus* (1896), a novel about the mammon worship of an unscrupulous San Francisco banker and his family, was serialized in the *Overland Monthly* from August 1895 to September 1896.

5. *Phaeton Rogers: A Novel of Boy's Life* (1881) was a boy's action and adventure novel. Rossiter Johnson (1840–1931), editor of *Appleton's Annual Cyclopedia* from 1883 to 1902, editor and author of many books and magazine columns, including the "Whispering Gallery," a monthly satirical column that appeared in the *Overland Monthly* from February 1898 to November 1899.

6. "An Odyssey of the North."

7. *The Son of the Wolf*, at this time under consideration by Houghton Mifflin.

8. In mid-October 1899 the Second South African War began. It was fought between Great Britain and the two Dutch Boer Republics, the Transvaal and the Orange Free State, over which the British Empire claimed authority.

9. Possibly William W. Jacobs, "Three at a Table," *San Francisco Sunday Examiner Magazine*, July 30, 1899.

To Cloudesley Johns

962 East 16th. st.,
Nov. 11, 1899.

Dear Cloudesley:—

Ha! ha! The mendicant *Overland*, eh? It's my belief that said mendicancy is no new departure. They may, however, have become more nervy. I doubt if they would have made such a munificent offer, had you been situated nearer at hand. They would have made you a cheap offer instead. That's the way I found them. For "To the Man on Trail," I received five dollars (agreed upon). Then you will notice that in the following month I did not publish. I was waiting to see Bridge[1] with the idea of getting a series published—that is, if I could get better rates. This he agreed to, but they were nothing to boast of—sold at a song. And then it kept me busy dunning them for my paltry due. They only pay for the two or three best articles each month—so I am informed. A glance at the remainder will show the type of contributor. It is said that *The Overland* broke the publishing House of Valentine up, and before that, some other publisher. I have it on hearsay, that Charles Green, the late associate editor and present incumbent of the Oakland Free Library librarianship, was behind something like a couple of thousand salary with them.

Think of it! Of the seven articles they published of mine, I never received the pay for one without excessive dunning—in person and by letter. Did your "Post No. 12" come back?[2] If so, did they have anything to say? I am interested in this little racket of yours, for the third of this month I sent them a Ms. Said Ms. had been declined in the East till it was

positively filthy.[3] From the First class magazines it always had brought
with rejection a complimentary letter and expressed desire to see more of
my work. But they were evidently afraid of it, and of me. Of course, second rate publications had nothing to say. However, it was so worn out,
that I could not in common decency send it east again, and I was too lazy
to retype it. So I sent it to the *Overland*, stating the case, and informing
them that they could have it for twenty-five dollars. In the face of this
proposition to you I am wondering how they will act upon it.

My only experience in asking gratuitous contributions, was with the
S.F. Call. I assured them that I, like themselves, was in such absorbing
pursuit of the shekels that I couldn't think of it; that it would be as hard
for me to give it to them for nothing as it would be for them to pay me for
publishing it. They couldn't send me back the Ms. But they did the
proofs. Hadn't waited to see if I was willing. Then I watched for them.
Had saved the correspondence. If they'd dared to publish it I had full intentions of being paid or of sueing them for all it was worth—advertisement, if nothing else.

"This is the beginning of the end—you'll see—and within ten years the
British Empire will have followed its predecessors, the Greek, the Roman,
and the French."[4] Well, well, well. I'd like to talk with you for a few moments. It's simply impossible to take it up on paper. The day England goes
under, that day sees sealed the doom of the United States. It's the Anglo-
Saxon people against the world, and economics at the foundation of the
whole business; but said economics only a manifestation of the blood dif-
ferentiations which has come down from the hoary past.

This movement, dimly felt and working in strange ways is not to be
stopped in a day, or by a lesser people, or by a bunch of the same which
have become anachronisms. The Boers are anachronisms. There is no
place for them in the whirl of the world unless they whirl with it.

You say, if subjugated they will still be Boers. Do you remember the
Norman invasion of England? How long the Saxons held strictly apart?
And how in the end, the Saxon, as a Saxon, vanished from the face of the
earth? Took several centuries, but it was accomplished.

Why The British Empire is going back, but not to dissolution. I can
only conceive, taking all the factors into consideration, that it is only a
temporary affair. The big and increasing adverse balances of trade are
striking her hard just now. But they are easily understood. To pay them
she is being forced to get rid of her holdings in foreign funds and stock.
But it is not for long. But why is it? With the whole world, teeming with
natural and undeveloped resources, England, the supramacy of the seas
and the best enlightenment of the world hers, leaped at once into the van
of the trading nations—this at the time of the industrial revolution, at the
end of the last century and the beginning of this. This revolution the rise
of modern capitalism and the change from domestic manufacture to capitalistic or factory manufacture.

England was in the lead, and developed a capacity for supplying the markets of the world. This gave her great foreign holdings. Then the newer nations began to compete with her. Prussian beet sugar, heavily subsidized, knocked out England's East and West Indian cane sugars— not for home consumption but for world consumption. The U.S. for instance, in manufactures, is selling everywhere. Same with most countries. Beresford plaintively cries that China is beginning to manufacture, and that England must look sharp if she wishes to sell them the machinery by which to do so.[5] But what does this mean? That in a short while, China will not even have to buy her machinery. And again, that instead of consuming her product, there will be surplus product, cheaper than England's—will England buy it? Who will? All countries are getting in a similar position.

But—England, having lead the van, feels now the pinch first; but the others are racing into the same pickle. Only a little while. As it is, absolutely necessary, is the fight for foreign markets. Forced upon the world, inevitably, is an era of great colonial empire—but for a little while. Wish I could talk it over with you. Am knocking it out at lighting speed and cannot present it consecutively fully—or logically.

I don't envy you the 240,000 words you have to type. I quit writing forever if such a dismal fate should come up against me. Don't think I'd have the fortitude to face it. What's your brother fitting himself for? You say he is cramming for Stanford.

Fifty 1 d. stamps—that's sufficient for twenty-five ordinary Mss. isn't it? Have been thinking of trying the English market myself, but have been always delaying getting the stamps.

How can you begin two more novels? And how many have you still unfinished? Pshaw! I envy you. I can't see my way clear to commence my first. Got an acceptance from the *Review of Reviews*—do you know how they pay?[6] And say, besides *Munseys* and Tillitson and Sons, what is the storiette market? Are there many other publications that make a specialty of them?

I believe Brete Harte wrote a story of a natural fool who got along nicely till he struck it rich.[7] I'm hard at it. Am just finishing an ambitious Klondike yarn which is a failure, and before the twenty-fifth of this month have to write and read up for two essays and prepare for a speech before the Oakland Section. Haven't addressed an audience for three years; it'll seem strange.[8]

I have asked half a dozen well-read friends, but none of them have heard of the "Spider-ship" idea. Nor have I. It seems good, and with your Biercian power of handling the nasty and wierd you ought to make something good out of it. Go ahead.

With poem which I did not enclose, I send another by Rudyard K. Ship us it back and tell what you think.

How's that for Teutonic construction?

That *Truth-Seeker* isn't a softe hiytter—this is not archaic English. I meant that it is not a soft hitter. Still, while I like good virile English, I believe that all discretion and good taste should not be cast to the wind. Vituperation does not make converts; it is not logic; it has no appeal to the intellectual person; the bigot is but hardened in his iniquity by it. Some Swedish woman protests, from the highest, purest, motives, if totally mistaken in her views; and the *T.S.* slaps it into her without mercy. And the persons concerned her own dead mother or father—I forget which. I don't mind blasphemy; but that, to my mind, is greater than blasphemy is to the Christian's. If I had a sister, mother, or dear friend who had been treated as she has been, and if the *T.S.* editor was within walking distance, I'd thrash him or he'd thrash me.[9]

A truly noble mind would not descend to that. O, when comes to strong, well equipped men, in the rough and tumble of life, I don't mind how hard they hit back and forth; but this is not such an instance. Eternal fitness, you know.

Why my dear fellow, you, who would rather sing your country's songs, are somewhat didactic after all, controversial, etc. I'm afraid there's too much of Father Adam in you to be nothing but a singer.

I can't help but wonder that you took five dollar's worth of the paper for "The God that Failed."[10] Where the devil else could you have sent it?—outside of the infidel publications? I wonder what *Munsey's* thought on receiving it? O, I have it—you could have simply changed the ending and had his prayer answered. Then a myriad of Sunday School papers would have clamored for it. You might even have had it printed as a tract and sold several hundred thousand. It's all in the ending you see.

Joshing aside, I think it all right. Logically handled. How your description on scene and man's physical actions reminds me of Bierce!—a certain, bald, but essentially perspicuous method. Nothing ambiguous; nothing requiring a second reading to assure one of the writer's meaning. Do you wish this copy of the *T.S.* back? Or do you want the answer to an anarchist?[11]

Critical I always am when it comes to dissertative work, but in said "letter," I cannot find one objection. Whatever you have stated, I agree with. Though I do not know how deep you would go into it, as far as it went it was correct. Why don't you get in and systematically ground yourself in history, economics, biology, and the kindred branches? Omniverous reading will never do it. System you must have if any really available good is to come.

As to your suggestion regarding the finish of "To the Man on Trail": I had never been satisfied with that ending, though too lazy to even think for an instant of attempting to better it. Your ending could not be bettered, and I shall hasten to take advantage of it. Many thinks for same. It will then leave one with a pleasant taste in the mouth. The alliterative effect you mention strikes my gaudy ear; I shall certainly use it. I want you to read my "Odyssey of the North," when it comes out. Nov. *Atlantic*, bills it for December. But editors told me not till January.[12]

Jack London.

MS: CSmH; 7 pp., tls. Pbd: *L*, 65–68; *BJL*, I, 313–14.

1. James H. Bridge, editor of the *Overland Monthly*.
2. Johns's "Post No. 12—a Story of the Spanish War" was published in *Home Magazine*, June 1900.
3. "The Children of Israel" was sent to *McClure's*, the *Atlantic Monthly*, *Scribner's*, the *Independent*, *Harper's Monthly*, and *Short Stories* before being mailed to the *Overland Monthly* on November 1, 1899. The manuscript was never published.
4. Johns expressed hostility toward England over the Boer War, a sentiment that was widely shared in Europe.
5. In his *Break-up of China*.
6. "The Economics of the Klondike" was sent to the *American Monthly Review of Reviews* on August 19, 1899. Accepted on November 9, 1899, it was published in January 1900. JL received $30 for the article on December 18, 1899.
7. Probably "The Fool of Five Forks," *Macmillan's Magazine*, October 1874.
8. The Klondike story was "Siwash." Sent to *Harper's Monthly* on November 15, 1899, and rejected, it was published in *Ainslee's Magazine*, March 1901, and later included in *The God of His Fathers and Other Stories* (New York: McClure, Phillips & Co., 1901). The two essays were "The Question of the Maximum" and "The Shrinkage of the Planet." The former was sent to the *North American Review* on December 1, 1899; rejected there, it was accepted by *McClure's* on February 6, 1900, but was not published until January 1917 in the *Occident*. JL received $100 for the article, which was later included in *War of the Classes* (New York: Macmillan, 1905). "The Shrinkage of the Planet" was sent to *Dilettante* on December 30, 1899, where it was rejected. It was published in the *Chautauquan*, September 1900, and was later included in *Revolution and Other Essays* (New York: Macmillan, 1910). JL delivered a version of "The Question of the Maximum" before the Oakland Section of the Socialist Labor Party on November 25, 1899. In 1896, before he left for the Northland, JL occasionally spoke on socialism to crowds gathered in Oakland's City Hall Plaza.
9. *The Truth Seeker: A Journal of Freethought and Reform* was a weekly magazine edited by E. M. MacDonald and published in New York. Founded in 1873, it sought "to educate the people out of religion and superstition" and championed the antireligious position of Robert Ingersoll. Alice C. Conklin, the writer of "Christomania," a letter to the editor of the *Truth Seeker*, November 4, 1899, had expressed her sorrow for the magazine's agnostic staff and told of her religious experience at her mother's grave. When Conklin's letter was published, the editors appended cruelly sarcastic comments such as the claim that "evidently the daughter felt a keen enjoyment in attending the old lady's funeral."
10. Cloudesley Johns, "The God That Failed," *Truth Seeker*, November 4, 1899.
11. Probably Johns's "Socialism or Anarchism," *Truth Seeker*, November 4, 1899, a letter to the editor in which Johns defended the philosophy of socialism. He was replying to a letter by J. A. Wilson entitled "Fallacious Answers to Social Problems," *Truth Seeker*, September 30, 1899, which claimed that socialism would enslave the individual and destroy ambition. The debate between Johns and Wilson continued in the columns of the *Truth Seeker*: Wilson published a rejoinder, "Socialism or Anarchism?" November 18, 1899, to which Johns responded with "Socialism or Anarchism?" December 16, 1899.
12. The editors were right: the story appeared in the January issue.

To Cloudesley Johns

962 East 16th. st.,
Nov. 21, 1899.

Dear Cloudesley:—

Hard at it—mostly history and economics. And yet I don't work a tithe of what you work. Why should you work seventeen hours a day? As regards your writing you positively should not do more than six—four were better. But any excess of six cannot be good stuff. Of course, the arrival of typewriter with a huge stack of work to run through accounts for overtime now. But before the arrival of the typewriter what were you doing with those seventeen hours? Writing?—impossible to turn out good work at such rate. Then what? as I do not think you would persistently turn out bad work. What then? what did you do with the other eleven hours? Say four for cooking, eating, etc., and three for post-office duties, what of the other four? Read? What? Aye, there's the rub. I shall take the liberty of forwarding to you by this mail some presumptious advice I was lately guilty of.[1] A certain portion, in line with preceding paragraph, applies to you, which same I leave to your discrimination to discover. Compositors mixed the tenses on me, besides divers other mistakes. All of which amounts to nil. I dashed it off at a white heat any way. The *Editor* has itself listed as "paying liberally." I thought I'd find out what they conceived "liberal" to mean. They were also listed as paying— no they were not either. They said on acceptance that I would receive pay promptly on publication. I dunned them the other day and am still waiting returns. Kindly return *Editor* to me as I wish file to be complete.

I read *Edwin Drood* when I was a little fellow, and was so disgusted at the break-off that I have never possessed an atom of respect for it since.[2] You see, I can remember nothing about it save something to do with a Lascar and with an opium den. Tell me, am I mistaken in those two items? Have I dug them up from something else?

You write very differently than do I. Every day sees what I have composed, all typed and ready to be submitted. I never polish. I write anywhere from ten to two hundred words in long hand, glance over it, and slap it through the machine. Then I repeat the maneuver.

I never pity anybody but my self. Life is too short.

The Overland declined my offer on specious grounds. Twenty-five dollars was stiff under the circumstances. However, I have placed a yarn with them to come out in the Christmas number.[3] O they're great people, of great heart; but heart and finance do not usually go together. Let us know how you come out with them.

Many thanks for English stamps; I shall proceed to exploit them.[4] And you, I suppose you will gather the sinews of war from the mother country, exploiting her as she is exploiting the world. Apropos of this I send clippings by Bierce, etc. I admire Bierce for the stand he takes.[5] Very few American educated people have little else but rancor for England—a rancor which is bred by the school histories and the school traditions. All of which are utterly wrong. I have to laugh when you call Kipling "a narrow hidebound, childishly pettish, mean, little man." Not that some of it is not true (or whatever I mean), but at the thought of the clipping I enclose with this. Any masculine who delights in taking down a woman's back hair will find a warm welcome in my heart. And especially so of a man who would in any way merit some of the adjectives you have showered upon him. He really is a man, you know. Yes, by Jove, he is. Why I could have hugged him—supposing it to be true, and as it seems to me if there is but one scrap of truth in the whole sensation-article, that one is the back hair episode.

Find return of Wilson's letter. Keep me informed of the outcome. I'd like to see them tackle you.[6]

Find, with *Editor*, when it comes along, some more proofs of yours truly, taken down by the sounding sea. Also one of the young woman who sometimes accompanies me in my far from conventional rambles. Last Sunday, threatening rain, we wandered off into the hills, cooked our dinner (broiled steak, baked sweet potatoes, coffee, etc, crab, French bread, and a patty of dairy butter), and were a couple of gypsies. To-morrow we may jump on our wheels and ride off forty or fifty miles. And yesterday we may have taken in the opera and dined fashionably. Never the same, except the camera, which same I am slowly mastering.

Haven't much of an opinion on the "Odyssey." Cutting out nearly three thousand words in the beginning, descriptive of the camp, the mailmen, dig-drivers, and policemen, cut me up as well. Luckily I refused to touch the "Odyssey" proper at all. I think it is good, though I only half realized what I conceived it to be. Be sure and tell me what you think of it.

O I was only joshing about the "God that Failed." What I evedently failed to convey was that it was so blasphemous that I couldn't possibly see where you could have rid yourself of it had you rejected the offer of the *Truth-seeker*.

Yes; I read *A New Magdalen*[7] when I was about twelve, and then shocked a very nice young lady by starting to discuss it with her.

Don't know who Rogers is—never heard of him before. But the "Prospector" was good, excellent.[8]

When England is so decadent as to lose her colonies, then England falls. When England falls the United States will be shaken to its foundations, and the chances are one hundred to one that it ever recovers again. Why, England is our greatest purchaser, and our greatest maker of markets, and the only nation which is not deep down hostile to us. Germany, France, Austria and Russia can supply the world with all that the world needs, if only they could get a chance by having England and the United States eliminated from the pro-position. And once one were eliminated the ruin of the other were easy. But England is not going to fall. It is not possible. To court such a possibility is to court destruction for the English speaking people. We are the salt of the earth, and it is because we have it in us to frankly say so that we really are so. No hemming or hawing; we state the bald fact. It is for the world to take or leave. Take it may, but it shall always leave us.

Nations do not fall before military prowess. Bad economics or killing competition is what kills them. Rome did not fall before the superior ability of the Germanic tribes. Bad economics had destroyed her warrior class; for centuries her armies had been recruited from among those self-same barbarians. She had ceased to reproduce her own citizens. No body cared to have children. She was empty. She did not fall in the end. Simply became empty and was filled up by the flood of emmigration from the north. The United States could defend herself against overwhelming odds—aye, in the hey day of economic integrity—but with such things in smash, which also smash the timber of her citizens—why she would assuredly fall.

So? Why the United States never had but one fight in its history; that was when it fought with itself. England never bothered much with her. Read up history and you will find that England's hands were full of other things, and preferring other matters, she *let* the colonies slip away. Do you really think we whipped the whole of England in the Revolution? Or in 1812, when her hands were full with Napoleon, and she was fighting in every quarter of the globe? Mexico was play. But that civil war was a war, a death grapple. And all hail to the south for the fight it put up against stiff odds.

You little know Canada. Why don't those other European countries, standing by themselves, fall? Because, they are but ostensibly alone. In reality they stand together—whenever it comes to bucking the Anglo-Saxon.

If cash comes with fame, come fame; if cash comes without fame, come cash.

I shall be pleased to see you when you drop in on me. Only I shall not devote myself to trying to knock out of you the fallacies ingrained in your youth. Just let us know a couple of days in advance of your coming. And then come.

I shall send clippings with *Editor*.[9]

Jack London.

MS: CSmH; 6 pp., tls. Pbd: *L*, 68–71; *BJL*, I, 314–16.

1. "On the Writer's Philosophy of Life."

2. Charles Dickens, *The Mystery of Edwin Drood* (1870). The novel was left uncompleted at Dickens's death; the lascar and opium den appear in its opening scene.

3. "The Wisdom of the Trail," *Overland Monthly*, December 1899.

4. From time to time Johns gave JL English stamps sent him by an acquaintance in England. JL used these stamps in submitting his manuscripts to English publishers.

5. Ambrose Bierce supported the British position in the Boer War in his column "The

Passing Show," *San Francisco Examiner*, October 22, 1899. He wrote: "The British empire would be a fool to let a petty, semi-savage and hopelessly unprogressive state to stand in the way of her dominion in South Africa."

6. See the preceding letter, n. 11.

7. Wilkie Collins, *The New Magdalen* (1873), a sentimental social allegory about a clergyman's sexual double standard.

8. An article entitled "The Prospector," by J. M. Goodwin, appeared in the August 1899 *Overland Monthly*.

9. JL wrote this sentence in longhand.

To Cloudesley Johns

962 East 16th. st.,
Dec. 5, 1899.

Dear Cloudesley:—

First letter-writing I have done for quite a while. Have been very busy. Have not had an evening at home for nigh on to two weeks, what with suppers, speaking, functions, and last but not least, FOOTBALL. Did you see what we did to Stanford? In case that benighted region in which you reside has not yet received the score, let me have the privilege of blazoning it forth. Thirty to nothing, Berkeley.

It was magnificent, to sit under the blue and gold and [see] the Berkeley giants wade through the Cardinals, and especially so when one looks back to the times he sat and watched the Stanfordites pile up the score and hammer our line into jelly. Do you care for football? In case you do not, I shall not permit my enthusiasm to bore you further.

Say? I am acquainted with Nan Byxbie,[1] one of the new space-writers on the *Call*. Her name you have probably seen in recent issues if you read that paper. I coached her up in versification and a little bit on style at odd intervals; besides we know each other very well. If the *Call* does not dig up your Ms., shall I see her about it?

Heaven save us from our friends! Last Sunday evening I spoke before the San Francisco Section. Unknown to me, and on the strength of divers newspaper puffs which recently have appeared, they posted San Francisco, and also perpetrated the enclosed hand bill. I knew nothing about it till just the moment before I was to go on the platform. Can I sue them for libel? Please return it, as I, also, have a collection.

I have not got to your *Truthseekers* yet, nor to anything else, but I will tear out and send you that portion you wish as soon as I read it. My reading table is banked with books and magazines and it makes me shudder everytime I look at them.

Am sorry you sent for the December *Atlantic*. The November Number announced the December table of contents, in which was my "Odyssey." But it has been evidently deferred.

So I'm a source of inspiration, eh? I thought that was the prerogative solely of the fair sex. But now that I've gone and inspired you, I don't think I should be defrauded of the fruit of my labor. Go ahead and publish it, but throw some carbon sheets into your typewriter and send me a copy.

228,000 words! Why I verily believe that's more than I have written in all my life (correspondence barred). Of course one should do one's own typing. I do all my polishing on the machine.

You say you are contemplating coming to Oakland somewhere near the end of the year. If you do I am afraid we won't meet each other. I expect to spend my holidays down country, and shall depart thereto as soon as I have caught up in my reading and work. It's a year-old promise, made because of neglect on my part last Christmas, and I cannot break it. If you could delay your coming till January I should be very pleased, for then we would be sure to meet.

I see you do not believe in what is called an adverse balance of trade. Very good. Yet I am sure you apply it in your own case; for the man [who] makes a practice of buying more than his pocket book contains usually goes bankrupt.

Why is it that England has such a grip over the material resources of the world, drawing interest from almost every country under the sun, and with that interest buying the grub of other countries? The answer is simple. Because she spent her spare money by invested it abroad. The man who lives over the contents of his purse never has any money to invest. The United States had to borrow money from abroad to develop a large portion of her resources. These foreign securities drained a huge tide of interest from the States. But the last several years America has been buying back her securities held abroad. And why has she been doing this? or rather, how has she been able to do this? Because her balances of trade had at last grown favorable. If she exports half a billion of dollars more than she imports, this half a billion must be paid to her in gold. And with this gold she has bought back her securities, also had part of it to invest in her own territory and in other countries. O yes, "I know that if we were denied the privilege of sending away a third of our food products we would have less to eat."

O, sure; there never was a fanatic on any subject who did not believe he had logically deduced or induced his conclusions from thoroughly correct premises.

As I said, I was a very little boy when I read *Edwin Drood.* Your criticism of my *Editor* article is exactly my own criticism. We could not disagree on that if we tried. By the way. There were 1750 words in it. The *Editor* was billed to pay liberally, and they told me on acceptance, promptly. It was published last October, I received for it five dollars which came to hand day before yesterday.[2]

O Lord! Goodbye.

Jack London.

MS: CSmH; 4 pp., tls. Pbd: *L*, 71–73; *BJL*, I, 316–17.
   1. Pseudonym of Ernestine Conghram.
   2. In his record of magazine sales, JL reported December 4 as the date he received payment.

To Cloudesley Johns

962 East 16th. st.,
Dec. 12, 1899.

Dear Cloudesley:—
   A short letter, for I depart down country. Write me, care Edward Applegarth, Jr.,

Corner Elm and Asbury sts.,
San Jose,
Calif.

I shall come back to Oakland after the holidays. Until then a truce to production and to the machine.
   How shall I say? Well, only this, do for goodness sake do some digging at evolution, some real hard digging. As for your theory, pardon my harshness, it is absurd. That self-same evolution, had you studied it in its esentials and not in the popular way, would have prevented you perpetrating the atrocity. What have you done? Builded up a theory on a few false analogies. Us reaching the summit more rapidly—why we have been the slowest, and, to adopt a true analogy, because ours is the highest is because it has been the slowest, just as man with his fourteen to sixteen years of adolescence is a higher order of being than the dog with its short year of puppyhood. The black has stopped, just as the monkey has stopped. Never will even the highest anthropoid apes evolve into man; likewise the negro into a type of man higher than any existing. But had you turned the other way you would have found a more youthful race and the only one which can scientifically answer to your hypothesis: namely, the Slav. The negro, like the Red, has been passed by. The Slav has not yet been reached. He may never be reached.
   But don't try to prove things too exclusively by analogy. It is the common belief that death is the correlative of life. That whatsoever lives must die. Yet this is not so. Why the life cells, or rather, germ cells, which leave your body when in the arms of a wanton, lived, yea, they lived when your ancestors were fishes in the sea, when they were reptiles in the dirt, when sex was unknown, when they were nothing but palpitating masses of formless life.
   The female is the passive, the male the active factor in the carrying on of the function of reproduction. This is a popular conception. Yet, in lower forms of life, certain lower forms, not all, the female is far larger than the male, the more predatory and ferocious. She alone possesses the

prehensile organs of reproduction. She it is who pursues the resisting male, holds him firmly, rapes him in short, that she may breed her kind. Watch out for analogies.

I started in to write a short letter, and I'll have to. Am going to take a run up to 'Frisco next week from San Jose and I'll find out what Nan Byxbie has discovered relating to your ms. I wrote her about it this mail—I mean manuscript at *Call.*

You mistake. I do not believe in the universal brotherhood of man. I think I have said so before. I believe my race is the salt of the earth. I am a scientific socialist, not a utopian, an economic man as opposed to an imaginative man. The latter is becoming an anachronism.

Nay, nay, bankruptsy (how is it spelled?) is not an ideal state, at least for me. It's horrible, too horrible for words. Give me the millions and I'll take the responsibilities.

Later on I shall forward you an article of mine on the "Question of the Maximum," which contains within it, though not the main theme, the economic basis for imperialism or expansion. This, I know, is directly opposed to the current ethics. But it is the one which will dominate the current ethics.

Good night,
Jack London.

P.S.—Is the enclosed page the one you wished torn out and sent to you?

J.G.L.

MS: CSmH; 3 pp., tls. Pbd: *L*, 73–74; *BJL*, I, 317.

To Anna Strunsky

962 East 16th. st.,
Oakland, Calif.,
Dec. 19, 1899.

My dear Miss Strunsky:—[1]

Seems as if I have known you for an age—you and your Mr. Browning. I shall certainly have to re-read him, in the hope after all these years of obtaining a fuller understanding.

What did I start in to write you about, anyway? Oh! First, that toasting the old year out-affair—does it take place on the last Friday or Thursday of the month; and secondly—well, it doesn't matter. I have forgotten.

Please don't carry a wrong impression of my feelings regarding Hamilton.[2] Because I happen to condemn his deficiencies is no reason that I do not appreciate his good qualities, nor that I should not love him. Indeed I do. Do you remember how I said I ran down the street after him on a circus day, cut engagements, etc.? My feelings and personal liking swayed me there; but in summing up the man I set such things to one side and perform the operation with the cold-bloodedness of the economic man. I hope you will understand. My regard for him is such that were I to accumulate a treasure I think I would advertise for him in the agony columns throughout the United States and bring him to me, give him a home, a monthly allowance, and let him live out his life whatsoever way he willed.

You said at parting that you also were a literary aspirant. I may be able to help you, perhaps—not in the higher criticism but in the more prosaic but none the less essential work of submitting Ms. Through much travail I have learned the customs of the "silent sullen peoples who run the magazines."[3] Their rates, availability, acceptability, etc. Should you stand in need of anything in this line (economic man), believe me sincerely at your service.

Of course, I do not know what lines you deem yourself best fitted for; however, as I sat there listening to you, I seemed to sum you up somewhat in this way: A woman to whom it is given to feel the deeps and the heights of emotion in an extraordinary degree; who can grasp the intensity of transcendental feeling, the dramatic force of situation, as few women, or men either, can. But, this question at once arose: Has she expression? By this I mean simply the literary technique. And again, supposing that she has not, has she the "dig," the quality of application, so that she might attain it?

In a nut-shell—you have the material, which is your own soul, for a career: have you the requisite action to hew your way to it?

Let me see—I had so much to say, and now I have forgotten it. New Years Day, down country, I read "Andrea del Sarto." Splendid, seems but feeble praise. How delicately and with what virility he touches upon the deepest truths of life. Now, if you will read that to me the next time we are together, I shall understand and appreciate. The good things of life must grow upon one. With each impact they are invested with greater significance. It haunts me that I have the title of the poem wrong. Anyway, it's the "faultless painter."[4]

I was out to Berkeley the other day, taking my friends through, and I was clad in the disreputable comfort of a sweater. It is well we did not meet. Tell me of your new life. My interest is great. Will Berkeley caress you, I wonder? I imagine it to be far colder than Stanford. Why, I cannot tell. It just seems so.[5]

Yours very cordially,
Jack London.

P.S.—I shall send this by your San Francisco address. Let me have your new one. And also when I may call. The first Fridays in every month, also every week the Mondays, Wednesdays & Sundays are usually engaged, though sometimes, under pressure, I break them.

J.L.

MS: CSmH; 3 pp., tls. Pbd: *L*, 74–75; *BJL*, I, 322–23.

1. Anna Strunsky (1878–1964), a Russian Jewess who had attended Stanford University and who, like JL, was a socialist. She met JL in the fall of 1899 at a lecture given by Austin Lewis at the Old Turk Street Temple in San Francisco. For her reminiscences of JL, see her "Memories of Jack London," *The Bowery News* (June 1962), pp. 8–9.

2. Frank Strawn-Hamilton.

3. See JL to Johns, March 7, 1899.

4. Following its title, Robert Browning's "Andrea del Sarto" has the parenthetical comment "(Called 'The Faultless Painter')."

5. Anna Strunsky enrolled in the University of California in January 1900; she attended school there for less than a year.

To Anna Strunsky

962 East 16th. st.,
Oakland, Calif.,
Dec. 21, 1899.

Dear Miss Strunsky:–

Surely am I a barbarian, lacking in cunning of speech and deftness of touch. Perhaps I am only a Philistine. Mayhap the economic man incarnate. At least blundering and rough-shod, lacking even that expression which should properly voice my thoughts. I call for a trial by jury. I throw myself on the mercy of the Court. Nay, after all is said and done, I plead not guilty.

"Somehow it is a new note to me, that of being seen as 'aimless, helpless, hopeless,' and I am uneasy under it all."

I rarely remember what I say in letters, sometimes retaining only vague recollections of what I do not say; but in the present case I am sure I said nothing like the above. I speculated on you as impartially as had you been a hod-carrier, a Hottentot, or a Christ. It was a first speculation; it dealt with but one portion of your being. And as I could not divorce Christ or the Hottentot from the rest of humanity as having nothing in common with it, so I could not divest you of the weaknesses which I know your fellows to suffer from. But such weaknesses are not to be classed under your three-fold caption, "aimless, helpless, hopeless." I granted aim. I then asked myself whether you had the qualities by which to realize it. I did not answer that question, for verily I did not nor do I know. I was even more generous. I granted the basic qualities, all-necessary for attainment, and only questioned the existence of the medium by which they could be made to meet with their proper end. And that question I did not answer (to myself) for I did not know, nor do I know.

This is my case. I call for your verdict.

Somehow I am like a fish out of water. I take to conventionality uneasily, rebelliously. I am used to saying what I think, neither more than less. Soft equivocation is no part of me. As had I spoken to a man who came out of nowhere, shared my bed and board for a night, and passed on, so did I speak to you. Life is very short. The melancholy of materialism can never be better expressed than by Fitzgerald's "O make haste!"[1] One should have no time to dally. And further, should you know me, understand this: I, too, was a dreamer, on a farm, nay, a California ranch. But early, at only nine, the hard hand of the world was laid upon me. It has never relaxed. It has left me sentiment, but destroyed sentimentalism. It has made me practical, so that I am known as harsh, stern, uncompromising. It has taught me that reason is mightier than imagination; that the scientific man is superior to the emotional man. It has also given me a truer and a deeper romance of things, an idealism which is an inner sanctuary and which must be resolutely throttled in dealings with my kind, but which yet remains within the holy of holies, like an oracle, to be cherished always but to be made manifest or be consulted not on every occasion I go to market. To do this latter would bring upon me the ridicule of my fellows and make me a failure. To sum up, simply the eternal fitness of things.

All of which goes to show that people are prone to misunderstand me. May I have the privilege of not so classing you?

Nay, I did not walk down the street after Hamilton—I ran. And I had a heavy overcoat, and I was very warm and breathless. The emotional man in me had his will, and I was ridiculous.

I shall be over Saturday night. If you draw back upon yourself, what have I left? Take me this way: a stray guest, a bird of passage, splashing with salt-rimed wings through a brief moment of your life—a rude and blundering bird, used to large airs and great spaces, unaccustomed to the amenities of confined existence. An unwelcomed visitor, to be tolerated only because of the sacred law of food and blanket.

Very sincerely,
Jack London.

MS: CSmH; 3 pp., tls. Pbd: *L*, 76–77; *BJL*, I, 323–24.
  1. See JL to Johns, July 5, 1899, n. 4.

To Anna Strunsky

962 East 16th. st.,
Oakland, Calif.,
Dec. 27, 1899.

My dear Miss Strunsky:–

I am surprised. And pleased beyond measure. So preposterous would it have seemed, that I could not even have canvassed the thought as to your caring for Kipling. Why I could hardly believe my ears when you claimed as among the finest lines of "Mandalay," "O ship me somewheres east of Suez, etc."[1] He is so many-sided that the general public finds plenty to admire in him, but your caring for him in other ways—ways in which I thought it possible for but a few world-roughened spirits—astounds me. And puzzles me. How? I ask, How? Not by what right, but by what means have you come to comprehend? Surely, from what little I know of your life, I may safely predicate, absolutely, that you know nothing of much with which he deals, cannot have experienced the feelings or personal conditions he portrays. "Where there aren't no ten commandments and a man can raise a thirst"[2]—How? how? I ask. And then it comes to me this way:— Are you one of those favored spirits who vibrate, by some subtle faculty to states or conditions of which they are in reality ignorant; who, by some occult divination or sympathy may feel with those of which they can know nothing, ring true to that which it would seem is not in them but of which by some incomprehensible way they may partake?

Pardon me for having ventured to analyze you, but mankind is my passion, and the search after potentiality and the realization thereof, my hobby. Thinkers do not suffer from lack of expression; their thought is their expression. Feelers do; it is the hardest thing in the world to put feeling, and deep feeling, into words. From the standpoint of expression, it is easier to write a *Das Capital* in four volumes than a simple lyric of as many stanzas.

A Truce to lecturing. Typewriters, while very excellent in their way, are a very poor medium for conversation. The mouth were better formed for expression than the finger-tips. May I see you next Friday night? Candidly, I may some time steal you or certain portions of you for exploitation between covers, unless you hasten to get yourself copyrighted. Which is to say, preliminarily, that I should like to sum you up some more.

Very cordially yours,
Jack London.

MS: CSmH; 2 pp., tls. Pbd: *L*, 77–78.

1. "Mandalay" (1890), l. 43: "Ship me somewheres east of Suez, where the best is like the worst."

2. "Mandalay," l. 44.

To Anna Strunsky

962 East 16th. st.,
Oakland, Calif.,
Dec. 29, 1899.

My dear Miss Strunsky:—

Just a line to thank you, for I too, after much unseemly hesitancy, am going away for a few days.[1]

Expression? I think you have it, if this last letter may be any criterion. How have I felt since I received it? How shall I say? At any rate, know this: I do agree, unqualifiedly, with your diagnosis of where I missed and how. If I recollect aright, it was my first and last attempt at a psychological study.[2] I saw that I had much before me yet to gain before I should put my hand to such work. I glanced over several pages just before sending, noted the frightful diction and did not dare go on to the meat of it. I knew, I felt that there was so much which was wrong with it, that the ending was inadequate, etc., and that was all. But you have given me clearer vision, far clearer vision. For my vague feelings of what was wrong, you have given me the why. It is you who are the missionary.

I am down in the dust to Jaky[3] for an unpardonable wrong. But my extenuation is my youth and inexperience. It was absurd at the time I wrote it to think of accomplishing such a thing. It really was false-winged, you see, that flight of mine. Not only have you shown me my main flaw, but you have exposed a second—the lack of artistic selection.

And above all, you have conveyed to me my lack of spirituality, idealized spirituality—I know not if I use the terms correctly. Don't you understand? I came to you like a parched soul out of the wilderness, thirsting for I knew not what. The highest and the best had been stamped out of me. You know my life, typified, mayhap, by the hastily drawn picture of the forecastle. I was troubled. Groping after shadows, mocking, disbelieving, giving my own heart the lie oftentimes, doubting that which very doubt bade me believe. And for all, I was a-thirst. Stiff-necked, I flaunted my physical basis, hoping that the clear water might gush forth. But not then, for there I played the barbarian. Still, from the little I have seen of you my lips have been moistened, my head lifted. Do you remember "It was my duty to have loved the highest; it was my pleasure had I known"?[4] Pray do not think me hysterical. In the bright light of day I might flush at my weakness, but in the darkness I let it pass.

Only, I do hope we shall be friends.

"Only not all Jews haggle and bargain"—there, surely, you did me wrong. My glimmering adumbrations bespoke far more than that. But there—remember I have misunderstood you a score of times and trampled rough-shod over as many sensibilities. Jaky and his wife did exist, did keep a second hand store, were fanatical(?) in their quest after knowledge. I helped them a little in English. Jaky, or his prototype, having abandoned night high school in dispair, afterward corresponded with me in order that I might correct his work.

I see this "just a line" has grown. Please do not answer till after your examinations. Know that I pray for the best possible best. And please let me know the outcome, for I shall be as anxious almost as yourself. And further—no—what's the use?

Oh! during the collapse after they are over with, should you run across a January *Atlantic Monthly*, look up my "Odyssey of the North." The first two sections were reduced by nearly three thousand words on bequest of the editor, and it so broke my heart in cutting them out that I simply mangled it. You see, I had endeavored to supply most of the atmosphere before the odyssey proper began, and such wholesale pruning, months after it was written, took all the spirit out of it. The odyssey proper I strove to invest with a certain rude epic swing—of course it's all idealized.

Again praying that I may be informed of the outcome, just whether it is or it isn't, I am,

Very sincerely,
Jack London.

MS: CSmH; 3 pp., tls. Pbd: *L*, 78–79; *BJL*, I, 325.
   1. JL was going to visit the Applegarths in San Jose.
   2. Apparently JL had sent Strunsky a sketch based on the life of a Jewish merchant.
   3. The central character in JL's sketch.
   4. Alfred Tennyson, "Guinevere," *The Idylls of the King* (1859), ll. 652–54: "It was my duty to have loved the highest: / It surely was my profit had I known: / It would have been my pleasure had I seen."

To Cloudesley Johns

[Oakland]
[? December 1899]

Dear Cloudesley:–

Here I am, at the machine. Have just run up to keep an appointment with my dentist—the ninth and last visit of torture within thirty days. Am going back on Saturday to stop over the New Year. Shall be back again by the fourth. If you get that substitute, shall expect you somewhere about that time. Find enclosed statement concerning your "Preservation of the Forests."

Also your last to Mr. Wilson.[1] I was far better pleased with it than with your preceding answer, or at least the preceding one I saw—whether the two are coincident I do not know. I should not care to rush madly into controversey with you as antagonist. You display powers which would lead one to wish the illuminating spectacle of a public encounter between you and Ambrose Bierce. "These great Anarchists were eventually ripped to shreds by flying lead and scattered all over their damned possessory rights"—why that is indeed worthy of the gentleman whose name I have just mentioned.

In haste. Should you write me before date of my expected return, address down country.

Jack London.

MS: CSmH; 1 p., tls.
   1. See JL to Johns, November 11, 1899, n. 11.

1900

On honeymoon bicycle trip, April 1900 (JL State Park)

To Anna Strunsky

962 East 16th. st.,
Jan. 15, 1900.

Dear Miss Strunsky:–

Have been home from my trip and gone away again, just returning last evening to find your letter. Also was tied with a couple of guests, who are now playing chess as many feet away, and appealing as often every minute to my decision. So whatever is choppy please forgive.

I hardly know what I can say on paper, and wish I could have seen you last night. But know this: your idea of education does not end with the sheepskin. That much goes without saying. The university is simply to prepare. The credit one should earn is not a high standard in the college work in itself, but a high standard in the work one is to ultimately do in the world, and for which the university has made fit. It is a matter of common knowledge that the one who captures the prizes for scholarship and the fellowships, rarely does anything in his or her after-life. The fact that he is capable of making of his brain a machine, militates against his being capable of the higher individual initiative in the years to come. Surely you cannot help measuring yourself against your fellows, and surely you cannot find aught to be ashamed of in the ideals which you cherish, the knowledge you have gained, the life you have led and the work you have done for the world—nothing, save that you have failed to be an intellectual machine and to learn—not your lessons (which you have learned)—but the lessons which have been set before you by others. Who are they that they should set these lessons? and who are you that you should receive them? Ah, yes, for the common run of humanity, it is proper that these lessons should be set and learned—but there are other souls which should not be so hampered. And when I see such souls wasting their time over work which is unnecessary or less necessary than other work which they need, which they should be doing, and which if they do not do then they may never do, why it always makes me sad. When you spoke of cramming algebra, simply to gain so many credits to your course, I felt for the moment toward you as I would toward a bright young fellow preparing to bring his razor and his throat in disastrous propinquity. It was all wrong, every bit of it. And in one way I am almost glad that Stanford has turned out as it did. Glad for the soul of Anna Strunsky that it is so. And at the same time sorry am I for the heart of Anna Strunsky, and the pride. Believe me, I do know the suffering entailed, and I do also know that I have not the moral bravery to face the music as you are doing.

But you do know, I know you do, that one's works are not measured by a college career and record but by a whole life, in which the former plays no part save that of preparing. The university, after all, is such a limited audience when the whole world is waiting to hear. You register to-day, at Berkeley. Is it as a special? Heartily I hope so. You escape the trammels, and I know you are well capable of setting your own lessons. But how metallic this all is! I wish I could have seen you last night.

Thank you for "The Feet of the Young Men."[1] I was about to quote from it, but find I must needs quote all, it is so good. Find enclosed the picture of Mary Antin.[2] I wish it were not profile.

It's too distracting, these guests of mine. I must give up writing this. However, let me hear of you, your new address, and when it may be convenient to have me call.

Oh! I also enclose one of Kiplings poems—a favorite of Hamilton's. He had suffered from insomnia himself and so, was never tired of repeating the lines.[3]

Most sincerely,
Jack London.

MS: CSmH; 3 pp., tls. Pbd: *L*, 83–84.

1. By Rudyard Kipling (1897).

2. Mary Antin Grabau (1881–1949), Jewish writer and social worker, who immigrated to America from Russian Poland in 1894. Her writings about the lives and customs of European Jews include *From Plotzk to Boston* (English trans., 1899), *The Promised Land* (1912), and *They Who Knock at Our Gates* (1914).

3. Frank Strawn-Hamilton. The poem may be Kipling's "The City of Sleep," which includes the refrain "But we—pity us! Oh, pity us! / We wakeful; ah, pity us!"

To Anna Strunsky

962 East 16th. st.,
Jan. 21, 1900.

Dear Miss Strunsky:—
    O Pshaw!
Dear Anna:—

There! Let's get our friendship down to a comfortable basis. The superscription, "Miss Strunsky," is as disagreeable as the putting on of a white collar, and both are equally detestable. I did not read your last till Friday morning, and the day and evening were taken up. But at last I am free. My visitors are gone, the one back to his desert hermitage, and the other to his own country. And I have much work to make up. Do you know, I have the fatal faculty of making friends, and lack the blessed trait of being able to quarrel with them. And they are constantly turning up. My home is the Mecca of every returned Klondiker, sailor, or soldier of fortune I ever met. Some day I shall build an establishment, invite them all, and turn them loose upon each other. Such a mingling of castes and creeds and characters could not be duplicated. The destruction would be great.

However, I am so overjoyed at being free that I cannot be anything but foolish. I shall, with pitfall and with gin, beset the road my visitors do wander in; and among other things, erect a maxim rapid-fire gun just within my front door. The sanctity of my fireside shall be inviolate. Or, should my heart fail me, I'll run away to the other side of the world.

Find enclosed, review of Mary Antin's book. Had I not known you I could not have understood the little which I do. Somehow we must ever build upon the concrete. To illustrate: do you notice the same in excerpt from her, beginning, "I thought of tempests and shipwrecks."[1] How I would like to know the girl, to see her, to talk with her, to do a little toward cherishing her imagination. I sometimes weep at the grave of mine. It was sown on arid soil, gave vague promises of budding, but was crushed out by the harshness of things—a mixed metaphor, I believe.

"Like most modern Jewesses who have written, she is, I fear, destined to spiritual suffering." How that haunts one!

Ho! ho! I have just returned from the window. Turmoil and strife called me from the machine, and behold! My nephew,[2] into whom it is my wish to inculcate some of the saltiness of the earth, had closed in combat with an ancient enemy in the form of a truculent Irish boy. There they were, hard at it, boxing gloves of course, and it certainly did me good to see the way in which he stood up to it. Only, alas, I see I shall have to soon give him instructions, especially in defense—all powder and flash and snappy in attack, but forgetful of guarding himself. "For life is strife,"[3] and a physical coward the most unutterable of abominations.

Tell me what you think of Ms. It was the work of my golden youth. When I look upon it I feel very old. It has knocked from pillar to post and reposed in all manner of places. When my soul waxes riotous, I bring it forth, and lo! I am again a lamb. It cures all ills of the ego and is a sovereign remedy for self-conceit. "Mistake" is writ broad in fiery letters. The influences at work in me, from Zangwill to Marx, are obvious. I would have portrayed types and ideals of which I knew nothing, and so, trusted myself to false wings. You showed me your earliest printed production last night; reciprocating, I show you one written at the time I first knew Hamilton. I felt I had something there, but I certainly missed it. Some day, putting it at the bottom of the deepest of chests, I shall reattempt it. Tell me the weak points, not of course in diction, etc. Tell me what rings false to you. And be unsparing, else shall I have to class you with the rest of my friends, and it is not complimentary to them if they only knew it.

One has so much to say that the best course is to not say anything.

Paper was made for business correspondence and for invitations; while the tongue is too often geared at too high a pitch to adequately carry on its labors.

Very sincerely,
Jack London.

P.S.—Your Stanford address? I have forgotten it. Is it "Stanford," "Stanford University," or "Palo Alto"?

MS: CSmH; 3 pp., tls. Pbd: *L*, 84–85; *BJL*, I, 326–28.
    1. *From Plotzk to Boston*, p. 70.
    2. Johnny Miller.
    3. Rudyard Kipling, "The Ballad of Fisher's Boarding House," l. 73: "Since Life is strife, and strife means knife."

To Cloudesley Johns

962 East 16th. st.,
Jan. 22, 1900.

Dear Cloudesley:—
    Have pawned my wheel, bought stamps, and got things in running order again. Find enclosed Wells, Fargo, receipt of package. I see on it that they have only put Los Angeles. At the office I addressed it with my own hand to Palmdale. Hope they have not made a mistake and sent it on to the city.
    How did you get on? Let us hear about it. Am indeed sorry that you had such a miserable visit; but unluckily for both, you caught me at my lowest ebb. Of which nothing more can be said. Have to get in a dig now—have jumped my stint to 1500 words per diem till I get out of the hole.

In much haste, and as ever, sincerely,
Jack London.

MS: CSmH; 1 p., tls.

To Anna Strunsky

962 East 16th. st.,
Jan. 29, 1900.

Dear Anna:—
    Say, then, Wednsday, 12:30, at the Library—University Library of course. Just be anywhere; I'll find you. Ah! the physical basis—you a lunch and I an appetite. "Because the gods may may not permit me to see you again many times." How now? More tumultuous changes?
    Am rushed. Proofsheets rolling in, and cut again.[1] Have just finished forty-eight pages of same, the clocks are striking twelve, and I have yet a

double day's work before me and the evening engaged. Please pardon brevity. Wednsday at the library.

Very sincerely yours,
Jack London.

MS: CSmH; 1 p., tls.
    1. Presumably, proofs for *The Son of the Wolf*; see JL to Houghton, Mifflin & Co., January 31, 1900, n. 1.

To Cloudesley Johns

962 East 16th. st.,
Jan. 30th. 1900.

Dear Cloudesley:—
    Am hard at it. Have not missed a day in which I have turned out at least 1500 words, and sometimes as high as 2000. How's that? And at the same time I have broken no engagements, gone on with my studying, and corrected daily from 16 to 48 pages of proofsheets. Sometimes forty-eight hours pass without my even stepping foot on the ground or seeing more of out-doors than the front porch when I go out to get the evening paper. Hurrah for Hell!
    Find enclosed the replies to "Man with the Hoe."[1] Please forward them to Edward Applegarth Jr.,
Cor. Elm & Asbury sts.,
San Jose,
Calif.
When you have done with them.
    Many thanks for your sending me "The Red wolf."[2] May I keep it a while?—long enough to read to some friends, to take a copy of, and to send down to Ted's sister?[3] Then return to you? Also thanks for newspaper and magazine catalogue.
    Will strive to find out what the "Yellow Dwarf" is.[4]
    So you fell! Sensible lad! The damn dollars do carry some weight after all. I am frankly and brutally consistent about money; you are neither, nor are you consistent.[5] Which reminds me, nothing of importance has turned up yet, but before the last of February I shall send you your fotos.
    He doesn't remember which literary *Digest*, is not sure if it was a *Literary Digest*,[6] but if it was it was in the last couple of numbers. Tell us about your being pulled. Did they turn you loose after you had missed the train, or did they take you to the city prison?[7] Give particulars. Am interested. Well, tra la. Have lots to do.

Jack London.

MS: CSmH; 1 p., tls.
    1. Markham's poem received high praise from such writers as Hamlin Garland, William

James, and Joaquin Miller, while other critics denounced it for being pessimistic, irreligious, and radical. See also JL to Johns, April 17, 1899, n. 14.

2. Bliss Carman, "The Red Wolf" (1893), a poem in which the narrator lives in dread, throughout the year, of the "Red Wolf of Despair" lurking at his door.

3. Mabel Applegarth.

4. In "The Red Wolf," the poem's narrator is also beset by an imaginary beast, "low and humped and foul," which he calls the "Yellow Dwarf" and characterizes as his "servitor and lord," because it constantly reminds him of the "Red Wolf" and prevents him from once again experiencing "God's great peace."

5. *Munsey's* had accepted Johns's "The Stage Driver's Proxy" on condition that he provide a happy ending. Johns later withdrew the story from *Munsey's* after the unrevised version was accepted by the *Puritan* (1897–1901), an illustrated women's magazine owned by Frank A. Munsey; in 1898 Munsey had bought *Godey's Lady's Book* and merged it with the *Puritan*. Johns's story was published in the *Puritan*, July 1900. See JL to Johns, March 1 and July 23, 1900.

6. The *Literary Digest* was a monthly magazine featuring current poetry, book reviews, and humor, published in New York from 1890 until 1938.

7. Johns "rode the rods" aboard a freight train to and from Oakland. Apparently he was caught by the police on his trip home.

To Houghton, Mifflin & Co.

962 East 16th. st.,
Oakland, Calif.,
Jan. 31, 1900.

Gentlemen:—

In reply to yours of January 25th. requesting additional biographical data.[1] I see I shall have to piece out my previous narrative, which, in turn, will make this choppy.

My father was Pennsylvania-born, a soldier, scout, backwoodsman, trapper, and wanderer.[2] My mother was born in Ohio. Both came west independently, meeting and marrying in San Francisco, where I was born January 12, 1876. What little city life I then passed was in my babyhood. My life, from my fourth to my ninth years, was spent upon Californian ranches.[3] I learned to read and write about my fifth year, though I do not remember anything about it. I always could read and write, and have no recollection antedating such a condition. Folks say I simply insisted upon being taught. Was an omniverous reader, principally because reading matter was scarce and I had to be grateful for whatever fell into my hands. Remember reading some of Trowbridge's works for boys[4] at six years of age. At seven I was reading Paul du Chaillu's *Travels*, Captain Cook's *Voyages*, and *Life of Garfield*.[5] And all through this Period I devoured what Seaside Library novels[6] I could borrow from the womenfolk and dime novels from the farm hands. At eight I was deep in Ouida[7] and Washington Irving. Also during this period read a great deal of American history. Also, life on a Californian ranch is not very nourishing to the imagination.

Somewhere around my ninth year we removed to Oakland, which, to-day, I believe, is a town of about eighty thousand, and is removed by thirty minutes from the heart of San Francisco. Here, most precious to me was a free library. Since that time Oakland has been my home seat. Here my father died,[8] and here I yet live with my mother. I have not mar-ried—the world is too large and its call too insistent.

However, from my ninth year, with the exception of the hours spent at school (and I earned them by hard labor), my life has been one of toil. It is worthless to give the long sordid list of occupations, none of them trades, all heavy manual labor. Of course I continued to read. Was never without a book. My education was popular, graduating from the grammar school[9] at about fourteen. Took a taste for the water. At fifteen left home and went upon a Bay life. San Francisco Bay is no mill pond by the way. I was a salmon fisher, an oyster pirate, a schooner sailor, a fish patrolman, a longshoreman, and a general sort of bay-faring adventurer—a boy in years and a man amongst men.[10] Always a book, and always reading when the rest were asleep; when they were awake I was one with them, for I was always a good comrade.

Within a week of my seventeenth birthday I shipped before the mast as sailor on a three top-mast sealing schooner. We went to Japan and hunted along the coast north to the Russian side of Bering Sea. This was my long-est voyage; I could not again endure one of such length; not because it was tedious or long, but because life was so short. However, I have made short voyages, too brief to mention, and to-day am at home in any fore-castle or stokehole—good comradeship, you know. I believe this com-prises my travels; for I spoke at length in previous letter concerning my tramping and Klondiking. Have been all over Canada, Northwest Ty. Alaska, etc. etc, at different times, besides mining, prospecting and wan-dering through the Sierra Nevadas.

I have outlined my education. In the main I am self-educated; have had no mentor but myself. High school or college curriculums I simply se-lected from, finding it impossible to follow the rut—life and pocket book were both too short. I attended the first year of high school (Oakland), then stayed at home, without coaching, and crammed the next two years into three months and took the entrance examinations, and entered the University of California at Berkeley.[11] Was forced, much against my in-clinations, to give this over just prior to the completion of my Freshman Year.

My father died while I was in the Klondike, and I returned home to take up the reins.

As to literary work: My first magazine article (I had done no news-paper work), was published in January, 1899; it is now the sixth story in the *Son of the Wolf*.[12] Since then I have done work for the *Overland Monthly*, the *Atlantic*, the *Wave*, the *Arena*, the *Youth's Companion*, the

Review of Reviews, etc. etc., besides a host of lesser publications, and to say nothing of newspaper and syndicate work. Hackwork all, or nearly so, from a comic joke or triolet to pseudo-scientific disquisitions upon things about which I knew nothing. Hackwork for dollars, that's all, setting aside practically all ambitious efforts to some future period of less financial stringency. Thus, my literary life is just thirteen months old to-day.

Naturally, my reading early bred in me a desire to write, but my manner of life prevented me attempting it. I have had no literary help or advice of any kind—just been sort of hammering around in the dark till I knocked holes through here and there and caught glimpses of daylight. Common knowledge of magazine methods, etc., came to me as revelation. Not a soul to say here you err and there you mistake.

Of course, during my revolutionaire period I perpetrated my opinions upon the public through the medium of the local papers, gratis. But that was years ago when I went to high school and was more notorious than esteemed. Once, by the way, returned from my sealing voyage, I won a prize essay of twenty-five dollars from a San Francisco paper over the heads of Stanford and California Universities, both of which were represented by second and third place through their undergraduates.[13] This gave me hope for achieving something ultimately.

After my tramping trip I started to high school in 1895. I entered the University of California in 1896. Thus, had I continued, I would be just now preparing to take my sheepskin.

As to studies: I am always studying. The aim of the university is simply to prepare one for a whole future life of study. I have been denied this advantage, but am knocking along somehow. Never a night (whether I have gone out or not) but the last several hours are spent in bed with my books. All things interest me—the world is so very good. Principal studies are, scientific, sociological, and ethical—these, of course, including biology, economics, psychology, physiology, history, etc. etc. without end. And I strive, also, to not neglect literature.

Am healthy, love exercise, and take little. Shall pay the penalty some day.

There, I can't think of anything else. I know what data I have furnished is wretched, but autobiography is not entertaining to a narrator who is sick of it. Should you require further information, just specify, and I shall be pleased to supply it. Also, I shall be grateful for the privilege of looking over the biographical note before it is printed.

Very truly yours,
Jack London.

MS: InNd; 4 pp., tls. Pbd: *L*, 86–88; *Mentor*, 12–14.
   1. Houghton Mifflin had accepted *The Son of the Wolf* on November 1, 1899. Presum-

ably the request for biographical data was for advertising purposes. For another description of JL's early life, see JL to M. Applegarth, November 30, 1898.

2. John London (1828–97), JL's stepfather. He was born in Clearfield County, Pennsylvania, fought in the Civil War, and lived in Iowa before coming to California with three of his nine children. He married Flora Wellman on September 7, 1876. See JL to M. Applegarth, November 16, 1898, n. 1.

3. Actually dirt farms in Emeryville, Alameda, San Mateo County, and Livermore.

4. John Townsend Trowbridge (1827–1916), popular writer of boys' stories and didactic narrative poems. He was a regular contributor to *Our Young Folks* and *Youth's Companion*. Among his best-known works are *Cudjo's Cave* (1864), the *Jack Hazard Series* (1871–75), and the *Silver Medal Series* (1877–82).

5. Probably either *Lost in the Jungle* (1870) or *Stories of the Gorilla Country* (1868), both subtitled "Narrated for Young Children," by Paul Belloni du Chaillu (1831–1903), French writer of romantic adventure stories; James Cook, *The Voyages of Captain James Cook* (1842); William M. Thayer, *From Log-Cabin to White House: The Story of President Garfield's Life* (1881).

6. The Seaside Library was a series of inexpensive reprints of more than two thousand popular romance and adventure novels, begun in 1877 by the publisher George Munro.

7. The pseudonym of Marie Louise de la Ramée (1839–1908), English novelist and writer of children's stories. Her novel *Signa* (1875) was one of JL's favorite books in his youth. See JL to Humble, December 11, 1914.

8. John London died on October 15, 1897.

9. Cole Grammar School, in West Oakland.

10. See JL to Johns, March 30, 1899, n. 7, and JL to the Corresponding Editor, *Youth's Companion*, March 9, 1903.

11. JL neglects to mention that both Bessie Maddern and Fred Jacobs tutored him for his college entrance examinations. See JL to E. Applegarth, September 13, 1898, n. 3, and November 14, 1898, n. 1.

12. JL's first magazine article was actually "Two Gold Bricks," *Owl*, September 1897, published while he was in the Klondike; he evidently did not know about this publication. "To the Man on Trail," published in the *Overland Monthly*, January 1899, is the fifth, not the sixth, story in *The Son of the Wolf*.

13. JL refers to "Story of a Typhoon off the Coast of Japan."

To Anna Strunsky

962 East 16th. st.,
Feb. 3, 1900.

Dear Anna:—

Saturday night, and I feel good. Saturday night, and a good week's work done—hack work of course. Why shouldn't I? Like any other honest artisan by the sweat of my brow. I have a friend who scorns such work.[1] He writes for posterity, for a small circle of admirers, oblivious to the world's oblivion, doesn't want money, scoffs at the idea of it, calls it filthy, damns all who write for it, etc. etc.,—that is, he does all this if one were to take his words for criteria. But I received a letter from him recently. *Munsey's* had offered to buy a certain story of him, if he would change the ending. He had built the tale carefully, every thought tending toward the final consummation, notably, the death by violence of the chief character. And they asked him to keep the tale and to permit that character, logically dead, to live. He scorns money. Yes; and he permitted that character to live. "I fell," is the only explanation he has vouchsafed of his conduct.

All of which reminds me—the most cleverly written article of the month is to be found in the February *Atlantic Monthly*. "Journalism as a Basis for Literature," by Gerald Stanley Lee.² If you should run across the magazine, read it. In a certain way it eulogizes Kipling, saying, among other things: "The fact that Mr. Kipling is not dead is the most heroically artistic thing about him"; "Kipling is an artist because he respects the passing thing, because he catches the glimmer of the eternal joy upon it and will not let it pass"; "His secret is that he took hold of something that nobody wanted him to do, and did it better than anyone wanted him to do it." His, Mr. Lee's, portrayal of the nineteenth century, "moment-mad," "turning all eternity upside down in the present tense," etc., is a splendid bit of writing, and as true as it is splendid. O you must read it by all means.

In the same magazine, modeled after "Childe Harold to the Dark Tower Came,"³ you will find a poem by Clinton Scollard,⁴ called "The Gray Inn."

Find under this cover, Alfred Austin's sonnet.⁵ It will bear thinking upon. Perish the thought!—but then, you know, it really will.

I have been looking over my book and find next Thursday evening open. Friday evening I am expecting a letter shortly to decide. It may be free, and it may not. But Thursday evening is. If you are free also, may I call upon you? And please let me know about time in the evening would best suit you.

And if you can have it at hand, may I look at some of your work? If you do, some time I'll reciprocate and let you see some of my dark-hidden earlier productions.

Sometimes I run across some of my pot-boiling work, though as a rule it is lost to me forever. Here are a couple. Please return, as they sometimes serve to chasten one's spirit. I send them to you in much the manner of a lawyer's brief. Do you wonder, turning out such stuff, that I sometimes grow bitter? O, but only for a moment, and then it all seems a joke again. Life is good, isn't it?

Poetry? What wouldn't I give just to be able to sit down and write ambitious work? But then it doesn't pay, and I don't. One must try one's hand for so long in order to get the touch, and the many attempts have no market value. And then, you know, at other times I lose faith in any co-operative commonwealth; cannot see how, after all, there will be incentive. And when I am feeling this way it seems inevitable that new inducements to strive will have to be offered in certain intellectual branches, or else it will fail as far as those branches go. Do you ever have doubts that way?

How one wanders! I shall stop.

Most sincerely yours,
Jack London.

P.S. Please let me have your real, condensed address. I find I am incapable of shortening it on the envelope and at the same time retaining the belief that the letter will be safely delivered.

J.G.L.

MS: CSmH; 3 pp., tls. Pbd: *L*, 88–89.
   1. Cloudesley Johns.
   2. Gerald Stanley Lee (1862–1944), a Congregational clergyman who wrote on issues of the day. In this article, Lee argues that Kipling, unlike most of his contemporaries, was able to survive in "the whirlpool of journalism . . . instead of being carried with it" by his great strength and ability as an artist and a journalist. Lee concluded: "The modern world makes extraordinary demands upon the artist, but Kipling has mastered them."
   3. JL mistitles Browning's "Childe Roland to the Dark Tower Came."
   4. Clinton Scollard (1860–1932), American poet and associate of the Canadian poet Bliss Carman. Painstaking versification and a strain of lyrical escapism characterized Scollard's verse at this time.
   5. Probably "Love's Wisdom" by Alfred Austin (1835–1913), English poet, journalist, and critic, and poet laureate from 1896 until his death. The poem (typescript, presumably by JL, CSmH; also Austin, *Soliloquies in Song* [1882]) begins, "Now on the summit of Love's topmost peak / Kiss we and part; no farther can we go" and concludes "Heaven of my Earth! One more celestial kiss, / Then down by separate pathways to the vale."

To Cloudesley Johns

962 East 16th. st.,
Feb. 10, 1900.

Dear Cloudesley:—
   Many thanks for *Philistine*[1] and for clippings. The former I especially enjoyed, nor did I fail to appreciate your vicarious criticism of the dining club.[2] Wow! How he did give it to Harry Thurston Peck.[3] What do *you* think about marriage being made more difficult, and divorce correspondingly easy?[4]
   No I won't forget the fotos, though, as yet, nothing important in the way of checks has arrived. However, I have had quite good success with *McClure's*. You remember my mailing that story of a minister who apostasizes?[5] And the vile sinner who did not? *McClures* accepted it if I would agree to the cutting of the opening and the elimination of certain swearwords. Of course I agreed, as it was an affair of 6000 words. Two days after that came an acceptance, from *McClure's*, of the "Question of the Maximum"—that socialistic essay I read to you. What do you think of that for a rather conservative house? I mean conservative politically. They said, however, that had I written them first concerning the article they would have told me that It was unavailable, but that the article itself was something different, and that they could not let it go. Also promised to

publish it between July or August, if not sooner.[6] But, say, I thought they paid on acceptance. That's over 11000 words and nary a cent. Do you have any idea as to what their rates are? Can they be less than 12 dollars per thousand? They also wanted to see more of my fiction, wanted to have me submit a long story if I had one, and if I had a collection of short stories they wanted to examine them for publication.

Have finished the *Son of the Wolf* proofsheets—251 pages of print in it.

Yes; I have noted the change in the editorship of the *Arena*,[7] but I did not note it until after your kind postal arrived, and it was the postal which made me look it up. I wonder if they will ever pay.

"I have told you that I consider absolute pauperism almost as objectionable as wealth." Now, say, I wonder if you mean it? Of course you are inconsistent. Of course you sacrificed (serially) your name and workmanship by changing the story. And further, you did it for money. You can't defend yourself, you know you can't. Why not come out and [be] brutally frank about it like I am? You are doing the very same thing when you write hack-work. *Press* or *Journal* and *Black Cat* prize stories—money, that's all. Simmer yourself down and sum yourself up in a square way for just once. Be consistent, even though you be vile as I in the matter of dollars and cents.

You simply excite my curiosity when speaking as cursorily of your arrest as you did.[8]

Have lost steerage way in the matter of writing. Have done twenty-two hundred words in five days, and gone out every night, and feel as though I can never write again. Isn't it frightful? O Lord! Who wouldn't sell a farm and go to writing! Say, I think I have stuck *Munsey's* with a thirty-two hundred word essay.[9] I wonder if it can be possible? *Wave* has not ponied up yet.[10] Do you want that *Philistine* back again? I have loaned it, and if you do I will get it back, if not, let it pass along the line.

Have evolved new ideas about warfare, or rather, assimilated them. If my article is published soon, upon that subject, I shall send it to you.[11] Any, to make it short, war as a direct attainment of an end, is no longer possible. The world has seen it's last decisive battle. Economics, not force, will decide future wars. Of course all this is postulated of war between first class powers, or first class soldiers; not frontier squabbles. Nor would I classify the fighting in the Transvaal as a squabble. Unless there is a grave blunder, and unless the British do not too heavily reinforce, it will be found that Neither British nor Boors can advance.[12] Which ever side advances, advances to its own destruction.

Good bye,
Jack London.

MS: CSmH; 2 pp., tls. Pbd: *L*, 90–91; *BJL*, I, 328–29.

1. *The Philistine: A Periodical of Protest*, perhaps the most influential of the little magazines of revolt in the 1890's; edited and published from 1895 to 1915 by Elbert Hubbard

and after 1899 written entirely by him as well. *The Philistine* took aim at the literary, religious, political, and educational establishment in its witty but biting critical essays.

2. Johns sent JL a copy of *The Philistine* for January 1900; in it, an untitled article on dining clubs concluded "the Dining Club is a vain effort to secure culture by going cross lots . . . and is a barren jactancy and pride-inflated antic of America's bourgeoisie" (p. 39).

3. Harry Thurston Peck (1856–1914), editor of the *Bookman* from 1895 to 1902. Peck had written a critical article entitled "Robert G. Ingersoll," *Bookman*, September 1899. A response in *The Philistine*, January 1900, attacked Peck's lack of charity in assessing Ingersoll: "You were the fice who sought out the last resting place of a good man and great and lifted a leg over the wreaths with which love had garlanded his grave" (p. 47).

4. An untitled article in *The Philistine*, January 1900, pp. 58–62, suggested this course.

5. "Sturges Owen, Apostate," published as "The God of His Fathers" in *McClure's*, May 1901, and later included in the collection of that title. JL was paid $120 for the story.

6. For the publication history of "The Question of the Maximum," see JL to Johns, November 11, 1899, n. 8.

7. John Emery McLean had become editor of *Arena*, which had accepted JL's "The Road." See JL to Johns, July 29, 1899, n. 5.

8. See JL to Johns, January 30, 1900, n. 7.

9. "First Aid to Rising Authors," published December 9, 1900, in *Junior Munsey Magazine*, a juvenile monthly magazine that featured stories and articles on literature, published by Frank A. Munsey in New York from 1887 until 1902. It had originally been called the *Quaker*.

10. *The Wave* had published JL's "A Daughter of the Aurora" (later included in *The God of His Fathers*) in its Christmas number for 1899. JL received ten dollars in August 1900 after dunning the magazine.

11. "The Impossibility of War," *Overland Monthly*, March 1900. For the article's source and earlier submission history, see JL to Johns, February 16, 1900. On April 5, 1900, the *Overland Monthly* paid JL $7.50 for the article.

12. At this time, the Boer War had become something of a standoff. However, on February 11 British forces 40,000 strong began their march on Blomfontein.

To Anna Strunsky

962 East 16th. st.,
Feb. 10, 1900.

Dear Anna:–

By solemn covenant agreed, you are in my debt a letter. Therefore, and time pressing, this is very short. I sometimes make and receive war through the mails in the form of bombarding and being bombarded by magazines and all sorts of erratic literature. I send you with this mail a January *Philistine*. After it was sealed and addressed, I reflected that the friend who had sent it to me had blue-pencilled it, and that you were liable to think the marks were mine and to try to puzzle out their significance. So I am writing this. You will note in one place how he (friend) volleys away at me regarding club dinners, etc. Most of the rest is a bolstering up of his own opinions, and so you see in such way one conveys more argument and better presented than he could by writing a letter himself. I imagine the construction of this last sentence is rather vague. Elbert Hubbard, the editor of the *Philistine* is rather a curious and at the same time a splendid character.[1] At least the world is better than had he never lived.

When you are done with it, please mail it in some sort of way to
Miss Mabel Applegarth,
Corner Elm & Asbury sts.,
San Jose,
Calif.

Saves times you know—that is if you are not disinclined. In latter case remail it to me.

Very sincerely,
Jack London.

MS: CSmH; 2 pp., tls.

1. Elbert Hubbard (1859–1915), charismatic author, editor of *The Philistine*, and printer. Following the example of William Morris, Hubbard founded and directed the Roycroft Shop in East Aurora, New York. He was renowned as well for his magnetic discourse and his unconventional dress. For a brief correspondence between JL and Hubbard, see JL to Hubbard, June 26, July 27, and ? August 16, 1911.

To Anna Strunsky

962 East 16th. st.,
Feb. 13, 1900.

Dear Anna:—

To be your taskmaster? Good! I love power, to dominate my fellows. I shall stand over you with a whip of scorpions and drive you to your daily toil. Like Pharoah of old, I shall hold you in bondage, and in the end, you will send plagues upon me, and amid signs and portents and great tumult, depart, leaving behind a wake of devastation and terror.

A most fascinating outlook, is it not? I love such things, and doubt not that prophecy will be fulfilled. However, fun aside, I'll do it. But, first of all, the first time I have you to myself you must be prepared for a lecture. I'll not be sparing, and I promise you I'll handle you without gloves. We'll get right down to the naked facts of life, adjust our compasses and set our course. And then—why if anything happens, it's the fault of the mariners.

I do not know you very well, so I may make mistakes and do you many injustices; so you must forgive all such things in advance. It's safest, you know, to obtain indulgence before you sin. Also, remember this, there will be divers things in which I am unqualified to teach you anything. And also this, that, after all is said and done, everything depends upon yourself.

I shall mail this directly, in the hope that you will receive it before you leave Glenholm Wednesday morning. I would put a special delivery upon it, but the Post Office is too far away. It's too bad that your best day for leisure comes on Wednsday. My Wednsday afternoons and evenings are always taken up.[1] So I shall be unable to come, and believe my sincerity when I state that I regret the fact. However, let me know when I may see you. And if, in the interim, you should perpetrate anything (vernacular for writing), please send it to me. Much wisdom lieth in deliberation.

What am I writing? Letters all morning. Shall now amend a boy's story for the *Youth's Companion* which they have accepted on the condition that I change certain things.[2] Isn't that inspiring? However, *McClures'* have become interested in my work, and are begging me to give them first glance at whatever I write. They accepted a 6000 word story of mine the other day on condition that I should change the opening and eliminate the profanity.[3] I agreed, telling them to go ahead and do it them selves. Gave them *carte blanche*, in fact. Just imagine permitting somebody handling *your* work that way. That is what is called art.

Also, in trying to find a time when I can see you, don't hit upon Sunday. A week from this Tuesday (to-day) or a week from the forthcoming Thursday, would suit me very well, either day or evening. How about you? I am expected out to Glenholm Shrove Tuesday—whenever that is. I don't know, but I've got it down in my book. But that would hardly suit for me to gird on my panoply of war and drag you at my chariot, while if the plagues descended it would certainly make it unpleasant for the theatricals.

Very sincerely,
Jack London.

ms: CSmH; 3 pp., tls. Pbd: *L*, 91–92.

    1. JL opened his house to his friends—mostly Bay Area writers, artists, and socialists—on Wednesdays. He supplied food and drink, and hosted card games, poetry and prose readings, and other activities. These Wednesday open houses became very popular, especially after JL moved to a larger house on 15th Street in April.

    2. "The Lost Poacher," *Youth's Companion*, March 14, 1901; later included in *Dutch Courage*. For the requested change, see the next letter.

    3. "The God of His Fathers."

To Cloudesley Johns

962 East 16th. st.,
Feb. 16, 1900.

Dear Cloudesley:—

Have you been reading *Tommy and Grisel*? By Barrie. It's coming out serially in *Scribner's*, commencing with the January number.[1] I never read serials, but being enticed into just glancing over it, I found I could not lay it down. So I am stuck to the job for a year. Read it by all means. You remember Edith Wharton's "Tragedy of the Muse"? It is the first of a collection of eight stories under the title of *The Greater Inclination*. And they are all as good. Have just finished it.

Your *Call* and *Wave* rackets reminds me of what happened to me recently. Last fall I lost a fourty-six hundred word story with *Collier's Weekly*. I wrote them, after due time, and they gave me a full-page letter explaining that it had never reached them, and that they had no record of it. To show them I still had confidence, I later on sent them another. It too became overdue and I trailed it. And lo and behold, the other day arrived both Mss. The first one I had long since retyped.[2]

Yes; that mirage city is seen at Muir Glacier, but only at a certain time along in mid-summer. I don't believe that the city has ever been identified, so any city would suit. Candidly, it's all a newspaper freak yarn in my estimation, having a foundation, perhaps, in mirage manifestations, but nothing more. Just like any desert.

Why should Oom Paul[3] be sacred to you? Is he a demi-god? By the way, I heard a noted politician, who prefixes Honorable and Colonel to his name, the other evening in a public pro-Boer meeting instance Bryce[4] as one of the many English scholars and philosophers who were opposed to England's S.A. policy. When he had done, another man arose, and quoted from Bryce to this intent: "The Dutch took with them to South Africa the habits and culture of the Seventeenth Century, and since then have developed backwards."[5]

And our friend Whittaker[6] got up and whopped it to the right honorable, and before he was done had about three times the applause. How's that for a Pro-Boer meeting and an unemotional speaker?

O hell! you're incorrigible. Why do you wish to go to Paris? Education? Do you then believe that wise traveling and plenty of it will educate, or only in the case of a world's exposition? And if the former, how may you travel decently so as to be able to afford that mode and method which will be the better educator, unless you have money?

My dear fellow, had I not been "an animal with a logical nature" I should not be here to-day. It is only because I was so that I did not perish or stagnate by the wayside. I have been called stern, cold, cruel, unyielding, etc., and why? Because I did not wish to stop off at their particular station and remain for the rest of my days. Money? Money will give me all things, or at least more of all things than I could otherwise possess. It may even take me over to the other side of the world to meet my affinity; while without it I might mismate at home and live miserably till the game was played out.

Is it correct grammar to say, "It *is* become a battle?" What say you?

Shall send you *Philistine* soon; also "Red Wolf"; also your fotos. Got an acceptance from *Youth's Companion* the other day—qualified—if I would make the opening a little longer. So will get check about twenty-second to twenty-fourth. You remember the *Wave*? I sent them yesterday a brief note, enclosing with it half a dozen pawn checks and a two cent stamp. I am wondering what they will do.

"I should like to see your article explaining away the inefficiency of the

Briton in war." There you are unjust. However, you will see it if you look up the *Overland* for March. It's merely a *resume* of another man's book.[7] The article was refused respectively by the *Call, Chronicle,* and *Examiner.* I wish you would look over it in an endeavor to find me the reason of said refusals.

Please return enclosed *McClure* note.[8] It's precious as pearls. And let us hear what you think about what they think, and what my policy should be toward them.

Find herewith foto, my sister (one of them), had the photographer reduce them from the original, and then she presented me with a fist full of them. I have been getting rid of them slowly through the mails. Only got about six left now, and expect to finish them in about a couple more days.

I've got the shakes, almost in collapse; so until next time.

Jack London.

Applegarths make Yellow Dwarf[9] out to be the "fear of want." Anna Strunsky & myself (principally Anna Strunsky) made it out that the "Wolf" was the concrete expression for not only want but misfortune in general. While the Yellow Dwarf is the concrete expression of man's own forebodings and morbid apprehensions (whether there be cause or not). The one is the objective, the external; the other the subjective, the internal. The co-ordination in two forms black despair. What think you?

MS: CSmH; 3 pp., tls. Pbd: *BJL,* I, 329–30.

1. James M. Barrie's *Tommy and Grizel* appeared from January to November 1900 in *Scribner's Magazine,* an illustrated monthly that contained literature and articles on history, art, travel, and other popular topics; it was published in New York from 1887 to 1939. Barrie's serial, a veiled autobiography, dealt with a successful writer's exposure of the weaknesses of an artistic temperament: being overwhelmed by popular success and unable to escape from the childhood experiences that he used for the subject of his work.

2. "The Man with the Gash," which appeared in *McClure's,* September 1900 (see JL to Johns, March 1, 1900), and probably "At the Rainbow's End," which JL submitted on September 21, 1899, and "trailed" on February 1, 1900, and which was published in the *Pittsburgh Leader,* March 24, 1901. Both stories were included in *The God of His Fathers.*

3. The nickname given to Stephanus Johannes Paulus Kruger (1825–1904), President of the Republic of South Africa from 1883 to 1900. At this time Kruger was in Europe trying to persuade European powers to intervene in the Boer War.

4. James, Viscount Bryce (1838–1922), Regius Professor of Civil Law at Oxford from 1870 to 1893, who later held a number of political and diplomatic posts in the British government. In the preface to the third edition of *Impressions of South Africa* (1899; orig. pbd. 1897), Bryce maintained that the Dutch in South Africa were not conspiring to overthrow British authority there. The pro-Boer meeting JL describes has not been identified.

5. In *Impressions of South Africa* (pp. 420–21), Bryce wrote: "Severed from Europe and its influences two hundred years ago, the Dutch have, in some of the elements of modern civilization, gone back rather than forward."

6. Herman ("Jim") Whitaker (1867–1919), an English writer and socialist who moved to Oakland with his wife and six children in 1895. He was in charge of the cooperative grocery store operated by the Oakland section of the Socialist Democratic Party. JL met and befriended Whitaker through the Oakland section; Whitaker taught JL to box and to fence, and in return JL helped him get a start as a writer.

7. "The Impossibility of War" was based on the six-volume work by Ivan S. Bloch, *The Future of War*. The last volume of this work, containing Bloch's conclusions on the impossibility of war, was translated into English by R. C. Long (1899).

8. Perhaps the note from *McClure's* mentioned in the preceding letter and JL to Johns, February 10, 1900.

9. See JL to Johns, January 30, 1900, nn. 2, 4.

To Cloudesley Johns

962 East 16th. st.,
Feb. 17, 1900.

Dear Cloudesley:—

Thanks for Julian Ralph's "Picture of new War Problems."[1] Find it herewith returned. If it has interested you, I am sure my article will, for I treat the machinery of war at length, and then go into the economic and political aspects. The world will learn a great lesson from the Transvaal War. I am intending to write an essay entitled "They That Rise by the Sword" shortly. And just you wait till I come out with my "Salt of the Earth."[2]

So, when you are doing your best work you only do about four or five hundred a day. Good. Most good. I hope you will live up to it. I insist that good work can not be done at the rate of three or four thousand a day. Good work is not strung out from the inkwell. It is built like a wall, every brick carefully selected, etc. etc.

You are always working me up with your mysteries. If you are monkeying with established traditions, and at the same time not monkeying with religion, pray let me know what you are monkeying with. If it is so terrible, not even if you were famous, could you get it published save on your own press, nor circulated by any but third-rate distributors. Why Ruskin, at the height of his fame, and turning out his best work in the *Cornhill*, had the series of essays stopped in the middle by Thackeray because they were daring.[3] And daring, mark you, not for their attacks on religion, but for their attacks on the prevailing school of political economy. The same Thackeray refused one of Elizabeth Barrett Browning's best poems because it was *risque*.[4] I'm afraid Thackeray was a snob, a cad, and a whole lot of other things which he in turn has so successfully impaled for the regard of the British reading public.[5]

Herewith from McClure himself.[6] Use it in giving me opinion I asked for in last letter.

Jack London.

MS: CSmH; 1 p., tls. Pbd: *L*, 94; *BJL*, I, 330.

1. Julian Ralph (1853–1903), American journalist. In 1900, Ralph was a war correspondent in South Africa covering the Boer War. The article JL mentions has not been identified.

2. JL never wrote "They That Rise by the Sword." "The Salt of the Earth" was published in *Anglo-American Magazine*, August 1902.

3. Serial publication of the essays on political economy that would become Ruskin's *Unto This Last* (1862) was discontinued in October 1861, after only four issues, by Thackeray, editor of the *Cornhill Magazine*, apparently because of critical outcry at the essays and the heterodox opinions they expressed.

4. In the spring of 1861, Thackeray rejected Elizabeth Barrett Browning's "Lord Walter's Wife."

5. JL refers to Thackeray's *The Snobs of England. By One of Themselves.*

6. Samuel S. McClure (1857–1949), founder of the McClure Syndicate and editor of *McClure's* magazine from 1893 to 1929.

To Anna Strunsky

962 East 16th. st.,
Feb. 20, 1900.

Dear Anna:—

You have done me a great wrong. I hardly know whether I can ever forgive you; for you have put into my life a great unrest which will continue for at least a year to come. Yes; out of the largeness of my heart I will forgive you, for I do believe that you did it without malice aforethought. You remember,—O surely you do,—that evening at Glenholm when you told me of Barrie's new story? It's your fault. It was because of you that I looked up the January *Scribner's* and could not lay it down again until I reached "to be continued." Your fault that I did likewise with the February number. Your fault that I am unhinged, my life thrown out of joint, and that I can hardly contain myself until the March Number arrives. No; on second thought I shall never forgive you. NEVER!!! But say, isn't *Tommy and Grizel* splendid? Barrie is a master. And in the whimsical delineation of character do you not notice a trace of Dickens at his best?

Now I feel comfortable. Nobody ever "Mr. London's" me, so every time I opened a letter of yours I felt a starched collar draw round my neck. Pray permit me softer neck-gear for the remainder of our correspondence.

Now about Thursday. I have to be down in Oakland at two o'clock in the afternoon. An old chum of mine,[1] (Class of 1900, U.C.), who died on the way to Manila, has come home. I have to attend the funeral. But the morning is free. Can I see you at any time between 9:30 A.M. and 1 P.M.? Tramp if the weather prophet be gracious, or anything you wish. Reply immediately on receipt of this so that I may know.

Most sincerely yours,
Jack London.

MS: CSmH; 2 pp., tls. Pbd: *L*, 94–95.

1. Fred Jacobs.

To Anna Strunsky

[Oakland]
[? February 1900]

Dear Anna:—

There! I hope you do not consider yourself so unconventional as to have merited this boxful of my regard. I blush yet, when I think of Saturday night. You had me on the hip, and scored hard. And I deserved it, every bit. It's wrong to make excuses, but I deserve this. To put it into few words, as I have said before, I am cursed with friends. Believe me, I am not an egotist. Were I, I would not be sending you this box which abounds in frailties and mistakes. But the excuse: I am cursed with friends. I have grown accustomed to their clamoring for my company, and unconsciously feel that my presence (to them) is desirable. This mood is dangerously apt to become chronic. Need I say it so manifested itself Saturday night? And need I say that your company has ever been a great delight to me? That I would not have sought it had I not desired it? That (like you have said of yourself), when you no longer interest me I shall no longer be with you? Need I say these things to prove my candor?

As to the box. Please take good care of the contents. And don't mix them up, please. I haven't written any poetry for months. Those you see are my experiments (studies in structure and meter), and though they be failures I have not surrendered. When I am financially secure, some day, I shall continue with them—unless I have prostituted myself beyond redemption.

To-day I am just learning to write all over again. When you can display as many failures, and have yet achieved nothing, then it is time for you to say that you cannot write. You have no right to say that now. And if you do say so, then you are a coward. Better not begin unless you are not afraid to work, work, work, to work early and late, unremittingly and always.

These are but a few of my failures, poetical and prose. I managed to rummage them out in one pile. I have many more stowed away but cannot take the time to locate them. Unless the house burns down I shall find them someday. And believe me, Anna, I am doing thus to you what I have done to no other person, and sheerly with the desire to encourage you. "O Haru"[1] I once showed to Whittaker for encouragement, but that is all. Other of the attempts, at the time of their perpetration, may have been shown to friends; but no one has seen anything like such a bunch of them. Do you show them to no one. Like the leper, I have exposed my sores; be gentle with me, and merciful in your judgement. And remember, they are for your encouragement. Anna, you have a good brain, also magnificent emotional qualities (this you have doubtless been assured of many times), and in so far you are favored above women in possession. But carry Strawn-Hamilton before you. No system, no application. Carry

also Mr. Bamford's quoted warning from Watson's "Hymn to the Sea."[2]
Don't apply what you have, wrongly. Don't beat yourself away vainly. Etc.
This was not the lecture I intended giving you; that was on other lines.

But Anna, don't let the world lose you; for insomuch that it does lose
you, in so much you have sinned.

Jack London.

MS: CSmH; 2 pp., tls. Pbd: *L*, 92–93.
   1. An unpublished short story (MS: CSmH), "O Haru" is the tale of a beautiful geisha
who waits for a decade while her lover is gone overseas to make his fortune. Although he
returns changed and without wealth, they marry. He soon becomes dissatisfied, however,
and because of his profligacy she is forced to go back to work. Despondent over her reversal
of fortune, she visits a shrine of Buddha and is inspired by the concept of Nirvana. With her
last few coppers, she buys all of an old woman's sparrows and sets them free; then, in one
last great dance, she performs hara-kiri and releases herself from life.
   2. Frederick Irons Bamford (1853–1928), professor and chairman of the English Department at Hesperian College in Woodland, California; associate librarian of the Oakland
Free Library from 1895 to 1918; a founder of the Ruskin Club. JL met Bamford at the
library in 1895. For an account of their relationship, see *Mystery*. Bamford may have quoted
William Watson (1858–1935), "A Hymn to the Sea," *Father of the Forest, and Other Poems*
(1895), ll. 80–81: "Thou, with punctual service, fulfillest thy task, being constant; / Thine
but to ponder the Law, labour and greatly obey."

To Cloudesley Johns

962 East 16th. st.,
March 1, 1900.

Dear Cloudesley:—
   You incorrigible!

> "Oh do not write for gold alone,
>   And do not write for fame;
> To self be true though still unknown
>   To all the world your name.
> Write on, the message is divine
>   Since from your soul it springs,
> While angels read each glowing line,
>   And guard you with their wings."

There, now! You can swear at me just as hard as you please. But say,
joshing aside, did the person who perpetrated the above do it for gold, or
was he a dam fool? Query(?)

I am glad that you have at last discovered *Bab Ballads*,[1] and shall look
for them with pleasure, great pleasure. I saw a most complimentary
though brief reference to them somewhere the other day. So they are not
entirely forgotten. No thanks; Wilson isn't worth a fifty word roast.[2]

"Does Matter Think," by Wm. H. Maple: Now that is striking and
very much like a strayed sheep or lamb in its *Truthseeker* bad company. It

is striking and excellent, but why? Because he is a man who has grounded in the fundamentals, and appears striking to those who have not. Why the man positively reeks of Herbert Spencer interpreted by Prof. Haeckel.[3] Not that I am impugning his article; far from it. But he has simply put into his own words what he has learned from them, and he has done it well.

Spencer was not openly, that is, didactitcly favorable to a material basis for thought, mind, soul, etc., but John Fiske has done many queer gmnastics in order to reconcile Spencer, whose work he worships, to his own beliefs in immortality and God.[4] But he doesn't succeed very well. He jumps on Haeckel, with both feet, but in my modest opinion, Haeckel's position is as yet unassailable.[5]

Dam you an your opium. Your analogies are insidiously and invidiously false, and yet you have the nerve to forestall me and denie me the write of so condemning them! Well, well. "You will think this comparison ridiculous if I leave it here, so I will explain that I am not comparing the substances (gold, opium) but the habits, and they are similar." Bah! This is so palpably in error that I am sure on reading it in cold blue type that you cannot fail to see it.

Well, if there is plenty more in your "Theorist"[6] like that which you quoted loosely about love, I don't see why it shouldn't succeed. No; I see not the slightest reason that the book should fail because of such things, but see reasons that (if it keeps up as well throughout), it should prevail. If you should ever get a chance, read Max Nordau's essay, "The Natural History of Love." It's thought is similar to yours, and it also goes down to the physical basis or the physiological basis. God! He does arraign fiction writers and the average man or woman in society on account of their love-making ways, etc.[7]

Am working busily away; have to finish a *McClure's* story, an *Atlantic* story, and my speech before the Oakland Section for the Eleventh of this month. Then I positively must write a *Black Cat* story. As yet haven't even worked out a plot, or idea.[8] Was going to send them my "Man With the Gash," but *McClure's* accepted it. It was the Ms. which I recently told you of—lost at *Collier's Weekly*, etc. and returned after I had taken a duplicate from the original longhand. Been refused by all sorts of publications and now *McClure's* are to publish it in the magazine. They paid me well. The two stories and essay which they accepted aggregated fifteen thousand words, for which they sent me three hundred dollars—twenty dollars per thousand.[9] Best pay I have yet received. Why certes, if they wish to buy me, body and soul, they are welcome—if they pay the price. I am writing for money; if I can procure fame, that means more money. More money means more life to me. I shall always hate the task of getting money; every time I sit down to write it is with great disgust. I'd sooner be out in the open wandering around most any old place. So the habit of money-getting will never become one of my vices. But the habit of money spending, ah God! I shall always be its victem. I received the three hundred last Monday. I have now about four dollars in pocket, haven't moved,[10] don't see how I can financially, owe a few debts yet, etc. Hows that for about three days?

Am going to 'Frisco to-morrow, when I shall procure your fotos, take one for myself, and send the rest along to Harold.[11] Sorry I have delayed you so long.

Bosh, man. When I come out with my "Salt of the Earth" you will not make me squirm. Naturally I shall look to details in any event; but you, if you were wise, would not attack me on details. Don't you see; if you attack a man verbally on details, and if he is fool enough not to force you down to fundamentals, why you will make him squirm to the vast mass of ordinary unthinking creatures which will applaud you. But a thinking man, would see the shallowness of such attack and go away sorry for the other fellow because he permitted you to attack his details. But, when you attack details in cold print it falls flat. See how flat the *Truthseeker* controversies are to real thinking people. No-body ever goes down to lay foundations. They all seize bricks from the parapets and towers and assault each other vigourously. There is certainly vigor, life, etc., but not intellectual battle. Compare the controversey of men like Spencer and Huxley,[12] etc., etc., to the ordinary newspaper controversies between correspondents. Can't you see the difference? Surely you do.

Apparently you had me on the hip in that little matter regarding how many words to write per day. Let us drop details, and come down to frank opinions. Opinions which are generalized and virtually unqualified. Opinions in few words, voicing your candid belief. Answer me this: Do you think a man can write two or three thousand words as well per day as one thousand? Do you think a man working twelve hours per day at writing can or will turn out as excellent work as though he worked three hours per day? Which will require most going over and polishing, hasty writing and voluminous, or slow writing and not so voluminous? Now I am not asking you to fly off and tell me the exceptions. I am asking you to generalize all data and all cases which may be known to you under one general head. "The greatest good for the greatest number"[13] sort of a way.

No, no; if you had been at that meeting Whitaker would not have been a worthy foeman for you, but you, attacking his details, would have been an unworthy foeman of his. You would have said nice bright sharp things which would have caught the minds of the popular unthinking audience, and you would have received more applause. But Whittaker's position would not have even been attacked. And you, if you be a thinker, in the silence of your chamber after the excitement had died away, could not possibly assure yourself that you had been true to yourself, to Mr. Whitaker, or to the question discussed. You would know that you had shunned the deeper phases and principles and turned your brain, in the way of the demogogue, to the catching of the popular approval. And if you thought long in the silence of your chamber, and if you have a conscience, you would become ashamed of yourself and what you had done. Such work, whether by priest or politician, has held back this world many a weary year.

You certainly have *Munsey* hard and fast in that *Puritan* story.[14] Of course, only morally, legally they have you. Let us hear how it comes out. I don't think you could get any magazine to publish such a thing and give names.

Find herewith "Concerning One Wilson." Pardon me, but since it appeared to me that you would not have to send it anywhere I took the liberty of indicating corrections on first page only. I believe such matters count when they catch the editor's eye. It was frightful on Wilson, your letter, and surely the *T.S.* was wise in not publishing it. If a man, in controversey, becomes undignified, he certainly is beneath your notice, and you likewise lose your dignity if you do notice him. And surely, if he remains dignified, you are the last in the world to become undignified. Life is strife, but it also happens to stand for certain amenities.

I am inclined sometimes to think you are right about Bliss Carmen and the Yellow Dwarf. Does he know?

Do you want Loomis's "The Hero Who Escaped" back?[15]

I shall take care of War Clipping, and by next writing shall return "Red Wolf." Pardon my delay in answering, but have been very busy. Nor have I written to anyone till yesterday. Sold *Youth's Companion* a four thousand word story which they say is the best I have yet sent them; that makes two since you were up.[16]

Well, good bye.

Jack London.

MS: CSmH; 6 pp., tls. Pbd: *L*, 95–98; *BJL*, I, 330–31.

  1. See JL to Johns, July 29, 1899.

  2. J. A. Wilson. See JL to Johns, November 11, 1899, n. 11. Johns had sent JL "Concerning One Wilson," his latest, unpublished retort.

  3. Ernst Haeckel (1842–1919), German biologist and proponent of organic evolution. JL probably refers to his *The Evolution of Man: A Popular Exposition of the Principal Points of Human Ontogeny and Phylogeny* (1896).

  4. Unlike Herbert Spencer, his philosophical mentor, John Fiske (1842–1901) wanted to reconcile belief in God and a divine plan with scientific determinism.

  5. Haeckel's staunch monism was enunciated in *The Riddle of the Universe* (1899–1900), in which he maintained that organic and inorganic matter were united, that the soul was not immortal, that there was no personal God, and that man did not have free will.

  6. Johns's projected novel.

  7. Max Nordau (1849–1923), Hungarian writer, art critic, and physician. In "The Natural History of Love," *Paradoxes* (1886), Nordau argued that people naturally have an instinctive sense of the qualities they desire in a mate "to ensure in a union with the latter the perpetuation and improvement of [their] own qualities in [their] offspring." But the effect of the "light literature of the day" was to substitute morbid and romantic images for an individual's own "organic ideal," resulting in bad choices and disastrous marriages.

8. The *Black Cat* story was "The Minions of Midas." Never published in *Black Cat*, it appeared in *Pearson's*, May 1901, and was later included in *Moon-Face and Other Stories* (New York: Macmillan, 1906). See JL to Johns, March 24, 1900.

9. According to his magazine sales record, JL received $180 from *McClure's* on February 26, 1900: $80 for "The Man with the Gash" and $100 for "The Question of the Maximum." He was paid $120 for "The God of His Fathers."

10. Originally "haven't not moved."

11. Harold, California.

12. Thomas Henry Huxley's disagreement with Herbert Spencer over the morality presented in Spencer's *The Principles of Ethics* (1879–93) caused a four-year rift in their friendship.

13. Jeremy Bentham's doctrine of utility.

14. See JL to Johns, January 30, 1900, n. 5.

15. Charles B. Loomis, "The Hero Who Escaped," *Century*, February 1900, a humorous short story in which the hero of an unfinished romantic novel escapes from the sheets of the manuscript before he is fated by the author to marry the stereotypical heroine and live happily ever after.

16. On January 22, 1900, JL sent "Chased by the Trail" to *Youth's Companion*, where it was not published until September 26, 1907. On February 3, 1900, JL submitted "The Lost Poacher," which was published March 14, 1901, and later included in *Dutch Courage*.

To Cloudesley Johns

962 East 16th. st.,
March 10, 1900.

Dear Cloudesley:—

How now? Wherefore the blues? Thought such things did not prevail in such a magnificent climate as Harold's. Everybody been jumping upon you at once? I know I have done my share of the jumping; but without animus. Only I wish I had reserved my jumping until you were in the best of spirits. It would have had better effect. Let me know when you are all right again; then I'll do it some more.

Honestly, though, rubbing with the world will not harm you if you take the rubs aright. Not only wild and wooly rubbing, but intellectual rubbing. The most healthful experience in the world for you who are rather versatile and universal, would be bumping into specialists who would handle you without gloves. Such has been for me the best education in the world, and I look for it more and more. Man must have better men to measure himself against, else his advance will [be] nil, or if at all, one-sided and whimsical. The paced rider makes better speed than the unpaced.

I can sympathize with you in your disgust for Harold. A year of it would drive me mad, judging from the pictures. Outside of your own work what intellectual life can you have? You are thrown back upon yourself. Too apt to become self-centered; to measure other things by yourself than to measure yourself by other things. If there were plenty of physical action and adventure (constant) in the Harold life, then for a year or so it would not hurt you. But as it is, it's unhealthful. Man is gregarious, and never more so when intellectual companions are harder to find than mere species companions. Get out by all means, if you feel the call that way. If you do not, then it were wiser not to; for without the call you will but lay up trouble against yourself.

As to being worthy of Whitaker—I simply took your statement of details and figured that you would live up to it. No; I am not contemptuous of you. Rather (frankly) pitiful for you. If I see a man with a good brain who simply won't get down and dig, who won't master fundamentals, I cannot help but pity him. So it is with you. You refuse to systematize yourself; refuse to lay a foundation for your life's work; say that such is not your temperament, etc; and in short are cowardly. Why, by what right do you say you cannot master first principles? And not only will you not master them, but you persist in holding forth views (no matter how correct they may be), but views which you have not right to hold forth; you have not qualified yourself to hold forth. This action may be forgiven in a youth who is just assailing the world, but not in a man grown. Especially when that man grown has no reason, (valid) to present for not qualifying. It is cowardly to say, "My ancestors made me thus; it is useless for me to try to make myself otherwise."[1]

Forgive me for lecturing you; but my intentions are of the best. I cannot bear to see a man misuse a good brain. Your rabidness against religion is one of the proofs of misuse. If you had discovered the place in this world which by rights you should be able to qualify for, you could not so spend your time. Life is only so long, and to fly against gods and devils is only permissible for very young men who have but received their manumission from superstition. This reaction, for them, is permissible, if they let the reaction work itself out and not become chronic.

Damit! I can't do anything but lecture to-day.

I am only averaging about 350 words per day, now, and cant increase the speed to save me; but, it's either very good work, or else it is trash; in either case I am losing nothing, for I am measuring myself and learning things which will bring returns some future day.

Have to speak Sunday, also Thursday, also very shortly before the Social Democracy of San Jose; so am rushed.[2] Haven't commenced my *Black Cat* story yet; hardly know if I shall have time to enter the competition.

I don't think that Roberts is the writer of the "Prospector." I read or tried to read a volume of short stories by some Canadian writer the other day, and think the man was Roberts.[3] I may be mistaken; but if so, the work is very crude.

Have just finished reading *Forest Lovers* by Maurice Hewlitt.[4] Read it by all means if you ever get a chance. Have made the acquaintance of Charmian Kittredge,[5] a charming girl who writes book reviews, and who possesses a pretty little library wherein I have found all the late books which the public libraries are afraid to have circulate. If you run across *A Man and a Woman*, by Stanley Waterloo, read thou it also. He's the fel-

low who wrote the *Story of Ab*, the review of which you sent me somewhere about a year ago. The Oakland librarians were studying as to
whether they would permit it to circulate or not, and gave it me to read
for my judgement.[6] It's good.

If you will read in Spencer's *First Principles* the chapter under the caption of "The Transformation and Equivalence of Forces," you will come
pretty close to seeing what god Spencer believed in.[7]

Yours in haste,[8]

MS: CSmH; 4 pp., tl. Pbd: *L*, 98–100; *BJL*, I, 332.

1. In the margin Johns later wrote: "I said nothing of the kind. I refused to [? hear of]
Jack's conception of 'first principles.' Later each of us admitted that the other was partly
right. C. J., 1918."

2. JL delivered a version of "The Question of the Maximum" in San Jose on March
14.

3. Probably George G. D. Roberts (1860–1945), Canadian newspaper editor, English
professor, historian, poet, and fiction writer. See also JL to Johns, November 21, 1899, n. 8.

4. Maurice Henry Hewlett, *The Forest Lovers; a Romance* (1898), a novel dealing with
the pure and ideal love of a gallant young knight, Prosper le Gai, and Isoult, the woman he
learns to love after he rescues her from the villainous Galors.

5. Clara Charmian Kittredge (CKL) (1871–1955), then an editorial assistant and photographer for the *Overland Monthly*. She had met JL when she accompanied her aunt and
foster mother, Ninetta Eames, to interview JL for Eames's article "Jack London," *Overland
Monthly*, May 1900. In 1905 she became JL's second wife.

6. Stanley Waterloo (1846–1913), American writer. His romantic novel, *A Man and a
Woman* (1892), is the story of Grant Harrison, a man sought after by many women, and the
one woman who truly loves him. It was considered risqué for its time.

7. JL probably refers to Spencer's concept of the "Unknowable." Through the Unknowable all things come into being, Spencer said, but in itself it is beyond human comprehension.

8. At the bottom of this letter Johns later noted: "So much haste he did not even sign it
'Jack'; yet he covered more ground than he realized. I want to write something about this
letter. C. J., 1918."

To Anna Strunsky

962 East 16th. st.,
March 10, 1900.

Dear Anna:–

You wicked girl! Wherefore have you delayed sending that *Philistine* on
down the line? Rise up and do that which you have left undone.

Haven't read the *Gadfly*[1] yet; but have just finished Maurice Hewlitt's
Forest Lovers. Have you read it? If I can retain my grip upon it I shall
lend it you the next time we meet.

Did you receive package?

In haste, also your creditor by two letters,

Jack London.

P.S. Find herewith Markham's "Ode to Lincoln."[2] Please return.

J.G.L.

MS: CSmH; 1 p., tls.

   1. Ethel L. Voynich, *The Gadfly* (1897), a best-selling novel about an idealistic young man, called the Gadfly, who was willing to sacrifice everything to overthrow the tyranny of the Catholic Church. Running through the novel is a romantic subplot involving the Gadfly and Gemma, who was also an idealistic revolutionary.
   2. Edwin Markham, "Lincoln, the Man of the People," in *Lincoln and Other Poems.*

To Cloudesley Johns

962 East 16th. st.,
March 15, 1900.

Dear Cloudesley:—

   Your *Wave* episode reminds me of my *Journal* one.[1] Letter concerning same find herewith and please return. I have sold 2000 words for one dollar and a half; but the work was bad and I would do the same again. But I can't exactly see it when I am offered three fifty for 2200 words of very good work.[2] I wonder what such people think a fellow lives on.

   Received *Bab Ballads* but haven't had a chance to run over any of them with the exception of "Gentle Alice Brown." Many thanks for the same. Let me know where to send them in Los Angeles somewhere about the first of April as you indicated. Also received *The Death of Ivan Illiich.*[3] Read half way through it on the way down town just now; will tell you how I like it when I have done.

   Find herewith two of your own clippings on war. *The Philistine* will be forwarded you shortly from San Jose. Find also some clippings I thought would interest you from my file which I went over the other night. Please return. A recent clipping, "Art Vs. Money," I don't want.

   No, no; Cloudesley; you do me wrong. When I say I feel sorry that you with your good brain won't get in and ground, I am not prompted to do so because you deny my gods (this was your explanation). Don't misconstrue my frankness. I said neither more nor less than I thought.

   You wax amusingly sarcastic over the first principles I mentioned, as though there was connected with them some great ambiguity or vagueness due to my manner of using them. I know, down in your heart that you knew, in a very general way, what they meant. But let me, for the moment, be concrete.

   To be well fitted for the tragedy of existence (intellectual existence), one must have a working philosophy, a synthesis of things. Have you a synthesis of things? Do you write, and talk, and build upon a foundation which you know is securely laid? Or do you not rather build with a hazy idea of "to hell with the foundation." In token of this: What significance do the following generalities have for you:— Matter is indestructible; motion is continuous; Force is persistent; the relations among forces are persistent; the transformation of forces is the equivalence of forces; etc. etc.?

And if you do find in these generalities some significance relating to the foundation (way down), of your philosophy of life, what general single idea of the Cosmos do they (which are relative manifestations of the absolute), convey to you? How may you, therefore, without having mastered this idea or law (they are all laws), put down the very basic stone of your foundation? Have you every thought that all life, all the universe of which you may in any way have knowledge of, bows to a law of continuous redistribution of matter? Have you read or thought that there is a dynamic principle, true of the metamorphosis of the universe, of the metamorphoses of the details of the universe, which will express these ever-changing relations? Nobody can tell you what this dynamic principle is, or why; but you may learn *how* it works. Do you know what this principle is? If you do, have you studied it, ay, carefully and painstakingly? And if you have not done these things, which have naught to do with creeds, or dogmas, with politics or economics, with race prejudices or passions; but which are the principles upon which they all work, to which they all answer because of law; if you have not, then can you say that you have a firm foundation for your philosophy of life?

I never said you could not master first principles; but I did say that you would not, and pitied you. Well?

My dear fellow, if you haven't described to me your temperament, laid such stress upon your heredity, etc., what have you done? You have told me that you can do this in study, that you can't do that in study, etc. O pshaw!

Do you not expose your view of things in all its narrowness, when you say that religion and empire are man's greatest curses? O, but you do. Had you studied that basic law, that law of laws, hinted at above, and studied it as your mind is capable of doing, why then you would not be guilty of such folly as in your statement of man's curses. Don't think all this dogmatic on my part; I simply state it baldly because it would take too much time to show you wherein you err. It will require you to do many weary an hour and night of study (which you can do), to learn it yourself. I couldn't write it in months—that which you require to study to so obtain that result.

"Screaming nonsense!"—my article on war.[4] You amuse me. Permit me to demolish you. What do you know of the new Mauser rifles which are not as yet even in use in South Africa? They have only recently been tested in Holland.[5] Let me demolish you out of your own mouth. Can you conceive of a man pointing, without removing from shoulder, a gun in any given direction for one second, or moving it, during that second at an approximately same elevation for a second? (This isn't sharpshooting, but repelling a rush attack of a body of men.) Also, can you conceive that man is capable of pressing a finger steadily (no clicking, no removing or ejecting of shells on his part) upon a trigger for one second? And can you conceive a man capable of inventing a devise, which, under steady pressure, will deliver six blows sufficiently heavy to explode by impact six caps set in the ends of six cartridges? If you cannot conceive these things, then I do sincerely pity you; it would be then the fault of your ancestors.

Did you think that it was necessary for a sharpshooter to shoot so rapidly as all that? Did you think I was fool enough to think so? Cloudesley, Cloudesley! You say that you firmly believe that any position which can be approached at double-quick can be carried at the point of the bayonet by a body twice the strength of the defenders. Cold steel, mind you. Do you happen to know that Hiram Maxim writes his name with a Maxim gun upon a target at two thousand yards?[6] Cold steel!

You misunderstood the whole trend of my article, which meant first the struggle between first class soldiers of the first class European powers, and said powers are on about an equal war-footing. Secondly, my aim was to show, and I did show, that war being so impossible, that men would not go up against each other to be exterminated, but that a deadlock would happen instead. This bringing in the economic factor. Because I stated that warfare was so deadly, I did not state that it would be applied. Rather would the deadlock occur. Read my article again. You missed the whole drift of it.

Here comes Whittaker. I have to speak over in Alameda in an hour, so must quit.[7]

No; the *Bulletin*, for which thanks, was not written by a friend from data furnished by yours truly. It was simply one of the many advertisements put out from Houghton Mifflin & Co., from data furnished by myself.[8] But why were you so carefull to inform me that the data was furnished by myself? Did you fear I might forget the fact?

I expect to have a try at the *Black Cat* in a couple of days, if only the damned plot will come. Am too busy now to think upon it.

Goodbye, and forgive haste, Most sincerely yours,

Jack London.

MS: CSmH; 5 pp., tls. Pbd: *L*, 100–102; *BJL*, I, 332–34.

1. On January 3, 1900, JL was paid two dollars by the *American Journal of Education*, a weekly published in Boston, for "What Are We to Say?" and "Strange Verbs." The articles had been submitted on May 18, 1899; JL received notice of their acceptance on July 26, after they had been published in the issue of July 13.

2. JL was offered $3.50 for "Husky—the Wolf-Dog of the North" by *Home* magazine on February 13, 1900; he refused the offer on March 10. He later sold the story to *Harper's Weekly* for twenty dollars; it was published June 30, 1900.

3. Leo Tolstoy, *The Death of Ivan Illych* (1884).

4. "The Impossibility of War."

5. JL later speculated about the effect of the 6 mm Mauser automatic repeating rifle in "Each Record Broken Adds to Country's War Strength," *San Francisco Examiner*, July 21, 1901.

6. Sir Hiram Stevens Maxim (1840–1916), Maine-born engineer and inventor, who developed a single-barrel gun with a completely automatic action. In the Boer War both sides used the 37 mm Maxim Vickers (Pom-Pom) gun.

7. JL was to deliver "The Question of the Maximum" to the Alameda branch of the Social Democratic Party.

8. See JL to Houghton, Mifflin & Co., January 31, 1900.

To Anna Strunsky

962 East 16th. St.,
March 15, 1900.

Dear Anna:—

"A Creed" is fashioned obviously after the quartrians of Fitzgerald, but is a new production, being culled from *The House of the Hundred Lights*.[1]

Did I ever speak with you about "Anarchy"?[2] Or was it some one else?

Regarding box (I am in a rush), please remember that I have disclosed myself in my nakedness—all those vain efforts and passionate strivings are so many weaknesses of mine which I put into your possession. Why, the grammar is often frightful, and always bad, while artistically, the whole boxful is atrocious. Now don't say I am piling it on. If I did not realize and condemn these faults I would be unable to try to do better. But—why, I think in sending that box to you I did the bravest thing I ever did in all my life.

Say, do you know I am getting nervous and soft as a woman. I've got to get out again and stretch my wings or I shall become a worthless wreck. I am getting timid, do you hear? timid! It must stop. Enclosed letter I received to-day, and it brought a contrast to me of my then "unfailing nerve" and my present nervousness and timidity. Return it, as I suppose I shall have to answer it some day.

Didn't speak last Sunday after all. Fetter[3] made a mistake, or somebody made a mistake, for he got it into his head that he was to speak March 11th, instead of February 11th, as per enclosed syllabus. I have to speak in Alameda to-night—"Question of the Maximum." Might as well work it for all there is in it, before it is published.

Am thinking about moving—getting cramped in my present quarters; but O the turmoil and confusion and time lost during such an operation!

Freda and Mrs. Eppingwell have fought it out, and I have just reached the climax of the scene with Floyd Vanderlip in Freda's cabin. I did not treat it in the way I suggested. Instead of her wasting a sacredly shameful experience upon a man of his stamp, I had her appeal to him sensuously (I think it handled it all right). So the conclusion of the story is only about a day away from now. Then hurrah for the East—if McClure accepts it it will mean about one hundred and eighty dols.[4] He (McClure) sent me a photograph, large and framed, yesterday, and when I could find no free place upon my walls to hang it, I decided to perambulate. Almost wish a fire would come along and burn me out. It would be quicker, you know.

Will write you better next time. Am in a rush. And next week see if you and I can arrange a meeting. Let's hear from you soon.

Hastily.

Jack London

MS: CU; 2 pp., typs. (Strunsky). Pbd: *L*, 103; *BJL*, I, 335–36.

    1. Frederick Ridgley Torrence, *The House of the Hundred Lights* (1900), a poem of one hundred quatrains.

    2. See JL to Johns, April 22, 1899, n. 10.

    3. Probably a fellow socialist in the Bay Area.

    4. Freda Moloof, Mrs. Eppingwell, and Floyd Vanderlip are characters in "The Scorn of Woman," *Overland Monthly*, May 1901, included in *The God of His Fathers* as "The Scorn of Women." Freda Moloof, "The Turkish Whirlwind Danseuse," was a real belly dancer in Dawson, Alaska. Despite the hopes JL expressed here, *McClure's* did not accept the story, and the *Overland Monthly* paid only $20.

To Anna Strunsky

[Oakland]

[? March 16, 1900]

Dear Anna—

Have just finished reading "Gadfly."—that is, yesterday; and spent the night weeping and moaning in my sleep. Seeking the cause gave no trouble.

Say, when you come over to see us, would you mind bringing along that box of my efforts which you have? And in the meantime would it be too much bother to ask you to mail me that letter I received from some lad in Washington. I have not yet answered it, and I have not the boy's address; while I think it is time that I did.

And further, when you come make arrangements so that you can stop to dinner. I can see you to the train; and from there to your door will be safe traveling. And let us know in advance when you are coming, else most likely we will be engaged elsewhere and so have the pain of missing you.

Most hastily,

Jack London.

P.S. I often think about you and your project, though, what of the Ex's.[1] I suppose it's too early to ask after what you may have done.

J.G.L.

MS: CSmH; 1 p., tls.

    1. The University of California examinations.

To Anna Strunsky

962 East 16th. st.,
March 17, 1900.

Dear Anna:—

I left home this afternoon about fifteen minutes before your special delivery arrived. I returned early (8:30) and found it awaiting me. I would thoroughly have enjoyed going, and strangest to say and best to say, I had the evening to myself and could have just as well as not.

So be it,
Jack London.

MS: CSmH; 1 p., tls.

To Cloudesley Johns

962 East 16th. st.,
March 24, 1900.

Dear Cloudesley:—

Am pulling out on my wheel for San Jose;[1] so pardon rush. You did not say where to send *Bab Ballads* in April.

I cannot comprehend how you so utterly misunderstood my last letter (controversially), but more anon.

I, at the eleventh hour, from a chance newspaper clipping, caught the motif for a *Black Cat* yarn. Behold, it is finished and off. How's this for a title: "The Minions of Midas"? That's what I afflicted it with. 5000 words in length. I did not write it for a first second or third prize, but for one of the minor ones. I knew what motif was necessary for a first prize *Black Cat* story, but I could not invent such a motif.

Return clippings with exception of "Creed" and clipping from *Detroit Journal*. I have taken a copy of "Creed" while the other is good for you to read[2] and yet not worth my keeping in file.

Shall be back next Tuesday 27th.

Very truly,
Jack London.

MS: CSmH; 1 p., tls. Pbd: *BJL*, I, 337.
  1. JL was going to visit the Applegarths.
  2. Originally "good for you not to read."

To Maitland L. Osborne

962 East 16th. Street,
Oakland, Cal.,
March 24, 1900.

Mr. M. L. Osborne: [1]

My Friend,—In reply to yours of March 19th, in which you kindly offer to give a review of my book and ask for data. Find herewith a couple of clippings which may be of use to you; also, I shall supplement them where I may imagine it to be essential.

Please do not be led away by the error in one of them relating to my birthplace. I was born in San Francisco and am a Californian by birth as well as residence. I was twenty-four years old last January. I lived on Californian ranches until my tenth year, when my family removed to Oakland, a city, I believe, now boasting eighty thousand inhabitants. By fits and starts I acquired a grammar school education, but rough life always called to me, my whole ancestry was nomadic (its destiny being apparently to multiply and spread over the earth), so at fifteen I, too, struck out into the world. I did not run away. My people knew the strain in the blood, so I went with consent. I first went faring amongst the scum marine population of San Francisco Bay, where I got a most adventurous experience, and one (like all the rest) which I have never regretted. I there learned the rudiments of seamanship, handling small craft in the sternest of weather, till, the month I was seventeen, I was fitted to ship before the mast as an able seaman. Went to Japan seal-hunting on the Russian side of Bering Sea, etc. It was the longest voyage I ever took (seven months); life was too short to admit of more. But I have taken many short ones, and have served in divers forecastles, stoke-holes, etc., and am at home anywhere.

When I turned eighteen, having taken an interest in economics and sociology, I went tramping (to the manner born), throughout the United States and Canada. Since then have continued those studies, but in a more conventional and theoretical way.

I dabbled at high school, took a brief fling at the State University, but failed to complete my freshman year (not failed from a scholarly standpoint), and hurried away with the first rush into the Klondike. Have mined and camped through the Sierras and other places, etc. Never having been unwise enough to learn a trade, I have worked at all sorts of hard labor.

When in the Klondike my father died, and I returned to take charge of the family. Have never been rash enough to put out a sheet anchor in the form of a wife. But when I returned from the Klondike I resolved to make the fight of my life by making my living with my pen. This was precarious, for my assets were nil, and my liabilities legion. I was also a beginner, knew nothing of markets, methods of editors, needs, or how to furnish those needs. My literary life is thus about fourteen months old, during which time I have striven to find myself, from the writing of triolets to blank verse, and from feature articles for yellow journals to really ambitious short stories. Consequently I have turned out a vast deal of hack work. And little ambitious work. Nor have I yet been so financially situated that I could try anything long.

The Son of the Wolf, as you will discover, is a collection of short stories. These were written to supply a pressing need for cash, and were published principally in the *Overland Monthly* of San Francisco; also in *Atlantic Monthly*. Then they were collected (nine of them), and submitted successfully to Messrs. Houghton, Mifflin & Co.

These gentlemen will supply you with electrotypes of myself, I doubt not, though you may have to ask for them. The *Overland Monthly*, April, (if the article is not delayed) will probably furnish you with further data should you need it. Said article is to be written by Mrs. Ninetle Eames,[2] who knows me personally, but I do not know what she intends saying in it.

Thanking you for past and present kindnesses, I beg to remain,

Very sincerely yours,
Jack London.

SOURCE: "What Jack London Told of Himself," *Los Angeles Evening Express*, February 14, 1917.

1. Maitland Leroy Osborne, associate editor of the *National*. His "Jack London and 'The Son of the Wolf,'" a favorable review of JL's short story collection, appeared in the *National*, May 1900.

2. Ninetta Wiley Eames (1852–1942), then a writer for the *Overland Monthly*. After the death of her sister Dayelle Wiley Kittredge in 1877, Eames acted as foster mother for her niece CKL. Eames's article appeared in May 1900. See JL to Johns, March 10, 1900, n. 5.

To Ninetta Eames

962 East 16th. st.,
Oakland, Calif.,
March 26, 1900.

My dear Mrs. Eames:—

Your letter came to hand in this morning's mail, so you see, had it not been for my opportune visit, I should have failed to come last Saturday afternoon or evening. The Gods are kind. I am all ready to pull out on my wheel for San Jose as soon as I have finished this. Find herewith answers to questions.

As regards brothers and sisters, they are only half, and are of little importance, as you some day may chance to learn.[1] I do not mean that they themselves are of little importance, but insomuch as they concern me they are.

When I return from down country I shall be delighted to run out your way and to bring Mr. Whittaker along. Tell Miss Kittredge I have her *Forest Lovers* and *Tess*[2] safe and sound, and that I shall return them speedily now; also, that my enjoyment of them has been keen.

Very sincerely yours,
Jack London.

MS: CSmH; 1 p., tls.

1. Although John London, JL's stepfather, had nine children, only three, Charles, Ida, and Eliza, went to California with him; Charles died shortly after their arrival. For JL's attitude toward his siblings, see JL to M. Applegarth, November 30, 1898.

2. Thomas Hardy, *Tess of the D'Urbervilles* (1891).

To Ninetta Eames

1130 East 15th St.,
Oakland, Calif.,
April 3, 1900.

My dear Mrs. Eames:—

Must confess you have the advantage of me. I have not yet seen my book, nor can I possibly imagine what it looks like. Nor can you possibly imagine why I am going to beg off from going out to your place next Saturday. You know I do things quickly. Sunday morning, last, I had not the slightest intention of doing what I am going to do. I came down and looked over the house I was to move into[1]—that fathered the thought. I made up my mind. Sunday evening I opened transactions for a wife; by Monday evening had the affair well under way; and next Saturday morning I shall marry[2]—a Bessie Maddern, cousin to Minnie Maddern Fiske.[3] Also, on said Saturday, as soon as the thing is over with we jump out on our wheels for a three days' trip, and then back to work.

"The rash boy," I hear you say. Divers deep considerations have led me to do this thing; but I shall over-ride just one objection—that of being tied. I am already tied. Though single, I have had to support a household just the same. Should I wish to go to China the household would have to be provided for whether I had a wife or not.

As it is, I shall be steadied, and can be able to devote more time to my work. One only has one life, you know, after all, and why not live it? Besides, my heart is large, and I shall be a cleaner, wholesomer man because of a restraint being laid upon me in place of being free to drift wheresoever I listed. I am sure you will understand.

I thank you for your kind word concerning the appearance of *The Son of the Wolf*. I shall let you know when I am coming out, and now, being located, want you and yours to come and see me and mine. Will settle when I get back. Wedding is to be private.

Send announcement later.

Very sincerely yours,
Jack London.

MS: CSmH; 2 pp., tls.
    1. To escape the cramped quarters in the bungalow on 16th Street, JL had rented a seven-room, two-story house on 15th Street for himself and his family.
    2. JL married Bessie Maddern on April 7.
    3. Minnie Maddern Fiske (1865–1932), actress associated with the new dramatic realism; she starred in the New York productions of several Ibsen plays.

To Cloudesley Johns

1130 East 15th st.,
Oakland, Calif.,
April 3, 1900.

Dear Cloudesley:—

Thanks for the stamps.[1] And by the way, before I get on to more serious things, let me speak of the *Son of the Wolf*. For fear you invest in a copy if I don't, I want to tell you that I shall send you one as soon as they come to hand. There is only one advance copy on the Coast, and I haven't seen that one yet. They say it is all right.

You must be amused, lest you die. Here goes. You will observe that I have moved. Good! Next Saturday I shall be married. Better? Eh? Will send announcement of the funeral later.[2]

Jack London.

MS: CSmH; 1 p., tls. Pbd: *BJL*, I, 338.
    1. English stamps. See JL to Johns, November 21, 1899, n. 4.
    2. Johns wrote at the bottom of this letter: "My reply was:— Jesus H. Christ! Cloudesley."

To Anna Strunsky

1130 East 15th. st.,
Oakland, Calif.,
April 6, 1900.

Dear Anna:—

How glad your letter has made me.[1] It was rather sudden. I always do things that way. I have been so rushed that I have forgotten whether you were on the list of those I did write to, or did not. You see, I had several hours to devote to letter writing, started in, and part way through was called away. This is the first letter I have written since, and I do not know whether I had got to you or not.

Am going away for several days. Will write you more fully on my return. Are you in the mood, in the near future, to take advantage of that invitation to dinner Mrs. Stein[2] extended you and I? For a thousand reasons I think myself justified in making this marriage. It will not, however, interfere much with my old life or my life as I had planned it for the future. Find herewith clipping concerning my prototype, Edward Howard Griggs.[3]

In haste,
Jack London.

MS: CSmH; 1 p., tls.
1. Apparently Strunsky had written to congratulate JL on his coming marriage.
2. Probably the Mrs. M. D. Stein, 811 Pierce Street, San Francisco, noted in JL's magazine sales records.
3. Edward Howard Griggs (1868–1951), author and professor of ethics at Stanford University from 1893 to 1898. His books include *The New Humanism* (1900), *Moral Education* (1904), and *The Philosophy of Art* (1913). In referring to Griggs as his "prototype," JL is probably thinking of the career as a public lecturer Griggs started in 1899.

To Cloudesley Johns

1130 East 15th. st.,
April, 16, 1900.

Dear Cloudesley:–

Why certainly you may defer congratulations till April 7th. 1910. Permit me to felicitate you upon your last letter bar this one I am answering.[1] We all had a good laugh over it and enjoyed it immensely. I was away on the little wedding trip when it arrived, and my sister (you met her), looked at it and said she'd give ten dollars to see what you had to say. And it was worth it.

No, I'll not answer it. Am not laconic enough.

Find herewith clippings, which same you need not return. I am sure I never have sent them to you before. You'll enjoy the one on Stevenson.

Say, I've been watching anxiously for the beginning of the end of that mighty empire "Great Britain," but somehow the signs don't seem favorable yet.[2] What's gone wrong with your prophecy machine anyway? Fire your weather clerk and hire me. I'm more reliable. Even though my prophecies do not suit the popular majority.

Got settled down to work to-day, and did the first thousand words in three weeks, and hereafter the old rate must continue. Say, A year ago I wrote a two thousand word skit or storiette called "Their Alcove." First, second, and third raters refused out of hand. Sent it to the *Woman's Home Companion*,[3] and without a word of warning, and in quick time, came back an acceptance accompanied by a twenty dollar check. Most took my breath away. Did you ever try them with any of your work?

Will write you better next time, now that I am at last settled down. Until then, or rather, until I hear from you,

Most cordially yours,
Jack London.

MS: CSmH; 2 pp., tls. Pbd: *BJL*, I, 341.
1. On April 12, 1900, Johns wrote JL (CSmH): "May I defer my congratulations of you and Mrs. Jack for ten years? Then I shall hope to tender them—Thursday, April 7th, 1910. Don't forget: try to expect them." For his earlier response, see JL to Johns, April 3, 1900, n. 3.
2. On March 13 the British troops had captured the Boer stronghold at Blomfontein. There were no other major developments in the war until May 31. See JL to Johns, May 26, 1900, n. 1.

3. *Woman's Home Companion*, a monthly magazine published from 1874 until 1957, was originally intended to appeal to a female readership, featuring articles on fashion, food, and housekeeping. When Arthur T. Vance became editor in 1900, he broadened the appeal of the magazine by including illustrations, fiction, and articles on public affairs.

To Anna Strunsky

1130 East 15th. st.,
April 16, 1900.

Dear Anna:–

Well, I'm back and just going through the process of getting things in shape and settling down to work. I have to speak next Friday in San Jose, and am tangled up for Sunday, but may I see you some evening the latter part of next week, say Thursday evening April 26 or Friday evening April 27th.? Saturday day is engaged with the Ebell,[1] or I would suggest that—no, you go home on Saturdays do you not?

Also, Mrs. Jack, as well as myself, wishes to thank you for your most kind letter of some time since, which same I do not remember whether I replied to or not.[2]

Got in my first day's work to-day—the first in three weeks, and have done my full stint of 1000 words. Am I not virtuous?

Very sincerely yours,
Jack London.

MS: CSmH; 1 p., tls.
1. The Ebell Club, a women's organization in Oakland that had a book section for discussing literature. The address JL delivered on April 28 was entitled "Methods of Literary Workers."
2. See JL to Strunsky, April 6, 1900.

To Cloudesley Johns

1130 East 15th. st.,
May 2, 1900.

Dear Cloudesley:–

I enjoyed your annotations of Paltry Bungler's article, which, of course, I could not consider seriously as a whole. At the same time I must confess that you did strike some true notes. As for Poultney Biglow's article, my opinion of which you asked, I can say that I thought it very good and very honest.[1] I don't believe the man was a hypocrite when he wrote it, and further, It is known that he has been well over the ground he writes about. I thought he was very moderate and quite just, while, naturally, I could not agree with him utterly.

"The White Silence seemed to sneer"[2]—no, I hardly think I find such things complete; they are more thought out. However, to a certain extent their genesis is swayed by the mood of the story or the mood of the setting or the mood of the man, which, certainly, I must also be feeling at the time of writing. No; at the moment I get a good phrase I am not thinking of how much it will fetch in the market, but when I sit down to write I am; and all the time I am writing, deep down, underneath the whole business, is that same commercial spirit. I don't think I would write very much if I didn't have to.

You seem to think that if Russia and England played the Kilkenny cat act,[3] there would be peace in the world and all would be well with us. If that should happen, it would be quickly emulated in part by continental Europe, in so far that the United States would be the cat. But it is not going to happen. You dear Anglophobist, study the statistics of import and export, and find out what country we rely upon mainly for our foreign trade. And tell me what would happen to us were that market destroyed by Russia or any other combination of world powers. Don't allow fancies or prejudices to run away with your thinking apparatus until you have laid the proper economic basis. You will find that economics, not ethics, plays one of the strongest leading parts in the drama of the races.

What the hell did the *New York Press*[4] want all rights for anyway? Am glad you made them come down. I am still waiting pay on the Pleasure of Vance of the *Home*.[5] What pay did you say he gave you for that story of yours which he published long ago? "Zebro"?

That was a pretty muddle you got yourself into by forgetting that most laconic of letters you wrote me on receipt of news of my intended marriage. I must confess, I, too, was muddled, for one or two letters to come, till you finally straightened yourself out. Ted[6] wanted to know what you would say; so I sent said letter on to him.

Am busy, so will have to quit. Have to speak to-night in 'Frisco, and I am not yet prepared. Also, now that the book is out, have been racing around a good deal in order to do my best for it locally. You understand. Business, you know.

                                                              Jack London.

Please return "Poor Old Kentucky"— Did I return you your war clippings you loaned me?

MS: CSmH; 2 pp., tls. Pbd: *L*, 104.

1. Poultney Bigelow (1855–1954), lawyer, historian, editor of *Outing Magazine* from 1886 to 1888, and correspondent for *The Times* (London) during the Spanish-American War. In 1900 he was writing articles on aspects of America's presence in the Far East for *Harper's Monthly* and on the Boer War for *The Independent*. JL may refer to his "Kruger and Steyn," *The Independent*, April 12, 1900, which contrasts Kruger's boorish personal habits and "narrow and uneducated mind" with the qualities demonstrated by Martin Steyn, President of the Orange Free State: "shrewd, deliberate, clean, in good taste." Bigelow concluded: "Kruger is a noble soul, but he has lived two hundred years beyond his time. . . . Today, however, he is the representative of a hopeless cause, a dead issue. . . . Kruger's gone—but Steyn is alive in flesh, blood and spirit."

2. JL quotes from the concluding sentences of "The White Silence": "The White Silence seemed to sneer, and a great fear came upon him. There was a sharp report; Mason swung into his aerial sepulchre; and Malemute Kid lashed the dogs into a wild gallop as he fled across the snow."

3. According to legend, the Kilkenny Cats fought together to the death.

4. The *New York Press*, a daily newspaper published from 1887 until 1916, had probably just accepted Johns's story "The Rocks"; see JL to Johns, August 18, 1900.

5. Arthur Turner Vance (1872–1930), editor of *Home Magazine* from 1898 to 1900 and of the *Woman's Home Companion* from 1900 to 1907. JL was awaiting payment for "Through the Rapids on the Way to Klondike," *Home Magazine*, June 1899.

6. Ted Applegarth.

To Anna Strunsky

1130 East 15th. st.,
Oakland, Calif.,
May 2, 1900.

Dear Anna:—

How sorry I am! Friday I am chairman at the Ruskin Club dinner and cannot possibly escape.[1] Thursday I speak in 'Frisco, and Saturday am bound out to dinner. So there! However, may I put you down for afternoon and dinner on Wednsday, May 9th.? Write and let me know if this is convenient.

How enthusiastic your letters always make me feel. Makes it seem as though some new energy had been projected into the world and that I cannot fail gathering part of it to myself. No; God does not punish confidence; but he grinds between the upper and the nether millstone all those of little faith and little heart, and he grinds them very fine. Of course you will succeed—if you will work—and certainly you seem to suffer from a superabundance of energy. Apply this energy, rightly and steadily, and the world will open its arms to you. You are all right; the world is all right; the question is: will you have the patience to gain the ear of the world. You will have to shout loud, for the world is rather deaf, and you may have to shout long. But the world sometimes opens its ears at the first call. May it be thus with you.

Jack.

MS: CSmH; 1 p., tls. Pbd: *BJL.*, I, 341–42.

1. The Ruskin Club, begun on December 9, 1898, at Maison de L'Opera in Oakland, was a group of Bay Area intellectuals, most having socialistic leanings, who met to discuss economic and political topics. The club was founded by Frederick I. Bamford, Austin Lewis, and A. A. Denison; JL was a charter member.

To Cornelius Gepfert

1130 East 15th. st.,
Oakland, Calif.,
May 5, 1900.

Dear Con:—[1]

You must pardon my long delay in answering yours of March 12th., but I have had a lot of public speaking to do; also have been busy moving, and to top it all off, have just been getting married and taking a honeymoon. There! I know you will forgive it all now.

Need I say how surprised I was to hear from you? I think not. But there was no reason for you to have given me all the details in order for me to identify you. "Con" would have been sufficient.

Do you remember a young fellow at Stuart River—Mason? I have been corresponding with him for some time; and I now owe him a two month letter. Also, in the cabin back of the one you and Rett occupied,[2] you will remember there were some Swedes and Norwegians. One of them, Emil Jensen, is in San Francisco, and occasionally comes over to see me. I stopped with him in Dawson before I went down the river.

You ask after Thompson[3]—the last I heard of him he was still in the Klondike, with wilder schemes than ever in his head, and smoking good cigars while doing nothing. Sloper,[4] the carpenter, came out the summer you and I did, but a little later. As soon as he arrived in 'Frisco, his wife instituted divorce (he came out broke), and I was present as a witness throughout the trial. She got left.

Thank you for your solicitude concerning my teeth—I have had three sets since I came out, and broken two of them. The present one seems very good. Makes quite a difference in a fellow, a set of teeth.[5]

Let us hear from you again, and what you are doing, and if you plan any more adventures into the "new and naked lands"?[6] Have you read my book *The Son of the Wolf*? They are all Klondike Stories, collected, and I am busy wondering how the Klondikers, who know all about it, will take them. If you read them, tell me what you think of them, and don't be chary of whatever adverse criticism comes into your mind. You see, I have had to take liberties, and to idealize, etc. etc. for the sake of the artistic effect, and often from the inherent need of the tales themselves, and for their literary value.

Do you remember John Thorson—one of the crowd that went with me to Dawson in the fall of the year on the last water? He's up in Eastern Oregon, cashier of a bank, and I have corresponded somewhat with him.

Well, let's hear from you again, and I promise I shall not be so long in replying another time,

Most cordially yours,
Jack London.

MS: CU; photocopy of 2 pp., tls.
1. Cornelius M. Gepfert, a Klondike friend of JL's at Stewart River who returned to the Yukon to prospect for gold.
2. JL ran Rett's boat through the White Horse Rapids en route to the Klondike. Rett and his wife subsequently lived in a cabin near JL on the Stewart River.
3. Fred Thompson.
4. Merritt Sloper.
5. See JL to Johns, February 22, 1899.
6. Rudyard Kipling, "The Sea-Wife," in which the fifth stanza runs "The good wife's sons come home again / With little into their hands, / But the lore of men that have dealt with men / In the new and naked lands."

To Cloudesley Johns

1130 East 15th. st.,
May 26, 1900.

Dear Cloudesley:—

O Well, if you think the United States can stand alone against the rest of the world (commercially and politically), why I can't convince you otherwise What do you think of the Boers now?[1] Do you see any further signs of disintegration in the British Empire? Why did not hostile Europe attack England in her bad hour? There's a few nuts to crack.

But a truce to funning. I got a ten dollar check from the *Home Magazine* the other day,[2] and a request for more Ms. and a promise of greater promptitude on their part. I guess not. I dunned them a dozen times or so.

As regards the clipping concerning the Texas Pagan, I merely sent it to show you in what esteem such rabid tomfoolery *Truthseeker* rot was regarded by the average man. The critic was the average man. Not that I won't acknowledge good stuff sometimes gets into the *Truthseeker*, but that such stuff is like a lamb lying down with the raging roaring ramping lions. It only gets there by mistake. Again, the *Truthseeker* may do some good for lower minds, but I am sure you have no place in its columns and that it should have no place on your table. The person who tolerates such stuff simply lacks in perspective and should be pitied for shortsightedness and not condemned for his sins, as the Texas Pagan was by the critic who was an average man. The Critic also lacked perspective, but not so much as the Pagan.[3]

Where you missed in "Betsy" was the too large portion which you allotted to men. The human element was to great and too strong for one to get in sympathy with the machine. Who could think of Betsy when the engineer lay on his back in the cactus? Don't you see? Toward the very end, after the men leap off and Betsy goes on the bridge alone, you begin to strike it, but you began too late. In a case like that the human must be eliminated, or as little used as possible. Am I right?

What prophecy was it, concerning yours truly, in *The Land of Sunshine*, which you did not think would be fulfilled?—the immaturity of Saxonism which was only an immaturity and might be expected to pass away because of that? Or what was it?[4]

Never mind sending back "Kentucky." I have since raked up another copy of it.

O, I received a very nice letter the other day from Charles Warren Stoddard, in which he mentioned you, also that you had written him about me.[5] He writes a crisp letter, doesn't he?

Am glad you have been enjoying yourself. Hope to be doing so myself before long, if only the dollars would come in. There I go, eh?—Commercialism.

Send enclosed clippings back, please, when you are done with them.

Jack London.

MS: CSmH; 2 pp., tls.

1. On May 3 Field Marshal Lord Roberts and the British troops began their march on Pretoria from Blomfontein. On May 31 they entered Johannesburg, and on June 5 they captured Pretoria. Roberts formally declared the Transvaal a British colony on September 1.

2. JL received payment for "Through the Rapids on the Way to Klondike" on May 14.

3. An untitled notice in *Truth Seeker*, May 12, 1900, announced: "The latest thing in Freethought literature from America is 'Sinai' and 'Olympus' by a Texas pagan, a series of 'Parallels in Heathen Thought and Hebrew Scripture.' The book is in a rather jocular vein throughout, which will make it interesting reading to 'the man in the street.'"

4. Two articles by Charles F. Lummis in the May 1900 issue of the *Land of Sunshine* discussed JL and *The Son of the Wolf*: "In Western Letters" praised the stories in this collection as "strong, elemental, and unusually well poised." He added: "Here and there is a crudity; and the general keynote of the conqueringness of the Saxon savors a whit of youth—an immaturity, however, shared by many whose heads are grey, outside at least. But the general grip and swing of things . . . are fine and muscular, and not at all unbearded. For a first book, it seems to me one of very direct promise." Later in the same issue there was a briefer notice of *The Son of the Wolf* in the column "That Which Is Written"; here Lummis wrote that the stories in this collection are "sure to take hold upon anyone with the real breath of life in him," and "the young Oaklander has every right to be proud of them."

5. Charles Warren Stoddard (1843–1909), a California poet, editor, and author of travel narratives. After journeying to Hawaii and Tahiti, he wrote *South-Sea Idylls* (1873), *Hawaiian Life* (1894), and *The Lepers of Molokai* (1885); JL borrowed the last title for an article in *Woman's Home Companion*, January 1908. From 1889 to 1902 Stoddard was professor of English at the Catholic University of America. He probably met Johns while a guest at Eagleswood, the estate of Johns's grandfather.

To Anna Strunsky

[Oakland]
[? May 1900]

Dear Anna:—

Just a line in haste. I have dispatched your story to Bliss Perry,[1] accompanied by a personal letter. Do not expect to hear from it inside a month or six weeks. And do not expect it to be accepted—the *Atlantic* is the most finicky fastidious magazine published. But the judgement of Bliss Perry is what is wanted—and not his judgement concerning that particular story so much, as his judgement concerning you, your capabilities, and your promise. Understand? When it comes back, I wish to have a try with it at Hamilton Wright Mabie, who is editor of the *Outlook*, and who occupies a foremost place in American letters[2]—but for his personal opinion, not for publication. Of course, should they wish it for publication, all the better. But don't expect it. Besides, what a miracle it would be, a first effort accepted.

Mr. Whittaker has had a story accepted by the *Overland*, which I consider very encouraging.[3] But let me tell you that anything you write would be accepted by the *Overland*, and further, that I wish you to fly your kite far higher than that.

O Anna, don't disappoint me. You have got everything; all you need is to work and work, and to work with the greatest care. Go ahead. Am very glad you have started another story, and I cannot down my impatience or curiosity concerning its motif or location. Also, read you the latest best fiction to get well in hand the modern touch—and all the various little tricks and diversities of style. And also, you, go ahead and master the typewriter so that you can turn out neat, clean, manuscript for yourself. If you can, type next story before you bring it over to me. That will be practice on the machine, and will also make our common task of revision much easier.

Whoever retyped your Ms. which I have sent off, did it well. It was a pleasure to run over it—economy, you know. Typographical errors use up much of the reader's energy, which otherwise would be spent upon the thought itself.

Find herewith a letter concerning the "Gadfly." I know you will like it, so I take the liberty of sending it.

I may drop in on you Saturday night, and then again I mayn't—it all depends if I go to 'Frisco on that day. And I should go.

McClure's have accepted "Grit o' Women," and "The Law of Life."[4]

Most hastily,
Jack London.

P.S.—Need I say I should like to see a certain letter, eliminating ten years, however; or better, hear its contents by word of mouth?
P.S.—In your work, don't let anything which jars your ear, pass you. Get it harmonious then.

J.L.

MS: CSmH; 2 pp., tls.
1. Bliss Perry (1860–1954), editor of the *Atlantic Monthly* from 1899 to 1909; later professor of English at Williams College, Princeton, and Harvard.

2. Hamilton Wright Mabie (1845–1916), literary critic and, from 1884 to 1916, associate editor of the *Outlook*, a monthly magazine published from 1870 until 1935, which featured articles on religion, public affairs, and arts and letters.

3. "A Tale of the Pasquia Post," *Overland Monthly*, July 1900.

4. "Grit of Women," *McClure's*, August 1900, later included in *The God of His Fathers*; "The Law of Life," *McClure's*, March 1901, later included in *Children of the Frost* (New York: Macmillan, 1902).

To Cloudesley Johns

1130 East 15th. st.,
June 2, 1900.

Dear Cloudesley:—

What do you think of the Boers now? Do you remember their brags that they and their women would die in the last ditch? That they would blow up Johannesburg? Destroy Pretoria? Make a howling desolation of the Transvaal before they were conquered? Do you remember these brags? And if so, what do you think of them now. And how do you incline concerning Ambrose Bierce's statement that the Boers were a warlike people but not a military people.[1] That they had failed in every siege they had attempted. That, were they actually besieged in Pretoria, the British engineering ability alone would have crushed and defeated them. Do you think this so, or not?

Now, Cloudesley, I not only grant, but have sung the praises of the Boers—at least the potential praises. They are strong, most strong. Theirs is the strength of good stock which is stuck close to the soil. There are no one, or two, or three removes among them. They are all close to the soil. They are potentially strong. Three or four generations more, and they will be splendid people. But they are a handful and will be swallowed up—as I have contended all along. A century from now their children's children will unite (they'll be mixed well anyway), with the sons sons of the present Tommy's to conquer more of the world for the Anglo-Saxons. And were they to-day a hundred millions instead of a few paltry thousands, why there would be a problem for the world and the Saxon, greater than the Slav. But, unhappilly (for your sake and theirs) they are very small and quite lost in the vast centralizing forces now at work in society.

You say you do see further signs of the disintegration of the British Empire—please tell me those signs.

As regards the *Truthseeker*—I stated that some good stuff did stray into it, but that it was like a lamb lying down with the lions, or like a saint among sinners. And further, a person who is capable of doing good stuff should not wander into such bad, narrow-sighted, fanatical, flat-headed company. They do do it, but they must not expect praise for it.

Never mind the Texas Pagan—my standpoint stands none the less, and I am sure you must have grasped it—what I said about lack of perspective, not being broad-minded, not understanding the laws of social evolution, etc. There are some people, lamentably, who never will understand, who never will get perspective, but that is no reason that those who have the capacity should not develop it and get a better comprehension of life.

Have you heard anything from the *Black Cat* yet? A fellow I know in 'Frisco was informed by them two weeks ago that he was in the charmed circle—when they wrote him concerning his status and asking if his idea, story, etc, was original in whole and part, and unpublished. I, however, have not heard from them, so am looking for Ms. to come back.[2]

Have sold a couple of hundred more dollars worth of good stuff to *McClure's*—at least I think it is good—"The Grit of Women," and "The Law of Life."[3]

Got the proofsheets of A *S.F. Examiner* story in and am correcting them. Probably be published in a Sunday or so. Story, "Which Make Men Remember."[4] If you run across it, tell us what you think of it. It's a newspaper story and maybe a little more.

Ted's grandmother died the other day and was brought up to Oakland for interment. They stopped over night with me afterward.

So! I am married, and I cannot start to Paris in July,[5] dough or no dough—That's why I got married.

But none the less I heartily envy you your trip. I'm think mabbe I'll take a vacation on the road this summer just for ducks and to gather material, or rather, to freshen up what I have long since accreted.—how would you judge of my use of that last word?

Smart Set?[6] I may go in for one of the lesser prizes. Can't tell yet. *Outing* has asked a bunch of Northland stories of me and I am busy hammering away at them just now.[7]

I should like to look over your "Philosophy of the Road," of which you say you have 17000 words done.[8] Could you possibly send me up a few sheets of it. The subject is a fascinating one, isn't it.

Jack London.

MS: CSmH; 3 pp., tls.

1. Probably a reference to Bierce's column "The Passing Show," *San Francisco Examiner*, May 27, 1900. In it Bierce claimed that the British had superior numbers and material resources but were not superior in courage and enterprise; the Boers, he said, were good fighters but not good tacticians.

2. "The Minions of Midas."

3. *McClure's* paid JL $300 for these stories.

4. In the *Sunday Examiner Magazine*, June 24, 1900, the story was entitled "Uri Bram's God"; it appeared as "Which Make Men Remember" in *The God of His Fathers*.

5. For the Exposition.

6. *Smart Set* was a monthly literary magazine published from 1900 until 1930. To encourage contributors, Col. William D'Alton Mann, the publisher, offered prizes for novels, short stories, poems, sketches, and jokes.

7. "Jan, the Unrepentent," *Outing*, August 1900; "Where the Trail Forks," *Outing*, December 1900. Both stories were also included in *The God of His Fathers*. *Outing*, published from 1882 until 1923, was a monthly magazine that featured articles on recreation and sports but also included some fiction and poetry. JL also submitted "Housekeeping in the Klondike" and "Siwash" to *Outing*, but neither was accepted by that magazine.

8. Presumably a study of tramping, an experience with which Johns was familiar.

To Ida M. Strobridge

1130 East 15th. st.,
Oakland, Calif.,
June 2, 1900.

Dear Idah M.:—[1]

You will pardon my way of address, I am sure, but I am poor at reading handwriting, and further, last night an obstinate chunk of kindling hit me in the eye and well nigh closed it, so that I really cannot at present make out your name. Also, I do not know your status—which side, wrong or right, of matrimony you are on.

So, dear Idah M., I wish to thank you for your kind letter, also Mr. Elwyn Hoffman[2] for his postscript. I think you were both right in your argument. Surely one cannot help appreciating the friends he makes through the printed page, nor hailing them with delight. I do not know much of your country, though I once beat my way up to Reno to the state fair when I was a boy, and later, I tramped through on my way east. If you lived along the railroad then I may have slammed your back gate in search of breakfast—in some of those little greasewood sagebrush towns I am sure I slammed every gate [before] my stomach or I called quits. I remember bunking three days in the round house at Winnemucca, and I pushed coal for the fireman to Carlin. How do you people manage to live up there? I have often marvelled over that point. And if you do scratch a living, how then do you then manage to exist? Or, are there little valleys and secluded nooks way off from the railway where Nature smiles just a wee little bit?

"Lassen Meadows" sounds all right.

Thanking you all for your kindness, I am,

Most Cordially
Jack London.

MS: CSmH; 1 p., typs.

1. Ida Meacham Strobridge (1855–1932), a writer of Western local-color stories who was born near Oakland. She apparently lived near Reno at this time, but later moved to the Arroyo Seco art colony in Pasadena, where she operated the Artemesia Bindery. In addition to stories in *Land of Sunshine*, Strobridge published three books: *In Miner's Mirage-Land* (1904), *The Loom of the Desert* (1907), and *The Land of the Purple Shadows* (1909).

2. Elwyn Irving Hoffman (?1870–?1949), San Francisco writer. Hoffman published most of his work in California newspapers and magazines.

To Cloudesley Johns

1130 East 15th. st.,
Oakland, Calif.,
June 16, 1900.

Dear Cloudesley:—

To commence with, you do me wrong. When you asked if I thought you could do the "Philosophy of the Road," I had no idea of what it was to be, that is, how it was to be treated, and so, did not have the slightest idea concerning whether you could do it or not. Further, when I wrote you, I overlooked that query—that was all. Had I remembered I would have spoken as I have spoken at the head of this paragraph. I do take a little of it back. I did think at the time that by experience you certainly were fitted for it.

It is a fascinating subject. It has itched me for long, and it is often all I can do to keep away from writing on it. However, I have been and am still laying aside notes on it,[1] so that, some day, saturating myself with the life again, I will go ahead. But as you say, it is infinite.

But Cloudesley, do you think you are handling it just right? I don't forget that they were written for "Stories and Sketches of the Road," nor that you say they will have to be re-written; but still I ask, are you going about it right. You are treating it in much the manner Wyckoff treated the *Workers East and West*.[2] But he treated it scientifically, and empirically scientifically, if I may use the phrase. And for that matter, he dealt more with the workers than with the tramps; but the method of treatment still applies. As it seems to me, you are to dry. You are not, from your choice of subjects or topics, treating it as he treated it. Therefore your style should be different. You are handling stirring life, romance, things of human life and death, humor and pathos, etc. But God, man, handle them as they should be. Don't you tell the reader the philosophy of the road (except where you are actually there as participant in the first person). Don't you tell the reader. Don't. Don't. Don't. But HAVE YOUR CHARACTERS TELL IT BY THEIR DEEDS, ACTIONS, TALK, ETC. Then, and not until then, are you writing fiction and not a sociological paper upon a certain sub-stratum of society.

And get the atmosphere. Get the breadth and thickness to your stories, and not only the length (which is the mere narration). The reader, since it is fiction, doesn't want your dissertations on the subject, your observations, your knowledge as your knowledge, your thoughts about it, your ideas—BUT PUT ALL THOSE THINGS WHICH ARE YOURS INTO THE STORIES, INTO THE TALES, ELIMINATING YOURSELF (except when in the first person as participant). AND THIS WILL BE THE ATMOSPHERE. AND THIS ATMOSPHERE WILL BE YOU, DON'T YOU UNDERSTAND, YOU! YOU! YOU! And for this, and for this only, will the critics praise you, and the public appreciate you, and your work be art. In short, you will then be the artist; do not do it, and you will be the artisan. That's where all the difference comes in. Study your detestable Kipling; study your Beloved's[3] *Ebb Tide*. Study them and see how they eliminate themselves and create things that live, and breathe, and grip men, and cause reading lamps to burn overtime. Atmosphere stands always for the elimination of the artist, that is to say, the atmosphere is the artist; and when there is no atmosphere and the artist is yet there, it simply means that the machinery is creaking and that the reader hears it.

And get your good strong phrases, fresh, and vivid. And write intensively, not exhaustively or lengthily. Don't narrate—paint! draw! build!—CREATE! Better one thousand words which are builded, than a whole book of mediocre, spun-out, dashed-off stuff.

Think it over and see if you catch what I am driving at. Of course, if you intend what I have called a scientific paper, then don't do anything of these things I have suggested. They would be out of place. But if you intend fiction, then write fiction from the highest standpoint of fiction. Don't be so damnably specific, adding dry detail to dry detail. Put in life, and movement—and for God's sake no creaking. Damn you! Forget you! And then the world will remember you. But if you don't damn you, and don't forget you, then the world will close its ears to you. Pour all yourself into your work until your work becomes you, but no where let yourself be apparent. When, in the *Ebb Tide*, the schooner is at the pearl island, and the missionary pearler meets those three desperate men and puts his will against theirs for life or death, does the reader think of Stevenson? Does the reader have one thought of the writer? Nay, nay. Afterwards, when all is over, he recollects, and wonders, and loves Stevenson—but at the time? Not he.

Do the wheels in Shakespeare creak? When Hamlet soliloquizes, does the reader think at the time that it is Shakespeare? But afterwards, ah afterwards, and then he says, "Great is Shakespeare!"

Do you see what I mean? Now please don't fall upon what I have written in spirit other than with which it was written. I've hammered it out hastily, and not done it justice, I know, but it has all been sincere.

I can't speak of the good points in the Mss., for I have devoted my space to generalities. But you show a good grasp of psychology, which will or should be a wonderful aid when you get the right method. But I can't go into that. Haven't time. Have to get ready to go out and want to get this off first.

However, let me thank you for sending me the Mss.

I shall not answer the rest of your short letter, though I appreciated it all and would like to.

Jack London.

MS: CSmH; 4 pp., tls. Pbd: *L*, 107–9; *BJL*, I, 343; *Mentor*, 15–17.
    1. Later used as the basis for *The Road*.
    2. Walter Augustus Wyckoff (1865–1908), professor of sociology at Princeton; *The Workers: An Experiment in Reality*, in two vols., *The East* (1897) and *The West* (1898). To learn firsthand about the life of the unskilled worker, Wyckoff, posing as a common laborer, traveled from Connecticut to California between 1891 and 1893. *The Workers*, his account of his observations, was considered an important contribution to the sociological literature; its realistic reports of the conditions of workers' lives also increased public awareness of the need for more adequate welfare programs.
    3. Robert Louis Stevenson.

To Ida M. Strobridge and Elwyn Hoffman

1130 East 15th street,
Oakland, Calif.
June 17th., 1900.

Dear Idah:–

I certainly may, since I am safely married and you are several years my senior; and yet further, because you live in Nevada.

Why Kansas should come in for so much opprobrium (I know I've mis spelled it!) while Nevada is on the map, I cannot see. Probably, I suppose, because nobody knows anything about its existence.

There, there! I'm hammering it into Nevada because I haven't had my vacation yet, and must have my fling at anything that smacks of large airs and great spaces—whereof Nevada certainly excels.

How I envy you up in your mountain camp on your rawhide bed, dating letters "Wednesday, 'bout 3 o'clock," and raising your doubts to Allah as to when they may be posted.

So your star became a milky way, eh? And I hope it turns into a whole sidereal system before you are done with it. Then you shall pull up stakes and trek from your lofty kopje down here, or most anywhere else to God's country.

When you talk of your saddle horse it makes me pine for the day when I am to learn to ride. For, do you know, I haven't the slightest knowledge of horses, yet think I would take to them immensely. I once journeyed to Yosemite Valley, accompanying a camping party in wagons—myself on horse most of the way. And in the Valley had several weeks of trail work with horses, but it was all so short, and so good, that I have forgotten all about them, and would now approach one much in the way a summer tourist does a cow.

To make up for them, however, I bike. Ever bike? Now that's something that makes life worth living! I take exercise every afternoon that way. O, to just grip your handle bars, and lay down to it (*lie* doesn't hit it at all), and go ripping and tearing through streets and roads, over railroad tracks and bridges, threading crowds, avoiding collisions, at twenty miles or more an hour, and wondering all the time when you're going to smash up—well, now, that's something. And then home again after three hours of it, into the tub, rub down well, then into a soft shirt, and down to the dinner table, with the evening paper and a cigarette in prospect—and then to think that tomorrow I can do it all over again! Doesn't it almost compensate for a vacation?

I see you have a cosmopolitan nature akin to mine. And that's the only kind of a nature to have in this good old world. The rut—the well-greased groove—bah! Have breadth and thickness, as well as length to one's life!

And you hail from near Oakland. No; from "the valley over the hills from Oakland." Livermore? Sacramento? San Joaquin? I've been somewhat over all of them.

Tell me; is the Humboldt House between Wadsworth and Winnemucca? If so, I was put off there one midnight, from the Overland, and pulled out half an hour later on a fast freight.[1]

I happened to mention that I was married. Now, you refuse to 'fess up, till you know my views as to which is the wrong side and which the right of matrimony. Can't you guess now? Or does the statement of my condition render my point of view more doubtful? How is it anyway?

Dear Elwyn Hoffman:

Say; she said to ask you if she wasn't old enough to be my grandmother at least; if not my great-grandmother. Now, I don't believe it. And I won't; even if you back her up. So you'd better be square.

You spoke of stacks of unfinished MSS. Let me tell you how I write. In the first place I never begin a thing, but what I finish it *before* I begin anything else. Further; I type as fast as I write, so that each day sees the work all upon the final MS. which goes for editorial submission. And *on* the day I finish the MS. I fold it up and send it off without once going back to see what all the previous pages were like. So, in fact, when a page is done, that is the last I see of it till it comes out in print. Of course, sometimes I have to hunt back for the spelling of the name of some character, or for just how an incident occurred; but otherwise I don't go back. I think it pays.

So you were on the *Vancouver World*! I tramped through Vancouver in '94, and spent several weeks there. And finally worked my passage out of there and down the coast on the *Umatilla*.[2] Remember her? I always liked Vancouver. I was never given a handout there in all the time I slammed back gates—always was "set down" to tables. I was only refused twice, and both times because I came out of meal hours. And, further, at each of said places I was given a quarter of a dollar to make up for the refusal. Fine town! Eh? What do you think? Though I suppose the tramps have since worked it out pretty well.

No; I'm damned if my stories just come to me. I had to work like the devil for the themes. Then, of course, it was easy to just write them down. Expression, you see—with me—is far easier than invention. It is with the latter I have the greatest trouble, and work the hardest. To find some thought worthy of being clothed with enough verbiage to make it a story, there's the rub!

I have a dozen fields I'd like to tackle. Fascinating ones, and practically virgin; but I am afraid I shall have to stick to the Northland for some time yet.

Say! Idah Meacham Strobridge said in a previous letter that you made poetry. If you happen to have clipped poems, would it be asking too much to give me a glance at them? You see, I know very little about periodical literature—I have been away so much; and, when at home, am so busy.

Thanking you both for your kindness and good wishes, believe me, sincerely yours,

Jack London.

ms: CSmH; 4 pp., typs.
    1. See JL's "Hoboes That Pass in the Night," *Cosmopolitan*, December 1907; later included in *The Road*.
    2. In 1894 JL worked his way back to San Francisco from Vancouver as a coal stoker on the Pacific Steamship Company's *Umatilla*, the same ship on which he booked passage from San Francisco to Port Townsend, Washington, on his way to the Klondike in 1897.

To Charles Warren Stoddard

1130 East 15th. st.,
Oakland, Calif.,
June 21/00.

Dear Mr. Stoddard:–

Find here a photograph which I think the best ever taken of me—the most like, perhaps, or the most flattering. I don't know which. Am very sorry, but the photograph taken out in the hills I cannot forward to you now. The plate has been loaned to a friend who wished to experiment with it, and has not yet come back. The one I am sending you is an amateur effort, and better than any of the professional ones.

So you think "The Son of the Wolf" the best. I always considered it so as far as unity and sustained effort go, but on the whole have always thought the "Odyssey of the North" the best.

You have been down in the South Seas, haven't you?[1] That's where I've always longed to go, and somehow never made it. Have, however, been south of the Sandwich Islands and into the tropics, and taken on water at coral islands to the S.E. of Japan, but the taste I got has only served to make me hungry ever since. What a good old world this is, after all, when one is not planted like a barnacle in one place, "and can't get 'ence observin' things until 'e dies."[2]

Faithfully yours,
Jack London.

MS: ViU; 1 p., tls.
    1. As a traveling correspondent for the *San Francisco Examiner,* Stoddard lived in Hawaii from 1881 to 1884 and made two earlier trips to Hawaii and Tahiti between 1868 and 1873.
    2. Kipling, "Sestina of the Tramp-Royal," ll. 5–6: "But must get 'ence, the same as I 'ave done, / An' go observin' matters till they die."

To Anna Strunsky

Santa Cruz,
Dear Anna:—   July 3/00

I am virtuous to-day. Am writing about twenty letters in an endevor to be free for a week. So just a line.

But do you write me, & let me know how Shakespeare & "Consciousness of Kind" are getting along. Also, yourself.

Have been swimming every day, & have a glorious dose of sunburn. Find clipping herewith, apropos of our discussion at Mrs. Stein's.[1] Tell me what you think of it.

                                                                Jack London.

Forgot to enclose clipping.
Did you get your Stetson book[2] all right?

                                                                Jack London.

MS: CSmH; 3 pp., als.
    1. Possibly Mrs. M. D. Stein; see JL to Strunsky, April 6, 1900.
    2. Probably either *Sea Drift* (1899) or *The Fortune of the Day* (1900), books of poems by Grace Ellery Channing Stetson (1862–1937). Stetson occasionally published poetry in *Land of Sunshine.*

To Elwyn Hoffman

1130 East 15th. st.,
Oakland, Calif.,
Dear Elwyn:—   July 23/00.

You will pardon my long delay I hope. I have been away on a wandering vacation, and very little writing did I do, and very few letters were forwarded to me. I have now about fifty or sixty to answer. Yours is the twenty-third so far. And I see I owe you for two.

Many thanks for the Vancouver fotos. I was not as familiar with the place as were you, but I enjoyed your letter immensely. As did also I and some friends the selections from your poems sent to me by Idah Strobridge. We liked especially "Three Things that stir My Heart." I found I had to explain to my plains friends the "cool fresh morning breeze"—at least the one I knew up in the Sierras and also in the big foothills.

One fault I find with your work—the very thing that Idah Strobridge praises—you do not go over. Poetry is rarely written in such way. A verse which will not scan certainly needs going over. Likewise with a phrase that jars or a figure that does not ring true. You understand.

So you are expecting to migrate down this way, eh? Well, when you do, drop in and see me, though I won't have any time for running around for some time to come. Expect to devote the next five months to the writing of a novel for McClure Phillips Co. They have agreed to give me an income of One twenty-five per month till the thing is done.[1] So I've got to work.

But don't forget to look us up when you come, and if I may be of service to you in any way, please do not fail to let me know.

Must chop off, and take up letter twenty-four, which is to Idah Strobridge, and which must be likewise short. So believe me,

Faithfully yours,
Jack London.

MS: CSmH; 2 pp., tls.
1. S. S. McClure agreed to pay JL an advance against royalties of $125 per month while he wrote the novel *A Daughter of the Snows*, which McClure later sold to J. B. Lippincott Co. for publication in 1902. JL eventually worked off his debt to McClure, Phillips & Co., the publishing house McClure founded in 1899, by sending them material for publication in *McClure's Magazine* and *The God of His Fathers*. See JL to Strunsky, April 1, 1902.

To Cloudesley Johns

1130 East 15th. st.,
July 23/00.

Dear Cloudesley:—

Back from vacation at last! And hard at it. This is thirty-fifth letter. Ye Gods!

No; I did not get hold of June number of *Home Magazine*.[1] Can you forward me it? I'll return. I have, however, seen your story in *Puritan*, and I have puzzled much, yet I do not see exactly the necessity for the man's dying. Tell us what makes it seem necessary to you.[2] But anyway, I read the story hastily, riding in a rig with a party of jolly people, so I'm sure I didn't do it justice. I'll look over it to-night when I won't be interrupted.

Did I tell you McClure has bought me (as you would call it), but as I would say, has agreed to advance me one hundred and twenty-five per month for five months in order that I may try my hand at a novel? Well, it is so, and I start in shortly, though filled with dismay in anticipation.

Did you read that storiette of mine "Semper Idem; Semper Fidelis"?[3] About fifteen hundred words, dealing with a man who cut his throat, bungled it, was cautioned by the doctor at the hospital as to how he bungled it, and who went out, profited by the advice, and did it successfully? Well, I have sent it everywhere. At last sent it to *Black Cat.* I would have sold it for a dollar. But the *Black Cat* gave me a sort of poor mouth, said it had hospital stuff to last it two years, etc., and that under the circumstances it could only offer me fifty dollars for it. Say! Most took my breath away. A fifteen hundred word sketch, "The Husky," I refused to sell some time ago for $3.50, and *Harper's Weekly* bought it for twenty dollars.[4] Say, those hang fire Mss. seem the best after all.

Jack London.

MS: CSmH; 2 pp., tls. Pbd: *BJL*, I, 344.
    1. Arthur T. Vance wrote a favorable review of *The Son of the Wolf* in *Home Magazine*, June 1900. Also in this issue was Johns's "Post No. 12—a Story of the Spanish War."
    2. "The Stage Driver's Proxy." See JL to Johns, January 30, 1900, n. 5; and JL to Strunsky, February 3, 1900.
    3. "Semper Idem," *Black Cat*, December 1900, later included in *When God Laughs and Other Stories* (New York: Macmillan, 1911).
    4. See JL to Johns, March 15, 1900, n. 2.

To Anna Strunsky

1130 East 15th. st.,
July 31/00.

Dear Anna:—

Comrades! And surely it seems so. For all the petty surface turmoil which marked our coming to know each other, really, deep down, there was no confusion at all. Did you not notice it? To me, while I said "You do not understand," I none the less felt the happiness of satisfaction—how shall I say?—felt, rather, that there was no inner conflict; that we were attuned, somehow; that a real unity underlaid everything. The ship, new-launched, rushes to the sea; the sliding-ways rebel in weakling creaks and groans; but sea and ship hear them not; so with us when we rushed into each other's lives—we, the real we, were undisturbed. Comrades! Ay, world without end!

And now, comrade mine, how long are those Shakespere papers to keep you from "Consciousness of Kind"? You know how anxiously I wait the outcome, and how much you must have improved. And Anna, read your classics, but don't forget to read that which is of to-day, the new-born literary art. You must get the modern touch; form must be considered; and while art is eternal, form is born of the generations. And O, Anna, if you will only put your flashing soul with its protean moods on paper! What you need is the form, or in other words, the expression. Get this and the world is at your feet.

And when are we to read "The Flight of the Duchess"?[1] And when are you coming over?

Jack.

MS: CSmH; 1 p., tls. Pbd: *L*, 109; *BJL*, I, 344–45.
   1. Robert Browning, "The Flight of the Duchess" (1845). For JL's plans to use this title, see JL to Brett, November 21, 1902, and JL to Strunsky, December 6, 1902.

To the Editor, *New Magazine*

1130 East 15th. st.,
Oakland, Calif.,
August 4/00.

Dear sir:—
   Some time ago you asked to see some of my work. At the time I was just going away on vacation, but I am now back again, and here goes. I hardly can imagine what you will think of Ms. enclosed herewith, as I don't know what to think of it myself. However, to get things on a proper basis, let me commence by saying that my work is very irregular, and I can never tell the value of anything of mine until from six months to a year have passed by. So I really don't know whether "Siwash" is rot or not. That is for you to decide, and please do not be a bit easy about so deciding.[1] If unavailable, just ship it back and I'll try something else for you.
   Incidentally, I wish to say that one thing that militates against the Ms. being worth anything, is the fact that it is all really so. I knew the characters well, was in the tent when the story was told by Tommy during the absence of Molly. And Molly really did bring back a load of pots and pans.[2]

Very truly yours,
Jack London.

MS: Kingman; 1 p., tls.
   1. The *New Magazine* rejected the story.
   2. Tommy, the narrator, tells the story of his daring elopement with the bride-to-be of a Siwash chief and of his happy seven-year marriage to her, until she died in childbirth. Molly, an American woman "playing a desperate single-hand in the equally desperate Klondike rush of '97," makes an unsuccessful attempt at backpacking through an Arctic blizzard laden with kitchen utensils.

To Elwyn Hoffman

1130 East 15th. st.,
August 8/00.

Dear Elwyn:—
   I think I forgot last time to acknowledge receipt of your picture. Let me do so now, and thank you heartily for it. And find herewith one of me— about the best I have ever had. I don't remember whether I sent you a copy of the same some time since or not. If I have, It won't make much difference.

I'll send you one, soon, of myself and wife in swimming, taken down at Santa Cruz.

O Lord! I never resent it, even if other people resent my criticism of their work (though I never for one moment dreamed from reading your letter that you had resented. Far from it). In fact, the only adverse criticism of any value, is the kind that hurts. I speak from experience; also, of the many I have criticized, I have always noted a marked improvement just subsequent to my handling them brutally. And you know I have had and still have no end of friends whose work I look over—and some of them as hypersensitive as are made.

When you said, regarding my work, that my writing table was too near my dictionary, you meant, I suppose, that I unduly strained my vocabulary, did you not? And if so, you were certainly right. In the collection of tales there are about one hundred polysyllable words I would like to be able to strike out; though of course at the time they suited me immensely. In my later work I am sure you will not find me groping after strange and ungodly words. Nay, nay.

So you're working in a mine, eh? And it seems you're not over strong. Do you stand it all right? But even if you do stand it all right, it's still miserable. I hate hard work (God wot I've done enough of it myself), and suppose I'll do lots more. But the saving grace with my experience has been that most of the hard work was congenial. But with such work it's the loss of time I lament most of all. One only has so much life given him at best, and each hour of uncongenial work seems to represent one-hours suicide of one's life. And if one works hard all his days, then he has been committing suicide all his life. O well, so be.

Sincerely yours,
Jack London.

ms: CSmH; 2 pp., tls.

To Cloudesley Johns

1130 East 15th. st.,
August 18/00.

Dear Cloudesley:—

So you are at last alive, and also bringing about the birth of the *Theorist*.[1] How do you like midwifery?

I like "The Rocks" as well if not better than anything else of yours I have read. Of course you'll not bear me out in it, if for nothing else, just for perversity's sake. Though the illustration of the "Rocks" was rich, wasn't it? I think the story was too good for the *New York Press*. It should have been published in some of the good magazines. What did they pay you for it—I mean how much per thousand?

Haven't commenced novel, yet.[2] Too busy with other things.

But will be at it soon, now.

McClure's have not given me one word of advice, instruction, etc., nor asked one word of information about what, which, why, when, and where, about whom and what, my novel is to be. Yes, I'll confess the "have to" part of it will bother me—until I get started. It would almost as much anyway, the only difference in this case being that I feel sort of bound in honor. I'm sure you'll understand. Because it is impossible for me to get far enough ahead of the game by my short story work, so that I can get the time to write a long novel, and because I see fit to receive royalties in advance, is no reason, surely, for being branded as an Esau. Now don't you think so?

Shall send you a foto soon, of my wife and I in swimming at Santa Cruz.

Jack London.

P.S.—I send back magazines this mail. Just before my vacation I read your "Post No. 12" but mixed it with something else by the time I was back from vacation. I liked it, also, and those several words you cut out, in the copy you sent me, were wonderfully effective. Wish I had you to go over my Ms. & cut out— But then I'd fight.

MS: CSmH; 2 pp., tls.
1. Johns's projected novel.
2. *A Daughter of the Snows.*

To Elwyn Hoffman

1130 East 15th. st.,
Aug. 25/00.

Dear Elwyn:—

Thanks, and thanks again, for the fotos of your den and The Hill.[1] I have enjoyed them very much. How I envy you that capacity for making something neat and pretty and a delight with your hands! I can't do such things to save me. If I should attempt it, it would be most harrowing to my soul, my nerves would be on edge, and ere I had done I would have broken and smashed and jumped upon the whole aborted effort. I can't do it, simply can't. And yet, how I wish I could!

I have just recently invested in a camera, and I can't do any work at all with it, and I can't find the time to learn. Though I signalized the Sabbath to-day by shooting a dozen plates or so at my sister's year-old baby.[2] I received some fotos of Idah Strobridges den last week about the same time yours arrived, and it is plain she knows the business.

Some friends have just arrived, and I shall be so busy for several days to come that I will be unable to do any letter writing, so I'll chop off here and get it under way at once.

In to-morrow's mail I send you a copy of *The Son of the Wolf*. I haven't got to the swimming photograph yet, but will handle it with the pictures of the baby.

I quite agree with you as to the use of words, and I agree because I have sinned greatly in the past, and because I feel it in my bones that I shall occasionally in the future.

But my friends are clamoring, and I must quit.

Jack London.

MS: CSmH; 2 pp., tls.
   1. Probably the name of Hoffman's residence in French Corral, California, a mining town in western Nevada County. See JL to Hoffman, September 18, 1900.
   2. Irving Shepard.

To Anna Strunsky

1130 East 15th. st.,
August 30/00.

Dear Anna:—

Monday is the only evening of next week which Bessie and I can spend with you of the evenings you suggested. Wednsday at home, you know,[1] and Friday, Ruskin. Mr. Whittaker and his wife will be over on Monday likewise. We'll come together most likely. I only saw Mr. Murphy once, but I liked him ever so much. He strikes me as strong.

My thanks for the tickets, and regrets for the added trouble of getting two more. Mr. Whittaker and Mrs. Whittaker decided they wanted to come, too. Am sorry I put you to so much trouble.

I hardly know where you have got those *Letters* to already in your impetuous way. You only have given me hints in your notes, and I don't know where you have traveled to. We must have a long talk about it. Some afternoon or evening by ourselves, preferably at my place. What do you say? We must have fully discussed it, and have everything thoroughly mapped out before we commence.[2]

Will see you Monday, then.

Jack.

MS: CSmH; 1 p., tls.
   1. See JL to Strunsky, February 13, 1900, n. 1.
   2. JL and Anna Strunsky coauthored *The Kempton-Wace Letters* (New York: Macmillan, 1903). The *Letters* constitute a debate on the nature of love between the characters Dane Kempton, poet and teacher at Stanford, and his foster son Herbert Wace, a graduate student in economics at the University of California. (The debate is sparked by Wace's decision to marry.) Strunsky wrote Kempton's letters, supporting romantic love, whereas JL, as Wace, approached love from the standpoint of a scientific materialist. In her "Memoirs of Jack London," *The Masses*, July 1917, Strunsky observed: "[JL] held that love is only a trap

set by nature for the individual. One must not marry for love but for certain qualities discerned by the mind. This he argued in *The Kempton-Wace Letters* brilliantly and passionately; so passionately as to again make one suspect that he was not as certain of his position as he claimed to be" (p. 16). For the beginnings of the project see JL to Johns, October 17, 1900.

To Elwyn Hoffman

1130 East 15th. st.,
Sept. 5/00.

Dear Elwyn:–

I am glad you liked the book,[1] and since you have faith, perforce I also have faith that some day there will come to me through the mails a book with "Elwyn Hoffman" on the title page. I am a deep-dyed materialist, and yet none the less I have a great faith in faith. Faith directly does nothing; but indirectly it marshals forces, and forces those forces to work toward the desired end. In fact, faith determines the direction in which one will spend his energy, and compels the expenditure of all one's energy in that direction. Do you catch me? I am rather vague.

So you have met Maynard Dixon.[2] What do you make of him? I have only met him a couple of times, and those times perfunctorily. While I liked him at once, I at the same time drew the conclusion that he was sort of hyper-sensitive. Did he strike you in this way?

Dialect stories? What do I think of them? I really haven't any opinion, though I have found many of them tedious and irritating. For, on the other hand, I have read some very splendid ones. The one mistake, it seems to me, in dialect stories, is that the writer is prone to subordinate substance to form. And this is easy, for many a story, which as a story would fall, goes, and goes because of its dialect.

Jack London.

MS: CSmH; 1 p., tls.
1. *The Son of the Wolf.*
2. Dixon, who illustrated *The Son of the Wolf*, had illustrated Hoffman's "The Keeper of the Camp," *Land of Sunshine*, January 1899.

To Cloudesley Johns

1130 East 15th. st.,
Sept. 9/00.

Dear Cloudesley:–

So am I up against it—and just got started against it. Have or rather am winding up the first chapter of novel.[1] Since it is my first attempt, I have chosen a simple subject and shall simply endeavor to make it true, artistic, and interesting. But afterwards, when I have learned better how to handle a sustained effort, I shall choose a greater subject. I wish I were done.

That bit of Oliver Herford was cleverly done,[2] but I am sure it was not precisely true. There are a number of Le Gallienne's quartrains which I like better than corresponding quartrains of Fitzgerald's.[3] Perhaps the literary mentors will not bear me out in this, but none the less, so far as I am concerned, it is so. I am forwarding the bit of verse to Ted.[4]

Am beginning to take exercise once again. Indian clubs,[5] jumping, etc, every day, wheelrides every day, and baths three to four times per week— swimming I mean. Am just back from practicing in diving, and am stiff and sore with practicing front and back somersalts. (I don't know how to spell the name of the act, so do it phonetically.) Expect to take up fencing later on, and the gloves, and shooting. It is Voltaire, I believe, who said: "The body of an athlete and the soul of a sage; that is happiness." I am trying to assimilate Spencer's philosophy just now, so there is a chance that I may yet attain to happiness.[6]

Jack London.

MS: CSmH; 1 p., tls. Pbd: *BJL*, I, 345.

1. *A Daughter of the Snows.*

2. Oliver Herford (1863–1935), English-born artist and humorist. His works include *The Bashful Earthquake, and Other Fables and Verses* (1898) and *Alphabet of Celebrities* (1899). The work to which JL refers has not been identified.

3. Both Le Gallienne and FitzGerald published English poetic versions of *The Rubáiyát of Omar Khayyám.*

4. Ted Applegarth.

5. Bottle-shaped metal or wooden clubs used for exercising the arms.

6. The words "I may yet attain to happiness" were handwritten.

To Anna Strunsky

1130 East 15th. st.,
Sept. 9/00.

Dear Anna:–

Don't forget that tomorrow evening you are to take dinner at Mr. Whittaker's. Now you don't know where his place is, I am sure; for he moved some time ago. So what do you say to coming to my place in the afternoon so that you and I can settle down and discuss the book?[1] I shall look for you anyway.

If you cannot come in the afternoon, however, then you must find your own way out to Mr. Whitaker's (though I would much prefer it the other way). Take the broad guage boat; get off at Broadway station; enquire for the Piedmont cars; tell the conductor of the Piedmont car to let you off at Laurel st; and go down the slight hill on Laurel st. to number 100—that is where Mr. Whitaker lives.

But do try to come out to my place in the afternoon.

Jack.

MS: CSmH; 1 p., tls.
1. *The Kempton-Wace Letters.*

To Anna Strunsky

1130. East 15th. st.,
Sept. 15/00.

Dear Anna:—

How glad I was to receive Dane Kempton's letter! And for the first of all the letters, it was far better than had I dreamed of. It is so hard to commence. Later, ah later, when we have come to realize the characters, then it will be inevitable; the very realization of our personalities will not permit us to wander from the predestined course, or to wonder what the next act or thought should be. If we be at all artistic, and have any sense of proportion in our souls, we cannot err. The living breathing souls we have created shall master us, and dictate to us, mere instruments of their manifestation. Do you see? And hence, now, the beginning, the period of creation, everything depends upon us. Here is where our toil and travail come in.

I shall make carbon copies of all the letters (Dane Kempton's and Herbert Wace's), so that both you and I shall have the complete file on both sides for constant reference. This will be very necessary, I am sure.

You will find I have altered Dane Kempton's letter somewhat, here and there, in little places. But I have striven to do so O so slightly. Only where I deemed strength and ambiguity demanded. For instance: you will notice, page 2, "It was no stepping down from the mountain top." Then you went on with "but rather greater flight, etc." Now it seemed to me a mixed metaphor to commence with, and further, that it weakened by stating the converse. I cannot go further into detail.

But remember, Anna, these alterations are not irrevocable. I must not cramp you for the very truth of it. It is impossible that there be the slightest common ring in the letters of Dane Kempton and the letters of Herbert Wace. We must be ourselves. So see, girl, that whatever alterations I make, I make with this understanding. And in the end, even on such things, your verdict shall be final.

Oh! One thing more. The story hinted at near close of letter—is it the great love story of Dane Kempton's life? And if so, is it good art to bring it in here at the commencement? Or rather should he not be goaded, through my madness of position and because of his great love for me, and his fear—should he not, I say, be goaded or impelled—absolutely, strenuously impelled—to lay naked before us his most sacred possession? Do you catch my drift? Let me hear what you conclude.

Keep up your splendid phrasing. "cramped little note blurted out nothing"; "the joy and the song"; "I seek and find and keep"; "the dear dead"; "frank and demanding"; "glory departed"; "the human hungered"; "fastidiousness of tone"; etc. etc. etc. Keep up, I say, the strength of phrase, but mark well, *don't strain after it.*

I appreciated keenly the suggestion you make of major and minor points, and thank you. And do we both do this to one another. Else will many a splendid point for reply be lost. Keep you a scratch book, and jot down suggestions and notes as they come to you—both for yourself and for me.

There were 615 words in this first letter. The length will pick up (as it should), as we get deeper into it.

The idea of Miss Stebbins[1] writing at end two letters, one to me and one to you, is excellent.

You will note that I have put you into Vernon Chambers, London. Later on you may change to the country—or other places, if you see fit.

As for me—shall we be definite as to what University? And if so, remember I know nothing about Stanford, and hence, verisimilitude of atmosphere would be lacking. I doubt the expediency of making it definite at all; and if so, think Berkeley better. Also, remember thou, I have a little bit of patriotism left in me.

I have a bad cold; have been dosing myself for twelve hours with whiskey; hence there is added unto me a bad headache. When I first received Dane's letter I was just finishing second chapter of novel, so put Dane aside until to-day. To-day or to-morrow I shall make Wace's reply. I want you to see second chapter of Novel, and pass judgement. Next week, Herbert's first, and Dane's second, should be through the machine; so it were well that you come over again. Wednsday if you can make it. Thursday and Friday I have to speak.

Jack.

MS: CSmH; 3 pp., tls. Pbd: *L*, 110–11.
1. Hester Stebbins, the fiancée of Herbert Wace. Being both poet and social scientist, she unites the qualities of the two men. The final letters Strunsky proposes were to be written after Stebbins broke off her engagement to Wace, having realized that he had never loved her.

To Elwyn Hoffman

1130 East 15th. st.,
Sept. 18/00.

Dear Elwyn:—
Are those lines yours:

> His work is a lash on the hide of him,
>   A breaking wheel to his soul,
> Who knoweth it, dark by the side of him,
>   A goad, but never a goal!

I think they are splendid, with a certain strength which reminds me of Kipling. But I have read almost all of his, so I don't think he can claim them. Did you? Did you?[1]

Thanks for data about Dixon. So you knew him quite well, for three years. The world is very small after all.

I am pegging away steadily at my novel, and also at the series of letters I have attempted. Besides I have been going about everywhere altogether too much. The week is half gone, yet I have to deliver two speeches, and attend two club suppers before another week is come.[2] Also, think of it! to-night I am going to the Circus![3] If that won't be rest, what will?

Thanks for addressed envelope enclosed with your letter. I take herewith and for all time the tip. Candidly, you usually superscribed your letters

"The Hill."
French Corral, Calif.

and I so addressed mine to you, and they carried. Will sin no more.

Jack London.

MS: CSmH; 1 p., tls.

1. The lines were indeed by Hoffman. See JL to Hoffman, October 27, 1900.

2. JL delivered "Romance" to the Adelphian Club of Alameda on September 21; his second speech has not been identified.

3. The Ringling Brothers Circus opened at the Exhibition Grounds in Oakland on September 18.

To Charles S. Pratt

1130 East 15th. st.,
Oakland, Calif.,
Sept. 18/00.

My dear Mr. Pratt:—[1]

I wish to thank you for your kind letter. Of course I thoroughly understand refusal of "Sea Sprite,"[2] and believe me, keenly appreciate your reference to "My Deceased Wife's Sister." That story has been a delight to me for three or four years, and it shall always be.

"The Sea Sprite" is an ancient effort, and chiefly an interest to me because of its almost countless refusals. Of all my work, it is, in that particular, my banner Ms. Each rejection is a birthday, and my love grows with its birthdays.

But seriously, it was with no view regarding its special fitness to *Little Folks*, that I sent it to you. And had I known you had liked the "White Silence," I am sure I would not have sent it at all. Again thanking you for your kindness, I am,

Very sincerely yours,
Jack London.

MS: ViU; 1 p., tls.
    1. Charles Stuart Pratt (*b.* 1854), co-editor from 1897 to 1907 and editor from 1907 to 1909 of *Little Folks,* an illustrated children's magazine published in Boston from 1897 until 1926.
    2. JL submitted "The Sea Sprite and the Shooting Star," a poem of seventeen six-line stanzas, to eight magazines between April 13 and August 27, 1900. The manuscript, retired after it was rejected by *Little Folks,* was published as a leaflet in 1932 by the Jack London Amateur Press Club.

To Anna Strunsky

[Oakland]
[? late September 1900]

Dear Anna:—
    Find here letter No. 2. and I must plead guilty to the same feelings which you were under when you wrote me. I don't know what to make of it. Seem all at sea. Feel that I am all wrong, that I am not building characters as I should, or even writing letters as they should be written. But I suppose the whole thing will grow, in time. Any way, it's a very good method for getting a fair conception of one's limitations.
    What do you think of my making a poet of Hester?[1] Should it be poet or poetess? I detest poetess. Is there such a word as "lyricist"? There is the word "lyrist," meaning the same thing, but I do not like it. Do you catch my new school possibly to be founded by Hester?—Poetry of a Machine Age. I may exploit it in later letters. Do you, Dane Kempton, behold that I have not told you anything about Hester physically? I don't like the wind up, the treatment of the minor conflict. It seemed as though I begged the question, and yet I couldn't conceive a way of arguing it out. To me it seems almost unarguable. I do not know. Perhaps not. Can't tell.
    Well, let's hear from you, I can't write any more. Was interrupted to-day, and have extended writing into the night, and am dead tired. Also am fighting a bad cold.

Goodnight, dear,
Jack.

And Do please criticize unsparingly, especially errors in taste. 1709 words in Letter No. 2.

MS: CSmH; 1 p., tls. Pbd: *BJL,* I, 359–60.
    1. In Letter 2 from Herbert Wace to Dane Kempton, Wace describes Hester as follows: "Preeminently she is a poet—this must be always understood. She is the greater poet, I take it, in this dawning twentieth century, because she is a scientist; not in spite of being a scientist as some would hold. How shall I describe her? Perhaps as a George Eliot, fused with an Elizabeth Barrett, with a hint of Huxley and a trace of Keats" (*The Kempton-Wace Letters,* p. 9).

To Anna Strunsky

[Oakland]
October 1/00.

Dear Anna:—

I don't know what you will make of this. At least I have postponed the main issue, of course, while really bringing forward the fundamental issue. In this case I think it better for the reader that we work from the universal to the particular—it will be clearer and arouse more sympathy with all parties concerned.

Behold! I have opened this letter in one mood, written myself into a passionate another mood, and stopped short. Wherefore, to-morrow expect another letter from Herbert Wace.

Your letter was splendid. It made me faint-hearted. So, as usual, I am afraid of the one I have just completed.

I had intended writing you from day to day, but have been so busy and had numerous interruptions. Also, I did not dare read your Dane Kempton letter; for I was in a certain mood in the novel, and it was too great a risk to run to throw myself out of that mood until the chapter was done. The chapter was finished yesterday. And I have worked away at the letters to-day.

Do come over Wednsday (afternoon and night), I am expecting no one in the afternoon, and not that I know of in the evening, and we have so much to discuss.

The appreciation of Grant Allen made me love Richard Le Gallienne.[1] How different from the gutter attack of Robert Buchanan on Kipling and Besant![2]

Am I right in substituting "spasms" for "fits"? And "Elizabeth Barrett" for "Mrs. Browning"? You deliver final judgement, remember.

Top of p. 12. "and 'vows have been made for me' in this connection I shall neither sleep nor dream again." Is this not ambiguous? What will the reader think you really mean? Think it over.

Bottom of p. 12. "you still seemed to think defense of an arrangement that made for our separation to be necessary." Poor structure. The reader will absolutely have to go over it 2 or 3 times to get its meaning.

Where shall I look in Wordsworth for "dedicated spirit,"[3] etc.

Remember, on your typed copy of the letters, make all corrections, suggestions, etc., and on margin pencil heavily in blue red or black so that it will at once attract our attention when we go over.

Have finished *The Ring and the Book*, "Half-Rome," the "Other-Half-Rome," and am just opening "Tertium Quid."[4] It is a revelation to me. How can I ever thank you!

Let us know if you can come Wednsday.[5] Bessie sends love.

Great Haste
Jack.

(1155 words)

MS: CSmH; 2 pp., tls. Pbd: *L*, 111–12.
    1. Richard Le Gallienne, "Grant Allen," *Fortnightly Review*, December 1899, was a personal appreciation of Grant Allen and a sympathetic evaluation of his works.
    2. Robert W. Buchanan wrote a stinging criticism of Kipling in "The Voice of the Hooligan," *Contemporary Review*, December 1899, in which he claimed that Kipling's works were "contemptible in spirit and so barbarous in execution" (p. 782). Buchanan's criticism of Sir Walter Besant (1836–1901), British novelist, has not been identified.
    3. *The Prelude*, book 4, l. 337, quoted in the second Kempton letter.
    4. "Tertium Quid," in *The Ring and the Book*, offers an impartial view of the story of Pompilia after both halves of Rome have given their opinions.
    5. Apparently Anna Strunsky did not visit JL on Wednesday, October 3, since he wrote to her that day.

To Anna Strunsky

1130 East 15th. st.,
October 3/00.

Dear Anna:—

If it's bad art, the latter part of letter, it shall be cast out. I introduced it in an effort to further build up Herbert Wace before the main issue is taken up. I hardly know whether I am justified in doing so. I thought also that it might serve to relieve things in a way. The thing really occurred at Berkeley in 1897, Edlin being the socialist in question,[1]—only they did not fase him at all. His endictment stood unchallenged. They were not able to take up the defense.

As for the first part of the letter, it should have been finished yesterday, but I was too sick to work on it, and to-day has been almost as bad; so I cannot vouch for the first part even.

I've had a bad cold for a week or so, and it has pulled me down. Then I was poisoned some time ago, and not seeming to work out of my system, I had recourse to powerful medicine and took double and triple quantity. So between the two I was knocked out for a day or so.

While I think of it, Weber tells me he had *Fables in Slang*.[2] Pratt, a mutual friend, is lying in hospital with both ankles broken, and needs reading matter. *Fables* would just suit him. Would it be asking too much for you to mail it over to me? Come next Monday by all means, to my place. Whitaker will be up. Come in the afternoon, not later than three. If it's windy, all of us will go sailing; if warm, swimming at Alameda; if cold and calm, swimming at Piedmont Baths. What say you?

I must go to San Francisco soon, some day, and will talk over the trip to Land's End later to bring it in on that day.

Bring your Wordsworth with you when you come. What did Hyndman say?[3] Have you the letter? I am indeed gratified.

Quite agree with you, Besant made a worse than poor defense;[4] my blood boiled as I read it and I wanted to rush into the arena myself. He meant well, but—

Here come some people, so good night,

Jack.

MS: CSmH; 2 pp., tls. Pbd: *L*, 112–13.

1. William Edlin (1878–1947), called the "Freshman Socialist" during the fall semester of 1896 at the University of California, where he challenged his professors and various student organizations to debate political and economic topics. In 1897 Edlin published *The Coming Social Struggle*. He moved East in 1900 and for the rest of his career edited an assortment of newspapers, including the two most prominent Jewish papers in New York, *The Jewish Daily Forward* (from 1902 to 1903) and *The Day* (from 1915 to 1925 and from 1942 to 1947).

2. George Ade, *Fables in Slang* (1899). Weber has not been identified.

3. Possibly Henry M. Hyndman (1842–1921), author of *The Economics of Socialism* (1896) and other books on political and economic topics. Hyndman, a wealthy socialist, founded the Social Democratic Federation in London in 1884. He opposed the Boer War and Great Britain's imperialist policies.

4. Sir Walter Besant's defense of Kipling, "Is It the Voice of the Hooligan," *Contemporary Review*, January 1900, declares that Kipling is "worthy of our deepest admiration." He concludes: "It is enough for me and for those unnumbered millions to know that here is one who has a message to deliver which concerns us all: that he has people to present to us among whom we walk daily, yet have remained hitherto in ignorance of their ways and thoughts and speech: that he has taught the people of the Empire what the Empire means: that he has shown us below their rough and coarse exterior the manhood of soldier and sailor, of engine-man and lighthouse-man and fisherman. It is enough that he speaks as no other of his generation—these be the reasons enough and to spare why he is loved by old and young in every class and every country where is the language of the folk."

To Elwyn Hoffman

1130 East 15th. st.,
Oakland, Calif.,
October 5/00.

Dear Elwyn:–

Another hypersensitive creature! When I spoke as I did of your four lines, I meant it. I still mean it. I realize how difficult it is to speak the truth in these days when one's fellows are so prone to doubt by a shade more or less. It seems as though one is only capable of taking two tacks, that of praising and that of damning—both in the superlative. There is no middle course possible. If it is attempted it will not be believed. Henceforth—ah, no rash oaths!

Now that I've registered my kick I feel better. I am sure I would enjoy going to a hanging— No, I'll modify; I want to go to one very much.[1] My nerves I flatter myself are strong enough to study such human phenomena, and I have always been interested in the way men die. Some can do it finely, can they not?

What *Call* do you expect to get on?—the Daily? Weekly? or Sunday?[2]

You remind me of a correspondent from Southern California.[3] Though you would quarrel gloriously ere the first fifteen minutes were up, I am sure. I shall take the liberty of exchanging your last letters with each other (please send the one you get back). Your criticism is just—the style of the "Odyssey"[4] would not do for a long-drawn tale.

Jack London.

MS: CSmH; 1 p., tls.
    1. See JL to Strunsky, February 11, 1902, and JL to Johns, February 23, 1902.
    2. Hoffman apparently had sought employment at the *San Francisco Call.*
    3. Cloudesley Johns.
    4. "An Odyssey of the North."

To Cloudesley Johns

1130 East 15th. st.,
Oakland, Calif.,
October 5/00.

Dear Cloudesley:—

So you're back at Harold ere this. If you could only take a suck of Mark Twain's ink, couldn't you write an article on that white elephant post office of yours!

"Clear-eyed I looked and laughed, and climbed no more."[1] That is one of my favorite lines in his rendering, one of my most favorite.

Have you read George Ade's *Fables in Slang*? They're rich. If I can borrow the copy I'll send it down to you. I send you by this mail a copy of the *International Socialist Review.*[2] The first really respectable American Socialist publication. Read it and tell me what you think of it. It is well worth a dollar per year to a socialist who wishes to keep thoroughly in touch with the movement.

I read *Tale of Two Cities* the other day, and at the time thought that Carlyle had got much of his style from Dickens, or vice versa since I did not know which antedated the other. As for the *French Revolution*—I shall always consider it a wonderful production, though faulty philosophically in many places.[3] But none the less wonderful for all that. I tried to read it once, with a rather vague knowledge of the Revolution. Had the good sense to discover that I was not ready for it and laid it aside. Then I read about fifteen or twenty works on the Revolution, thoroughly steep myself in it, and then went back to Carlyle. Then I understood. It does set one's teeth on edge, and it is freaky and abominable and all that, but—as you say, "there are things mixed into it all through." And again, there must be some connection between the form and the substance. Take many of his best things (phrases, thoughts, judgements, etc), and clothe them conventionally and see how flat they would fall.

I have a correspondent somewhere at the opposite end of California to you, and I think you and he would war gloriously on sight. I am taking the liberty of exchanging your last letter with his. Send his back when you are done. I won't give you any tips about him; so tell me what you make of him.

"Berry's Cottonwoods"[4] has not yet arrived.

Have fifteen thousand words of novel ready for press. And also pegging away at my volume of letters and have (betwixt myself and collaborator) nearly seven thousand words of that.

Jack London.

MS: CSmH; 2 pp., tls.

1. Richard Le Gallienne, *The Rubáiyát of Omar Khayyám*, stanza 60, l. 240. See JL to Johns, March 30, 1899.

2. The *International Socialist Review* was initiated in Chicago in July 1900 by the Charles H. Kerr Company.

3. In the preface to *A Tale of Two Cities* (1859), Dickens acknowledged his debt to Carlyle's *A History of the French Revolution* (1837): "It has been one of my hopes to add something to the popular and picturesque means of understanding that terrible time, though no one can hope to add anything to the philosophy of Mr. Carlyle's wonderful book."

4. One of Johns's stories.

To Elwyn Hoffman

1130 East 15th. st.,
Oct. 8/00.

Dear Elwyn:–

Can you come over and see me this evening, Monday evening. Three or four of us are going either swimming or sailing this afternoon. If you could make my place by three o'clock this afternoon I should be very happy, for then you could join us. My treat. But if you cannot, try and get here, say, by 6:30, in time for whatever sort of a lunch we may manage to dig up on our return. I do hope you can make the afternoon; but if not, then the evening surely.

At least one of the two or three will charm you I know. Everything informal of course. If you prefer soft shirt, wear one. I shall probably be in sweater.

Try and make it, do.

Hastily,
Jack London.

P.S.—*Ainslie's* have just informed me that they are willing I should have bookrights, but that they preferred the story should not come out in bookform for at least six months after magazine publication.[1]

MS: CSmH; 1 p., tls.

1. JL's "The Great Interrogation" was to be published in *Ainslie's Magazine*, December 1900; it was later included in *The God of His Fathers*. *Ainslie's* was a general illustrated

monthly magazine that featured short fiction; it was published in New York from 1897 until 1926.

To Cloudesley Johns

1130 East 15th. st.,
Oct. 17/00.

Dear Cloudesley:—

Yes, I have just been trying the English Market myself, these last few weeks, thanks to your English stamps. No, I did not make the mistake in mailing Ms. Find herewith an editorial letter from *Pearson's*. Note the "American flavor." [1]

Didn't I explain my volume of letters? Well, it's this way: A young Russian Jewess of 'Frisco and myself have often quarrelled over our conceptions of love. She happens to be a genius. She is also a materialist by philosophy, and an idealist by innate preference, and is constantly being forced to twist all the facts of the universe in order to reconcile herself with her self. So, finally, we decided that the only way to argue the question out would be by letter. Then we wondered if a collection of such letters should happen to be worth publishing. Then we assumed characters, threw in a real objective love element, and started to work. Of course, don't know yet how it will turn out. We're both doing some very good work—in spots; but we are agreed, in case they merit it, to go over when we are done.

I see you complain against *Tale of Two Cities*. Why, under the sun? What's wrong?

I send you "Berry" in a couple of days. Mr. Whitaker has borrowed it to read, but will bring it back shortly.

I never heard of Kennedy, or his book. [2] How is it there are no reviews any where else? I should like to see it some day, and I will when I can raise the price. Clipping (for which same thanks), was from *Sunshine*, I presume?

Find here a poem by 'Gene Field. It's a page which Scribner's send out with his complete works, but which is never bound. [3]

I can't see it. To me "The Rocks" was quite a deal better than "Berry." Better in handling and better in theme. What think you? Agree with me or with *N.Y. Press*? You have painted the landboomer all right, and the sucker too.

"The widow is gathering nettles for her children's dinner; a perfumed seigneur, delicately lounging in the OEil de Boeuf, hath an alchemy whereby he will extract from her the third nettle and call it rent." [4]

The above is Carlyle's; let it go. I shall give you better, which is as monstrous as anything he ever wrote (style), and as characteristic. Read it aloud. Don't quarrel with his generalizations in the reading,—just read it aloud. Then find fault with it if you can.

I shall commence excerpts on top of next page.

Jack London.

MS: CSmH; 2 pp., tls. Pbd: *L*, 113–14; *BJL*, I, 346.

1. Possibly "Editorial: Better Roads," *Pearson's*, July 1900, signed by C. Arthur Pearson. Arguing for the improvement of highways, it cited a letter from a farmer in Camden, New Jersey, that detailed the economic benefits of good roads.

2. Bart Kennedy, *A Man Adrift* (1900). The review in *Land of Sunshine* concludes: "Its strength is in its apparently true pictures of life as a deck-hand, oyster-dredger, coal-shoveler, miner, hobo and various utilities Mr. Kennedy writes about in his autobiography. There is a suspicion in us that he was at one time hobo 'pardner' of a youth already much better known to fame and much likelier to grow therein—Jack London."

3. Eugene Field (1850–95); *The Writings in Prose and Verse of Eugene Field* (1898–1901), published by Charles Scribner's Sons. The specific poem referred to by JL has not been identified.

4. Thomas Carlyle, *History of the French Revolution*, vol. 1, book VI, chap. 3.

To Elwyn Hoffman

1130 East 15th. st.,
Oakland, Calif.,
Oct. 27/00.

Dear Elwyn:—

I can hardly say how happy I was when I found that you had not come Monday night after all. You see, it was this way: We waited probably half an hour, hoping you might show up for the boating trip. Then we went sailing with the intention of being back by six or half past. Very good. But we got stuck on a mud bank and did not get back until—I forget now—but somewhere around nine o'clock or after. And all the time we worrying for fear that you had come and found us away. Evidently the god that watches over me had his eyes open at that time.

There the man goes, more hypersensitive than I thought him! It was the inference from what I said that your lines were an imitation of Kipling! Great God! If I had thought so I should most likely have kept my mouth shut. You do me very scant justice—nay, you do me no justice at all. A man doesn't take a ship to sea without a compass. He must have something to determine where he is at. Any piece of writing ever produced, more nearly resembles one thing than another. How may we be able to judge of anything else. We are so made that on receiving an impression or sensation we at once and unconsciously proceed to classify that impression or sensation. The babe new born does that. And I simply did the same, found your bit of verse recalling Kipling to me more than it did Tennyson, Keats or Shelly. Wherefore thou hasty man?

Oh! I have read on a bit in your letter! And I find it richer. Take the second page (which I send back in preference to copying).

On the first page I am accused of having said that your verse reminded me of Kipling. I plead guilty. I did say that. Then on first page you draw the inference that I had meant that you had imitated Kipling. Then on the second page, you forget that it was merely the inference that *you* drew, and succeed in so twisting the charge around that it appears that I said you had imitated Kipling. Preposterous! Poor logic!

And further, on the second page, you do me all justice, by your argument, though you do not mean it. A suggestion can only remind one of that which is suggested. "So with my verse," you say. Of course. It suggested Kipling, reminded of Kipling, I said that it did, and then had the pleasure of having my words twisted about until I found myself charged with having said you had imitated Kipling. Look your letter over; read your own words for yourself, and then see if I have not been grievously handled.

As for myself, there is no end of Kipling in my work. I have even quoted him. I would never possibly written anywhere near the way I did had Kipling never been. True, true, every bit of it. And if several other men had never existed, Kipling would never have written as he did.

But a truce to the contention. I know you will not hold that a suggestion is not a reminder, so there is no more about it.

How are you getting along, anyway? I have been down to Fresno[1]— just got back this morning.

I wish I could have had you over a number of times first following your arrival. Now everything is somewhat dead. I am making engagements with myself and camera and dark room, and so crawling out of others. Wednsday nights am always at home. Mondays if you warn me in advance—Monday nights.

Would you like to attend a Ruskin Club supper—informal—no dress or anything of that sort of stuff. We shall hold the supper at the Hotel Metropole, Oakland, at 6:45 P.M. I think President Wheeler of University of California is to be a guest among others.[2] Let us know if you care to come (socialism), so that I may turn your name in to the secty. The dinner takes place Friday evening, November 9th.[3] You come as my guest, of course.

Lets hear from you, and how and what you are doing.

Jack London.

MS: CSmH; 3 pp., tls.
    1. JL delivered "The Question of the Maximum" to the Parlor Lecture Club in Fresno on October 24.
    2. Benjamin Ide Wheeler (1854–1927), president of the University of California from 1899 to 1915. Wheeler was unable to attend the meeting because he was entertaining a visiting professor from Oxford.
    3. At the meeting, JL spoke on the balance of trade.

To Cloudesley Johns

1130 East 15th. st.,
Oct. 27/00.

Dear Cloudesley:—

Am just back from delivering a lecture at Fresno, and have to go out and deliver another in an hour, so this must be just a line. Aren't the *Black Cat* perpetrations hideous! I don't know what to make of the people who served as judges.[1] It seems more of a nightmare to me, when I think of it.

I send you this mail or next, foto of my wife and I swimming at Santa Cruz.

Keep the magazine by all means. I sent it you to keep.

Jack London.

MS: CSmH; 1 p., tls.
  1. The winners of the *Black Cat* competition, to which JL and Johns submitted stories, had apparently just been published.

To Cornelius Gepfert

1130 East 15th. st.,
Oakland, Calif.,
Nov. 5/00.

Dear Con:—

Yours of October 10th. at hand. How lively the Dawson mails are now. In fact, by postmark, your letter arrived in Oakland October 29th. Pretty good time, eh? I was away when it came, down in Fresno delivering lectures and taking a vacation.

I shall delay sending this letter for a day or so, now that I think of it, so that I may enclose foto of myself and wife, taken last summer vacation down by the sea. My sober expression, nay, savage, is due to the fact that I had a small boy manipulating the camera on the bank, and that he was very awkward.

So you are back in Dawson? It was quite a surprise to me. There must be some charm about the North which draws men back again and again. I can hardly contain myself, so strongly do I desire to go back. And I shall soon, probably next year—I mean a year from now. I had planned going in this fall, but have been too busy writing an unexpected novel for McClure's. Then next year wish to make a San Francisco sociological study, in form of novel, so that I expect to be pretty busy.[1]

If you run across Thompson,[2] give him my regards.

Lucky fellow! Three hundred dollars for a Henderson Creek claim! How much would you give for one now? No; I never realized a cent from any properties I had interest in up there. Still, I have been managing to pan out a living ever since on the strength of the trip.

Yes, California is quite different to where you are just now. At the present moment it is going on midnight, in November. I am in my shirt sleeves, pegging away at the typewriter. All the doors and windows are open, and I get up once in a while and go dabble in the dark room washing prints—one of which prints I expect to send to you.

This afternoon I was swimming. Think of it!

I am glad you like my book.[3] Of course, there is a peculiar atmosphere to it, which many a Klondiker will hardly recognize. But those same Klondikers, I fear, are largely unable to see the romance of the country. Nay, though they live romances they are not aware of it.[4] Have you run across any copies of the book on the inside? I am curious.

I thank you for your most kind offer to help me in any way in collecting data, etc, and I thank you heartily. I hardly know, however, unless you should run across the ingredients of a good short story. You know it is the merest suggestions that count—I rarely handle plots, but nearly always do handle situations. Take the different ones of my stories which you may recollect, and you will see that they are usually built about some simple but striking human situation.

But you might do this, if it is not asking too much. When on a jaunt down to Dawson, if you should run across any good fotographs of the country, dogs, dog-teams, water, ice, snow, hill, cabin, raft, steamboat, ice-run, jam, etc. etc., scenes, why buy them and send them out to me, and then I will send in the cost of transportation and purchase price. Of course, if it is possible to send them out by the mails. I haven't any fotos of the country, and if I were lucky enough to get hold of any I should prize them most dearly. I haven't ceased kicking myself yet for not having taken a camera in with me in '97.

Well, good luck to you, Con, and a happy Thanksgiving.

Most cordially yours,
Jack London.

Oh! Was it Brett you went into the country with? Anyway, you'll remember the man and woman who went in his boat with you from Stewart River to Sixty Mile. Howard Hall the man's name was. Well, I received a letter from him a short while back. He is in New York.

 MS: CU; photocopy of 3 pp., tls.

1. JL never wrote his sociological study of San Francisco.

2. Fred Thompson.

3. *The Son of the Wolf.*

4. See "The Gold Hunters of the North," *Atlantic*, July 1903, later included in *Revolution*, for similar comments on the Klondikers' inability to see the romance of the country.

(*Right*) John London as constable of Brooklyn township in Oakland, ca. 1886 (Russ Kingman)

(*Below*) Flora Wellman London, ca. 1896 (Trust of Irving Shepard)

The earliest known photo of JL, ca. 1884 (JL State Park)

JL and his dog Rollo,
Oakland, 1886 (CSmH)

Mabel and Ted Applegarth, ca. 1885 (CSmH)

Ted Applegarth, ca. 1898 (Noto

Dyea, August 8, 1897.

Dear Mabel: — I am laying on the grass in sight of a score of glaciers, yet the slight exertion of writing causes me to sweat prodigiously.

We lay several days in Juneau, then hired canoes & paddled 100 miles to our present quarters. The Indians with us brought along their Squaws, papooses & dogs. Had a pleasant time. The 100 miles lay between mountains which formed a Yosemite Valley the whole length, & in many places the heights were stupendous, Glaciers & waterfalls on every side. Yesterday a snow slide occurred & the rumble & roar extended for fully a minute.

I expect to carry 100 lbs to the load on good trail & on the worst, 75 lbs. That is, for every mile to the Lakes, I will have to travel from 20 to 30 miles.

First page of the letter of August 8, 1897, to Mabel Applegarth (CSt)

(*Left*) In Klondike garb, posed for Ninetta Eames's article in the *Overland Monthly*, spring 1900
(Trust of Irving Shepard)

(*Below*) With Bessie Maddern and Mabel Applegarth possibly on JL and Bessie's honeymoon bicycle trip, 1900 (Noto)

A pawn ticket (JL State Park)

INTEREST MUST BE PAID MONTHLY

TREAGER'S LOAN OFFICE

Money loaned on goods of
all Descriptions

862 WASHINGTON ST., BET. 7TH AND 8TH
OAKLAND, CAL.

Unredeemed Pledges Sold for Amount Loaned and Interest   Highest Cash Price Paid for Old Gold
Fine Watch Repairing and Jewelry Manufacturing a Specialty

No. 1037   *Rambler*   Oakland, Cal.

Description   *Bicycle*

Amount loaned ($ ....)   .... Dollars

Name .... or bearer.

The Pledgor in consideration of the premises and as a part of the same transaction hereby expressly waives the demand of performance provided for by Section 3001 of the Civil Code of California and also the notice of sale provided for by Section 3002 of said Civil Code. All loans by the month. The Pledgor also agrees that the Pledgee shall not be responsible for any loss by fire, water, the act of God, the public enemy, or robbery.

For Value Received, I hereby promise and agree to pay to TREAGER'S LOAN OFFICE the above sum of money and interest in U. S. Gold Coin.   *Jack London*   (seal)

Pledges are forwarded to any part of the U. S. if this ticket and money are sent by express   (seal)

In his Oakland study, ca. 1901 (Russ Kingman)

Cloudesley Johns (CSmH)

Elwyn Hoffman (CSmH)

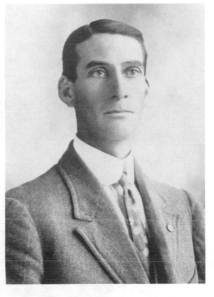

Anna Strunsky (CSmH)

Anna Strunsky and Herman (Jim) Whitaker
in a play at Camp Reverie, Forestville,
California, 1901 (Russ Kingman)

JL and Bessie in Santa Cruz,
California, ca. 1900 (CSmH)

(*Above*) Charmian Kittredge,
ca. 1898 (Trust of Irving Shepard)

(*Left and below*) Inscriptions in
CKL's copy of *The Kempton-
Wace Letters* (ULA)

To Charmian:—

"..., my Beloved, fill the
            Cup that clears
..-day of past Regrets
            and future Fears:
To-morrow!—Why,
    To-morrow I may be
myself with Yesterday's
    Seven thousand Years."

Jack.

The Bungalow,
June 6, 1903.

The Kempton-Wace Letters

To my Wife —
One hour of love is
worth a century
of science.

Mate.

Feb. 28, 1906.

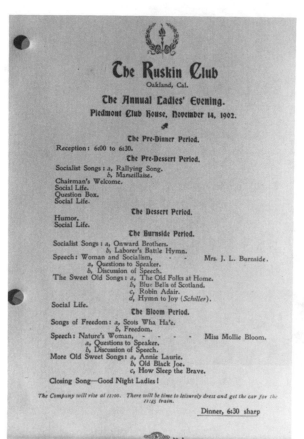

Program for the November 14, 1902, meeting of the Ruskin Club (JL State Park)

(*Below left*) Frederick Irons Bamford (CSmH)

(*Below right*) Ninetta Wiley Eames Payne (CSmH)

To Elwyn Hoffman

1130 East 15th. st.,
Oakland, Calif.,
Nov. 13/00.

Dear Elwyn:–

Was most sorry that you could not come to the Ruskin. We had Dr. Jordan there,[1] to say nothing of the rest of college Profs. and professional men. And a very interesting evening it was. I shall hope, however, that somewhere in the future you will feel able to come and see and hear us wrangle.

I wonder if you found that house on the Sunday trip to Oakland which you mentioned?

Drop over and see us when you can. Am not going out much, now— too rushed. Have so much study I must accomplish, in addittion to my regular work, to say nothing of the camera, that I am lucky when I get over five hours sleep in the twenty-four. As often as not I get nearer four.

Find herewith several fotos—the Velox ones are my first attempt, and you will notice they are too dark.[2] Am learning slowly, however.

Haven't heard anything of Idah M. for a coon's age. Have you?

Jack London.

MS: CSmH; 1 p., tls.
1. David Starr Jordan spoke to the Ruskin Club on books that had influenced his life.
2. Velox prints have been screened for halftone photoengraving.

To Anna Strunsky

1130 East 15th. st.,
Nov. 15/00.

Dear Anna:–

I see our letters cross each other on the way. And by your letter I see more clearly than ever what a mess the whole thing has been. "Woman called the creature of a lower evolution, weaker, inferior, unfit." "An insult to every woman in the world."

O Anna, it is all so unjust!

As to Sunday evening. I don't think I can possibly come. It is the third lecture of Austin Lewis' at the Unitarian Church, and I have attended neither of the other two. Also, I have sworn solemnly to myself that I would go and hear him this coming Sunday. And I really must. It is not just to him, otherwise. You will certainly understand.

And now that I have disappointed you, do not you do likewise with me. Do come, please, next Monday. We shall expect you.

Yours, with great haste, and not a little bitterness and sorrow,

Jack.

MS: CSmH; 1 p., tls.

To Elwyn Hoffman

1130 East 15th. st.,
Nov. 22/00.

Dear Elwyn:—
Thanks for the kind way in which you received my amateur attempts—the criticisms from some of my friends were rather stiff. I suppose I'll learn in time, only I can't find the time in which to learn. I get rushing along, and usually don't arrive at the dark-room part of the day's work until one or two in the morning.

Yes, just received a letter from Idah the other day after a long silence. Her mother has been sick, she is advertising the place for sale, and eastern men are there preparatory to bonding her gold properties. That's all her news I believe. I have just written her telling her what an unsociable fellow you are. Came once, was bored by me for an hour, and wouldn't even stop for dinner—that's your record.

Well, nothing much going on. Am approaching the forty-thousand mark in the novel and am damn well sick of it.

Drop over and see us whenever you feel inclined. Don't expect to be entertained, though. We usually fight and box and fence around Monday evenings, and Wednsday evenings sometimes there's a hetereogenous crowd, and sometimes only yours truly.

Jack London.

MS: CSmH; 1 p., tls.

To Cloudesley Johns

1130 East 15th. st.,
Nov. 22/00.

Dear Cloudesley:—
What a time you're having with the "Undertakers of the Desert." [1] You should have gathered by this material enough for a story about it, and a good one. It seems striking enough to call forth personal letters right down the line. Evidently the terror tale, unrelieved by humor or pathos (properly the horror tale), is in bad odor with the editorial powers that be.

But, dear Cloudesley, do you expect me to think that Great Britain should assimilate the stiff-necked Boers before breakfast? The Anglo-Saxon and the Norman give a striking instance of absorption which required a century or so to consummate. We don't require so long to-day, but then we can't do it before even we have begun.

Election went the way I expected—would have voted for McKinley myself, had I thought Bryan had a ghost of a chance of winning. As it was, cast a straight socialist ballot. Bryan's dead, Pops. dead, Dems. dying—will be dead from four to twelve years from now—part flopping to Reps. and part to us.[2] And then there will be the capitalistic party and the socialist party (by whatever names you will), in the field. In the meantime commercial expansion against the ultimate marshalling of the races.

Until then—no, until next letter,

Jack London.

MS: CSmH; 1 p., tls.
   1. See JL to Johns, December 22, 1900.
   2. William McKinley defeated William Jennings Bryan for the presidency in 1900, as he had in 1896. The Socialist candidate was Eugene V. Debs, who was also his party's nominee in 1904, 1908, 1912, and 1920. Although Bryan was to run again as the Democratic candidate in 1908, after his defeat in 1900 support for the Populist Party, which had also endorsed him that year, dwindled, and the party was indeed dead before the end of the decade.

To Anna Strunsky

[Oakland]
Nov. 27th. [1900]

Dear Anna:—

I have been sitting here crying, like a big baby. I have just finished reading *Jude the Obscure*.[1] Perhaps it is not so great as *Tess*, but in a way it is greater. When are you coming over that I may lend it you? With two such books to his name Hardy should die content. Well may he look upon his work & call it good.

Jack.

MS: CSmH; 1 p., als.
   1. Published in 1896.

To Elwyn Hoffman

1130 East 15th. st.,
Oakland, Calif.,
Dec. 10/00.

Dear Elwyn:—

Well, how goes it? At your last writing evidently very badly, but better now, I hope. You seem to be in the dumps, the blues, or something. So am I, I get them regularly, and thereby am greatly flattered. It is a penalty, you know, which must be paid by the higher organisms. Ergo, I am a higher organism. You know what Huxley says:

"The constant widening of the intellectual field indefinitely extends the range of that especially human faculty of looking before and after, which adds to the fleeting present those old and new worlds of the past and future, wherein men dwell the more, the higher their culture. But that very sharpening of the sense and that subtle refinement of emotion, which brought such a wealth of pleasures, were fatally attended by a proportionate enlargement of the capacity for suffering; and the divine faculty of imagination, while it created new heavens and new earths, provided them with the corresponding hells of futile regret for the past and morbid anxiety for the future. Finally, the inevitable penalty of over-stimulation, exhaustion, opened the gates of civilization to its great enemy, ennui—the stale and flat weariness where man delights not, nor woman either, when all things are vanity and vexation, and life seems not worth living except to escape the bore of dying."

It is from his *Evolution and Ethics*.[1] Read the essay; it will hurt no one, and do much good.

This is the penalty we pay for being higher organisms, but it is not always paid. I know many bright, talented fellows, and women too, who escape the futile regret and morbid anxiety by addressing themselves to the work of ameliorating so many factors in present-day society which are causes of futile regret and morbid anxiety. Look at the socialists, for instance—men who immolate self upon the altar of the Cause, and so immolating self, forget self, and exchange the pains of self for the pleasures of struggle and altruism. Now don't say this is all bosh. I have been so blue as to have spent a day contemplating suicide, and gone forth in the evening to lecture before some socialist organization,—or even before some bourgeois organization,—and in the battle forgot self, been uplifted out of self, and in the end returned home happy, satisfied. The thing works; it's bound to. Too much introspection is unhealthy. Man is a gregarious animal, and when he shuns his fellows he is bound to become morbid, abnormal. Would he seek happiness, let him forth to his brothers, "Who are neither children nor gods, but men in a world of men."[2]

Think it over, Elwyn.

Most sincerely yours,
Jack London.

MS: CSmH; 2 pp., tls.
1. Thomas Henry Huxley, *Evolution and Ethics: The Romanes Lecture* (1894), p. 55.
2. Rudyard Kipling, "England's Answer to the Cities" (1896), l. 30.

To Cloudesley Johns

1130 East 15th. st.,
Oakland, Calif.,
Dec. 10/00.

Dear Cloudesley:—

Kim, of course, as you have learned ere this, is appearing in *McClure's*.[1] What do you think of the opening installment?

I am full of interest for "The Undertakers of the Desert." If you have a spare copy, send it along. I remember reading one of yours in which the black specks come drifting in and drifting in from the desert to the solitary cabin where the tragedy is—is that the story in question? The *drifting* (of the specks), has impressed me and stuck by me strongly ever since. One of those one words in all the language which fits the case.

Apropos of the Boers—what do you think of Salisbury throwing down the gauntlet to the world yesterday or the day before, when he informed the nations that pleading for arbitration would not be tolerated by England and would be received as an act of hostility; and that it was England's firm intention to crush the Boer till not the least iota of disobedience or national liberty remained?[2] You peace lovers! You who say war is past—what of the forty millions of new warships the U.S. has ordered? Of the money England is now spending to make her artillery the best in the world? Eh? What of the sweeping victory the other day when the people of the United States signified their overwhelming approval of the political and geographical expansion of the United States; stamped democratically with the seal of their approval the proposition the U.S. hold all territory gained by her since '98? Eh?[3]

So many of you are prone to stand for the things which should be, abstractly considered, for the things you would like to have; and so standing; to mistake desire for the accomplishing fact. While I—I stand with those who say, it would be better if we could have what you stand for; we abhor and condemn much that flourishes to-day; but unhappily it must come, must endure for long ere the desired position is obtained. In other words, that the desired condition can only be obtained as the resultant of present forces, and while present forces in their evolution contain much which is abstractly wrong, they are relatively right, and must be.

You can't get away from the materialistic conception of history, Cloudesley. Ideas do not rule, never have ruled; where they have apeared to rule, it was merely because economic or material conditions were such as to have first generated the ideas, and secondly, to have been in harmony with the working of them. I send you something this mail bearing upon the subject. Of course, it is a pamphlet, but if so inclined, you would some time profit by running across and reading Achille Loria's *Economic Foundations of Society*.[4] The work is faulty in many places, but it is good.

Jack London.

MS: CSmH; 2 pp., tls.

1. Rudyard Kipling's *Kim* was published serially in *McClure's* from December 1900 to October 1901; it appeared in book form in 1901.

2. Robert Arthur Talbot Gascoyne-Cecil (1830 to 1903), third Marquess of Salisbury, Great Britain's prime minister from 1885 to 1892 and from 1895 to 1902. On December 6 Salisbury reaffirmed to Parliament that there would be no deviation in Great Britain's policies toward the Transvaal or the Orange Free State: neither would ever be granted independence, and war must proceed to ensure the British position in South Africa.

3. A reference to the election of the expansionist McKinley as president. Under McKinley's secretary of war, Elihu Root, the army was enlarged, officer training schools were established, and the federal government assumed the supervision of the National Guard.

4. Trans. Lindley M. Keasbey (1899). According to the translator's preface, "[Loria] divides social evolution into two distinct stages, the precapitalistic and the capitalistic. . . . [He describes] three epochs, the slave-economy, the serf-economy, and the wage-economy, and proceeds to show how the 'connective institutions of society,' morality, law, and politics, have been consistently dominated through those stages by a capitalistic spirit" (p. ix).

To Cloudesley Johns

1130 East 15th. st.,
Dec. 22/00.

Dear Cloudesley:—

"The Place of Truth"—doesn't such criminal negligence disgust one. There can be no excuse when the whole verse is regular to lose out one complete foot. It's damnable.

Yes, there is a bit of pathos in "The Undertakers." But it is such a little bit, considered from the standpoint of the reader. Don't you see, your pathos is only potential. The story contains all the possibilities of pathos, but those possibilities are not exploited. There are many reasons that they are not.

First, and above all, you approached the thing wrong. There are scores of ways of handling any subject, any situation, only one of which is the best. In my opinion, you did not choose the best. I mean, now, the point of view. Your man who dies is the particular; the world,—your readers, the universal. You, in writing the tale or sketch, meant to apply the particular to the universal. To have been true, to have been artistic, you should have applied the particular, *through the particular*, to the universal. You did not do this. You applied the particular, *through the universal*, to the universal. Let me explain. You took the point of view of the reader, not the main actor in the tragedy. You approached the tragedy and the main actor through the reader, instead of approaching the reader through the tragedy and the main actor. Or, to be plainer (even if I am mixing things up), the reader does not get inside that man and contemplate the whole thing through his soul. The reader stands apart and looks on. This should not be. For instance, the reader did not look through the man's eyes; the reader did not see, as he saw, or should have seen, the buzzards drifting in.

I cannot be plainer without bringing up something concrete. Yesterday I corrected proofsheets of a story for *McClure's*.[1] It was written some eight months ago. It will be published in the February number. Do look it up, so that you may understand more clearly what I am trying to explain. It is short, applies the particular to the universal, deals with a lonely death, of an old man, in which beasts consummate the tragedy. My man is an old Indian, abandoned in the snow by his tribe because he cannot keep up. He has a little fire, a few sticks of wood. The frost and silence about him. He is blind. How do I approach the event? What point of view do I take? Why, the old Indian's, of course. It opens up with him sitting by his little fire, listening to his tribesmen breaking camp, harnessing dogs, and departing. The reader listens with him to every familiar sound; hears the last draw away; feels the silence settle down. The old man wanders back into his past; the reader wanders with him—thus is the whole theme exploited through the soul of the Indian. Down to the consummation, when the wolves draw in upon him in a circle. Don't you see, nothing, even the moralizing and generalizing, is done, save through him, in expressions of his experience.

As to the finish of your sketch, you err. You should have chopped off at "and still newcomers wheeled lazily above the buttes, and black specks appeared against the desert sky." That is your proper ending. And have the man lying there, helpless, panting, and watching these black specks. So will the reader lie there, panting, and watch—through his eyes, always through his eyes, looking out from the door of the cabin upon the visible heat. As you have it, the reader does not look out through his eyes, from the door of the cabin. What does the reader do? Why the reader is perched up somewhere on a butte, or in mid air, and looks down and into his eyes and into the cabin door. Don't you see?

I have sent the story off as directed, several days ago; but do, please, consider these things and try to rewrite it, entirely rewrite it.

Again, I know that you can stomach my criticism without offense. Your style—don't be so halty and disconnected. Diversify your sentence structure. Sentence after consecutive sentence of yours are identical in structure, and sometimes almost in length. Quick, snappy sentences, short and crisp and curling, are oftentimes excellent for action. But if, in inaction, or minor action, you have employed them, when you come to major action, great action, they are worthless and worse than worthless.

Still again, as to phrasing. You do not cultivate it enough; you are too bald. Too rarely do you hit upon a good phrase such as "dignified birds of horror." (I could name several others.) But too rarely. Sit down and grope after them, hammer them out in sweat and blood, endure your share of the travail of birth. Don't have so many still-borns.

Oh! One other thing, Cloudesley. You are at the same time a miser and a prodigal. You are penurious of words, and spendthrift of substance. The art of omission is of tremendous importance, but must not be misunderstood. Out of the many details, many features, select only the most salient one—but, God, man! when you have selected that one, shove it along for all it is worth. In a sketch, such of yours, a score of major features may be salient, and a thousand minor ones. Yours to select the one major one, and the several minor ones. But then do not neglect the minor, while all the time subordinating them to the major. For instance, how lavish you were with the episode of the spring disappearing and leaving him more lonely. That phase dismissed in a couple of short sentences! Why, you should have taken that up somewhere along near the opening, insinuatingly, craftily, all the time and all the time preparing the poor unconscious reader for it. Let him, in the midst of the vast desert, come to it as to a human for consolation, to stretch beside it and think of the past, to moralize. Weave it into him till it is a part of him,—and then, when it disappears, there is your minor tragedy consummated without ever a word being said for that matter. The tragedy is obvious. The mere statement that it has disappeared is enough. No need to say that he is lonelier; no need, if your preparatory work has been well done. Christ! Pathos! You have all the pathos in the world in that one incident; but you did not bring it out, work it up. It is still only potential. Can you catch what I am driving at?

Yes, after much delay, I captured *Cosmopolitan* prize.[2] I flatter myself that I am one of the rare socialists who have ever succeeded in making money out of their socialism. Apropos of this, I send you a copy of a letter received day before yesterday from Brisben Walker.[3] Of course I shall not accept it. I do not wish to be bound. Which same you do think I am. Not so. McClure's have not bound me, nor will they. I want to be free, to write of what delights me, whensoever and wheresoever it delights me. No office work for me; no routine; no doing this set task and that set task. No man over me. I think McClure's have recognized this, and will treat me accordingly. Aside from pecuniary considerations, I think they are the best publishers, or magazine editors, in their personal dealings that I have run across.

Whites cannot thrive in Philipines.[4] Well, did you ever hear of the control of the tropics, by the dominant white races, from their seats in the temperate zone?—a latter day slavery, if you will. Certainly. The negro in the South is holding up his hands even now and having the shackles of the new slavery bound upon him. Such is destiny. The exploitation of lesser breeds in non-caucasian latitudes will become an anachronism—when there are no lesser breeds.[5]

You read "Evolution of Class Struggle." And found nothing in it with which to disagree. What is that little tract? Only a throwing of the light of the "materialistic conception of history" upon one phase of human development. If you had addressed that portion of your letter, which dealt with the potency of the idea, to Noyes, he would have smiled and told you to go and read Achille Loria's *Economic Foundations of Society*, or Karl Marx's *Das Kapital*. Where do they put the idea? Bah, it is of little account. Whence does the idea come? From the economic structure of the society. Your idea cannot escape coming. It is imperative that it shall come, inevitable. But not come because it is intrinsically an idea, but because it cannot help itself. The thing is to deep for me to go into in a correspondence, but read it up, you. Read also, Draper's *Intellectual Development of Europe*,[6] if you want to know about the materialistic conception of history.

Your idea does not crystalize material conditions, but is crystalized by material conditions. All evolution, all change, is from without, in; not from within, out. The fundamental characteristic of all life is IRRITABILITY. In the other words, capacity for feeling pressures from without. Life itself is an equilibrium, between what is within and what is without. A change from without in the pressures, and the organism's equilibrium is overthrown. Possessing irritability, it may be able to respond to the changed pressure and so establish a new equilibrium. If it does, it continues to live. If it fails, it dies. Life is equilibrium. If all forces which impinged upon an organism were constant, you would have a constant organism. There would be no change. There would be no development. The economic pressure, from without, forces the change, forces the idea, causes the idea.

Yes, do please send me a copy of "The Path of the Destroyer."[7] No, I have seen *Review of Review*'s notice of *Cosmopolitan* essay.[8] Thanks just the same.

War—what did I hold? Read up my *Overland* resume of Bloch's book.[9] I held that war, as a direct means of ganing the desired end, was worthless; that it was now only the indirect means. That behind it was economics, which exerted themselves through it, and accomplished the desired end through it. "Not battles, but famine," I said. I do not ask you to occupy my old ground; for I wish to still occupy it myself. But while we are on this question of occupying ground, let me show you an example of your straddling propensities. In one portion of your present letter you are for "boosting natural selection" out of the way. In another, you say war is a splendid necessity, preventing stagnation, etc. Well, can you reconcile the two statements?

Speaking of illustrations, did you see how beautifully *Ainslie's* did by my story in December number?[10] Incidentally, without asking my permission, here and there they succeeded in cutting out fully five hundred words, which I shall reinsert when published in book form. I suppose the one hundred and twenty-five they paid for it was considered sufficient justification for mangling.

Jack London.

MS: CSmH; 7 pp., tls. Pbd: *L*, 114–18.
    1. "The Law of Life."
    2. See JL to Johns, June 12, 1899, second letter, n. 4.
    3. John Brisben Walker (1847–1931), owner and publisher of *Cosmopolitan* from 1885 to 1894 and its editor from 1886 to 1905. On December 13, 1900, Walker offered to retain JL to write for *Cosmopolitan* on an annual basis.
    4. JL repeats an assertion Johns made in an undated letter, presumably written in mid-December 1900 (CSmH).
    5. In his undated letter Johns wrote: "I admit evolution—as opposed to revolution—but it may be boosted, & '*natural* selection' taketh now a back seat. Also I am convinced that exploitation of lesser breeds in anti-caucasian latitudes has become an anachronism, best recognized as such by nations not founded upon it, even though *extermination* of ditto breeds in higher latitudes be inevitable & essential to the material welfare of the race which averages best & strongest now."
    6. John William Draper, in the introduction to *History of the Intellectual Development of Europe* (1869), asserts: "Social advancement is as completely under the control of natural law as is bodily growth. The life of an individual is a miniature of the life of a nation. . . . No one, I believe, has hitherto undertaken the labour of arranging the evidence offered by the intellectual history of Europe in accordance with physiological principles, as to illustrate the orderly progress of civilization or collected the facts furnished by other branches of science with a view of enabling us to recognize clearly the conditions under which that takes place." Draper attempts to "ascertain how far [Europe's] progress has been fortuitous and how far determined by primordial law" (p. 1).
    7. A story by Johns, published in *Home Magazine*, December 1900.
    8. "What Competition Costs Us," *American Monthly Review of Reviews*, December 1900.
    9. "The Impossibility of War."
    10. "The Great Interrogation," illustrated by W. V. Cahill.

To Anna Strunsky

1130 East 15th. st.,
Dec. 26, 1900.

Comrade Mine:—

    Thus it was I intended addressing you a Christmas greeting, saying, as it seemed to me, for you, the finest thing in the world. But it was impossible. For a week I have been suffering from the blues, during which time I have not done a stroke of work. Am writing this with cold fingers, at six in the morning—going for a day on the water, fishing, shooting, etc., to see if there are any curative forces left in the universe.

    Ah! We refuse not to speak, and yet we speak brokenly and stumblingly! True, too true. The paradox of social existence, to be truthful, we lie; to live true, we live untruthfully. The social wisdom is a thing of great worth—to the mass. For the few it is a torment, upon it they are crucified—not for their salvation, but for the salvation of the mass. I grow, sometimes, almost to hate the mass, to sneer at dreams of reform. To be superior to the mass is to be the slave of the mass. The mass knows no slavery; it is the task master.

But how does this concern you and me? Ah, does it not concern us? We may refuse not to speak, yet we speak brokenly and stumblingly—because of the mass. The tyranny of the crowd, as I suppose Gerald Stanley Lee would put it.[1] As for me, just when freedom seems opening up to me, I feel the bands tightening and the rivetting of the gyves. I remember, now, when I was free. When there was no restraint, and I did what the heart willed. Yes, one restraint, the Law; but when one willed, one could fight the law, and break or be broken. But now, one's hands are tied, one may not fight, but only yield and bow the neck. After all, the sailor on the sea and the worker in the shop are not so burdened. To break or be broken, there they stand. But to be broken while not daring to break, there's the rub.

I could almost advocate a return to nature this dark morning. A happiness to me?—added unto me?—Why you have been a delight to me, dear, and a glory. Need I add, a trouble? For the things we love are the things which hurt us as well as the things we hurt. Ah, believe me, believe me, "I have not winced or cried aloud."[2] The things unsaid are the greatest. Surely, sitting here, gathering data, classifying, arranging; writing stories for boys with moral purposes insidiously inserted; hammering away at a thousand words a day; growing genuinely excited over biological objections; thrusting a bit of fun at you and raising a laugh, when it should have been a sob—surely all this is not all. What you have been to me? I am not great enough or brave enough to say. This false thing, which the world would call my conscience, will not permit me. But it is not mine; it is the social conscience, the world's, which goes with the world's leg-bar and chain. A white beautiful friendship?—between a man and a woman?—the world cannot imagine such a thing, would deem it as inconceivable as infinity or non-infinity

(Thursday morning)

A cold, miserable, shivery day, yesterday, but I brought back a fair catch of fish. I shall be

(Friday morning)

So far did I take up the broken screed yesterday, when breakfast called. But before breakfast was over a friend dropped in—most unusual thing. But ere he had been gone five minutes, another dropped in, and another, and then two, and—well, that is the history of the day. Further, received a telephone from Bamford[3] asking me to come and see him, important, and I went.

Now I shall try and finish. I'll come over in the afternoon, Saturday. (Have just come back from your call at the phone.)

So, until to-morrow,

Jack.

MS: CSmH; 3 pp., tls. Pbd: *L*, 118–19; *BJL*, I, 347–48.

1. JL refers to Lee's "The Dominance of the Crowd," *Atlantic*, December 1900. Lee wrote: "This is the main fact about this modern world: that it is a crowded world, that in the nature of the case its civilization is a crowd civilization. . . . Any man who makes the attempt to interpret anything, either in art or life without a true understanding of the crowd principle as it is working to-day, without a due sense of its central place in all that goes on around us, is a spectator in the blur and bewilderment of this modern world . . . helpless in it, and . . . childish and superficial in it."

2. See JL to Johns, April 22, 1899, n. 7.

3. Frederick I. Bamford.

1901

Lecturer at Camp Reverie, Forestville, California, June 1901 (CSmH)

To Cloudesley Johns

1130 East 15th. st.,
Jan. 5/01.

Dear Cloudesley:—

Regarding Talcott Williams on "Change in Current Fiction," must say I cannot agree with him, and that a canvass of the majority of recent books will totally disprove his averages.[1] He says nothing can be done with a book of fifty thousand. *The Son of the Wolf* had only 49,000, and it make a dollar and a half book of fair size. I hate to go into a book of more than 100,000. What do you think about it?

I stand convicted on the buzzards. My treat. The principle I outlined is all right, though it does not apply in this particular case.

I have written probably one hundred and ten thousand this year, against your ninety-odd; but I think that I loafed or did other things less, and that each thousand took me longer than each of your thousands did you.

To tell you the truth, Cloudesley, I haven't had any decent work published recently—work which I would care to have you read—socialistic essay excepted,[2] and that I was unable to get a whack at in the proofsheets.

Your "plowing" repeated in "Destroyer" sketch[3] is certainly right. "At this season"—wouldn't it damn you. "Not so" is correct. "Not as" is vile grammar. "So" also accompanies the negative. "As," the positive. I am *as good* as you. I am *not so good* as you. That's the rule, anyway, and if I were you I'd fire it into *Home Magazine* editor. Why, sometimes my ear demands that I turn a positive "as" into a "so"; but never have I felt impelled to do the opposite. The bad use of "so" in such instances as this, is chronic with ninety-nine percent of newspaper men, about ninety of editors, and about fifty of first class writers.

I liked the sketch. I was taken by it right into the country described. Yet I do not think the *motif* was exploited as fully as it might have been or should have been.

I am indeed sorry that I cannot help you out just now. Almost any other time I would have been able to. But, you see, Christmas is just past. Further, a friend[4] has taken up writing with seven children and an un-

developed ability, which said friend I have been helping to finance. Another, both ankles broken badly some time since. Then my mother, to
whose pension I add thirty dollars each month, got back in her debts and
I have just finished straightening her out to the tune of thirty-six dollars.
She just got five more extra ones to-day. And my Mammie Jennie (negro
foster mother) came down upon me for December quarterly payment of
interest on mortgage, and delinquent taxes. Furthermore, within a week I
expect my wife to be confined.[5] Just the wrong time, Cloudesley, old man.
January check *non est*, and I have been going along on borrowed money
since before Christmas.

Jack London.

MS: CSmH; 2 pp., tls. Pbd: *L*, 119–20; *BJL*, I, 349.
   1. Talcott Williams (1849–1928), leading American journalist, from 1912 to 1919 first
director of the Columbia School of Journalism; "The Change in Current Fiction," *American
Monthly Review of Reviews*, December 1900. Williams claimed: "A story of 50,000 words
is too long for a magazine and too short for a book. Anything short of 100,000 words offers
serious difficulties, because it fits no special sale. The right length is a story which reaches
150,000 words and does not pass 200,000. The reader will accept more from some authors,
but he dislikes a larger measure from any."
   2. "What Communities Lose by the Competitive System."
   3. "The Path of the Destroyer."
   4. Herman Whitaker.
   5. Their first child, Joan, was born on January 15.

To Elwyn Hoffman

1130 East 15th. st.,
Jan. 6/[01].[1]

Dear Elwyn:—

   As regards Markham.[2] Poverty of rhythm and richness of phraseology
do mark his work. But that is not the whole tale. Further, his very expression and phrasing are empoverished. But, on the other hand, his greatest
claim on the present, and on posterity, is the substance. After all, it is the
substance that counts. What is form? What intrinsic value resides in it?
None, none, none—unless it clothe pregnant substance, great substance.
There is where Markham steps in. Of course, I grant it is well to have
both substance and form, but it is better to have substance alone, than
form alone.

   Now that you have broken the ice, come and see us again. I should like
to have you meet Miss Anna Strunsky some time. She is well worth meeting. Further, she lives in 'Frisco,[3] and at her place you may meet all sorts
of people. I told her, when you first came down, that I had a friend whom
I imagined was not well acquainted in the city, and that I wished to make
it pleasant for him. Of course, I did not entertain myself, and only went
out on invitation (which usually precluded my taking any one with me)—

I have no places where I call, you know. So she promised, in fact it was on her initiative, that she would like to have you come to her place now and again. Debating clubs (literary, etc.) meet there. Also, she has her exoteric circles and her esoteric circles—by this I mean the more intimate and the less intimate. One may pass from the one to the other if deemed worthy.

She it was who went sailing with us that Monday I asked you over in order that you might meet her. She loves Browning. She is deep, subtle, and psychological. She is neither stiff nor formal. Very adaptive. Knows a great deal. Is a joy and a delight to her friends. She is a Russian, and a Jewess, who has absorbed the Western culture, and who warms it with a certain oriental leaven.

Jack London.

MS: CSmH; 2 pp., tls.
    1. Misdated "Jan. 6/00."
    2. Edwin Markham.
    3. JL recorded two San Francisco addresses for Anna Strunsky in his address book (CSmH): 901 Golden Gate Avenue and 974 Sutter Street.

To Anna Strunsky

[Oakland]
Sunday Morning,
Jan. 6/[01].[1]

Dear Anna:—

I had intended writing you yesterday, asking you to come over Monday evening and go with me to that equal suffragist club before which Whittaker was to read.[2] Then Tuesday I could have taken your pictures. But I had forgotten Mrs. Cowell's lectures.[3] Then your letter came. Also found out that Monday was not the night and that we would have our regular boxing bout.

So Saturday, but come early, in the morning, so that I may take advantage of the sun. This, then, be the qualification: if I do not telephone you otherwise. Possibly, ere that time, the boy—I do pray for a boy—shall have arrived.[4] In which case, you must come. So, Saturday, early, be it understood, unless I telephone. My birthday. A quarter of a century of breath. I feel very old.

Of the New Comer, I thank you for what you say. It will be in itself a dear consummation. Then must come the patient determining. And, O Anna, it must be make or break. No whining puny breed. It must be great and strong. Or—the penalty must be paid. By it, by me; one or the other. So be.

I shall be glad to go in for the Ibsen circle. I need more of that in my life.

Do bring the two photographic plates from Mrs. Stein's.[5] I am getting soft; I must box more.

Jack.

MS: CSmH; 1 p., tls. Pbd: *L*, 120–21; *BJL*, I, 349–50.

   1. Misdated "Jan. 6/00."

   2. Whitaker spoke on objections to women's suffrage at a meeting of the Seventh Ward Political Equality Club in Oakland on January 10. JL also gave his views on this subject at the meeting. See JL to Johns, June 23, 1899, for his views opposing women's suffrage.

   3. Possibly S. Emma Cowell, an American dramatic reader popular in the 1870's and 1880's.

   4. According to Joan London, her father was so unhappy his child was a girl that he referred to her as "it" for the first few days (*JL Times,* 227).

   5. Possibly Mrs. M. D. Stein.

To Joseph C. Rowell [1]

1130 East 15th. st.,
Oakland, Calif.,
Jan. 23/01.

Dear sir:—

   The other evening Prof. Armes [2] spoke to me concerning the alcove of California writers in the U.C. Library, and I shall be indeed happy to contribute my small quota. I have had only one book published so far, *The Son of the Wolf.* And unhappily, I have none on hand just now. But this mail I am writing Messrs. Houghton, Mifflin & Co., to send me a few copies, and as soon as they arrive I shall start one, autographed I believe, to you. But do tell me, please, how and where and on what leaf one is supposed to write the autograph. I am lamentably ignorant.

Very sincerely yours,
Jack London.

MS: CU; 1 p., tls.

   1. Joseph Cummings Rowell (1853–1938), librarian at the University of California.

   2. William Dallam Armes (1860–1918), professor of American literature at the University of California, and an occasional speaker at the Ruskin Club.

To H. Gaylord Wilshire

Oakland, Cal.,
Jan. 23, 1901.

Dear Comrade:

   Find herewith coin cards containing fifty cents in silver, for which please send me *The Challenge* [1] at above address for one year. I saw the first copies this morning and send in my subscription at once. There is a snap and go about your new venture which I must say I like, to say nothing of its intrinsic worth. I know I shall get my money back many fold ere the year is out.

Fraternally yours,
Jack London.

SOURCE: "From America's Kipling," *The Challenge*, February 6, 1901.
    1. H. Gaylord Wilshire (1861–1927), socialist and millionaire land developer in the Los Angeles area. He began *The Challenge* as a weekly socialist magazine in 1900. Later in 1901 Wilshire moved the magazine from Los Angeles to New York, and published it as the monthly *Wilshire's Magazine*, which continued until 1915.

To J. H. Eustice[1]

1130 East Fifteenth street
Oakland, Cal.
Jan. 29, 1901.

Dear Sir—

In accepting the nomination for Mayor, at the hands of the Social Democratic party, I feel constrained to add a few words concerning the forthcoming election.[2]

A striking feature of recent municipal elections has been one of remarkable similarity in the platforms of the various parties. All the platforms, not omitting the Social Democratic, have contained strong demands for the municipalization of public utilities. So expressed, it would seem, therefore, that the common wish of the community was for municipal ownership. And it would seem, furthermore, since all parties have demanded it, that long ere this a fair share of public utilities had passed into the hands of the people of Oakland.

So it seems, but as a matter of fact not so. There has been some hemming and hawing, no doubt; and that was all that was to be expected. It could not have been otherwise, considering the parties into whose keeping were entrusted the affairs of the city. They could have done nothing more than they have done; nor is it in the nature of things that they should.

Between the national creed and the municipal creeds of either of the old parties there is little or nothing in common. The little in common is, in the last analysis, that they are capitalistic. The interests of capitalism are their interests, and that is all. On the other hand there is much in conflict. When a party nationally champions gold, expansion, the trusts and the big capitalist it is certainly very inconsistent for the same party to municipally champion public ownership, to the detriment of the large capitalist and the benefit of the proletariat. The same holds for the other party when it goes into municipal politics, for, though it opposes gold, expansion, the trusts and the large capitalist, it cries out unavailingly for the salvation, not of the proletariat, but of the small capitalist who is being crushed out by the inexorable industrial evolution. So, election after election, we see the same inconsistency flourish, the same paradox, which, strive as they will, cannot be fused into the honest truism.

But the municipal platform of the Social Democratic party does not stand unrelated as something quite different from the national platform; for, after all, it is merely a part of a great world philosophy—an economic, political and social philosophy, reared on sound ethical, and humanely ethical, foundations. Its one great demand is justice, or, in other words, an equal chance for all men. Just as we today have civil equality before the law, and political equality at the polls, so it is a matter of simple justice that we should also have equality of opportunity in industrial life. For, without the last the first and second often come to naught. The law is many-sided. That which it measures to the poor man is not always what it measures, under precisely similar circumstances, to the rich corporation. Of this there is no discussion. It has been substantiated, under oath, before too many a Congressional and State investigation committee. As regards political equality it is much the same. One vote counts as much as another; but the machine counts for something more, and when the wealth of the country is back of the machine the equality of the unorganized, incoherent, moneyless working class vanishes in thin air.

So when we Social Democrats draft our municipal platform we demand that which our national platform demands, that which we demand the world over, namely, equality of opportunity. True our immediate municipal demands partake of the nature of palliatives; but on the other hand they are consistent with the great fundamental demand. This cannot be said of the old parties.

Incidentally, in closing, it is meet that we congratulate ourselves for the work we have already done. For it is we, the Socialists, working as a leaven throughout society, who are responsible for the great and growing belief in municipal ownership. It is we, the Socialists, by our propaganda, who have forced the old parties to throw, as sops to the popular unrest, like demands, and unwittingly to aid us in the education of the people.

Fraternally yours,
Jack London.

SOURCE: "London Accepts the Nomination," *Oakland Tribune*, February 5, 1901.

1. J. H. Eustice, secretary of the City Executive Committee of the Social Democratic Party.

2. Along with most other Oakland socialists, JL had left the Socialist Labor Party for the Oakland Social Democratic Party, organized at the beginning of 1901; see Foner, *Jack London*, p. 45. JL was the first candidate the new party ran for mayor. He received only 245 votes in the fall election, which he lost to the wealthy Populist John L. Davie.

To Cloudesley Johns

1130 East 15th. st.,
Oakland, Calif.,
Feb. 4/01.

Dear Cloudesley:—

Not dead, but rushed as usual. Have got down to my regular five hours and a half sleep again and running by the clock. Am just answering a whole stack of letters (you'll say I'm apologizing for not having written sooner—but not so, rather for the shortness of this.)

Well, there's no accounting for things. I did so ardently long to be a father, that it seemed impossible that such a happiness should be mine. But it is. And a dam fine, healthy youngster. Weighed nine and a half pounds at birth, which they say is good for a girl. Up to date has shown a good stomach and lack of ailments, for it does nothing but eat and sleep, or lie awake for a straight hour without a whimper. Intend to call her "Joan." Tell me how you like it, what associations it calls up.

Tell me what kind of answer Vance made to your scorcher of Jan. 4th.[1] I am most interested to hear. However, as regards editing the "Destroyer," is there any necessity of drawing me into it. I do not remember what I wrote about it, but nevertheless, if you want to quote me, go ahead. I should rather not, though.

As regards "bumming by force from peoples inhabiting lands we cannot thrive in? Does not our modern slavery serve to deteriorate us, affecting our own government? While counting the profit you must not ignore the loss."—as regarding this I hardly know what to say. Do you not realize that whatever is "is right and wise." Certainly it may be made wiser and more right in the natural course of evolution (and then again it mayn't), but the point is that it is the best possible under the circumstances. Given so much matter, and so much force, and beginning at the beginning of things as regards this our world, do you not know that it could not have worked out in any other way, nay, not in the least jot or tittle could it have been other than it has. We may make it better; and then again we may not.

As Dr. Ross[2] somewhere says: "Evolution is no kindly mother to us. We do not know at what moment it may turn against us and destroy us." Don't you see; I speak not of the things that should be; nor of the things I should like to be; but I do speak of the things that are and will be. I should like to have socialism; yet I know that socialism is not the very next step; I know that capitalism must live its life first. That the world must be exploited to the utmost first; that first must intervene a struggle for life among the nations, severer, intenser, more widespread, than any ever before. I should much more prefer to wake to-morrow in a smoothly-running socialistic state; but I know I shall not; I know it cannot come that way. I know that the child must go through its child's sicknesses ere it becomes a man. So, always, remember that I speak of the things that are; not of the things that should be.

Find enclosed *Cosmopolitan* letters.[3] I stood off first one & wrote to *McClure's.* They have agreed to go on with me, giving me utter freedom. So you see, at least they have not bought *me* body & soul.[4] Honestly, they are the most human editors I ever dealt with. When I think about them, it is more as very dear friends, than people I am doing business with.

However, in refusing *Cosmopolitan* offer, which means giving up freedom, I think I have acted for the best. What think you?

Please return letters.

Jack London.

I send *Fables* this mail.[5] Also "Charge to Company." You fixed the latter up much better, very much better.[6] The former please return quickly, as half a dozen are clamoring for it.

MS: CSmH; 3 pp., tls. Pbd: *L*, 121–22; *BJL*, I, 350–51.

    1. Arthur Turner Vance, to whom Johns had sent a letter protesting the *Home*'s editing of "The Path of the Destroyer." See JL to Johns, January 5, 1901.

    2. Edward Alsworth Ross (1866–1961), former professor of sociology at Stanford and an occasional speaker at the Ruskin Club. On November 13, 1900, he was forced to resign from Stanford for advocating restriction of immigration from Japan. In 1901 he published *Social Control: A Survey of the Foundations of Order.*

    3. Beginning with this sentence, the remainder of the letter is handwritten.

    4. See JL to Hoffman, July 23, 1900, n. 1; JL to Johns, December 22, 1900, n. 3.

    5. Probably George Ade's *Fables in Slang.*

    6. See JL to Johns, February 22, 1899.

To Cloudesley Johns

1130 East 15th. st.,
Feb. 13/01.

Dear Cloudesley:–

Well, I am on the home stretch of the novel,[1] and it is a failure. This is not said in a fit of the blues, but from calm conviction. However, on the other hand, I have learned a great deal concerning the writing of novels. On this one which I have attempted, I could write three books of equal size showing wherein I failed, and why, and laying down principles violated, etc. O, it's been a great study. I shall be at work finishing it for the rest of the month—you know I always finish whatever I begin. I never leave a thing in such a state that in the time to come haunting thoughts may creep in—"If I only had gone on," etc.

McClure's are getting ready to bring out a second collection of Klondike stories[2]—not so good as the first, however.

March I shall take a vacation, and April I intend writing my long-deferred "Salt of the Earth." So get ready to burn me up and go to collecting data.

I see you laugh at me and my optimistic philosophy. So be. I only wish you would study up the materialistic conception of history, then you would understand my position.

No, won't want "Mayor of Jacktown thing."[3]

Jack London.

MS: CSmH; 1 p., tls. Pbd: *BJL*, I, 351–52.

    1. *A Daughter of the Snows.*

2. *The God of His Fathers.*
3. A notice by "Yorick" in the *San Francisco Evening Post*, January 26, 1901, claimed: "I understand that as soon as Jack London is elected mayor of Oakland by the Social Democrats, the name of the place will be changed. The Social Democrats, however, have not decided whether they will call it London or Jacktown."

To Cloudesley Johns

1062 First Avenue,
Oakland, Calif.,
March 15/01.

Dear Cloudesley:—

Note by above address that I have moved.[1] Last seen of old house there was a foot and a half of water under it, and the back yard a lake. Am much more finely situated now, nearer to Oakland, with finer view, surroundings, air, etc. etc. Do you remember Lake Merrit?—a body of water which you might have seen from the electric cars on the way to my place from down town. I am located right near it, and believe, with a sling shot from the roof of the house, that I could throw a stone into it.

Shall have the novel done in ten days, now—N.G. But I know I shall be able to do a good one yet.

Say, do you recollect telling me about that story of your mother's which was published in the last issue of *Godey's,*[2] and which Munsey refused to pay for, but which Munsey later republished? How did it ever come out? What did you do about it?

Mr. Whitaker is selling some of his work, now—*Ainslie's, The S. S. McClure, Munsey's,* etc. etc.[3] He's picking up.

Thanks for samples from scrap collection. I liked them, and better, I like the way you have arranged the collection. It's very neat and handy. Well, nothing doin'.

Jack.

MS: CSmH; 1 p., tls. Pbd: *BJL*, I, 352.
1. The Londons had moved to Villa La Capriccioso, owned by the sculptor Felix Peano.
2. Jeanie Peet, "The Justice of Colomare," *Godey's Lady's Book* (April 1898). The last issue of *Godey's* was actually August 1898.
3. In addition to the three magazines mentioned by JL, Whitaker sold his work to the *Overland Monthly, Harper's, Cosmopolitan, Arena,* and other periodicals.

To Edward Applegarth

1062 First Avenue
Oakland, Calif.
Mar. 19/01.

Dear Ted:—

I'll arrive at your place somewhere along Friday, Sat. or Sunday.—stop 2 or 3 days. (Novel is done, but have to go over it.) Do you think out a *motif* for a Fourth of July story for *Youth's Companion*.[1] Scene must be Klondike, or at sea, or frontier somewhere. It must involve rough life or adventure, but must not be weird or humorous.

Jack.

MS: CSmH; 1 p., als.
    1. JL did not publish a Fourth of July story in *Youth's Companion* in 1901, but "The 'Fuzziness' of Hoockla Heen" appeared in the July 3, 1902, issue of the magazine.

To Anna Strunsky

[Oakland]

Dear Anna:—   [? March 1901]

Your letter is a splendid, a delicately splendid, addition to the book.[1] I am anxious to see it in type (of course the book, but I mean your letter). I want to see it shape up.

While I could not answer yours, it nevertheless impelled me to work, and find here my attempt at re-writing my first letter. I have been two whole days on it, and working hard. From the trouble I have had with it, and from its original horribleness, I now know that I shall have to write it a third time (at the general revision), ere it is worth looking at. However, I send it for what it is worth. How bad my first letters were I never dreamed. I know now.

You will notice that I have devoted little space to Hester, and more space to other and unimportant things. I have described her mental characteristics, her intellectual constitution, that which appeals to the non-loving Herbert Wace. For the reader I have already opened the breach between you and me. When the book opens we are both aware of the slipping away, vaguely aware; one certain function of the book will be to differentiate us so that the breach becomes sharply defined. I change my landlord to my friend Gwynne. I shall develop a love experience for him, which shall culminate in one of the inserted letters—naturally the love experience will be evidence on my side of the contention.

Am rushing this to catch the postman. Sunday afternoon at 901.[2]

Jack.

MS: CSmH; 1 p., tls. Pbd: *BJL*, I, 359.
    1. *The Kempton-Wace Letters*.
    2. Strunsky's address in San Francisco, 901 Golden Gate Avenue.

To Cloudesley Johns

1062 First Avenue
Oakland, Calif.
April 1/01.

Dear Cloudesley:—

The novel is off at last, and right glad am I that it is. The very first thing I shall do, now, will be the "Salt of the Earth." I do not know whether it will be a success (from standpoint of writing), and if it is I do not know whether I can find publication. But if these things come out all right, you'll then have your chance to fire back at me. But there are others. Almost every one I know very intimately, are threatening to come back at me on the same thing. So there should be something doing.

You have heard me speak often of Strawn-Hamilton, the genius, tramp, socialist, etc. etc. He has been back some time now, and has gone into the labor movement. Two months ago he organized the cooks and waiters of San Francisco.[1] To-day they are seventeen hundred strong, with six thousand dollars cash in the treasury. He is their walking delegate (business agent), and gets five dollars a week carfare and a hundred a month salary, besides having an assistant secretary, etc. So things move along.

I never can understand why it is you cannot leave go that Postoffice. How is it?

I send herewith a letter from *Town Topics*. They are paying two dollars for jokes now, and if you have any it wouldn't be a bad idea to send them along. I do not know much about joke writing, but I wouldn't send jokes in a bunch. I sent four triolets (the only four I ever wrote), to *Town Topics*. They took one, and sent three back. Later I re-sent one of the triolets: they took it. Later I resent another; they took it. But they balked on the fourth.[2]

Yes, I should like ever so much to have some of those pastescraps—the more the merrier.

Your remarks concerning my stuff in the *Writer* was the first I had heard of its being published.[3] I did not know what to make of your criticism, and bided judgement until I had read what I had long before written—written long before I was married. I have just now read the stuff and I cannot see that your criticism is merited. Pray where am I "illogical and unscientific"?

You remember my advice long ago (this is not apropos of the previous paragraph, but of your letter in general)— By all means shake Harold, and come somewhere and live in the center of things. In this day one cannot isolate oneself and do anything. Get you a big city anywhere, and plunge into it and live and meet people and things. If you believe that man is the creature of his environment, then you cannot afford to remain way off there on the edge of things.

Jack London.

MS: CSmH; 2 pp., tls. Pbd: *L*, 122–23; *BJL*, I, 352–53.
1. JL gave an account of the strike of the San Francisco cooks and waiters in "Wanted: A New Law of Development," *International Socialist Review*, August 1902; this article was later included in *War of the Classes*.
2. See JL to Johns, March 15, 1899, n. 3.
3. "The Question of a Name," *Writer*, December 1900. *Writer*, founded in Boston in 1887, was a monthly magazine that gave help to beginning authors.

To Anna Strunsky

[Oakland]
April 3/01.

Dear Anna:–

Did I say that the human might be filed in categories? Well, and if I did, let me qualify—not all humans. You elude me. I cannot place you, cannot grasp you. I may boast that of nine out of ten, under given circumstances, I can forecast their action; that of nine out of ten, by their word or action, I may feel the pulse of their hearts. But of the tenth I dispair. It is beyond me. You are that tenth.

Were ever two souls, with dumb lips, more incongrously matched! We may feel in common—surely, we ofttimes do—and when we do not feel in common, yet do we understand; and yet we have no common tongue. Spoken words do not come to us. We are unintelligible. God must laugh at the mummery.

The one gleam of sanity through it all is that we are both large temperamentally, large enough to often understand. True, we often understand but in vague glimmering ways, by dim perceptions, like ghosts, which, while we doubt, haunt us with their truth. And still, I, for one, dare not believe; for you are that tenth which I may not forecast.

Am I unintelligible now? I do not know. I imagine so. I cannot find the common tongue.

Large temperamentally—that is it. It is the one thing that brings us at all in touch. We have, flashed through us, you and I, each a bit of the universal, and so we draw together. And yet we are so different.

I smile at you when you grow enthusiastic? It is a forgivable smile— nay, almost an envious smile. I have lived twenty-five years of repression. I learned not to be enthusiastic. It is a hard lesson to forget. I begin to forget, but it is so little. At the best, before I die, I cannot hope to forget all or most. I can exult, now that I am learning, in little things, in other things; but of my things, and secret things doubly mine, I cannot, I cannot. Do I make myself intelligible? Do you hear my voice. I fear not. There are poseurs. I am the most successful of them all.

Jack.

MS: CSmH; 2 pp., tls. Pbd: *L*, 123–24; *BJL*, I, 353–54.

To Cloudesley Johns

1062 First Avenue
Oakland, Calif.
April 8/01.

Dear Cloudesley:—

Thanks for slips. I'm open to as many as you can spare. I am using them for precisely the same thing you do, so thanks for the idea, too.

I am sending you herewith pictures of the youngster at three weeks and two months.

Every man, at the beginning of his career (whether laying bricks or writing books or anything else), has two choices. He may choose immediate happiness, or ultimate happiness. This is a fact you nor nobody else can deny. He who chooses ultimate happiness, and has the ability, and works hard, will find that the reward for his effort is cumulative, that the interest on his energy invested is compounded. The artisan who is industrious, steady, reliant, is suddenly, one day, advanced to a foremanship with increased wages. Now is that advance due to what he did that day, or the day before? Ah, no, it is due to the long years of industry and steadiness. The same with the reputation of a business man or artist. The thing grows and compounds. He is not only "paid for having done something once upon a time," as you put it, but he has been paid for continuing to do something through quite a period of time. Is this not true of the veriest gambler, who first loses to his victim, deferring payment for such expended energy until the end?

However, Cloudesley, I grasp what you meant to say. You meant "Unethical" instead of "unscientific." Science deals with the things which are; ethics deals, usually, with the things which ought to be. Ethically, perhaps (only perhaps), it might be better to have only immediate happiness; but *actually*, ultimate happiness is a potent thing which must be considered.

O no. My "incentive" is not the "assurance of being able some day to sell any sort of work on the strength of a name." Every year we have writers, old writers, crowded out—men, who once had names, but who had gained them wrongfully, or had not done the work necessary to maintain them. In its way, the struggle for a man with a name to maintain the standard by which he gained that name, is as severe as the struggle for the unknown to make a name.

Jack London.

MS: CSmH; 2 pp., tls. Pbd: *L*, 124–25; *BJL*, I, 354.

To Cornelius Gepfert

1062 First Avenue
Oakland, Calif.
April 19/01.

Dear Con:—

I often think of you, up there in the Northland, and wonder when I shall go back. For go back I certainly shall, and I pray the day be not far distant. But, as you say, things must be changed.

I have finished the novel, sent it East, and word of its acceptance has already come back. It will be published next fall by McClure, Phillips & Co. In the meantime immediate serial publication is being sought for it.[1] Also, in a month or so I shall have another collection of short stories brought out.[2] Let me know if you will be still in the Klondike a couple of months from now; if you will, I'll send it to you.

Been moving house (note change of address above), and am just about fairly settled down now in the new quarters. How different from moving the few traps of an Alaskan camp!

By the way, photographs have not yet arrived. I presume, however, that only letters leave the country, as of yore, and that packages will not travel until the river breaks.

Must cut this short, as I'm going to a funeral right away.[3]

Sincerely yours,
Jack London.

MS: CU; photocopy of 1 p., tls.
  1. McClure offered *A Daughter of the Snows* to the *Saturday Evening Post*, but the novel was rejected and never appeared serially. See JL to Hoffman, July 23, 1900, n. 1.
  2. *The God of His Fathers.*
  3. For John Layne.

To Cloudesley Johns

1062 First Avenue
Oakland, Calif.
April 19/01.

Dear Cloudesley:—

I agree with you in some of your criticism of "The Law of Life," but not in all. For instance, "What was that?" Remember, the words occur, not in the writer's narrative—in such a place your criticism would hold good. But the words do occur in the mind of the Indian. He *thinks* them. And that it is the most natural thing in the world for a person to so think when something unknown or unusual occurs, you cannot deny.

Certainly, science deals with potentialities—with what will be as well as what has been and is.[1] But that does not effect my position in the slightest. Note again, science deals with what *will be* not with what *should be*. It is all the difference between preached ethics and practiced ethics. The one deals with the conduct which ought to be; the other with the conduct which is to be. Also, when I said science deals with what is, I perhaps was in error not to include past and future of the verb. I thought it understood.

You did not answer my choices of immediate and ultimate happiness; nor my sober steady artisan raised to a foremanship. Can you answer them in the light of your argument? I doubt it.

"In 1889 my grandmother, hypnotized by the seductive eloquence of a highly evolved land shark"—well?[2]

Kim is all right—if, as you say, he can keep it up.

Did I tell you?—novel is accepted to be brought out this fall. In the meantime immediate serial publication is being sought.

Enjoyed your resignation almost as much as will the Fourth Assistant.[3]

Have to go and read a poem over a coffin to satisfy the whim of a man who was quick and is now dead, so so long.[4]

Jack London.

MS; CSmH; 2 pp., tls. Pbd: *BJL*, I, 355.
 1. In a letter to JL, April 13, 1901 (CSmH), Johns said: "Science deals with potentialities as well as with facts; with what will and must be as well as with what is. If a thing is so unethical that it cannot endure, I class as unscientific any attempt to defend it."
 2. Thus begins the second paragraph of Johns's letter of April 13; however, he did not develop the idea.
 3. Johns had resigned from the post office in Harold and moved to Los Angeles.
 4. At the service for John Layne, JL read William Cullen Bryant's "Thanatopsis."

To Anna Strunsky

1062 First Avenue
Oakland, Calif.
[? April 1901]

Dear Anna:—

An imperative engagement which I thought for the corresponding time in May, I suddenly find occurs in April; so I shall be unable to be with you all next Tuesday evening.

Novel is accepted; publish in the fall; I'm meanwhile trying to sell it for immediate serial publication.

Pardon haste,
Jack.

MS: CSmH; 1 p., tls.

To Anna Strunsky

[Oakland]
May 9/01.

Dear, dear Anna:—

And how did you get home Tuesday? My heart was full of you all evening. I hope no further strain was put upon you.

Do come Saturday afternoon for the fencing. And do bring the completed letter with you. The two samples I sent to *McClure's* have come back.¹ The letter from them is very amusing. It puts us on our mettle. We must do something big with those letters for spite. I depend on you.

Hope Burgess² was not wrathful. How do you like the new machine? I am just trying it.

Jack.

MS: CSmH; 1 p., tls.

1. Apparently JL had offered *The Kempton-Wace Letters* to *McClure's* for serial publication.

2. Possibly Gelett Burgess (1866–1951), Massachusetts-born author of humorous verse and stories. From 1895 to 1897 Burgess edited *The Lark*, a little magazine in San Francisco published by the literary coterie known as Les Jeunes.

To Anna Strunsky

[Forestville, California]¹
[? June 1901]

Dear Anna—

Just a line, as they are all waiting for me to go swimming. Your Dane Kempton letter is O.K.

First thing I do when I get back will be to answer it. Do not expect to be back till after the Fourth. Ferguson is a bully fellow, & the more I see of him the more I like him, & so would it be with you.

Jack.

MS: CSmH; 1 p., als.

1. On June 14 and July 11, JL lectured at Camp Reverie in Forestville, California, about twelve miles northwest of Santa Rosa on the Russian River. The residential camp operated during the summer of 1901 and provided daily lectures in addition to outdoor activities.

To Cornelius Gepfert

1062 *First Avenue*
Oakland, Calif.
July 12/01.

Dear Con:—

Your Klondike Views came to hand, for which same I am indeed grateful. They are splendid. Am just back from vacation, and am just going out to do some special rush work for the *S.F. Examiner*.[1] So I must cut this short. I presume, ere this, that you have safely arrived home.

That picture of the White Horse makes a fellow's blood tingle as one looks at it, doesn't it?[2] I'd like to make another run through it before I die, and another run I hope to make, too, some day. Well, must chop off. However, give us the news and gossip. I met Thompson's brother a couple of weeks ago, and though younger, he looks like our Thompson and talks like him.[3] Thompson is still in the country, I believe. Hear anything of Jim Goodman?[4]

Sincerely yours,
Jack London.

MS: CU; photocopy of 1 p., tls.

1. JL was commissioned by the *San Francisco Examiner* to report on the Third National Bundes Shooting Festival (or Schuetzenfest) sponsored by the National Shooting Bund, at Shell Mound Park in Oakland. In all, he wrote ten Schuetzenfest articles (published in the *Examiner* from July 15 to July 24) for which he received $200.

2. The White Horse Rapids, a treacherous area south of Lake Laberge on Thirty-Mile River in the Yukon Territory. For JL's account of shooting these rapids, see "True Stories—A Klondyke Adventure. A Klondiker Tells the Story of an Exciting Boat-Ride Through the White Horse Rapids and the Box Canyon of the Yukon River," *Home Magazine*, June 1899.

3. Fred Thompson's brother was deputy county clerk for Sonoma County in Santa Rosa; JL may have met him while in Forestville.

4. "Big Jim" Goodman, one of JL's Klondike partners, was the model for Big Bill Wilson in "Like Argus of the Ancient Times," *Hearst's Magazine*, March 1917, and is mentioned in "True Stories—A Klondyke Adventure."

To Cloudesley Johns

1062 First Avenue
Oakland, Calif.
July 12/01.

Dear Cloudesley:—

Have lost your Los Angeles address, so send this via Harold. Am just back from vacation. Took a longer vacation than I intended. No, much as I would like to, will be unable to foregather with you in L.A.

A man hit three or four times with a club I would consider beaten with a club. Three or four hoofs grinding into a man would constitute trampling for me. Trampling, in your psychology, seems to carry with it malice aforethought. It must be done with vicious and premeditated intent. All of which is not so.

As for the father of Mirabeau, he was trampled and he lived to tell of it, for, a cavalry charge sweeping over the field, his servant covered his master's head with a large camp kettle and fled. Mirabeau came out of it trampled, and for the rest of his days, besides all the other contrivances, he wore a silver tube in his throat.[1]

"Trampled *into* the earth" is used figuratively. For that matter, did you ever hear of a "handful of men"? What kind of a handful? Whose big hand? Don't quarrel with figures, my son-with-the-too-literal-soul.

Here the man comes to fix the typewriter—make changes in the letters, etc, so must chop off.

Jack London.

MS: CSmH; 2 pp., tls.

1. At the Battle of Cassano in 1705, Jean Antoine, Marquis of Mirabeau, was shot through the arm and neck, then trampled. Because the tendons in his neck were severed, he needed a silver stock around his neck to enable him to hold up his head. JL has mistaken him for Victor Riqueti (1715–89), Marquis de Mirabeau, father of Honoré Gabriel Riqueti (1749–91), Comte de Mirabeau, French revolutionary and political leader.

To Anna Strunsky

[Oakland]

My Little Collaborator:—
July 24/01.

Yes, and the Yellow is dead[1]—at least for some little time to come. For all I know, I may be doing prize fights next.[2]

Explanations are hardly necessary between you and me, but this case merits one I think. Didn't get home till the middle of the day, Monday. Went to see my mother, sister, etc. Tuesday went to Santa Cruz to speak.[3] Came back Wednsday and pitched into work on back correspondence. All the time intending to take up reply to Dane Kempton's last and surprise you with it. But the *Sunday Examiner* rushed me Thursday to have a freak story in by Friday noon.[4] And Thursday also the *Daily Examiner* clamored to see me instanter. Put daily off, finished Sunday work on time, and on Friday also went to see *Daily Examiner*. They proposed the Schuetzenfest to me. Saturday I started reply to Dane Kempton and paid bills. And on Sunday took up the Schuetzenfest and have been at it steadily for ten days, publishing in to-day's *Examiner* the last of that work. My whole life has stood still for ten days. During that time I have done nothing else. Why, so exhausting was it that my five and one-half hours would not suffice and I had to sleep over seven.

And just now, to-day, as I sat down to send you greeting, along comes yours to me. I kind of looked for you to be over to-day, though little right had I to, and I have now given up that idea.

And further. I find I must do something for *McClure's* at once, or they will be shutting off on me.[5] So I am springing at once into a short story, which will be finished by end of week, and then the letters. You know I have striven to be on time, so forgive me do this once. Tell you what I'll do, if you don't expect to be out—see you on Friday afternoon. Won't be able to stop to dinner, though, for have to go to 6:30 supper.[6] If I do miss the supper, will be dropped from the rolls, for it will have been my third consecutive absence.

Haven't finished *Aurora Leigh* yet, but it is fine, greater, I think, than Wordsworth's (*Excursion* is it?)[7] from the little you read me of it.

Jack.

MS: CSmH; 2 pp., tls. Pbd: *L*, 125–26; *BJL*, I, 356.
1. JL had completed the "yellow journalism" of the Schuetzenfest articles.
2. JL did report a fight, later that year, the James J. Jeffries–Gus Ruhlin bout, in "Gladiators of the Machine Age," *San Francisco Examiner*, November 16, 1901.
3. On July 9, JL delivered the lecture "Competitive Waste" at the Opera House in Santa Cruz.
4. "Girl Who Crossed Swords with a Burglar Tells How Athletic Training Saved Her Life," *San Francisco Examiner*, American Magazine Supplement, July 21, 1901.
5. JL was paying off his debt for advances against royalties on *A Daughter of the Snows*; see JL to Hoffman, July 23, 1900, n. 1. "Nam-Bok the Unveracious" was sent to *McClure's* on August 3, 1901. After being rejected by *McClure's* and several other magazines, it was accepted by *Ainslee's* on January 14, 1902; JL received $100 in payment on February 27. The story was published in August as "Nam-Bok, the Liar" and was later included, under the original title, in *Children of the Frost*.
6. Of the Ruskin Club.
7. Elizabeth Barrett Browning, *Aurora Leigh* (1856); William Wordsworth, *The Excursion* (1814).

To Anna Strunsky

[Oakland]
[? mid-September 1901]

Dear Anna:—

Must see you and talk over the letters. *McClure's* have dropped me so I am free lance again. You must come over and see us before we move. I forgot—we are to move the latter end of the week. So Do come Wednsday afternoon early before any body chances to be here so that we may have the talk to ourselves. That is if you can. If you can't, drop a postal at once, otherwise silence consents.

We move Friday.[1] I think the new place will be far more comfortable. The view, at least, is splendid. Further, it is not a bit harder to get to from San Francisco, than is the present place.

I shall have the reply to your good letter waiting for you Wednsday if you can come.

Jack.

MS: CSmH; 1 p., tls.
1. In mid-September JL moved his family from Villa La Capriccioso to a house at 56 Bayo Vista Avenue in the foothills above Oakland.

To Anna Strunsky

1062 First Avenue
Oakland, Calif.
[? mid-September 1901]

Do come over on Wednsday. The letter is ready for you. While you will not like it as an artistic production, I am sure you will like its attitude, for it gives you all the room in the world. I have also flatly & fully opened the discussion, & laid down, in a sketchy way, the physiology or natural history of love.

Jack.

MS: CSmH; 1 p., als.

To Elwyn Hoffman

56 Bayo Vista Avenue
Oakland, Calif.
Sept. 18/01.

Dear Elwyn:—

It must indeed be a small philosophy which cannot accept the assasination of McKinley as a very natural sociological phenomenon,[1] and which cannot say that no generalization has been shattered or even in the slightest effected. What of it, my dear Elwyn? The death of the chief servant of the dominant class in society cannot change in the slightest the destiny of that society. The socialists do not stand for such deeds, principally, I think, because the deaths of a thousand presidents would be of no avail.

The president is dead. What of it? We have another president in his place, and so we will continue to have like presidents until society, economically ripe, compasses the inexorable change which is coming.

What do I think about such deeds? I am sorry that McKinley is dead, as I am sorry that John Smith or Jack Davis of some place I have never heard of before are dead. Law and order are not in danger, nor is the "perpetuity of our institutions," as the politician puts it, in danger. So I have no feelings there. I wonder by the way, if society takes into sufficient account these Wolves of Europe and Wolves of America[2] it is breeding, and if it would forget blood-lust for a moment to speculate upon the reasons for such a breed.

As for Czolgosz, I am sorry for him. He has been so bred. He is the fruit of society, and for society he suffers. He has suffered and must suffer far more than McKinley, who died full of honors, on the down slope of life, with his name on the lips of men and a fair record behind him. But Czolgosz has suffered in the hands of the police, must still suffer, and then must die a shameful death.—Why? Ah, do you tell me why, Elwyn, you who do not study sociological affairs and yet dare sarcastic utterance about that which you know nothing. How do I feel? How do you feel? Do you know why you feel? Or are you the slave of a mob-emotion, as are seventy-five millions in these United States to-day? Come, tell me, you who are audacious enough to philosophize without data or thought.

How do I feel? I feel that the ministers of Christ's gospel might better pray for the soul of poor Czolgosz than to shriek for his blood as they are doing. How do I feel? I feel the keenest upon the cry of blood-vengeance which has gone up so high and wide that it needs must drag out the hearts of every man or woman who belongs to the same sect (so called) as did Czolgosz. The act was unplanned, in the first place, and in the second place he belonged to the Reds, to the extreme wing of the movement. Yet look at the men and women who have been rounded up, without the slightest cause, by the minions of the frightened capitalistic society.[3] Do you remember Morton, the anarchist you met at my place? He was editor of *Free Society*, the paper of which Isaak is now editor and for which editorship he now rots in jail in Chicago.[4] Morton, had he remained editor, would now be in Isaak's place. Whom did Morton ever harm but himself, and that by a too Christlike devotion to the cause of humanity.

Do you remember the Haymarket affair?[5] Without the slightest un-manufactured evidence, seven strong men were selected out of the anarchists of Chicago in order that the blood-cry of society might be satisfied. I know a woman in San Francisco, one of the sweetest truest women ever made. She knew the Haymarket prisoners as I knew Morton, and not only that, she was rounded up and a prisoner herself. An experience for a delicate, sensitive woman sufficient to wreck her, and wrecked she was. You will remember Governor Altgeld afterward pardoned the two anarchists serving life sentences,[6] for he had examined the evidence and seen that these friendless ones, as well as those executed, had been convicted without the slightest relevant evidence—blood-lust as low as that of the reddest Red. Furthermore, it was a deed of revenge, vengeance, while the deeds of the Reds, mistaken though they be, are prompted by the highest motives. By the way, Altgeld, because he did pardon the life-timers, was killed politically and has since been damned by the name, "anarchist."

As a socialist I have not the slightest sympathy for the anarchistic philosophy; it is diametrically opposed to socialism. We stand for all law, the anarchists stand for the abolition of law. So to me their arguments are vain and their remedies futile. None the less, as a man, for the anarchists as men, I have all the sympathy in the world. They do not hate so much as they love. They (the Reds) kill that good may come of it. Of course they are wrong, but they mean the best, and they hazard life and liberty for the Cause, and that is more than you and the thousands who clamor for their blood are brave enough to hazard for the welfare of the human.

How do I feel, Elwyn? How do you feel, when one man is execrated for the vilest spawn upon earth, because forsooth he killed a man, and when his execrators clamor to tear him limb from limb, to rip his heart out dripping from his breast, etc, etc, all of which I have heard good American citizens proclaim? Blood? Who clamors for blood the loudest? the poor devil of an anarchist, or the decent, law-abiding, law-upholding Americans who would subvert law and order that they might lave their hands in his blood?

Now, Elwyn, I'd like to know how you feel about it.

Ever sincerely,
Jack London.

MS: CSmH; 5 pp., tls.

1. The anarchist Leon Czolgosz (1873–1901), Detroit-born son of Polish immigrants, shot President William McKinley on September 6, 1901, at the Pan-American Exposition in Buffalo. McKinley died on September 14. Czolgosz was convicted for the murder and was electrocuted on October 29, 1901, in Auburn, New York.

2. Anarchist terrorists.

3. After his arrest, Czolgosz said he had been converted to anarchism by the words of Emma Goldman, but he did not claim affiliation with any anarchist group. He had acted alone, he said, and had decided on the assassination three days before. Disbelieving his confession, for several weeks police sought evidence of an anarchist conspiracy. The public outcry at the assassination was immense. Throughout the nation anarchists were denounced from the pulpit and individually harassed; there was a call for reform of the immigration laws; and Czolgosz was the target of mob demonstrations. At the time, like the socialists (with whom they were sometimes associated), American anarchists were members of small, diverse groups and were often foreign immigrants. "Reds" appears to have been a popular term for anarchists, especially those with Marxist or revolutionary leanings.

4. Abraham Isaak, German immigrant and anarchist. With his wife Maria, Isaak published an anarchist weekly, *The Firebrand*, in Portland, Oregon; later he renamed the paper *Free Society* and moved first to San Francisco, then to Chicago. On the night of September 6, Isaak and eight of his associates had been arrested in Chicago. Most of them were later charged with conspiracy to assassinate the President, but the charge was eventually dropped for lack of evidence.

5. On May 4, 1886, during a protest in Chicago's Haymarket Square against police brutality to striking workers, a bomb exploded in the front ranks of the police, who thereupon opened fire into the crowd. Seven police were killed and 67 wounded; the number of citizens wounded or killed is unknown. Eight anarchists were brought to trial for the bombing. All were convicted, and four were subsequently executed.

6. John Peter Altgeld (1847–1902), Judge of the Superior Court in Chicago from 1886 to 1891 and Governor of Illinois from 1893 to 1897. He pardoned three of the anarchists— Oscar Neebe, Samuel J. Felden, and Michael Schwab—because he felt that they had not been fairly tried.

To Cornelius Gepfert

56 Bayo Vista Avenue
Oakland, Calif.
Sept. 22/01.

Dear Con:–

Behold, I have moved. Am all in the chaos of settling down in new quarters. Have a great view, now, a clean sweep of the horizon—San

Francisco across the bay, Goat, Angel, and Alcatraz islands, the Golden Gate and the Pacific, to say nothing of the Contra Costa and Berkely hills. Writing has not been up to much lately, but I should surely do good work here.

To make matters better, I am quite close to a writer friend,[1] who agrees with me politically and philosophically, and with whom I can not only discuss things literary, but with whom I can also fence and jump and box. In which latter art I am somewhat rusty.

If you are ever down this way, do look us up. Latch-string's always out.

Should another rush take place up North would I join the procession? Well, I guess yes. I think my chance to go in as a correspondent would be excellent, and say, wouldn't I collect material for fiction work and take photographs galore! I'm just itching to be off, but I run two households steadily,[2] and very often a couple more, and so the nimble pence must come tripping in month by month.

What are you doing besides enjoying yourself, now that you are back in civilization once more? Nay, there is not a soul who can appreciate the comforts of civilization unless they have first roughed it in the Northland sense of the word. Pardon mistakes, please, for I am dozing off with a score of letters yet to answer. One cannot move house and hammer the machine at the same time.

I see your letter is on a typewriter. Are you somebody's secretary, or has the North coughed up enough dust for you to employ a secretary?

Did you ever hear of the man Stevens in the Klondike, and if so, of what became of him. If you will remember when you first landed at Stewart, Stevens had a woman and a camp across on the opposite bank of the Yukon. He was a wild sort of chap, and either a man of marvelous adventures or marvelous imagination.

> Yours sincerely,
> Jack London.

MS: CU; photocopy of 3 pp., tls.
  1. Herman Whitaker.
  2. Shortly after JL moved to 1130 East 15th Street, he also rented a small cottage for his mother a block away to prevent friction between Bessie and Flora London. Subsidizing multiple households was to be a financial strain for the rest of his life.

To Anna Strunsky

56 Bayo Vista Avenue
Oakland, Calif.
October 3/01.

Dear You:—

I have just finished reading your review.[1] I cannot say how good it is, how splendid. I can only thank you silently. You have been in my thoughts all day and I have been wondering, wondering—and now comes *Impres-*

sions and I hear you in your written speech. Well, to break the silence for a moment, yours is by far the best review the book has received. And by that I do not mean the lauding and the discreet silences, but I do mean the sympathy.

As I say, wondering. I should have written you long since, but I have been so busy; also looking each day for a letter from you. I did take the time to write to Morton when the papers announced the arrest of the whole colony[2]—but that was all.

In the last twelve days I have done over eleven thousand words, and that's the rate I have, and am keeping up. "Writer's cramp," you know. Do run over and see us some day—any day—when all is well. The rest is bound to do you good. And stop all night—we've a little more room in our new quarters.

And O, before I close, Whitaker has sold a story to *Harper's Monthly*[3] for one hundred dollars, a story which had been refused divers times by lesser publications.

I am to proceed right now to a review of *Foma Gordyeeff* for *Impressions*.[4] Have you read it yet? I am saving it for you to read first of all if you haven't. It is a wonderful book. I wish I could allow myself the freshness of a whole day to it instead of going at it, as I now shall, jaded and tired.

Let's hear from you,
Jack London.

MS: CSmH; 2 pp., tls.

1. Strunsky reviewed *The God of His Fathers* in *Impressions*, October 1901, calling the work a classic and JL an artist. *Impressions* was a literary magazine published in San Francisco as a monthly from 1900 until 1902, then as a quarterly until 1905. It featured book reviews and articles on literary criticism.

2. JL probably refers to the arrest of Isaak and his associates.

3. Probably "Lost Kirk," published in *Harper's*, February 1902.

4. JL reviewed *Fomá Gordéeff* (1899) by Maxim Gorky, in *Impressions*, November 1901.

To Cloudesley Johns

56 Bayo Vista Avenue
Oakland, Calif.
October 9/01.

Dear Cloudesley:–

Note change of address. Am now living out on the hills. Yours of September 28th. was a most pleasant surprise. Well, how did you fare? But then there is hardly any need for me to ask. I should surely know, at least in a general sort of way. I sort of looked for more postals from you during your trip. However, better this than none. And how's New York? Are you going to settle down to writing for the winter?[1] I nearly shipped across on a cattle boat when I was on the road, but somehow didn't.

Am free lance again. Have just finished a 3700-word defense of Kipling against the rising tide of adverse criticism.[2] Did you see the attack in current *Cosmopolitan*?[3] What did you think of it? And I wonder what you'll think of my article . . . if it is ever published or if you ever read it.

Mr. Whitaker, whom you will remember, is still pegging away with his wife and seven little ones. *Harper's* have just accepted for one hundred dollars a story of his which had gone to the rounds pretty thoroughly. He's going to make it.

Did you know C. A. Moody, of *The Land of Sunshine*?[4] He dropped in here day before yesterday. Didn't know of your trip, and I told him of it, and of your arrival at New York.

Well, Haven't much news. Am hard at it. That series of letters with Miss Strunsky is three-fifths through. That is to say, we have three-fifths of a book done. Though the Lord only knows what publisher will dare to tackle it. Also, am hammering away at a series of Klondike tales, which I shall assemble under the title *The Children of the Frost*. They are all to be from the Indian approach, you know.

Well, I shall await a letter from you with interest.

Jack London.

MS: CSmH; 2 pp., tls. Pbd: *BJL*, I, 357.

  1. In September Johns "rode the rods" hobo-fashion to New York, where he planned to peddle his stories to magazine editors and publishers. He stayed in New York for two years, supporting himself with various jobs.
  2. "These Bones Shall Rise Again." After being rejected by several magazines, this article was published in *The Reader*, June 1903; it was later included in *Revolution*. In payment, JL received $30 on June 2, 1903.
  3. C. E. Russell, "Are There Two Rudyard Kiplings?" *Cosmopolitan*, October 1901. Russell criticized Kipling's realism and failure to provide moral uplift, saying, "An artist may properly enough seek to create effects of pity, horror, sadness, pain; but to create effects merely depressing and disconcerting is new in recognized literature, and its permanence may be held open to doubt" (p. 656).
  4. Charles Amadon Moody, coeditor of *Land of Sunshine* (later *Out West*). With Charles F. Lummis, he wrote book reviews for "That Which Is Written," a standing column in the magazine.

To Anna Strunsky

[Oakland]
[? October 1901]

Dear Anna:—

I am impelled. If Porter Garnett[1] answers you in *Impressions* I shall answer him. I shall have the last word, and shall sum up the controversey. And as one who has also published criticisms in *Impressions*,[2] and hence am reflected upon by those on the other side—why I shall be perfectly justified in entering the lists. And I promise you I "won't do a thing to them."

Last night was a good night with Browning. I should like some time to be with you so long as to be sated; then I would not be hungry when you went away. I look straight out of my window to where you live, you know, and it is a distraction.

However, yours,
Jack.

MS: CSmH; 1 p., tls.

1. JL seems to be confusing Porter Garnett (1871–1951), drama and literary critic for several Bay Area periodicals including the *San Francisco Call* and the *Argonaut*, with Gelett Burgess, the author of "Upon Pseudo-Literary Criticism," *Impressions*, October 1901. In his article Burgess notes his repulsion for book reviewing and the commercial reviewers who "tear [books] to tatters." He concludes: "No man with brains enough to write a book has either time or inclination to criticise another's." Strunsky responded to Burgess's article in "Upon Literary Criticism," *Impressions*, November 1901. She agreed that pseudo-literary critics should not be defended but maintained that not all criticism should be condemned: "It all resolves itself down to a consideration of the value of literature. If literature is vital, if there is identity between the Logos and the Life, between the written story and that which tells itself out in the facts of blood and nerve and world-stuff, then is the claim of literature upon our best effort vital; then is no man too great to become its interpreter and expositor. So it is that by the side of the commercial book reviewer we find our Henleys and Howells, we find our critics, the men who neither snarl nor fawn, but who teach."

2. In addition to *Fomá Gordéeff*, JL had reviewed *The Octopus* in *Impressions*. See JL to Johns, April 30, 1899, n. 15.

To Cloudesley Johns

56 Bayo Vista Avenue
Oakland, Calif.
Nov. 8/01.

Dear Cloudesley:—

Of course the painter has to quit painting bears, but he has first to gather together his itinerary and select his route. (Say, is this what they call a mixed metaphor?)

Anyway, it's the same old story. A man does one thing in a passable manner and the dear public insists on his continuing to do it to the end of his days. O the humorists who try to be serious!

How was yours a surprise? Did I imagine you had wings and halo and golden fiddle? Nay, nay. When a man dissappears on the road, and the days go by and the days go by, why that man becomes a memory. And when, suddenly, that memory takes to itself form, as it were, embodies itself in a material letter, stamped and addressed and delivered by a post-man, why of course it is a surprise. My dear sir, when you permit yourself to be swallowed up by the road, consider yourself a memory. Only tyros do otherwise. (Now! Come back at me!)

Did I ever tell you of that letter series Miss Strunsky and I are writing? Well, we've got past the forty-thousand mark and the goal is in sight. Gee! I wonder how you'll jump upon it. My contention is the same as I heard you make once: that propinquity determines choice. Yet I am sure you will be after my scalp before you finish it . . . that is, if we can entice a publisher into getting it out.

Whittaker has just sold a story to *Cosmopolitan*.[1] Rah for Whitaker! O, he's going at it scientifically.

I wouldn't mind being with you next spring when you pull out for the old countries.

Cosgrave[2] mentioned having several interesting conversations with you, and that he expected to get some tramp work from you. How is it coming on?

Jack London.

MS: CSmH; 2 pp., tls. Pbd: *BJL*, I, 357–58.
    1. Probably "Saga of 549," *Cosmopolitan*, January 1902.
    2. John O'Hara Cosgrave (1866–1947), Australian-born journalist. Cosgrave was a reporter for the *San Francisco Call* before becoming editor and publisher of *The Wave* in 1890. In 1900, he joined *Everybody's Magazine* as managing editor; he was its editor from 1903 to 1911.

To Cloudesley Johns

56 Bayo Vista Avenue
Oakland, Calif.
Dec. 6/01.

Dear Cloudesley:—

Nothing doing. Am hammering away in seclusion, trying to get out of Alaska.[1] Guess I'll succeed in accomplishing it in a couple of years.

By the way, the book of letters is not based upon your proposition at all. Said proposition is merely a phenomenon of love, of which there be many phenomena. The book goes down deeper, and my side, at least, shows why very many other things are besides your proposition. And, in fact, when I say your proposition, I do not mean to say that we have used your characterization of that proposition, and when I say that I mean to say that the phenomenon your proposition characterized is a very old one and has been recognized and put into print many times ere you and I were born. Leaving out the evolutionists, I can refer you to Max Nordau's essay on Love which occurs in his *Paradoxes*.[2] The same thing is handled there at length.

And yet furthermore, the particular proposition or epigram upon which "The Theorist" is founded, in our letters will occur among so many many other propositions that it can not hurt in the slightest any subsequent publication of your book. Not that your epigram has been used at all. For it hasn't.

In trying to give you a comprehension of the nature of the letters, I recollected your epigram and knew that by mentioning it you would get the whole point of view it stood for. That was all.

Wyckoff is not a tramp authority.[3] He doesn't understand the real tramp.

Josiah Flynt is the tramp authority.[4] Wyckoff only knows the working-man, the stake-man, and the bindle-stiff. The profesh are unknown to him. Wyckoff is a gay cat.[5] That was his rating when he wandered over the States.

Well, good luck on the way to Cuba! Wish I were with you. I am rotting here in town. Really, I can feel the bourgeois fear crawling up and up and twining round me. If I don't get out soon I shall be emasculated. The city folk are a poor folk anyway. To hell with them.

                                                                    Jack London.

MS: CSmH; 3 pp., tls. Pbd: *L*, 126–27; *BJL*, I, 358.

   1. JL finished his first version of "To Build a Fire" and sent it to *Youth's Companion* on December 15, 1901. He received $50 for the story on February 17, 1902; it was published on May 29. For the distinction between this and the second version of the story, see JL to Gilder, December 22, 1908.

   2. "The Natural History of Love."

   3. Wyckoff had just published *A Day with a Tramp and Other Days* (1901). For JL's earlier comments on Wyckoff, see JL to Johns, June 16, 1900.

   4. Josiah Flint Willard (1869–1907), a former hobo who published books under the pseudonym "Josiah Flynt"; author of *Tramping with Tramps: Studies and Sketches of the Vagabond Life* (1899).

   5. In "The Road" JL defined "profesh" as a "Simon-pure tramp, hence professional. . . . [The profesh] are looked up to as the aristocracy of their underworld" and "bindle-stiff" as a tramp with a "predilection to carry his bed [i.e., blanket, or 'bindle'] with him." In "Road-Kids and Gay-Cats," published in *The Road*, JL defined "gay cats" as "short horns, chechaquos, new chums or tender feet. A gay cat is a new comer on The Road who is a man grown, or at least a youth grown." He does not define "workingman" or "stake-man," though it is likely that he is referring to a tramp who performs common labor for subsistence money rather than begging, stealing, or victimizing others for money.

To Dan Murphy

                                                        56 Bayo Vista Avenue
                                                        Oakland, Calif.
                                                        Dec. 17/01.

Dear Dan:—[1]

   Since last writing you, I learn that Reynolds[2] is marketing my stuff. This was an unauthorized act on the part of McClure, Phillips, & Co. I had sent them three stories in rapid succession, the tacit and operating understanding being that if unavailable they were to be returned to me. This was what had been done before with my stuff. But this time, neither returning to me or consulting me, they handed the three stories over to Reynolds.

   I am just sending this little word in order that you may not think I am not playing fair.

                                                        Sincerely yours,
                                                        Jack London

MS: Kingman; 1 p., als.
   1. Dan Murphy, evidently acting as a literary agent for JL in Britain.

2. Paul Revere Reynolds (1864–1944), who founded the first American literary agency, Paul R. Reynolds & Son, in New York in 1893.

To Anna Strunsky

[? Oakland]
[? 1901]

Dear Anna—

I have been in dispair over this letter. Four days I have devoted to it, and the thing is still ridiculous. Well, well, there will have to be no end of revising when we have finished. Don't be hurt at flippancy in letter—that will be revised too. The great thing after all is to get the letters shaped. I grip your hand, dear heart, for your encouragement from San Rafael.

Jack.

MS: CSmH; 1 p., als.

To Anna Strunsky

[? Oakland]
[? 1901]

Dear You:–

I have just taken up and read the latter part of the letter. It's great—some of the very best, if not the best, work you have done in the whole series. The amateurishness seems to have utterly vanished. The ending is splendid—"For what do you hope?"—I really cannot, on the spur of the moment, imagine how I am to answer it.

Jack.

MS: CSmH; 1 p., als.

To Anna Strunsky

[? Oakland]
Saturday Evening. [? 1901]

Sister:–

Girl! Girl! Why do I write to you? It is so inadequate, so incoherent. I am brimming over. I could talk all the night to you, and yet the half would not be told. Where shall I begin? Of the much to be said what may I choose to form the little I may say?

Refrain from thinking of his identity! When I knew ere I even glanced at his letter? My heart goes out to him. In my own fashion, in my thoughts all day, I have prayed for him. Ay, prayed for him as I have not for you. Pardon me; he needs it most. Do you not see? He suffers from he knows not what; fears and hopes he knows not what. It is more exquisite. But you—you know. You have no hope; your fear and pain is out of knowledge. It is not a crisis in your life; in his, it is. True, a minor one, but he mistakes it for a major, and suffers just as much as though it were. So I have prayed for him all day.

Do I look down and speak from a lofty peak of egotism, which I mistake for wisdom? I do not know. Only it does seem that I speak from out the lost years.

But you have not been forgotten, dear. I have thought of you more, if I prayed less. I know how all this must work upon you, all this which is heart-breaking. I know that you feel too much for your own good; too much for whatever or whoever is at stake. This should not be, but it is your way. Blame? No one is to blame, no one. Listen! Here are you absolved: "You have taught me to see clearly, to think honestly, to live clean and purely, to cherish high ideals, to strive for noble ends. . . . Him whom you have taught to love the beautiful and good."

What more would you? Again: "I did not play with this man's soul. I was too careful of it. I wished so to strengthen him, to help him. . . . And I did wish to do good by this boy. I pledged myself that since we served the same cause and our work lay together I would make him love the things I loved."

Blame? Then blame the springtime, blame the trade wind, blame the stars in their rounds. For all these things be allotted and neither man nor star may veer to right or left.

And it is not bad, Anna, any of it. Nobody is hurt, unless it be you. And you do not count in this. It is the man, and he certainly has not been hurt. It is a good letter he has written, with the strain in it which would be in yours and mine did we write in our pain. But the strain and the pain are good. Forever heart-hurt? Ah, his is a stronger breed, and a braver. He mistakes the moment for the eternal, that is all. He will grow. He is no Dante, to mourn an impossible Beatrice and squabble futilely for Guelph or Ghibbeline.[1] He is a worker, for the Great Cause, and he is so made that he must work. The process may be painful, but he will live it through and come out better. Do you not see?

Again, though I know him but slightly, it yet seems to me what we call the puppy love—the false dawn, the promise of potentiality, the glimmering adumbration of the greatness to come in the fulness of time. May I speak out of my own experience? Is it right?—but, well, I have never told but one woman that I loved her.[2] Did I love her? There was no love greater, so I thought. She was more than mortal. I remember, we were eating cherries one day. Lying on my back and looking up I saw that the black juice had discolored her lips. I hailed it with delight. An omen that we were drawing closer together, that she was stripping off her immortality. Let me see, how was it? I came out of the great rough ugly world and stumbled

upon her as in a garden. Culture? I knew none—had dreamed of it perhaps, but dreamed dimly. But she was surrounded with it, saturated in it,
was a product of it? Can't you imagine the result, remembering always
that she was also woman? The inevitable. I thought it was the greatest
thing in the world. In reality, it was the puppy love, which affects each
according to the time and season and the blood which runs in his veins—
the false dawn, the glimmer.

It was a great love, at the time. I mistook the moment for the eternal.
See, we were in danger once, a day of danger; and often and often her life
lay in my grasp. The slip of a hand, the crash of a rock, the snap of a rope,
and she had been gone. And often and often and just so often did I swear
to myself, should it so happen, that I would follow her in the plunge.
Loose my grip on all life, on all joy, on all the future, and follow her; for
life and joy and future were embodied in her, were her—at the time. It
was a great love.

But see! Time passed. I grew. I saw immortality fade from her. Saw her
only woman. And still I did not dream of judging. Time passed. I awoke,
frightened, and found myself judging. She was very small. The positive
virtues were hers, and likewise the negative vices. She was pure, honest,
true, sincere, everything. But she was small. Her virtues led her nowhere.
Works? She had none. Her culture was a surface smear, her deepest depth
a singing shallow. Do you understand? Can I explain further? I awoke,
and judged, and my puppy love was over. I have not seen her for long; I
hear of her rarely; and out of it all, pity only remains.

Can I show the bearing? To almost all of us it comes. For all I know, it
may have come to you. If so, you will comprehend. It comes in various
ways, and goes in various ways, but it is ever the same in principle. And
may this not be so with him by whom you are saddened almost into
marrying?

To marry? Suppose I had? or she had? Work it out for yourself. To
marry? for you? And give the lie to everything you have stood for? Better
that you died, now; better for you, and better for him. Ah, it is an awkward thing to play with souls! As yet, you have not played. But did you
marry, then would the play begin, the play with his soul. Am I right? You
are judge.

And yet again. Taking it for granted that he will endure the process and
come out the better, a yet greater responsibility is laid upon you. Try to
follow me. Remember that we all grow; that some grow faster than
others; that some stop growing before others. Take the woman I spoke of.
She had bloomed and blossemed ere our lives crossed. Thereat was I
amazed, for I was a raw young shoot. But—I grew, and passed her, and
out of it all pity only remains. It is not sweet to remember, sweet to revert
to. It is a tragedy, rather, for her and for me. For me, there is no uplift, no
strength. For her, what? O, the pity of it! the pity of it!

Now for you and for him. Your growth has been greater than his—why, in his very letter he quotes your Browning, your phrases. Your growth has been greater; it must stay greater. Do you not see? You dare not let him pass you. For your sake you dare not. Nor for his sake. Let him not come to say, "Poor blind mole! I mistook a glow-worm for a star. There are no stars."

When he says "You must write and produce the wonderful fine-souled works your heart and brain conceive. The future will empty horns of plenty at your feet and your brow be wreathed with laurel," he says, Behold! the star!

You dare not, cannot, do else than remain the star. As his vision grows clearer, you must grow brighter. If not—I shrug my shoulders; the world shrugs its shoulders; *he* shrugs his shoulders. And he is the worse for the shrug.

So here we have it. This is the danger. Not now, though, for there is no hurt, no lessening of faith; but then—then is the time he has need of all his faith. Will he retain it? Will he be better, stronger, greater? It is for you to say.

If I have put too much of myself in this letter, it is because I have felt with you, and with him. My hand on your head, Anna.

Jack.

MS: CSmH; 5 pp., tls.

1. The Guelphs (pro-papacy) and Ghibellines (anti-papacy) were opposing political factions in thirteenth-century Italy and Germany.

2. Mabel Applegarth.

1902

In London's East End, posing as a stranded American sailor, 1902 (Calif. State Parks)

To George P. Brett

56 Bayo Vista Avenue
Oakland, Calif.
January 4/[02].¹

Dear Sir:—

In reply to yours of December 27th., concerning work on hand.² I have a novel,³ but McClure, Phillips & Co., are to publish it. At present they are seeking serial publication for it. I have never written anything else of any length.

However, I have a series of Klondike short stories under way. Forty thousand words are done, and I have about ten or fifteen more thousand words to do to complete the series, which I call by the general title, *The Children of the Frost*. At present, those completed are waiting or seeking serial publication. I should be glad, when they have received serial publication, to submit them to you for publication on both sides⁴—that is, if you care to look at them.

Sincerely yours,
Jack London.

MS: NN; 1 p., tls.
  1. Misdated "January 4/01."
  2. George Platt Brett (1858–1936), English-born president of the Macmillan Company. Brett wrote JL on December 27, 1901 (CSmH), to solicit longer manuscripts not suitable for serial publication that Macmillan might publish in both England and America. He said that JL's stories "seem . . . to represent very much the best work of the kind that has been done on this side of the water."
  3. *A Daughter of the Snows.*
  4. Of the Atlantic. Macmillan had offices in London and New York.

To Elwyn Hoffman

56 Bayo Vista Avenue
Oakland, Calif.
January 4/[02]¹

Dear Elwyn:—

You are quite an analytical cuss, aren't you. The way you analyzed all the possible reasons for my sending you the Emma Goldman clipping is admirable.[2] The laughable part comes in, after all your analyzing, when you decide you will say nor more about it because you don't know what I wish you to say in reply.—"If I knew your wishes in the matter I should probably write at more length." Rats! What wishes should I have in the matter.

Now to put a stop to your analyzing. I had heard that you were no longer up country, did not know where you were, and did not care to write a letter which might go questing vainly after you through the mails. So I sent clipping, via Idah,[3] merely to locate you. Incidentally the clipping was apropos. We had been corresponding about McKinley's assassination. Further, I thought the clipping an interesting human document, a document which should have been of interest to any person in the world, not matter what their political belief might be. So there you have it.

Come over and see us some Wednsday. Always at home. Then we may talk it over. Concerning my reporting of prizefights and dabbling in yellow journalism we certainly must talk it over.[4] Of all places, the charge there of inconsistency is least merited. Of course, when you measure me by your own standards I appear inconsistent, but how about when you measure me by my own standards? What do you know of my standards concerning prizefighting and yellow journalism? Pray what do you know? But come on over. You may run across George Sterling here, a poet you will surely like to meet.[5] Find enclosed a poem by him, which same please return.

No, I did not know of your lines in the *News Letter* and *Town Talk* until you mentioned them.[6] Then I sent over for copies. By the way, in one or the other of them, your little missile developed into a boomerang and both of us got hurt. I had a hearty laugh over it. Did you?

Why, damn it man, I am taking it all in the best of good nature. I am laughing in this letter, even as I laughed up my sleeve when I wrote you hotly when you were up country. You had thrown yourself open and I chose to land with several short-arm jolts (there are my prizefighting tendencies cropping out). While I don't agree with you in your political and sociological views, that doesn't make you less a man in my estimation. And while I certainly do not agree with you in your personal judgements on me, I can only like you the better for holding them. You might not hold any at all, and then that would be hell.

As for the socialistic and anarchistic atmosphere which surrounds me, if it is so distasteful to you that you cannot come, I can only take it as a token of your supreme and bigotted insularity. Further, I know that you know so little about either anarchy or socialism that what little you do know is even more criminal than utter ignorance.

Get off at Broadway station, and take Piedmont electric cars. Get off electric cars at Bayo Vista Avenue, and walk between two and three block to my place—two story house with lawn and row of leafless poplars in front.

Sincerely yours,
Jack London.

P.S.—You note my prizefight and lecture in the one week; did you also note my review of Markham's poems in same week?[7] Do express an opinion on them in relation to the other two items.

MS: CSmH; 4 pp., tls.
1. Misdated "January 4/01."
2. The Emma Goldman clipping has not been identified. Goldman (1869–1939), Russian-born anarchist, met JL through the Strunsky sisters, Anna and Rose, probably in 1899. For her recollections of JL, see her *Living My Life* (1931).
3. Ida Strobridge.
4. JL refers to his account of the Jeffries-Ruhlin fight and his Schuetzenfest articles, all commissioned by the *San Francisco Examiner*.
5. George Sterling (1869–1926), New York–born poet. Sterling moved to Oakland in 1890 to work in the real estate office of his uncle, Frank Havens. He met JL in 1901, and they became lifelong friends. Sterling was the model for Russ Brissenden in *Martin Eden*.
6. In a humorous poem entitled "A Letter to Jack London," *Town Talk*, November 30, 1901, Hoffman chided JL for prostituting his literary talent by writing newspaper articles. *Town Talk* was a San Francisco weekly urban magazine published from 1892 until 1921, which featured literature and society gossip. Hoffman's "lines" in *News Letter*, a San Francisco weekly literary magazine published from 1856 until 1928, have not been identified.
7. A review of *Lincoln and Other Poems*. See JL to Johns, April 17, 1899, n. 14.

To Anna Strunsky

[Oakland]
January 5, 1902.

Dear, Dear You:—

Your greeting came good to me. And then there was the dear little token for Joan. And it all impresses me with how much I am and always shall be in your debt. You do not know—you, you!

You look back on a tumultuous and bankrupt year; and so I. And for me the New Year begins full of worries, harassments, and disappointments. So you? I wonder?

I look back and remember, at one in the morning, the faces I saw go wan and wistful—do you remember? or did you notice?—and I wonder what all the ferment is about.

I dined yesterday, on canvasback and terrapin, with champagne sparkling and all manner of wonderful drinks I had never before tasted warming me heart and brain, and I remembered the sordid orgies and carouses of my youth. We were ill-clad ill-mannered beasts, and the drink was cheap and poor and nauseating. And then I dreamed dreams, and pulled myself up out of the slime to canvasback and terrapin and champagne, and learned that it was solely a difference of degree which art introduced into the fermenting. And I thought of you, and I wondered.

Sordid necessities! For me Yorick has not lived in vain.[1] I am grateful to him for the phrase. Am I incoherent? It seems very clear to me.

And now to facts. Bessie wants me to ask you, if, on January 12th., we can stop all night, and if we can put Joan to bed also. You see, in Piedmont here, we have to leave San Francisco an hour earlier than we used to on account of the street cars. And Bessie cannot bring herself to be away from Joan a whole night.

Jack.

MS: CSmH; 2 pp., tls. Pbd: *L*, 127; *BJL*, I, 367–68.

1. Yorick was the pseudonym of a satirical columnist for the *San Francisco Evening Post* who occasionally made stinging but humorous comments on JL's writing. See JL to Johns, February 13, 1901, n. 3.

To Cloudesley Johns

56 Bayo Vista Avenue
Oakland, Calif.
January 6, 1902.

Dear Cloudesley:–

But after all, what squirming, anywhere, damned or otherwise, means anything? That's the question I am always prone to put: What's this chemical ferment called life all about? Small wonder that small men down the ages have conjured gods in answer. A little god is a snug little possession and explains it all. But how about you and me, who have no god?

I have at last discovered what I am. I am a materialistic monist, and there's dam little satisfaction in it.

I am at work on a short story that no self-respecting bourgeois magazine will ever have anything to do with.[1] In conception it is really one of your stories. It's a crackerjack. If it's ever published I'll let you know. If not, we'll wait until you come west again.

As regards "effete respectability," I haven't any, and I don't have anything to do with any who have . . . except magazines. Nevertheless I shall be impelled to strong drink if something exciting doesn't happen along pretty soon.

My dear boy, nobody can help himself in anything, and heaven helps no one. Man is not a free agent, and free will is a fallacy exploded by science long ago. Here is what we are:—or, better still, I'll give you Fish's definition: "Philosophical materialism holds that matter and the motion of matter make up the sum total of existence, and that what we know as psychical phenomena in man and other animals are to be interpreted in an ultimate analysis as simply the peculiar aspect which is assumed by certain enormously complicated motions of matter." That is what we are, and we move along the line of least resistance. Whatever we do, we do because it is easier to than not to. No man ever lived who didn't do the easiest thing (for him).

Or, as Paschal puts it: "In the just and the unjust we find hardly anything which does not change its character in changing its climate. Three degrees of an elevation of the pole reverses the whole jurisprudence. A meridian is decisive of truth; and a few years, of possession. Fundamental laws change. Right has its epochs. A pleasant justice which a river or a mountain limits. Truth this side the Pyrenees; error on the other." [2]

Nay, nay. We are what we are, and we cannot help ourselves. No man is to be blamed, and no man praised.

Yes, Cosgrave wrote me instanter about the letters.[3] I am afraid they're not for him. They would be utter Greek. Say, Cloudesley, did you ever reflect on the yellow magazinism of the magazines? Cosgrave says I ought not to write for the *Examiner*. And in the same breath he says he will take what I write if I write what he wants. O ye gods! Neither the *Examiner* nor *Everybody's* wants masterpieces, art, and where's the difference in the sacrifice on my part?

You mention Sedgewick of *Leslie's*.[4] Do you mean weekly or monthly *Leslie's*? And what his initials?

Well, in six days I shall be twenty-six years old, and in nine days Joan will be one year old. Did you know we had named her Joan?

Jack London.

MS: CSmH; 4 pp., tls. Pbd: *L*, 128–29; *BJL*, I, 369–70.

1. Probably "Bâtard," which JL sent to *Cosmopolitan* on January 17, 1902. He received $141.25 on May 27, 1902; the story was published in June, with its offensive title changed to "Diable—a Dog." It was included in *The Faith of Men and Other Stories* (New York: Macmillan, 1904) with the original title restored.

2. Blaise Pascal, *Pensées* (1670), no. 294.

3. JL had probably approached John O'Hara Cosgrave about publishing *The Kempton-Wace Letters* serially in *Everybody's*, a general illustrated monthly magazine published in New York from 1896 until 1929.

4. Ellery Sedgwick (1872–1960), editor of *Frank Leslie's Popular Monthly Magazine* from 1900 to 1905 and of the *Atlantic Monthly* from 1908 to 1938. Johns had probably been in contact with Sedgwick regarding the publication of his short story "Mr. Judd Was Awake" in the March issue of *Frank Leslie's*.

To Elwyn Hoffman

56 Bayo Vista Avenue
Oakland, Calif.
Jan. 8/02.

Dear Elwyn:—

Now I have you hip and thigh! In your last letter you charge me with being inconsistent. Very good. In this letter now in hand you plead ignorance of my standards, even marvel that I should happen to have any, and tell me that anyway you prefer to measure me by your own standards. How then under the sun could you ever call me INCONSISTENT? Have you lost the meaning of words?

And I suppose you have me on the hip concerning Markham, you old, old man, who would deny me the fresh enthusiasms of youth. I delight in appreciation. I have reviewed several books, now. They have all been appreciations. When I have become a critic (God forbid!) then shall I say harsh things. Markham has not the wonderful rhythm, say, for Instance, that Watson has in his "Hymn to the Sea." [1] What of it? I had only so much time and space, and I could better employ it in telling the good I found in Markham than in coldly calculating the precise quality of his rhythm and so doing, belittle the untold good. [2] A disquisition on style, my dear boy, and a carping caviling disquisition, would draw nothing but carpers and cavilers to read Markham, and his good would be no good for them.

You quoted from a letter of long ago concerning Markham. [3] Will you kindly quote me the context? A part quotation is often a damnable crime. And anyway, whether it is in the context or not, take this from me: Always have I held substance greater than form: always have I said, "Keep your canons; give me the results."

Don't forget to send me context. Sorry you can't come over right away. I'll have forgot what it's all about if you delay too long.

                                                                Jack London.

MS: CSmH; 2 pp., tls.
    1. See JL to Strunsky, ? February 1900, n. 2.
    2. In his review of *Lincoln and Other Poems*, JL remarked: "[Markham's] power is his own, his treatment his own. While he is remarkable for his largeness of grasp, a vivid concreteness characterizes his work. His phrases ring like trumpet calls; and there is an epic sweep in his conceptions and his figures. And his figures, always clean, clear-cut, have in them all the primitiveness of the elements and the earth."
    3. See JL to Hoffman, January 6, 1901.

To George P. Brett

56 Bayo Vista Avenue
Oakland, Calif.
January 16/02.

My dear sir:—

Yes, I shall with pleasure place *The Children of the Frost* in your hands. You ask as to when it may likely appear. It is all so indeterminate that I dare not set a date. You see, I cannot figure on the serial publication of the different tales at all. One magazine may publish in a month. Another magazine may delay six or eight months. As for myself, the work is almost done, there being but two or three more stories to write. [1]

I am especially glad to publish with you, for then I get a hearing on both sides. *The Son of the Wolf,* for instance, was brought out in the United States by Houghton, Mifflin & Co. I sold the English copyright to Ward, Locke & Co., who, up to this time, I believe, have not brought it out.[2] Possibly they are waiting on the chance of my becoming famous twenty years hence. This may be all very well for them, but it's tough on me.

> Sincerely yours,
> Jack London.

MS: NN; 2 pp., tls.

1. "The Sunlanders" was sent to *McClure's* on September 9, 1901, and then to *Ainslee's* on October 2, 1901. JL declined the *Ainslee's* offer of $100 on October 20, 1901; the story was subsequently sent to *Everybody's* and *Pearson's* on November 7, 1901, and the *Saturday Evening Post* on November 21, 1901. On December 20, 1901, JL decided to accept the *Ainslee's* offer of $100 for the American serial rights and $50 for the English serial rights to "The Sunlanders." However, since JL did not wish to delay publication of the forthcoming *Children of the Frost* in which this story would appear, *Ainslee's* accepted his promise to provide another story in place of "The Sunlanders." On March 6, 1903, JL sent them a story titled "The Hobo," which was published in the October 1903 issue of *Ainslee's* under the title "Local Color." "The Death of Ligoun" was sent to *Outing,* March 4, 1902; to *McClure's,* March 31, 1902; to the *Saturday Evening Post,* January 5, 1902; to *Collier's,* June 21, 1902; and to the *Atlantic,* July 19, 1902. Like "The Sunlanders" it was included in *Children of the Frost* without serial publication.

2. On May 29, 1900, JL accepted the offer of Ward, Locke & Company to buy the English copyright of *The Son of the Wolf* for £25. For its eventual publication, see JL to Brett, April 28, 1902.

To Anna Strunsky

[Oakland]
Jan. 16/02.

Dear You:–
Good luck with the work. As I sit here, I wonder how you are over there, & try to conjure up you & your room. I succeed with you, but fail on the room.
Got a Letter from Greer, who asks to be remembered.

> Jack.

MS: CSmH; 1 p., als.

To Anna Strunsky

[Oakland]
Jan. 18/02.

Dear Anna—
Good for your Henley stand! I am sending you his article on Steven-

son. I honor him for having written it. A brave soul! I hope you make a stand for his stand.[1]

Have just finished your birthday letter. It is splendid. You are getting a big grip on written words. And I am whistling over my work at the way the *Letters* are coming on. We must finish them on this lap. I begin a reply to-day to your last in the series. But, Oh! won't we have to lick those first letters into shape!

As for my not having read Stevenson's letters[2]—my dear child! When the day comes that I have achieved a fairly fit scientific foundation and a bank account of a thousand dollars, then come & be with me when I lie on my back all day long and read, & read, & read, & read.

The temptation of the books—if you could know! And I hammer away at Spencer and hackwork & try to forget the joys of the things unread.

Jack.

MS: CSmH; 3 pp., als. Pbd: *BJL*, I, 371.

1. Strunsky was to deliver a speech on W. E. Henley to the Woman's Press Association; it was later published as "On the Principle of Loyalty in Biography," *Impressions Quarterly*, March 1902. In it, she defended Henley's biographical sketch of Stevenson, "R. L. S.," *Pall Mall Magazine*, December 1901, against charges of disloyalty. Henley was responding to Sir Graham Balfour's *The Life of Robert Louis Stevenson* (1901), which he considered false but which was loved by Stevenson's admirers.

2. Sidney Colvin, ed., *The Letters of Robert Louis Stevenson to His Family and Friends* (1901).

To Anna Strunsky

Dear You:–

[Oakland]
Jan. 22/[02].[1]

On Sunday I had the Herbert Wace letter half completed. But I have been busy on *Examiner* business[2] ever since. From Sunday I did not return home till late last night.

To-morrow, Thursday, I go to San Quentin with Hymen.[3] I have just written him, for divers reasons, not to bring Mary[4]—can explain to you when we meet.

Am in a rush. However, on Friday shall finish letter and send it to you. In this mail, in two envelopes, I send you three untyped letters. Exercise your dire & shaking fist on the machine & in counting up the words. It is much better for us to precisely know where we stand so far as concerns number of words.

Hastily,
Jack.

MS: CSmH; 1 p., als.
1. Misdated "Jan. 22/01."
2. Possibly "Governor Taft Tells Jack London about Filipinos and Philippines," *San*

Francisco Examiner, January 22, 1902, an interview with William Howard Taft, Civil Governor of the Philippines from 1901 to 1904.

3. Hyman Strunsky (*d.* 1942), Anna's brother. He wrote on political and economic topics for magazines and later became a staff member of the *New York Call*, a socialist daily newspaper. JL probably visited San Quentin to arrange to see a hanging. See JL to Strunsky, February 11, 1902, n. 1.

4. Probably Mary Strunsky, Hyman's first wife.

To George P. Brett

56 Bayo Vista Avenue
Oakland, Calif.
Jan. 30, 1902.

Dear Mr. Brett:

My hearty thanks for *Little Novels of Italy*[1]—a favorite book of mine which I did not possess. I think "A Madonna of the Peach Trees" one of the world's short story masterpieces.

Unfortunately, I haven't any copy of the stories already written of *The Children of the Frost*[2]—that is, no *readable* copies, as witness my fist in this letter.

The idea of *The Children of the Frost*, is the writing of a series of tales in which the reader will always look at things from the Indian's point of view, through the Indian's eyes as it were. Heretofore the viewpoint in my Northland stories has been that of the white man's.

Thanking you for your kind interest & hoping that California may soon open her arms to you,[3] I am, sincerely yours—

Jack London.

MS: NN; 1 p., als. Pbd: *L*, 129.

1. Maurice Henry Hewlett, *Little Novels of Italy* (1899), published by Macmillan. "Madonna of the Peach-Tree," one of the stories in the collection, is a tale of a late-medieval Veronese love triangle, an ambiguous "supernatural" apparition, and an outcast wife; in an unexpected reversal at its end, the handsome young friar rather than the aged husband is revealed to be sexually impotent.

2. In a letter to JL of January 23, 1902 (CSmH), Brett asked for manuscript copies of the stories to be included in *Children of the Frost* so that he could read the collection before sailing on February 8 for England, where he planned to arrange for English publication of the book.

3. Brett noted in his letter of January 23 that he had planned to visit JL in California during the Christmas holidays, but that illness had prevented his trip.

To Anna Strunsky

[Oakland]
[? January 1902]

Dear You:—

Just received program of Womans' Press Association, which has you down for Tolstoy. Stand by you Henley. You're doing them the favor, you know, and it is you who gives the *time* and suffer the strain. Stand by it!

Your letter just arrived. Haven't had time to glance at it, as I am writing immediately. But I know the major portion of it, and there is no need for disappointment, much less "bitter" disappointment.

Jack.

MS: CSmH; 1 p., als.

To Elwyn Hoffman

56 Bayo Vista Avenue
Oakland, Calif.
Feb. 1/02.

My dear Elwyn:—

You go to a philologist and get him to explain to you the meaning of the word "inconsistent." After that you will never be guilty of the indiscretion of first calling a man inconsistent and then asking him what his standards are. It's up to you.

The context I asked for made me solid, eh? Again it's up to you.

I return Clifford Richmond's letter. Some time previously I had sent him a few names in a friendly sort of way. That's good, isn't it, that phrase?

I enjoyed your dig at Burgess [1] very much. It was clever.

But then,—and ah! Elwyn, there you miss,—what's it all worth? Cavil, & carp, & critize, bark & snap, and what does it amount to? You're none the better for it. The world is not. Bierce, & Yorick & Hoffman cause only pain. They do not help the world along "in a friendly sort of way." They read the letter of the Law and are damned forthwith. The joy of the Spirit they know not.

I have said that substance was greater than form. Let me now say that motives are the things to judge by, not acts. The poor soul, rightly impelled, may blunderingly execute. But we must measure him, not by what he did do, but by what he tried to do.

Jack London.

MS: CSmH; 2 pp., als.
   1. Gelett Burgess.

To Anna Strunsky

[Oakland]
Feb. 5/02.

Dear You:—

I have been unexpectedly rushed, and so rushed that Miss Boyle utterly slipped my mind. [1] But I am writing her this mail, telling her that I shall be at her studio next Wednsday.

But—but—dear girl, how often are these telephone messages and nervous consents to be repeated? May there not be a selfishness on the man's part which you must not overlook? O, true, true. "A man will protect the woman he loves against every other man in the world except himself; this he leaves to her."[2]

And who am I to say aught, only—well, you understand. You are only a little girl, and yet you are the world's desire, you proud-breasted woman.

Well, am expecting to move.[3] I wonder if you will like the place. I shall say nothing about it, waiting to see your like or dislike in your eyes.

I am sorry Radke[4] came in that morning. To you I have stuttered & failed to tell my inmost thought on the two questions at issue. Did I not stutter I am sure you would think less harshly of me. I am frank enough & bold enough to claim that I understand your side better and give you fuller measure of justice than do you understand mine or give me.

Jack London.

MS: CSmH; 2 pp., als.

1. Possibly Gertrude F. Boyle, who had an art studio at 609 Sacramento St. in San Francisco.

2. "A man would always protect a woman against every man but himself. That task he left to her." (Ella Wheeler Wilcox, "Men or Women as Friends," in *Men, Women, and Emotions*, p. 36.)

3. The Londons were moving to the Worcester bungalow on Blair Avenue in the Piedmont Hills above Oakland. The house was recommended to JL by George Sterling and was located near Sterling's home.

4. Theodore Radtke, member of the Executive Committee of the Oakland Social Democratic Party and Socialist nominee for treasurer of Oakland in 1901.

To Elwyn Hoffman

56 Bayo Vista Avenue
Oakland, Calif.
Feb. 7/02.

Dear Elwyn:—

Ah, I see. The critic hates to be criticized. Had I attempted to outflank you, it would have been fair; but I met your frontal attack with frontal attack. What more would you?

As for your "unanswerable" arguments, I fail to see them. Please give a brief resumé of them.

As for your argument on motives, permit me to tell you that it is rot— the sort of stuff schoolboys are guilty of in debating societies when they try to score "points."

(Damn points! That's the whole trouble between us.) You're after the letter of the law. A vain thing & profitless.

As regards socialism, you are densely ignorant of it. As regards "carp, cavil, criticizes, bark & snap," you fail to understand that such words, so grouped, do not embrace all the different meanings of the word "criticize." It is because you are after the letter of the law that you thus misunderstand. You would twist & distort the whole English language in order to interpret the letter. And of what profit?

You bark & snap at men.

The socialist criticizes principles & systems which make men, as you were made with your proletarian position in society & your bastardized bourgeois ethics.

And the socialist not only makes destructive criticism, but hand in hand goes his constructive criticism. He is doing something to make the world better, & he is swinging the world his way. And what the hell are you doing? How are you making the world better? or swinging it? or doing anything in it except exist?

You stand for the persistence of the established. You would have crucified Christ & burned Bruno[1] just as to-day you vote the Republican ticket.

Sincerely yours
Jack London.

MS: CSmH; 3 pp., als.
1. Giordano Bruno.

To Anna Strunsky

56 Bayo Vista Avenue
Oakland, Calif.
February 11/02.

Dear You:

It is because you are "dear you" that it is made very hard for me. I am unable to express the counter impulses and dictations which run riot in me at this moment. Impulses—to grant. Dictations—to deny. Believe me, it is far far easier to yield to the impulses than to obey the dictations. The woman in me pleads, but my manhood reasons. And, strongest of all, over and above your dear face I see myself, demanding me to be true to myself, to be consistent. I am sure your esteem for me would be less were I untrue to myself in order to be true or kind to you. Do you catch me? I know not why, but the thing so shapes itself that it is not you I must face and consider, but myself. All that I have stood for, and preached and thought (which is I), rises up before me to judge. And I, careless and wanton though I may have always appeared, do secretly respect myself. Without that respect I go to pieces. And believe me, for one of my mould I realize how easily I may go to pieces.

But I cannot say my thought. I become incoherent. Possibly you may grope and catch me. I pray you do, though you remain unconvinced. To strive to answer, as I have just given over striving, were the truer way, but I fail of it.

Superficially, I may easily say many things. If I believed it were wrong, I should not go.[1] Believing it right, honestly believing it right, dare I not go? I do thank you for one thing: you do not ask for your sake. It would make it harder than it is. But you are generous enough to put the request on the fairest possible basis. But it does hurt to be told that I do not stand close enough; that I must always believe my way is far enough from yours never to run counter. And it is not the statement, but the truth of the statement that hurts. And there's the paradox—why do I, who am so little of you, find so much in you? And we are coldly independent of each other. But, as I think, it seems not so. Possibly in no way have I affected you, possibly in only a little way have you affected me. But a little way with some, in the very nature of things, turns out to be a great deal.

Behold! I have lived! Ah, but don't you see? We are so different, that to live we must live differently. Is it necessary that we should be like to be friends? Is it not well that we should reach out hands to each other, like captains of great hosts, in alliance?—neither of us compromising, neither of us giving over or diminishing? Surely such things can be, and are. Is it meet that friends lose themselves in each other? Away with such friendships!

And how have I lived? Frankly and openly, though crudely. I have not been afraid of life? I have not shrunk from it. I have taken it for what it was at its own valuation. And I have not been ashamed of it. Just as it was, it was mine. And as I have not been afraid of life, so have I a frankness with death. I am not afraid to die, and for that reason I am not afraid to see men die. And by "afraid" I do not mean the ordinary meaning of fear. I am not afraid that it will hurt me to see men die. I have seen men die. It was of value to my living that I should see them die. And whatsoever I take I am willing to give. All the world, if it so wishes, may come and see me die.

I am a sentient creature. To live is to experience sensations. To see living is to know living—so dying. I shall be unable to reflect upon my own death, even though I, too, ripen and fall from a gallows tree. And being denied the intellectual value of my own death, I must seek to get those values before my death from the deaths of others. There is such a wonder in it all.

You have not faith enough in me. You fear that if I should see a man sordidly die that it will pollute me—"coarsen" you said. Possibly you meant it. How coarsen? My whole life rises up and says no. I have seen far worse and viler than a legal execution. The legal execution could only be anti-climactic. If I am coarse (as I am), then I am. The worst has been wreaked upon me. What is done, is done.

O God! you can't understand. My manhood to your womanhood may be all wrong, but to stand up, on my two feet, and face life as it is, to have no fear, to see death come to others with as calm and equal poise as when I shall see it come to me, to be unafraid, undismayed, to have no poltroony, no femininity (which is mawkish in a man though good in a woman) to not cover up my eyes but to look bravely out, to take life and the things of life just as I know myself to be a mere thing of life—but you cannot understand; nor can I tell you. How can I tell you?—tell you of the things slowly and subtly grown in me, of the long upbuilding of what I am, of my last and inmost self from which I cannot get away. Why to tell you this, were to have you live with me from the cradle, to dream with me my boy-hood's fancies, to do things with my hands and face things with my face, to buck with men, to think as I have thought at masthead or solitary wheel, to drink long nights and days away, to sleep under blanket with men that were MEN, to learn to grow sick at cowardice and to honor a brave man above an honest man, to honor men unafraid—and how can you understand when I cannot tell you.

On the other hand, I fail to see the difference between laughing and joying in a system wherin a man is hanged, than in seeing that man hanged. And you and I—we all laugh and joy. When you dare to walk home by sidewalks lighted by the Law, then are you a party to the crime committed by the Law when it hangs a man. Nothing remains but to find some mountain top or coral reef utterly outside the domain of man's Law, or else to quit living. But if you dare accept the gaslight on the corner then you must accept the murders the Law commits, for you are part of that Law, by your accepting the gaslight on the corner and the policeman on the crossing you live in this community of people, and by living in this community of people you help to support the Law which this community makes, and when you help to support the Law it means that you pay your share of the rope which is bought to hang the man. Quit or stay with it— that's the proposition. I, for one, stay with it, and staying with it I am neither afraid nor ashamed of it. I do not purpose to live in the front par-lor with the blinds drawn. I want to see the kitchen and the scullery. By God! the man who is afraid to take the fish off the hook or the guts from the bird he expects to eat is no man at all. Neither the fish nor the bird were intended for him. He has no right to them. Let him quit eating. Or, if he will eat, let him get in and unhook and gut. We are no cleaner be-cause we have someone else to do our dirty work for us.

Do we want fruits and vegetables? well and good. Let us work for them. But while we are working for them we must eat fish and birds? Very true. Then, so long as the fish and birds are good enough for our bellies, let them be not unclean for our hands. And rest assured that the Law that protects you from insult and assault on the open street is stained with the blood of the man it hangs at San Quentin. What if that man's eyes rest on you or me? Do they not rest upon us five miles or five thousand miles away? I am not afraid to look that man in the eyes. Why should I be afraid? Do I coarsen by looking him in the eyes? Then do I coarsen more by staying away afraid to look him in the eyes, afraid that I will be hurt by looking him in the eyes. Believe me, only a bastard sympathy can be generated on couch cushions. "Tender feelings" after all are pleasurable. I should rather look with my own eyes and feel sick. Then I might feel sick ever after when a man is hanged.

But why go on? Am I bending to convention by baring my soul? I only wax heated anyway. The primordial beast lifts up its head and roars—of what good?—ten thousand generations seem to separate us. And anyway, though you may point the way to the New Jerusalem, I shall build the road thereto. And while you eat your fish and birds, and though you despise me, I shall unhook and gut. And it will taste good in your mouth and your hands will be as dirty as mine.

I did not write the letter I intended to write.[2] I went astray somehow. I wished to meet your sweetness with sweetness, and instead have called upon all that was harsh & unlovable in my nature. I am grateful, and I do appreciate that you care enough for me to wish me not to do anything no matter how great or small. But—but possibly the first page of this letter, is, after all the clearest expression of what I mean. I cannot. Had you, before I dreamed of going, said "Never go to a hanging," I would have promised to please you. But coming afterward, the whole thing seems changed. I should be ashamed of myself. I would rather go, and then, to make it easier for you, never see you again, than to not go & have your favor showered upon me a thousand-fold. Not that I hold a hanging above your favor, much less your favor a thousand-fold; but that there is something else which I must hold above all if I would hold you or anyone or anything at all.

Jack.

MS: CSmH; 6 pp., tls. Pbd: *L*, 129–32.

1. JL was going to San Quentin to witness the hanging of Isaac Daily, which occurred on February 21. For JL's desire to see a hanging, see JL to Hoffman, October 5, 1900. On January 9, 1900, Daily had taken his bicycle to Lemuel Metz for repair of a flat tire, for which Metz agreed to extend him credit. The next day Daily returned for more repairs to his bicycle and argued with Metz over the amount of the charges. He left the shop, only to return a half hour later with a shotgun and kill Metz. Daily pleaded insanity but was convicted of murder.

2. Beginning with this sentence, the remainder of the letter is handwritten.

To Anna Strunsky

[Piedmont]
Feb. 18/02.

Dear Anna:—

Your letter has worried me greatly,—as much for itself, and almost as much for the fact that I have been plunged head under heels in moving and have been unable to scribble off even a postal.

Am moved. You must come & see us at very very first chance. The next time you go home. Next Sunday. What do you say?

Jack.

P.S. Come out to the very end of the Piedmont car-line, & then inquire for me. (I am living where the Squire's & Fagins used to live.)

MS: CSmH; 1 p., als.

To Elwyn Hoffman

Piedmont, Calif.
Feb. 23/02

Dear Elwyn:—
Behold! I have moved! You must come out and see me. I am living in the country, and yet am within 24 minutes of the heart of Oakland. Take Piedmont cars & ride to the very end of the line. I am four minutes' walk from the very end of the line. Any of the houses should be able to direct you to my place.

As for the argument—your last letter has thoroughly convinced me that I am an ass and you Solon[1] & Solomon rolled into one. I can only say that you go through life missing life. Your attitude is all wrong—

Jack London.

MS: CSmH; 1 p., als.
    1. Solon (?638–?558 B.C.), Athenian statesman.

To Cloudesley Johns

Piedmont, Calif.
Feb. 23/02.

Dear Cloudesley:—
Behold! I have moved! Wherefore my long silence. I have been very busy. Also, I went to see a man hanged yesterday. It was one of the most scientific things I have ever seen. From the time he came through the door which leads from the death-chamber to the gallows-room, to the time he was dangling at the end of the rope, but 21 seconds elapsed.

And in those twenty-one seconds all the following things occurred: He walked from the door to the gallows, ascended a flight of thirteen stairs to the top of the gallows, walked across the top of the gallows to the trap, took his position upon the trap, his legs were strapped, the noose slipped over his head drawn tight and the knot adjusted, the black cap pulled down over his face, the trap sprung, his neck broken, & the spinal cord severed—all in twenty-one seconds, so simple a thing is life and so easy it is to kill a man.

Why, he made never the slightest twitch. It took fourteen and one-half minutes for the heart to run down, but he was not aware of it. ⅕ of a second elapsed between the springing of the trap and the breaking of his neck & severing of his spinal cord. So far as he was concerned, he was dead at the end of that one-fifth of a second. He killed a man for twenty-five cents.

You ask what else beside matter moves. How about force? Waves of light, for instance?

We'll have to reserve the free will argument till God brings us together again. I've got the cinch on you.

Did you go in on the *Black Cat*? I went in for a couple of stories, though I have little hope of pulling down even the least prize.[1] I imagine I can sell the stuff somewhere else, however.

Lord, what stack of hack I'm turning out! Five mouths & ten feet,[2] and sometimes more, so one hustles. I wonder if ever I'll get clear of debt.[3]

Am beautifully located in new house. We have a big living room, every inch of it, floor & ceiling, finished in redwood. We could put the floor space of almost four cottages (of the size of the one you can remember) into this one living room alone. The rest of the house is finished in redwood, too, & is very, very comfortable. We have also the cutest, snuggest little cottage right on the same ground with us, in which live my mother & my nephew. Chicken houses & yards for 500 chickens. Barn for a dozen horses, big pigeon houses, laundry, creamery, etc. etc. A most famous porch, broad & long & cool, a big clump of magnificent pines, flowers & flowers & flowers galore, five acres of ground sold the last time at $2000 per acre, half of ground in bearing orchard & half sprinkled with California poppies; we are twenty-four minutes from the door to the heart of Oakland and an hour and five minutes to San Francisco; our nearest neighbor is a block away (and there isn't a vacant lot within a mile), our view commands all of San Francisco Bay for a sweep of thirty or forty miles, and all the opposing shores such as San Francisco, Marin County & Mount Tamalpias, (to say nothing of the Golden Gate & the Pacific Ocean)—and all for $35.00 per month. I couldn't buy the place for $15,000. And some day I'll have to be fired out.

Jack London.

MS: CSmlI; 5 pp., als. Pbd: *L*, 132–33; *BJL*, I, 372–73; *Pictorial Life*, 110.

   1. The *Black Cat* was offering a total of $10,285 in prizes in a story contest closing on February 26, 1902. JL sent "Moon-Face" to the competition on February 7, 1902; after several rejections it was accepted by the *Argonaut* on June 29, 1902, and published July 21. He was paid $15 for the story in the fall of 1902. "The Shadow and the Flash" was sent to the competition on February 21; after seven rejections the story was accepted by the *Bookman* on April 1, 1902, and published in June 1903. JL received $50 for it on May 29, 1903. Both stories were included in *Moon-Face*.

   2. Bessie, Joan, and Flora London, Mammie Jennie Prentiss, and Johnny Miller.

   3. JL was to be free of debt for only a short time in 1904 after his return from the Russo-Japanese War. Then, he had almost four thousand dollars in the bank.

To Anna Strunsky

Dear You:—

Not including your letters to be inserted, in the regular series we have now 45,032 words already done.

This letter of mine is not up to much. The second half, relating to my loves, I had expected to do good work on, but the *Examiner* interruption and the trip to San Quentin somehow threw me out & I could not get the swing again.

Good luck for the Henley lecture.

Jack.

MS: CSmH; 1 p., als.

To Anna Strunsky

Piedmont, Calif.
March 14/02.

Dear, dear You:—

Why should I, how could I, be angry? I who know you so well? I have been wondering, and wondering, and each day intended to write you, (but your postal each day bade me wait till the next day brought the letter); but have been too rushed. I find myself forced to get up at four o'clock now, in order to turn out my day's work. And of course, so long as tradesmen bicker & landlords clatter, that long must the day's work be turned out.

Also, Joan has been under the weather, my sister's boy on the edge of dying for a number of days, my other sister very close to death herself,[1] and the many & varied demands have consumed every minute of my time.

Do run over & see us when you're in town. We are nearly settled now, & things will be more comfortable. Arrange before you come to stay the night. It will be delightful here this summer.

I had something more to say, but have forgotten.

Anyway,
Jack.

MS: CSmH; 2 pp., als. Pbd: *BJL*, I, 373.
   1. Irving Shepard and Ida Miller.

To Anna Strunsky

Piedmont, Calif.
March 22/02.

Dear You:—

Many happy returns of the year, since I am too late for the day. And after all, it is the year that must count, & not the day. May it be a full year.

And may it be an empty one, too—empty of heartache, and soul sickness, and the many trials which have been yours in the past twelve months.

Day by day I look out across the bay to a nook in the Marin shore where I know San Rafael clusters, and I wonder how it fares with you and how you are doing.

I would suggest, if things continue to go badly there, that you gather together your belongings, gypsy fashion, and seek a change. New scene, new inspiration, perhaps, you know. Also, do not worry. Things are not worth worrying over, except bills and rent. Other things do not count.

My sister and little boy are out here now.[1] By the time the boy was convalescent it seemed as though the mother was ready to die. So I sent a hack and carted them up here into the hills, where they are changed creatures already.

And say, next Sunday, to-morrow, what's the matter with running over to see us? Charmian Kittredge, charmingly different from the average kind, is liable to be here. Perhaps you will like her. Also, Jensen,[2] an old Klondike friend (the sailor whose letters I once showed you), is to be here. Also, possibly several others who will pitch quoits, & fence, & what not. Also, I am scheduled, in the company of Jim & George,[3] to take hasheesh as a matter of *scientific* investigation.

And when you come, if come you do, make arrangements to stop the night with us. Do come.

Jack.

MS: CSmH; 2 pp., als. Pbd: *BJL*, I, 374.
    1. Eliza and Irving Shepard.
    2. Emil Jensen.
    3. Herman Whitaker and George Sterling.

To Cloudesley Johns

Piedmont, Calif.
March 26/02.

Dear Cloudesley:—

Certainly, force moves matter. It is the movement of matter that manifests force. But explain this to me: The sun is in a state of combustion. It gives off heat. Heat is not matter, though it is liberated from matter. Heat is a form of energy. It is a force. Now the heat of the sun comes to the earth. Now the heat of the sun that we feel on the earth is not the matter of the sun. And now, since the heat that was in the sun, and is on the earth, must have traveled, via matter, to get here. But the point is, this heat, or energy, or force, came from the sun to the earth.

Force gives motion to matter. Surely that which gives motion must move. Here is a current of force. (It is flowing, no matter how.) Into this current is put a piece of iron, and all the molecules of the iron are swung about & put in such order that the iron is magnetized. Here were molecules of matter, altered or moved by a current of force. But withdraw the piece of iron from the current. Are we then to suppose that the current of force is no longer there?

Damn your callous heart! I'll never tell you where or how I am living. It's plain to see you are not a domestic animal, else would you have sympathized with me. Let me add this to the description, however, in the words of Gelett Burgess: "the floors are flat, the windows obvious."

Have got another collection of stories done, *Children of the Frost*, though they are waiting publication at various magazines.

Jack London.

MS: CSmH; 2 pp., als.

To Anna Strunsky

Piedmont, Calif.
Saturday.
March 29/02

Dear You:—

I had intended to write you a good long letter for yourself, but people have come, must shave now or never, and have some toning to do in dark room. You have hardly been out of my thoughts since last you were here, and I have been haunted by a half-fear lest you were hurt by my not going with you to tea with that English lady. And all week I have wrestled with that story part of which you read.[1] I finished it last night—10,000 words.

But, do you know, leaving out the letters to be inserted, we have now 50,000 done on the book!

I must get a letter from you saying that you are coming to California, and also, somewhere in your Stanford letters a hint must be given to the effect of our meeting, which meeting I should imagine must precede your meeting with Hester.[2]

What ho! now, for the revision! You must come & live with us during that momentous period. It's glorious here, more like a poppy dream than real living.

Jack.

Let me know if letter fits, or if another is needed.

MS: CSmH; 2 pp., als. Pbd: *BJL*, I, 375.
1. JL had completed "The Story of Jees Uck." After being rejected by *McClure's* and *Cosmopolitan*, it was accepted by *Smart Set* on May 19, 1902, and published in the September 1902 issue. JL received $100 for it on June 24, 1902. It was later included in *The Faith of Men*.
2. Hester Stebbins, in *The Kempton-Wace Letters*.

To Anna Strunsky

[Piedmont]
[? March 1902]

Dear You:—

I have just finished reading your last letter, Dane Kempton, preparatory to replying to it. And before replying, I must tell you that I feel the letters will *go! Go! Go!*[1]

Your last is good, is great! You do get your position stated better than I had thought it possible it could be stated. Come to-morrow. The reply will await you. How goes the novel? I must see & hear of it, all of it.

Jack.

MS: CSmH; 1 p., als. Pbd: *BJL*, I, 375.
1. JL underlined the second "Go" twice, the third three times.

To Anna Strunsky

Piedmont, Calif.
April 1/02.

Dear, Dear You:—

Why, certainly. I see no reason why Mrs. Harton should not receive copy, and there is no reason why you should not be the subject matter. All the world's copy, for that matter, and you are exceptionally good copy. I would ask no better.

I like the "insert" letter that arrived to-day. By all means develop Barbara.[1] What an addition she'll make to the book! We're winding up the home stretch, girl, don't you know it? We're winding up! And then the revision!

Have been enquiring about the typing of manuscript. Think it will come to about fifty dollars all told—maybe cheaper.

I am confident we can get a first class house to bring out the book, though it will take hard work, possibly, to get serial publication.

Got news to-day about my failure-novel.[2] It will never see serial publication. But Lippincotts will take it off McClure's hands and bring it out themselves in book form. They will advance $750 on the royalties. Of course, I'll not touch the money. It will go to pay off part of my indebtedness to McClure's. Nevertheless I am $750 richer this evening than I was this morning.

As usual, am in a rush. Bound for business meeting of Ruskin.[3]

> Thine,
> Jack.

MS: CSmH; 3 pp., als.

1. Barbara, in *The Kempton-Wace Letters*, was Herbert Wace's sister. She lived with Dane Kempton in London.
2. *A Daughter of the Snows.*
3. The Ruskin Club.

To George P. Brett

Piedmont, Calif.
April 16/02.

Dear Mr. Brett:—

Here's some idea of the *Children of the Frost*:

"Nam-Bok the Unveracious"	5,500	words.
"Li Wan the Fair"	6,500	"
"The Sun Folk"	8,000	"
"In the Forests of the North"	6,800	"
"The Law of Life"	2,700	"
"Keesh, the Son of Keesh"	4,000	"
"The Master of Mystery"	4,100	"
"The Death of Ligoun"	3,700	"
"The Sickness of Lone Chief"	3,000	"
	45,000	"

The first four are sold and waiting serial publication. The fifth and sixth have received serial publication, the seventh is seeking serial publication, as are the eight and ninth which were written within the past month. I expect shortly to write one or two more, when the collection will be complete.[1] It should be in your hands by early fall. The two previous collections, *The Son of the Wolf* and *The God of His Fathers*, contained respectively 49,000 and 50,000 words.

In connection with *The Children of the Frost*, I should like to know if it is in line with the Macmillan Company's policy to sometimes make an advance on royalties? And if so, could two hundred dollars be advanced me now on the royalties of *The Children of the Frost*? Now I do not mean this as a guarantee necessary before the book can go to you. Whether you can make any advance or not, the book goes to you, for I have said it. The point is, that if you can make the advance, things will be made easier for me. And this is the reason: I have no income, and my expenses are about $150 per month. This sum I manage to get from my magazine work. But, beginning next week, I shall put in about thirty days writing and revising a book manuscript,[2] so that during that time I shall be earning no ready money. This book, by the way, has been promised to Bliss Perry for the *Atlantic*, (if serially available), and for Houghton, Mifflin & Co., which firm brought out my first book.

It hardly seems necessary for me to state that two previous collections of short stories have earned me much more than two hundred dollars apiece.

The tramp story,[3] which you mention, is only the first one of a series which I have discontinued. It is with the *Atlantic* just now, or I would let you see it, though, really, I have become chary of letting anyone see it. As for sea novels, I am waiting to make a lucky strike some time, when I can devote a few months to them. You see, though once a sailor myself, I have gone stale on sea men and sea atmosphere, and I have control enough not to attempt such work until I have refreshed myself. My plan is, when I can see expenses clear for half a dozen months, to take passage on sailing vessel almost anywhere, and with typewriter and paper along, to do my work in the thick of it.

Thank you very much for Mrs. Atherton's new book,[4] which I have just received and which I look forward to reading with pleasure.

Yours very sincerely,
Jack London.

MS: NN; 2 pp., tls. Pbd: *L*, 134–35.
    1. The stories in *Children of the Frost* were first published as follows: "Nam-Bok, the Unveracious," *Ainslee's*, August 1902 (see JL to Strunsky, July 24, 1901, n. 5); "Li Wan, the Fair," *Atlantic*, August 1902; "In the Forests of the North," *Pearson's*, October 1902; "The Law of Life," *McClure's*, March 1901; "Keesh, Son of Keesh," *Ainslee's*, January 1902; "The Master of Mystery," *Out West*, September 1902; "The Sickness of Lone Chief," *Out West*, October 1902. "The Sun Folk"—later retitled "The Sunlanders"—and "The Death of Ligoun" were not published serially; see JL to Brett, January 16, 1902, n. 1. Also included was "The League of the Old Men," *Brandur Magazine*, October 4, 1902.
    2. *The Kempton-Wace Letters*.
    3. "The Tramp" was rejected by the *Atlantic* and subsequently accepted by *Wilshire's Magazine*; it was published in the February, March, and April 1904 issues of *Wilshire's* and was later included in *War of the Classes*. In a letter to JL of April 7, 1902 (CSmH), Brett wrote that Macmillan's San Francisco agent, Mr. Goodyear, had mentioned to him that "The Tramp" had been returned to JL by the *Atlantic*. Brett wished to peruse the manuscript to see if he could make any use of it.
    4. Possibly Gertrude Atherton's *The Conqueror: Being the True and Romantic Story of Alexander Hamilton*, published by Macmillan in 1902.

To Anna Strunsky

Piedmont, Calif.
April 24/02.

Dear You:—
    I doubt whether I shall be able to make over to San Francisco Friday evening for the reception. If I can, and if agreeable to you, should like to

stop all night and bring you back with me in the morning *early*. Don't expect me, though I may turn up.

I need not tell how disappointed I was at your non-arrival. But you must come Saturday, & we must pitch in & get off the letters. Tuesday I received a letter from the Century Company. They own *St. Nicholas*. For *St. Nicholas*, some time ago I condensed a boy's story of 20,000 words to 14000 words. They now want me to expand it to 40,000 words so that they may bring it out as a book in the early fall.[1] They wanted me to go to work right away so as to get it into the printer's hands. I explained what I was doing, and that as soon as I finished *our* letters, I should take up their work.

Until Saturday, and maybe Friday,

Jack.

MS: CSmH; 1 p., als.

1. JL had written *The Cruise of the Dazzler* as a serial for *Youth's Companion*, to which it was submitted on October 28, 1899. The story was rejected there, however. On July 14, 1900, it was accepted by *St. Nicholas*, an illustrated children's magazine featuring stories, poems, and sports articles, published in New York from 1873 until 1943. JL was paid $250 for the work, which appeared in July 1902. The Century Company published it in book form in October 1902.

To Corresponding Editor, *Youth's Companion*

Piedmont, Calif.
April 24/02

Dear sir:–

I cannot imagine what led Mr. Reynolds to submit a story like the "One Thousand Dozen" to the *Companion*.[1] He certainly received no instructions from me to do so. The eternal unfitness of such a story for the *Companion*!

Ere this, you will have received my "long" short story, "In Yeddo Bay."[2] Also my "Fish Patrol" proposition.[3] In the latter thing, I think the field is as yet untouched.

Very sincerely yours,
Jack London.

MS: ViU; 1 p., als.

1. "The One Thousand Dozen" was published in the *National*, March 1903, and later included in *The Faith of Men*. The morbid irony of this story, in which the protagonist hangs himself after the failure of his scheme to sell eggs at exorbitant prices to the Klondikers, would make it unfit for young readers. See also JL to Putnam, November 11, 1902, n. 2.

2. "In Yeddo Bay," *St. Nicholas*, February 1903; later included in *Dutch Courage*.

3. JL was probably negotiating with *Youth's Companion* for serialization of the adventure tales of San Francisco Bay later published as *Tales of the Fish Patrol*. JL wrote seven stories between April 1902 and February 1903. *Youth's Companion* paid $75 for each and published them from February 11 to May 11, 1905.

To George P. Brett

Piedmont, Calif.
April 28/02.

Dear Mr. Brett:—

I am returning you herewith the signed agreement of *The Children of the Frost*.[1] It is eminently satisfactory. I am now at work on the last story in that series, and will have it off to the magazines ere another week is out. Also, within a week or ten days I shall be able to dispatch to you duplicates of nearly all, if not all, the stories, so that they may be available for illustration and for copyrighting in England. I will enclose with them a list of the ones which are to receive serial publication in England.

I feel very confident that the complete manuscript will be in your hands in time for October publication. The Century Company expects to bring out a book of mine this fall, a boy's story expanded from one to be published soon in *St. Nicholas*, and Lippincott's are bringing out a novel I wrote a year ago, this fall or winter. In England, Isbister & Co., are bringing out the *God of his Fathers*, and they have bought the English copyright of *Son of the Wolf* from Ward, Lock & Co and expect to bring same out this fall or winter.[2]

That's the way I stand with my work just now, with, in addition, the book I am at present working on and of which Houghton, Mifflin & Co., have been promised the first sight.

I do not know whether *Children of the Frost* is an advance over previous work, but I do know that there are big books in me and that when I find myself they will come out. At present I am just trying to find myself and am busy gripping hold of life.

Yours very sincerely,
Jack London

MS: NN; 2 pp., tls. Pbd: *L*, 135.
1. The contract JL signed with Macmillan provided him, in addition to the $200 already advanced by Brett, a $300 advance upon publication, 15 percent royalties on the first five thousand copies sold, and 20 percent thereafter.
2. Isbister published both books in 1902.

To H. Perry Robinson[1]

[Piedmont]
April 28/02.

Dear sir:—

I was glad to receive the copies of *The God of His Fathers*, which I liked very much, and for which I thank you heartily. I am awaiting the clippings feverishly, for from the two I have managed to get hold of, it seems that you on your side of the water have caught my underlying motive better than the average American reviewers caught it.[2]

You mention in your letter sending for plates of the book to print from in England. Will you tell me what, if any, difference this makes in your arrangement with McClure's for the English copies.

Concerning the novel which they have, I can tell you this: Lippincott's are to bring it out in the United States this fall. I have but recently signed the contract with them, they advancing $750 royalties.

By the way, some time ago I wrote a long short story for the *St. Nicholas* juvenile magazine. Century Company has just written me, asking me to expand it by twenty thousand words, fetching it up to forty thousand, so that they may bring it out in book form this fall. I have agreed to this, and shall do the work very shortly. I presume they will only publish in America (the contract has not yet arrived), and so I am wondering if you have a market for a boy's adventure story in England? If you have, I should like to have you bring the book out.[3] Regarding this, if you are inclined to chance the book, we could deal personally, I retaining my right in American contract to dispose of British rights. And so, what would be the terms on which you would handle the British side of it? I imagine it should be a case of royalty and not outright sale of copyright.

Of course, it must be understood that this is distinctively a juvenile book, good for boys of from eight to eighteen, and that it is in no way an adult book.

Yes, I have long since made up my mind to see England and the Old Countries (I have started twice, but never succeeded in making it). And some day I hope walk into No. 16 Tavistock Street and shake hands with you.

Please let me know your will in the boy's book, and please do not delay sending the clippings. Thanking you for your kindness, I am,

Sincerely yours,
Jack London

MS: CSmH; 2 pp., cctl.

1. H. Perry Robinson (*b.* 1859), managing director of the English publisher Isbister & Co. from 1901 to 1904. Robinson had lived in America from 1883 to 1900, working as a journalist and gold miner. For Robinson's response to JL's work, see JL to Brett, November 21, 1902.

2. The two clippings from English periodicals were probably the anonymous reviews "Fiction: *The God of His Fathers*," *Academy and Literature*, March 1, 1902, and "Short Stories: *The God of His Fathers*," *Athenaeum*, April 5, 1902. In the former the reviewer remarked: "It would not be fair not to treat [*The God of His Fathers*] with some seriousness, but Jack London's loud and swaggering disregard for the simplest rules of realism is a temptation to jocosity . . . he writes on the whole very well and forcibly, [but] his eloquence is a fiery steed that sometimes runs away with him." In the latter the reviewer claimed that the book was a volume of "exceptional merit with strongly dramatic stories."

3. An English edition of *The Cruise of the Dazzler* was published, not by Isbister & Co., but by Hodder and Stoughton in 1906.

To George P. Brett

Piedmont, Calif.
May 2, 1902.

Dear Mr. Brett:—

I have managed to get together duplicates of the stories in *The Children of the Frost*, and I am expressing them to you this day. At the beginning of each I have given a brief history of where published, in what publisher's hands, etc.

As you requested, I am sending them to you now for copyright in England and for illustration. I should like to have them back again, before getting ready for print, as they are wholly unrevised and I have many crudities to smooth up. They are not ready for print as they stand.

I am now at work on the last one of the series: "The Perplexity of Imber," [1] and shall have it completed shortly.

Sincerely yours,
Jack London.

MS: NN; 1 p., als.
1. Retitled and published serially and in *Children of the Frost* as "The League of the Old Men."

To Frederick I. Bamford

Piedmont,
May 6/02.

Dear, dear Comrade:—

I stretch out my hand to you across the land. [1] You are very near. Let me sit with you awhile, dumbly, sharing your pain and breathing you hope. There is the world yet, the patient, long-suffering world for which you have done so well and still shall do well.

For you & the Cause,
Jack London.

MS: JL State Park; 1 p., als. Pbd: *Mystery*, 181.
1. Bamford was grief-stricken over the death of his youngest and favorite sister, Maggie, in Minneapolis a few days earlier.

To Dan [? Murphy]

Piedmont, Calif.
May 12/02.

Dear Dan:—

Here's a yarn, not top notch, for England. I think I shall dispose of it to the *National* on this side. [1]

It's one in the book, *The Children of the Frost*, which Macmillan Company is to bring out this fall, so, if salable in England it must be published not later than October.

The God of His Fathers, I understand, is being received cordially in England, where *The Son of the Wolf* is to be brought out this fall. Lippincotts bring out the novel this fall, and if all goes well, Century Company will at same time bring out a boy's book of mine.[2]

Then there is *The Book*. Anna Strunsky is now visiting me, and we have begun the revision.

Sincerely yours, and hastily,
Jack London.

MS: Batchelder; 1 p., als.

   1. "The Master of Mystery" was sent to the *National* on May 12 and was rejected there. It was then sent to *Out West* on June 10, where it was accepted and published in the September issue. JL received $15 for the story on October 3.

   2. *The Cruise of the Dazzler.*

To Mr. and Mrs. C. C. Behringer

[Piedmont]
May 18, 1902.

My dear Mr. and Mrs. Behringer:[1]

   From the rather excited state of mind I left you in this afternoon, I imagine that your wits were strayed too far to grasp what I tried to tell you. Also, I wish to let you know that my P.O. address is Piedmont, Alameda county. To this address please send out my entire bill, to my last dealings with you, not forgetting to give me credit for the six loaves of bread in payment of which I left thirty cents on your counter.

   Now, you are both of you quite good ordinary folk, with little business ability and less tact. I do not purpose to be exceeding hard to you, but I do intend to teach you a little lesson in business and manners. You lied to me and beat about the bush for four days and then left me in the hole. This lying to me, and beating about the bush, and leaving me in the hole is really unpardonable. And being so treated, I could hardly continue to deal with you. That is to say, by your own action you disconnected yourself from me so far as business is concerned. I therefore do not longer include your bill among my living bills, and it is my living bills I always make a point to pay first. So I set your bill among my general and back bills. Now, my general and back bills (few though they be) have never pressed me while they have been uniformly courteous and kind. None of them ever lied or left me in the hole. So it is incumbent on me to treat them with the same courtesy and kindness, and they will be paid before you are paid.

   In the end, which may be one month away or twelve, I shall certainly pay you. You will be as certain of the few dollars I owe you as you are certain of the sun rising to-morrow—that is, if, from now on to that time, you are courteous and gentlemanly and ladylike, if you misbehave, if you overtalk yourself, if you attempt to blacklist or to cause trouble for me in any possible way, why then you forfeit all chance of ever getting a cent out of me. As regards blacklist, by the way, you know how utterly worthless such a proceeding is. You could blacklist me from now until Doomsday, and on the strength of my dealing with dozens of far more responsible firms than yours I could get all the new credit I wished.

I have never had to treat but one other person as I am now treating you. I gave that person the same terms I am now giving you. But he preferred to kick over the traces and play rough with his mouth, so he never got a cent. On the other hand, while I refused to pay him, at the very time, I went back and paid a bill of my father's, a bill which had been run long before I was of age, a bill which had become outlawed in fact, a bill which had no legal claim upon me at all.

You said you would get it out of me to-day. Well, dear Mister-Mistress Behringer. I have shown you the only possible way in which you can get it, and that way is by keeping your tongue between your teeth, by saying nothing and by being courteous. Do not delude yourself by thinking that you can possibly get it out of me in any other way. In this connection I wish to refer you to your own words to-day. You said that no one had ever talked to you the way I had. That being so, you can only conclude that I am a different kind of a man from any you ever met. Possibly that is because I talk right up to the handle and say what I mean instead of lying over a telephone. And that being so, it were well that you take to heart what terms I have laid down. Also, if you are sensible at all, you will profit by this thing and keep the lock off your door. Also, if you feel inclined, present this letter to a lawyer and see if you can entice him into taking the case on a contingent fee. You know you could not afford to buck me out of your own pocket. Find a lawyer who will read this letter and dig into his own pocket to fight me, and then go ahead and God bless you.

Cordially yours,

Jack London.

SOURCE: "To Man He Owes Jack London Writes," *San Francisco Examiner*, May 29, 1902.

1. C. C. Behringer, a grocer, who had dunned JL over the telephone for a bill of $35 run up at his store. Behringer read JL's letter aloud at a meeting of the Retail Grocers' Association in Oakland on May 27. According to the *Examiner*, the Association, "not knowing what else to do, has had the letter placed on file." Subsequent publication of the letter in several Bay Area newspapers apparently so angered JL that he refused to pay the bill.

To Lurline Lyons

Piedmont, Calif.
June 2/02.

Dear Lurline:—[1]

Your picture received. It is great. We are all wild over it. That man Genthe[2] is all right, and so are the people who have their pictures taken by him & who give them to their friends.

We were sorry you were not able to come & see us before you went away. We know, of course, that you are having a good time down at the tail-end of the state, and we wish we were with you or you with us.

Oh, by the way, look up Mrs. Idah Meacham Strobridge. Tell her I sent you and she will make you very welcome. She is out in the "Lummis Colony,"[3] and lives in a famous house, or rather, in a house she has made famous by her own personality. Her address is:

Mrs. Idah Meacham Strobridge,
231 East Avenue Forty-One,
Los Angeles.

I was out sailing Saturday with Mr. Eames, Mrs. Wylie & Beth & Esmond, & Charmian & others.[4] We had a fine time.—Bess & Joan send their love, and I send mine—

Jack.

MS: CSmH; 2 pp., als.

1. Lurline Lyons (*b.* 1881), CKL's cousin.

2. Arnold Genthe (1869–1942), German-born photographer. Genthe had a studio in San Francisco from 1898 to 1911. Along with Mary Austin and George Sterling, he was one of the first to settle in the artist colony in Carmel-by-the-Sea, where he built a house in 1905. For Genthe's reminiscences about his relationship with JL, see his *As I Remember* (New York, 1936), pp. 49–50, 74–75.

3. The Arroyo Seco art colony in Pasadena. Charles F. Lummis had one of the first houses on the banks of the Arroyo and established the Arroyo Seco Foundation in 1885 for the preservation of the area's natural beauty.

4. Roscoe Eames (?1846–1931), business manager for the *Overland Monthly* and husband of Ninetta Eames. Mrs. Wiley and Beth and Esmond, CKL's aunt and cousins.

To Anna Strunsky

Piedmont, Calif.
June 2/02.

Dear You:—

I do not know whether you will be here or not this afternoon, but do come to-morrow anyway.

I am head over heels in work or else I would be over to you again. I was out sailing Saturday, and you were with me. You are with me always.

Jack.

Oh, the entire proofs of *The Children of the Frost* came to-day, neatly arranged as a paper-cover book. You must see it.

MS: CSmH; 1 p., als.

To Anna Strunsky

Piedmont,
June 7/02.

Dear You:—
I am sending this by special delivery so that you may receive it before Sunday. People are coming here in the afternoon, and I must do a day's work in the morning. I deny myself in not going to you, & Sunday remains a very miserable day to look forward to. Nevertheless, I shall see you & be with you all day.
Bills are beginning to press, & I am behind in all my work. Just now I am hammering out juvenile stuff—the Fish Patrol stories for the *Youth's Companion*. The proofsheets of the novel[1] are giving me endless trouble. It is terrible to doctor sick things. Last night was business meeting of Ruskin. In morning did day's juvenile work. Expected to get off 7 pages of proofs in afternoon & go down town on business. At one o'clock I started in on proofs (7 sheets) at quarter past five I finished them. Every batch seems the worst till the next batch comes along.
How I looked for you Tuesday afternoon. I felt sure you would come. Can you come Monday or Tuesday of next week?
I shall be with you Friday afternoon the 13th., but do let us see each other before that.
Your very miserable Sahib.

Second Tuesday in June, June 10th, is night you are billed for the lecture at 528—27th. st. Can you not be here that afternoon, and stop with us that night after the lecture?[2]

MS: CSmH; 3 pp., als. Pbd: *BJL*, I, 377.
1. *A Daughter of the Snows.*
2. The address 528 27th Street, Oakland, was the home of a Mrs. Shannon and apparently a gathering place for the Second Ward Political Equality Club. JL had addressed the group there on April 9, 1901, on "What Communities Lose by the Competitive System."

To Anna Strunsky

[Piedmont]
June 10/02.

Dear, Dear You:—
I shall be over Friday afternoon. I am doing 2000 words a day now, &

every day, and my head is in such a whirl I can hardly think. But I feel. I
am sick with love for you and need of you.

The Sahib.

MS: CSmH; 1 p., als.

To George P. Brett

Piedmont, Calif.
[June 18, 1902]

My Dear Mr. Brett:—
   The proofs of *Children of the Frost*, have been to hand some time now. I
like the type & arrangement very much.
   I shall delay going over the proofs, for several weeks more, if I may, for I
am quite rushed on proofs of a novel Lippincotts are bringing out, and in
finishing a boy's adventure story for the Century people.[1]
   Also, one of the *Frost* stories, "Li Wan, the Fair," was utterly re-written
for the last six or seven pages, the revised copy of which is in the hands of
the *Atlantic* awaiting publication. I shall write them to-day for a duplicate of those pages.[2]

Very truly yours,
Jack London.

P.S.—Oh. I want to ask a favor. Lippincotts, on the title page of novel,
under my name, were kind enough, on my request, to put: "Author of
The Son of the Wolf, and *The God of His Fathers*." Could the same be
done on the title page of *The Children of the Frost*.[3]

MS: NN; 2 pp., als.
   1. The expanded version of *The Cruise of the Dazzler*.
   2. In a letter to Bliss Perry of June 18, 1902 (IaU), JL asked for copies of the last three
pages of the revised manuscript of "Li Wan, the Fair."
   3. Brett complied with JL's request.

To Anna Strunsky

[Piedmont]
June 20/02

Dear, dear You:—
   I have been trying to write you a line ever since your visit, in which I
saw so little of you. Last night I thought I would surely be able to, but
after knocking out 2400 words, typing them, and doing 100 pages of
proofs, I fell asleep in my chair. It was midnight when I finished the proofs.
   Tuesday I expect to have this boy's stuff done & off, and Tuesday I expect some great thing or other from you. So I leave Tuesday evening open
for whatever you have in mind.

[Sahib][1]

MS: CSmH; 1 p., al.
    1. Apparently the signature was cut off this letter.

To Anna Strunsky

[Piedmont]
July 3/02

Dear, dear You:—

I am wondering and wonder what you are doing, and as usual am too rushed to write. For three months I have been steadily dropping behind in all my work, & I have sworn a great vow to catch up. Yesterday I worked eighteen hours, and did clean up quite a lot—the same the day before, & day before that, etc.

Can I see you next Monday afternoon? And if so, will you get Hyman[1] or somebody to get tickets for whatever good is playing, & I'll return for same when I come over.

How unsatisfactory it is to meet you out among people, & how I enjoyed the look of you the other night.

Sahib.

MS: CSmH; 1 p., als. Pbd: *BJL*, I, 377.
    1. Hyman Strunsky.

To Edward S. Holloway

Piedmont, Calif.
July 11/02

Dear Mr. Holloway:—[1]

I think your "yarn," as you call it, is fine. Only, in my mind, it is not a yarn. It is a study, delicately & cleanly written, and considering the form you couldn't have done better. Believe me, I'm a great slasher, but there's nothing to slash in it. You certainly did what you set out to do, and you as surely did the psychology a whole lot better than most writers could have done it.

I have been sick with "Grip"—think of it! Grip in the middle of summer.

Yes, I should like very much to have your House consider future work of mine. Just now, I have nothing on hand or in sight. A book, just completed, will soon be starting for Houghton, Mifflin & Co., to whom it has been promised a long time. Macmillans are to bring out a collection of tales this fall, & Century Company a juvenile.

I return copy of *Delineator*[2] this mail.

I am looking forward with interest to receiving Yohn's[3] color reproductions.

Sincerely yours,
Jack London.

MS: CSf; 2 pp., als.
    1. Edward Stratton Holloway (1859–1939), art director of J. B. Lippincott Co. His "yarn" may have been a story sent to JL for a critique.
    2. *The Delineator* was an illustrated monthly magazine for women published in New York from 1873 until 1937.
    3. Frederick C. Yohn (1875–1933), who did the color illustrations for *A Daughter of the Snows*.

To Anna Strunsky

[Piedmont]
[? July 11, 1902]

Dear You:—
    Very Sick, but recovering. Had La Grippe. Came down with it next day after I saw you, and by ten o'clock was out of my head. So my valiant determination to catch up with my work has come to grief. Have not done a stroke all week.
    How you slip away from me!

Jack

MS: CSmH; 1 p., als.

To Cloudesley Johns

Piedmont, Calif.
July 12/02

Dear Cloudesley:—
    You must have been having one hell of a time. Aren't you disgusted with metropolitan life?[1] If you aren't you ought to be. I am, & I've never seen it.
    This world is made up chiefly of fools. Besides the fools there are the others, and they're fools, too. It doesn't matter much which class you & I belong to, while the best we can do is not increase our foolishness. One of the ways to increase our foolishness is to live in cities with the other fools. They, in turn, would be bigger fools if they should attempt to live the way you & I ought to live. Wherefore, you may remark that I am pessimistic.
    Speaking of suicide, have you ever notice that a man is more prone to commit suicide on a full stomach than on an empty one? It's one of nature's tricks to make the creature live, I suppose, for the old Dame knows she can get more effort out of an empty-bellied individual than a full-bellied one.
    Concerning myself, I am moving along slowly, about $3000 in debt, working out a philosophy of life, or rather, the details of a philosophy of life, and slowly getting a focus on things. Some day I shall begin to do things, until then I merely scratch a living.
    Between you & me, I wish I had never opened the books. That's where I was the fool!

Well, some one is going down town, so I'll shut off & give them a chance to mail this. I am just staggering along under an attack of "grip."

Jack London

ms: CSmH; 3 pp., als. Pbd: *L*, 136; *BJL*, I, 377–78.
   1. See JL to Johns, October 9, 1901.

To Anna Strunsky

The Desert,
Nevada,
July 18/02

Dear, dear You:—
   Just a line to let you know that all is well, that I am exceedingly warm, that the train is wobbling, and that I am thinking of you.
   Do thank Cameron for me, for coming to see me off.[1] It was good of him. How I wished you could have come with him!
   But perhaps our good bye was the better way.
   I send you herewith the first installment of those letters Bliss Perry mentioned to me.[2] Truly, they make me happy. Ours are so very, very much better. We've done something, little one, you & I.
   I hold you in my arms.

Jack.

Write me, care of American Press Association, New York City.

ms: CSmH; 2 pp., als.
   1. Cameron H. King, Jr., a mutual friend and fellow socialist who lived in San Francisco. On commission from the American Press Association, JL was en route to South Africa to interview government officials and to report on post–Boer War conditions.
   2. Probably Baroness Bettina von Hutten, "Our Lady of the Beeches," *Atlantic*, July–October 1902. The July and August installments of this story were written, in part, as love letters.

To Herman Whitaker

New York City,
July 23/02.

Dear Jim:—
   I was most grievously disappointed in my S.A. trip. But shall cross over to England & the Continent for a couple of months.[1]

Mr. O. J. Smith,[2]
American Press Association,
45 Park Place,
New York City.

   I recommended you to him to day, in reply to his desire for humorous stories—which I imagine are similar to those accepted by *Harpers*.

He is starting a magazine, & wants good stuff for it. Don't think of sending him anything but good stuff. You see, it was for this magazine that I was to be sent to S.A.—& so you can see that connections with him may be valuable, especially if the thing arrives, & any way as President of the Am. Press. Ass.

Pardon my hasty scrawl.

Jack London.

MS: CSmH; 2 pp., als.

1. JL's trip to South Africa was canceled because the South African officials he was to have interviewed had left Capetown for Europe. Instead, he traveled to England on money advanced by the American Press Association with the idea of writing a book about the London slums. (See the following letter and JL to Brett, September 29, 1902.) The literary result of his stay, in London's East End, is *The People of the Abyss* (New York: Macmillan, 1903).

2. Orlando J. Smith (1842–1908), former midwestern newspaper editor, president of the American Press Association from 1882, and publisher of *Brandur Magazine*.

To John Spargo

Hastings-on-Hudson,
July 28/02

Dear Mr. Spargo:—[1]

Am hastening across to England, or would stop in & see you. Your letter just forwarded from California.

"The Question of the Maximum" was an old lecture, & I sent it to you because my conscience was pricking me, & to show you that at least I meant well.

Shall be glad to tell how I became a socialist, & I think it may differ very interestingly from the causes given by most men.[2] But of this later, when I return from abroad several months hence.

I may do some writing of the London slums, possibly a book, though as yet everything is vague & my main idea is to get a vacation.

Think you had better return the manuscript to my California address,

Hastily & sincerely yours,
Jack London.

MS: VtU; 2 pp., als.

1. John Spargo, member of the editorial board of *The Comrade*, an illustrated socialist monthly magazine published in New York from 1901 until 1905.

2. "How I Became a Socialist" was published in *The Comrade*, March 1903; later included in *War of the Classes*.

To Cloudesley Johns

New York Press Club
Tuesday [July 29, 1902]
1:05 P.M.

Dear Cloudesley:—

It's a damned shame we missed each other. I sail to-morrow morning for Liverpool. I received your letter last night at 8 o'clock at the Harvard Club [1]—too late to write you.

So I came to-day, at 11:30 A.M., to the Press Club. I gave my card to the man who seems to run things where the letters are. I told this man I wished to see you, & that you would find me in the Club rooms. And then, in the club rooms I sat me down & waited until now—one hour & a half.

Then I interrogated the man who seems to run things, and he said that you had got your letters but had neglected to take my card, which was with them. Also he said that he was sorry, and that it was your fault.

I don't like the man who seems to run things.

Write me, care of

> Am. Press. Association,
> 45 Park Place,
> N.Y.C.

Jack London.

MS: CSmH; 3 pp., als.
   1. JL stayed at the Harvard Club while in New York.

To Anna Strunsky

New York Press Club
July 29/02.

Dear You:—

Just to say I received your ink-beteared letter, that I sail to-morrow, that I am waiting for Cloudesley Johns,[1] & that I love you.

The Sahib.

MS: CSmH; 1 p., als.
   1. According to Johns in "Who the Hell Is Cloudesley Johns?" he did meet briefly with JL before JL sailed on the *Majestic*. At their meeting JL gave him ten dollars.

To Anna Strunsky

RMS Majestic
July 31/02

Dear You:—

I am thinking of you to-day, as you speak at Pacific Grove. It is 6:30

P.M. here, which is 3 P.M. with you, and possibly you are speaking at this present moment. Well, good luck be with you, comrade. I know you will do well.

I sailed yesterday from New York, at noon. A week from to-day I shall be in London. I shall then have two days in which to make my arrangements and sink down out of sight in order to view the Coronation from the standpoint of the London beasts.[1] That's all they are—beasts—if they are anything like the slum people of New York—beasts, shot through with stray flashes of divinity.

I meet the men of the world, in Pullman Coaches, New York clubs, & Atlantic-liner smoking rooms, and truth to say I am made more hopeful for the Cause by their total ignorance & non-understanding of the forces at work. They are blissfully ignorant of the coming upheaval, while they have grown bitterer & bitterer toward the workers. You see, the growing power of the workers is hurting them & making them bitter, while it does not open their eyes.

"There are many to-morrows my love, my dove; but there is only one To-day."[2]

This may be bettered.

"There are many To-morrows, my love, my dove, and we will make them all To-days."

I am doing quite a lot of essay work aboard ship, and so, until you hear from me in London,

The Sahib.

MS: CSmH; 4 pp., als. Pbd: *L*, 136–37; *BJL*, I, 379.
    1. The coronation of Edward VII took place on August 9. See *The People of the Abyss*, chap. 12.
    2. Joaquin Miller, "The Voice of the Dove" (1893), ll. 3–4.

To George P. Brett

[RMS Majestic]
August 5/02

Dear Mr. Brett:—

In the rush & excitement of New York, I quite forgot to come & see you & get the letters of introduction you had kindly mentioned.

But on the steamer they came at once to hand, also the copy of the *Virginian*.[1] Unhappily, I was denied the pleasure of reading the *Virginian* on the trip across, for I had already read the very first copy obtainable in California. It's the biggest cowboy story yet written, and I imagine, ever to be written. And it was well illustrated, too, which is an unusual thing, it seems to me, with books.

Thanking you for your kindness, I am,

Very sincerely yours,
Jack London.

MS: NN; 2 pp., als.
    1. Owen Wister, *The Virginian; a Horseman of the Plains*, published by Macmillan in 1902. The book was illustrated by Arthur I. Keller.

To Anna Strunsky

London,
Aug. 16/02

Dear Anna:—
    No letters from you or anyone at all since I arrived in England, & I have been here 9 [da]ys.[1]
    [Am] settled down & ha[rd] at work.[2] The whole thing, all the co[nd]itions of life, the in[t]ensity of it, eve[ry]thing is overwhelming. I never conceived such a mass of misery in the world before.
    With regards to every one,

Jack.

MS: CSmH; apcs.
    1. Brackets indicate letters supplied where JL's postcard has deteriorated.
    2. JL rented a room at 89 Dempsey Street in Stepney in the East End.

To Cloudesley Johns

[London]
Aug. 17/02

Dear Cloudesley:—
    Your letter forwarded from California, just received. I enjoyed it immensely. I am located in the East End & am hard at work. Have finished 6000 words.
    Latter part of this week I go down into Kent to do the hop-picking.[1]
    Been in England 11 days, & it has rained every day. Small wonder the Anglo-Saxon is such a colonizer.

Jack London.

MS: CSmH; apcs. Pbd: *BJL*, I, 380.
    1. JL's journey is reflected in *The People of the Abyss*, chap. 14.

To Anna Strunsky

89, Dempsey Street,
Stepney, E., London.[1]
Aug. 21/02

Dear, dear You:—
    Have not received a letter from you since I arrived in England—all of two weeks now, plus voyage of eight days. On receiving this, again address mail care of American Press Association.

Enclose letter from *Atlantic*.[2]

Macmillan, I presume, have it[3] in their hands now. Will write you more fully later on. Am rushing through my work. Have book 1/5 written & typewritten. Expect to be done in five weeks from now. Then a vacation on the Continent & home!

Am rushing, for I am made sick by this human hell-hole called London Town. I find it almost impossible to believe that some of the horrible things I have seen are really so.

The Sahib.

MS: CSmH; 1 p., als.
    1. In the original letter, this is two lines, Stepney E./London.
    2. JL may have approached the *Atlantic* about serial publication of *The Kempton-Wace Letters*.
    3. The manuscript of *The Kempton-Wace Letters*. See JL to Brett, September 3, 1902.

To George and Caroline Sterling

London,
Aug. 22/02

Dear George & Carrie:—[1]

How I often think of you, over there on the other side of the world! I have heard of God's Country, but this country is the Country God has forgotten that he forgot.

I've read of misery, and seen a bit; but this beats anything I could even have imagined. Actually, I have seen things, & looked the second time in order to convince myself that it was really so. This I know, the stuff I'm turning out will have to be expurgated or it will never see magazine publication. I won't write to you about the East End, & I am in the thick of it. You will read some of my feeble efforts to depict it, some day.

I have my book over one-quarter done and am bowling along in a rush to finish it & get out of here. I think I should die if I had to live two years in the East End of London. Love & regards to everybody—

Jack London.

MS: CLU; 1 p., als. Pbd: *L*, 137.
    1. Caroline Rand Sterling (1880–1918), George Sterling's wife. They had met while she was working as a secretary in the real estate office of Frank Havens and were married in 1896.

To Anna Strunsky

London,
August 25/02

Dear You:—

Saturday night I was out all night with the homeless one, walking the streets in the bitter rain, and, drenched to the skin, wondering when dawn would come. Sunday I spent with the homeless ones, in the fierce struggle for something to eat. I returned to my rooms Sunday evening, after 36 hours continuous work and short one night's sleep. To-day I have composed, typed & revised 4000 words and over. I have just finished. It is one in the morning. So, no matter how inadequately I may state what I wish to say, & no matter how cold I may appear, please remember that I am worn out & exhausted, and that my nerves are blunted with what I have seen and the suffering it has cost me.

Your W.C.T.U. letter, and your letter from San Francisco, arrived together about ten o'clock this evening. I read the one, overjoyed; plunged into the other (you know I have received nothing from you for a month), plunged into the other, and brought up, innocently, unexpectedly, and all in a heap at the quick, sharp rise to the climax.

You are ever quick to harshness. You are one of the cruelest women I have ever know. I have insulted "our" friendship—let it go, it is a past issue. But I have insulted "your" love (the distinction was invidious), and I have "lied" to you. Also, you have "pitied" me and my children. Please do not pity Joan. There you have me in my most vital spot. I would rather be called liar, even by you, a thousand times; I would rather be a liar, even to you, a thousand times, than to have you pity Joan. Do with me what you will; but leave Joan's soul alone.

To return. I have insulted your love by lying to you. I try to follow your mind processes, to see where you develop that lie. I may answer it here, if I divine correctly I shall certainly answer it. I expect a child to be born to me shortly.[1] Work back nine months. Come ahead again to the time at the Bungalow when we held speech upon a very kindred subject. Bearing these two periods in mind, if you have a superficial knowledge of things sexual and physiological, you will fail to discover any lie. If you have not this knowledge, & I do not think you have, consult some woman who has.

Shall I tell you what I have been guilty of? Not of lying, but of keeping my word. I shall never be anything but soft underneath and hard outside. Whoso penetrates to that softness involves themselves in confusion and misery. I promised that I would not tell you of any expected child. I promised, that is all. I promised, & I kept my word.

But this witholding has nothing to do with what you call the lie.

Possibly, you may not be able to understand the explanation I have given. I shall be quite frank in order that you may. Long, long after a child is conceived, a man may know his wife, long past the time spoken of at the Bungalow. That is all. Or if there be more, you must tell me, for I cannot see.

I should have been angry; but I am too jaded & lifeless to rise to it. "Do not fear, I shall not speak of this again." I could only say that to a person whom I wished wantonly to insult. I could never say it to you. Yet you say it to me, & I can only smile and say to myself that it [was]² written by a very cruel woman, by a woman who is as cruel as she is tender & soft, who is as harsh as she is sensitive, who can wound others in degree equal only to her own capacity for being wounded.

And the Sahib is dead, and forgiven as the dead are forgiven. Poor devil of a Sahib! He should have been all soft, or all hard; as it is he makes a mess of his life and of other lives. Do you know, life is cheap here in London Town. I never dreamed it could be so cheap. And its very cheapness and unworthwhileness has given me the most astounding blues I have ever experienced. The whole world draws away; you draw yourself away; and I can see nothing save a wee creature known as "Joan." Possibly she is too young to draw away. I do not know.

And you beg my pardon for your "impetuousness that wrung that 'I love you'" from me. Then I do not love you, and I have spent months building up a wonderful tissue of lies. *Wasted* months, and years, for, not loving you, the thing is purposeless. Only one other significance could attach itself to this wonderful tissue of lies, and as I did not seek that thing, the months & years were truly purposeless and wasted.

Now is that reasonable? I leave it to you.

Too great a capacity for happiness is equivalent to being born to sorrow. I am of that sort, and I imagine you are, too. O to be a swine, wallowing in its sty and undergoing the sweet process of fattening for market! And who shall say it were not best?

Well, I am wandering, so good night, dear. I may say "dear," for your impetuousness this time is of another order.

                                                                                Jack

MS: ULA; 5 pp., als. Pbd: *BJL*, I, 380–81.
    1. JL's second child, Bess (usually called Becky), was born on October 20, 1902.
    2. JL wrote this word, then crossed it out.

To Anna Strunsky

                                                              [London]
                                                              August 28/02
Dear You:—
    I am just out from the casual ward of the workhouse, where I spent last night and to-day,¹ & where I should have spent to-night, only, having gathered the material, I risked fourteen days in jail by running away. Well, I'm away, and a day ahead.

    I wrote you late the other night, right after receiving your most impetuous letter. I think I made explanation, then, but I know that I have really been waiting ever since for "a laughing & protesting next." Perhaps this is a "laughing & protesting next" (O the irony of it!), for I believe I was rather rough in the reply I made. I know I was very blue & tired when I wrote it, and as it was sealed & posted at once, I had no chance of re-reading it. Did you re-read yours? I wonder?

I have been reading it over. I have read it over a score of times. I am quite lost & breathless each time I lay it down.

"Your letter was cold enough and long enough in arriving to enlighten me of itself, & I beg your pardon for having been so impetuous in my letters. It wrung that last 'I love you' from you."

I wonder if this is a result of the W.C.T.U. orgy? Of course I am cold. When I get warm I make a mess of it, as per instance above. It doesn't suit me to be warm. I am unfit for it. Yours was the last clean, pure warming I shall ever receive, I imagine. It was the fire of sunset. Henceforth night, and the electric lamp? This is not a threat, believe me, it is mere wondering. Though this I do know, by duty or desire, or both, & by these only, may I bribe myself to continue being. You can live by theory, and therein you approach perfection. I blunder at living by theory. At first I did too much living by practice. They failed "to catch me when I was young."

This book I am plunging through with, will not be a great book. In two weeks and a couple of days I have done almost half of it. It is written, first, for money; second, in its own small way, for the human good. It is not constructed as a book should be constructed, but as a series of letters are written—without regard to form.

By the middle or end of next week I shall be down in Kent among the "hoppers."—hop-pickers. Here one will find life at about its lowest.

I have seen men's eyes here, & women's, that I was almost afraid to look in—not because of the viciousness therin, nor the sensuality, or anything of the sort, but because of the utter lack of all these, because of the supreme bestiality or unhumanness. I should not like to be God. Nor, if there be a God, should I like to be a West-Ender.

Why, I repeatedly ask forgiveness of my body for the vileness I have dragged it into the last two weeks, and of my stomach for the vileness I have put into it. And so I am wandering again. Good night—

Jack.

MS: Neville; photocopy of 3 pp., als.

1. Workhouses, financed by local rates and managed by local Boards of Guardians, were required to house and feed the local poor and disabled. They were also required to maintain casual wards to provide short-term relief to destitute transients. A number of casual wards, especially in populous districts, were notorious for their filthy and harsh conditions. For JL's comments on these casual wards, see *The People of the Abyss*, chap. 17.

To George P. Brett

London, England,
September 3/02.

My dear Mr. Brett:—

Do you remember when *The Children of the Frost*, was proposed for publication, that I stated some of the stories had already received magazine publication, & that some of them were waiting magazine publication. I have just recollected two of these, unpublished up to the time of my leaving the United States. One, "In the Forests of the North," with *Pearson's Magazine*, should be published in September or October; the other, "The Sunlanders," I think ought to come out in the September *Ainslee's*.

Can you see about them. You see, I received $150.00 each for the serial rights of them, & if the book came out without their having been published serially, the magazines could land on me for the $300.00 plus cost of illustrations prepared.[1]

I am at work on my East-End-of-London book. Half of it is already written. Ere this you should have received the Love-Letter-Series from *Atlantic Monthly* via American Press Association.

I have not yet availed myself of the introductions you so kindly sent me, having devoted myself entirely to the book. To write half of it in three weeks & at the same time collect the material, doesn't give much time for anything else. But I shall avail myself of the introductions, when the book is done.

Very sincerely yours,
Jack London.

MS: NN; 2 pp., als.
    1. On "The Sunlanders" publication, see JL to Brett, January 16, 1902, n. 1.

To Frederick I. Bamford

London, England,
Sept. 9/02

Dear Comrade:—

Your kind letter at last at hand. Thanks, best thanks to the Ruskin for its good wishes.

Things are terrible here in London, & yet they tell me times are good and all are employed save the unemployable. If these are good times, I wonder what bad times are like?

There's no place like California, & I long to be back. The book is 2/3 written, & the material for the remaining 1/3 is collected. With best love—

Jack London

MS: JL State Park; apcs. Pbd: *Mystery*, 182.

To Anna Strunsky

Stepney, E.
Sept. 9/02

Dear You:—
Your letter of August 19th. has just arrived and it has made me quite happy to hear from you.—Shall I go on in the above vein? For in such way does your letter begin & go on. I suppose it's sending me the "news."

Now I feel impelled to wax witty, but you are so dead serious that I won't. I'll be serious, too. If you are unable to send more than the "news," why, really, I don't care for the "news," and to do without the "news" would not be quite so embarassing to me as you seemed to imagine in your letter before this.

Sending the "news." I honestly believe there is as much "Tommy" in you as in me,[1] and that you, being more of an artist, & also being a woman, carry it off far better than I can. Yours, whatever it may have to be, is always true, genuine; mine always becomes clownish & culminates in ridiculousness.

Jack.

MS: CSmH; 1 p., als.
    1. A reference to the protagonist of Barrie's *Tommy and Grizel*. See JL to Johns, February 16, 1900, n. 1.

To Cloudesley Johns

East London,
Sept. 22/02.

Dear Cloudesley:—
Yours of Sept. 9th. received. I quite agree with you that not to be a free agent is hell. But I don't quite follow you when you say the particular lies in not being able to blame anybody, anything, and not even yourself. I don't see how that will help matters in the least. If you throw me down & break my back, of course I can blame you; but that doesn't mend my back.

I am glad you liked "Nam-Bok the Unveracious." The idea of it always appealed to me (including the satire),[1] but I was not satisfied when I wrote it. I feel that I missed somewhere.

By the way, you mentioned that one of the *Ainslee* people cherished a belief that I was a regular son-of-a-gun. Can't you give me some of the details? Also, anything further about the McClure blacklist? Sometimes I grow quite curious, you know.

In another week I shall have finished my book of 60,000 words! It's rather hysterical I think. Look up a brief article of mine in the *Critic* somewhere in the last numbers.' Also tell me how you like the "Story of Jees Uck" in current *Smart Set*.

You're the greatest fellow for landing a man, as you have landed me on the whole proposition.

Jack London

MS: CSmH; 1 p., als. Pbd: *BJL*, I, 381.
  1. The story includes a satire in the mode of Plato's "The Allegory of the Cave"; a young Indian who has been lost at sea returns to his tribe many years later to tell wonderful tales of the white man's civilization. These seem so farfetched to the natives that they suspect him of being a "shadow" from the world of the dead; therefore, they send him back to the sea and the "shadow-world" from which he came.
  2. "Again the Literary Aspirant," *Critic,* September 1902. The *Critic,* a monthly magazine featuring articles on literary topics and book reviews, was published in New York from 1881 until 1906.

To Anna Strunsky

East London,
Sept. 28/02

Dear You:—

The book is finished! I typed the last word of the last chapter ten minutes ago—63,000 words. Now I shall have to move out of this room I have occupied seven weeks. Shall I give you the last paragraph?

"When the people who try to help, cease their playing and dabbling with day nurseries and Japanese art exhibits, and go back & learn their West End and the sociology of Christ, they will be in better shape to buckle down to the work they ought to be doing in the world. And if they do buckle down to the work, they will follow Dr. Barnardo's lead,[1] only on a scale as large as the nation is large. They won't cram yearnings for the Beautiful & True & Good down the throat of the woman making violets for three farthings a gross, but they will make somebody get off her back and quit cramming himself till, like the Romans, he must go to a bath and sweat it out. And to their consternation, they will find that they will have to get off that woman's back themselves, as well as the backs of a few other women and children they did not dream they were riding upon."

I am afraid that I have hit out too strongly right along to get serial publication.[2] But, try as I would, I could not curb my wrath enough to make it sufficiently innocuous for a bourgeois publication.

Sept. 28.
Later.

I have just come back from a meeting of the East End socialists, where I had a tilt on the floor with one Freidburg, an Impossiblist and a correspondent of Austin Lewis'. The English socialists seem to be on the verge of a split similar to what we went through in the United States. The Impossiblists and the Opportunists are marshalling to arms, and their next conference may see the split brought about.[3] Freidburg, by the way, has been expelled, and it is the consideration of his case at the conference that is liable to bring things to a head.

Sept. 29/02.

Your letter, telling of how you received *Atlantic*'s rejection, and a letter from Macmillan's, have both arrived together. So you see, though we fail of serial publication, we get the stamp of one of the largest, most widely known, & reputable publishing houses in the world. If you will remember, it was they who refused Miss Peixiotto's book.[4] So you are recalled from your rustication.

I should advise you to plug right in, and get over the difficulty of those last two letters. As you love me, do not put it off till the eleventh hour. I know it is dispiriting to tackle, but the Macmillan seal of approval should at least balance it off. Any other touches you see fit to make won't hurt it any. I am to suppose that I have carte blanche in making arrangements with the publishers. Of course, advantage or disadvantage, blunder or happy stroke, will be shared equally between us.

What rot this long-distance correspondence is! About the time you are receiving harsh letters from me, I am receiving the kindest letters from you. You have never had the advantage of seeing a prizefighter knocked out. It is a good asset for one's education in the world. But should you have seen such a man, panting, exhausted, dazed, bewildered, terrific blows landing upon him from above, below, and everyside, and his own arms flying out madly, blindly, threshing the air crazily,—then you would understand my condition when I received that frightful letter from you. My arms flew out madly, blindly, that is all. And I am sorry. I should have taken the knock-out clean & not put up any defense.

And now it is all over and done with. So be it. Henceforth I shall dream romances for other people and transmute them into bread & butter.

Did I tell you I had finished the book? I did yesterday afternoon. I shall move to-morrow to the West End, where I shall stay a week. Then take my run on the Continent,[5] return to England, then home to New York & arrange for the publication of the *Letters*. Continue writing me, please. My mail will be forwarded.

Jack.

MS: CSmH; 5 pp., als.

1. Thomas John Barnardo (1845–1905), founder in 1867 of the East End juvenile mission for destitute children and in 1870 of the boys' home in Stepney, which developed into an organization of nine separate institutions, known as "Dr. Barnardo's Homes." Barnardo believed that outcast children could be molded into useful citizens if removed from their degrading environment, exposed to the proper religious influences, and given vocational training.

2. *The People of the Abyss* was only partially serialized, in *Wilshire's Magazine* from March 1903 to January 1904.

3. The division among English socialists may have been a split between Fabian and either revolutionary or Utopian socialism. For a similar split in other countries, see JL to Johns, June 23, 1899.

4. Jessica B. Peixotto (1864–1941), social economist and professor of sociology and economics at the University of California, from 1904 to 1935. Peixotto had received her Ph.D. from Berkeley in 1901 and was its first woman professor. JL met her through Austin

Lewis, and he may have attended some of the informal gatherings of Bay Area liberals and radicals at her home. The book Macmillan rejected may have been her doctoral dissertation, *The French Revolution and Modern French Socialism*, which Crowell published in 1901.

   5. During October, JL took a three-week tour of France, Germany, Italy, and Holland. For an episode from this tour, see JL to Vance, July 18, 1906.

To George P. Brett

East London
Dear Mr. Brett:—   Sept. 29/02.

   Yours of Sept. 16th. just to hand. Of course, I shall not delay the publication of the book on account of the story *Ainslee's* have not published,[1] though it means a clean loss to me of $150.

   I expect to return in a couple of months via New York, and as you suggest, I can then arrange with you concerning the publication of the *Letters*. I think there is quite a chance for them to make a hit, as they are out of the common, deal with the most popular subject under the sun, and deal with it so radically and roughly that heated disagreement & discussion may be aroused.

   Concerning this East End book, I want you to have first chance at it for book publication. It is not a novel, by the way, but a dive by me into the Under-World and a narration of the people, things, & conditions I encountered. I send you this mail a couple of pictures of myself in diving costume. I pose as the seafaring man who has lost his money & clothes & can't find a ship. Being a sailor of old time, I am able to carry it off and mingle indiscriminately with all kinds of people. I have taken a number of photographs, which should make good illustrations for a book. The title I have chosen is *The People of the Abyss*. And, by the way, last night I wrote the last word of the last chapter. The book is done, & it contains 63,000 words. I am now going to take my long-deferred vacation. Mr. Smith,[2] who is publishing the *Brandur Magazine*,[3] had the promise of first chance at it for serial publication before I left New York.

   As you know, I have taken this trip to England, & shall take the vacation on the Continent, on moneys advanced to me by Mr. Smith; so that the running of my household in California has been largely on a basis of credit, and will be for a couple of months or more to come. So I should like to know if you can find it compatible with your policy to advance another $150 to my wife should she require it, the same to be charged to my account against future work of mine to be brought out by you? If you should find that you are able to do this, kindly write directly to Mrs. London, informing her of the fact. As you know, she has received from me full powers of attorney, and her signature to anything is mine.

   Please send a copy of *The Children of the Frost*, addressed to me care of

Thomas Cook & Son,
Ludgate Circus, E.C.
London.

I shall then be able to receive it on my return to England from the Continent.

I leave the East End to-morrow, & move to the West End, where I shall be able to present the letters of introduction you kindly gave me.

Very truly yours,
Jack London.

MS: ViU; 3 pp., als.
   1. "The Sunlanders."
   2. O. J. Smith.
   3. *Brandur Magazine* was a short-lived magazine of fiction and essays, published in New York from September 2 to October 11, 1902.

To George P Brett

Texas,
Nov. 9/02.

Dear Mr. Brett:—

When I left you Thursday,[1] I went to the American Press Association to get Ms. of *People of the Abyss*. I found that they had, after all, submitted it for serial publication. However, should it come back to them, they will at once forward it to me.

In the meantime, I have duplicate copy in my baggage. As soon as I arrive in California I shall get hold of it, revise it at once, & forward to you. So you will receive it by November 20th., if not a day or so sooner.

By N.Y. letters (which I have just opened on the train), I learn that Miss Anna Strunsky is now on her way to New York.[2] She is my collaborator in the *Letters*. She will come & see you, for she wishes to re-write the last two letters of the book & to do some general revising.

I am sure you will find her charming. She is a young Russian-Jewess, brilliant, a college-woman, etc.

By the way, I feel inclined somewhat to differ with the idea that the *Letters* may not make a hit. They are just the sort of stuff to arouse a whole lot of interest & agreement & disagreement among the critics; and this once aroused, the subject (Love), is likely to make the book go far with the reading public. The thing with the book, as I see it, is that it will hit big or not hit at all.

Well, in four days I shall be in California & hard at work again.

Very truly yours,
Jack London.

MS: NN; 4 pp., als. Pbd: *L*, 138.

1. JL had arrived in New York on November 4 and met with Brett on Thursday, November 6.

2. Strunsky had left California to visit relatives in New York.

To Anna Strunsky

Texas,
Booming West,
Nov. 9/02

Dear Anna:—

What an unlucky mischance! I changed my plans suddenly in Holland; returned to England; changed plans suddenly in England and sailed for New York; stopped in New York just long enough to get started West; carried my mail (held in New York) on the train to read; and on the train, rushing West, I opened your letters and learned that at that very moment you were rushing East.

I have just written to Mr. Brett, President of Macmillan Company, telling him that you will come to get manuscript and revise same.

Now, dear you, do not be disheartened when you meet this Mr. Brett and hear him speak of the *Letters* just incidentally. Remember that he publishes more books each month than he has time to read, that he is saturated in books, books without end, and saturated from a business standpoint.

Just to show you, I'll tell the following. On my way to England I outlined the book to him, told him how you & I chanced to write it, etc. On my return, speaking of the *Letters*, he was quite surprised to learn that I had had a collaborator. So there you are. I doubt if he has even read them. Instead of reading them, he has relied on the judgement of his "readers."—professional readers.

For that matter, look at my experience. Major Smith, of the Am. Press Association, who was heartily in sympathy with my East End project, told me that he was very sorry, but that he had not read a line of the Ms.

He was to publish the stuff in the *Brandur*, but the *Brandur* has suspended, so I doubt if I shall be able to get serial publication.

The thing for you to do when you see Mr. Brett, is to inspire him with confidence in the letters, as I know you to be well able to do. For I do believe that there is a big hit in our work if it is given only half a chance.

I am sending this care of Isadore Strunsky,[1] though hoping you have delayed your departure from California.

[Jack][2]

MS: CSmH; 6 pp., al.

1. Strunsky's uncle in New York.

2. Apparently the signature was cut off this letter.

To Frank Putnam

Piedmont, Calif.
Nov. 15/02

Dear Mr. Putnam:–[1]
   Am just replying to yours of Oct. 21st. & 23rd. Concerning this story you have accepted, I am afraid there is some mistake about it. You see, Mrs. London has been marketing my manuscripts during my absence, and by some mischance she has sent off to you "The One Thousand Dozen"—or a duplicate copy of it rather.
   In the meantime, the original copy has been in the hands of Mr. Watt & Son for the English, & possibly for the American market.[2]
   So will you kindly hold the copy you have, & do nothing toward printing it till I receive advice concerning it from England?
   Now for the Christmas sentiment for the December *National*. I am all in a whirl since my return home, and I can think of nothing. So just say anything you like & stick my name to it. I feel so good, and love America and things American so much, that I can endorse anything on the subject.[3]
   All right, I'll take you up on your offer to bet the drinks that the Slav beats us out 500 years from date, and "I'll take a swig with you in hell," Frank Putnam,—or in Chicago.

Don't fail me,
Jack London.

MS: CU; 2 pp., als.
   1. Frank Putnam, managing editor of the *National Magazine*.
   2. JL sent the manuscript of "The One Thousand Dozen" to A. P. Watt & Son on May 28, 1902. Watt sold the story to the *Graphic Magazine* for three guineas per thousand words, an offer JL accepted on February 27, 1903. On August 21, 1903, JL sent Watt the corrected proofsheets of the story, and on August 31, after paying a commission to Watt, he received £19 4s. "The One Thousand Dozen" was stolen by the *Windsor Magazine*, however, and published in its July 1904 issue; it never appeared in the *Graphic*. The story was published in the *National* of March 1903. See JL to Putnam, February 27, March 9, March 16, and March 25, 1903; January 17, January 31, and March 7, 1905; and JL to Chapple, July 22, 1905. For an account of this episode, see James E. Sisson, "'No Disgrace to Be Poor,'" *Bancroftiana*, April 1983, pp. 1–2.
   3. In a letter to JL of November 22, 1902 (CSmH), Putnam wrote that this permission to include JL in the "Christmas Sentiment Party" in the December *National* arrived a few days too late.

To George P. Brett

Piedmont, Calif.
November 21, 1902.

Dear Mr. Brett:–
   A couple of days ago I expressed you the revised duplicate manuscript of the *People of the Abyss*. The slight delay in dispatching it was due to

the fact that I was out on a newspaper detail[1]—buckling down to the grind as soon as I won home—

This *People of the Abyss*, as you will speedily learn on looking over it, is simply the book of a correspondent writing from the field of industrial war. You will notice, while it is often unsparingly critical of existing things, that it has proposed no remedies and devoted no space to theorizing— It is merely a narrative of things as they are.

Ere this you will have met Miss Anna Strunsky, and been pleased with her I am sure. Of course, she will be one of the contracting parties in getting out this book of letters, though she is content to let me arrange the thing for her.

Now, concerning myself and the work I wish to do, I should like to have a good talk with you. The hurry and bustle and unwonted confusion of traveling and racing around post haste is over with, and I think I can say what I wish to say somewhat more coherently than when I was rushing through New York.

In the first place, I want to get away from the Klondike. I have served my apprenticeship at writing in that field, and I feel that I am better fitted now to attempt a larger and more generally interesting field. I have half a dozen books, fiction all, which I want to write. They are not collections of short stories, but novels. I believe I can turn out a novel now. The novel Lippincotts published this fall[2] was written by me over two years ago, at the beginning of my writing. At that time the twenty short stories I had written constituted my literary experience. Not only was that novel my first novel, but it was my first attempt at a novel. I have done a great deal of studying and a great deal of thinking in the last two years, and I am confident that I can to-day write something worth while.

Besides others, for which I have been gathering material a long while, I have three books which I should like to write as soon as I can get at them. The third book, with which I shall bid for a popularity such as Bellamy[3] received, (yet a quite different popularity), I shall write last, in the meantime preparing for it while I write the other two. The first of these two I have thought of calling *The Flight of the Duchess*. It will be in the Here and Now, and though situated in California, it will not be peculiarly local, but will be really a world-story which might take place anywhere in the *civilized* world. It will end happily. The second is a sea story, or, better, a sea study. I have thought of calling it *The Mercy of the Sea*, though I am not altogether satisfied with the title— It will be almost literally a narrative of things that happened on a seven-months' voyage I once made as a sailor. The oftener I have thought upon the things that happened that trip, the more remarkable they appear to me. Looking back, they hardly seem real. I can no more say that this story will end happily than can I say that it will end unhappily. It is, in fact, a sea-tragedy, and not to end it as it did end would be a distinct disappointment to the reader.[4]

Now here comes the rub. I have no income save what my pen brings me in the magazine and newspaper field. Just as you advanced royalties to me on *The Children of the Frost*, so the royalties have been advanced on my other books recently brought out. In the four months I have been away, my stock of articles and stories has been disposed of to the magazines; so I return home without these assets, without income, and with nothing before me but to sit down and write up another stock of magazine articles and stories. Of course, this means the work of months, and then continual work to keep the stock replenished. Without a certain sure income, it is impossible for me to sit down and write a book. The returns from a book, from the moment of beginning the first chapter, do not arrive for a year or two, but the tradesmen's bills arrive the first of each month.

That you may understand how I happen to be thus situated, let me give you a brief biographical note. When I was ten years of age I was selling papers on the street. From then on, I worked for my living. At fifteen I left home to shift for myself. I worked with my hands at many things. I grew up to a early manhood without any education to speak of. When I first began to write I had no art-concepts whatever. So I have mainly educated myself in the last several years while at the same time I was learning to write, and on top of it all, trying to get a living from my writing. When I returned from the Klondike I began to write. But when I returned from the Klondike I found my father dead and my mother in debt. I was a young fellow who had never been rash enough to anchor himself by marrying. Nevertheless I found myself with a household on my shoulders. I buckled down and began to write to support that household and at the same time to educate myself. Finding myself anchored with a household, I resolved to have the compensations of a household, and so I married and increased my household or the weight of my anchor. But I have never regretted it. I have been well compensated— Nevertheless, as a result, I have no income save what I earn with my pen from day to day, and the tradesmen's bills are larger and more insistent than they would be were I all by myself in the world.

We live moderately. One hundred and fifty dollars per month runs us, though we are seven, and oft-times nine when my old nurse and her husband[5] depend upon us. Now, if I am sure of this one hundred and fifty dollars per month, I can devote myself to larger and ambitious work. And here is the proposition I wish to advance for your consideration. If you find it practicable to advance me $150. per month for one year, say beginning with December 1st., 1902, I guarantee to have in your hands *The Flight of the Duchess* and *The Mercy of the Sea* by December 1st., 1903. In addition, I shall by that time have completed two other books which are now nearly done.

One book is a collection of Klondike stories,[6] similar to the ones I have already brought out. 33,000 words of it are already written, all of which, save the last story written, have been published in the magazines. They were written off and on during the time the *Children of the Frost* was being written. To complete them I have but 17,000 words to write, and nearly half of this amount I owe to *Ainslee's Magazine* in return for the story they gave up so that *The Children of the Frost* should not be delayed.[7]

The other book is a series of connected boy's stories, *The Fish-Patrol Stories*, which I had nearly completed for the *Youth's Companion* before I went to England last summer. A couple of weeks' work will finish them. This book will compare favorably with *The Cruise of the Dazzler*, a juvenile which the Century people are bringing out this fall and which is going well.

So the account, if you met my proposition, would stand something like this on December 1st., 1903:

From you.	From me.
	New Collection of Klondike Stories.
	Fish-Patrol Stories.
$1800.	*The Kempton-Wace Letters.*
	The People of the Abyss.
	The Flight of the Duchess.
	The Mercy of the Sea.

That is to say, against your $1800. I will balance six books. Granting an average earning power of $300. to each book, the six books will equal the $1800. Of course, either *The Flight of the Duchess* or *The Mercy of the Sea* may sell well enough to wipe out the $1800. Also, from the way I shall write *The Flight of the Duchess* I know that it will have a serial value of a thousand dollars at least—this in case it's serial sale be necessary to balance the account. On the other hand, *The People of the Abyss* already has $150. advanced on it, and the royalties from the *Kempton-Wace Letters* will be divided between Miss Strunsky and myself. These last two items I do not think will alter the balance when it is considered that I have placed the average earnings of each of the six books at $300.

My idea is this: balancing the books against the $1800., does away with financial risk on your part and gives me a year's trial with the experiment. Please let me know what you think of my proposition as soon as you conveniently can.[8]

Of course, my hope, once I am on my feet, is not to write prolifically, but to turn out one book, and a good book, a year. Even as it is, I am not a prolific writer. I write very slowly. The reason I have turned out so much is because I have worked constantly, day in and day out, without taking a rest. Once I am in a position, where I do not have to depend upon each day's work to keep the pot boiling for the next day, where I do not have to dissipate my energy on all kinds of hack, where I can slowly and deliberately ponder and shape the best that is in me, then, at that time, I am confident that I shall do big work.—

While this letter is traveling to you, I shall be at work on the sort of story magazines buy. Should you view my proposition favorably, telegraph me, and I shall at once start to work on *The Flight of the Duchess*.

There was one matter upon which I wished to speak with you, but I forgot in my rush West through New York. In England, I found Mr. H. Perry Robinson, President of Isbister & Co., most enthusiastic over my work. Every book I had written he had brought out or got possession of, with the one exception of *The Children of the Frost*. He had pioneered the English market for me. The copyright of my very first book had been bought by an English house, which seemed afraid to publish it. All the English houses seemed afraid, or, at least, they were all loth to play pioneer. But Mr. Robinson got hold of my second book and made the initial attempt. And he worked hard that I might get a good hearing. He ploughed the ground, he was the first to plough it, and he ploughed it well. Then he bought in the first book, which had been lying around England for so long, and brought it out.[9] Since then he has procured the English rights of my other books and is preparing to bring them out. When I met him, he put the case fairly and squarely before me. He was the first to take me up in England; he had performed the labor of introducing me; in order to introduce me well he had foregone immediate profits, sinking them into the publishing, with the idea of building up greater mutual profit for both of us; and because of all this he looked upon my future work as honestly his to publish.

Now I have explained to you the errors and confusions through which I have waded in acquiring what little experience I have of publishing. Living out here on the edge of things, utterly ignorant of the whole thing, I simply butted around blindly in the dark till I knocked holes through somehow and saw daylight. I believe, now, that the first period of my career has been completed, and that I am about to enter a second period. And on the publishing side of this second period, I think I shall be able to avoid the errors into which I previously blundered. I think I am starting off without being handicapped by my own confusion and ignorance and by all that confusion and ignorance entail. What I want is to have everything clear and straight, and in the following statement I hope to get everything clear and straight:

To have Macmillan Company, and no other house, bring out my American books (if they should wish to). To have Isbister Company, and no other house, bring out my English books. In the case of Isbister, I had much rather it had been the Macmillan Company too, but it seemed to me to be Isbister's by right of work performed. I give over to them from a sense of justice. In their favor, I may say that they agree to give me the same royalties, whatever they be, that I receive in America.[10]

In trying to be just to Isbister & Co., I do not think I have been unjust to the English Macmillans or to you. As I understand it, the two houses are quite separate, financially separate, though they work together in a friendly way. So that I do not financially hurt the American Macmillans, who interested themselves in me, when I give the English rights to the Isbisters; nor do I wrong the English Macmillans, who did not interest themselves in me as the Isbisters did. You know the difficulties that oft-times beset the author in dealing with publishers, and this is, I hope, my last difficulty.

My difficulty this fall of three books coming out at the same time, was unavoidable, and was because I was ignorant and had no definite arrangement with anybody. The Lippincott novel, written long previously, was altogether out of my hands. While the Century juvenile[11] was a serial written a good while before for *St. Nicholas* (written before the novel, even). And when the *St. Nicholas* people bought it, at that early date, they asked for and received the book rights for the Century Company. So it happened that these two books, written at different dates and altogether out of my control, unfortunately came out at the same time you brought out *The Children of the Frost*. Not only was the simultaneous publication of these three books unfortunate from a standpoint of sales, but it gave rise to a feeling that I had become unduly prolific and was turning out regular machine stuff.

In conclusion, I can only hope that I have not wearied you with this lengthy recital. Also, I want to say, "Keep an eye of those Kempton-Wace letters." There is a bigger chance for a hit in them than they are given credit for. First, the subject, love, is one that possesses not only undying interest, but the most wide-spread interest. We are given more to an analysis of our emotions these days than ever before, while the tendency of of the American reading public is so strong towards things scientific, that a scientific discussion of love is bound to arouse interest. Further, though I may be wrong, it is my belief that the book is quite original in both its treatment and subject matter.

Sincerely yours,
Jack London.

MS: NN; 9 pp., tls.

1. JL's latest newspaper work was "Simple Impressive Rite at Corner-Stone Emplacement of Hearst Memorial Mining Building," *San Francisco Examiner*, November 19, 1902.

2. *A Daughter of the Snows.*

3. Edward Bellamy (1850–98), author of the socialist Utopian romance *Looking Backward* (1888). This book was a publishing sensation, selling over a million copies and giving rise to a spate of Bellamy Clubs devoted to discussing the author's ideas.

4. Neither *The Flight of the Duchess* nor *The Mercy of the Sea* was ever written; notes for *The Flight of the Duchess* are at CSmH.

5. Jennie and Alonzo T. Prentiss.

6. *The Faith of Men.*

7. See JL to Brett, January 16, 1902, n. 1.

8. Macmillan agreed to JL's terms but gave him two years to write six books. They were *The Kempton-Wace Letters* (published in May 1903), *The Call of the Wild* (July 1903), *People of the Abyss* (October 1903), *The Faith of Men* (May 1904), *The Sea-Wolf* (October 1904), and *Tales of the Fish Patrol* (1905).

9. For the first two books, see JL to Brett, April 28, 1902.
10. For the terms of JL's contract with Macmillan, see JL to Robinson, December 11, 1902. Isbister published *The Kempton-Wace Letters* (1903), *The People of the Abyss* (1903), and *A Daughter of the Snows* (1904).
11. *The Cruise of the Dazzler.*

To Anna Strunsky

Piedmont, Calif.
Nov. 25/02

Dear Anna:—

I feel better. The time you have taken in your trip across the continent does away with the closeness of the shave by which we missed each other in New York.

Saw your people last week.[1]

Have won home, more in debt than ever, with less in prospect, and so am buckled down to the grind. Have already been out on an *Examiner* detail. Just now, am trying to catch up with a neglected correspondence of Alpine outlines.

I am waiting anxiously to hear how you find Mr. Brett. I stir him up each time I write him, telling him there is a big hit in the *Letters*. Let us know how everything is going with you. Will write better next time.

Jack.

MS: CSmH; 1 p., als.
1. Elias and Anna Hurowich Strunsky, Anna's parents, who lived in San Francisco.

To Anna Strunsky

Piedmont, Calif.
December 6/02

Dear Anna:—

I am so glad you like Mr. Brett, and overjoyed to hear the readers' opinions of the *Letters*. You see, I came through New York in too great a rush to hear those opinions. Of course they are "eminently publishable," etc. etc. Quite agree with them; but if only Mr. Brett can raise the faith in their making a hit, why I am confident that they will make a hit. You see, Mr. Brett's faith is necessary, not that they may be published, but that they may be *pushed* after they *are* published. There is a chance for them to make a hit without being pushed, but being pushed will greatly increase this chance.

Every letter I write to Mr. Brett I insist upon their large chance for success. I remember writing to him in my last letter, (written sometime before I reached yours, in which I learned that he thought I had lost interest in the *Letters*)—in this last letter I remember opening a *spurring* paragraph thus: "Keep an eye on those Kempton-Wace letters. There is a bigger chance for a hit in them than they are given credit for."—and then I went on to show why there was that bigger chance for a hit.

Concerning title & precedence of authors' name, Anna, I leave to you.[1] You know I want you to appear in the manner which will be most advantageous to you. That is my wish in the matter. But, recollecting back, I do not know whether you wanted your name to appear before mine or after mine. Also, whether it should be *Kempton-Wace* or *Wace-Kempton Letters*. I leave this to you. Let me know upon what you decide.

By the way, can't you think out a better title for the book? Not only better commercially, but better artistically. I have been vainly racking my brains for that title. There is such a title, if we can only find it.

To my mind, it seems absolutely impossible to interlard a series of Hester's letters. You see, the book would be neither one thing nor the other. As it is, it is a straightforward, consecutive series of well-argued letters on Love. It is not Love Letters. To interlard love letters would not only not make it a book of Love letters, but would destroy it as a book of Letters on love. It would be a broken-backed, unconsecutively argued hodge-podge. Do you see what I mean?

Further, and mark well, the public is sated with *Love Letters*, while that same public has not had any letters on Love at all.

All goes well. I am hard at the grind again. Though I have just received a telegram from Mr. Brett which makes me financially [secure] for some months to come, I am getting ready to write a novel to be called *The Flight of the Duchess*! similar motive to Browning's.

I enclose a letter from a Hollander I met in Latin Quarter, to whom I sent a couple of my books. How would you like to know him?

Jack.

MS: CSmH; 5 pp., als. Pbd: *L*, 143–44.
    1. The first edition of *The Kempton-Wace Letters* was anonymous. When the book was reprinted in September 1903, the authors' names appeared in alphabetical order.

To George P. Brett

Piedmont, Calif.
December 11, 1902.

Dear Mr. Brett:—
    I am sending you herewith signed contract. I cannot say how glad I am that you have made the period of contract two years instead of one year, giving me a year to a novel instead of six months. In token that I am taking it seriously, carefully, and without haste, I shall deliberate long over *The Flight of the Duchess*, and over two or three other motifs for novels. Some time in January I shall send you the scenario of *The Flight of the*

Duchess, or of whatever else I may decide upon in place of it, or maybe two or three scenarios for you to select from.

You have the full list of books by me, written, or partly written, or projected, and there is none in other publishers' hands, nor have I any arrangements with other publishers whatsoever concerning above books and future work.

Collection of Klondike Stories—I have already brought the 33000 words written up to 43000 words. This leaves me only about 7000 words left to complete the book. So I shall certainly have the manuscript in your hands by July, 1903. There is, of course, a chance that it may be short, say one story; but even in this case, vurtually the whole manuscript will be in your hands.

The Fish Patrol Stories—I shall finish them, and have manuscript in your hands by July 1903. It comes in conveniently that you do not expect to bring them out till fall of 1904, or till 1905, because the *Youths Companion* I do not think will run them till 1904. You see, they like to make announcements a year ahead, especially of anything like a series of stories, and as they are not yet completed, and as they are unannounced for 1903, there is no chance for them before 1904 for serial publication. Of course, I am quite willing to have an additional clause put in the contract, agreeing (in event of discontinuance of contract), to publish no books[1] elsewhere till these six books or their equivalents have been brought out by you. If you wish to put in such a clause, I am perfectly willing to sign it. I am prompted to this solely by the *Fish-Patrol Stories*, for the *Youths' Companion* sometimes holds stuff a long time before it brings it out.

Kempton-Wace Letters—Miss Strunsky has written me that she is about starting to work to add about fifteen thousand words from the woman, Hester Stebbins. I am thoroughly in accord with this plan of hers. It is excellent. In the book, as so far written, two fundamental aspects of love have been presented; but she will cap them by presenting the third aspect, which is, from what I understand from her letter, the intuitive aspect—the heart-love of woman as opposed to the two different kinds of head-love of the man. I am confident that there is nothing published that will be anything like it. I am overjoyed that you have so far decided to bring it out in the spring.

People of the Abyss—I see you have set this off till next Fall. Being correspondent-stuff, I believe that serial publication, far from hurting it, should enhance its value when published in a book. If you have no objection to the plan, I should like to submit it to a couple of publications. And if you have no objection, will you send the manuscript in your possession to the *New York Independent*? I shall write them to-day advising them of its possible coming. By the way, I have a few photographs which may go to illustrate it should you so decide, and possibly that very tough picture of me in East End garb might not make a bad frontispiece.[2]

I have a copy of the *People of the Abyss* manuscript, which is now on its way west to me. If you wish it, I can revise it and put it in your possession in place of the one I am asking you to send to the *New York Independent*. However, I should like to keep this duplicate copy in my possession, for I am sometimes called upon to give lectures out here, and I have matter for a number of lectures in it—social reform lectures, etc, you know.

I have several thousand words to do to finish this Klondike short story I am now at work upon.³ Then I shall put my undivided thought upon *The Flight of the Duchess* and other motifs for novels till I have made my choice. Depend upon it, I shall put the best that is in me into the work of the next two years; and the one thing, above all, that I shall avoid, is haste.

Sincerely yours,
Jack London

MS: NN; 3 pp., tls. Pbd: *L*, 144–46.

    1. Originally JL typed "nothing," then made a handwritten correction to "no books."

    2. Instead of the picture of JL in "East End garb," a photograph of indigent men sitting on a park bench was used as the frontispiece to *The People of the Abyss*.

    3. "The Marriage of Lit-Lit." This story was sent to the *Atlantic* on February 2, 1903, where it was rejected. It was published in *Frank Leslie's Popular Monthly*, September 1903, and was included in *The Faith of Men*.

To H. Perry Robinson

[Piedmont]
December 11, 1902.

Dear Mr. Robinson:–

I have just signed a contract with Macmillan Company, and am writing off to you so that everything may be clear. You know, I have really been making my living from the magazines and newspapers these last several years, and thus situated I have been unable to tackle long and more ambitious work. The returns from a book, from the moment one begins the first chapter, rarely arrive before at least two years, while the tradesmen's bills arrive the first of each month. To try my hand at a book, I had to be financially secure for a few months at least. This the Macmillans have made me, and it is in the contract I have just signed that they have made me secure. I wish to give you one clause in that contract, and also the way it was brought about—I mean the clause.

I rushed through New York, hardly speaking two words with Mr. Brett, and it was not till I arrived home that I wrote him that you were to have the English publication of my books. I quote from my letter to him anent this:

    "In England I found Mr. H. Perry Robinson most enthusiastic over my work. Every book I had written he had brought out or got possession of, with the one exception of *The Children of the Frost.* He had pioneered the English market for me. The copyright of my very first book had been bought by an English house, which seemed afraid to publish it. All the English houses seemed afraid, or, at least, they were all loth to play pioneer. But Mr. Robinson got hold of my second book and made the initial attempt. And he worked hard that I might get a good hearing. He ploughed the ground, he was the first to plough it, and he ploughed it well. Then he bought in the first book, which had been lying around England for so long, and brought it out. Since then he has procured the English rights of my other books and is preparing to bring them out. When I met him he put the case fairly and squarely before me. He was the first to take me up in England; he had performed the labor of introducing me; in order to introduce me well he had foregone immediate profits, sinking them into the publishing, with the idea of building up greater mutual profit for both of us; and because of all this he looked upon my future work as honestly his to publish. I may say that he agrees to give me the same royalties, whatever they be, that I receive in America."

Now comes the clause, in response to this, in the contract:

"This agreement relates to America only. The English market on said works is to be in the hands of the Macmillan Company for negotiation but it is first of all to offer said works, on terms to be dictated by said Jack London, to the Messrs. Isbister & Company of London, and in the event of the Messrs. Isbister & Company refusing the terms quoted the books are then to be published at the hands of any other London publisher who may be willing to make the best offer for them. After making arrangements for the English market as above the Macmillan Company is to furnish the English publisher with proofsheets of its editions of the works in question, together with blocks of the illustrations, if any, for which illustrations the English publisher is to pay half cost, but the Macmillan Company is to have no further responsibility in regard to the publication of the books for the English market nor is the Macmillan Company to be responsible for any payments due said Jack London under the terms of the English agreements."

Macmillans are to bring out that Love-Letter book I told you about, they are to bring it out next Spring, if their plans do not change, which I do not think likely. So it might be well for you to arrange to bring it out at the same time. If it makes any kind of a hit, each market then has a chance to react upon the other and increase interest and sales.

The East End book, *The People of the Abyss,* Macmillans expect to bring out next Fall. This also might well come out at the same time on your side.

In the next two years I expect to write two novels. These, of course you will have the English rights for. Also, I have another collection of Klondike tales, which are all written with the exception of about eight thousand words. My novels, however, will not be situated in the Klondike.

You have now two unpublished books of mine, *The Dazzler*, and *Daughter of the Snows*. I should suggest that you watch your chance to work these in between, and to follow Macmillans with simultaneous publication of the books they bring out.[1] Once you have caught up, there will be no difficulty to stay caught up, for I hope I shall not be so apparently prolific as I have been. I say apparently prolific, for in reality I am not. I am not a fast writer, and my present overplus of books just now is due to two things, first, the lumping together of several books written through several years, and second, to the fact that I am a slow but pre-eminently steady worker. Four thousand words a week (working hard all week), is a splendid week's work for me; but fifty-two weeks of such work will turn out a couple of hundred thousand words—equivalent to three or four books the size I turn out.

Very sincerely yours,
Jack London

MS: CSmH; 3 pp., cctl.

1. Isbister failed in mid-1904, and so published neither the planned books nor *The Cruise of the Dazzler*. See JL to Brett, April 3, 1904.

To Anna Strunsky

The Bungalow,
Dec. 20/02

Dear Anna:—

How can one answer such a charge? If I say that you have an utterly aborted view of student life at Stanford, how can you reply? How can you prove that your view is not utterly aborted? So it seems to me with this charge that I have no Alaskan local color.[1]

Here is a man who has spent years in Alaska, and has not seen any of the things I have seen. What is one to do about it? One cannot make him see these things.

All I can say of such a man is that he is not an artist in any sense. That he were a poor man did he possess no more than a million dollars for each grain of imagination in his nature.

On top of this, what puzzles him is artistic selection. It is not the things I have used which bothers him (though he is unaware of it), but it is the co-existent things which I have not used. In art (if I beggar the term), with him it is not the sin of commission but the sin of omission. I should not omit. When I have drawn a picture in few strokes, he would spoil it by putting in the multitude of details I have left out.—Again, he does not know this. His trouble is that he does not see with a pictorial eye. He merely looks upon a scene an sees every bit of it; but he does not see the true picture in that scene, a picture which can be thrown upon the canvas by eliminating a great mass of things that spoil the composition, that obfuscate the true beautiful lines of it. There is no color scheme in the scene he sees, no line scheme, no tone scheme, no distribution of light & shading, nothing that may be gained by elimination.

He does not understand that mine is not *realism* but is *idealized realism*; that artistically I am an emotional materialist. My speech, in short, is alien to him.

Further, he has no comprehension of things subjective. Take, for instance, "In a Far Country." There the description of the silence, & cold, & darkness, & loneliness, is subjective. Anent this, when I say "the passive mastery of the slumbering ages," it is Greek to this man who prates of having studied aboriginal sociology & ethnology.

Still further, he charges me with the sins of my illustrators. Never, in one written word of mine, will he find a Thlinket canoe of the coast on the waters of the upper Yukon. The illustrator did that, as he has done divers others strange things.

To sum it up—difference in point of view is the difference between this man & me. We were born into the world with different eyes, that is all, & we use them differently. What think you would be his criticism of our *Letters?*[2]

Thank Mr. Lanosberg for me for his kind interest in my behalf. I give him my word that the color is all right, and if his eyes are anything like mine, he can go there & see little else than what I saw.

If you can make anything out of the material I have given, why my blessing on you & go ahead. Sign your name to it.

Take men like Sam Dunham & Joaquin Miller, poets & artists[3]—they have been unstinted in the praise of my atmosphere.

Why does not this man specify? Is my temperature wrong? my landscapes & river scapes? & mountainscapes? the food men eat? the way they travel? the sleds, canoes & boats they use? the dogs they drive? the hardships they undergo? and so forth & so forth.

The only specification he made relates to what an illustrator wrongfully pictured, not to what I have written.

No snow here, Christmas is at hand, the sun is laughing, the poppies are rearing their heads, out of my window humming birds are flashing & other birds singing.

No, Dear Anna, I am neither in joy nor sorrow. I closed certain volumes in my life on a certain day in London. These volumes will remain closed. In them I shall read no more.

Yes, & I have happiness in Joan—great, wonderful, glorious Joan. I have rushed swiftly through life. I am fifty years old to-day. The mystery of man & woman is behind me. I am deep in the mystery of father & daughter. You do not understand this. You are about seventeen to-day. And between seventeen & twenty-seven you will linger until you die. You will never get beyond the man-and-woman mystery. Theoretically, at least, you will remain always lost in it.

Like Mr. Dahl, in some things you see with eyes different from mine. You epitomize your race, as I epitomize mine. You are subjective, in the last analysis; I am objective. You toy with phantasmagoria; I grasp the living facts. You pursue mirages, unsubstantialities, subtleties that are vain & worthless; I seize upon realities and hammer blindly through to results.

Behold, my seed comes after me. I am joyed with it, satisfied. Still you pursue, wrestling with angels & demons without end, when all the wrestling is without avail. Not so, you say, and I am coward to sit down & leave the fight. And I reply: so be it. I am so made, as you are otherwise made. I prefer least to nothing. You prefer nothing or all to less.

Yours is the first news I had of bringing out the *Letters* anonymously. I have not made up my mind on it, though I am quite willing that they should be brought out anonymously. There is a far greater chance for them to make a hit that way, I think, though our project is known to so many that our secret is bound to come out in the end. Even so, a good idea.

How goes the Prologue? I am impatient to see it.

Jack.

MS: CSmH; 9 pp., als.

1. JL was probably responding to "Jack London's 'Local Color,'" *New York Times Saturday Review of Books and Art*, December 6, 1902, by William H. Dall (1845–1927), a "Yukon pioneer of the sixties." Dall was at that time honorary curator of mollusks at the American Museum of Natural History, a paleontologist with the U.S. Geological Survey, and a professor of invertebrate paleontology at Wegner Institute of Science in Philadelphia.

2. JL underlined "*Letters*" twice.

3. Samuel Clarke Dunham (1855–1920), author of *The Goldsmith of Nome, and Other Verse* (1901) and *The Men Who Blaze the Trail, and Other Poems* (1913); Joaquin Miller, pseudonym of Cincinnatus H. Miller (?1841–1913), Oregon-born California poet and author of "frontier poetry," including *Pacific Poems* (1870) and *Songs of the Sierras* (1871).

To George P. Brett

Piedmont, Calif.,
Dec. 30/02

Dear Mr. Brett:—

I am writing you this in bed, where I have been placed on my back for a week to come through a petty little accident, which accident is as painful as it is petty.[1]

I learn you expect to be in San Francisco on Jan. 2nd. & 3rd. Of course, situated on my back, I shall be unable to run over & see you. But if you have the time, and have nothing else to do, and are so inclined, why run over & see me and take pot luck. If you do come, I can promise that you will be amply repaid by the view, than which there is none better in the world.

How to get here. Time, less than an hour's travel from San Francisco to my door. Take Ferry boat to Oakland. Get off at Broadway and right there take electric car marked "Piedmont Avenue." Ride to the end of the line, where you will find yourself less than five minutes' walk from my place. Either the conductor of car, or the people who live where you get off the car, will tell you where I live.

I think your idea excellent, & shall write a final & hopeful chapter for *People of Abyss.*[2] I shall speak with you or write you later concerning this and other suggestions of yours.[3]

Have just finished reading the *Cecilia* you sent me. Also *The Battle with the Slum.*[4] In this latter I was especially pleased when Riis pointed out the deadness & hopelessness that characterize the East-London slum, and added that there was life & promise in our American slum—"yeast" in our slum, as he called it.

Thanking you for the pleasure these books have given me, & hoping that I may possibly see you, I am

Sincerely yours,
Jack London.

MS: NN; 3 pp., als.

1. See JL to Strunsky, January 20, 1903.

2. In a letter to JL of December 17, 1902 (CSmH), Brett wrote: "The last chapter of your book should be, I think, an optimistic chapter, a chapter pointing out the possibilities of amelioration of the terrible conditions that you set forth."

3. Brett, in his letter of December 17, also suggested that JL not criticize Edward VII directly, that he make more explicit the reasons why work in the lead trades was "frightfully dangerous," and that he focus more pointedly on the criminal element in London.

4. F. Marion Crawford's *Cecilia, a Story of Modern Rome,* and Jacob Riis's *The Battle with the Slum* were published by Macmillan in 1902. Jacob August Riis (1849–1914), Danish-born journalist, author, and reformer, wrote about conditions in the New York slums.

1903

Portrait for the December 1904 issue of *The Argonaut* (CSmH)

To Anna Strunsky

Piedmont, Calif.
Jan 7/[03]¹

Dear Anna:—

I have lost a week or so in bed. Am now sitting up. Mr. Brett came out to see me. Told me he would not be able to get to Stanford. Rose came over with Mary & Max to see me.² Rose is beautiful. Was she not well named?

Have thoroughly revised the *Letters*, yours & mine, though in yours I mainly confined myself to suggesting. Wherever I have pencilled a suggestion to you, do you decide one way or the other, & then erase my suggestion.

Same day this is mailed to you I express (Wells Fargo) the *Letters'* to you. At once, as soon as they arrive, let me know that you have received them.

Shall send fotos of Joan & Bess as soon as I can get around to the making of them. Quite a good likeness of you, the one you enclosed of yourself.

Do tell me whether you care for the *People of the Abyss*. Unless you have a different copy of it than I have, my closing remarks were not cut out. But some of the stuff in the middle was expurgated.

Say, don't tell Wilshire that I received $2000 cash for rights in dog story.³ I[n] his last letter to me he said that the finances of the magazine were such that he did not think he would be able to pay me for rest of serial publication of *Abyss*.⁴ If he thinks it has made my position a little easier (and it is none too easy), he may make no effort to give me further payment for what his magazine is publishing of mine. You understand.

By the way, the contract you signed with Macmillan Company is for the U.S. only. I feel quite certain that you & I will receive the same royalties from England from Messrs. Isbister & Co. If they are not willing to pay same royalty, then, very probably, the English Macmillans will bring out the book. (This Isbister proposition is due to certain publishing arrangements I have on that side of the water.)

Jack.

MS: CSmH; 3 pp., als.

  1. Misdated "Jan 7/02."

  2. Rose Strunsky, Anna's younger sister; Mary Strunsky; and Max Strunsky (*d.* 1957), Anna's brother, an orthopedic surgeon.

  3. In a letter of January 30, 1903, to George Brett (NN), JL wrote: "*Wilshire's Magazine* a radical publication, is willing to handle at once my *People of the Abyss*. This means, of course, several hundred dollars to me. The book itself is so radical that I dispair of finding serial publication for it in the orthodox magazines. Also, the time between now and the fall book-publication is too short to seek regular serial publication and obtain it even if the orthodox magazines would consider the matter." JL's "dog story" was *The Call of the Wild*, which was serialized in the *Saturday Evening Post* from June 20 to July 18, 1903.

  4. Between March and November 1903, Wilshire paid JL $337 for the portion of *The People of the Abyss* published in *Wilshire's Magazine*.

To Anna Strunsky

[Piedmont]
[? mid-January 1903]

*   *   *

Mr. Brett's opinion was against the prologue—likewise my opinion. I read the Prologue carefully, and found, good as it was, that to put it in was also to put in that stubborn obstacle we labored so long to remove & finally succeeded in removing—namely, the delay in introducing the reader to the meat of the matter. You remember how hard we worked to start right & the start not to confuse the reader by too long an opening. This the Prologue would undo for us, so it is best, I am sure you will agree, to let the Prologue go.

However, it was well done. The introduction of Edna Warwick[1] was good, and the letters were truly the love letters of a woman uncertain that she was loved.

Now, Anna, Mr. Brett wants to bring the book out in March, or not later than April at the latest. So do you go over your letters for the final revision as rapidly as you can, and without delay turn them in to him. You see, after they are set up & printed, the proofsheets will have to be gone over by you & me. All this takes time and there is no time to spare.

From our talk, Mr. Brett seems to have gathered a great deal of faith in them. It is his intention to put them on the market well. They are to be published anonymously, which gives a chance for mystification & to make a hit. This is his idea. Also, after they have made their hit, say six months after publication, he will let our names come out as the perpetrators.

I would suggest, for the sake of the reader, that you head all your "London" letters "London," either with the house address in or out as you happen to see fit.

Anything you may see wrong in my letters please correct.

In Letter VI, is not the name spelled "Tolstoy" rather than "Tolstoi"? I think he writes it himself the first way.

How about the way Dane Kempton signs his letters? Look at opening, "Ever your friend." Would Dane, more than father to me, so end a congratulation to me upon my engagement?

The very first letter of all really has no indication that it is written in England.

Mr. Brett thought the end was left hanging in the air because he did not read the two last letters—the two Hester Stebbins' letters you have in your possession. See that these two go in.   Jack.

MS: CSmH; 3 pp. fragment of 4 pp., als.
    1. Edna Warwick was a character who appeared only in the deleted prologue of *The Kempton-Wace Letters*.

To George P. Brett

Piedmont, Calif.
Jan. 20/03.

Dear Mr. Brett:—
    I have finished revising the *Kempton-Wace Letters*, following your suggestions as largely as possible; and some time since have forwarded them to Miss Strunsky for her final revision. I have thought the matter over and have decided against the Prologue. Miss Strunsky has been informed of this.
    By the way, half the royalties on this book fall to her; so would it not be well to furnish her a contract to that effect? She has said nothing about it, & I make the suggestion because I know how little she bothers her head about matters of business.
    Concerning the first novel I write, I have made up my mind that it shall be a sea story. But it shall not be *The Mercy of the Sea*, which same is a tragedy, unrelieved by love, comradeship, or anything else.
    I am on the track of a sea story, however, which shall have adventure, storm, struggle, tragedy, and love.[1] The love-element will run throughout, as the man & woman will occupy the center of the stage pretty much of all the time. Also, it will end happily. The *motif*, however, the human motif underlying all, will be what I may call *mastery*. My idea is to take a cultured, refined, super-civilized man and woman, (whom the subtleties of artificial, civilized life have blinded to the real facts of life), and throw

them into a primitive sea-environment where all is stress & struggle and life expresses itself, simply, in terms of food & shelter; and make this man & woman rise to the situation and come out of it with flying colors.

Of course, this underlying motif, will be *underlying*; it will be subordinated to the love motif. The superficial reader will get the love story & the adventure; while the deeper reader will get all this, plus the bigger thing lying underneath.

As I say, I am on the track of this story, and it is slowly taking shape. By the first or tenth of February, if I do no hear otherwise from you, I expect to have it well enough in hand to begin the first chapter. But believe me, I am not rushing it, & I intend to take plenty of time over it.

Sincerely yours,
Jack London.

P.S.—Please send me five copies of *Children of the Frost*, charging same to my account. I do not know, but I imagine so small a number may be more cheaply mailed than expressed.

MS: NN; 3 pp., als.
  1. *The Sea-Wolf.*

To John Spargo

Piedmont, Calif.
Jan. 20/03

Dear Mr. Spargo:—

Yes, I shall be only too glad to furnish you with a "How I Became a Socialist."[1] But, unfortunately, cannot do it right away. I returned to California to find a heap of accumulated work waiting me; and to cap it all have lost two weeks through an accident.[2] So that I have positive engagements which I am back in and which will require the hardest work to meet.

However, I think I can wade through them in a couple of months, when I shall give you the "How I Became" story.

It is rather strange on the part of the publishers, their not sending a copy of *Daughter of the Snows* for review; but publishers I have given up long ago. You never can understand them. Besides, you did not miss much. I have done better work, I am confident in my short stories, say *The Children of the Frost*.

Sincerely yours,
Jack London.

MS: VtU; 1 p., als.
  1. See JL to Spargo, July 28, 1902.
  2. See the following letter.

To Anna Strunsky

Piedmont, Calif.
Jan. 20/03

Dear Anna:—

I thank you sincerely for my birthday present, and heeded contents marked.[1] After all, as I think about it, there *are* two sides to it. But the dead are dead, why worry about them.

I was very sorry to decide against the Prologue. I hardly think, however, considering that superficial thing the *general reading public*, that we have made a mistake.

I have received word that Isbister & Co., will bring the letters out next fall, though I shall write them to-morrow, suggesting next spring simultaneous with the American publication.

I do not know whether Steinberg is alive; but have written him & shall soon know.

My accident? A heavy box of books fell on me, striking me in a vital place. Then cold settled in the wound and I was left helpless in bed. That is all. I am well on the road to health, now, though I shall be unable to jump, box, or ride a bicycle for some months to come.

I am enclosing herewith, letter from an Englishman. Throw away when you are done with it. In previous letters of his, written to English Editors enquiring about me, he waxed very inthusiastic over my Klondike work. Unhappily, I destroyed those letters. This man Dall returns to the attack, & the only thing to be done is to let it go.[2] He changes from local color being all wrong to folk-lore being all wrong; but he does not specify. There's no doing anything with such a man. Concerning folk-lore, perhaps the greatest liberties I have taken with it is to remove it from a known place several hundred miles into an unknown place where white men have never been. This is surely pardonable, or permissible; rather— and any way, Mr. Dall has never been to the unknown place to know whether the folk-lore given obtains there or not.

Jack.

MS: CSmH; 2 pp., als.

1. Strunsky may have sent JL a copy of W. E. Henley's *Hawthorn and Lavender* (1901), a collection of his poetry. See JL to Strunsky, February 3, 1903.

2. See JL to Strunsky, December 20, 1902. The *New York Times Saturday Review of Books and Art*, January 3, 1903, carried a letter to the editor entitled "Jack London," from "L.," which refuted Dall's earlier letter. It undoubtedly was written by Anna Strunsky, since it used the arguments and even the words of JL's letter of December 20. Dall, in a second letter, published in the *New York Times Saturday Review*, January 10, 1903, under the title "Jack London's Indians," refuted the claims made by "L." and maintained that JL's Indians were "melodramatic white men in . . . disguise" (p. 26).

To George P. Brett

Piedmont, Calif.
Jan. 27/[03][1]

Dear Mr. Brett:—

In reply to yours of January 22nd.

Concerning conclusions reached with Isbister & Co., Mr. Robinson agreed to give me same royalties as I received in America. In your letter intended for him you ask a royalty of 20%. If I recollect rightly, in your contract the royalty is 15% on first 5000, and 20% on all Sold over 5000. This being so, it seems to me your proposition to Isbister & Co., must be modified accordingly.

Concerning payment down on publication of one hundred pounds on account—while it would be highly gratifying to me, I do not know enough of the English market to know whether it can stand it.

However, I do not see why some sume should not be advanced—as to how much, I leave to your judgement.

By the way, Isbister & Co., have an account against me of ten pounds; so whatever agreement may be made, you may expect them to deduct this sum of ten pounds.

Sincerely yours,
Jack London.

MS: NN; 2 pp., als.
1. Misdated "Jan. 27/02."

To Cloudesley Johns

Piedmont, Calif.
Jan. 27/03

Dear Cloudesley:—

So you've been oystering?[1] And at a beautiful time of the year— November, on the Atlantic seaboard! How did you like it? I note that you are non-committal in your postal.

A line from Stoddard,[2] telling me that you had dropped in on him, led me into looking for your arrival in California at any time. When are you coming West? If you are not, then go on East, but don't stop in that man-killer New York. Mate with the "wind that tramps the world."[3] Do anything except stay in that "fierce" burg. It will kill anybody with guts, even you.

If you hit California you must drop in on me & stop for a spell. I am always hard up, but I'll never again be as hard up as during your previous visit. You see, I do not have to worry about grub from day to day. I'm doing credit on a larger & Napoleonic scale. And gee! if at any moment I should die, won't I be ahead of the game!

By the way, I think your long-deferred congratulations upon my marriage are about due. I have been married nearly three years, have a couple of kids, & think it's great. So fire away. Or, come & take a look at us, and at the kids, & then congratulate!

When I was in England, you told me that *Ainslee's* had moved to Fifth Avenue, to number *156*. I was unable to comprehend the connection between *156*—Fifth Avenue & the change in the management & policy.[4] Enlighten me.

I think, In previous letter, I asked you some other question. Which same I have forgotten & you have not answered.

Jack London.

MS: CSmH; 2 pp., als. Pbd: *BJL*, I, 371–72.

1. Johns had left New York for Baltimore to find work. There he signed on the *John G. Mitchell*, an oyster dredger, as a crewman from November 1902 through January 1903.
2. Johns visited Charles Warren Stoddard in Washington, D.C., on his way back to New York.
3. Rudyard Kipling, "Sestina of the Tramp-Royal," l. 30.
4. *Ainslee's*, after its sale in October 1902 by Street & Smith to the newly formed Ainslee Magazine Company, changed from an 80-page, general interest, illustrated monthly to a 160-page fiction magazine.

To Anna Strunsky

Piedmont, Calif.
Feb. 3/03

Dear Anna:—

Thank you very much for Weda Addick's letter.[1] She must be a splendid woman, and I know you must be glad to know her.

I regret very much my remark on the Henley markings. You see, two projecting slips of paper, marking very apposite passages, could lead me into imagining nothing else than that they had been recently inserted. I did not dream that they had lingered in their precarious situation for so long a time, and their prominence & appositeness seemed advertisement of a challenge which I could not quite let pass. Again, I say I regret my remark & ask your forgiveness.

News of Mary's death did not reach me till a week afterward, when Cameron called me up by telephone and told me.[2] You see, I am quite a hermit these days, going nowhere & seeing nobody. I have been in San Francisco but once since my return, & then it was to see your people. Between my crippled condition and the excessive delayed work it heaped upon me, I have been unable to see your people since Cameron told me the sad news. I have written a short letter to Hymen, & hope to get over soon.

It hardly seems realizable that Mary is dead. My last memory of her is of the beginning of the new year, when, with Max & Rose, she came in out of the cold night, rosy & full of life, to pay a visit at my bedside. Well, so be it. It is the way. And so long as we can do the thing bravely when our turn comes, all is well.

I hear all kinds of flattering bits of news concerning you from Don & Wilshire,³ & know that you are glowing & rampant, living always at the pitch of life as is your way, pleasuring in your sorrows as ardently as in your joys, carelessly austere, critically wanton, getting more living out of hours & minutes than we colder mortals, God pity us, get out of months & years. Child, how one envies you. For child you are, as essentially a child as saliently you are a woman.

I have re-read what I have written. Believe me, there is no sting in it—only envy, honest envy, for one who will always titillate with desire, & with a thousand desires, who is content to pursue without attaining, and who enjoys more in anticipation than do others who grasp and satisfy and feel the pangs of hunger that is sated and yet can never be sated. Am I wrong? I hope not. For insofar as I am wrong, that far will sorrows be built up for you which I would rather were not built—

                                                                    Jack London

MS: CSmH; 3 pp., als. Pbd: *BJL*, I, 388–89.
    1. Weda Cook Addicks (1858–1937), friend of Walt Whitman. Addicks composed musical settings for Whitman's poems and often sang at his lectures.
    2. Mary Strunsky, Hyman's wife; Cameron King, Jr.
    3. Probably Gaylord Wilshire; Don has not been identified.

To George P. Brett

                                                                    Piedmont, Calif.
                                                                    Feb. 12/03
Dear Mr. Brett:—

I am beginning at once to revise *The People of the Abyss*. It will be in your hands very shortly. And thank you very much for the trouble you have taken in arranging the copyright.

By the way, you remember you found me at work on a story when you visited me. This story I had begun immediately on my return from England & before my contract with you was signed. It is large enough to make a book, and of course I shall want you to bring it out some day if it should prove available.

I have just received word from the *Saturday Evening Post*, Curtis Pub. Co. They have virtually accepted it for serial publication, and we are now discussing the price for American serial rights. They also expect to cut it down some few thousand words. Watt & Son are handling English serial rights.¹

It is an animal story, utterly different in subject & treatment from the rest of the animal stories which have been so successful; and yet it seems popular enough for the *Saturday Evening Post*, for they snapped it up right away. They were the first people I offered it to.

Now, to the point. With the money I shall receive from the serial publication of this story, the title of which is *The Call of the Wild*, I expect to do two things. (1), Pay off some of my debts. (2)—Take what is left, engage cabin passage in a sailing vessel for the South Seas, take a typewriter, plenty of paper & ink, and the plot for my sea story[2] along, and thus get the sea atmosphere on which I have during the last several years gone stale.

My method of work will be precisely the same as when I am home. Each morning I shall write, and spend the rest of the day knocking around deck, talking, & soaking in atmosphere.

Do you like my idea?

Of course, I shall not start for a month at least. And of course, if I do start, household would be run on monthly check of $150.00 from you. Checks made out, as usual, in my name, for I always leave Mrs. London with powers of attorney.

When may I expect the proofsheets of the *Kempton-Wace Letters?*

Sincerely yours,
Jack London.

MS: NN; 3 pp., als.
    1. See JL to Strunsky, January 7, 1903, n. 3. *The Call of the Wild* was never serialized in a British magazine.
    2. *The Sea-Wolf*.

To George P. Brett

Piedmont, Calif.
February 16/03.

Dear Mr. Brett:—

Am sending you herewith "The Story of Jees Uck." It is something like ten thousand words in length, and I think may possibly be suited for your series of small booklets. It was published in the *Smart Set* some time ago. I had intended it for next collection of Klondike tales, which, as you know, is nearly complete. This collection of tales, the title of which I am thinking of making *A Hyperborean Brew* (so named from the title of one of the stories), you will not be able to publish for nearly two years; so, bringing out "The Story of Jees Uck" in your series of booklets—will it prevent it later on being included in the larger collection?[1]

I hope you will like this "Story of Jees Uck." At the time it was published serially I was gratified to receive a letter from a man who had lived wild life, and who was so convinced by the story that I could not unconvince him that I had never lived with a native wife, for only by so living, he contended, could I have got the experience necessary to write the story.

According to your request, I am also informing you that I have this day expressed the revised copy of *The People of the Abyss* to you, so that no delay may occur in rushing it into print.

I have wholly cut out the references to the King of England in the coronation chapter, have softened in a number of places, made it more presentable in many ways, and added a preface and a concluding chapter. In this concluding chapter I have surely been optimistic (as I really am), though I have seriously challenged the political managing class of England.[2] The point I make, that political machinery racks itself out and must be replaced by newer and improved political machinery, I have also touched in the preface.

Do you remember that photograph of myself I sent you in my slumming clothes—would not this photograph make a good frontis-piece?[3]

Also, I have a few photographs, which I took, which are now with the copy being serially published. Later on, when we see how these photographs reproduce, would it not be well to consider the advisability of putting a few of them in the book?

Again advising you that *The People of the Abyss* has been expressed to you to-day for purposes of immediate copyright.

Very truly yours,
Jack London.

MS: NN; 2 pp., tls. Pbd: *L*, 146–47.
   1. "The Story of Jees Uck" was not published in Macmillan's "Little Novel" series.
   2. See JL to Brett, December 30, 1902, nn. 2, 3.
   3. See JL to Brett, December 11, 1902, n. 2.

To Cloudesley Johns

Piedmont, Calif.
Feb. 21/03

Dear Cloudesley:—

Well, I must say, from your letter, that my predictions concerning you & New York came pretty close to being verified. And I'm glad to hear you're shaking its dust from your shoes by May. Do it, by all means. The city life is too unnatural & monstrous for us folk of the West. To hell with it. There's more in life that what the social shambles offers.

Do, by all means, stop over & see us.[1] I hope, by May, to have a sloop on the Bay & be writing a sea novel![2] You & I can have some fine voyaging together—

Jack London.

MS: CSmH; 1 p., als. Pbd: *BJL*, I, 387.
   1. Johns visited JL in April on his way to Los Angeles from New York.

2. JL bought a 38-foot sloop, the *Spray*, with some of his earnings from *The Call of the Wild*.

To Bailey Millard

Piedmont, Calif.
Feb. 21/03

Dear Mr. Millard:—

I have indeed appreciated the many good notices you have given me, for which same I thank you heartily. When are you going to give me something of which I can say the good word, say in the *Examiner*?[1]

The book on the London slums will be published next fall by the Macmillan Company. I have only two typewritten copies—one of which is in their possession, for they are rushing the book into print for copyright purposes. The other copy is in the hands of *Wilshire's Magazine*, which is publishing it serially beginning with March. However, I shall see that you get an advance copy of same.

I shall be only too glad to look you up at Larkspur some day. Thanks for the kind invitation; also thanks for turning my sociological review over to the Sunday Editor of the *Examiner*.[2]

Yes, I knew you had given up the Sunday Editorship, and was glad. It seemed to me that I never saw a man more paradoxically situated than you were, with all your delight in good literature and fresh open life, jammed in a howling city at the editorial desk of the Sunday supplement.

Jack London

MS: OrU; 2 pp., als.
1. Millard had published two books: *She of the West* (1900), a collection of stories; and *Songs of the Press* (1902), a book of poetry.
2. Possibly a reference to "What Shall Be Done with This Boy?" *San Francisco Examiner*, American Magazine Section, June 21, 1903. In this article JL described a juvenile delinquent, Edgar Sonne, who lived in the Boys and Girls' Aid Society home in San Francisco. He concluded that the boy was unable to be cured of his behavioral problems because of his "starved body . . . [and] starved brain." JL suggested that once the boy's physical condition had been improved, "we will build up the mind and the moral nature until they become healthy, wholesome and good."

To George P. Brett

Piedmont, Calif.
Feb. 25/03

Dear Mr. Brett:—

According to your suggestion, I am expressing you to-day the complete manuscript of *The Call of the Wild*. As you will see, it is somewhat different from anything I have yet done.

It has to be set up and copyrighted one time or another, and to avoid a possible hitch in simultaneous serial publication, of course now is the best time of all, & I thank you for the suggestion.[1]

I am also expressing you to-day the complete manuscript of the *Fish Patrol Stories*. You see, while pursuing the plot of my sea story I am at the same time cleaning up my desk, so that when I commence the sea story there will be no other things pressing upon me or worrying me.

As I told you some time ago, a long & indeterminate time will elapse before the *Youth's Companion* prints the *Fish Patrol Stories*, but I am sending them to you so that they may be set up & copyrighted the same as *The Call of the Wild*.

Concerning these *Fish Patrol Stories*, I have an idea for you to consider. You know, boys are such literal-minded creatures, that a map of the ground covered in the seven Fish Patrol adventures should be just the thing for them. Just a sketch map in black & white for frontispiece. Will you please tell me what you think of this. Of course, I could furnish the map later on. The book, I suppose, would be published as a dollar juvenile.[2]

Very truly yours,
Jack London.

 MS: NN; 3 pp., als.

1. In his letter to JL of February 19, 1903 (CSmH), Brett wrote: "If you have not an extra typewritten copy [of *The Call of the Wild*], perhaps you could let me see a proof as it is sent to you from the serial publishers; and this, by the by, ought to be attended to because in case the serial publication in England is not simultaneous with the serial pubication here there is danger of one copyright or the other being lost; i.e. the copyright here or the copyright in Great Britain, so that a story ought either to be set up and copyrighted as a whole before serial publication begins, or the serial dates should be made to coincide on both sides."

2. A sketch map of San Francisco Bay, San Pablo Bay, and Suisun Bay served as the frontispiece to *Tales of the Fish Patrol*, which was published in a standard $1.50 clothbound edition.

To Frank Putnam

Piedmont, Calif.
Feb. 27/03

Dear Mr. Putnam:—

At last I can write you definitely concerning the "One Thousand Dozen." It has been sold in England to the *Graphic*.[1] The *Graphic*, as is its custom, retains the right of setting date of serial publication. That this publication may be simultaneous, the *National* must accept the *Graphic's* date.

In this connection, write to

Messrs. A. P. Watt & Son,
Hastings House,

Norfolk Street,
Strand,
London W.C.

They will inform you of the date decided upon by the *Graphic*.

By the way, this "One Thousand Dozen" is a pretty long yarn—nearly 7000 words. What may I expect to receive for it from the *National*?

And why can't you send me a copy of the *National* every once & a while so that I may see how things are going with you?

Sincerely yours,
Jack London.

MS: CU; 2 pp., als.

1. Probably the *National Graphic*, a weekly general-interest magazine published in London from 1869 to 1932. For the beginning of JL's correspondence on "The One Thousand Dozen," see JL to Putnam, November 5, 1902.

To Frank Putnam

Piedmont, Calif.
March 9/03

Dear Mr. Putnam:—

Just received your check for $20.00 for "1000 Dozen."

Now let me be entirely frank with you. Almost needless to state, as a starter, I am hard up. Through the failure to publish of a projected magazine, the trip to England I made last year, & the stuff I wrote on the trip, has put me in the hole for a thousand dollars. My debts are clamorous, & I am trying to write a novel which, as you know, is not an immediately remunerative undertaking, while I have a household of nine people that wears clothes & eats three square meals per day.

There are 6,800 words in the story for which you have sent me twenty dollars. I can sell this story to a railroad magazine and received just $204.00 worth of transportation over its roads.

As I said, I am entirely frank with you, & want to put the case plainly before you. All the money my mother possesses was loaned to me to keep the household going while I was in England. It was three hundred dollars. Now my mother, who came from the East when she was a child, who is old, & has never been back to the old home & the old places & faces, wants to go back once before she dies. It is her intention to take her grandson with her. And she has asked me to return the three hundred dollars I borrowed from her. As I say, she is old, & her heart is set upon the trip, & I have no three hundred dollars.

Now, & here's where I throw myself on your generosity, if I can sell this story you have for $204 transportation, I can turn this transportation over to my mother, borrow another hundred dollars somewhere, & let her make her trip.

Not only does it mean a great deal to her, but it means a great deal to me in my present precarious financial position. It means to me the difference between $20.00 & $204.00. This difference is a profit of $184.00 which the *National* could not make out of my story, & which I can make out of my story, which the *National* would not be justified in making out of my story, & which I should be justified in making out of the work of my head & hand.

I have put the case plainly & honestly. I am sending you herewith your check for twenty dollars, & asking you kindly to return the manuscript.

I can only say how sorry I am for all this trouble I have caused, and in extenuation can say that it is all because I am poor. It is no disgrace to be poor, but, believe me, it is often damned inconvenient.

Sincerely yours,
Jack London.

MS: CU; 5 pp., als.

To the Corresponding Editor, *Youth's Companion*

[Piedmont]
March 9. 1903.

Dear sir:—

Your letter of March 4th. enquiring about actual conditions upon which were built the *Fish Patrol Stories*.

Let me frankly state, first of all, the knowledge from which I write. I, when a young fellow of from fifteen to seventeen, was for a good while one of the oyster pirate fleet. My sloop, *The Razzle Dazzle* was an oyster pirate sloop. With the rest of the fleet, grown men, convicts, and what-not, I have raided the oyster beds when I was fifteen and sixteen, both in my sloop, and, when she was wrecked, in the actual sloop *Reindeer* with one, Nelson, a man who was shortly afterward shot by officers of the law at Benecia. He was shot and killed upon another sloop, which, at the time, he was running.

In fact, the oyster bed raid I have described in one of the stories, is almost literally a narrative of an actual raid. The watchmen had been placed on the beds as the tide was falling, and left there without a skiff. When the oyster pirates, in small boats, which they dragged a long distance across the mud, arrived, they forced the two watchmen off into the water, but did not molest them. The only departure from truth is that the raid was successful and that not one of the pirates was captured.

Later on, this Nelson and myself, in the *Reindeer*, were up in Benecia with a load of oysters, when we were approached by one of the Fish Patrolmen with a proposition which caught our fancy, and for some months afterward the *Reindeer*, Nelson, and myself, took an active part in the raids on the law-breaking fisherman. The way we captured the big Chinese fleet of shrimp-fishers in the first story "White and Yellow,"[1] [is] again almost a literal narrative of what actually happened, even to the refusal of the Chinese to bail the *Reindeer* until she was just about ready to sink.

Big Alec, the King of the Greeks, in story by that title,[2] was an actual man. I have not even changed his name. or nickname. He had a record of several men killed by him, but, aided by all the Greeks, with money, etc. he beat the cases. He actually came down to Benecia with his ark, told Charley and me that he was going fishing Chinese Sturgeon-line in the Bight at Turner's Shipyard; but, such was his reputation, Charley and I left him alone, instead of, as in story, capturing him. Later on, Big Alec (I was in Japan at the time), killed two sailors, under most dramatic circumstances, escaped the authorities, and has never been heard of since. Let me give you the facts of this killing. A feud was on between these two English sailors (deserters), and Big Alec. Everybody knew of this feud. The people on the wharf at Martinez, in broad day, saw Big Alec sailing along in one direction, and the two sailors sailing along in an opposite direction. The point where the two boats would pass was hidden from the people on the wharf by a wheat ship lying at anchor. The people saw the two boats disappear behind the wheat ship. After a while they saw Big Alec's boat appear as he continued on his way. They watched for the boat with the two sailors to appear. It never appeared. In the short space of time while behind the wheat ship, Big Alec had killed these two men, sunk their boat with them in it, and gone on as though nothing had happened. Charley told me the details of this affair when I returned from my voyage to Japan. He had dragged for and finally recovered the scuttled boat with the two dead occupants.

"The Seige of the Lancastershire Queen"[3] is founded on a certain amount of fact. Charley and I, in the salmon-boat of a captured Vallejo Greek, came upon the two men with the sturgeon line outfit, chased them round and round a wheat ship, and lost them by having them sheltered by the captain of the wheat ship. We gave them up, the story captured them. But, we captured other fishermen in the same water, for the same offense, sailing along our side of the triangle in a faster boat. Also, we have had them beat us ashore, when we returned, dragged for their line, and raised it with over a thousand pounds of sturgeon on the hooks. And when the men claimed their line we arrested them and convicted them.

"Charley's Coup"[4] is imaginary insofar as the story goes, but is based upon the fact that it was an old trick of the fishermen to leave their nets drifting and go ashore, and when the Fish Patrol attempted to confiscate their nets, to fire with their rifles from the shore.

"Demetrios Contos"[5] is a fiction which exceeds the truth. For, in point of fact, Demetrios Contos would have left me to drown had the story actually occurred. But the pride in a fast boat, and the flaunting of the Fish Patrol is certainly true to life.

"Yellow Handkerchief"[6] is a fiction insofar as he chased me around through the mud. But I actually did take the helm of his junk, outpoint the *Reindeer*, have them cast off the tow-line, and beat them into San Rafael Creek. Yellow Handkerchief, however, did not escape, but went to jail with his crew.

I have written of the years 1891 and 1892 in San Francisco Bay and up the rivers. The fishermen were then a wild crowd, as they still are a wild crowd. The oyster pirates are gone. The Chinese shrimpers remain, for, backed by the powerful Seven Companies, which hired for them the best legal talent to be obtained, they beat all our efforts to convict them by carrying the cases from court to court and by outgeneraling the mediocre city attorneys who usually fought our cases for us.

There is not so much shooting, etc, going on now among the Greeks and Italians as formerly, and they have been pretty well brought under the heel of the law. Though, as I say, they are a wild lot yet. George, one of the cowardly patrolmen mentioned in first story of series, was stabbed, after I left the Fish Patrol, by a revengeful Greek. In the old days dead fishermen were brought in lying across their nets, and pitched battles, such as was fought around Big Alec's ark, were fought.

I know that Charley, three other men, and myself, have raced for our lives down the Martinez wharf, pursued by a howling mob of fishermen, because we had just arrested two of their number red-handed. We escaped in our salmon boat, and when the trial later took place in Martinez, we attended with a reinforcement of fighting men in case of trouble. But the trial was a farce. Martinez was to a large extent a fishing town, fishermen innumerable were challenged by us, but solid jury of fishermen remained at the end, and brought in "Not Guilty" without leaving their seats, when as I say, the culprits had been caught red-handed.

So I certainly do vouch for the conditions which obtained among the fishermen ten years and more ago, and I should be glad to have all letters of enquiry referred to me. By the way, there in the East with you, the Chesapeake oyster pirate war is not yet forgotten.

Sincerely yours,
Jack London

MS: CSmH; 5 pp., cctl. Pbd: *L*, 147–49.
    1. "White and Yellow," *Youth's Companion*, February 11, 1905.
    2. "The King of the Greeks," *Youth's Companion*, March 2, 1905.
    3. "The Siege of the 'Lancashire Queen,'" *Youth's Companion*, March 30, 1905.
    4. "Charley's 'Coup,'" *Youth's Companion*, April 13, 1905.
    5. "Demetrios Contos," *Youth's Companion*, April 27, 1905.
    6. "'Yellow Handkerchief,'" *Youth's Companion*, May 11, 1905.

To George P. Brett

Piedmont, Calif.
March 10/03

Dear Mr. Brett:—

I am glad you like the *Call of the Wild*; but, unfortunately, I cannot accept your offer for all rights in it.[1] You see, the *Saturday Evening Post* bought the American serial rights of it, and already have sent me over half of the proof-sheets; while Watt & Son are handling the English serial sale of it.

The whole history of this story has been very rapid. On my return from England I sat down to write it into a 4000 word yarn, but it got away from me & I was forced to expand it to its present length. I was working on it when you came to see me in January. At the time I had made up my mind to let you carry the uncompleted duplicate away with you; but somehow the conversation did not lead up to it & I became diffident. Then I sent a copy to the *Saturday Evening Post* and they at once accepted it.

They have paid me three cents a word for the American serial rights. This was the money I intended dividing between my debts and my South Sea trip. But when it arrived last week, my debts loomed so large & the South Seas loomed so expensive, that I compromised matters and bought a sloop-yacht for San Francisco Bay. It is now hauled out & being fitted up. I shall live on it a great deal, and on it I shall write the greater part of my sea-novel. The sloop is old, but it is roomy & fast. I can stand upright in the cabin which is quite large. I'll send you a picture of her some time.

I did not like the title, *The Call of the Wild*, and neither did the *Saturday Evening Post*. I racked my brains for a better title, & suggested *The Sleeping Wolf*. They, however, if in the meantime they do not hit upon a better title, are going to publish it in the *Post* under *The Wolf*. This I do not like so well as *The Sleeping Wolf*, which I do not like very much either. There is a good title somewhere, if we can only lay hold of it.[2]

The *Saturday Evening Post*, as first buyer, reserved the right of setting date for simultaneous serial publication in England & America, so they would be the ones to write to in this connection. Of course, they will illustrate it.

I should have been glad to close with your offer, both for the sake of the cash & of the experiment you mention;[3] but, as I have explained, the serial right has passed out of my hands. As a book, however, under the circumstances as they are, you may succeed in getting a fair sale out of it.

I shall shortly make a rough sketch of the map for frontispiece of *Fish Patrol Stories*. The difficulty with *Youth's Companion* is that they may not publish it serially for a good time to come.

Will you please send me five copies of *Children of the Frost* (if they have not already been sent), and also, One copy of *Guns, Ammunition, and Tackle*,[4] & charge to my account.

Sincerely yours,
Jack London.

MS: NN; 5 pp., als. Pbd: *L*, 149–50.
   1. In his letter to JL of March 5, 1903 (CSmH), Brett offered to buy the entire copyright of *The Call of the Wild* for $2000 cash.
   2. The novel was serialized as *The Call of the Wild*.
   3. Brett wrote in his letter of March 5: "I would like to try an experiment with the story, i.e., publish it in a little different form to the ordinary run of stories and possibly this might help, not only the book itself, but the general reputation of your books as well."
   4. Capt. A. W. Money, Horace Kephart, W. E. Carlin, A. L. A. Himmelwright, and John Harrington Keene, *Guns, Ammunition, & Tackle*, which, according to the *National Union Catalog*, was not published by Macmillan until 1904.

To Anna Strunsky

Piedmont, Calif.
March 13/03

Dear Anna:—

I quite wondered if you were ever going to write to me again. And I should have wondered more, only I have been head over heels in work, getting things cleaned up, books partly finished, etc, so that I might start in on the sea novel for Mr. Brett.

You found him reading the manuscript of what was probably my dog story. I started it as a companion to my other dog story "Batard," which you may remember; but it got away from me, & Instead of 4000 words it ran 32000 before I could call I halt. I hope you will like it when it appears.

I wrote Hyman a letter which he must have received just about the time he arrived in San Francisco. I have been unable to get over and see him. I go no where any more. Since my return I have been to San Francisco but twice & do not dream of when I shall again go there.

I have just finished writing two lectures, each 6000 words long & something like the "Tramp." They are "The Scab" & "The Class Struggle."[1] Of this, however, do not tell Mr. Brett, for he may think I am neglecting his work which I really am not.

I can hardly contain myself, looking forward to seeing the *Letters* in print. Be sure, to question anything & everything in mine that strikes you as wrong.

Oh, by the way, I have lost a friend. Jim Whitaker has cancelled my name from his list and even cut me in public. For what reason I cannot imagine, for he has said nothing to me at all, though I have heard he was incensed because I told Leonard D. Abbot[2] when I was in New York that he (Whitaker) was a backslider from the Cause.

Funny topic to end a letter with,

Jack.

MS: CSmH; 3 pp., als. Pbd: *BJL*, I, 388.

1. JL had delivered "The Tramp" at the Academy of Sciences in San Francisco on January 19, 1902; to the Pacific Coast Women's Press Association in San Francisco on February 25, 1902; and to the Fourth Ward Equality Club in Oakland on May 17, 1902. He delivered "The Scab" twice in the Bay Area: in Oakland at the temple of the Tribe of Ben Hur on April 5, 1903, and in San Francisco at the Alhambra Theater on December 18, 1904. "The Scab" was published in the *Atlantic Monthly*, January 1904. JL gave many presentations entitled "The Class Struggle," including one at Harmon Gymnasium, University of California, on January 20, 1905. "The Class Struggle" was published in the *Independent*, November 5, 1903. All three essays were included in *War of the Classes*.

2. Leonard D. Abbot (1878–1953), English-born socialist and associate editor of the *Literary Digest* from 1897 to 1905. JL referred to him as "St. Leonard."

To Cloudesley Johns

Piedmont, Calif.
March 16/03

Dear Cloudesley:—

By all means, if anything comes your way, buy a ticket and get "hauled out to the Coast." You know what our spring is, it will do you good. And as for summer, if you have been left in any way weak, that damned humid heat won't help you any.

I should be sending you a ticket with this, but for the fact that I have just previously gone the limit with the money-lenders to keep things going. You see, buying the sloop just about swamped me.

But in a letter I received from Sedgewick[1] yesterday, he says: "Our friend Johns is not very well, and I am urging him strenuously to return to California. I hope we shall be able to get him off this week."

I shall write him this mail, in case he has not yet got you off, and tell him to go ahead and that I'll be ready for you at this end.

Get your ticket for *Oakland*, and you certainly will get on your feet up here on the hill at our shack.

Take the *Piedmont* Avenue cars, at Seventh street & Broadway, (Oakland), and ride to the end of the line. If conductor or motorman cannot direct you, ask at the first house. Five minutes walk to my place.

If you have any "horror" stories, submit them to *Bookman*.[2]

I have the following, in a letter from *Bookman*:—"Don't you happen to have up your sleeve a dramatic tale with plenty of battle, murder, & sudden death—a story with real horror in it. Remember the more gore the better."

Jack London.

MS: CSmH; 3 pp., als.

1. Ellery Sedgwick.

2. *Bookman*, an illustrated literary magazine that featured book reviews and current American literature, was published in New York from 1895 until 1933.

To Frank Putnam

Piedmont, Calif.
March 16/03

Dear Mr. Putnam:—

To say that your letter of March 11th. flabbergasted me is to put it mildly. It was the one thing editors had never done to me before, & the one thing I did not expect ever would be done to me.

As you will remember, I was in England when "1000 Dozen" was submitted to you. It was submitted to you by *mistake* on the part of my wife, as I *explained* to you. English agents told me, while in England, that English *Pearsons* liked the story & would take it if American *Pearsons* would take it. Did both English & American *Pearson's* take it, I should have received about $175.00 for it.

Imagine my surprise, on my return home, to find a letter of acceptance from you. I at once sat down & wrote you, explaining the matter, & asking you, not to *publish*, but to hold the story.

I let you *hold* it, because I was sorry to disappoint you, and thought English *Pearson's* might finally take it & American *Pearson's* let it go.

This letter of mine you acknowledged, and by the words of your acknowledgement showed that you clearly understood that it was my wish for you to do nothing with the story till you heard from me again.

This was the state of affairs, & I trusted to it. The very mail that I received news of the purchase of English serial rights by *Graphic*, I wrote you, telling you to go ahead, but to get date of English publication in *Graphic* from my English agents. But it was all too late. You, and I must say that it be called nothing else than "deliberate"—you deliberately went counter, you had, rather, deliberately gone counter to my request and already published the story.

Now here's where I stand. I have worked two weeks, writing a story, roughly, of 7000 words. If you have quiered the English sale of it (which I am something more than fairly certain you have), then for my two week's work & my 7000 words I received $20.00. This is a rate of $40.00 per month, and it will not keep a household of nine souls out of the poorhouse.

To show you what I am confident you have lost me, I enclose letter from Watt & Son. You will see it amounts to $105.00 roughly. If this is lost, will the *National* stand good for it to me? For you see, it is lost through no error on my part, through no mutual error on our parts, but through a direct disregard of my wishes which I had conveyed to you months previously.

Concerning the last letter you received of mine, in which I returned your check & asked for manuscript, of course it is all out of the running. I thought it was funny that the *National* was paying in advance for its stuff, but even then I could not conceive that it had published the story. It never entered my head. It was too impossible.

As you are no smug fat editor of one of the *big*[1] magazines, but one of the lean & hungry writer-folk like myself, I know that you will thoroughly understand the part I have played throughout the transaction. In the first place I have been right up to the handle and frank. Even when I saw a chance to get $200.00 for American serial rights instead of your $20.00, I told you all the reasons, showed you how badly I needed it. And what writer-man would not exchange, if he could, twenty dollars for ten times twenty dollars?

In this letter, as in previous ones, I have talked right up to the handle. Do not feel unduly hurt if I have been harsh, for it is up to you, and what's to be done if the manuscript comes back from England?

Sincerely Yours,
Jack London.

P.S.–Please return me the letter of Watt and Son.

MS: CU; 6 pp., als.
  1. JL underlined this word twice.

To George P. Brett

Piedmont, Calif.
March 20/03.

Dear Mr. Brett:–

You have, ere this, received fifteen or sixteen photographs of London scenes for illustrating the *People of the Abyss.* Just after mailing these illustrations to you, I received your letter of March 12th.[1] Following your suggestion, I have written a letter to England, to Mr. Robinson,[2] which I enclose to you herewith. If satisfactory to you, it may be sealed and mailed. You will notice that I have made a point of having the cost of these photographs sent to me. I do this because I have long since been impressed with the fact that when work is done for a large company the price is usually "socked" on. Of course, in the event of the photographs being taken, I shall have to fall back on you to pay for them.

James Russell Lowell's poem at beginning of book is only an extract from a much longer poem.[3]

The legend used at the head of Chapter XIX, is merely an extract from Tennyson's very long poem, *Locksly Hall Sixty Years After.*[4]

The only entire poem in the book is Longfellow's "Challenge" at end of the book. I do not know when it was written,[5] nor can I learn the name of the publishers who own his copyrights. If this could be learned for me, I shall at once write them for permission to use the poem.

Following your suggestion I have made the book uniform by putting legends at the heads of all the chapters—which same I like much better than the old way.

I have made the legend changes, etc, in proof-sheets I have received from the printers. You mention sending me an extra copy of the book, asking me to let you have "any corrections to the book marked in this extra copy."

Beyond putting in the legends at heads of chapters, and duly accrediting the one By Tennyson to him, I have not, and do not expect to make any other changes in the book that will amount to more than a word in a place, and not more than ten words altogether. I like the looks of the book very much.

Sincerely yours,
Jack London

MS: NN; 2 pp., tls.

1. In his letter of March 12, 1903 (CSmH), Brett inquired if JL knew someone who could provide photographs to illustrate *The People of the Abyss*.

2. JL probably wrote H. Perry Robinson to persuade Isbister & Co. to publish *The People of the Abyss* in England.

3. "A Parable" (1848), ll. 33−48. In his letter of March 12, Brett asked if this poem and the other poems JL used as chapter legends might be out of copyright.

4. *Locksley Hall Sixty Years After* (1886), ll. 217−18; 223−24.

5. Longfellow's "Challenge" was published in 1873.

To Anna Strunsky

Piedmont, Calif.
March 23/03

Dear Anna:−

I am sending you this mail the first batch of proofsheets. I had expected them to come from you, but they have come, instead, from the printer.

They seem very clean, & I have made very few corrections.

A couple of places I have made suggestions to you. Whether you follow them or not, in either event rub out what I have written in pencil.

Should you see any errors in my letters, change said errors yourself.

When you have done, forward them at once to the printer, whose address you will find on first page of proofs. (Don't delay.)

What has come of the four bits of poetry we intended to place at the first of the book?[1]

Also, please write & let me know that you have received the proofs I am now sending you—

Jack.

MS: ULA; 1 p., als.

1. See JL to Strunsky, April 6, 1903.

To Anna Strunsky

Piedmont, Calif.
March 23/03

Dear Anna:—

I am sending you this mail, under separate cover, the proofs you just sent me & which I have just received & gone over this morning.

As I do not think the ink typographical corrections are yours, why this copy, with ink typographical corrections, should be the one returned to the printers. If the typographical corrections are yours (as I now think they are), why it should likewise be the copy you send to the printers.

So, place in this copy the corrections I placed in my copy sent you yesterday (if they pass muster with you). The point is, *let the ink-typographically-corrected copy, contain both your corrections & mine and send that copy in.*

Next proofs I receive direct from printer I shall put aside, and then, when I receive proofs from you, embody my corrections with yours.

Jack.

MS: ULA; 1 p., tls.

To George P. Brett

Piedmont, Calif.
March 25/03

Dear Mr. Brett:—

I have telegraphed you to-day accepting your offer for *The Call of the Wild.*[1]

I had thought, previous to receiving this last letter from you, that my already having disposed of serial rights had knocked in the head whatever plan you had entertained for the publishing of the book. I cannot tell how glad I am to find that I was mistaken.

I am sure that pushing the book in the manner you mention will be of the utmost value to me, giving me, as you say, an audience for subsequent books. It is the audience already gathered, as I do hope you will gather in this case, that counts.

Concerning title, I must confess to a sneaking preference for *The Call of the Wild.*[2] But, under any circumstance, I want the decision of the title to rest with you. You know the publishing end of it, and the market value of titles, as I could not dream to know.

You may send the contract along at your convenience for me to sign. And I cannot convey to you the greatness of my pleasure at knowing that the book has struck you favorably; for I feel, therefore, that it is an earnest of the work I hope to do for you when I find myself. And find myself I will, some day.

Concerning the *Kempton-Wace Letters*, I am rushing the proofs through as fast as they arrive.

The covers you mention sending will probably arrive in this afternoon's mail, when I shall at once state my preference.

As the *Letters* come out anonymously, they should not collide with the dog story at all.

Sincerely yours,
Jack London.

P.S.—Do you remember what I told you of the nationality of Joseph Conrad? It was correct. He was a Polish boy who ran away to sea from Poland.[3]

MS: NN; 3 pp., als. Pbd: *L*, 150–51.

1. In a letter to JL of March 19, 1903 (CSmH), Brett said that Macmillan would "still pay two thousand dollars in full for the remaining rights in the copyright of [*The Call of the Wild*]."

2. Brett, in his letter of March 19, wrote: "I may say that *The Wolf* seems to me to be a bad title, and *The Sleeping Wolf* not a great deal better: indeed I am coming to like *The Call of the Wild* better the more familiar I become with it and I suspect in the end that I shall like that title for the story pretty well." In his letter of March 5, 1903 (CSmH), however, Brett had written: "It is a title which, it seems to me, the public would not understand until after they had read the book, which is the wrong end about of going to work. I hope something else will occur to you, as I like the story very well indeed, although I am afraid it is *too true to nature* and *too good work* to be really popular with the sentimentalist public."

3. Joseph Conrad (1857–1924), born Teodor Josef Konrad Korzeniowski in Russia of Polish parents. Conrad joined the crew of a French ship in 1874. For JL's appreciation of his work, see JL to Conrad, June 4, 1915.

To George P. Brett

Piedmont, Calif.
March 26/03

Dear Mr. Brett:—

I am returning you this mail the covers of *The Kempton-Wace Letters*. I am confident that I like the darker cover.

As a test to my judgement, I have shown the two covers to about a dozen people who were at the house last night, carefully concealing my own preference; and one & all, & each alone, not swayed by knowledge of the judgement of others, decided that they liked the dark cover better.

As for myself, I could hardly imagine a more appropriate cover than the dark one—[1]

Sincerely yours,
Jack London.

MS: NN; 1 p., als.

1. See JL to Strunsky, May 29, 1903.

To George P. Brett

Piedmont, Calif.
April 2/03

Dear Mr. Brett:—
I am sending you herewith signed contract for *Call of the Wild.*

I notice, on outside of paper book brought out for copyright purposes, that the title is printed *Call of the Wild.* To me this seems far less effective than *The Call of the Wild.* Somehow, the "The" seems to give it a different & more definite meaning.

I am Waiting until you send the suggestions you mentioned, before I begin correcting the proofs of *Call of the Wild.*

I think I sent you the proofs of *People of the Abyss,* expressed to you on March 23rd. You should, ere this, have received them. They were sent Wells Fargo.

There is a very slight possible chance that they were expressed to the printers, but on looking over my Wells Fargo shipping receipts I find none in the name of the printers, but all in your name.

I shall look forward with interest to the English photographs.

I have been away a week, making my first cruise on the *Spray.* I beat down with her from the mouth of the Sacramento, through Suisun Bay, & into Carquinez Straits in the teeth of a sou'west. Under double-reefed mainsail & bonneted jib, (storm canvas), we were repeatedly knocked flat.

Jack London.

MS: NN; 2 pp., als.

To Anna Strunsky

Piedmont, Calif.
April 6/03.

Dear Anna:—
Telegram received. I have no copy of the quotations lost by the printers. So book will have to go without them. Too bad!

Yes, I remember Jack Crawford, or, at least, I think I do. And we must have met if he remembers me (this in charity).

Am in tremendous rush. Hope you'll make this out. Wilshire was out to see me, with Rose, the Wallings, etc. etc.[1] All went to Ruskin Annual Dinner together.

I am sending this mail Hyman's pictures. I did my best with them, and though I am troubled because they are no better, I feel, at least with my apparatus, that they could not be bettered. An accident happen to one of them, for which I hope Hyman will forgive me. Tell him to drop me a postal announcing their safe arrival.

Oh, how far away is July.

Jack.

MS: CSmH; 2 pp., als.
1. Gaylord Wilshire; Rose Strunsky; probably the family of wealthy socialist William English Walling, who married Anna Strunsky in 1906.

To George P. Brett

Piedmont, Calif.
April 10/03

Dear Mr. Brett:—

I am mailing you, under separate cover & registered, the corrected proofs of *The Call of the Wild*.

I have not added to it, or cut out from it; but merely contented myself with minor alterations.

I have searched in vain for appropriate legends for the various chapters. I do not believe they exist. I have even tried to compose some myself, but not being a poet, have failed lamentably.

You will remember that the one legend I used, was placed at the beginning both of the first & last chapters.[1] This I have cut out from the last chapter. Also, I have removed it from the head of the first chapter & placed it opposite on the blank Page. This may not be the most appropriate way of placing it—which same I leave to you; but I feel that it will be very appropriate in some otherwise vacant page previous to the beginning of the first chapter.

Concerning the oaths.[2] Inside the back cover I have given the pages & lines of the book wherein oaths occur. I have a feeling that some of the less vigorous one (two or three at any rate), should remain. But I have been both loth & unable to tackle their elimination. This I leave to you, and you have my full permission to do whatever you please with all the oaths in the book—only, if possible, I pray you leave me two or three.

Is it asking too much to have placed on inside title page, under my name: "Author of *The Son of the Wolf, The God of His Fathers, The Children of the Frost*"?[3]

If the *Sat. Eve. Post* illustrations are not used by you, I wish then to call especial attention of the artist to page 183, on which page he will find the portrait of Buck depicted in words.[4]

With these proofsheets, my desk is at last clean. I have already worked out plot, characters, details, etc., of it, and shall start in now on the actual writing of the Book.[5]

Sincerely yours,
Jack London.

MS: NN; 4 pp., als.
1. The first stanza of John Myers O'Hara, "Atavism" (1902): "Old longings nomadic

leap, / Chafing at custom's chain; / Again from its brumal sleep / Wakens the ferine strain."
See JL to O'Hara, July 25, 1907.

2. In a letter of April 1, 1903 (CSmH), Brett asked JL to "remove [the] few instances of profanity in the story, because, in addition to the grown-up audience for the book, there is undoubtedly possible for it a very considerable school audience." As a result, the strongest oath uttered in the novel is "by Gar."

3. Macmillan did not list these other titles.

4. The illustrations for the book version of *The Call of the Wild* were by Philip R. Goodwin and Charles Livingston Bull.

5. *The Sea-Wolf.*

To Cloudesley Johns

Piedmont, Calif.
April 24/03

Dear Cloudesley:—

Sedgwick has accepted "Marriage of Lit-lit," if I put a "snapper" on the end of it. As it's already sold in England I guess I'll obey.

As you will understand, with abbreviated thumb am not writing at length.[1]

I wanted to give you a copy of *Daughter of the Snows*, but forgot. Remind me if I forget again, & I'll send you one a little later.

Am mailing you both to-night *Daughter of Snows* & *People of Abyss*. Return latter at early convenience.

Jack London

MS: CSmH; 1 p., als. Pbd: *BJL*, I, 391.
    1. See the following letter.

To Anna Strunsky

Piedmont, Calif.
April 24/03

Dear Anna:—

This is the first writing I have done for some time. Easter Sunday I elected to cut off the end of my thumb, and not finding the piece, have had a painful wound to heal.

Mabel Applegarth has been spending a couple of weeks with us—likewise Cloudesley Johns.

Am glad you liked the dog story. Have a heart beating in the end of my thumb, so—

Jack London.

MS: CSmH; 1 p., als. Pbd: *BJL*, I, 391.

To Cloudesley Johns

Piedmont, Calif.
May 5/03

Dear Cloudesley:—

Thank you very much for your criticism.[1] The proofs are in, but I shall save your points (almost all of which I bow to) until I get another whack at the proofs, which I will get when I place the illustrations in it.

My thumb is growing nicely—quite a chunk of new & very tender meat on the end of it. We went out sailing yesterday, and about everybody aboard, & there were fifteen, ran into it. It's throbbing to-day.

Please send me C. W. Stoddard's address.

My regards to your mother & Bert.[2] Have started the sea novel, & expect to swing along 5000 word per week till it is completed—

Jack London

MS: CSmH; 1 p., als. Pbd: *BJL*, I, 391–92.
  1. Of *The People of the Abyss.*
  2. Herbert Heron Peet.

To Cloudesley Johns

Piedmont, Calif.
May 12/03

Dear Cloudesley:—

What do you think of the chess editorial? I am afraid that the writer makes a huge mistake, forgetting that life has as inexorable limits as chess has.[1]

The love letters[2] are published. Shall send you a copy as soon as I get some.

Jack London.

Hermits picture is on the wall above my desk. How sad you look.

MS: CSmH; 1 p., als.
  1. In the *San Francisco Examiner*, May 5, 1903, an editorial entitled "No Napoleonic Chess Player on an Air Cushion" took issue with Israel Zangwill's statement "The Napoleon of the future will be an epileptic chess player, carried about the field of battle on an air cushion." The editorial writer asserted ([p. 16]): "Chess is a weak game for it admits all kinds of rules and all kinds of foreordained impossibilities. The man that makes the world's great success will not be bound by rules. The great men of the world are great because they refuse to admit impossibilities."
  2. *The Kempton-Wace Letters.*

To George P. Brett

Piedmont, Calif.
May 18/03.

Dear Mr. Brett:—

Enclosed letter from the *Sat. Evening Post* concerning date of publication of *The Call of the Wild*.

There is a short review of mine, of *Social Unrest & Benevolent Feudalism*, in the May number of the *International Socialist Monthly Review*.[1] I tried the Hearst papers with the same review, but they were shy. Still, it is published where it is bound to reach a peculiarly fit portion of the reading public.

By the way, have you decided to use that yarn of mine, "The Story of Jees Uck," in that series of long short stories you are bringing out?[2]

I received a copy of the *Kempton-Wace Letters*. In addition to the several complimentary copies coming to me, could a dozen more copies be sent to me and be charged to my account?

I have to thank you for *The Water Fowl Family*,[3] which you recently sent me. It will make a splendid addition to my reference library.

I have been experimenting with a Rotary Neostyle duplicator,[4] and send you herewith a sample of proofs which I have taken in the course of getting seven manuscript copies of the sea novel upon which I am at work. In this connection, & concerning copyrighting, I want information.

From what you have told me, I realize that rushing a book into print for copyright purposes, long before it is to come out, makes it an expensive course because of its having to lie in type for so long. If I take sufficient copies of a book or short story, can these manuscript copies be copyrighted in England & American and thus save the cost of lying a long period in type?

Of the sea novel, I am making seven copies,—which I figure to use for you & the English publishers, for the magazine editors, & for copyright purposes.

Now, will you tell me how I should go about to get the work copyrighted? or where I can get information on the subject? Or whether I could send the copies to you and have the copyrighting done through you?—& if so, if more than one typewritten copy is necessary in England or in America?

Also, what is the expense of copyrighting a book? & a short story?

Very truly yours,
Jack London.

MS: NN; 3 pp., als.

1. John Graham Brooks, *The Social Unrest* (1903); William J. Ghent, *Our Benevolent*

Feudalism (1902). Both books were published by Macmillan. JL's review was "Contradictory Teachers," *International Socialist Review*, May 1, 1903.
    2. See JL to Brett, February 16, 1903.
    3. Leonard C. Sanford, L. B. Bishop, and T. S. Van Dyke, *The Water Fowl Family* (1903), published by Macmillan.
    4. An early version of the mimeograph machine.

To Cloudesley Johns

Piedmont, Calif.
May 29 1903

Dear Cloudesley:—

When are you coming up? Am just in from a cracking good trip in which I blew the *Spray*'s sails to ribbons. Am waiting ashore now while new ones are being bent. I find that I can work splendidly upon her.

Nothing doing, no news, nothing. Thumb is getting along, & have finished 30,000 words of sea story. When it is done am going to send you a ms. copy for criticism (if you don't mind), before I submit it.

Jack London

MS: CSmH; 1 p., als. Pbd: *BJL*, I, 392.

To Anna Strunsky

Piedmont, Calif.
May 29 1903

Dear Anna:—

Your friend must be a woman worth knowing.

My disappointment in the cover of our book is keen. The dark green cover, which both you & I selected, was far better.[1] I don't know why Brett made the change. He said nothing to me about it.

In your letter you say that Cameron[2] asked at the Macmillan store for the book. Is Cameron in New York? My regards to him if he is.

I am waiting anxiously for the reviews. In this connection you must be prepared for all kinds of rot adverse & eulogistic. Don't let it effect you.

My thumb is slowly growing. I shall be able to take the bandages off in another six weeks.

I spend a good deal of time out on my boat, where I am largely writing my sea novel. Have just come in from a trip, during which I blew my sails into ribbons. Am waiting ashore while new sails are being bent.

Shall write you more coherently next time.

Jack.

MS: CSmH; 2 pp., als.
    1. The cover of the first edition of *The Kempton-Wace Letters* was grayish blue with a

black-edged border of bird and flower decorations on cover and spine. The front-cover lettering was white, and the spine lettering, gilt. See JL to Brett, March 26, 1903.
    2. Cameron King, Jr.

To Blanche Partington

Piedmont, Calif.
Jun 12 1903

Dear Blanche:—[1]
    Just my luck. Mrs. London pulled out for Glen Ellen yesterday,[2] and I pull out on the yacht Monday for parts unknown.
    But I hope you'll be able & inclined to indefinitely extend your invitation.
    Please accept a copy of the *Letters* I am sending you this mail. And, if you survive them, let me know what disagreement you have with my argument.

Sincerely yours,
Jack London.

MS: CU; 1 p., als.
    1. Blanche Partington (*d.* 1951), a native of the Isle of Man who came to California in 1891. As music and drama editor for the *San Francisco Call*, she had become acquainted with JL through "the Crowd," JL's circle of artistic friends in the Bay Area. The Crowd in its later years, when it centered in Carmel, is described in Franklin Walker, *The Seacoast of Bohemia* (San Francisco, 1966). A discussion of the Crowd in its early days is included in Andrew Sinclair, *Jack: A Biography of Jack London* (New York, 1977), pp. 67–72.
    2. Bessie London and her daughters had gone to spend the summer in Glen Ellen in the Sonoma Valley (the Valley of the Moon). They stayed in one of the guest cabins at Wake-Robin Lodge, owned by Ninetta Eames and Edward B. Payne, an editor at the *Overland Monthly*.

To Charmian Kittredge

[Glen Ellen]
June 18 1903

I see that what I spoke of worries you.[1] It would worry me equally, I am sure, did it come from a friend. But the very point of it was that I did not know what it was. If I had, I should not have brought it up. If you will recollect, it was one of the lesser puzzles of your make up to which I merely casually referred. None of your guesses hits it. I have seen and measured your "inordinate fondness" for pretty things and for the correct thing. These are logical and consistent in you, and the fact that they are arouses nothing but satisfaction in me. I referred to something I did not know, something I felt as I felt the vision of you crying in the grass. Perhaps I used the word "conventionality" for lack of adequate expression, for the same reason that I spoke from lack of comprehension. A something felt of something no more than potential in you and of which I had seen no evidences. If you fail to follow me I am indeed lost, for I have strained to give definite utterance to a thing remote and obscure.

You speak of frankness. I passionately desire it, but have come to shrink from the pain of the intimacies which bring the greater frankness forth. Superficial frankness is comparatively easy, but one must pay for stripping off the dry husks of clothing, the self-conventions which masque the soul, and for standing out naked in the eyes of one who sees. I have paid, and like a child who has been burned by fire, I shrink from paying too often. You surely have known such franknesses and the penalties you paid. When I found heart's desires speaking clamorously to you, I turned my eyes away and strove to go on with my superficial self, talking, I know not what. And I did it consciously,—partly so, perhaps,—and I did it automatically, instinctively. Memories of old pains, incoherent hurts, a welter of remembrances, compelled me to close the mouth whereby my inner self was shouting at you a summons bound to give hurt and to bring hurt in return.

I wonder if I make you understand. You see, in the objective facts of my life I have always been frankness personified. That I tramped or begged or festered in jail or slum meant nothing by the telling. But over the lips of my inner self I had long since put a seal—a seal indeed rarely broken, in moments when one caught fleeting glimpses of the hermit who lived inside. How can I begin to explain? Perhaps this way. My child life was uncongenial. There was nothing responsive around me. I learned reticence, an inner reticence. I went into the world early, and I adventured among many different classes. A newcomer in any class, I naturally was reticent concerning my real self, which such a class could not understand, while I was superficially loquacious in order to make my entry into such a class popular and successful. And so it went, from class to class, from clique to clique. No intimacies, a continuous hardening, a superficial loquacity so clever, and an inner reticence so secret, that the one was taken for the real, the other never dreamed of.

Ask people who know me today, what I am. A rough, savage fellow, they will say, who likes prizefights and brutalities, who has a clever turn of pen, a charlatan's smattering of art, and the inevitable deficiencies of the untrained, unrefined, self-made man which he strives with a fair measure of success to hide beneath an attitude of roughness and unconventionality. Do I endeavor to unconvince them? It's so much easier to leave their convictions alone.

I tell you this, and in the telling I am not at your feet in shame. I am glad of it! glad of it! For you did so greaten, and my love for you did so greaten, that the struggle you felt was coming was no struggle at all. I was vanquished before the battle. It was inevitable that it should be no struggle, just as everything between us has been inevitable.

And yet, dear Love, had you been less in anything that struggle would have come. Had you failed by a hair's breadth in anything, had you made but the one coy flutter of the average woman, or displayed the fear or shock of the average woman, we should have struggled, and somewhat sordidly it is true, instead of lifting up our eyes to the Gates of Morn as we are doing now and going onward and upward, hand in hand, into the blazing light.

You might have won that struggle, dear; and you might have lost. Your dear sweet will,—and it is as big as you,—might have been broken, and it might have broken mine. In any event it would have meant hurt and grievous wrong.

But I thank "whatever Gods there be,"[2] that it was not so destined. For I did not know ALL that was in you, my Great One; I did not know all that was in me. I know now, and I am so glad, so glad.

If I could only make it clear just where you greatened and passed beyond and rose above my first intention! But you were so frank, so honest, and, not least, so unafraid. Had you been less so, in one touch, one pressure, one action, one speech, I think I should have attempted to beat down your will to mine.

Ah, I remember so many things. When we rode side by side, on a back seat, and I suggested "Haywards," and you looked me in the eyes, smiling, not mocking, with no offended fastidiousness in your face, no shock, no fear, no surprise, nothing but good nature and sweet frankness—when you looked me thus in the eyes and said simply, "Not tonight."

When you said you could be "game."

When you said that you were not afraid to go all the way with me, were you and I alone concerned.

Speech fails me. A thousand things demand to be said, and to be said at the same time, like some great chord, in order to tell you all you are to me and why you are all this to me. I doubt if I ever succeed in telling you all.

You do well to trust in me, and I shall "figure" well. We shall live life together, dear. Yours now to wait, mine to work, though it be work that shall wring my heart strings. You understand, you understand. And know, though I do not need to tell you, that it shall be right, all of it; that should I hurt my honor I hurt yours; that, like you, I can be truer to you than to myself, even though it meant for me to forego you forever and ever— which it will not, shall not, mean; and that in being true to you, and only by being true to you, may I be true to myself.

I reach out my hand to meet yours across the hills and hours, Love, and our hearts touch with our fingers, and you are real and beside me and all about me now.

MS: CSmH; 2 pp., typs. This letter and many of the subsequent letters to CKL exist in typescripts prepared by her. The letters appear sequentially, without salutation, complimentary close, or signature.

1. For JL's account of the events of this period and the beginnings of his love, see JL to C. Sterling, September 15 and 29, 1905.
2. W. E. Henley, "Invictus," l. 3.

To George P. Brett

Glen Ellen,
Sonoma Co., Calif.
June 19/03

Dear Mr. Brett:—

Mrs. London & the children are up here camping in the woods, and I have run up to make them a visit.

I have just received the first clippings of a dozen or so newspaper reviews of the *Kempton-Wace Letters*.[1]

These reviews strike me as extremely favorable. (Have you seen them?) It seems to me that everything is ripe for the book to make a hit, if we strike while the iron is hot. There are no really big sellers on the market now, and it seems to me that the book has a likely chance of becoming a big seller in this quiet interval and of surging into the summer season at the top of the list. The reviews are eminently favorable. Many of them predict a big success for the book, first, because of the popularity of the subject, and second, because of the refreshingness, the dignity, and the style with which the subject is handled.

Do tell me, please, what you think of the way in which the book has started out.

I know, myself, that it has started far more promisingly than any of my other books have ever started.

Very truly yours,
Jack London

MS: NN; 2 pp., als.
1. Most of the early reviews of *The Kempton-Wace Letters* were positive, citing the elegant writing style and sensible philosophy as the book's strongest points.

To Charmian Kittredge

[Glen Ellen]
Monday June 1903

I do not know whether I shall hear from you, whether or not you will come to me tonight; but this I do know—that I love you.

And this also do I know—that you *will* come to me, some time, some where. It is inevitable. The hour is already too big to become anything less than the biggest. We cannot fail, diminish, fall back into night with the dawn thus in our eyes. For it is no false dawn. Our eyes are dazzled with it, and our souls. We know not what, and yet WE KNOW, WE KNOW,

WE KNOW. The life that is in us knows. It is crying out, and we cannot close our ears to its cry. It is reaching out yearning arms that know the truth and secret of living as we, apart from it and striving to reason it, do not know. O my Golden-Eyed Great One! we give and live, we withhold and die.

You may laugh and protest, but you ARE big. A thousand things prove it to me—to me who have never needed the proof. I knew—knew from the first. I who, have felt and sounded my way through life like some mariner on a fog-bound coast, have never felt or sounded when with you. I knew you from the first, knew you and accepted you. This is why, when the time for speech came, there was no need for speech.

There is the Lesser Law, and the Law—the one for lesser creatures; the Law itself for the great ones only, for you and me. We ARE the Law. It is what speaks from within us. It is that which proudly proclaims "Tuesday!" while the Lesser Law shamefacedly says "Monday." Ah, my Golden-Eyed One! the lips were reluctant. They knew the wrong they did. It was the heart spoke true.

I do not know whether you will come tonight, and, such is the certitude of our tangled destiny, I hardly think I care. Did I doubt, it would be different. But it must be so, I know, not sooner or later, but soon. It is the will of your life and mine that it shall be so, and we are not so weak that we cannot keep faith with the truth and the best that is in us.

You are beside me, now. My arms are about you. I kiss you on the lips, the free frank lips I know and love.

MS: CSmH; 1 p., typs.

To Charmian Kittredge

[Piedmont]
June 1903

Monday night found me thus: No telephone, no letter; she will come. And then, as Monday night wore along, I wondered what was the matter, wondered if my *feel* of you had been wrong; for I had felt so strongly and so surely that I would have staked my life upon it, staked all that I am and hope to be. And then came the call from you, and then the delayed and blessed letter. And I saw what I already knew, that all I had said of you in my Monday letter was true.

I have been wondering why I love you, and I think, in dim ways, that I know. I love you for your beautiful body, and for your beautiful mind that goes with it. It is the very frankness of your mind, I think, that gives the greatness. Never mind our earlier intercourse, where frankness could well have been a pose, but beginning very recently, you have shown the frankness that could not possibly have been posed. Had you been coy and fluttering, giving the lie to what you had always appeared to be by manifesting the slightest prudery or false fastidiousness, I really think I should have been utterly disgusted. It would have been to me a terrible belittling of you. But you were not! you were not! You were great through it all! You are more kin to me than any woman I have ever known.

"Dear man, dear love"—I lie awake, repeating those phrases over and over. To you I can say nothing greater than dear woman, dear love.

MS: CSmH; 1 p., typs.

To Charmian Kittredge

[Glen Ellen]
[early] July-03

Do you know a happy moment you have given me?—a wonderful moment? When you sat looking into my eyes and repeated to me: "You are more kin to me than any woman I ever knew." That those words should have shaped to you the one really great thought in the letter, the thought most vital to me and to my love for you, stamped our kinship irrevocably. Surely we are very One, you and I!

Shall I tell you a dream of my boyhood and manhood?—a dream which in my rashness I thought had dreamed itself out and beyond all chance of realization? Let me. I do not know, now, what my other loves have been, how much of depth and worth there were in them; but this I know, and knew then, and knew always—that there was a something greater I yearned after, a something that beat upon my imagination with a great glowing light and made those woman-loves wan things and pale, oh so pitiably wan and pale!

I have held a woman in my arms who loved me and whom I loved, and in that love-moment have told her, as one will tell a dead dream, of this great thing I had looked for, looked for vainly, and the quest of which I had at last abandoned. And the woman grew passionately angry, and I should have wondered had I not known how pale and weak it made all of her that she could ever give me.

For I had dreamed of the great Man-Comrade.[1] I, who have been comrades with many men, and a good comrade I believe, have never had a comrade at all, and in the deeper significance of it have never been able to be the comrade I was capable of being. Always it was here this one failed, and there that one failed until all failed. And then, one day, like Omar, "clear-eyed I looked, and laughed, and sought no more."[2] It was plain that it was not possible. I could never hope to find that comradeship, that closeness, that sympathy and understanding, whereby the man and I might merge and become one for love and life.

How can I say what I mean? This man should be so much one with me that we could never misunderstand. He should love the flesh, as he should the spirit, honoring and loving each and giving each its due. There should be in him both fact and fancy. He should be practical in-so-far as the mechanics of life were concerned; and fanciful, imaginative, sentimental where the thrill of life was concerned. He should be delicate and tender, brave and game; sensitive as he pleased in the soul of him, and in the body of him unfearing and unwitting of pain. He should be warm with the glow of great adventure, unafraid of the harshnesses of life and its evils, and knowing all its harshness and evil.

Do you see, my dear one, the man I am trying to picture for you?—an all-around man, who could weep over a strain of music, a bit of verse, and who could grapple with the fiercest life and fight good-naturedly or like a fiend as the case might be. Don't you see, dear love, the all-around man I mean?—the man who could live at the same time in the realms of fancy and of fact; who, knowing the frailties and weaknesses of life, could look with frank fearless eyes upon them; a man who had no smallnesses or meannesses, who could sin greatly, perhaps, but who could as greatly forgive.

I spend myself in verbiage, trying to express in a moment or two, on a sheet of paper, what I have been years and years a-dreaming.

MS: CSmH; 1 p., typs.
    1. For a fictional portrayal of JL's dream of the perfect Man-Comrade, see his "The Heathen," *London Magazine*, September 1909, included in *South Sea Tales* (New York: Macmillan, 1911). See also JL to Johns, April 17, 1899.
    2. For the quote and its source, see JL to Johns, March 30, 1899.

To Charmian Kittredge

[Glen Ellen]
[early] July 1903

I am filled with a great pride. It seems to me somehow that all my values have been enormously enhanced. And do you know why? Because you love me. O God, that's the wonder of it, the wonder of it, that you should find me worthy of you! Oh, believe me, dear, I have reason for this very great pride.

And it is so much greater because it has not the novelty of being for the first time loved. I may say to you, what I would not dare to say to any one else in all the world, what, because of my self-consciousness, I have rarely said to myself—and then felt shame that I had said it—and that is, that it is my ill fortune, or good fortune, as you please, to win love easily. It has caused me some happiness, some vexation, and a great deal of worry and anxiety. Nor have I bid for it; it simply seemed to fall my way.

It is true, I have known the little thrills of gladness which come of knowledge of being loved; but never have I known pride, much less such a pride as now possesses me, and all because you love me.

Oh, don't you see, dear one, the wonder of it, the greatness and the glory? For look you, how different it would have been, how much less in every way, had you been a pretty, shy-shrinking creature, sweetly innocent and ignorant, dreaming vaguely and beautifully of life and knowing nothing of life. There could not possibly have been pride in the fact. It would have been pleasing to me that such a sweet pleasing creature should care for me—pleasing as that a flower should yield up to me its fragrance, pleasing and nothing more.

But YOU, YOU, who are so much more, who know life and have looked it squarely in the face, who are open-eyed and worldly wise, and mature in thought and knowledge, that YOU should love me, of all men, and find that in me which is worthy of your love, is the awful, almost terrible, miracle. Pride? Oh, if you could but know the pride I take in this!

And now, confession. And yet I confess what you already know, what you knew from the very first and from moment to moment through all its changes. But it will relieve me to tell you how my love has greatened. When first I broke silence, it was with the intention of making you my mistress, or, rather, of trying to make you my mistress. Oh, believe me, believe me, I loved you then, but I loved you so much less than now, because I did not know how much greater you were then as now.

I reasoned that I was bound in a miserable chain of circumstance, which I was too selfish to break—both from fear of hurting myself, and of hurting others which would likewise have been hurt to me. Had I been free, of course it would have been different from the very first.

But I was not free, and so I thought: being bound thus and so, if I can win her love we shall establish this relation. It will mean tragedy to both of us, but it will mean happiness also, and why should we not in our brief little lives take this happiness? And so I could conceive of this relation lasting for some time, for a long time possibly, when, at the end, you would marry, and we would break it off and drown everything in final tears and regrets, and be thereafter naught but good friends.

MS: CSmH; 1 p., typs.

To Cloudesley Johns

Glen Ellen,
Sonoma Co., Calif.
July 2/03

Dear Cloudesley:–

Here I am, camping & knocking out 1500 words per day seven days in the week.

If you're coming to see me, come just the same. Am only 2 1/2 hrs. ride from San Francisco. So bring your traps right on up to camp here. Have a girl to do the cooking, plenty of grub, and plenty of blankets. So come along.

Expect to stay here for a month yet. Then for the sloop![1]

Drop a line, telling when you are coming, so that I can be at Glen Ellen to meet you.

You remember the rig we rode in the day I cut my thumb. Five [of] us were coming in on it, same road, down hill, horse hitting it up—when king-bolt broke & we spilled. I had five different places on arms & legs in bandages, also a stiff knee. Am almost recovered now!

No, the Kempton letters were written entirely by Anna Strunsky, though the ear-marks of each are to be found in the other's work—unconscious absorptions of style, I suppose.

Jack London.

MS: CSmH; 3 pp., als. Pbd: *BJL*, I, 395.
   1. The *Spray*.

To George P. Brett

Glen Ellen,
Sonoma Co., Calif.,
July 8/03

Dear Mr. Brett:—

I am enclosing herewith a duplicate of a private letter from Julian Hawthorne to Mr. Wilshire.[1] You will notice that he speaks of the book as written by one mind—so that he does not guess the identity at all. The last time he reviewed anything of mine he slated me good & hard.

I notice with pleasure that you have been shoving the book hard.

Very truly yours,
Jack London

MS: NN; 1 p., als.
   1. Julian Hawthorne (1846–1934), author and critic; son of Nathaniel Hawthorne. He probably wrote his comments on *The Kempton-Wace Letters* in his letter to Gaylord Wilshire. Previously Hawthorne, in a scathing review titled "New Books: A Daughter of the Snow [*sic*]," *Wilshire's Magazine*, February 1903, pp. 84–87, called that book "a crude and incoherent novel" and stated that if JL were "satisfied with his present level of performance, there is little hope for him" (p. 87).

To George Sterling

Glen Ellen,
July 8/03

Dear George:—

As It was in the Beginning[1] came last night. I began at once reading aloud from it. All were delighted, and I am delighted that you, and no one else, should have sent it to me. I don't know, but some how I always feel indebted to you for an endless number of pleasant things & happy hours.

Find enclosed a duplicate of a private letter from Hawthorne to Wilshire.

> Love to all,
> Jack London

MS: CCC; 1 p., als.
  1. Joaquin Miller, *As It Was in the Beginning* (1903).

To Joaquin Miller

> Glen Ellen,
> Sonoma Co., Calif.,
> July 11/03

Dear Joaquin Miller:—

It's great! It's great! You know what you are singing about, and you have sung it as only you could sing.

I am writing the *Examiner* for the privilege of reviewing it, if said privilege has not been given elsewhere.[1]

It is truly a song of the West, and all the strength, & health, & joy, & beauty of the West, our West, is in it.

I do not congratulate you. My hand is on your shoulder and you know that I mean more than congratulations can say.

> Jack London.

MS: CU; 2 pp., als.
  1. JL's plans for a review did not come through.

To George Sterling

> Glen Ellen,
> July 11/03

Dear George:—

When I began reading aloud from *As It was in the Beginning* I made a note to write a congratulatory letter to Joaquin. This letter was in process of fulfillment when your letter arrived suggesting same.

I am also writing *Examiner*, if it has not already been given elsewhere, for privilege of reviewing same. I am sure he deserves a page.

No, I don't approve of Pegasus ploughing, if he *can* fly. But I believe in his plugging like hell in order to fly.

Thank Blanche Partington for the advertisement of the *Letters*. Macmillan Company is evidently trying to shove it.

What Freda[1] told you rather puzzles me. I was younger & less serious in the North perhaps; but this I know, that in these later day you have frequently given me cause for honest envy. And you have made me speculate a great deal. You know that I do not know you,—no more than you know me. We have really never touched the intimately personal note in all the time of our friendship. I suppose we never shall.

And so I speculate & speculate, trying to make you out, trying to lay hands on the inner side of you, the self side of you—what you are to yourself in short. Sometimes I conclude that you have a cunning & deep philosophy of life, for yourself alone, worked out on a basis of disappointment & disillusion. Sometimes, I say, I am firmly convinced of this, and then it all goes glimmering, and I think that you don't want to think, or that you have thought no more than partly, if at all, and are living your life out blindly and naturally.

So I do not know you, George; and for that matter I do not know how I came to write this.

Jack

MS: CCC; 4 pp., als.
1. Sterling may have met Freda Moloof in Oakland, where she occasionally danced. See JL to Strunsky, March 15, 1900, n. 4.

To George P. Brett

Piedmont, Calif.
Jul 24 1903

Dear Mr. Brett—

Indeed, indeed you have made a beautiful little book of the dog story. Not only is it the first book of mine which has been adequately illustrated, but I think it is about the most beautiful of its kind I have ever seen. The color printing is the most satisfactory I have yet seen. The decorative scheme, too, seems most appropriate.[1]

I have just finished getting off the 25 copies you sent me, to my various journalistic friends. I took the liberty of making each copy a presentation book on the idea that they would carry farther & to better advantage.

I should like to have ten additional copies for my personal friends. Can these be sent me soon & be charged to my account.

I should like to get possession of two or three of the original drawings for the book—say the frontispiece, or Francois, or Perrault, or To the Death, or—well, or any of them. Will you let me know, please, how I may do this? By purchase? By writing to the artists who made them? Or how?

I am writing appreciation to the three men and addressing them under cover of your house.

I was away up in the mountains when Mr. Carpenter[2] arrived in California, but managed to run down & meet [him][3] at the Bohemian Club.

I like him very much, and am sorry my camping trip prevented me seeing more of him.

Sincerely yours,
Jack London.

P.S.—I have the sea novel about half-done, now, and, as usual, do not know what to make of it. This I do know: it will be utterly different in theme and treatment from the stereotyped sea novel.

MS: NN; 4 pp., als.
    1. See JL to Brett, April 10, 1903, n. 4. Charles Edward Hooper decorated *The Call of the Wild*.
    2. Probably George Rice Carpenter (1863–1909), professor of English at Columbia University. Brett had sent Carpenter manuscript copies of *The People of the Abyss* and *The Kempton-Wace Letters*, and Carpenter had advised against publishing either work.
    3. Originally "meet me."

To Cloudesley Johns

Piedmont, Calif.
July 24/03

Dear Cloudesley:—
    Just a line to let you know I am suddenly back from camping, that my affairs are all in confusion, that I do not know yet what I shall do, that I need & can use no help other than my own strength may give me, and that you do not come North till you hear from me again.

Jack London

MS: CSmH; 1 p., als.

To Charles Warren Stoddard

Piedmont, Calif.
July 24/03

Dear Charles Warren:—
    I thought I recognized Cloudesley's mother in "Little Mama"; but as I knew her only through his description, I was not sure.
    And I *knew* that Paul was you, & that it was all real.
    Dane Kempton was written by Anna Strunsky, a young Russian Jewess, & the most brilliant woman I have ever known. Of course, the anonymity is bound soon to be spoiled; for we were too well known together on the Coast.
    Just now she is traveling in Europe.
    Am sending you, in the midst of great confusion, *Call of the Wild* & *Children of the Frost*. This, I think, makes your file of my books complete.

With all the love in the world, & a man's love,

Jack London.

MS: PBL; 2 pp., als.

To Cloudesley Johns

[Piedmont]
July 29th. [1903]

Thank you, old man. Am moving house & splitting up, just now. Poor, sad little Bungalow!

Should I need you I will call upon you unhesitatingly.

Jack London.

MS: CSmH; 1 p., als. Pbd: *BJL*, I, 397.

To George P. Brett

1216 Telegraph Ave.
Oakland, Cal.
Aug 10 1903

Dear Mr. Brett:—

I am expressing you to-day one-half of sea-novel with synopsis of un-written half.

As you will note by change in address above, I have been moving house and so was unable to get synopsis done until now.[1]

I hardly know whether the sea novel will lend itself readily to serial publication, but shall be very, very glad if it does.

The book will contain between 90,000 & 100,000 words.

You ask me to quote price for serial publication. I hardly know what to say. I know far less about selling a novel serially than does Mr. Gilder about buying a novel serially.[2] All I know, however, is that I am getting a minimum rate of three cents a word from the best magazines, where my best work goes. This is what I received from the *Call of the Wild*. In case the novel should prove available for the *Century*, I do not know whether Mr. Gilder would buy it for a lump sum, or pay a rate per word for the quantity he published.

Sincerely yours,
Jack London.

MS: NN; 3 pp., als.
    1. JL had rented a six-room flat at 1216 Telegraph Avenue, which he shared with Frank Atherton and his wife. In addition, he rented a house at 919 Jefferson Street, Oakland, for his mother and Johnny Miller.
    2. Richard Watson Gilder (1844–1909), editor of the *Century Magazine* from 1881 to

1909. Gilder paid $4000 for serial rights to *The Sea-Wolf*, which appeared in the *Century* from January to November 1904. See JL to Brett, September 2 and 10, 1903, and to Johns, September 5, 1903.

To George P. Brett

1216 Telegraph Ave.
Oakland, Cal.
Aug 10 1903

Dear Mr. Brett—
   Thank you for a squint at Mr. Greene's kind letter, which I am returning as you request.
   I do hope you'll make a strike on that dog story, for you have been such help to me that I want to see you getting some adequate return.
                                        Sincerely yours,
                                        Jack London.

MS: NN; 1 p., als.

To Fannie K. Hamilton

1216 Telegraph Ave.
Oakland, Cal.
Aug 14 1903

Dear Fannie K. Hamilton:—[1]
   Thank you, and indeed thank you for *Tales of Unrest*.[2] Now is my Conrad complete. I have glanced at the first tale, & been compelled to choose between it & my day's work, and have nobly put it down until bed-time.
   As you will notice by above address, the Bungalow is no more. I never loved a habitation so greatly in my life. And alas! it is no more. Ere this you may have heard things concerning me in the Eastern papers. At least believe this of me: that whatever I have done I have done with the sanction of my conscience, that I have performed what I consider the very highest of right acts.
                                        Sincerely yours,
                                        Jack London.

MS: CU; 1 p., als.
   1. Fannie K. Hamilton, newspaper feature writer and reporter. Hamilton interviewed JL at the Bungalow in early 1903; the interview, including a description of the house, was published in "Jack London: An Interview," *Reader*, August 1903.
   2. Published in 1898. The first tale in Conrad's book was "Karain: A Memory."

The hop pickers, JL and "Bert,"
England, 1902 (Trust of Irving Shepard)

Johnny Miller (CSmH)

At a military checkpoint in Korea during the Russo-Japanese War, 1904 (CSmH)

JL's caption: "Some of my friends"; Korea, 1904 (CSmH)

Removing a splinter for daughter Joan (JL State Park)

With daughters Bess (Becky) and Joan, ca. 1905 (CSmH)

George Sterling (CSmH)

Caroline Rand Sterling (CSmH)

At the Bohemian Grove, 1904 (CSmH)

Joaquin Miller, George Sterling, and Charles Warren Stoddard (CSmH)

The photographer (CSmH)

Cartoon views of JL (CU)

Jack London Reveals Himself Gradually in the Hum of a Newspaper Office.

At Wake-Robin Lodge, Glen Ellen, California, with
his dog Brown Wolf, ca. 1905 (CSmH)

Outside Wake-Robin Lodge, ca. 1905 (CSmH)

Letter of January 26, 1905, to an unnamed correspondent (JL State Park)

To George P. Brett

1216 Telegraph Ave.
Oakland, Cal.
Aug 15 1903

Dear Mr. Brett:—

[I]¹ have a number of sociological and economic essays, all of them right up to date in their facts and conditions, and written in a popular style. In fact, they are sufficient to make a book of from forty-five to fifty thousand words.²

I am wondering if such a book would be available, and if so, if you would care to figure upon where you could fit it in among my others you are bringing out.

Some of the essays are particularly and most essentially up to date, dealing with the very industrial conditions which are at present occupying the most prominent place in the public mind, as instance, "The Scab," and "The Class Struggle." Concerning this last, which is awaiting publication in the *N.Y. Independent*, Mr. Hamilton Holt³ wrote me that he could "truthfully say that it was the best & clearest exposition of the industrial situation & tendencies he had ever seen."

Another of the essays is a recent *Cosmopolitan* prize winner.⁴

Though I am compelled to say it myself, every last one of the essays is bright, interesting, and bound to arouse disagreement and discussion.⁵ I have put my best thinking & work into them.

I have just seen copies of the second edition of *The Call of the Wild*. I like the new cover immensely. You have improved splendidly upon an already splendid book. But in this connection I need say nothing. I notice that all the reviews speak highly of the get-up of the book. I do hope that you will get a good return for all the labor and trouble you have taken with it.

Sincerely yours,
Jack London.

P.S.—I may say this of the batch of essays: they are studies which I have made in the course of attempting to grip hold of this gigantic, complex civilization of ours. And I am attempting to grip hold of it in order to exploit it in fiction, in what, if I succeed, will be the biggest work I shall ever do. It is a great field, and it is really & practically virgin.

MS: NN; 4 pp., als.
1. Originally, "If."
2. *War of the Classes.*
3. Hamilton Holt (1872–1951), managing editor of the *Independent* from 1897 to 1913 and its editor and owner from 1913 until 1921. The *Independent*, published in New York from 1848 to 1928, was a weekly Congregationalist magazine that contained illustrations and secular articles on current events, especially the reform movement.

4. "What Communities Lose by the Competitive System." It was not included in *War of the Classes*.

5. In addition to "The Scab" and "The Class Struggle," *War of the Classes* contained "The Tramp," "The Question of the Maximum," "A Review," "Wanted: A New Law of Development" (*International Socialist Review*, August 1, 1902), and "How I Became a Socialist."

To Cloudesley Johns

1216 Telegraph Ave.
Oakland, Cal.
Aug 21 1903

Well, Good luck to you, old man.[1] If you love, that is all there is to it. I thought you donned my Herbert Wace philosophy rather squeamishly.

And so we go zigzagging through life. When we first knew each other we were on the same tack. Then I filled away on the other tack and married. Now I have come about once more, and I find that you have put your helm down & are away on the opposite tack. May your reach be a longer one than mine—much longer.

Jack London.

MS: CSmH; 1 p., als. Pbd: *BJL*, I, 397.

1. Johns probably had told JL of his engagement to Mazie Brosenne of Los Angeles. In 1904 the engagement was broken off.

To Elwyn Hoffman

1216 Telegraph Ave.
Oakland, Cal.
Aug 23 1903

Dear Elwyn:—

Sorry to hear you are having such bad luck with your work. Nothing to it, I suppose, but to keep plugging away. Or, if you have to do other work, why don't you go in for journalism. I should think there would be better pay in reporting, & easier work, than in ordinary manual labor. Why don't you tackle it?

My own affairs are somewhat in confusion, as you may imagine, & I am so pressed for time I cannot write a longer letter. But if I can do anything for you, sing out.

Luck be with you—

Jack London

MS: CSmH; 1 p., als.

To Cloudesley Johns

1216 Telegraph Ave.
Oakland, Cal.
Aug 26 1903

Dear Cloudesley:—

Yes, I shouldn't mind living for a while in Los Angeles; but, you see, I'm settled, am three months behind in all my work, letting my contracted work go and hammering away at hack in order to catch up with a few of my debts, and do not see my way to getting even with my work for all of a year hence.

Hard-a-lee with me will not affect my work—in fact, I am confident it will be far otherwise.

I laugh when I think of what a hypocrite I was when, at the Bungalow, I demanded from you your long-deferred congratulations for my marriage—but, believe me, I was a hypocrite grinning on a grid.[1]

Concerning your affair, let me say this: it's all right for a man sometimes to marry philosophically, but remember, it's damned hard on the woman.

Jack London

ms: CSmH; 3 pp., als. Pbd: *L*, 151–52; *BJL*, I, 398.

1. See JL to Johns, April 16, 1900, n. 1, and January 27, 1903.

To Merle Maddern

1216 Telegraph Ave.
Oakland, Cal.
Aug 28 1903

Dear Merle:—[1]

No, I had not thought of the ending you suggest. It might do, but I doubt. You see, he could sing only the *song* of the wild, not the *call* of the wild. There is a distinction. The song of the wild was the call to him, but he could not very well sing his own call.

I am so glad you liked the story.

The only reason I named him Buck was that years before I had filed away among my notes as appropriate dog names, "Buck & Bright." I had thought of using them some time on a pair of dogs. But when I looked over my list of dog-names for a good one for my hero, I chose Buck—I guess because it was stronger than Bright.

We know little or nothing about what dogs think. But then we may conclude from their actions what their mental processes might be, and such conclusions may be within the range of possibility.

With love,
Jack.

MS: CCamarSJ; 4 pp., als.

1. Merle Maddern, Bessie London's niece and the daughter of William A. Maddern and Corinne M. Maddern. During the writing of *The Kempton-Wace Letters*, she acted as a go-between, delivering JL's and Anna Strunsky's notes on her bicycle. Later she became a successful actress in New York.

To Charmian Kittredge

[Oakland]
Tuesday, Sept 1/03.

The memories of last night with you are good. There seemed to enter a sort of placidity, a restfulness born of perfect intimacy & sureness, such as I have never had with you before. Oh, you are good, my Dear One, so good, so good—the feel of you, the touch of you, mind & body.

Yes, we must have been planned for each other from the beginning—at least you for me. You meet me so on every side of me. I have met so many women, who had this side, or that side, or the other side; but none had every side. Here they missed, and there they missed, just where you hit and hit. I dreamed in vague ways of you long & long ago, and then I gave over dreaming. And then you came, when I did not look for you, realizing it all in beautiful flesh and blood.

We are so alike in so much, that, as you have remarked, perhaps we are too alike to be for each other. But there is a great difference between us, which, in connection with our likeness, makes us pre-eminently for each other, and that difference is your essential femininity and my equally essential masculinity. There is where our great unlikeness comes in. You are, when all is said & done, of women the most womanly; and I, I hope, am somewhat of a man. Unlikeness attracts, and here is where we are attracted irresistibly—this is what gives us our wonderful physiological affinity, that makes the feel of our flesh good and a joy. Without this, no matter how tremendous our spiritual affinity, life together could mean nothing to us but irk and irritation & almost hatred.

Don't you see, we balance off so well. The feel of flesh & spirit are both good with us. You, as well as I, I know, have met people whom we liked intellectually but the feel of whose hands was repulsive. And we have met people the feel of whose flesh was a pleasure, such as we might experience when feeling a splendid dog or horse; but at the same time, with these same people, there was no feel of the mind or spirit at all. They were beautiful & joyful animals only. But you & I, ah, dear dear Love, we are perfect animals, and we have our measure of soul too and we love, we perfectly love, as man & woman were made to love. "God made our bodies each for each, & put your hand into my hand." [1]

Dear hand, dear Love.

Monday letter O.K.

MS: CSmH; 8 pp., al.

1. Arthur Symons, "Magnificat," in *London Nights* (1895), ll. 15–16. The precise quote is "He made our bodies each for each, / Then put your hand into my hand."

To George P. Brett

1216 Telegraph Ave.
Oakland, Cal.
Sep 2 1903

Dear Mr. Brett:—

Concerning my separation from Mrs. London, I have really nothing to say except that the *Kempton-Wace Letters* have nothing whatever to do with it.[1] That the causes of the separation have been operative long previous to the writing of the book. As the reporters could not ascertain the real reason, they dug one out of the book, that is all. So far as the public is concerned I have no statement to make except that the *Kempton-Wace Letters* play no part whatever in the separation.

I am enclosing herewith an amplification of the synopsis of the sea novel, also a copy of the synopsis, so that both may go to Mr. Gilder together.[2] I shall return you his letter in a couple of days if I may be permitted, or pardoned, rather, the liberty of holding it that long.

He has my full permission to blue pencil all he wishes, and, while it is practically impossible to give any synopsis of such a novel as this, I have striven to show him that the situation, because of the characters themselves, will not permit of anything offensive. Furthermore, in this there is no alteration of my original conception of handling the story. I elected to exploit brutality with my eyes open, preferring to do it through the first half and to save the second half for some thing better. I am taking plenty of time on the book and shall not rush it. In fact, because of the changes in my life which have just been occurring, yesterday morning is the first actual work on the book I have done in a month. But there are no more interruptions in sight, and I shall now proceed steadily with it. I shall have it finished by the first of December.

Mr. Gilder's offer for the serial rights is satisfactory.[3] If he should take the book, I can have the final copy of the first installment in his hands in a month, or in two months, just as he elects.

Mr. Gilder speaks of rough drafts. I do not make any. I compose very slowly, in long hand, and each day type what I have written. My main revision is done each day in the course of typewriting the manuscript. This manuscript is the final one, and as much time is spent on it as is spent by many a man in making two or three rough drafts. My revisions in proof-sheets are very infrequent, chopping a word or a phrase out here, putting in one or the other there, and that is all. So that, for me, a rough draft is an impossible thing.

You can say to Mr. Gilder, however, that I shall be very amenable to any suggestions he may make concerning the serialization of the novel. I am absolutely confident myself, that the American prudes will not be shocked by the last half of the book.

Cosgrave[4] is the most conservative and conventional of editors. He wrote me concerning the novel and I thought I'd make him shy at it. Work of mine he has refused for *Everybody's*, I have sold promptly, and right on top of it, to the *Atlantic*.

Personally, and outside of money considerations, I should greatly like to see the novel serialized in the *Century*. It means much in the way of advertisement and of bringing me into the notice of the clique of readers peculiar to the *Century*.

Very truly yours,
Jack London

MS: NN; 2 pp., tls. Pbd: *L*, 152–53.

1. In his letter to JL of August 27, 1903 (CSmH), Brett wanted to know if the newspaper reports that *The Kempton-Wace Letters* had caused JL's separation from Bessie were true. In the *New York Herald*, August 16, 1903, an article entitled "*Kempton-Wace Letters* Cause of Divorce Suit" speculated that JL's relationship with Strunsky during their collaboration was sexual as well as professional. Elsie Martinez, wife of artist Xavier Martinez, member of "the Crowd," stated in "San Francisco Bay Area Writers and Artists" (MS: CSmH) that Strunsky "was very much in love with [JL], yet claimed there was no affair, which we all believed. Bessie had told us of the evening when Anna and Jack were working on *The Kempton-Wace Letters*. She found her sitting in Jack's lap. That was enough for Bessie. . . . Jack once confided to Sterling that he wouldn't marry her because he was pure Anglo-Saxon and she was Semitic, although he loved her" (p. 131).

2. Gilder wrote Brett on August 26, 1903 (CSmH), that "the dead level of sickening brutality" in the first half of *The Sea-Wolf* was causing him difficulty.

3. See JL to Brett, August 10, 1903 (first letter), n. 2.

4. John O'Hara Cosgrave.

To Cloudesley Johns

1216 Telegraph Ave.
Oakland, Cal.
Sep 5 1903

Tell you what I'll do. I'll take a flying trip down to Los Angeles, say somewhere in January—if not December, as soon as my sea novel is done and providing the *Century* takes it serially for 1904. The dicker is now on, and the only thing Gilder hesitates about is the last half (unwritten) wherein a man & woman are all by themselves on an island. I have just tried to assure him that I won't shock the American Prude, and, anyway, that he can blue-pencil all he wants.

If *Century* doesn't take the novel, why, when I get done with it I'll have to plunge into hackwork up to my ears to escape bankruptcy. If *Century* does take it, why then I can take a vacation.

As for living in Los Angeles—nay, nay. I am wedded to 'Frisco Bay.

I should like to take the ride you mention. I love motion and can never go too fast.

Darned if I know anything about the *Century*. Never sold them anything. But $100.00 for 7000 words is pretty small.

No, haven't seen Aug. *Metropolitan.*[1]

I wouldn't care much for a woman capable of saying: "A woman can lose everything, even her loved ones & her life, & still be rich in her purity." I may respect her, but I could not admire her. She is a little cloudy & small in her ethical concepts even though it be not her fault.

Jack London

MS: CSmH; 5 pp., als. Pbd: *BJL*, I, 398–99.

1. Johns published "In the Heat Mist" in the *Metropolitan Magazine*, August 1903. The *Metropolitan* was an illustrated monthly magazine published in New York from 1895 until 1924.

To Edwin Markham

1216 Telegraph Ave.
Oakland, Cal.
Sep 5 1903

Dear Mr. Markham:—

Thank you for your kind offer to lend me the "Prattle" scrap books.[1] I did not want them to look over, but for a present to a friend, the dearest friend I have in the world, and a deep and ardent admirer of Bierce. I, personally, while I like a great deal of Bierce & of Bierce's work, would put little or no value on his "Prattle"; so, since it is a present, I do not find myself able to go beyond one hundred dollars. I should esteem it a great favor, if at any time your "sordid necessities" impel you to sell, to give a chance at the four scrap books for one hundred & one dollars. This is, you see, an increase on your standing offer.

Thank you heartily for the kind words you said for the *Kempton-Wace Letters.*

Sincerely, your friend
Jack London

MS: NNWML; 3 pp., als.

1. JL wrote Markham on July 5, 1903 (NNWML), to ask if Markham would care to sell his file of the "Prattle," a regular column on a variety of topics that Ambrose Bierce had written for the *Wasp* and later for the *Examiner* between 1887 and 1896. Apparently JL wanted to buy the collection for George Sterling.

To Anna Strunsky

1216 Telegraph Ave.
Oakland, Cal.
Sep 5 [1903][1]

Dear Anna:—

As usual, hard at work. It's been so long since I had a *real* vacation that I hardly know what such a thing would be like. Even when I was in Europe last year, instead of resting I wrote a book. Well, in about a year I am starting off around the world, and I expect to take seven years in going around, if not longer.[2]

How you must be enjoying yourself![3] For you surely have the capacity for feeling pleasure as well as pain to a tremendous degree.

Our Book—I haven't the least idea how it has sold; but, when all is said & done, it has been received far more favorably than might have been expected. It is a good book, a big book, and, as we anticipated, too good & too big to be popular—

Jack London.

MS: CSmH; 2 pp., als. Pbd: *BJL*, I, 399.
   1. Incorrectly stamped "1908."
   2. For JL's plans for a seven-year voyage, see JL to Millard, February 18, 1906.
   3. Strunsky was vacationing in New York.

To George P. Brett

1216 Telegraph Ave.
Oakland, Cal.
Sep 10 1903

Dear Mr. Brett:—

I am enclosing herewith Mr. Gilder's letter which you asked to have returned. I have also, this day, sent you telegram giving permission to print authors' names on title page of second edition of *Kempton-Wace Letters*; and giving permission to Mr. Gilder to use *The Triumph of the Spirit* as serial title for sea story, but suggesting, in place of it, *The Sea Wolf* or *The Sea Wolves*.

Frankly, I do not like Mr. Gilder's title at all. The very thing he feared about the last half of the sea novel (the making of a tract of it), I fear about his title. It seems to breathe a purpose, an advertisement of a preachment; in fact, it might do for the title of a tract—or, at least, that is the way it strikes me.

The Sea Wolf is a strong and brief title.

I have also expressed you to-day that collection of essays, which I have thought of calling *The Salt of the Earth*.[1]

I am indeed grateful to you, Mr. Brett, for your efforts in behalf of my sea story. It is a good thing to have it come out in the *Century*, and I hope the additional synopsis I forwarded will clinch the matter.

Sincerely yours,
Jack London.

MS: NN; 3 pp., als. Pbd: *L*, 153–54.
    1. Changed to *War of the Classes*.

To George P. Brett

1216 *Telegraph Ave.*
Oakland, Cal.
Sep 16 1903

Dear Mr. Brett:—

I shall have first final installment of *Sea Wolf* in Mr. Gilder's hands by Oct. 4th., and shall follow it up rapidly with succeeding installments.

To help me in revision, I expect to have a couple of friends look over, suggest, & criticize; so I need the copy now in Mr. Gilder's hands. Can it be returned to me at once?

Thank you for the arrangement of payments you have suggested to Mr. Gilder. It is quite satisfactory to me.

I am putting in my best licks on the novel, and so far it is not showing the least sign of disappointing me.

Very truly yours,
Jack London

MS: NN; 2 pp., als.

To Blanche Partington

1216 *Telegraph Ave.*
Oakland, Cal.
Sep 19 1903

Dear Blanche:—

Am glad you like the Lee essays.[1] I thought they would interest you.

Now concerning this meeting Mrs. Crawley.[2]

Friday, Sept. 26th., I have to lecture here in Oakland, not more than a dozen blocks from the Macdonough. Of course, I'll be done before the play is out, so I could run around and meet you and the rest.[3] I should prefer your Sunday proposition; but, unfortunately, I have agreed to go down to Santa Clara on 27th. with Howard, the Spring Valley Water Works Man; so that is prevented.

Nothing remains, but to meet you & the others Friday after the theatre, and I am indeed grateful for the privilege.

Now—information. Between lectures, prize-fights, & one thing and another, I have but one free night next week—Saturday night, Sept. 26th. Is *Everyman* played that night? And if so, where? I certainly *must see* it if I can.[4]

And now, George and Carrie and the rest are going sailing with me on the *Spray* Sunday Oct. 4th. I have already spoken to Phyllis. Will you & Gertrude and John come along?[5] Data as to where & when, later.

Jack London.

MS: CU; 4 pp., als.
   1. Possibly Gerald Stanley Lee, *The Lost Art of Reading* (1902).
   2. Probably Constance Crawley (1880–1919), an actress best known for her Shakespearean roles.
   3. At this time, *East Lynne* was playing at the Macdonough Theatre in Oakland.
   4. The Charles Frohman production of the medieval play *Everyman*, directed by Ben Greet, was playing at Lyric Hall in San Francisco.
   5. George and Carrie Sterling; Phyllis Partington, well-known soprano, who sang with the Chicago Lyric Opera Company and the Metropolitan Opera under the stage name "Peralta"; Gertrude Partington, painter and illustrator, who later taught at the California School of Fine Arts; John ("Jack") Partington, piano player in California mining-town saloons, who later worked as a detective, in motion-picture production, and in theater management. Phyllis and Gertrude were Blanche Partington's sisters; John was her youngest brother, whom she had virtually reared.

To Cloudesley Johns

1216 Telegraph Ave.
Oakland, Cal.
Sep 21 1903

Dear Cloudesley:—

You say you'll be away in December & first half of January. May I send you, right away, the first half of sea novel for criticism? Let me know right away.

I have to start the first four or five chapters East at once, so I'll miss your advice for that much of the serial publication, but I have it for all the book & the remainder of the serial publication. At least, I hope I shall.

Your *Cattle Den* must be a whopper from what you say of it—"34 characters besides supes & 7 *motifs*."

I'm sending you, this mail, a copy of *Call of the Wild*. You don't seem to care for the *Daughter of the Snows*. I don't blame you. I wonder how you'll like the *Sea Wolf*. I'll bet you'll wonder how the *Century* dares to publish it.

Jack London

MS: CSmH; 2 pp., als.

To Robert U. Johnson

1216 Telegraph Ave.
Oakland, Cal.
Sep 22 1903

Dear Mr. Johnson:—[1]
I haven't telegraphed you any title[2] because I have been unable to devise one. I have racked my brains, and racked my brains, in vain.

I appreciate keenly your reasoning, and your need for a title which will suggest the second half of the book. I know precisely what you want and why you want it; but for the life of me I can't give it to you.

There must be such a title, but it won't come into my mind.

My chief objection to *The Triumph of the Spirit* is that I at once associate it with tracts. It would make a very good title for a tract, don't you think? It seems to advertise a moral, I think, and to me such a thing is more wicked than to advertise a sin.

Possibly, as I work along through the last part of the novel, an appropriate title will come to me, and if it does I'll telegraph it to you at once.

In the meantime, I shall be only too glad to receive any suggestion from you.

Sincerely yours,
Jack London.

MS: CU; 4 pp., als.
  1. Robert U. Johnson (1853–1937), associate editor of *Century*.
  2. For *The Sea-Wolf*.

To Charmian Kittredge

[Oakland]
Thursday, Sept. 24/03.

Nay, nay, dear Love, not in my eyes is this love of ours a small and impotent thing. It is the greatest and most powerful thing in the world. The relativity of things makes it so. That I should be glad to live for you or to die for you is proof in itself that it means more to me than life or death, is greater, far greater, than life or death.

That you should be the one woman to me of all women; that my hunger for you should be greater than any hunger for food I have ever felt; that my desire for you should bite harder than any other desire I have ever felt for fame and fortune and such things;—all, all goes to show how big is this our love.

As I tell you repeatedly, you cannot possibly know what you mean to me. The days I do not see you are merely so many obstacles to be got over somehow before I see you. Each night as I go to bed I sigh with relief because I am one day nearer you. So it has been this week, and it is only Monday that I was with you. To-day I am jubilant, my work goes well. And I am saying to myself all the time, "To-night I shall see her! To-night I shall see her!"

My thoughts are upon you always, lingering over you always, caressing you always in a myriad ways. I wonder if you feel those caresses sometimes!

Our love small! Dear, it might be small did the love of God enter into my heart, and the belief in an eternity of living and an eternity of the unguessed joys of Paradise. But remember my philosophy of life & death, and see clearly how much my love for you & your love for me must mean to me. Ah Love, it looms large. It fills my whole horizon. Wherever I look I feel you, see you, touch you, and know my need for you. And there is no love of God to lessen my love for you. I love you, you only & wholly. And there are no joys of a future life to make of less value the joy I know & shall know through you. I clutch for you like a miser for his gold, because you are everything and the only thing. Remember, I must die, and go into the ground, and cease to feel and joy & know; and remember, each moment I am robbed of you, each night & all nights I am turned away from you, turned out by you, give me pangs the exquisiteness of which must be measured by the knowledge that they are moments and nights lost, lost, lost, forever. For my little space of life is only so long. To-morrow or next day I cease forever; and the moment I am robbed of you and the night I must be away from you will never, never come again. There is no compensation. It is all dead and utter loss. So I live from day to day like an unwilling prodigal. I am wasting my substance and I cannot help it—nor am I wasting it even in riotous living. My fortune of life is only so large. How large I know not, but no matter how large, the sum of the hours & moments which compose it is determined. Each lost moment, is a moment squandered. My fortune is diminished that much without return. And so, day by day, helplessly, I watch the bright-minted moments flowing out and see the day of my bankruptcy approaching which is the day when I shall have no more moments and perforce must die.

But it is even harder. For I know I am twenty-seven, at the high-tide of my life and vigor; and I know that these wasted moments now are the brightest-minted of all my moments.

I have not wandered through all this in order to plead for something I have not & might have, but to show how large to me, in the scheme of life, bulks this love of ours.

MS: CSmH; 13 pp., al.

To Charmian Kittredge

[Oakland]
Monday, September 28, 1903

Ah, Sweet, I have already and long pondered the fact that you have witheld nothing from me of your belief in me and your love for me. It has meant much to me,—all to me,—that you have not said: "Thus far he shall know me; the rest of myself I reserve for myself." I know I matched you, only matched you, in the utterness of my surrender. Indeed, indeed, we are blessed above mortals!

I always held, always I say, that there were rare loves, such as the Browning love,[1] once in a generation of folks. But I little dreamed that such a love would be my love affair. And it is, it is! Nor am I inflated with vainglory when I say it. I am merely filled with a pure and simple pride, and a reverent wonder.

Truly, as you say, it takes two. And it took you to meet me and bring out the best that was in me. I, for myself, know that I feel myself a better man since I have known you. My dear wonderful one. I thank you, I thank you.

I was talking yesterday with a man from Japan. He has verified my plan of going to live, first, in Kobe. There is frost in the winter time in Kobe, but no snow. There are enough white people—a cosmopolitan crowd of a couple of thousand to interest us and make us feel not quite bereft of our own kind.

How dearly intimate you grow to me as I plan the little details of our house-keeping! We shall live on the hill that slopes down to the city and the ocean. We shall certainly have a piano if such a thing is rentable. We shall have two or three servants and a couple of the ponies if they are at all ridable. And we shall have a second *Spray* on the bay, and make long cruises, with a couple of Japanese sailors and a Japanese maid for you— where will we make those cruises? In that wonderful dreamland, the Inland Sea. Think of it, dear love of mine.

But dearest of all, will be you by my side.

MS: CSmH; 1 p., typs.
  1. Between Robert and Elizabeth Barrett Browning.

To Charmian Kittredge

[Oakland]
Tuesday, Sept. 29/03

Just a line, dear—and not tit for tat. I have to hurry away to take Joan to the dentist.

Just received a letter from Anna. She has known of the separation for some weeks, so she says. But this is the first time she has mentioned it. But believe me, trust me, my own girl, all will be well in that direction. I am overwhelmed with thankfulness in that she has taken it in quite sisterly fashion. I quote:

"Cameron[1] sent me a newspaper clipping some weeks ago. I am sorry for all the unhappiness, and I am strong in my faith. You never meant to do anything but the right and the good—poor, ever dear, dreamer! You never will do wrong. I cried over the news, half in gratitude for your strength and half in sorrow, perhaps all in sorrow, for all the sadness with which you are weighted."

MS: CSmH; 3 pp., al.
   1. Cameron King, Jr.

To Charmian Kittredge

[Oakland]
Wednesday, Sept. 30, 1903

Yes, Mrs. Browning was very delicate physically, but Browning was a robust heavily-built man.

Do you know, I have always wanted to live clean all my life. And I have always felt, with rare exceptions, that I was living clean. And at the end of a watch of coal-shoveling, say, naked to the waist and black as an Ethiopian, I have felt that I was very clean.[1] Because of the very work I had just done. I felt clean—clean inside, and you know what I mean.

The most repulsive grossness to me, I think is a grossness of the tissues. I have watched club-men thus grow gross from high-living, from gluttony, in short, but, worst of all, this grossness seems never to stop there, but goes on into the face and seems to stamp the very soul.

I love good living and I am afraid of it; so I leave it alone, save at rare intervals, when it is very delightful and all that, as it is for a child to play with fire. These days I feel not only virtuous but very glad each time I sit down to a simple meal prepared by Maggie.[2] I know that it is for the good of my body and the good of my soul, and for the good of something more—for my love for you. Never so much as now, never so strongly as clean as you are clean, and you are very clean, my woman, clean inside!

I guess the watch'll have to keep till Friday. Friday—when I shall see you with the light again on your face and love you in the ways different from those of the woods!

And in different ways still I shall love you Thursday night in the good salt water. And in still other and different ways I shall love you forever and forever.

MS: CSmH; 1 p., typs.
  1. In 1894 JL had shoveled coal in the boiler room of the power plant of the Oakland, San Leandro & Haywards Electric Railway.
  2. Maggie Atherton, Frank's wife.

To Cloudesley Johns

1216 Telegraph Ave.
Oakland, Cal.
Oct 7 1903

Dear Cloudesley:—
  Thanks old man for the work you've done on the manuscript. It's just arrived. I'll send you some more, if I may, a little later. Do you want me to have a look at the *Cattle Den*?
  "Have a Smile" seems principally Crawley Jagson.[1]

Jack London.

P.S.—By the way, got a line from one, Van Loan, Standard Oil Co., Los Angeles, who had read "Local Color" & decided you were my model.[2] Said he had met you, wanted to meet you again.
  I dropped him your address. Then thought. And now I am wondering whether or not I did wrong.

MS: CSmH; 2 pp., als.
  1. "Crawley Jagson" was the pseudonym Johns had adopted when submitting humorous verse and paragraphs to the political humor magazine *Up to Date* in the late 1890's.
  2. Charles E. Van Loan, assistant bookkeeper for the Standard Oil Company in Los Angeles. Johns had read some of Van Loan's work and had encouraged him to become a writer. Van Loan did so, starting as a sports writer, sports editor, and special writer for the *Los Angeles Herald* and *Los Angeles Examiner*, and later selling stories to national magazines. He met JL through Johns at the Ascot Race Track in Los Angeles in January 1905. JL's "Local Color" was published in *Ainslee's*, October 1903, and later included in *Moon-Face*.

To George P. Brett

1216 Telegraph Ave.
Oakland, Cal.
Oct 8 1903

Dear Mr. Brett:—
  Yes, I think it would be much better to talk things over together. You mention being out in California in January. I Hope we do not miss each other, for I am considering a proposition to go East in that month & deliver ten lectures. The trip, as outlined, will take about a month, and will be as a vacation to me, also will be educational, and in a small way may have advertising value.[1]
  But at all events, if you miss me here, I shall make a point of seeing you in New York.

By the way, I have just remembered the "Story of Jees Uck," which you were going to bring out in your Little Novel series. Have you decided at all as to when it is to come out?[2]

I am very glad to hear the *Century* is likely to retain the title, *Sea Wolf*.

Very truly yours,

Jack London.

MS: NN; 3 pp., als.

   1. JL did not make a lecture tour in the East until 1905. On November 20, 1903 (NN), JL wrote Brett that he had definitely decided against going East and looked forward to visiting with him in California in January.

   2. See JL to Brett, February 16, 1903. In a letter to Brett of October 20, 1903 (NN), JL stated: "I am just as glad that 'Story of Jees Uck' is not to come out as a 'Little Novel.' It will fit quite well into my next collection of short stories."

To Cloudesley Johns

1216 Telegraph Ave.
Oakland, Cal.
Oct 9 1903

Say, Cloudesley:—

   Thursday, Oct. 22nd., I set sail in the *Spray* for a couple of months' cruising about the Bay, & up the Sacramento, San Joaquin & Napa rivers. Do you want to come along, just you & I?

   We can both get our writing in each day and have a jolly time. Also, I'll have a shotgun & rifle along and we can get in plenty of duck-shooting. It won't cost you anything, and if you need it, I can send you transportation. Also, I have that Smith-Premier typewriter, & if you can use such a machine you won't have to bring your own along.

   What d'ye say? Let's hear soon.

Jack London.

MS: CSmH; 3 pp., als. Pbd: *BJL*, I, 400.

To Charmian Kittredge

[Oakland]
Monday—Oct. 12/03.

   Five minutes, my love, & then I must shave & pull out for Frisco—beg pardon, San Francisco.

   Yesterday was very calm. Only two men & myself. They steered. I laid around in cabin & on top of cabin & thought, & thought, & thought of you—always you. And I thought of you as I had you & knew you mine on Saturday. Blessed day! And over & over I lived every moment of it, from the three bells to the parting. God! You do love me!

   I never needed any proof of it, yet each new proof is sweet, so sweet.

And this last proof is not alone sweet; it is heroic. You *are* brave, my own brave mate woman.

So long as you are alive I could never hit out on the Long Trail into the West without you. Did you die, & did I not die, too, I could *never, never*[1] hit that same *Long Trail*.[2] It would be impossible.

Lost the wind yesterday. Got home at 1:10 this morning.

Had I gone away, & been away from you these last two months, we could not have been as near or as dear to each other.—Next Thursday.

MS: CSmH; 4 pp., al.
    1. JL underlined each "never" twice.
    2. Kipling's poem "The Long Trail" (1892) describes embarking on an autumn voyage; its refrain repeats "the old trail, our own trail, the out trail . . . the Long Trail—the trail that is always new!"

To Cloudesley Johns

1216 Telegraph Ave.
Oakland, Cal.
Oct 13 1903

Dear Cloudesley:–

All right, old man. I shall look for you, then, on Oct. 21st.[1] You may desert or receive a dishonorable discharge, whichever you will, whenever you wish. If I were not confident that I'll get in just as much work in the *Spray* as on shore, I wouldn't be making the trip; because I simply *have* to get this sea novel done.

We ought both of us get in plenty of work, and have a good time, and get health & strength.

Jack London.

MS: CSmH; 2 pp., als. Pbd: *BJL*, I, 400.
    1. Johns joined JL on the *Spray* on October 21. For an account of their cruise, which lasted until early December, see his "Who the Hell *Is* Cloudesley Johns?" pp. 283–314.

To Charmian Kittredge

[Oakland]
Tuesday, Oct. 20/03

Last night was not an anti-climax, and I am glad, glad! Sunday night was so perfect that I knew it could not be exceeded. But last night was different, and I shall carry the memory of it with me up river, and down river, & on the Long Trail, and forever.

As sweet of you to send me the picture as the picture is sweet. Another side of the many-sided You—just pose, & bust, and arms, & bust most of all, but what a bust! Joaquin Miller should rave about it as he raved about his heroine's legs.

Do you know, dear, that I am smitten these days with a sort of shame in that you give so much to me and that I give you nothing. It is the woman that gives and the man that takes, & you have given me yourself and all that that means. Yours the risk, yours the terrible penalty that woman always pays if the world comes to know; mine is no risk, no penalty at all. God! You must love me! And I take all this, and give nothing. Is there not something I can do, or give, or risk, for you? I would willingly cut off a hand,—anything, in order to meet you half way and be as generous in my gifts as you are generous.

And now I must hie me away down town. My sister is to be here in an hour. I have just learned that her birthday has passed, forgotten by me, & I must get her something.[1]

Somewhere in mythology, in a strange land, fighting, a hero dies—"and dying remembered sweet Argos." And I, dying, will remember sweet Charmian.

MS: CSmH; 5 pp., al.
    1. Eliza Shepard's birthday was October 13.

To Blanche Partington

1216 Telegraph Ave.
Oakland, Cal.
Oct 22 1903

Dear Blanche:—

I'm so sorry that my arrangements prevented my seeing Mr. Edison and *Soldiers of Fortune.*[1]

You see, I was and am scheduled to sail, on the *tide*, this morning; and as my arrangements involved others, I could not alter them. Also, for same reason, could not cut my last night at home.

I should like very much to tackle such a play; but, you see, it is utterly impossible for some time to come. My arrangements with my publishers (and I'm three months behind), which extend for at least another year, prevent my turning my hand to anything else than the novels now projected & partly completed.

But I shall write a play some day, & I will![2]

Sincerely yours,
Jack London.

P.S.—I was sorry you were unable to make that Sunday cruise on the *Spray.*

MS: CU; 3 pp., als.
    1. Robert Edeson (1868–1931), prominent New York actor. Edeson starred in Augustus Thomas's stage version of the popular novel *Soldiers of Fortune*, by journalist and author Richard Harding Davis, which was playing at the Columbia Theatre in San Francisco.
    2. JL did not publish a play until 1906, when Macmillan brought out *Scorn of Women.*

To Charmian Kittredge

[On board the *Spray*]
[? October 27, 1903]

*   *   *

I had all sorts of horrible nightmares last night about you—Seemed you were in Paris, another man's wife, but that you loved me. That we spent a terrible, endless night trying to meet each other, & trying vainly. And then, at gray dawn, we met, in a park or garden. But we had just met, & our arms were about each other in the first embrace, when your maid gave the signal of warning and you had to fly. And while the day was yet young I had the pleasure(?) of being run down by your husband and a dozen friends, before your eyes, & of being killed before your eyes. At least, at the moment I was killed, I woke up, and was very glad to know that you were my wife and not another man's.

These lines of Symons seem to tell me all of our Greater Intimacy:

> "I drank your flesh, & when the soul brimmed up
>   In that sufficing cup,
> Then slowly, stedfastly, I drank your soul;
>   Thus I possessed you whole." [1]

And with this thought strong in my soul, I kiss you dear, and say good night.

But he is not the one small woman who means all the world to me, who is all the world and upon whom I base my hope of Paradise. If you can only make me happy, Love? Haven't you made me happy? Happy in ways more exquisite than I have ever experienced or dreamed that I might experience. It required you to show me just how much I could love and forget all else in the loving. Happy? The very thought of you is a happiness. Your name, the sound of it, the look of it is a joy to me. Yesterday I saw it, printed in blue, on the fly-leaf of the *Monk & the Dancer*. [2] I looked at it, at the look of it, & I was certainly entranced, for I spent a solid hour staring at it and thinking of you.

I mailed a letter to you Sunday, at Collinsville; but I guess there was no Sunday steamer to take it, so you did not receive it Monday.

We must do something. We cannot possibly wait a year after we have already lived through the one year and lived it apart. If a deep sea marriage is legal, or a Honolulu marriage, then we must have such a one. If not, then Nevada or California, it matters little which, for one or the other will show that we intend well (according to Mrs. Grundy's dictates), [3] and then, a year later we can celebrate the really legal marriage.— This for the world, for we are already married, my own woman, my wife—married as much as two souls can ever be married, and married far more than the vast majority of marriages which are made by the mummery of the legal ceremony. Dear, sweet Love, you are mine, I am yours, we are one, and there's no more to be said so far as you & I are concerned. Of course, there is the world. We will respect the world & the way of the world, but the world's way can never make us one iota more to each other or one iota more married than we are now.

But, oh, to have you mine with the world's sanction, so that your proud head shall not be bowed! To have you mine always & always & forever!

It makes me thrill with gladness when you tell how you hesitated and half turned back that night in the hammock. And I am more than glad that you did not turn back. Our way, our own way, the way we have come together, was the best. And yet, had you turned back, the result would not have been altered. My need of you was too great, too deep, too intrinsic, for me to have ever been contented with less than *all* of you. And, God! God! I have all of you, and I am loved as it is given to few men to be loved! I could pray, did I have aught to pray to. I have only you, & I am on my knees to you.

MS: CSmH; 11 pp. fragment of 13 pp., al.
   1. Arthur Symons, "From Stephane Mallarme," in *Images of Good and Evil* (1899), 9.1–4.
   2. Arthur Cosslett Smith, *The Monk and the Dancer* (1900).
   3. Mrs. Grundy, a symbol of conventional propriety, was originally a character in Thomas Morton's play *Speed the Plough* (1798).

To Lurline Lyons

On Board the *Spray*,
Stockton,
Nov. 10/03

Dear Lurline:—
   How often I have envied you up there in Glen Ellen this long summer! And in your *poppy* hat. Don't forget, it is to be mine when you get off the earth—if I haven't preceded you. But I won't. I intend to live forever and to be always young.

   I read with interest Mr. Montgomery's letters,[1] and I do thank you for letting me secure them; and I am glad he is not offended with me for my sermon, etc. It seems as though there are many who do things for Lurline's sake. He sent me the verses for your sake, and it was for your sake that I sermonized him. Well, it's worth it, dear Lurline.

   Don't speak of that "Coronation Day" lecture.[2] It was terrible. I had a most miserable cold, and I did neither myself nor the subject justice.

   And yet, in relation to the lecture, there is one thing in your letter I liked very much. I hope it will always be true of me. That I am without pose. It is so good and sweet for people always to be natural, to be just themselves. And it is for this, dear Lurline, that I liked you from the first, in those Camp Reverie days at the swimming hole & in camp. You were, and you are, always just yourself & just natural. It is the biggest & the best thing in the world to be.

My love to Aunt Netta & Uncle Edward,[3] and a goodly portion thereof to you.

Uncle Jack.

MS: CSmH; 5 pp., als.
  1. Percy F. Montgomery, whom Lurline Lyons married in 1904.
  2. JL delivered "Coronation Day" to the Pacific Coast Women's Press Club on October 12, 1903.
  3. Ninetta Eames. Edward Biron Payne, an editor at the *Overland Monthly*; he had earlier been a minister, and he became Ninetta Eames's second husband in 1910.

To Marshall Bond

[Alviso]
Dec 17 1903

Dear Marshall:—[1]

Lo and behold! I am just reading your letter of Oct. 12th.

About that time I jammed my unopened mail into a gun case and pulled out on a duck-hunting cruise of six weeks. During this cruise, of course, I opened my gun-case correspondence & answered it. Then I was home for a few days. During which time gun-case remained on the yacht. Last Monday pulled out on another cruise. Am now in lower end of the Bay near Alviso. To-day my partner,[2] cleaning guns, discovered your letter, crumpled up at very bottom of the case where it had been jammed by the gun. It is a miracle that it was ever found. Might have remained there for years.

Yes, Buck was based upon your dog at Dawson.[3] And of course Judge Miller's place was Judge Bond's[4]—even to the cement swimming tank & the artesian well. And don't you remember that your father was attending a meeting of the Fruitgrowers Association the night I visited you, and Louis was organizing an athletic club—all of which events figured with Buck if I remember correctly. As you say you expect to be in S.C. for Christmas I'll mail this to you there. Hope to see you soon. Have received a couple of letters from Del Bishop, & Charley Meyers looked me up recently—[5]

Sincerely yours—
Jack London.

P.S.—Was it a boy?[6]

MS: CU; photocopy of 4 pp., als. Pbd: *L*, 154.
  1. Marshall Bond, a gold miner from Santa Clara, California, whom JL met in the Klondike in 1897. For his relationship with JL, see Marshall Bond, Jr., *Gold Hunter: The Adventure of Marshall Bond* (Albuquerque, 1969), pp. 34ff.

2. Cloudesley Johns.

3. "Jack," a cross of St. Bernard and collie, owned by Marshall Bond and his brother Louis, a mining engineer.

4. Judge Hiram G. Bond, Marshall's father.

5. According to Franklin Walker, Del Bishop was "a pocket miner who appeared under his own name in *A Daughter of the Snows*"; Charley Meyers was portrayed as "a trader in London stories, a nameless French-Canadian, and an equally nameless Swede" (*Jack London and the Klondike*, p. 142).

6. Richard M. Bond, Marshall's brother, was born on November 5, 1903.

To George P. Brett

[On board the *Spray*]
Dec 20 1903

Dear Mr. Brett:—

This finds me out on the *Spray* duckhunting as usual.

Jan. 1. I am all engaged up—and can't break very well. But Jan. 2, I'll keep open for you all day & evening. Come & see me, or I'll go & see you, just as is most agreeable to you.

By that time, praise the Lord, I'll have the *Sea Wolf* finished.

Sincerely yours,
Jack London.

MS: NN; 2 pp., als.

To Robert U. Johnson

1216 Telegraph Ave.
Oakland, Cal.
Dec 20 1903

Dear Mr. Johnson:—

By the time you take the topmast off the foremast, and further reduce the butt by the dismasting, you will have a 65 or 70-foot spar, say 15 inches in diameter at the butt & weighing somewhere around 3500 pounds.

Rig a sheers out of the fore & main-topmasts thus ∧ . Put a hoisting tackle at apex of sheers. Carry this tackle to an improved crank windlass capable of lifting 3 tons (one man heaving), and something's bound to happen. If I couldn't step—not one mast, but both masts,—single-handed, it would be because I didn't have somebody to "hold the turn." Van Weyden has Maud to hold the turn, & he is going to put in both masts.[1]

I'd hate to be Maud Brewster, wrecked in company with your "sea dog" who would "want the whole shipyard to help."

Seriously, though, the thing can easily be done. And I consulted, in rigging my schooner at the very start, the shipyard men. They gave me the

igures, length, weights, powers of windlasses, etc. I am just in the thick of
stepping the masts now—and it proves up.

Faithfully yours,
Jack London.

MS: LNHT; 4 pp., als.
  1. See *The Sea-Wolf*, chap. 37, in which Humphrey Van Weyden, the protagonist, with
he help of heroine Maud Brewster, steps the masts of the *Ghost*.

1904

At Wake-Robin Lodge, Glen Ellen, California, ca. 1904 (JL State Park)

To George P. Brett

1216 Telegraph Ave.
Oakland, Cal.
Jan 7 1904

Dear Mr. Brett:—

I sail to-day.[1] Here's the rest of the *Sea Wolf.*

Tell me how it strikes you.

Letters to me by regular address—will be forwarded.

By arrangement, you are to send each month $127.50 to my wife—this beginning of course with the first of February. Will you also please send each month $22.50 to Miss Kittredge, beginning with first of February.

I enclose herewith the arrangement of the book of short stories.[2]

The last six of these stories I shall mail you, revised, from Honolulu. The first two I have not in my possession; you will have to obtain them in New York.

Don't fail to send proofsheets of book to Miss Kittredge. She and another friend will go over them—a Mr. Sterling, my best man friend, my comrade—and a man with an eagle eye for errors.

In all haste—

Jack London

MS: NN; 4 pp., als.

1. JL was going to Asia to cover the Russo-Japanese hostilities for the *San Francisco Examiner.* On January 7, 1904 (CSmH; also pbd. in *JL Reports,* 3), he wrote Cloudesley Johns a brief note: "Sail today for Yokohama. Am going for Hearst. Could have gone for *Harper's, Colliers,* & *N.Y. Herald*—but Hearst made best offer."

2. *The Faith of Men.*

To Cloudesley Johns

S.S. Siberia
Jan. 8, 1904[1]

Dear Cloudesley—

I have told Charmian to send you the last chapters of the *Sea Wolf.* It looks like war.[2] A wad of correspondents aboard.[3]

Jack London.

MS: CSmH; 1 p., als.
    1. Underlined twice.
    2. On February 8–9, 1904, ten Japanese destroyers surprised the warships of the Russian fleet anchored at Port Arthur, and the situation erupted into war.
    3. Also sailing on the SS *Siberia* were Bill Lewis and Oscar K. Davis of the *New York Herald*; Lionel James of the London *Times*; Frederick Palmer, Robert L. Dunn, and James H. Hare of *Collier's Weekly*; Willard Straight of Reuter's News Agency; Percival Phillips of the London *Daily Express*; Sheldon I. Williams of the London *Sphere*; Ashmead Bartlett, a noted English journalist; and other reporters.

To Charmian Kittredge

S.S. Siberia
Jan. 13/04.

Somewhat weak and wobbly, but still in the ring. Came down with a beautiful attack of La Grippe. Of course, didn't go to bed with it, but spent the time in a steamer chair, for one day half out of my head. And oh, how all my bones ache, even now! And what wild dreams I had! . . .[1]

Honolulu is in sight, and in an hour I shall be ashore mailing this, and learning whether or not there is war.

. . . Am, Grippe excepted, having a nice trip. The weather is perfect. So is the steamer. Sit at the Captain's table, and all the rest—you know.

MS: ULA; 1 p., typs. Pbd: *JL Reports*, 4; *BJL*, I, 403.
    1. JL's letters from Korea seem to have been edited in transcription, with asterisks used to mark omissions. Asterisks within the body of these letters have been normalized to ellipses; asterisks at beginning or end, however, have not been noted.

To Charmian Kittredge

S.S. Siberia
Jan. 15/04.

Well, we sailed yesterday from Honolulu. . . . Am still miserable with my Grippe, but getting better. Had a swim in the surf at Waikiki. Took in the concert at the Hawaiian Hotel, and had a general nice time.

Had some fun. I bucked a game run by the Chinese firemen of the *Siberia*, and in twenty-five minutes broke three banks and won $14.85. So, you see, I have discovered a new career for myself.

The war correspondents, the "Vultures," are a jolly crowd. We are bunched up at the Captain's table, now that the passenger list has been reduced by the lot who left at Honolulu. In fact, the trip to Honolulu had three bridal couples which sat at the upper end of the table. This is a funny letter—the correspondents are cutting up all around me; and just now I am being joshed good and plenty.

MS: ULA; 1 p., typs. Pbd: *JL Reports*, 4; *BJL*, I, 403.

To Charmian Kittredge

S.S. Siberia
Jan. 20/04

Quite a time since I last wrote. You'll wonder why. Well, know that I am the most fortunate of unfortunate men. The evening of the day we left Honolulu I smashed my left ankle. For sixty-five sweaty hours I lay on my back. Yesterday I was carried on deck, on the back of one of the English correspondents. And to-day I have been carried on deck again.

The smashed ankle is the misfortune; the fortune (which has prevented me from writing you) is the crowd of friends I seem to have collected. From six o'clock in the morning till eleven at night, there was never a moment that my stateroom did not have at least one visitor. As a rule there were three or four, and very often twice as many. I had thought, when the accident happened, that I should have plenty of time for reading; but I was not left alone long enough to read a line.

I am looking forward with interest to the sixth day, when, if the surgeon does not change his mind, I may put my foot to the deck and try to walk with the aid of crutches.

Of course, what you want to know is what the smash consists in. I was jumping and coming down from a height of three feet and a half. I landed on my left foot—having "taken off" with my right. But my left foot did not land on the deck. It landed on a round stick, and lengthwise with the stick. Stick about diameter of broom-handle. Of course, my foot went up alongside of my leg. My ankle was strained on one side, sprained on the other. That is, the tendons on the inside were stretched and ruptured, the bones on the outside ground against each other, bruising themselves and pinching the nerves—result, an irresistible combination.

Now I have two weak ankles. I fear me I am getting old. Both my knees have been smashed, and now both my ankles. It might be worse, however. What bothers me just now is that I don't know just how bad this last ankle is. Absolute rest, in a rigid bandage, has been the treatment, so not even the surgeon will know till I try to walk on it.

. . . Don't worry because I have let my worry out in this letter. Anyway, I'll be able to write you later, before we make Yokohama, and let you know more. I hope the report will be promising.

MS: ULA; 1 p., typs. Pbd: *JL Reports*, 4–5; *BJL*, I, 403–4.

To Charmian Kittredge

S.S. Siberia
Jan. 21, 04.

You should see me to-day. Quite the cripple, hobbling around on a pair of crutches. I can't stand on the ankle yet, but hope to be able to walk by the time we make Yokohama. Today is Thursday, and we expect to arrive next Monday morning. I hope war isn't declared for at least a month after I arrive in Japan—will give my ankle a chance to strengthen.

All hands are very good to me, and I might say I am almost worn out by being made comfortable. . . . I am in for a game of cards now, so more anon.

MS: ULA; 1 p., typs. Pbd: *JL Reports,* 5–6, BJL, I, 404.

To Charmian Kittredge

S.S. Siberia
Jan. 23/04.

Yesterday I dragged about on crutches to the boat deck and to tiffin, and to bed. To-day I have ventured without crutches. But I walk very little—just from stateroom to boat deck.

A young gale is on, but the *Siberia* is behaving splendidly.

P.S. The young gale is still growing.

MS: ULA; 1 p., typs. Pbd: *JL Reports,* 6; BJL, I, 405.

To Charmian Kittredge

S.S. Siberia
Jan. 24/04.

Just packing up. Shall be in Yokohama at six to-morrow morning. Ankle is improving. Am walking (very slowly, and limpingly, and carefully), without crutches. I just missed breaking the leg—so you can see what a twist it was. Hope the war holds off for a month yet.

MS: ULA; 1 p., typs. Pbd: *JL Reports,* 6; BJL, I, 405.

To Charmian Kittredge

[Japan]
Thursday, Jan. 28/04.

If you can read this. The train is joggling, and the temperature inside the car is 40. I am on the express bound for Kobe—where, on Jan. 31, if not sooner, I expect to get a steamer for Korea. I am bound for Seoul, the capital. Was pretty busy in Yokohama and Tokio. Arrived Monday, and have been on the jump until now, though this writing looks as though I were still jumping.

Ankle is getting better very slowly.

I called, and called, and called, for your letter which should have come on the same steamer with me. But no letter to date. Either it is lost or it missed the steamer.

MS: ULA; 1 p., typs. Pbd: *JL Reports*, 6; *BJL*, I, 405.

To Charmian Kittredge

[Japan]
Jan. 29/04.

You should have seen me plunging out of Kobe this morning, myself and luggage in three 'rickshaws, with push-boys and pull-boys and all the rest, and racing to catch the express for Nagasaki. No steamer out of Kobe till Feb. 3rd, so am going to try my luck at Nagasaki, twenty-two hours ride on the train and no sleeping car.

Weather is warmer down here. It was bitter cold up Yokohama-way.

Have caught beautiful glimpses of the Inland Sea to-day, the sea whereon you and I shall soon be sailing. I think, however, we'll say in May at the earliest—spend summer in Japan, and winter say in India.

If I do not refer to war doings, know that there is a censorship, and cables, etc. are held up.

MS: ULA; 1 p., typs. Pbd: *JL Reports*, 7; *BJL*, I, 405.

To Charmian Kittredge

Shimonoseki,
Feb. 3/04.

Still trying to sail to Chemulpo.[1] Made an all-day ride back from Naga-saki to Moji to catch a steamer, Feb. 1 (Monday). Bought ticket, stepped outside and snapped three street scenes. Now Moji is a fortified place.

Japanese police "Very sorry," but they arrested me. Spent the day examin-ing me. Of course, I missed steamer. "Very sorry." Carted me down coun-try Monday night to town of Kokura. Examined me again. Committed. Tried Tuesday. Found guilty. Fined 5 yen and camera confiscated.[2] Have telegraphed American Minister at Tokio, who is now trying to recover camera.[3]

Received last night a deputation from all the Japanese Newspaper cor-respondents in this vicinity. Present their good offices, and "Very sorry." They are my brothers in the craft. They are to-day to petition the judges (three judges sat on me in black caps) to get up mock auction of camera, when they will bid it in and present it to me with their compliments. "Very uncertain," however, they say.

Expect to leave for Chemulpo on the 6th or 7th inst.

MS: ULA; 1 p., typs. Pbd: *JL Reports*, 7; *BJL*, I, 405–6.

1. Chemulpo (now Inchon), Korea, a seaport east of Seoul, was the site of the second naval defeat of the Russians by the Japanese a few days after the battle at Port Arthur.

2. See "How Jack London Got In and Out of Jail in Japan," *San Francisco Examiner*, February 27, 1904.

3. For an account of this episode by Lloyd Griscom, then American Minister to Japan, see his *Diplomatically Speaking* (Boston, 1940), pp. 242–46. For a Japanese account, see Eiji Tsujii, "Jack London Items in the Japanese Press of 1904," *Jack London Newsletter*, 8 (May–August 1975), 55–58.

To Charmian Kittredge

On board Junk, off Korean Coast
Tuesday, Feb. 9, 1904.

The wildest and most gorgeous thing ever! If you could see me just now, captain of a junk with a crew of three Koreans who speak neither English nor Japanese and with five Japanese guests (strayed travelers) who speak neither English nor Korean—that is, all but one, which last knows a couple of dozen English words and with this polyglot following I am bound on a voyage of several hundred miles along the Korean Coast to Chemulpo.

And how did it happen? I was to sail Monday, Feb. 8th., on the *Kiego Maru* for Chemulpo. Saturday, Feb. 6th., returning in the afternoon from Kiokura, (where my camera had been returned to me)—returning to Shimonoseki, I learned *Kiego Maru* had been taken off its run by the Jap. Government. Learned also that many Jap. warships had passed the straits bound out, and that soldiers had been called from their homes to join their regiments in the middle of the night.

And I made a dash right away. Caught, just as it was getting under way, a small steamer for Fusan. Had to take a third class passage—and it was a *native* steamer no white man's chow (food) even first class and I had to sleep on deck. Dashing aboard in steam launch, got one trunk overboard but saved it. Got wet myself, and my rugs and baggage, crossing the Japan Sea. At Fusan, caught a little 120 ton steamer loaded with Koreans and Japs, and deck load piled to the sky, for Chemulpo. Made Mokpo with a list to starboard of fully thirty degrees. It would take a couple of hundred of such steamers to make a *Siberia*. But this morning all passengers and freight were fired ashore, willy nilly, for Jap. Government had taken the steamer to use. We had traveled the preceding night conveyed by two torpedo boats.

Well, fired ashore this morning, I chartered this junk, took five of the Japanese passengers along, and here I am, still bound for Chemulpo. Hardest job I ever undertook. Have had no news for several days, do not know if war has been declared and shall not know until I make Chemulpo—or maybe Kun San, at which place I drop my passengers. God, but I'd like to have a mouthful of white man's speech. It's not quite satisfying to do business with a 24 word vocabulary and gesticulations.

MS: ULA; 1 p., typs. Pbd: *JL Reports*, 8–9; *BJL*, I, 406–7.

To Charmian Kittredge

[Off the Korean Coast]
Thursday, Feb. 11, 1904.

On board another junk. Grows more gorgeous. Night and day traveled for Kun San. Caught on lee-shore yesterday, and wind howling over Yellow Sea. You should have seen us clawing off—one man at the tiller and a man at each sheet (Koreans), four scared Japanese, and the fifth too seasick to be scared. Of course, we cleared off, or you wouldn't be reading this.

Made Kun San at nightfall, after having carried away a mast and smashed the rudder. And we arrived in driving rain, wind cutting like a knife. And then, you should have seen me being made comfortable last night—five Japanese maidens helping me undress, take a bath, and get into bed, the while visitors, male and female, were being entertained (my visitors). And the maidens passing remarks upon my beautiful white skin etc. And this morning, same thing repeated—the Mayor of Kun San, the captain of police, leading citizens, all in my bed-room, visiting while I was being shaved, dressed, washed and fed.

And all the leading citizens of the town came down to see me off, and cheered me, and cried "Sayonara" countless times.

New junk, manned by Japanese—five—and not one knows one word of English and here I am, adrift with them, off the Corean Coast.

No white man's news for a long time. Hear native rumors of sea-fights, and of landing of troops, but nothing I may believe without doubting. But when I get to Chemulpo, I'll know "where I am at."

And maybe you think it isn't cold, traveling as I am, by junk. The snow is on the land, and in some places, on North slopes, comes down to the water's edge.

And there are no stoves by which to keep warm—charcoal boxes, with half a dozen small embers, are not to be sneered at—I am beside one now, which I just bought for 12 1/2 cents from a Korean at a village, where we have landed for water.

MS: ULA; 1 p., typs. Pbd: *JL Reports*, 9; *BJL*, I, 407–8.

To Charmian Kittredge

[Off the Korean Coast]
Saturday, Feb. 13, 1904.

Still wilder, but can hardly say so "gorgeous," unless landscapes and seascapes seen between driving snow squalls, be gorgeous. You know the tides on this Coast range from 40 to 60 feet (we're at anchor now, in the midst of ten thousand islands, reefs, and shoals, waiting four hours until the tide shall turn toward Chemulpo—30 ri, which means 75 miles—away).

Well, concerning tides. Yesterday morning found us on a lee shore, all rocks, with a gale pounding the whole Yellow Sea down upon us. Our only chance for refuge dead to leeward, a small bay, and high and dry. Had to wait on the 40 ft. tide, and we waited, anchored under a small reef across which the breakers broke, until, tide rising, they submerged it. Never thought a sampan (an open crazy boat) could live through what ours did. A gale of wind, with driving snow—you can imagine how cold it was. But I'm glad I have Japanese sailors. They're braver and cooler and more daring than Coreans. Well, we waited till eleven A.M. It was twixt the devil and the deep sea—stay and be swamped, run for the little bay and run the chance of striking in the surf. We couldn't possibly stay longer, so we showed a piece of sail and ran for it. Well, I was nearly blind with a headache which I had brought away with me from Kunsan, and which had been increasing ever since; and I did not much care what happened; yet I remember, when we drove in across, that I took off my overcoat, and loosened my shoes—and I didn't bother a bit about trying to save the camera.

But we made it—half full of water—but we made it. And maybe it didn't howl all night, so cold that it froze the salt water.

All of which I wouldn't mind, if it weren't for my ankles. I used to favor the right with the left, but with the left now smashed worse than the right, you can imagine how careful I have to be (where it [is] impossible to be careful) in a crazy junk going thro' such rough weather. And yet I have escaped any bad twists so far.

Junks, crazy—I should say so. Rags, tatters, rotten—something always carrying away—how they navigate is a miracle. I wonder if Hearst thinks I'm lost.

MS: ULA; 1 p., typs. Pbd: *JL Reports*, 10–11; *BJL*, I, 408–9.

To Charmian Kittredge

[Off the Korean Coast]
Monday, Feb. 15th, 1904.

Oh, yes, we waited four hours! When four hours had passed, wind came down out of the north, dead in our teeth. Lay all night in confounded tide-rip, junk standing on both ends, and driving me crazy what of my headache.

At four in the morning turned out in the midst of driving snow to change anchorage on account of sea.

It was a cruel day-break we witnessed; at 8 A.M. we showed a bit of sail and ran for shelter.

My sailors live roughly, and we put up at a fishing village (Korean) where they live still more roughly, and we spent Sunday and Sunday night there—my five sailors, myself—and about 20 men, women and children jammed into a room in a hut, the floor space of which room was about equivalent to that of a good double-bed.

And my foreign food is giving out, and I was compelled to begin on native chow. I hope my stomach will forgive me some of the things I have thrust upon it.—Filth, dirt, indescribable, and the worst of it is that I can [not] help thinking of the filth and dirt as I take each mouthful.

In some of these villages, I am the first whiteman, and a curiosity.

I showed one old fellow my false teeth at midnight. He proceeded to rouse the house. Must have given him bad dreams, for he crept in to me at three in the morning and woke me in order to have another look.

We are under way this morning—for Chemulpo. I hope I don't drop dead when I finally arrive there.

The land is covered with snow. The wind has just hauled ahead again. Our sail has come in, and the men are at the oars. If it blows up it'll be another run for shelter. O, this is a wild and bitter coast.

MS: ULA; 1 p., typs. Pbd: *JL Reports*, 11; *BJL*, I, 409–10.

To Charmian Kittredge

Chemulpo
Tuesday night, Feb. 16 [1904]

Just arrived. Am preparing outfit—horses, interpreter, coolies, etc. for campaign into the North toward the Yalu and most probably into Manchuria.[1]

MS: ULA; 1 p., typs. Pbd: *JL Reports*, 12; *BJL*, I, 410.
    1. See "Troubles of War Correspondent in Starting for the Front," *San Francisco Examiner*, April 4, 1904.

To Charmian Kittredge

Chemulpo,
Feb. 17/04

Am preparing to advance north—campaign to the Yalu and perhaps into Manchuria. I shall accompany. Am busy getting interpreters, coolies, horses, saddles, provisions, etc. Only four outside newspapermen here. The rest, a host, cannot get here.

SOURCE: *JL Reports*, 12. Also pbd: *BJL*, I, 410.

To Charmian Kittredge

Ping Yang,[1]
March 4/04

Have made 180 miles on horseback to this place. I shall be able to ride a little with you when I return, for it appears there are months of riding before me. I have one of the best horses in Korea—was the Russian minister's at Seoul before he went away.

Very little chance to write these days—am not writing enough for the *Examiner* as it is. Worked to death with the trouble of traveling.

Have received no more letters from you nor anybody.

Am pulling North soon for Anju and maybe the Yalu. Am now in the midst of accounts with correspondents, interpreters, mapus[2] and what not, so cannot think. I do not know when I shall ever be able to write you a real letter—lack of time.

But I'm learning about horses—last two days traveled 50 miles a day, and I was saddle-sore and raw.

Am living in a Japanese hotel crammed with soldiers. (Only three of us 1 English correspondent—1 American photographer.)[3] Am ordering whiskey just now for them.

MS: ULA; 1 p., typs. Pbd: *JL Reports*, 12–13; *BJL*, I, 411.
  1. Pyongyang, Korea.
  2. Korean grooms for the horses.
  3. Robert L. Dunn, a photographer for *Collier's Weekly*, and F. A. McKenzie, a correspondent for the London *Daily Mail*. (They appear as Jones and Macleod in JL's "Troubles of a War Correspondent in Starting for the Front.") For Dunn's account of JL in Korea, see "Jack London Knows Not Fear," *San Francisco Examiner*, June 26, 1904; for McKenzie's, see "The Little Brown Man Marching North with the Japanese Army," *Daily Mail*, May 30, 1904.

To Charmian Kittredge

[Pyongyang]
March 4th, 1904.

I think as to the quietness, strictness and orderliness of Japanese Soldiers it is very hard to find any equals in the world. If it were our boys they should have gone light-heartedly to all over the places and [we would] sure have heard for many a time about kicking up row, but such things never happen in Japanese and it is wonderful how they keep so orderly. Therefore no citizen in the town has any fear at all about them and women, bar, property and all the rest are quite safe. It is well known fact that in last China–Japanese war the Japanese troops on every occasion paid for all articles got off citizens and they are still continuing this method now. You will hear from all Coreans that "if they were Russians what might have happened!" I never [have] seen even a single Jap soldier who got drunk or acted violent, yet its infantry is perfectness itself, as can be judged by our General Allen's [1] saying that the Japanese infantry excels anyone else in the world. In fact, although each of them carries the necessary things weighing 42 pounds on the march the sign of distress never can be found on any of them. None bend forward, none stoop their body, none fall behind from the company, none to be seen re-arranging the strap, none to be attracting the notice by making disagreeable noise caused by the carrying articles not properly put on, and its orderliness and perfectness of company is just as same as with that of each individual. With no fault on individual and no delay on the work, they go straight on the aim. Japanese is the race who can produce real fighting, and its infantry is simply superb. But, on the other hand the cavalry, I think, is not the department they are well acquainted with, it seems something funny to our eyes. The horses are small and strong but they cannot be compared with ours, and the riding style is also very unseemly, holding the rein mostly with one hand, either with right or left. All the horses are untrained stallions, therefore when they start to fight each other, they cannot be managed by Japanese hands very well. For instance, few days ago when their horses started to fight each other at the front of hotel it was only separated by hand of General Allen after great difficulty. But they are also the soldiers, so I think the day will come, ere long, when they are able to ride on good Russian horses by capturing them, and then not take trouble by savageness of their horses anymore, etc.[2]

MS: ULA; 1 p., typs. Pbd: *JL Reports*, 13–14.
    1. Brigadier General Henry T. Allen (1859–1930), an attaché to the American legation in Seoul with the status of official military observer. He arrived in Korea on February 8 and left April 1.
    2. For JL's praise of the Japanese army, see "Japanese Army's Equipment Excites Great Admiration," *San Francisco Examiner*, April 3, 1904.

To Charmian Kittredge

Poval-Colli,
March 8/04

How the letters have roused me up! . . . Furthermore, they have proved to me, or, rather, reassured me, that I am a white man.

As a sample of many days, let me give to-day. Was forbidden departure by Gen. Sasaki at Ping-yang—argued it out through interpreters—vexations, delays, drive me mad. Should have started at 7 A.M. Scarcely started to load pack horses, when summoned by Japanese Consul—more interpreter—distraction—successful bluff—pull out late in afternoon.

Arrive at this forlorn village; people scared to death. Already have had Russian and Japanese soldiers—we put the finishing touch to their fright. They swear they have no room for us, no fuel, no charcoal, no food for our horses, no room for our horses, nothing—no grub for our mapus and interpreters. We storm the village—force our way into the stables—capture 25 lbs. barley hidden in man's trousers—and so forth and so forth, for two mortal hours—chatter and chin-chin to drive one mad.

And this is but one of all the days. One can scarcely think whiteman's thoughts. . . . As I write this, the horses are breaking loose in the stable— native horses are fiends, and I have desisted writing long enough to stir up the mapus.

I read your letters in the saddle as I rode along to-day, and it reminded me of a letter of mine you once read in the saddle. And the horse you were astride of was named Belle. The horse I was astride of to-day is named Belle. I named her. She is as sweet and gentle as yours, and she is the only sweet and gentle horse in Korea. She is an Australian barb, and have I told you she was the Russian Minister's at Seoul? She is gigantic compared with all other horses in Korea—Chinese, Japanese, and Korean horses— and excites universal wonder and admiration.

As I write this a cold wind is blowing from the North, and snow is driving. Also, before my door are groaning and creaking a hundred bullock-carts loaded with army supplies and pushing North.

My interpreter comes in with his daily report. Manyoungi, my Korean cook and interpreter, comes in with tea and toast.[1] Dunn sends down half a can of hot pork and beans—and there are a thousand interruptions.

MS: ULA; 2 pp., typs. Pbd: *JL Reports*, 14–15; *BJL*, I, 411–12.
   1. JL's interpreter was K. Yamada, a Japanese. See "Interpreters and How They Cause Trouble," *San Francisco Examiner*, April 26, 1904. Manyoungi, JL's valet, is described in "Troubles of War Correspondent in Starting for the Front." After the war, Manyoungi returned to America with JL and served him for three years.

To George P. Brett

[Near Anju]
[March 9, 1904]

Dear Mr. Brett:–
   Have just heard of change of title for collection of stories.[1] It is all right, & a more taking title than mine.
   Am now on the Road north of Ping-yang, *March 9/04*—not far from Anju, close to the very forefront of the Japanese advance, & detained by soldiers from proceeding further—

London.

Received in Seoul, Korea all O.K.[2]

MS: NN; 1 p., als.
   1. *The Faith of Men.*
   2. This entire letter is written at the bottom of a note of January 4, 1904, from the Macmillan Company, which requested that JL acknowledge receipt of an enclosed royalty check for $100.

To Charmian Kittredge

Sunan.
Wednesday, Mar. 9/04

Here we are—captured and detained, while the wires are working hot between here and Ping-yang and Seoul. I mean captured by Japanese soldiers who will not let us proceed North to Anju. And five more vexatious hours have just elapsed—chin-chin and delay galore.
   As I write this, a thousand soldiers are passing through the village past my door. My men are busy drawing rations for themselves and horses from the Army.
   Red Cross ponies, pioneers, pack horses loaded with munitions and supplies, foot soldiers, are streaming by. Captains are dropping in to shake hands and leave their cards, and then going on.
                    IMPORTANT. ANOTHER VEXATION!
   Just caught five body lice on my undershirt. That is, I discovered them,

Manyoungi picked them off, the while he interpreted for me an invitation from a Korean nobleman to come to his place and occupy better quarters! The nobleman looked on, while the lice were caught and I changed my clothes. Lice drive me clean crazy. I am itching all over. I am sure, every second, that a score of them are on me. And how under the sun am I to write for the *Examiner* or write to you!

Intermission—the horses, stabled within ten feet of me, have been kicking up a rumpus—kicking, biting, stampeding my Belle and my three other horses—and broken legs would not be welcome just now. I am advised to get my life insured. . . .

And the troops stream by, the horses fight—and mapus, cook and interpreter are squabbling 4 feet away from me. And the frost is in the air. I must close my doors and light my candles.

A Korean family of refugees—their household goods on their backs, just went by.

MS: ULA; 1 p., typs. Pbd: *JL Reports*, 15–16; *BJL*, I, 412–13.

To Charmian Kittredge

[Sunan]
[March 10, 1904]

This is one of many commands not heeded.[1] This was issued yesterday at Pingyang. I am now north of that city & in advance of General Sasaki.

The first command, had I obeyed it, would have held me in Tokio to this day, where are 50 other correspondents who did heed. I am prepared, however, to be held up by Japanese scouts at any moment & be brought back to Pingyang. But its all in the game. I am the only correspondent this far in advance. With me is Dunn, a photographer for *Collier's Weekly*.

Follow *Collier's Weekly* & you will see what I am seeing every day, and you will see the very things themselves.

In Pingyang are two other correspondents[2]—and that is all the regular correspondents[3] in Korea at present moment.

MS: CSmH; 2 pp., als. Pbd: *JL Reports*, 16; *BJL*, I, 413.

1. JL wrote this letter on a note from C. Shingo, Japanese acting consul at Pyongyang, dated March 9, 1904. The note reads: "I have the honour to inform you by the order that you would stay here until our Land Forces under Major General Sasaki proceed for the North."

2. Apparently McKenzie and Dunn. See "'Examiner' Writer Sent Back to Seoul," *San Francisco Examiner*, April 25, 1904.

3. JL used ditto marks for "correspondents."

To Charmian Kittredge

Sunan,
Mar. 11/04

Have just returned from a ride on Belle—doesn't that strike you familiarly? North I may ride for a hundred yards, and when I come thundering up at a lope the Japanese guard turns out on the run, presenting bayonets to me in token that I may proceed no further. East, West, and South I may ride as far as I wish, but North, where fighting is soon to begin, I may not go.[1] Nor may I go until I receive permission from Lieut-General Inouye,[2] commander of the 12th Division of 12,000 men, and just now at Seoul, a couple of hundred miles to the South.

. . . Your two letters I received several days ago were brought up, horseback, from Seoul. As I write I look out my door and a dozen feet from where I am sitting, see Belle munching away at her barley ration which I have drawn for her from the Army. She *is* a joy! . . . I am my own riding teacher. I hope I don't learn to ride all wrong. But anyway, I'll manage to stick on a horse somehow, and we'll have some glorious rides together.

MS: ULA; 1 p., typs. Pbd: *JL Reports*, 16–17; *BJL*, I, 414.
    1. For JL's account of his detention in Sunan, see "Koreans Have Taken to the Hills," *San Francisco Examiner*, April 17, 1904.
    2. Possibly Kaoru Inouye (1835–1915), one of the Japanese Gen-ro, elder statesmen who were guardians of the Imperial Constitution and advisors to the Emperor.

To Charmian Kittredge

Sunan,
March 12/04.

You needn't worry about my welfare. The Japanese are taking very good care of me. Here I am, 40 miles from the front, and here I stay. The only other newspaperman who reached this far, Dunn, has gone back.[1] So I'm farthest north of all the correspondents. Furthermore, no others may now pass out of Ping-yang.[2]

MS: ULA; 1 p., typs. Pbd: *JL Reports*, 17; *BJL*, I, 414.
    1. According to JL's account in "Koreans Have Taken to the Hills," Dunn had "gone back to Ping Yang to wake the dead in an effort to get permission to proceed."
    2. The transcriber added the following note: "He quotes several short poems from the Korean—and comments: 'These are sweet, are they not? They are the only sweet things I have seen among the Koreans!'"

To Charmian Kittredge

Ping-yang,
March 16/04

Here beginneth the retrograde movement. Have been ordered back 50 li[1] from Sunan to this place. Am now ordered back 540 li from this place to Seoul—the Japanese are disciplining us for our rush ahead and the scoop we made—and they are doing it for the sake of the correspondents who remained in Japan by advice of Japanese and who have made life miserable for the Japanese by pointing out that we have been ahead gathering all the plums.

540 li to Seoul and 540 li back = 1080 useless li I have to ride, plus 100, (Sunan and return) = 1180 useless li. Well, I'll become used to the saddle at any rate.

MS: ULA; 1 p., typs. Pbd: *JL Reports*, 17; *BJL*, I, 414–15.
    1. A *li* equals about one-third of a mile.

To Charmian Kittredge

Seoul,
March 18/04

Just arrived, fired hence from the North.[1] Pull out on a little side jump to Wei-hai-wei to-morrow morning early. Learn that a bunch of letters is chasing around after me up at Ping-yang. . . . Shall get them a week hence when return from Wei-hai-wei.

MS: ULA; 1 p., typs. Pbd: *JL Reports*, 18; *BJL*, I, 415.
    1. For JL's account of his frustration in Seoul, see "'Examiner' Writer Sent Back to Seoul."

To Charmian Kittredge

Seoul, Korea,
March 29/04

Here I am, still in Seoul, assigned to the first column but not permitted to go [to] the Front. None of the correspondents at front. All held back by Japanese, and in this matter we are being treated abominably.

. . . I have decided that I shall remain away no more than a year. Ten months from the time I left San Francisco, I shall cable Hearst to send out another man to take my place at the front—if I've got to the front by that time.

. . . Since writing you from north of Ping-yang at Sunan, I have not only received not one letter from any one else, but not one letter from you. . . . You, at least, have my miserable letters to the *Examiner* to read. Have never been so disgusted with anything I have done. Perfect rot I am turning out. It's not war correspondence at all, and the Japs are not allowing us to see any war. Photographs enclosed taken at table upon which I am writing this.

MS: ULA; 1 p., typs. Pbd: *JL Reports*, 18; *BJL*, I, 415.

To Cloudesley Johns

[Korea]
[? March 1904]

By God! Cloudesley! I wrote it, & two others went over it; but it took you to discover the Bible contradiction.[1] I'll fix it by having him quote from it.

Jack London.

MS: CSmI I, 1 p., als.
    1. According to Johns: "I found a startling error in the manuscript [of *The Sea-Wolf*], in which Jack had Wolf Larsen derisively reading passages from the Bible months after the ship had been searched vainly for a Bible when crew members insisted upon some religious service at a burial at sea" ("Who the Hell *Is* Cloudesley Johns?" p. 317).

To Charmian Kittredge

Grand Hotel,
Seoul, Korea,
April 1/04

And still no mail. . . . I'll never go to a war between Orientals again. The vexation and delay are too great. Here I am, still penned up in Seoul, my 5 horses and interpreters at Chemulpo, my outfit at Ping-yang, my post at Anju—and eating my heart out with inactivity. Such inactivity, such irritating inactivity, that I cannot even write letters.

Mark you, while inactive, I am busy all the time. What worries is that I am busy with worries and nothing is accomplished. Never mind, I may not ride beautifully or correctly, but I'll wager that I stick on and keep up with you in the rides we are to have together in the years to come.

Just now I'm riding all kinds of Chinese ponies, with all kinds of saddles, in all kinds of places (and some of the ponies are vicious brutes). I was out yesterday, without stirrups, and loped all over the shop with another fellow, down crowded streets, narrow streets, crooked streets, over sprawling babies for the ponies are hard-mouthed and headstrong (a thousand shaves), and live to tell the tale.[1]

MS: ULA; 2 pp., typs. Pbd: *JL Reports*, 18–19; *BJL*, I, 415–16.

1. Apparently JL enclosed with this letter a note from a Mr. James, written from Chemulpo. It read: "Your mare and the ponies are well looked after. Only a little influenza in her and she wants a lot more exercise. She is quite fat. Chin-chin, old chap. Yours as a Sourdough, James." At its foot was a note from JL's interpreter, K. Yamada: "For you don't returned within long time there happened trouble yesterday that I has been arrested to Japanese gendarme as reporting military secret to you and after 10 hours examined several questions, I could come back to my boarding house. Received telegram and I shall do your order. . . . [P.S.] If you don't come back I can't help plenty troubles." JL appended this comment: "These two letters, on same sheet, as indicative of some of my troubles. Here I am, compelled to remain in Seoul, my horses at Chemulpo. My interpreter, K. Yamada, left in charge of horses, arrested. My mare with influenza, and suffering from 'hay-belly,' which James mistakes for being with foal. Hay I had sternly forbidden, for I had learned effect on mare. James (an ex-Klondiker) and making a dash for Chemulpo, I asked to take a look at my horses" (*JL Reports*, 19–20; *BJL*, I, 416–17).

To George P. Brett

Seoul, Korea,
April 3/04

Dear Mr. Brett:–

I hear that Isbister & Co. has failed. If this is so, and they're out of business, somebody else will have to handle my books in London. Isbisters were giving me same rates I received in America. It would not be unfair for me to receive same rates from whatever other English house takes up my books. May I leave this to you?

I can't do anything myself out here. Haven't received a letter for a month & don't know what has become of all my mail. As yet, all I have received from Isbisters is ten pounds. I wonder if anything is coming to me. *The Son of the Wolf*, they bought from Ward, Locke & Co. so nothing to me from that. *The God of their Fathers*,—they got on an arrangement from McClure Phillips, so nothing there. *A daughter of the Snows*— same arrangement. But *The People of the Abyss, Kempton Wace Letters, Cruise of the Dazzler* they owe me for.[1] The first two on same rates I have with you, and *Cruise of Dazzler* on similar arrangement. Anything you can do in straightening this out will be appreciated I can tell you—of course, if they have failed & all the rest. I merely heard it as a rumor.

Now, concerning that book of essays of mine, *The Salt of the Earth*. From the way you spoke (in San Francisco) I had the feeling that you had read only the title essay. If this is so, would you mind glancing at some of the later-written essays, "The Scab," "The Class Struggle," "The Tramp," etc., with the object of a change of conclusion regarding the expediency of not issuing as a book for an indefinitely long time to come. The later-written essays, to me, seem to have a timely importance. I'll abide by what you say, but just give a second thought to them.

At this late date, all the correspondents are still held back from the front. While the rest remained in Tokio I made a dash for the front, traveled up the west Coast of Korea in sampans (8 days & 2 hard blows), & on horseback through the snow from Seoul to Ping-yang, and From Ping-yang to Sunan—which latter place, even now, a month after I was there, is only a half-day's ride from the fighting line. I was right up with the fun when arrested & ordered back by the Japanese military authorities.

Am now waiting in Seoul (under instructions), for the correspondents in Tokio to get permission to start & to overtake me. Then I may go on. Believe me, it has all the appearance, now, (so far as we are concerned), of a personally conducted Cook's tourist proposition.

When the *Faith of Men* is issued, please send twenty copies of same to my Oakland address, where I shall get them on my return.

Sincerely yours,
Jack London.

P.S.—I'm going to try, later on, to get accredited to the Russian side, and go over & see how they do things.

MS: NN; 7 pp., als. Pbd: *L*, 155–56.

1. JL set out the titles as a list, but carried on into the next paragraph. For his arrangements with Isbister, see JL to Robinson, December 11, 1902.

To Charmian Kittredge

Seoul, Korea,
April 4/04

Dearest—

Enclosed letters will tell you a tangled tale. I could kill the *Examiner* people. Of course there is a mail delivery in Korea, American Legations, & all the rest.

You will see that B.[1] has read all you have written me. You will see, after all, that my sister is standing by me. Believe me, even though she has made mistakes as well, there have been many mistakes & misunderstandings in the first few days after my departure.

Even when Eliza said in reply, "I am afraid it is,"—there was misunderstanding.—misunderstanding of her nature & her ways. I wish I had told her all when I left. My error.

I have told her all now, & asked her to write to you. I believe she will. Wait & see.

Surely I am right when I say I *know*[2] her. And right when I say she is so difficult to know—unapproachable, as it were—that the most mistaken impressions of her are the result. I wish I could talk to you for ten minutes.

When she writes you, I leave the rest to you. But when you read her letter, remember, oh remember, that unapproachableness of spirit which is hers, & that she has not expression of thought such as you have.

I have started the pressure for divorce, and I believe it will come off. It must come off. It shall come off.

Send me some pictures of you—I grow hungry, so hungry for you. And the campaign has not yet really begun.

And remember, I shall cable you "Mate" at Newton, Iowa.[3] Be sure & register yourself as such at Telegraph office.

If you need money (& if you love me), you will cable for it. Cable: "Mate wants" & the amount.

Dear, dear one.

MS: CSmH; 3 pp., al.
1. Bessie London.
2. Underlined twice.
3. On February 20, 1904, CKL, afraid of a scandal over JL's separation, had left California to visit Mrs. Lynette McMurray, the daughter of Edward B. Payne, in Newton, Iowa. She stayed in Iowa until July 29.

To Charmian Kittredge

Seoul, Korea,
April 5/04

I'm going out to ride off steam now on a jockey saddle and a spanking big horse, and if we don't kill each other we'll kill a few native babies or blind men. Had the horse out yesterday—hardest mouth—took half a block to bring it to a walk and half a dozen to hold it when I got off to pay a call. How I stuck on I don't know—but I never took the reins in both hands, a la Japanaise, nor did I throw my arms around his neck. Oh, I'm learning, I'm learning. I never had time in my life to learn to play billiards, but I'm learning now. I never had time to learn to dance, but if this war keeps on I'll learn that, too—only the missionaries don't dance, and the *Kresang* (Korean dancing girls) can't dance because the Emperor's mother is dead and the court is in mourning.

To-morrow night I give a reading from *Call of Wild* before foreign residents for benefit of local Y.M.C.A.—and I give it in evening dress!!! Custom of the country and I had to come to it. In Japan, however, one has to have a frock coat and top hat—imagine me in a Prince Albert and a stovepipe. Anyway, if Japan wins this war the Japs will be so cocky that white people will be unable to live in Japan. . . .

. . . Here's the horse, and I go. Say, I have learned a new swear-word (Korean), "Jamie." Whenever you want to swear just say "Jamie" softly, and people won't know you are swearing.

MS: ULA; 1 p., typs. Pbd: *JL Reports*, 20; *BJL*, I, 417.

To Charmian Kittredge

O-pay, Korea,
April 16/04

In the saddle again . . . and riding long hours. Roads are muddy. Was putting Belle in up to the shoulders as darkness fell last night. Have breakfast eaten and am under way at 6 A.M. It is now 9:30 P.M., and I have just finished supper and am going (in about one minute) rather tired to bed.

MS: ULA; 1 p., typs. Pbd: *JL Reports*, 20; *BJL*, I, 417–18.

To Charmian Kittredge

Anju House,
April 17/04

Plugging along in the race for Japanese Headquarters. Four men ahead of me, but expect to overhaul them, though I am bringing my packs along and they are traveling light. The rest of the bunch is left in the rear.

Beautiful long hours in the saddle, & beautiful mud. Had Belle in up to her shoulders more than once to-day.

Am prouder than a peacock—for I am able to keep her shoes on her, to tighten them when they get loose, & to put on a shoe when she casts & loses one. Of course, it is cold-shoeing, but they *work*! they *work*!

Wiju,
April 24th.

Well, I didn't overtake the four men ahead of me, though I caught up with them where they were stopped farther back along the road, and arrived here with them, where we shall stop for some time.

Now, to business. As I understand it, Macmillan's expect to bring out the *Sea Wolf* late this fall.[1] I shall not be able to go over the proofsheets. And you must do this for me. I shall write to Brett telling him this & asking him to get into communication with you.

In the first place, before any of the book is set up in print, you must get from him the original Ms. in his possession. Much in this Ms. will have been cut out in the *Century* published part. What was cut out I want put back in the book. On the other hand, many good[2] alterations have been made by you, & George,[3] & by the *Century* people—these alterations I want in the book. So here's the task—: take the Macmillan Ms., and, reading the *Century* published stuff, put into Macmillan Ms. the good alterations.

Furthermore, anything that offends you, strike out or change on your own responsibility. You know me well enough to know that I won't kick.

Haven't received a letter from you—&, for that matter, a letter from anyone for I don't know since when.

I hope to get hold of them in a month or so.

In previous letter I told you certain things, & on chance that it may not have reached you, I tell them again.

Register yourself at telegraph office at Newton, Iowa, as "Mate."— also, your house address.

Thus, I may cable you any time.

Also, when I am pulling out for California, I'll cable you. If it suits you, you could take your comfortable time in pulling back for California and yet be there a good time before I arrive.

Say I telegraph: "Mate, am coming," from the field here. It would take me between 30 & 40 days to get to 'Frisco. You, receiving this cable, could be in California between 3 & 4 weeks before I arrived. And then I could see you at once, on landing. Can you guess what that means to me?

Now, when you get back to Berkeley, register your name & address there as "Mate"; and, from last part of departure, say Japan, I could again cable you, giving this time the name of steamer on which I sail.

Presumably arriving in Oakland some time in the day, I should be out that evening to you. Will you occupy your old quarters? Or maybe go to Glen Ellen? Let me know. If Glen Ellen, register yourself there.

And now I'm off in haste to get this censored—a good 2-mile ride to headquarters & back 2 miles more.

Nevertheless, I dare to say I love you, love you, love you.

Jack.

P.S.—As I told you before, your letters to me are not read, so be kind as ever.

P.S.—A little, red rubber stamp on envelope will show the censor's mark.

MS: CSmH; 4 pp., als. Pbd: *L*, 156–57; *JL Reports*, 21; *BJL*, I, 418.
    1. *The Sea-Wolf* was published the first week of October.
    2. Underlined twice.
    3. George Sterling.

To George P. Brett

Wiju,
April 24, 1904

Dear Mr. Brett:–

Here I am, on the banks of the Yalu, waiting for the first big land fight. Can say I know a lot more about horses than when I started out.

As I understand it, you expect to bring out *Sea Wolf* late this year. I shall be unable to prepare same for printing, or to go over proofsheets. This, I shall have to put in Miss Kittredge's hands.

Much that *Century* cut out I should like in book; & on other hand, many *Century* alterations I should like to retain. So the thing to be done is this: Do you send the Ms. you possess to Miss Kittredge, & she will put in the *Century* alterations for the better. Then, when this is printed, please send her the proofs.

I am writing her this mail advising her fully what is to be done & promising her that you will enter into communication with her.

Her address is:

> Miss Charmian Kittredge,
> Care Mrs. Lynette McMurray,
> Newton,
> Iowa.

If you will mail me a copy of the *Faith of Men*, I shall be highly pleased. Address it to

> Jack London,
> War Correspondent,
> Headquarters,
> First Japanese Army,
> Japan.

Then it will be forwarded to me.

> Sincerely yours,
> Jack London.

P.S.—Any other good new novel to read would also give me joy.

MS: NN; 2 pp., als. Pbd: *L*, 157–58.

To Charmian Kittredge

> Headquarters 1st Japanese Army,
> Manchuria,
> May 6/04.

I am well, in splendid health, though profoundly irritated by the futility of my position in this Army and sheer inability (caused by the position) to do decent work.[1] What ever I have done I am ashamed of. The only compensation for these months of irritation is a better comprehension of Asiatic geography and Asiatic character. Only in another war, with a white-man's army, may I hope to redeem myself. It can never be done here by any possibility.

MS: ULA; 1 p., typs. Pbd: *JL Reports*, 22; *BJL*, I, 418–19.

1. See "Japanese Officers Consider Everything a Military Secret," *San Francisco Examiner*, June 26, 1904.

To Cloudesley Johns

First Japanese Army,
Antung, Manchuria,
May 8/04

Dear Cloudesley:—

Just a hello to let you know that all is well with me—physically. Am in splendid health. But mentally am suffering from a profound irritation.

My work? It is rot. Am hugely disgusted with it, but the insane state of affairs I find myself in, the restrictions, the inability in any way to get in touch with things (& not my fault)—make my stuff the rot it is.

It will require another war, & a whiteman's war, for me to redeem my-self. I'll never do it here.

Jack London.

MS: CSmH; 1 p., als.

To George Sterling

First Japanese Army,
Antung, Manchuria
May 8/04

Dear George:—

How often I think of you and the fresh California days in the open, the while I swelter here in a Chinese city breathing alike the dust of the living and the dust of the dead.

I am clean disgusted. My work is rotten. I know it, but so circum-scribed am I, so hedged about with restrictions, that I see little, hear but little more (& that unsatisfactory & ofttimes contradictory), [and]¹ in no way can manage to get in intimate touch with officers or men. I am an outsider, pent in one portion of the machine and from that restricted view watching the machine work. The result: Rot!

My love to Carrie—with due hesitancy I offer it.

To you my love with no hesitancy at all.

Jack.

MS: CO; 1 p., als. Pbd: *L*, 158–59.
  1. Originally "am."

To Charmian Kittredge

Headqrs. First Jap. Army,
Feng-Wang-Cheng, Manchuria,
May 17, 1904.

I have so far done no decent work. Have lost enthusiasm and hardly hope to do any thing decent. Another war will be required for me to redeem myself, when I can accompany our army or an English army. Well, time rolls on. In six weeks the rainy season will be here. The chances are that I'll pull out for some point in China where I can get in touch with a cable. And then. . . .

Do you know—beyond my camera experience at Moji[1] (mailed before the War) I do not know whether the *Examiner* has received one article of mine (I have sent 19) or one film (and I have sent hundreds of photographs). . . .

If I remain a whole year away, even so, one-third of it has passed.

MS: ULA; 1 p., typs. Pbd: *JL Reports*, 22; *BJL*, I, 419.
  1. See JL to CKL, February 3, 1904.

To Charmian Kittredge

Headquarters First Japanese Army
Feng-Wang-Cheng, Manchuria,
May 22, 1904.

My heart does not incline to writing these days. It could only wail, for I am hungry to be where you are, and disgusted at being here. War? Bosh! Let me give you my daily life.

I am camped in a beautiful grove of pine trees on a beautiful hill-slope. Near-by is a temple. It is glorious summer weather. I am awakened in the early morning by the songs of birds. Cuckoo calls through the night. At 6:30 I shave. Manyoungi, my Korean boy, is cooking breakfast and waiting on me. Sakai, my interpreter, is shining my boots and receiving instructions for the morning. Yuen-hi-kee, a Chinese, is lending a hand at various things. My Seoul mapu is helping in the breakfast and cleaning up generally. My Ping-Yang mapu is feeding the horses.

Breakfast at 7. Then try to grind something out of nothing for the *Examiner*. Perhaps go out and take some photographs, which I may not send any more for the Censor will not permit them to go out undeveloped and I have no developing outfit or chemicals with me.

I am at liberty to ride in to headquarters at Feng-Wang-Cheng, less than a mile away. And I am at liberty to ride about in a circle around the city of a radius little more than a mile. Never were correspondents treated in any war as they have been in this. It's absurd, childish, ridiculous, rich, comedy.

In the afternoon, the call goes forth, and we (the correspondents) go swimming in a glorious pool—clear water, over our heads, plenty of it. It all reminds me of Glen Ellen. A campfire at night, whereby we curse God, or Fate, and divers peoples and things which I shall not mention for the Censor's sake, and the day is ended.

Disgusted, utterly disgusted.

I have this day written the *Examiner* that in a month or six weeks (at outside) I shall pull out of the country and go to some place where I can get in direct cable communication with them; that my position here is futile; that there is no reason for my continuing here, and that, unless arrangements have been made for me to go on the Russian side, I shall return to the United States—unless they expressly bid me remain.

Now I don't think it is possible for them to make arrangements for me to go on the Russian side, so, my dear one, my very dear one, as you read this I may be starting on my way back to the States, to God's Country, the Whiteman's Country, and to You! Who knows? Who knows? At any rate, believe me . . . it would take a many times bigger salary than I am receiving to persuade me to put in the year in Japan much less pay for the year out of my own pocket. In the past I have preached the Economic Yellow Peril; henceforth I shall preach the Militant Yellow Peril.[1]

And just imagine the Censor reading all this. . . . Not a letter; not a line. I know not what is happening.

. . . I have no heart, no head, no hand, for anything. In preposterous good health, but ungodly sick of soul.

MS: ULA; 2 pp., typs. Pbd: *JL Reports,* 22–24; *BJL,* I, 419–20.

1. For JL's comments on the "economic" yellow peril, see "The Yellow Peril," *San Francisco Examiner,* September 25, 1904, and later, "A Bit of Data—on the Japanese Question," *Australian Star,* January 21, 1909, also published as "If Japan Wakens China," *Sunset,* December 1909.

To George P. Brett

Seoul, Korea,
June 4/04

Dear Mr. Brett:–

Yours of Jan. 23rd. just received. Am now turning back to the States, quite disgusted with the whole situation so far as it concerns a correspondent getting material. Our treatment has been ridiculously childish, and we have not been allowed to see anything. There won't be any war-book so far as I am concerned.[1]

I am glad I shall be able to revise the *Sea Wolf,* though I can't make up my mind, now, as to whether it would be advisable to shorten the description of the remasting of the schooner. I'll be better able to decide when I get back to white-mans land.

Yes, I have thought often, of that Indian race-story, but it's a stubborn thing, and the get-at-ableness of it has so far eluded me. It's a big thing—if it can be done, & if I can do it.

If all goes well, by the time you receive this I should be in California.[2]

Sincerely yours,
Jack London.

MS: NN; 2 pp., als. Pbd: *L*, 159.

1. JL had written Brett on June 1, 1904 (NN): "I doubt that my stuff will make a book. It's too worthless." The Russo-Japanese war continued into 1905, when Japan defeated Russia in decisive land (Mukden) and sea (Tsushima Strait) battles. See JL to Winship, September 4, 1905, n. 1.

2. JL left Asia in mid-June, sailing from Yokohama to San Francisco on the SS *Korea*.

To Charmian Kittredge

[Oakland]
Wednesday Morning,
July 6, 1904.

The fight is on. Am too busy to write love. Knew that George[1] had telegraphed you. Had no time to write. Bess is adamant. Tell you the case in a nutshell. Bess brought suit before the year was up. Couldn't therefore bring suit on ground of desertion, so brought it on ground of cruelty, etc., etc. She wanted to bring suit in order to get injunctions on all I possess, before I arrived on the spot, and so hold all I possess tied up until full year elapsed, when she could bring suit for separation and maintenance and have court give her a whack at all I possess in division of community property.[2]

She never intended to press suit for divorce, for she will not give me my freedom.

She offered to withdraw complaint for divorce if I would contract to buy her land and build her a home and give regular monthly support. When I asked for freedom she said nay. Then I said nay. There it stands.

Now this is the case. For the first time in my life I have a couple or four thousand dollars above my debts.[3] She intends fighting for cash. You know I don't give a whoop for money. She has started the expense of law, I'll help run up said expense of law. Result, neither she nor I shall see a penny of it. The several thousand will be dribbled out amongst the lawyers.

My English publishers have failed, all my American publishers have injunctions served upon them, likewise the *Examiner*, the Central Bank, the *Spray*, my books, carpets, and everything.

Now there is to be no suit for divorce—from present indications. You were not mentioned by name in complaint for divorce, (said complaint being only a bluff anyway). I see no reason why you should not return to California, for my troubles with Bess are bound to continue for a weary long while. You may crop up in the midst of it, you may never be mentioned. But elect to do as you see fit. If you remain away till divorce is granted, you may remain away for years, you may die and be buried away.

With this mail I shall send letter for transportation for you to California. If you should decide to come, let me know and I shall telegraph to New York for them there to forward you transportation (which above mentioned letter will have already arranged for).

In this matter I cannot impress upon you too strongly these several things: (1) Bess will not sue for divorce. (2) Quite a time must elapse before lawyers can get my few dollars and I go insolvent. (3) Though no divorce is sought your name may be brought in and a big scandal may be made of it. (4) Your name may not be brought in at all. (5) I shall almost believe that I am wild to see you. And, sixth and last, you must decide for yourself, for your own good, and not allow any thought of me and my selfish desire for happiness to influence you.

Mate

Write me at Flat[4] if you can see your way to it.

MS: ULA; 2 pp., typs. Pbd: *L*, 159–60.
   1. George Sterling.
   2. On June 28, Bessie London had filed suit for divorce on the grounds of cruelty and desertion and had petitioned for a restraining order against JL's publishers and the Central Bank of Oakland to prevent their making payments to him until the divorce had been settled. On July 12, after JL agreed to build Bessie a house and provide her with adequate alimony and child support, the restraining order was dropped.
   3. From money paid by Hearst for his war reports and from the *Century* for the serialization of *The Sea-Wolf*.
   4. At 1216 Telegraph Avenue.

To Frank Putnam

[Oakland]
July 6/04.

Dear Mr. Putnam:—
   Somewhere along in February or March, 1903, you will remember we had a correspondence concerning payment for my story "The One Thousand Dozen." In your letter of March 16th of that year, you stated that you could pay me in transportation, which same you had over several roads. It was a couple of hundred dollars worth of transportation coming to me, I believe. And I said to let it go until I needed it. Now I need it. I want transportation, first class, for Miss C. Kittredge, from Newton, Iowa, to Oakland, Calif. Can you let me have it? Will you telegraph me immediately?

And if you can arrange it, and telegraph me to that effect, when you in turn receive telegram from me will you at once send transportation to: Miss C. Kittredge, Care Mrs. Lynette McMurray, Newton, Iowa.[1]

Sincerely yours,
Jack London

MS: CSmH; 1 p., cctl. Pbd: *L*, 160–61.
   1. Putnam did not send the transportation. See JL to Putnam, September 13, 1904, n. 1.

To George P. Brett

1216 Telegraph Ave.
Oakland, Cal.
July 8/04

Dear Mr. Brett:–
   The *Sea Wolf* will never be dramatized by anyone else—it's not the right sort of thing.
   Mansfield's mad to offer $1000.00 for it; & I'm glad to take advantage of his madness to that extent.[1]
   It's a thousand or nothing, & the dramatization cannot at least hurt the sales of the book.
   I cabled acceptance of offer, as soon as I received it. Is it too late, now?
   Indeed, most hastily,

Jack London

MS: NN; 2 pp., als.
   1. In the *New York News*, June 11, 1904, an article entitled "Mr. Mansfield to Play 'The Sea Wolf'" stated that Richard Mansfield had bought a copy of *The Sea-Wolf* a few weeks earlier at a railroad-station newsstand and had been so impressed by the character of Wolf Larsen that he wanted to play the role on stage. Mansfield probably withdrew his offer, for on July 27, 1904 (ULA), JL wrote Cloudesley Johns: "Nobody is dramatizing the *Sea Wolf* that I know of, though I am quite willing to sell the privilege of so doing to anybody." In April 1904, B. D. Stevens, a New York theatrical producer and manager of Broadway actors, had contacted Brett to offer to buy dramatic rights to *The Sea-Wolf*, but because JL was overseas no agreement was reached.

To Cloudesley Johns

1216 Telegraph Ave.
Oakland, Cal.
July 8/04

Dear Cloudesley:–
   Am back, rushed to death, & trying to straighten things out. At present all money tied up (earned & to be earned) & don't know where I'm at.
   "Real portrait"—you'll have to describe more fully—at present can't recollect it—which one.
   Write you more fully later on.

Wonder if you'd care for a trip on the *Spray* a couple of months from now.

Jack London

P.S.—*Spray* tied up too.

MS: CSmH; 1 p., als. Pbd: *BJL*, II, 4.

To George P. Brett

1216 Telegraph Ave.
Oakland, Cal.
July 11, 1904

Dear Mr. Brett:—

Concerning the book publication of the *Sea Wolf*, I hardly see how you can bring it out in October. I have just sent back the October proofs to the *Century*, and it was patent that there must be a couple of installments to follow. All of which is merely by the way. I don't care myself, & if you can arrange it with the *Century* well and good.

Haven't you issued a paper-cover edition of *People of the Abyss*? And if so, couldn't I get several copies of same?

Also, please have sent to me and charge to my account the following:—

> 3 copies *Kempton-Wace Letters*
> 3 copies (cloth) *people of the Abyss*.
> 5 copies *Faith of Men*.
> 5 copies *Call of the Wild*.
> 3 copies *Children of the Frost*.

By the way, is the *Call of the Wild* still selling to any extent? You know, I don't know what has been happening during the last six months.

And now, if you think my selling-power has increased sufficiently[1] to warrant such an advance, I'd like to know if you can let me have $250.00 per month. If you can, please do it as follows: Send my wife a monthly check for $75.00, and me ditto for $175.00.

Frankly, this is what I am doing for my wife. In addition to check from you, I shall (and have been doing same in past), personally pay all unusual expenses such as Doctor bills, nurses, outings, etc. etc.

Also, with what I have earned as correspondent, plus what *Century* pays for *Sea Wolf*, I am setting about buying land and building her and the children a home after her own plans.[2] This will take all my little capital abovementioned, and also put me a bit into debt. But it will all be straightened up inside a year or so.

If an injunction has been served on you, it will soon be raised.

If you can see your way to the $250.00 per month, I'd like to have it begin the first of August.

Will you please have your bookkeeper send me the earnings of my different books up to date, and royalties advanced on same—in fact, full account.

And now, another idea for you to consider.—The *Sea Wolf* will make my tenth published book. If I can go on & develop in the next few years, & turn out a few successful books, there will be a good string of books & a fair possibility for uniform editions. Therefore this suggests itself: Why shouldn't you get the copyright on the several books you haven't published? I do not know enough about publishing to know whether it would be worth while or not.

The books are:

> *The Son of the Wolf*—Houghton, Mifflin & Co.
> *The God of His Fathers*—McClure, Phillips
> *A Daughter of the Snows*—Lippincotts
> *The Cruise of the Dazzler*—Century Co.

Please let me know what you think of all this.

You have arranged with Heineman for *Faith of Men* & *Sea Wolf*. Do you think I could now get a fair advance from them?

And by the way, I want to ask your advice. Isbisters are paying 6 shillings on the pound.

Isaac Pitman (or some similar publishers), who have taken hold of Isbisters, offer to take over my Isbister books & pay, not 6 shillings on the pound, but all that is coming. Their offer seems to imply, also, my future dealing with them. Now what do you think—would it be wiser for me to accept the six shillings, and get the books for myself? or to turn them over to Pitman?[3] I may here state that Isbisters own outright *The Son of the Wolf*, having bought it off Ward, Lock & Co, who bought it from Houghton, Mifflin.

I do not know how much is due me from Isbisters, but shall write to learn this mail.

Sincerely yours,
Jack London

MS: NN; 13 pp., als. Pbd: *L*, 161–62.

1. "Sufficiently" was written twice.

2. JL signed over to Bessie a lot at 519 31st Street in Oakland and contracted with C. M. McGregor to build a house there. According to their arrangement, she could keep this property as long as she remained unmarried.

3. Brett advised JL in a letter of July 20, 1904 (CSmH), to get his books back and turn over his English publishing affairs to William Heinemann & Co. of London.

To Corinne Maddern

Wake Robin Lodge,
Sonoma Co.,
July 18/04

Dear Corinne:—[1]

I'm not bothering my head over the letter taken to Bessie. I said in it for Will to do what he himself thought was right. Surely, one can ask and expect no more of any man.

But under all the circumstances I can not see my way to coming out to your place.

But do you drop in on me. Come to lunch or dinner at 1216.

I should like to see Merle's[2] imitation of Mrs. Fiske.[3]

Sincerely yours,
Jack London.

MS: Bernatovech; 2 pp., als.
1. Corinne M. Maddern, wife of William A. Maddern, Bessie's brother. She was editor of the dramatic page of *Club Life*, the San Francisco–based magazine of the California branch of the General Federation of Women's Clubs.
2. Merle Maddern.
3. Minnie Maddern Fiske.

To Anna Strunsky

1216 Telegraph Ave.
Oakland, Cal.
July 23/04

Dear Anna:—

Your 2 letters just to hand. You see, Cameron's letter to me gave me to understand that he was acting for you, & the content was such as to require an answer such as I gave. I am sorry, also amused as regards my telling or hinting of my approaching marriage. Either he imagined it, or you imagined it, or else he has some outside information which is news to me & which I should like to hear.

I do most earnestly hope that your name will not be linked[1] any more with my troubles.[2] It will soon die away, I believe. And so it goes. I wander through life delivering hurts to all that know me. And so one pays for the little hour—only, it is the woman who always pays.

Unspoilt in your idealism? And think of me as unsaved in my materialism. And why should we forget each other yet awhile? Why should we not always remember & know each other?

However, I am changed. Though a materialist when I first knew you, I had the saving grace of enthusiasm. That enthusiasm is the thing that is spoiled, and I have become too sorry a thing for you to remember.

Jack London.

MS: CSmH; 4 pp., als. Pbd: *L*, 162–63; *BJL*, II, 4.
    1. Originally, "be not be linked."
    2. See JL to Brett, September 2, 1903, n. 1. Articles in local and national newspapers had speculated that Strunsky was having an affair with JL, and Bessie London had originally named her as co-respondent in the divorce suit, although the allegation was later retracted. For Strunsky's account of the divorce, see Joan London, "The London Divorce," *American Book Collector*, 17 (November 1966), 31.

To George P. Brett

1216 Telegraph Ave.
Oakland, Cal.
Jul 24 1904

Dear Mr. Brett:–
    Yours of July 20th., to hand, & perfectly fair.
    Please prepare the supplementary agreement (mentioned bottom p. 3), and make the changed payment August 1st—$75.00 per month to Mrs. Jack London and $175.00 to me.
    I'll go ahead and see what I can do to get hold of books held by other American publishers, but, first, let me tell you how they stand, and do you then give me a line upon fair prices for them.
        Son of the Wolf:–Houghton, Mifflin & Co.,
            Feb. 29th./04—balance against me of $54.83
        Cruise of the Dazzler—Century Co.
            Sept. 30th./03—balance against me $9.25
        A Daughter of the Snows—Lippincotts
            —just about broke even, have no account.
        God of His Fathers—McClure Phillips
            July 13/04—Balance against me—$519.85
    I should imagine that these books, at least *Son of Wolf* & *God of Fathers* (if not the others), could be brought out in new editions & would sell well—(for they were originally read by very few)— Also, they might ultimately be brought out in paper covers—but you know more about this than do I.
    I am waiting word from Isbisters (or Pitmans), concerning what is due me on books they have published. I think, however, that I shall try to get them back & turn them over to Heinemann as you suggest.
    Have just received Nov. proofs of *Sea Wolf* from *Century*, & the book is wound up in that number.
    Have telegraphed today to Iowa for Macmillan proofs of *Sea Wolf*, & should have them in hand by end of the week. Then I shall immediately go over them. Can you set the latest date I can send them in to you?
                                        Sincerely yours,
                                        Jack London.

MS: NN; 6 pp., als.

To Anna Strunsky

1216 Telegraph Ave.
Oakland, Cal.
Jul 28 1904

Dear Anna:—

How glad I am that you intend finishing the novel.[1] I should be still more glad if you'll let me read what you've already done—if it's typed.

I expect to be in S.F. latter part of next week (do not know the precise day yet), and I'll run out to your place.

I'll let you know the day, either by phone or letter.

Jack.

MS: CSmH; 2 pp., als.
 1. Strunsky's *Violette of Père Lachaise* (1915).

To George P. Brett

1216 Telegraph Ave.
Oakland, Cal.
Aug 16 1904

Dear Mr. Brett:—

I am registering today, to you, corrected proofs of *Sea Wolf*. Somebody liberally be-sprinkled it with commas (which I have struck out). Please do not let anyone sprinkle the commas back again.

Sincerely yours,
Jack London.

MS: NN; 1 p., als.

To Blanche Partington

1216 Telegraph Ave.
Oakland, Cal.
Aug 16 1904

Dear Blanche:—

Mine was a keen pang of disappointment when you turned up missing Sunday morning.—Never mind, you can get a vacation & come & cook for a week when Kate and Marion[1] & the rest have all had their turns. Am I not generous?

Indeed, & I just wild to see *Candida*—but Aug. 18th. pull out with George for Jinks—get back Wednsday Aug. 24th.—how about Thursday, Friday or Sat. of that week?[2] Please let me know. *Superman*[3] is great—have finished third act.

Gee! I'd like to write half a dozen *real* plays, even if they were unactable & were never acted.

And you?—why don't you tackle a play? I'm ambitious for you, you see.

Jack.

MS: CU; 3 pp., als.
    1. Kate Partington (*d.* 1907), one of Blanche Partington's sisters, and Marian D. Sterling (*b.* 1885), one of George Sterling's sisters.
    2. George Bernard Shaw's *Candida* (1894) opened at the Columbia Theatre in San Francisco on August 22. JL and George Sterling were going to attend the annual High Jinks of San Francisco's Bohemian Club, held at the Bohemian Grove on the Russian River. In 1904 JL became an honorary member of this exclusively male social club of leading artists, writers, and businessmen. On August 22, on their way home, JL and Sterling stopped in Glen Ellen to visit CKL, who had returned to California on August 3 and was staying at Wake-Robin Lodge. Sterling left on August 23; JL remained one more day. There is no earlier record in CKL's diary of meeting JL after her return.
    3. Shaw, *Man and Superman* (1903).

To Blanche Partington

1216 Telegraph Ave.
Oakland, Cal.
Aug 24 1904

Dear Blanche:—
    Friday night be it, 8:15 at front of Columbia. But say—I returned home to find Cloudesley Johns came to see me & stop a few days. He's a Shawite, by the way. Now, can you make room for him to join us Friday night? Don't go out of your way to do so; and if you can't—why, an' you love me you'll say you can't, and he'll pay the penalty of making an unexpected visit by being debarred my precious companionship for an evening.

Sincerely yours,
Jack London.

MS: CU; 2 pp., als.

To Blanche Partington

1216 Telegraph Ave.
Oakland, Cal.
Aug 30 1904

Dear Blanche—
    All right, *Spray* trip postponed to Friday morning Sept 9th (or Thursday evening Sept 8); Let me know at once, & definitely, about this.
    That *Superman* is intended for you to keep.
    When astute critics like Stevens & Robertson cannot assimilate Shaw, how under the sun can a to-day's audience assimilate him?[1] The discovery is original with your own small self but you needn't get it copyrighted.
    Why shouldn't Shaw irritate you? Truth is usually the most irritating thing in life. No woman cares to hear herself called ugly, no man to hear

himself called cowardly, no spade to hear itself called a spade. "Vitality in woman is fury to create"[2]—if I were a woman I'd insist that vitality meant anything but that; I'd refuse to acknowledge myself a puppet of Dame Nature, I'd refuse to acknowledge that the surge of life in me was the clamor of life to be born. But then, I'm not a woman; neither is Shaw.

As a man, had I a few of the commoner illusions left to me, I'd be intensely obtuse to Shaw, or intensely irritated by him. I would not permit him to laugh at my illusions. All the optimism in me (which is the life germane) would rise up in revolt. Only the life survives that finds life good; and life can be found good only through illusion.

But you may ask me, therefore, how I manage to continue living, having lost the commoner illusions? And I answer, by replacing them by a single illusion, by an attitude of non-seriousness, by watching the serious worms writhe most seriously & by being amused thereby—George & Dick, for instance, over cards, Mrs. Grundy over morals,[3] Miss Partington over duty. The last is beautiful as well as amusing. I say, also, the last is amusing as well as beautiful. Were it not amusing, it would give me the hurt of tragedy. I know the amusement is illusion, but I insist upon the illusion; I must insist if I would continue to live. It is my last big illusion, the straw of the drowning man. For the same reason I cherish other illusions. The urge of the red blood in me toward woman is the urge of Dame Nature toward progeny. But I work off the red blood in me in other sense-delights, (heaving on ropes, diving from springboards, skylarking, & what-not), in[4] such moments of sense-delight I firmly believe that I am realizing & vindicating the life that is in me—illusion, of course illusion, but if you should tell me when at the summit of such delights that it was illusion, I should be offended & irritated & recoil from you (as you & other women recoil from Shaw), as something unhealthy that made not toward life & surviving.

And when I do obey the urge of the red blood toward women, I do so dreaming of the "deathless creature of coral and ivory"—[5] illusion, I know it is illusion; but for the time, at least, I must cherish the illusion if I would live.

I don't know where I am now—save that I have realized the paradox of being serious in the elucidation of my non-seriousness—illusion, but for a few moments it has served to make toward living by making me forget my living.

Jack

MS: CU; 13 pp., als.

1. JL was referring to reviews of *Candida*. Ashton Stevens's review was titled "Shaw Drama Proves Delicious Comedy," *San Francisco Examiner*, August 23, 1904. By contrast, Peter Robertson, in "First Production of Shaw's 'Candida,'" *San Francisco Chronicle*, August 23, 1904, described the play as being "of no consequence" and "tommyrot."
2. *Man and Superman*, Act I: "Vitality in a woman is a blind fury of creation."
3. George Sterling and Richard Partington (1869–1929), one of Blanche Partington's

brothers and a painter who taught at The Partington School of Magazine and Newspaper Illustration in San Francisco; for Mrs. Grundy, see JL to CKL, October 27, 1903, n. 3.

4. "In" was written twice.

5. *Man and Superman*, Act III: "The visions of my romantic reveries, in which I had trod the plains of heaven with a deathless, ageless creature of coral and ivory, deserted me in that supreme hour."

To Blanche Partington

1216 Telegraph Ave.
Oakland, Cal.
Sep 1 1904

Miss Partington & her duty are all right. It has *possibly* made her a nobler woman, but it has prevented her from living her own life & being herself to the uttermost.

Now, for the *Spray* trip. Madeline's coming, you, Kate, & Phyllis—that makes the women. Then Whitaker, Albrecht, maybe Johns, maybe Matthews, maybe neither & maybe both, & myself. George & Carrie are not to be persuaded.[1]

Everyone who comes must bring blankets enough to keep themselves warm—also, as the pillows have knocked around some time on the boat, the fastidious had better bring pillowslips. Whitaker says he'll bring enough bread to go nearly around.

I'll furnish coffee, tea, milk, sugar, beefsteak, butter, canned goods, etc., and anybody else can bring anything they like.

Now, everybody should be aboard Thursday night—this will enable us to catch the tide Friday morning at three—& have the whole beautiful morning for sailing. *Spray* will be lying as of old at Broad Guage pier, & people can come aboard at any hour Thursday evening even to time of arrival of last boat from S.F.

Now let me know definitely about this. I'll arrange it so that you shall sleep by yourself.

Jack.

MS: CU; 4 pp., als.

1. Laura Madeline Sterling (*b*. 1882), one of George Sterling's sisters; Kate and Phyllis Partington; Herman Whitaker; Herman ("Toddy") Albrecht, pioneer California photographer, married to Kate Partington; Cloudesley Johns; Ernest Matthews (1882–1920), JL's friend, married to Bessie London's sister Flora; George and Carrie Sterling.

To Blanche Partington

1216 Telegraph Ave.
Oakland, Cal.
Sep 5 1904

Dear Blanche:—

It is incinerated. I kept it 24 hrs. for re-reading and then promptly committed it to the flames. But I loved you for it, and felt it all true of you before ever I read it. I was even proud—not that your words backed my judgement, but that you had been so frank with me. It was an honor. And it put me more in touch with the human, for you are very human.

Oh, we'll feed all right. Most everybody to go on the trip will be here Wednesday night, when we'll talk final things over. Let me have word, roughly, what time to expect you Wednesday night—

Jack

MS: CU; 2 pp., als.

To Frank Putnam

1216 Telegraph Ave.
Oakland, Cal.
Sep 13 1904

Dear Mr. Putnam:—

Did you receive the letter I wrote you a couple of months ago concerning transportation?[1]

Jack London.

MS: CU; 1 p., als.

1. In a letter to JL of September 20, 1904 (CSmH), Putnam stated that because of personal problems he had turned over JL's request to the *National*'s business manager, who was unable to get the desired transportation.

To Frederick I. Bamford

1216 Telegraph Ave.
Oakland, Cal.
Sep 16 1904

Dear Comrade:—

I like the poem greatly; it has dignity and strength, & suits the times as well.[1]

Beyond my old criticism of breaking the swing by the marshalling of too many adjectives, I have nothing but minor suggestions to make.

And now one general suggestion—I have the feeling that you condense too much matter into too little form. Instead of so many thoughts, take fewer thoughts and expand them. I feel that you have enough meat in this poem to go to the making of four or five poems of equal length.

The objection is that too great a strain is thrown on the reader. He has to think too hard to be able to enjoy.

Jack London

MS: JL State Park; 3 pp., als. Pbd: *Mystery*, 182–83.
1. For the comments of Bamford's wife on JL's criticism, see *Mystery*, p. 183.

To Blanche Partington

1216 Telegraph Ave.
Oakland, Cal.
Sep 19 1904

Dear Blanche:–

Did you return Cowell's[1] essay? And if not, & if you still have it, will you send it along?

I don't think I explained why I had already seen *Marta*.[2] My delectable sister-in-law[3] is very anxious to get me interested in the stage. Incidentally she hath a daughter,[4] for whom she'd like to have me write something. Candidly, & without vanity, she likes to be able to introduce me to theatrical people, believing, no doubt, that it helps her standing with them—and she has a daughter and ambition for that daughter.

Well, she telephoned first part of week saying I must see *Marta*. Said I was full up. She insisted. Said Thursday night. She said O.K. Scarcely had hung up when your note arrived asking me to see *Marta*. Had but one choice in the matter, said yes, & called up sisterinlaw. Told her I couldn't come Thursday night. Hung up.

Then she called me up: (I had thought it all settled).

How about Saturday afternoon? she asked. (You see, when I had called it off & hung up I had no engagement with anybody but you.) How could I tell her, when she renewed invitation for Saturday, that I was going with you.

Well, I said I lectured in Vallejo Friday night, would be in that town Saturday morning, but that would make desperate effort to go to *Marta* Saturday afternoon, though I might arrive late. She said she'd wait. I said not to wait, in case I mightn't come at all. She said she'd wait anyway,—& hung up.

And I was engaged to go with you!

Imagine the quandary of an innocent & fairly truthful young man—possibly, a little-selfish young man. And I did want to go with you.

Behold, I called up my sisterinlaw and told her I'd manage to go Thursday night. And I went.

I don't know whether I should ask you to forgive me, or her.

Jack.

MS: CU; 6 pp., als.
1. Possibly S. Emma Cowell.

2. *Marta of the Lowlands* (1896), by the Spanish dramatist Angel Guimera, was a socio-logical tragedy dealing with the tyranny of an evil landlord. It was playing at the California Theatre in San Francisco.
3. Corinne Maddern.
4. Merle Maddern.

To Anna Strunsky

1216 Telegraph Ave.
Oakland, Cal.
Sep 19 1904

Dear Anna:—

I have given the Gorki essay a second & third reading, and I am driven to conclude the following:— That it is an early, amateur effort of his, filled with fire, some wonderful lines and thoughts, but not mature enough in handling to go.[1]

Do you just go over the similes he introduces to see the youthfulness of the effort.

So I feel that it is best to send it back to you. If I am wrong, forgive me.

Why, if you were to turn loose on an essay on Man, you'd do a thousand times better than this.

Possibly, my chief objection is the personification—I don't know, perhaps that's it. The American people to-day doesn't go much on personification.

No—I haven't tackled any play yet. I'm writing what I call a "Transcript from Life"— *The Game.*[2]

It is about prizefighting. When I finish it I'll send you a copy to read.

And what are you doing? I'm waiting for something from your pen & typewriter.

Jack.

MS: CSmH; 4 pp., als.
1. Strunsky, who was fluent in Russian, may have translated an essay by Russian writer Maxim Gorky (1868–1936), considered the father of Soviet literature. His work combined realism and a passion for social justice.
2. *The Game* (New York: Macmillan, 1905).

To Blanche Partington

1216 Telegraph Ave.
Oakland, Cal.
Sep 21 1904

Dear Blanche:—

Ah! and Alas! if I were only divinely kind instead of being merely self-ish! But if the satisfying of the desire I have to be with you be kindness, then I'm going in for kindness and all kindred philanthropies. I never knew before how easy it is to be good.

Seriously, I grow frightened to learn that another's strength rests ever so little on mine. I know my own weakness too well under the splendid farce that [1] conceals it. The strangest thing about it is that it is to you I have somehow looked this many a day, even when I knew you little, knew less of you, & perhaps guessed but little more. The thought of you was a tonic. It seemed to clear my brain and steady me. You had strength, you were brave—and, believe me, the thought of you has more than once shamed me.

And if you dare to tell me that this little confession of mine is "kind," I'll scarcely know how to forgive you.

Isn't Amateur Night on Friday? I have Monday and Friday evenings of next week clear. Cloudesley, I fear, will not be here. Please let me know when & where.

Any time you see a week-end free, somewhere a little ahead, let's try and get up another *Spray* trip. I'd like to get Gertrude [2] along, too, before she goes East.

Jack.

MS: CU; 4 pp., als.
  1. "That" was written twice.
  2. Gertrude Partington.

To Charmian Kittredge

[Oakland]
Sep 28 1904

Yours of 22th:–

I am keeping the letter I prefer to give to Eliza when she comes back from Santa Cruz, which will not be until the end of the week.

You must be taken physical culture, to have got that stiff neck.[1] Glad to know it—not the stiff neck, but the fact that you're exercising.

I'm waiting to hear whether it is to be Monday or Tuesday. I know I wait just as impatiently for these meetings as you do.[2]

Yes, you did very well, Sweetheart—& I didn't enjoy being honest with you, I assure you. But it's better so, & I do love you, I do, I do.

MS: CSmlI, 2 pp., al.
  1. According to her diary entry of September 24, CKL had gone swimming that day. Two days later she noted: "Feeling miserable—poison oak, cold in bladder—otherwise sick, and stiff neck."
  2. CKL made trips to Oakland and San Francisco on September 1, 13–14, and 22–23 to see JL. Her next trip was on Monday, October 3.

To Anna Strunsky

1216 Telegraph Ave.
Oakland, Cal.
Sep 28 1904

Dear Anna:—

Gee! And what a rain it must have been for people living in a tent! Almost an adventure for you, I should think.

Am anxious to see the Brown Peril—but not Sunday. After engaging the day with George Sterling, I engaged the night out at the Alhambra Theatre. And Saturday I go to Berkeley to hear Hamlet.

But might I not come & see you after the lecture?

Did you see my Yellow Peril article?[1] What did you think of it?

Jack.

MS: CSmH; 2 pp., als.
  1. "The Yellow Peril."

To Charmian Kittredge

[Oakland]
Sep 29 1904

Dear heart, Dear Heart—

And my (Tuesday) letter had not yet reached you. Surely it has ere this—and the Wednsday one as well.

No, dear, I have no particular trouble bothering me now.

I think, most probably, that you [and][1] I are in a very trying stage just now. The ardor & heat & ecstasy of new-discovered love have been tempered by time, on the one hand; and on the other hand we are denied the growing comradeship which should be ours right now. Instead, we must wait another year before we can enter upon this comradeship of daily intimacy—& the intervening period is bound to be full of worry & anxiety if we do not understand its significance.

Am I right?

Am sending you the *Game* under separate cover to Aunt Netta—please suggest corrections & return as soon as you can.[2]

Have been getting hold of some of Neitzsche. I'll turn you loose first on his *Genealogy of Morals*—and after that, something you'll like—*Thus Spake Zarathustra.*[3]

Sept. 28 O.K.

MS: CSmH; 4 pp., al.
  1. Originally "are."
  2. According to CKL's diary, during a visit in San Francisco on September 22, JL read her

a portion of *The Game*. She received the complete manuscript on September 29 and returned it with corrections the next day.

3. First published in 1887 and 1883–85, respectively.

To Charmian Kittredge

[Oakland]
Oct 4 1904

In many respects, last night was (to me) one of the most satisfying
times we have had together—at least in 'Frisco.[1] But then, we've had so
many satisfying times together.

Am beginning again to consider tackling a play.

A brief letter, Love-Woman—but it is written in Love by your Lover.

MS: CSmH; 1 p., al.

1. According to her diary, during their rendezvous on October 3, CKL read to JL and
practiced the piano.

To Blanche Partington

1216 Telegraph Ave.
Oakland, Cal.
Oct 4 1904

Dear Blanche:–

Thursday be it, at 8:10, in front of Lyric Hall,[1] your mother, Phyllis &
Gertrude. Ah, my old sea-training! You know, at sea, one has always to
repeat orders received, and to this day I do it, even with directions.

Jack

P.S.—Indeed, I should like to see *Joseph Entangled*.[2] Mansfield is still after
me, and so is Ethel Barrymore (if that's the way to spell it).[3] I'm beginning
to warm to the idea, & if I get the chance should like to try my hand at a
couple of curtain-raisers—perhaps as a beginning. Gee! I'd like to turn
out a good play just once!

Jack.

MS: CU; 2 pp., als.

1. The Ben Greet Players were performing *Everyman* at Lyric Hall in San Francisco.

2. *Joseph Entangled* (published in 1906), a comedy by Henry Arthur Jones.

3. See JL to Brett, July 8, 1904. JL had probably discussed with the actress Ethel Barrymore (1879–1959) the possibility of her playing Freda in the dramatization of "The Scorn
of Women." She did not act in the play.

To Cloudesley Johns

[Oakland]
Oct 8 1904

Dear Cloudesley:—
   I liked the clippings all right. Cleverly written. But the one about faking—surely you did not send it to me apropos of our telepathy disagreement? For it certainly has no bearing. Please do not forget that I am fairly scientific, & that I have a fair knowledge of fakes & fakirs.

Jack London.

MS: CSmH; 2 pp., als.

To George P. Brett

1216 Telegraph Ave.
Oakland, Cal.
Oct 10 1904

Dear Mr. Brett:—
   Gee! I'm glad to hear that the *Sea Wolf* promises to start off well. I hope for both our sakes that it proves a good seller.
   No, I'm pretty sure I'll have no spring book. In the three months since my return, I have written nothing at all, with the sole exception of story enclosed herewith [1]—which I hope may interest you as an attempt to do the ring. Please return it at your early convenience.
   I don't imagine I'll tackle a long effort until the beginning of the year. I expect to potter around the next couple of months writing several short stories, and trying my hand at a play [2]—not a serious big effort of a play, though I'd like some time to write a really big play.
   I enclose also, herewith, several replies to my proposition to buy plates. [3] It would not seem worth while to go further in the matter. Please return letters.

Sincerely yours,
Jack London.

MS: NN; 3 pp., als.
   1. *The Game.*
   2. *Scorn of Women.*
   3. JL was probably negotiating with other publishing houses to buy the plates of his previously published work. See JL to Brett, July 11 and 24, 1904.

To Anna Strunsky

1216 Telegraph Ave.
Oakland, Cal.
Oct 13 1904

Dear Anna:—

The movement of this is too rapid and sketchy. It is too much in the form of a narrative, and narrative, in a short story, is only good when it is in the first person.

The subject merits greater length. Make longer scenes, dialogues, between them.

And then you quit too suddenly, too abruptly. It is not *rounded* to its end, but chopped off with a hatchet.

You should elaborate the development of his apparent madness, his own psychology, the psychology of the cruelty of the East Side idealists—as you did for me by word of mouth.

My criticism is, in short, that you have taken a splendid subject and not extracted its full splendor. You have mastery of it (the subject), full mastery,—you *understand*; yet you have not so expressed your understanding as to make the reader understand. And this same criticism I would make in general of all your short stories.

Remember this—confine a short story within the shortest possible time-limit—a day, an hour, if possible—or, if, as sometimes with the best of short stories, a long period of time must be covered,—months—merely hint or sketch (incidentally) the passage of time, & tell the story only in its crucial moments—

Really, you know, development does not belong in the short story, but in the novel. The short story is a rounded fragment from life, a single mood, situation, or action.

Now don't think me egotistical because I refer you to my stories—I have them at the ends of my fingers, so I save time by instancing them. Take down & open *Son of the Wolf.*

The first eight deal with single situations, though several of them cover fairly long periods of time—the time is sketched and made subordinate to the final situation. You see, the situation is considered primarily—"The Son of the Wolf" in beginning is hungry for woman, he goes to get one; the situation is how he got one.

"The Priestly Prerogative" is the scene in the cabin—the rest is introductory, preliminary.

"The Wife of a King"—not a good short story in any sense.

"The Odyssey of the North"—covering a long period of time, is first person, so that long period of time (the whole life of Naas) is exploited in an hour & a half in Malemute Kid's cabin.

Take down & open *God of His Fathers.*

First story, single situation.

"Great Interrogation"—single situation in cabin where whole past history of man & woman is exploited.

And so on, to the last story, "Scorn of Women"—see in it how time is always sketched and situation is exploited—yet it is not a short story.

And so forth & so forth.

Am sending you "The Nose"[1] for a wee bit of a smile.

Jack London

MS: CSmH; 9 pp., als. Pbd: *L*, 163–64.

   1. "A Nose for the King," *Black Cat*, March 1906; later included in *When God Laughs*.

To George P. Brett

1216 Telegraph Ave.
Oakland, Cal.
Oct 25 1904

Dear Mr. Brett:—

I'm glad you liked the *Game*. I've been thinking it over, your suggestions, and I don't think I'd care to tackle a series of stories on the ring. Besides, it would be impossible to run this same character through the different stories; for he has his beginning and end right here in this one story.[1]

I guess it will have to go into a miscellaneous collection of stories— a number of which are already written—& be brought out that way some day.

Sincerely yours,
Jack London.

P.S. Thank you very much for Ghent's new book.[2] I am already started on it, & I know that I shall enjoy it hugely.

MS: NN; 2 pp., als.

   1. Joe Fleming, *The Game*'s protagonist, dies from head injuries after his last fight.

   2. Macmillan had recently published *Mass and Class: A Survey of Social Divisions*, by William J. Ghent (1866–1942), Indiana-born author of books on social reform and history of the American West. He was a frequent contributor to the *Independent* and a founder of the Social Reform Club of New York in 1894.

To Charmian Kittredge

[Oakland]
Oct 26 1904

You haven't said yet, how early Monday evening. Don't fail to let me know.

Not another word have I heard about divorce. Just our luck!—But anyway, we're pretty lucky to get a divorce at all.[1]

Have just had another stirring time, getting B. to sign an amended con-tract of my own amending. I didn't want the home to become the prop-erty of the children in case the mother married or died.[2] It's fixed all right now. Also, there were several minor changes.

I hope you'll have a good time on this trip down.

Until Monday, then, & maybe Monday morning—

Your Man.

Yours of Tuesday

MS: CSmH; 2 pp., als.
    1. JL's divorce hearing was Monday, October 31, at 10 A.M. After a piano lesson in San Francisco during the day, CKL joined him in the evening for a champagne celebration.
    2. See JL to Brett, July 11, 1904, n. 2.

To Robert U. Johnson

1216 Telegraph Ave.
Oakland, Cal.
Nov 2 1904

Dear Mr. Johnson:—

Just now, I am working on a play—but expect to knock out a couple of short stories when I have finished play.

I have done only 2 short stories since my return from Japan, one of which you saw—the other was merely a skit without merit.[1]

Sincerely yours,
Jack London.

MS: CCamarSJ; 1 p., als.
    1. *The Game* and "A Nose for the King."

To Cloudesley Johns

1216 Telegraph Ave.
Oakland, Cal.
Nov 15 1904

Dear Cloudesley:—

In middle of second act of Play, & hard at it (three acts—to be called *The Way of Women*).

The films are out just now, wandering around amongst the rest of the crowd & being printed from.

Haven't been out on *Spray* nor seen her since our last. Guess I'll sell her. Or else go on a trip when I finish this play (if there is an appearance of any money in it)—which trip should start say a month from now. Would you care to make it if I can see my way to it?[1]

Jack London

Am curious about those pictures you mention. Am looking forward to them.

MS: CSmH; 2 pp., als.
    1. For their eventual sailing trip, see JL to Brett, February 21, 1905, n. 1.

To George P. Brett

1216 Telegraph Ave.
Oakland, Cal.
Nov 17 1904

Dear Mr. Brett:—

Gee! The advance sales of the *Sea Wolf* make me feel good. Your letter telling of same caught me at a fiercely hard-up moment, with Christmas staring me in the face, heavy annual insurance on half a dozen policies waiting for me to pay first of January, and a few other debts. Will it be possible for you to advance me on *Sea Wolf* sales, right away, say about three thousand dollars?

Now as to the business talk you mention. I don't think I'll be in New York for a long time to come. On the other hand, I may run off, as a sort of recreation, next January for six weeks, and give a few lectures in the Middle West.—all this, however, is in the air. Possibly, we could have the talk by letter. What do you say?

This I must say for myself. As my earning capacity increases, my output diminishes. With all the top-notch magazines offering me from 8 to 10 cts. per word, I am writing nothing for them. *The Game* is not a magazine story—I don't expect to find a magazine that will dare touch it.[1]

This play I am experimenting with (to be three acts) I shall, in two days more have completed the second act, in 2 weeks the third act. Then a trip on the *Spray* & duck-hunting.

What did you think of our socialist vote?[2]

And by the way, not to utterly forget the *Salt of the Earth*, why couldn't that book be brought out this summer, after *Sea Wolf* has run its run?—That is, if it can be brought out without loss to you. You know I have a sneaking liking for it, and I have waited pretty patiently while my favorite child was set aside for my mongrel fiction children.

And also, would it be expedient, some time in the future, to bring out *People of the Abyss*, in paper cover to sell for 25 cts. or fifty cents?

It's good propagand to commence with. On the other hand, there is a likelihood that it may become a sort of sentimental-radical-reformer's classic. If it could be more generally read in paper cover, it might react and increase future sales again in cloth-cover. Tell me what you think of the idea.

And by the way, I don't know whether I've told you already why I am hard up. At any rate, (so that you may not think I am dissipating, blowing myself), my cash has principally gone to buying land and building & furnishing a home for my children and their mother.[3] Also, in legal tangle (brought about because of my absence in Far East), the lawyers got hold of my wife, & as a result they waded into me good and hard for the cash.

Sincerely yours,
Jack London.

P.S.—On next page I give several books published by you I'd like sent to me and charged to my account.

P.S. Some Time ago a Mr. Peluso wrote to you about translating *Call of Wild* into French.

Can you tell me how the correspondence turned out?[4]

Jack London.

MS: NN; 10 pp., als. Pbd: *L*, 164–65.

1. In America *The Game* was published serially in the *Metropolitan Magazine*, April–May 1905; in England, it ran in the *Tatler*, April 5–26, 1905.

2. As the Socialist candidate for President, Eugene V. Debs polled 402,283 votes out of some thirteen million votes cast in the 1904 election, which was won by the incumbent, Republican Theodore Roosevelt. For JL's analysis of the socialist vote, see his "Big Socialist Vote Is Fraught with Meaning," *San Francisco Examiner*, November 10, 1904.

3. See JL to Brett, July 11, 1904, n. 2.

4. JL wrote Brett on August 17, 1904 (ULA), that a French journalist named Edmund Peluso would be in touch about translating *The Call of the Wild*. Although JL endorsed the project, it went no further.

To George P. Brett

1216 Telegraph Ave.
Oakland, Cal.
Nov 19 1904

Dear Mr. Brett:—

Mr. Georges Dupuy[1] is a Frenchman, an artist, a journalist, & a man who knows Alaska better than I do. He has lived the life. He feels that he can make sympathetic translations into French of say *Faith of Men* or *Children of the Frost*. Incidentally, if no arrangements have been made for *Call of the Wild*, he'd like to tackle that.

He will write you this mail.

Will you please talk it over with him, the business arrangements, etc., and see what can be done.

I called him an artist, & by the word I mean not "painter" but "temperament." He *sees*.[2]

From my talks with him I see that he has the romance, the fire, the color, the idiom of the land.

This last thing, the idiom, is vastly important in the translation of any of my stuff. The mere scholar-translator, or literary-translator could never render the spirit of my language into another language.

Mr. Dupuy is on his way to Paris. I have taken the liberty of inviting him to call on you when passing through New York.

Sincerely yours,
Jack London.

MS: NN; 4 pp., als. Pbd: *L*, 165–66.
    1. A Klondike friend of JL. See JL to Dupuy, December 1, 1910.
    2. Underlined twice.

To Anna Strunsky

[Oakland]
[December 2, 1904]

        *   *   *

Austin Lewis called the Socialist-Vote article in *Examiner*,[1] "socialism of 1860." I'm afraid I've grown old & crystalized.

I have been working hard, & what of my physical afflictions have been a pretty good recluse. Am on third & last act of play, adapted from "Scorn of Women," & to be called *The Way of Women*. Not a big effort. Wouldn't dare a big effort. An experiment, merely.—Lot's of horseplay, etc., & every character, even Sitka Charley, is belittled.

Seems to me you promised to let me see some of your novel, & other things, & that I haven't seen.

Now I'll put you in debt to me by enclosing a couple of yarns I wrote a year or so ago. Please return soon, & send along some of yours.

Jack.

MS: CSmH; 3 pp. fragment of 5 pp., als.
    1. "Big Socialist Vote Is Fraught with Meaning."

To George P. Brett

1216 Telegraph Ave.
Oakland, Cal.
Dec 5 1904

Dear Mr. Brett:—
    I'm dropping you a line hot with the idea. I have the idea for the next book I shall write—along the first part of next year.
    Not a sequel to   *Call of the Wild*.
    But a companion to " " " ".
    I'm going to reverse the process.
    Instead of the devolution or decivilization of a dog, I'm going to give the evolution, the civilization of a dog.—development of domesticity, faithfulness, love, morality, & all the amenities & virtues.[1]

And it will be a *proper*[2] companion-book—in the same style, grasp, concrete way. Have already mapped part of it out. A complete antithesis to the *Call of the Wild*. And with that book as a forerunner, it should make a hit.

What d'ye think?

Jack London.

MS: NN; 3 pp., als. Pbd: *L*, 166.
1. JL refers to *White Fang* (New York: Macmillan, 1906). Evidently the idea for the book came from Flora Hines Loughead, "The Call of the Tame: An Antithesis," an article about a wolf-dog named Bones published in the *San Francisco Chronicle*, December 4, 1904. JL's annotated copy of the article is on file in the London Collection at ULA.
2. Underlined twice.

To Charmian Kittredge

[Oakland]
[? December 5, 1904]

Find here, and please return, the *motif* for my very next book.[1] A companion to *The Call of the Wild*. Beginning at the very opposite end—evolution instead of devolution; civilization instead of decivilization. It is distinctly NOT to be a sequel. Merely same length, dog-story, and companion story. I shall not call it "Call of the Tame," but shall have title quite dissimilar to *Call of Wild*. There are lots of difficulties in the way, but I believe I can make a crackerjack of it—have quit the play for a day to think about it.

May go East in January after all for two or three months—lecturing.

SOURCE: *BJL*, II, 12.
1. In her comments on this letter, CKL wrote that on December 6 she "received a handful of notes in the mail" along with JL's comments (*BJL*, II, 12).

To George P. Brett

1216 Telegraph Ave.
Oakland, Cal.
Dec 8 1904

Dear Mr. Brett:—
Received your check for $3000.00 on account of general royalties, and I can tell you it came in handy for Christmas.

Concerning *Salt of the Earth*. I'm glad you'll bring it out in the spring. If you'll return it to me I'll get in shape at once. I may possibly take out the "Salt of the Earth" essay, and change title.[1] Also, I'll bring the matter of the other essays rights up to date—and also revise thoroughly. Taking out "Salt of Earth" essay, will still leave 40,000 words.

Also, I'll write a preface. On the strength of the vote we socialists cast the other day,[2] and also on the strength of the aroused interest in socialism, there is a chance for a fair sale of the book. I can have the copy in for you early in January—if you send it on to me right away.

The *People of the Abyss*, like *How the Other Half Lives*, etc., is more of a popularly written book than *Benevolent Feudalism* & *Social Unrest*.[3] You see, it is largely narrative, & is certainly popular in treatment. Also I imagine I am better known to the reading public, because of my fiction, than Ghent or Brooks, who have done no fiction. I was thinking of a fifty-cent paper cover edition. The kind they sell on trains, etc. etc.

The Game I think is sold to the *Metropolitan* Magazine. They've made an offer, & we're now dickering.

But concerning adding 3000 or 4000 words to the *Game*. It's the hardest kind of work to do that adding, but I believe I can do it—simply recast the first portion of it, keeping a grip in accord with the last portion, which cannot be added to. You ask me to add & then you'll make estimates of it. Why not make estimates, on the basis that I have added (I'll do my end all right), and let me know what you think you can do with it?

It may interest you that I've won a *Black Cat* Prize—a minor prize, for it was a skit written, typed, & sent off in one day.[4]

I'm wondering how my companion story to *Call of the Wild* has struck you.

Say—if I should want to get an automobile somewhere along the first of next year, would it be decent for me to ask for another advance on royalties?

Sincerely yours,
Jack London.

MS: NN; 9 pp., als. Pbd: *L*, 167.
1. JL omitted this essay from *War of the Classes*, which was published in April 1905.
2. See JL to Brett, November 17, 1904.
3. Jacob Riis, *How the Other Half Lives* (1890), an exposé of the inhumane conditions that existed in New York tenements; for the other two books, see JL to Brett, May 18, 1903.
4. "A Nose for the King" tied for third prize, and JL received $350. For *Black Cat* prizes, see JL to Johns, March 7, 1899, n. 1.

To Cloudesley Johns

1216 Telegraph Ave.
Oakland, Cal.
Dec 8 1904

Dear Cloudesley:—

I had to tell *Black Cat* that the idea of my story was not original, having been told to me by a Korean. So I don't know whether my chance is spoiled or not.

I must tell you how much all the crowd liked the fotos of you & Bony. I had them on exhibition on the mantel for a week, & now they're pasted away in one of the albums devoted to the Crowd.

Sure, I'll come & stay with you—if I can bring Manyoungi! Only too glad.

Expect to be down in first part of January.

Under separate cover am mailing you a copy of book about Death Valley which may interest you. You may keep it.

Jack London.

P.S.—I went down to look at the *Spray* to-day. First time since that night we came in from Petaluma. Won't be able to get out on her this year.

MS: CSmH; 4 pp., als. Pbd: *BJL*, II, 13.

To Cloudesley Johns

1216 Telegraph Ave.
Oakland, Cal.
Dec 14 1904

By God! I'll be with you. Leave Oakland Dec. 31st.[1]

Yep, sent in $10.00 clip with *Black Cat* story.

Can't I get a watering-trough which Manyoungi could fill every morning? I never could stand a cold sponge.

Jack London

I've some *Sea Wolfs* ordered. You can wait, as you've read it anyway.

MS: CSmH; 1 p., als.

1. Johns had occasionally attended meetings of the Los Angeles Chapter of the Socialist Party and was instrumental in arranging for JL to give a party-sponsored lecture on January 8, 1905, at Simpson Hall in Los Angeles.

To George P. Brett

1216 Telegraph Ave.
Oakland, Cal.
Dec 17 1904

Dear Mr. Brett:—

In reply to your telegram asking me, if the *Game* appears serially to insist on its appearing in more than one installment. On the very contrary, I have been insisting on its appearing in one installment.

It would be absolute ruin to it to divide it. You see, it is a thing without plot, and must be read in one sitting.

Very truly yours,
Jack London.

MS: NN; 2 pp., als.

To Cloudesley Johns

[Oakland]
Dec 21 1904

Yes—met Miss Shaw—went to dinner.[1] Liked her better than any actress ever met.

Jack London.

P.S. Too bad for Connie.[2] Hope she gets back.

MS: CSmH; 1 p., als. Pbd: *BJL*, II, 13.
    1. JL met Mary Shaw, an actress playing in Shaw's *Mrs. Warren's Profession* in San Francisco, after a performance and, according to CKL, he considered her to be "the most intellectual actress he ever talked with" (*BJL*, II, 13).
    2. Constance L. Skinner (*d.* 1939), a poet, editor, and historian who worked for the *Los Angeles Examiner*; she was also a member of the Johns household.

To George P. Brett

1216 Telegraph Ave.
Oakland, Cal.
Dec 22 1904

Dear Mr. Brett:–
    In reply to yours of Dec. 15th.
    Yes, your idea about companion story to *Call of Wild* is precisely my idea. There must be no hint of any relation between the two. Even in title I had decided there should be not the slightest resemblance. I have figured on naming book after dog—*White Fang*, for instance, or something like that. Now I believe that that very title, *White Fang* has splendid commercial value.
    Of course, I shall have copy of story in your hands as soon as finished. In fact, I have already drifted into that custom—*The Game*, for instance.
    And now, speaking of *The Game*, and your proposition on same. You will remember that I was very averse to selling out all book rights to *The Call of the Wild*. Certainly, to-day, I am more averse than ever to doing such a thing. I really cannot see my way to do it.
    Yet I like your idea very much of the manner of bringing out *The Game*, and I cannot see why you cannot bring out *Game* as planned, on a royalty basis. I can promise to have it up to 15,000 words. Between you & me, I consider it the best short thing I have done. The motif is tremendous, the subject vastly more interesting to the average man & woman than they or you would think, while the novelty of it—well, it's pretty novel for a literary effort, that is all.
    You have, ere this, received my letter telling of serial publication of *Game* in one installment. This I believe to be absolutely essential to it's

serial publication. Also, I do not think being published in the *Metropolitan* in one installment will have so detrimental an effect on its book publication. An instance of this occurs to me right now—Maeterlinck's *Our Friend, the Dog*.[1] It was published in one installment, It is less than 15,000 words, & it is now out in book-form & doing well.

I shall go to work at once on *Salt of Earth* copy, & am pretty sure I'll have copy in to you by middle of January.

I am quite willing to accept 10% royalty on paper edition of *People of the Abyss*, and am very glad that you see your way to bringing it out at fifty cents.

I am afraid that I won't find time to look up automobiles for some months to come (and it takes time). At any rate not until after the middle of January. And I am grateful to you for your kindness in offering to advance me additional money after that date.

I received the little book, or booklet, you have got out of my life & work.[2] And now, could you send me about a hundred copies of it to have in stock? You see, I continually receive requests from newspapers, writers of articles, reviews, etc., on me or about me, for biographical data, etc.,— and could use these booklets to our mutual advantage.

Also, can you charge to my account & send me five copies of *Sea Wolf*.

Also, 10 copies of *People of the Abyss*—the old edition, the two-dollars-net, if possible. But ten copies anyway.

> Sincerely yours,
> Jack London.

MS: NN; 12 pp., als.

1. Maurice Maeterlinck (1862–1949), Belgian dramatist, essayist, and poet; best known for Symbolist plays such as *La Princesse Maleine* (1889) and *Pelléas et Mélisande* (1892). *Our Friend, the Dog*, published in book form in 1904, had appeared in the *Century Magazine* in January of that year.

2. Macmillan published a fifteen-page biographical and critical sketch entitled *Jack London, a Sketch of His Life and Work, with Portrait* (1905).

To George P. Brett

1216 Telegraph Ave.
Oakland, Cal.
Dec 26 1904

Dear Mr. Brett:—

In reply to yours of Dec. 20th. As I understand it, you merely sold, (exported) to England, some 500 copies of *Children of the Frost*.

Now I shall always believe that it is by far my best collection of short stories. Take a glance at [it] yourself & see. "League of Old Men" is one of my best two short stories. "Master of Mystery," "Death of Ligoun" etc. etc. are in technique, humor, etc., among my very best.

Now, under the circumstances, having had so little sale in England, would it not be feasible for say "Heineman" to bring out the book—after *Sea Wolf* has just about shot its bolt?[1]

What do you think?

Sincerely yours,
Jack London.

P.S.—Your Christmas gift has just arrived, & I appreciate as heartily as I thank you, which same I do now.

J.L.

MS: NN; 4 pp., als.
1. Heinemann never published *Children of the Frost*.

1905

JL and CKL, shortly after their marriage (CSmH)

To George P. Brett

Los Angeles, Calif.
Jan 6, 1905

Dear Mr. Brett:—

I am expressing to-day the revised copy of book of essays. I have been hard put to find a title, & have finally decided to call it: *The Struggle of the Classes.* The initial essay, you see, is entitled "The Class Struggle."

If you, or any of your people, should hit upon a better title, I should be glad for the opportunity to consider it.

The preface I mailed off yesterday to be expeditiously typed & forwarded to you. It should reach you as quickly as the copy of book.

With preface you will receive a table of contents, which will indicate order of essays in book.

Metropolitan & some English publication will have to set a simultaneous serial publication of the *Game*—& of this I am waiting to hear. Then I'll let you know at once.

I shall be back in Oakland in five days, & expect to start East by end of January, when I hope to see you.

White Fang, of course, is not begun yet, & cannot be begun until after Eastern trip. Then, with serial publication, I am afraid it will not be ready for book publication until next year.[1]

I am glad you see your way to bringing out the *Game* on a royalty basis. I feel that it is one of my best efforts. It is the unusual thing. Has novelty and all that. Also, it is all things to all people. Those who stand for prizefighting, will like it. Those who dislike prizefighting, will find it an endictment of prizefighting. Those who know nothing of prizefighting will be curious, etc. etc. Also, it has good healthy sentiment, love, etc.

Sincerely yours,
Jack London.

MS: NN; 6 pp., als.

1. In America *White Fang* was published serially in *Outing Magazine* from May to October 1906; in England it ran in *T.P.'s Weekly* from October 5, 1906, to February 8, 1907.

To Frank Putnam

1216 Telegraph Ave.
Oakland, Cal.
Jan 17 1905

Dear Mr. Putnam:—
   In all my miserable existence I never had such a miserable time as with the miserable "One Thousand Dozen." Read the enclosure and weep for [me].¹ Also return the enclosure.²
   And now it's up to you. What are you going to do about it?
   Please let me hear from you at your early convenience.

Very truly yours,
Jack London.

MS: CU; 2 pp., als.
   1. The page is torn where the word was written.
   2. For the mix-up over this story, see JL to Putnam, November 15, 1902. For the enclosure, see JL to Putnam, January 31, 1905.

To an Unnamed Correspondent

[Oakland]
Jan 26 1905

Dear Comrade—
   I can't read your letter. I've wasted twenty minutes, ruined my eyesight, & lost my temper, and I can't make out what you have written.
   Try it over again & more legibly.

Sincerely yours,
Jack London.

P.S. I can't even make out your name.¹

MS: JL State Park; 2 pp., als.
   1. Apparently the recipient of this letter returned it. The word "over" is written several times on both pages, and on the reverse is the message: "To Whom this may concern, J.L. in particular. I am sorry I wrote once to you and I paid the penalty—only a thing not a man still less a Socialist, will display such conceit as this with your signature signed writing [illegible] I beg your pardon, Caligraphics [material crossed out]. I only received the letter in question the other Day otherwise I would have long ago replied to it. Kindly remember Conceit is allways followed by the Downfall. My name you find on that by you to me addressed envelope. [Initials?]"

To Frank Putnam

1216 Telegraph Ave.
Oakland, Cal.
Jan. 31/05

My dear Mr. Putnam:—

Do you know, I have to pinch myself to see whether or not I am awake.

(1) I write a story of 6,800 words.

(2) For this story you send me $20.00.

(3) It looks as though it were up to me to dig down & pay to the *Graphic* over one hundred dollars—due to the blundering of the *National* or it's agents.[1]

(4) and lastly, you discover and explain to me a way in which I can balance accounts by selling you five hundred dollars worth of work for one hundred dollars.[2]

> Story—6800 words.   I did this work.
> Receive $20.00
> $105.00   pay out $105.00
> $125.00
>
> $125.00
>   105.00
> $ 20.00 for 6,800 words.
>
> $500.00
> $100.00
>
> $400.00 more loss.   Where in hell am I at anyway?

You say, Jan. 24th. 1905—"I should say at a guess that he (Mr. Chapple) forgot to notify his London agent concerning the prior sale of English rights in your story."

But you say, March 11, 1903—"I notified our English agent that your story had already been sold in England."

It seems to me it's up to you. And in the meantime you explain to me that the way you'll square it will be to give me $100.00 for $500.00.

Wake me up, Please.

I've dealt with magazines on both sides of the water for all these years, & I never had such treatment as this—slovenly & unbusinesslike is the mildest censure I can put upon it.

Now it's not up to me that Chapple is out of town. And it is not up to me to see Chapple about it. All my dealings & misdealings were with you. It's up to you to see Chapple. It's up to you to do your damndest in straightening this out and giving me some measure of justice.

Please let me hear from you at once and let me know what you are doing, or intend doing, in the matter.

Sincerely yours,
Jack London.

MS: CU; 8 pp., als.
    1. See JL to Putnam, November 15, 1902, n. 2, and JL to Chapple, July 22, 1905.
    2. In a letter to JL, January 25, 1905 (CSmH), Putnam suggested that JL write two articles on socialism in Europe and in America for which he would receive $100 from the *National*.

To Charmian Kittredge

[Oakland]
Feb 2 1905

Dear, dear Mate—
    Blanche Bates, in suggestion of making a struggle between Freda & Mrs. E. for Capt. E., violates the eternal art canon of *unity*.[1] It is *another* story.[2]
    I viol[at]ed all the conventional art-canons, but not one eternal art canon.
    I wrote a play without a hero, without a villian, without a love motif, & with two leading ladies.
    Mrs. Fiske has just telegraphed me to send on play immediately.[3]
    I'll bring books along.

Mate.

MS: CSmH; 3 pp., als.
    1. Blanche Bates (1873–1941), popular actress then starring in *The Darling of the Gods* at the Macdonough Theatre in Oakland. Bates was being considered for the role of Freda in *Scorn of Women*. Because JL showed unusual interest in her—repeatedly attending her performances, hosting a dinner in her honor, and meeting with her in her room at the Metropole Hotel—the *Los Angeles Examiner* published a story on January 27, 1905, under the headline "Reported Blanche Bates Will Wed Jack London." Mrs. E. and Captain E. were the Eppingwells, characters in *Scorn of Women*.
    2. JL underlined "unity" and "another" twice.
    3. Minnie Maddern Fiske had expressed interest in starring in the play. JL wrote to her on February 1, 1905 (CSmH), saying he had received her telegram and would send her a typed copy of the revised play within a few weeks.

To the Editor, *Ability*

Oakland, California
February 20, 1905

Dear Sir:[1]
    Every time a writer tells the truth about a manuscript (or book), to a friend-author, he loses that friend, or sees that friendship dim and fade away to a ghost of what it was formerly.
    Every time a writer tells the truth about a manuscript (or book), to a stranger-author, he makes an enemy.
    If the writer loves his friend and fears to lose him, he lies to his friend.
    But what's the good of straining himself to lie to strangers?

And, with like insistence, what's the good of making enemies anyway?

Furthermore, a known writer is overwhelmed by requests from strangers to read their work and pass judgment upon it. This is properly the work of a literary bureau. A writer is not a literary bureau. If he is foolish enough to become a literary bureau, he will cease to be a writer. He won't have time to write.

Also, as a charitable literary bureau, he will receive no pay. Wherefore he will soon go bankrupt and himself live upon the charity of friends (if he has not already made them all his enemies by telling them the truth), while he will behold his wife and children went their melancholy way to the poorhouse.

Sympathy for the struggling unknown is all very well. It is beautiful—but there are so many struggling unknowns, something like several millions of them. And sympathy can be worked too hard. Sympathy begins at home. The writer would far rather allow the multitudinous unknowns to remain unknown than to allow his near and dear ones to occupy pauper pallets and potters' fields.

Sincerely yours,
Jack London

SOURCE: *Mentor*, 77–78; also pbd: "Jack London to the Unknowns," *Ability*, April 1905, and "London Explains Why He Refused to Become a Critic," *Oakland Tribune*, November 28, 1932.

   1. According to Dale L. Walker, "this interesting letter was solicited of London by Gertrude F. Boyle, editor of the San Francisco magazine, *Ability*, which survived only a single issue. London was asked for his 'advice to unknown writers'" (*Mentor*, 77).

To Frederick I. Bamford

Walnut Grove.
Feb 21 1905

Dear Comrade—

Letter off to Miss Peres. Am dreadfully sorry my diatribe against the Club had such a woeful effect upon you, but by Golly I believe to be all true.[1] I become indignant every time I think of it. What the Ruskin wants is life (intellectual dynamic life), & then it rejects life when it is offered.

I wish I had never opened the books at all—not only biology, but Browning, Milton, Shakespeare, and all the rest, including that philosophic-charlatan, Emerson.

Sincerely yours,
Jack London.

MS: JL State Park; 2 pp., als. Pbd: *Mystery*, 183–84.

   1. JL had become disenchanted with the Ruskin Club, and, at a talk given at another club, he had criticized the Ruskin for becoming "too literary" (*Mystery*, 184).

To George P. Brett

On Board *Spray*,
Feb 21 1905

Dear Mr. Brett—

Yours of Feb. 8 just received. Yes, I cut out the trip East, and have gone off for a couple of months on the *Spray*.[1] Am just starting in *White Fang*.

Can you give me an idea of *Sea Wolf* sales.

I am having difficulty in selling *White Fang* serially. The leading magazines are willing to give me 10 cts a word for serial rights, & *Harpers* offer that much for American serial rights alone;—but all of them append the proposition that they are to publish the book. So in each case, so far, it is all off.

I see you have not congratulated me upon my engagement to Blanche Bates.[2] Why this cold unregard?

Concerning that remittance on account—I want it for an automobile, but I can't get the time to buy the automobile. One has to study up the proposition first. So just let that remittance go for a while. Will it be all right for me to wire for it when I want it?

Sincerely yours,
Jack London.

MS: NN; 3 pp., als. Pbd: *L*, 168.

1. On February 4 or 5, 1905, JL and Cloudesley Johns began a trip through the sloughs of the San Joaquin and Sacramento river deltas aboard the *Spray*. They were accompanied by JL's valet, Manyoungi, and dog, Brown Wolf; for a brief part of the cruise, Herman Albrecht joined them.

2. See JL to CKL, February 2, 1905, n. 1.

To Charmian Kittredge

[Aboard the *Spray*]
Feb 24 1905

Dear Mate—

Got to Stockton. Ran down yesterday to Oakland to get forgotten data for dog story, to get *Game*, which I must immediately expand, to get statistics, etc., for "The Class Struggle," full proofsheets of same which I must correct in next 48 hours. May I then send proofsheets to you, you, on your own responsibility to change grammar, bad construction, etc., & forward immediately to:

J. S. Cushing & Co.,
Norwood Press,
Norwood,
Mass.

Express the proofsheets.

Express one good copy of the play to Mrs. Fiske as soon as finished. Her address is:—

Mrs. Minnie Maddern Fiske,
Care *Dramatic Mirror*,
1432 Broadway,
New York City.

Will you also send a copy of the play to me? Never mind that. I'll be in Napa between 6th. & 10th., & between 10th. & 15th. shall run up to G.E. for that horseback ride. Can get copy of play then.

Also, shall bring "Revolution" for typing. Give "Revolution" Sunday night in Stockton from my handwriting—a nasty job.[1]

Glad, monstrously glad, you're improving so fast.[2]

No, I'm running for mayor.[3]

Yes, that was the Miss Peres, a French Jewess.

Yes, your envelopes have been coming to me all wide open.

Please send me the Freda letter—want it for my desk copy of book in which she is.[4]

"Cheap kerosene lamp," etc—accentuate contact of civilization & the wild. Bizarre contrast—and true.[5]

Also, please *mail* at once a copy of the play to England to:

Mr. James B. Pinker,[6]
Effingham Place,
Arundel st.,
Strand,
London, W.C.
England.

Enclose a note with it telling him it is my play about which I wrote him, & for him to proceed to try to market it. Now *do not seal*[7] the package. Don't mind what local post office people say. Just tie it securely and put postage on it at the rate of one cent for every two ounces & fractions of ounces. Also, do not enclose letter in package—that letter must go separate as first class sealed matter. Understand?

Freda warns Vanderlip of maid because it is part of her play to stir him up and also to restrain him—this prolongs & gives time. Also, it is the *very* thing almost any kind of a common prostitute would do.[8]

I have written this at the end of fully 40 letters. I don't have time to breathe these days.

May take Greek[9] up to Stockton & bring him down San Joaquin on *Spray*. He is no[t] well. Don't mention it, but write him a cheery line.

I asked cigar label what there was in it for me.[10] If he says nothing, I say go ahead anyway.

I had something else to say, & have forgotten it. Thanks for hanky. I *did* need it.

Your Own Man.

MS: CSmH; 11 pp., als.
    1. JL lectured to the Critic Club of Stockton on February 26.
    2. For the preceding two weeks, CKL had been suffering from neuralgia and an abscess in her left ear.
    3. JL was once more the Socialist Party's nominee for mayor of Oakland. See JL to Eustice, January 29, 1901, n. 2, and JL to Brett, April 27, 1905.
    4. Freda Moloof wrote JL two letters, dated July 10 and August 2, 1903 (CSmH), which he tipped in his personal copy of *The God of His Fathers*.
    5. JL refers to his description of Freda Moloof's cabin at the beginning of *Scorn of Women*, Act III.
    6. JL's English literary agent.
    7. JL underlined "not seal" twice.
    8. See *Scorn of Women*, Act II.
    9. JL's nickname for George Sterling.
    10. JL had probably been approached by a cigar company for an endorsement of their product. Apparently a Jack London cigar was eventually advertised; see JL to Lewis, August 8, 1911, n. 1.

To Frederick I. Bamford

On Board *Spray*,
San Joaquin River,
Mar 2 1905

Dear Comrade—
    I have a feeling that Miss Peixotto[1] said something about Socialism being the only live thing, etc., but I wouldn't stake my life on it. I believe she did, but I am not certain enough to say it as a fact of knowledge.

Yours for the Revolution,
Jack London.

MS: JL State Park; 1 p., als. Pbd: *Mystery*, 184.
    1. Jessica B. Peixotto.

To George P. Brett

[On board the *Spray*]
Mar 7 1905

Dear Mr. Brett—
    Am still out on the *Spray*. Just a hasty line in acknowledgement of yours of Feb. 27th.
    Yes—I go East lecturing next fall for three months.[1]
    No—I'm not going on the stage.
    White Fang is sold serially to *Outing*— Just got a telegram this morning from them. They had been trying like the devil to get the book.
    Haven't got around to the automobile yet.

Sincerely yours,
Jack London

MS: NN; 2 pp., als.
1. JL lectured throughout the Midwest and East in the fall and winter of 1905–6. For an account of this tour, see Donald R. Glancy, "Socialist with a Valet: Jack London's 'First, Last, and Only' Lecture Tour," *Quarterly Journal of Speech*, 49 (February 1963), 31–39.

To Frank Putnam

[On board the *Spray*]

Mar 7 1905

My dear Mr. Putnam:—

Have read yours of Feb. 23rd.[1] Some day I shall call upon you in Boston. I shall bring your letters along with me. One of several things will happen. You will either refuse to see me, or, if you see me, will either beg my pardon or stamp yourself a miserable cad.

Very truly yours,
Jack London.

MS: CU; 2 pp., als.
1. Putnam concluded his letter of February 23, 1905 (CU): "I owe you nothing. The *National* owes you nothing. Get off our doorsteps and quit yowling."

To an Unnamed Correspondent

Napa, Cal.

Mar. 9, 1905.[1]

Dear Sir:

You ask for my views on the water question as a candidate of the Socialist Party for Mayor.[2]

The class and the Party which I represent have absolutely no interest in this question as to which of the two Companies shall supply the city of Oakland with water. The motives of the Contra Costa Water Co. and of the Bay Cities Water Co. are identical, namely, to exploit the public. The City Government of Oakland has the power to fix the charges and regulate the tolls of the Contra Costa Water Co. They according to law have power to make it impossible for the present company to take any more money from the people than the service they render the people costs the Corporation. But a Capitalist political party or a Capitalist Government will never exercise such power. Capitalism rests entirely on the system of production for profit. Capitalist Parties and Governments must protect Capitalist Property and profits. To enforce this principle of law against the Contra Costa Water Co. would rob that Co. of the power of exploitation and thus destroy its value as capitalist property. The capitalist class will not do this for by so doing they would thus endanger the whole of capitalist property. The only political party that could deal with the corporations in the interest of the great majority is the Socialist Party, representing the revolutionary nonproprietary class whose material interests compel them to convert or transform the whole of capitalist property into collective property as soon as they have the power to do so. The position of the Socialist Party then is to let the capitalist class and capitalist parties settle this bond question to suit themselves. It is none of the business of the working class. Municipal ownership under capitalism is not a part of the socialist programme. Our business is to accomplish the Social Revolution. And in the language of Marx and Engels, "We disdain to conceal our views and aims and boldly declare that our ends can be attained only by the complete overthrow of all existing economic conditions. Let the ruling class tremble at this Proletarian Revolution. Workingmen of the world unite. You have nothing to lose but your chains and a world to win."[3]

Yours for the Revolution.

Jack London

 MS: CSmH; 1 p., typs. ("Dic. H.T.").

　1. On the original, "Sash Calmes, Oakland" is typed below the date.

　2. For JL's earlier comments on the municipal ownership of water works, see JL to the Editor, *Oakland Times*, August 12, 1896.

　3. The closing lines of *The Communist Manifesto* (1848).

To George P. Brett

[On board the *Spray*]

Mar 13 1905

Dear Mr. Brett—

Concerning pamphlet "The Scab" in your letter of March 3rd. No, I do not think that pamphlet publication of same can hurt sale of *War of Classes*.[1]

On the contrary, it reaches people who never read, or rather, who never buy $1.50 book.

The first paragraph of your letter explains this very point—You say "These concerns (socialist publishing houses), do not seem to be very successful in selling any considerable quantities of the high-priced publications."[2]

That's the very thing. Their patrons are the cheap-publication-buyers.

Of course I may be wrong in all this, and if so, am sorry & won't do it again.

But just the same I'd almost believe I'd like to bet a dollar against a dollar that no 5-cent-sale of "scab" will ever knock a $1.50-sale of *War of the Classes*.

By the way, when complimentary copies of *War of Classes* are sent me, can 20 additional copies be sent me charged to my account.

I received a letter from *Everybody's* asking to see *White Fang*, and I thank you for your kind offices in this. I don't remember whether I have already told you, but *Outing* has agreed to take serial rights only. So that's settled.

I may say that—

(1) I am running for Mayor of Oakland.

(2) I am not going on the stage.

(3) I am not going to marry Blanche Bates.

(4) I am going lecturing next fall (thought I'd have one try at it).

(5) And I am not going to do any of the other things mentioned in the papers.

Have been having a great time on the *Spray*, and have hardened up some. You ought to see my hands! & my broken nails—I carry no sailors.

Am going to bring the *Spray* back to her moorings now, & go up into the mountains until next fall—no telephones, no people, no engagements, nothing but work, sunshine, & health.

Sincerely yours,
Jack London.

MS: NN; 8 pp., als. Pbd: *L*, 168–69.

1. After "The Scab" appeared in the *Atlantic Monthly*, it was published as a five-cent reprint by the socialist publishing house Charles H. Kerr & Co. of Chicago; it was also included in *War of the Classes*.

2. JL had written Brett on February 25, 1905 (NN), asking him to consider an arrangement with Charles H. Kerr & Co. and the Comrade Co-operative Co. of New York for the distribution and sale of *The People of the Abyss* in Macmillan's proposed paperback edition.

To Ida Winship

1216 Telegraph Ave.
Oakland, Cal.
Mar 23 1905

Dear Ida—[1]

I came home to go to bed, where I have been lying ever since, awaiting operation. To-morrow I am carted away to hospital, & Saturday the surgeons will be gouging around in my anatomy—an old hurt of years' standing, which I hope will now be quite cured.[2]

Oh, darn the luck anyway—I'm always in revolt against set formulas, & for that matter, rarely understand them. What I understood from Mrs. Grant was that even at the eleventh hour she'd be glad to have Johns & me to dinner. I understood this not once, nor twice, but a number of times—"If you are stuck at Vallejo, run up for the dinner,"—an instance.

I did not understand it to be what it really was, a set & meaningless formula of politeness. My mistake, & my treat.

As regards our dress. We left the *Spray* on a mud-bank. We left in a rush, doubting that we could arrive by 6:30 because of the strong ebb tide against us. We did not stop to dress, nor think to dress—again we butted up against a formula.

Damn formulas.

Now, dear Ida, don't think I am in a huff. I'm not. I'm merely explaining. I am sorry it happened. Do you please present my apologies to Mrs. Grant, and thank her for her courtesy and kindness. Cut this out of this page & give it to her, telling her I'd write were it not for lying on my back in pain.

And now all thanks to you and Ed, for the jolly, jolly, happy time we had.

The doctor is here & I must chop off this screed.

Sincerely yours,
Jack London.

MS: Labor; 6 pp., als.
1. Ida Winship, wife of Napa County millionaire Ed Winship. JL had met the Winships aboard the *Siberia* in January 1904 on his way to Japan, and they became lifelong friends.
2. JL was to have a nonmalignant tumor removed at the Shingle Sanitarium in Oakland; he was released on March 31.

To George P. Brett

[Oakland]
March 31/05

Dear Mr. Brett—

I am just sitting up after a successful operation. Have been on my back for a couple of weeks before and after operation.

Am writing you this hurriedly, to say something about the *Game*.

I have seen only the illustrations of the first half of the *Game*, in the *Metropolitan*, and it seems to me that they would ruin the sale of any book ever written.[1]

Look at them yourself. They are preposterous.

I am going over proofsheets of *Game*, and, per your request, am again expanding it. This time I shall get in over a thousand additional words.

Please put me down for 20 extra copies of *Game*, to be charged to my account and to be sent to me.

Jack London.

P.S.—I've cut out the automobile, but I'd like to have a thousand dollars advanced to me as soon as convenient. Also, can I get any data on English sales of *Faith of Men*?

J.L.

MS: NN; 6 pp., als.
1. Henry Hutt, whose work appeared in *Life*, *Harper's*, and the *Saturday Evening Post*, illustrated *The Game* in both book and serial form. T. C. Lawrence provided the decorations for the volume. JL was apparently commenting on Hutt's illustrations depicting Joe

Fleming, the novel's hero, as an effete, upper-middle-class gentleman. See also JL to Brett, May 26 and June 20, 1905.

To Charles F. Lummis

Oakland, Calif.   ·
April 4, 1905

Dear Mr. Lummis—[1]

You and I are both fighters, and single-purposed fighters, too. So I am sure you will understand my position. If I have ten dollars a year to spare, I'd sooner put it into my fight than your fight.

Besides, you can get capitalists to contribute to your fight, but I'm damned if we can get capitalists to contribute to my fight.

I'm willing to give my countenance to your fight, but not to give my time nor my money.

Sincerely yours,
Jack London

SOURCE: *L,* 169.

1. Lummis, in addition to editing *Out West,* became the librarian of the Los Angeles Public Library in 1905. He had offered JL membership in the Archaeological Society of America. For the relationship between Lummis and JL, see Dudley C. Gordon, "Charles F. Lummis and Jack London: An Evaluation," *Southern California Quarterly,* 46 (March 1964), 83–88.

To Cloudesley Johns

1216 Telegraph Ave.
Oakland, Cal.
Apr 6 1905

Dear Cloudesley—

Bravo for you and the Revolution. The word that you are going actively into the movement and that you are to deliver your first propaganda lecture in July is, to me, the happiest thing you have done in many a day.[1] I am glad, glad.

Thanks for P.O. order for $25.00.

Yes, in a week from now, Charmian's address will be Glen Ellen.[2]

Wolf.

MS: CSmH; 2 pp., als.

1. Because of a cancellation by another speaker, Johns actually gave his first talk, entitled "No Compromise," at the party meeting in June.

2. CKL visited JL almost daily during his stay in the hospital and convalescence at home. On April 13 she rode Washoe Ban, a thoroughbred horse she had recently purchased, to Glen Ellen, arriving on April 14.

To George P. Brett

1216 Telegraph Ave.
Oakland, Cal.
Apr 9 1905

Dear Mr. Brett:–
   Will you please have the check for Mrs. Jack London (which is now $75.00 per month), increased to $100.00 per month, the first increase to go into effect the first of May check to Mrs. London.
   If necessary, deduct this additional $25.00 from my monthly check of $175.00, so that I shall receive $150.00 each month.
   I prefer, however, if you can see your way to it, that my monthly check remain at $175.00.

Sincerely yours,
Jack London.

MS: NN; 2 pp., als.

To Cloudesley Johns

1216 Telegraph Ave.
Oakland, Cal.
Apr 14 1905

Dear Cloudesley—
   Pictures I like very much—though not the expressions.[1] It's pretty hard to keep a decent face while tensing muscles, isn't it.
   Thanks for rattles[2]—already appended to skin.
   I have won Brown.[3] He has his liberty all the time now, & does not go to other house at all.

Jack.

MS: CSmH; 1 p., als.
   1. In a letter to Johns, April 11, 1905 (ULA), JL mentioned sending him "all the films I could get my hands on" and having sent "the Petaluma *Spray* trip films . . . off to the printers."
   2. Possibly from a rattlesnake.
   3. Brown Wolf, JL's dog.

To Ida Winship

[Glen Ellen]
Apr 20 1905

Dear Ida—
   Well, I'm in the country now,[1] & beginning slowly to ride.
   But oh, I'm so dreadfully behind in all my work, and I am doing a day and a half's work every day.

Here's that sweater foto.
Regards to Ed.

Jack London

MS: Kingman; 1 p., als.
    1. JL arrived in Glen Ellen on April 17. He and CKL shared a two-room cottage at Wake-Robin Lodge throughout the summer, a time she characterized in her diary as a honeymoon.

To Ada L. Bascom

[Oakland]
Apr 27 1905

Dear Miss Bascom.[1]
    In the matter of the dramatization of my story, "The Great Interrogation" it is understood that my name shall appear as collaborator and the proceeds from royalties of the play shall be divided equally between us. You have my permission to arrange for the production of the piece. But under no consideration is the play to be sold outright.[2]

Jack London

Copy of permission signed by me. *Apr 27 1905*

MS: CSmH; 1 p., tls.
    1. Ada Lee Bascom (Mrs. George Hamilton Marsden) adapted JL's "The Great Interrogation" for the stage; her version was presented at the Alcazar Theatre in San Francisco on August 21. Evidently JL advised Bascom and corrected her manuscript. See also JL to J. Gilbert, December 29, 1908; JL to Marsden, September 28, 1911; and JL to Noel, September 4, 1913.
    2. This sentence was handwritten.

To George P. Brett

1216 Telegraph Ave.
Oakland, Cal.
Apr 27 1905

Dear Mr. Brett:—
    War of the Classes received, and I like very much the way you got up the book.
    No, I wasn't elected mayor, but I was called an anarchist, and the straight socialist vote in Oakland was increased 300% in two years.[1]
    Please have book department send me the following books & charge to my account:[2]

Sincerely yours,
Jack London

P.S.—Mr. Brett, when am I to have a good photograph of you?—the best you've got.

MS: NN; 2 pp., als.
  1. JL received 981 votes, 736 more than in 1901. Because of his incendiary speeches, the *San Francisco Newsletter* of March 25, 1905, labeled him "a firebrand and red-flag anarchist," saying he should be arrested for treason.
  2. The list of books is not included with the original of this letter.

To Cloudesley Johns

[Glen Ellen]
Apr 28 1905

Yes, but the whole trouble with Hawthorne is his *conventional* mind.[1] He cannot understand things that are not, but which might be, or ought to be.

Jack.

MS: CSmH; 1 p., als.
  1. Although Julian Hawthorne had praised JL in "Jack London's Socialism" and "Jack London in Literature," *Los Angeles Examiner*, January 10 and 12, 1905, apparently JL was bitter because of Hawthorne's harsh review of *A Daughter of the Snows*. See JL to Brett, July 8, 1903, n. 1.

To George P. Brett

[Glen Ellen]
May 2 1905

Dear Mr. Brett:—
  I want to ask a favor of you. Mrs. Ninetta Eames is a very dear friend of mine. I call her "Mother," so you can see how dear and near she is. I have just learned that a week or so ago she forwarded your house a manuscript of hers (book Ms.) "Deseret."
  Mrs. Eames crossed the plains by wagon-train in the long ago, and knows thoroughly the life described in her book.
  Now the favor I am asking is this: that the book be given a thorough threshing out amongst your readers. It is one of those books that seems to puzzle publishers and put them in a state of indecision—so that they do not reject it off-hand, cannot make up their minds to publish it, and at the same time are disinclined to forego it.
  The Lothrop Company had it accepted just before the Company's failure.[1]
  The Century Company asked Mrs. Eames to revise it, promising thereupon to publish it, and then in some mysterious way fell down upon the promise. In short, a puzzling proposition to publishers.
  Just now, the interest seems keen in the matter of the Mormons & the early doings of the West, and there may be a chance for the book to make a fair hit.

I guess you've found ere this that I'm not one to ask favors of this sort. (It is the first time, and I don't believe I'll ever be guilty of it again.)

But I am so very *personally* interested in this matter, that as soon as I heard that the book had gone to your house, I sat down to write this letter.[2]

Sincerely yours,
Jack London

MS: NN; 6 pp., als.

   1. The D. Lothrop Company, founded in 1850, was consolidated with Lee and Shepard in 1904 to form the Lothrop, Lee and Shepard Company.

   2. Macmillan rejected Ninetta Eames's manuscript.

To the Editor, *Atlantic Monthly*

[Glen Ellen]
May 6 1905

Dear sir:—

Please find herewith, essay, "Revolution."[1] Before reading it, I wish you would take this one thing into consideration: It is an essay composed of facts. There is not one bit of prophecy in it. The number of the Revolutionists is a fact. The Revolutionists exist. Their doctrines exist just as much as they themselves exist. Their doctrines are facts. You will note that I do not say their doctrines are *right*. I merely state what their doctrines are, in the process of describing things that exist.

In conclusion, please remember that this essay is composed of facts.

Sincerely yours,
Jack London.

MS: ICU; 3 pp., als. Pbd: *L*, 170.

   1. Bliss Perry rejected "Revolution"; see JL to Perry, May 31, 1905. The essay was published in the *Contemporary Review*, January 1908, and later included in *Revolution and Other Essays*.

To Frederick I. Bamford

Glen Ellen
May 8 1905

Dear Comrade—

Most hearty thanks for your corrections of my pronunciation. This is one of my virtues: I *love*[1] to be corrected. And I keenly appreciate the kindness of such corrections.

I am glad you like the closing words of the preface.[2] In writing them I am no less a materialist; nor am I insincere. I see the force of the spirit, the power that comes of living up high to things that are unphilosophic, unreal, & illusory.

"And sent his progeny down through the generations to become even you and I." Isn't this the place which you suggest has a nominative after a verb?

But doesn't "become" take the nominative?

And now, a favor.

Can you find out for me the following:

(1) when do wolves mate?

(2) how long do they carry their young?

(3) What time of the year do they bring forth their young?

All this is data for a new book I am beginning—[3]

Sincerely yours,
Jack London

MS: JL State Park; 4 pp., als. Pbd: *Mystery*, 185.
1. Underlined twice.
2. To *War of the Classes*.
3. *White Fang*.

To Frederick I. Bamford

[Glen Ellen]
May 11 1905

Dear Mr. Bamford:—

Heartiest thanks for the Wolf information. The *Outlook* article is great. I should like to have about ten of the Week's Pamphlet.

I am sending you inclosed check for Seventy-five ($75.00) Dollars. Don't fret about it, and don't be in a rush about it, and take your own good time in returning it. I need not tell you how glad I am that you have come to this decision, for I know it will do you a world of good.[1]

Yours for the Revolution,
Jack London

MS: JL State Park; 1 p., tls. Pbd: *Mystery*, 186.
1. Bamford was about to enter Burke's Sanitarium in Santa Rosa for a rest.

To George P. Brett

[Glen Ellen]
May 11 1905

Dear Mr. Brett:—

Yes, I am very pleased at your suggestion of bringing out a 25¢ edition of *The War of the Classes*, and the one-half division of the profits is certainly acceptable to me.[1] I am very glad to have the book circulated in that fashion. It reaches the people it is intended to reach, and who as a class never buy a dollar and a half cloth book.

I am inclosing herewith a letter from Mr. Herman Albrecht, a friend of mine who is desirous of translating my stories into German. You will note that he says that American and English authors have no copyright protection in Germany. I am writing you to find out if this is so. Please let me know soon.

I am off in the mountains and hard at work. In a month's time I have had not one visitor, nor had a hat on my head. I ride from ten to twenty miles every day and am getting myself into the pink of condition. Also, I shall shortly begin my regular daily swim.

Outing has agreed to take *White Fang* at ten cents a word for American serial rights. But they do not expect to publish it in the magazine until the first part of 1906. So, while I am all ready to begin it, I have put back beginning it for a month or so, in the meantime turning out some short stories. I have sold one of them, "The Sun Dog Trail," to *Harper's*.[2]

My play, *Scorn of Women*, I have submitted to Mrs. Fiske. I have just received a letter from her in which she says that she is delighted with it, and that she has sent it on to her husband[3] for *his* reading, and that she will see me next month here in California, and talk it over with me. Of course, I do not know whether or not we shall come to any final arrangement, or whether she would find it sufficiently acceptable for acting.[4] Of course, this is just between you and me. I don't care to have the newspapers getting hold of the idea while it is yet unsettled.

Sincerely yours,
Jack London

MS: NN; 2 pp., tls.

1. Macmillan published the paperback edition of *War of the Classes* in 1906.

2. "The Sun-Dog Trail," *Harper's Monthly*, December 1905, later included in *Love of Life* (New York: Macmillan, 1907).

3. Harrison Grey Fiske, journalist, playwright, and his wife's manager. From 1901 to 1907, the Fiskes ran their own theater and company, in opposition to the Theatrical Syndicate, at the Manhattan Theatre in New York.

4. For the upshot, see JL to Fiske, August 2 and 4, 1905.

To the Corresponding Editor, *Youth's Companion*

[Glen Ellen]
May 11 1905

Dear sir:—

In reply to yours of May 3; I am glad you like my stories, and still continue to find use for them.[1] However, in the last year or so I have been doing very little short fiction, possibly half a dozen stories in that time. I note your offer of $200.00 for an available story of 2,000 words. But on the other hand, from all the large magazines, *Harper's*, *McClure's*, *Ainslee's*, *Outing*, *The Century*, etc., etc., I am receiving ten cents a word for my American serial rights, so it would scarcely be profitable for me to undertake *Youth's Companion* stories at half the rate I am receiving elsewhere. Besides, as I say, I am doing very little short-story writing now. But I hope that I shall never be so busy as quite to forget the *Youth's Companion*. I tell you, you pulled me out of some pretty tight holes when I was beginning my writing career, and filled an empty flour barrel more than once.

Sincerely yours,
Jack London

MS: CSmH; 1 p., tls.
    1. The short stories later collected in *Tales of the Fish Patrol* had just finished their run in *Youth's Companion*.

To Robert U. Johnson

Glen Ellen
May 18, '05

Dear Mr. Johnson:—
    Yes, I quite see your point of view in your letter of May 12, and largely agree with you. "The White Man's Way" is certainly not a short story with beginning, middle and ending.[1] Now that I look back, I can remember that my reason for sending it to you was that it was not bluggy nor horrible, and that you had stipulated that you did not want any bluggyness nor horribleness.
    I'll turn loose and try to do a real short story for you, and you may expect it along in the next several weeks.[2]
    Now concerning payment: when I wrote Mr. Gilder[3] a number of months ago, I stated the rate I was then receiving, which was eight (8¢) cents per word—rather, that was what I was being offered by the various magazines I was holding off, because at that time I was not doing any short fiction. I have only just now started in to do short stories—a few. In the meantime, my rate has been going up, though I have not been selling anything. This, as you will readily understand, is due to conditions outside of me, and to which I not only gracefully but gratefully yield. For instance, you will remember I made an offer of a short serial to you, some time ago. This same short serial of 40,000 words *Outing* recently took, paying me ten cents a word for the American serial rights only. Another instance: Since my statement that my rate was eight cents a word, *Collier's* has offered me $1,000 an article, for twenty articles about the United States, the subjects to be selected by myself. This offer, however, for a number of reasons, was declined by me.
    Now you have the situation in a nutshell. The question with me is not one of technicality nor legality, but of spirit. If the spirit of our correspondence of that date was of the nature that my rate with *The Century* would

be unchanging for all the future, or even unchanging for an indefinite future until such time that I should supply a short story, why I am quite willing to live up to it, and as to what the spirit of that correspondence was, I'll leave it to you. If you decide that it was eight cents a word for an indefinite future, eight cents a word goes, and I'll do my very best by the short story and you. Please let me know your judgment in the matter.

Now one other thing: You say, that you ought to have the story exclusively, independent of any English publication. Surely this is not based upon our correspondence of several months ago.

Now in the face of what has gone before in this letter, I am willing to suggest a compromise: Pay me ten (10¢) cents a word, and I'll forego the English serial rights. In the meantime, while I am writing the story for you, do you let me know what you think of the whole proposition.

Sincerely yours,
Jack London

MS: CSmH; 2 pp., cctl.

1. "The White Man's Way" was published, not by the *Century*, but in the Sunday magazine of the *New York Tribune*, November 4, 1906. It was later included in *Love of Life*. The story consists of a satiric dialogue between an unnamed first-person narrator and an old Indian, in which the uncomplicated mores of the Indian world are contrasted with the incomprehensible complexity of "the white man's way."

2. JL probably sent "All Gold Canyon," published in the *Century*, November 1905, and later included in *Moon-Face*.

3. Richard Watson Gilder.

To George P. Brett

Glen Ellen, Cal.,
May 26, 1905.

Dear Mr. Brett:—

As I am up here in the hills, away from all my letter-files and business papers, I don't remember exactly what time of the year the contract calls for, for a settlement of account. But I have a hazy recollection that it is somewhere along in the spring of the year. I should like to get from you a statement showing how much royalties has been advanced, the respective earnings of the various books, and how much is now coming to me.

I'll tell you why: For a long time I have been keeping steadily the idea in mind of settling down somewhere in the country. I am in a beautiful part of California now, and I have my eyes on several properties, one of which I intend to buy,[1] so I want to know how much money I possess in order to know to what extent I may buy.

Also, the situation is such, other men desirous of buying in at low figures, (and they have been waiting for years, some of them), etc., that I'd like to have a few thousands on hand in order to close immediately with any proposition that may be made. If I had to delay the putting up of the cash for the ten or twelve days necessary to get the money from you, there would be opportunity for the word to be carried to the rival would-be purchasers, and they might snap up the property themselves. So, I'd like to arrange with you, if possible, the two following things: (1) For you on receipt of telegram from me, to reply by telegram that money was being forwarded, and also, to forward money by mail. (Your telegram I could use to raise money upon immediately with some bank, and I guess, that would be cheaper than telegraphing a large sum directly to me. That's one thing I do not know much about—telegraphing money. It might not be as dear as I think, and it might be more expedient and practical for you to telegraph me the whole sum.)

(2) If the time is up or past for the annual settlement of account, I should like you, not only to send statement, but to send me balance due me along at the same time. And for that matter, if it is anywhere around time for settlement of account, and if you could find it in line with your policy, I should like the balance due me to accompany the statement of account.

I should prefer getting the money this way, in my hand, to the depending upon telegraphing for it.

Please let me hear as soon as you can, concerning the whole matter.

Sincerely yours,
Jack London

P.S.—I have just received the proofs of *The Game*, and I want to tell you how pleased I am with the way it is being illustrated, page by page. The effect is splendid. This running illustration of the text, in my belief gives life to the impressions of the reader.[2] In short, I like it immensely.

MS: NN; 2 pp., tls. Pbd: *L*, 170–71.
  1. See JL to Brett, June 7, 1905.
  2. *The Game* was illustrated by T. C. Lawrence's black-and-white line drawings and chapter frontispieces that depicted Death as a skeleton manipulating the plot; Henry Hutt's glossy color inserts portrayed scenes from the novel. See JL to Brett, March 31 and June 20, 1905.

To Frederick I. Bamford

Glen Ellen, Cal.,
May 28–1905.

Dear Mr. Bamford, dear friend:–

We are glad to hear that you are getting along so well and are so happy. It's too bad that you can only get your country in the expensive doses of the Sanitarium. Of course the baths and treatments are all right, but after all, they are not the main thing. The main thing is the country itself, and the fact that you are out of the high pressure of city life. If you could only manage some less expensive way of taking the country, you would be able to lengthen the dose. A tent, ten miles from a railroad station or a mail box, an axe to chop your own wood with, a bucket to carry your own water with, a couple of pots and a frying-pan to cook your own food in, and all the rest of the time for simply loafing, without meeting people who ask you to outline the life of Caesar, would be the one very thing for you. This is just my suggestion. I may not know anything about it at all, and I give it for what it is worth.

The thing is, to cease being intellectual altogether. To take delight in little things, the bugs and crawling things, the birds, the leaves, etc., etc. The thing is to get so keenly interested in decently cooking a pot of rice, that you will forget that there ever was a socialist revolution, or a library, or high school children getting books for collateral reading, or anything else under the sun except the one end—a decently-cooked pot of rice. You see what I'm driving at. The idea is capable of untold enlargement.

I was very much taken with *De Profundis*, but I'm not going to make you think any thoughts by telling you what I thought about it.[1]

Everybody here sends you love, in which I join.

Oh, by the way, next time we ride over to Burke's I sincerely hope that I shall meet one less person than I did last time—that woman who lugged you and me in out of the hay and the sunshine to sit in a stuffy room and talk little nothings, for instance. I haven't anything against this particular woman, but against her kind. I didn't ride over to Burke's to see her, but to see you. I didn't come to Glen Ellen to see people, but to get away from people. All this à propos of a line in your letter saying that there were some people over there who would like to meet me, and for me to come to the ten o'clock breakfast. When I come over, I shall come over to see you, and though quite willing and glad to meet Doctor Burke, would want to cut out all the rest. I consider such people vampires and I haven't any life-blood to waste upon them.

Frankly and sincerely yours,
Jack London

MS: JL State Park; 2 pp., tls. Pbd: *Mystery*, 187–88.
  1. Bamford had given JL a copy of Oscar Wilde, *De Profundis* (1905).

To George Sterling

Glen Ellen, California,
May 28, 1905.

Dear Greek:

Be sure and let me know when to look for you when you come up. Let me know in advance what train you are coming on, and let me know well enough in advance, so that in case I am not going to be there, I can head you off.

You see, I am planning to go down to see Mrs. Fiske some time during her stop in San Francisco, which will be somewhere in the first part of June, but precisely where in the first part of June, I do not know.

Regarding Lafler's scheme [1]—I think it's all right. I am willing to work for it, I am willing to write for it, and to pony up a share of the money necessary to start it. But on the other hand, plans of mine which have been maturing for some time would render it impossible for me to be the angel for the enterprise. I have long since given over my automobile scheme; it was too damned expensive on the face of it, and I have long since decided to buy land in the woods somewhere and build. I have just written MacMillan Company to get whatever balance I have coming from them, and also to find out how much more they can advance me on future work, in order to put through my land-buying and house-building enterprise. Of course, dear Greek, all the forgoing is between you and Lafler and me.

For over a year now, or rather, since my return from Korea, which is just under a year, I have been planning this home proposition, and now I am just beginning to see my way clear to it. I am really going to throw out an anchor so big and so heavy that all hell could never get it up again. In fact, it's going to be a prodigious, ponderous sort of an anchor.

To return to the question. While I am willing to get in and work for Lafler's paper should he start it, you will readily see I could not go in for being the main-finance-guy of it without smashing my already matured plans. It's up to Lafler and any enthusiastic co-workers he can gather immediately around him to hustle for the sum total of money necessary to start this paper and keep it going for the many months which in the nature of things are bound to intervene before it can attain a paying basis.

It's this way, George: I feel that I have done and am doing a pretty fair share of work for the Revolution. I guess my lectures alone before socialist organizations have netted the Cause a few hundred dollars, and my wounded feelings from the personal abuse of the Capitalist papers ought to be rated at several hundred more. There is not a day passes that I am not reading up socialism and filing socialistic clippings and notes. The amount of work that I in a year contribute to the cause of socialism would earn me a whole lot of money if spent in writing fiction for the market.

So now you see the situation as regards other plans, as well as my feeling in the matter, and I know you understand. Don't forget to let us know several days in advance, when you expect to come up.

                                                                Wolf.

MS: CSmH; 2 pp., tl. Pbd: *L*, 171–72.

1. Harry Lafler, an editor of the *Argonaut*, and Sterling were seeking financial backing for a new socialist periodical.

To Bliss Perry

[Glen Ellen]
May 31 1905

Dear Mr. Perry:—
Thank you for your kind rejection of May 25. Now this is not sarcastic at all, and I am thanking you for the best and most genuine rejection I ever received in all my life. Not only that, but I quite agree with you. My article certainly was not suitable for the readers of the *Atlantic*, and if I had thought of it at the time, given it but a moment's thought, I should never have sent it to you.[1]

Sincerely yours,
Jack London

MS: ULA; 1 p., tls.
  1. See JL to the Editor, *Atlantic Monthly*, May 6, 1905.

To George Sterling

Glen Ellen
Sonoma Co.—Cal.
June 1, 1905.

Dear Greek:
Nay, nay, I don't think you misconceived my financial status insofar as you thought that the *Sea Wolf* had made me at least $20,000. I guess the *Sea Wolf* made me about $15,000. Your misconception lies in how much of it I have on hand. You take advance royalties such as I am receiving from the Macmillan Company—$300.00 per month, or $3600 per year—and figure how rapidly they will eat into $15,000. Yea—yea, and figure how rapidly no end of other things will eat into $15,000. I have just come through hospital myself, and I guess I dropped a couple of hundred right there. I have just put one of my sisters[1] through five weeks of hospital: it is not the first time I have done this for her, nor will it be the last. The doctor bills that I have paid for Bessie and the two children have run up into many hundreds of dollars in the last year, to say nothing of nurses. My Mammy Jenny[2] has to send for the doctor once in a while. I pay for it. My mother has to send for the doctor now and again. It's up to me. I haven't said a word about dentists for myself and other people. I'll mention in passing the several hundred dollars that Bessie's lawyer hooked me up for. And I could go on for a half dozen more blessed pages reciting where my money has gone. Yesterday, for instance, I sent off a $10 check to help out a new socialist paper that is struggling for existence in Toledo, Ohio.[3] Just now I am coughing up $30.00 for the printing of the Appeal to the Supreme Court of an ex-convict who is lying in the County Jail with a

sentence of fifty years over his head.⁴ And so on, and so on—it just leaks away.

As the situation now is, I hope to be able to scrape enough money together to buy merely the land; then I'll either wait for a year or so to build, or else mortgage the land in order to build. I have not made up my mind yet.

I have been giving you all this hash of stuff in order that you may see my position and just how I stand. You're the only person in the world that I'd take the trouble for. The rest could go to the devil and I wouldn't care. But you, dear Greek, you I do want to know.

Oh, the little item of life-insurance comes into my head—I am carrying $20,000 insurance. It is in the endowment form. And if you know what *endowment* means, you can see how heavy that little item is.

I don't care a red [cent] how much the Lazar sheets roast me. It was merely in a humorous way that I decided that my hurt feelings were worth something.

I am sorry to hear that you are not coming up. I don't know when I'm coming down. I have to go to see Mrs. Fiske, but we have not yet arranged date of meeting. From your repeated trips to Carmel, it would strike me that something is doing down there. How is it? Have you got the land in sight yet, or are you still prospecting.⁵ Do let me know.

I have given your final line to Charmian, and she tells me she got a letter off to you day before yesterday.

No, I am afraid that the dream was too bright to last—our being near each other. If you don't understand now, some day sooner or later you may come to understand. It's not through any fault of yours, nor through any fault of mine. The world and people just happen to be so made.

As ever,
Wolf.

MS: CSmH; 2 pp., tl. Pbd: *L*, 172–73.
    1. Ida Miller.
    2. Virginia Prentiss.
    3. *The Socialist*.
    4. See JL to Johns, October 4, 1905.
    5. Sterling, disenchanted with bohemian life in San Francisco, bought a lot and built a house in Carmel.

To George P. Brett

Glen Ellen,
June 7 1905

Dear Mr. Brett:

Yours of the 1st just received. Now I'll tell you what I have done and what I want. I have found the land I want, and have closed the deal by paying $500.00, binding the bargain for a few days, when I must pay the balance, $6,500.00. The place was a bargain, one of those bargains that a man would be insane to let slip by. The entrance is a half-mile from a small town and two different railway stations. An electric road is soon to be constructed, when the running time to San Francisco will be cut down to an hour and a half. At present it is something like two hours and a half by the railroad. There are 130 acres in the place, and they are 130 acres of the most beautiful, primitive land to be found anywhere in California. There are great redwoods on it, some of them thousands of years old— in fact, the redwoods are as fine and magnificent as any to be found anywhere outside the tourist groves. Also there are great firs, tan-bark oaks, maples, live-oaks, white-oaks, black-oaks, madrono and manzanita galore. There are canyons, several streams of water, many springs, etc., etc. In fact, it is impossible to really describe the place. All I can say is this—I have been over California off and on all my life, for the last two months I have been riding all over these hills, looking for just such a place, and I must say that I have never seen anything like it.[1]

Woodchoppers were already at work when I snapped up the place. It had to be snapped up. Twenty years from now I'll wager it will be worth twenty times what I am now paying for it. In a few days I shall have to pay over the balance of $6,500.00. This I want to get from you as soon as you receive this letter. Also, I want you to telegraph me at above address as soon as the money is dispatched.

Now to business: I have made a rough calculation upon royalties advanced, and upon earnings of books. I say "rough calculation," because all my papers are down in Oakland; but I also made it a conservative calculation. Outside the regular monthly advances, I have received, I believe, a couple of thousand. Subtracting all royalties advanced from what I figure to be the royalties earned, there should be coming to me say $10,000—in this calculation I have taken no account of what the English earnings of a couple of the books would be, *The Sea Wolf* and *The Faith of Men*.

Now in the past, you made me advances on unearned royalties. The present situation is different; I am asking an advance on *earned* royalties. Of course, I understand according to contract that in present instance I am not supposed to touch the royalties of *The Sea Wolf* until nearly a year afterward. So I am compelled to call upon your good-nature to help me out.

I don't care to bother with getting San Francisco banks to discount your Note; so you can arrange it any way you wish, discounting your Note there in New York, and sending me the $10,000 as soon as you possibly can.

I say "as soon as you possibly can," because just now every moment counts. I have to go away in October,[2] and between now and then, with all the usual irritating delays, I must start building; when I have paid out that $7,000.00 for the place, there won't be very much left with which to build. But I can at least put up the barn and live in that until I can get the money together to put up the house. Incidentally, to-day, according to agreement with present tenant[3] who is leaving in order to put me into possession, I am to pay him something like $600.00 for his several horses, a couple of cows, mountain wagon, harnesses, plows, harrows, etc., etc. So you'll see I am pinching my ready cash down and shall be flat-broke until I get remittance from you.

This is to be no summer-residence proposition, but a home all the year round. I am anchoring good and solid, and anchoring for keeps, and it means a great deal to me. My lasting regret, in case the thing fell through, would be not the loss of the money already advanced, but the loss of the place itself. I could never find another place like it again, and I, who am a Californian, tell you this.

Sincerely yours,
Jack London

P.S.—In reading over this letter, I notice an ambiguity. In one place I mention your dispatching me $6,500.00 (for payment of the place), and later on I mention your sending me $10,000. Now what I want is the $10,000.00.

MS: NN; 3 pp., tls. Pbd: *L*, 174–75.
    1. JL purchased the 129-acre Hill Ranch from Robert P. Hill. This became the nucleus of JL's Beauty Ranch.
    2. On his lecture tour of the East and Midwest.
    3. The tenants were the Allens.

To Cloudesley Johns

Glen Ellen, Calif.
Jun 7 1905

Dear Cloudesley—
    Yea, verily, gorgeous plans. I have just blown myself for 129 acres of land. I'll not attempt to describe. It's beyond me.
    Also, I have just bought several horses, a colt, a cow, a calf, a plough, barrow, wagon, buggy, etc. etc. to say nothing of chickens, turkeys, pigeons, etc. etc. All this last part was unexpected, & has left me flat-broke. Also, I am expecting to receive, & dreading to receive, each moment, a notice from Bess that she wants several hundred dollars with which to buy a horse & surrey. I built her a barn, & promised her the money for horse & surrey as soon as she found them. And at any day she's liable to find them. I've taken all the money I could get from Macmillan to pay for the land, & haven't any now even to build a barn with, much less a house.

Haven't started *White Fang* yet. Am writing some short stories in order to get hold of some immediate cash.

Jack

MS: CSmH; 4 pp., als.

To Frederick I. Bamford

[Glen Ellen]
Jun 8 1905

Dear Mr. Bamford:

Many thanks for the beautiful excerpt from Watson.[1] It is splendid.

By the way, my proposition to you about cooking rice was literary, not literal.[2] It was a figure of speech, not a diet. I was merely trying to describe the simple life as I thought you ought to live it.

—Meat!—why, that's what I've been saying to you ever since I knew you! That instead of starvation, the very thing you wanted was meat. I am glad Dr. Burke agrees with me.

No, I haven't the Revolution speech with me. Certainly, my idea was not to modify, when I gave it at the U.C.,[3] but to make it a stinging blow, right between the eyes, and shake their mental processes up a bit, even if I incurred the risk of being called a long-haired anarchist.

I am afraid we shall not be able to ride up to Dr. Burke's again. I have just bought a lot of land here, horses, cows, colts, calves, pigeons, chickens, turkeys, plows, barrows, hay, etc., etc., and their possession and arrangement, building operations, etc., plus all my work, will keep me about as busy as I can jump, until I go East in October. I won't attempt to describe the place, but I just tell you that once you are here and see it for yourself, you'll say there's no place like it in all California. And come you certainly must, for any length of time you can, and if for no more, for a week-end anyway—after I've got the place in shape and the house put up.

Sincerely yours,
Jack London

MS: JL State Park; 1 p., tls. Pbd: *Mystery*, 189–90.
    1. Bamford sent JL the following excerpt from William Watson's "A Hymn to the Sea": "Sea that breakest forever, that breakest and never art broken / Like unto thine, from of old, springeth the spirit of man—Man who / Seemeth so easy to shatter, and proveth so hard to be cloven" (*Mystery*, 190). See also JL to Strunsky, ? February 1900, n. 2.
    2. See JL to Bamford, May 28, 1905.
    3. JL delivered "Revolution" at the University of California on January 20 and at the Unitarian Club of San Jose on January 25, 1905.

To the Editor, *San Francisco Examiner*

Glen Ellen,
June 14 [1905]

I never personally met Alexander McLean,[1] but I heard of his wild exploits from the men with whom I went seal hunting in 1893.

McLean had an exciting record of adventure and upon his deeds I based my Sea Wolf character. Of course, much of the Sea Wolf is imaginative development, but the basis is Alexander McLean. Alexander had a brother, Dan McLean, who also was a sealing captain and a petty adventurer of some note.

Jack London

SOURCE: "Jack London Telegraphs to 'The Examiner' About Alexander M'Lean the Original of His 'Sea Wolf,'" *San Francisco Examiner*, June 15, 1905.

1. Alexander McLean, captain of the sealing schooner *Carmencita* and the model for Wolf Larsen in *The Sea-Wolf*. McLean had been arrested in Victoria, British Columbia, on September 4, 1905, and fined $1,600 for poaching fur seal. See "London's Sealing Sea Wolf an Outcast on the Deep," *San Francisco Examiner*, June 15, 1905. In an article entitled "'Sea Wolf' Drowned; Savage of the Deep," *Chicago Record-Herald*, January 29, 1906, JL commented on McLean, recently lost in a storm in the Straits of Juan de Fuca, leading into Puget Sound: "I met him in 1898 [*sic*] off the coast of Japan, when he was seal hunting in a vessel of his own, and when I was a sailor on one of the other ships in the fleet. I myself never sailed with McLean, but knew much of him from the other men in the fleet. McLean had a big record as a rough character and was known as the worst man, so far as physical violence was concerned, among the seal hunters. He also had a brother, Dan McLean, who was almost as rough a customer as Alex. I spent several months on the cruise when I was brought into contact with him, and although I never knew McLean personally to any extent, I gathered a great deal of information and gossip about him."

To George P. Brett

Glen Ellen, Calif.
Jun 20 1905

Dear Mr. Brett:—

My hearty thanks for the two checks aggregating $8322.28, which came safely to hand.

As I understand it, this is but a partial account, and that when the proper time arrives, the full statement of our whole account, everything up to date, will be sent me.

The place I have bought is indeed a beautiful part of California, and I shall only be too glad of a chance to prove to you the wisdom of my selection by having you come and look at it yourself. Which reminds me, by the way, of your doubt as to the advisability of any man who has a part to play in the world, tying himself down by the purchase of real estate in any part of the country, no matter how beautiful and no matter how productive; and also your proposition that it is not usually profitable to the absentee owner. When I lived in Oakland on the Heights where you visited me, I was something like an hour's run from San Francisco—in fact, a number of minutes over an hour's run. I am now, in present location, a few minutes more than two hours' run from San Francisco, and in a year or so when the new road is completed, I shall be an hour and a half's run from San Francisco. It's not so very remote, nor inaccessible, and in view of the fact that I always resolved that California should be my home, I scarcely see the possibility of any unwisdom entering into my purchase. I shall always be free to come and go, even to the ends of the earth. Also, I was very careful to buy a place out of which no profit possibly could be made. On the land or absent, I'll never be bothered by a profit or loss account so far as the place is concerned. It will run itself so far as firewood and pasture for a couple of horses and a cow is concerned. And there is nothing that I could possibly sell off of it except the scenery. I told you in my previous letter that it would be worth in twenty years twenty times what I have paid for it. It was one of those bargains that one stumbles on to in much the same way that one finds a gold mine. The architect whom I have had over the place, a man who knows California and land values thoroughly, seemed quite confident that in ten years, considering all the factors of the situation, it would be worth a hundred thousand. I am not quite so sanguine as he, and so I am content to say that it will be worth one hundred and forty thousand in twenty years. It will be the second ten years that will jump up its value. Well, never mind, just wait until you see it for yourself.

I have made a number of changes, according to the suggestions of Mr. Heinemann,[1] for the English copies of *The War of the Classes*. I can't see how Mr. Heinemann can get finicky over the fair name and fame of Rockefeller or Collis P. Huntington,[2] whose misdeeds are pretty historically correct by this time; but so be it, Mr. Heinemann does get finicky, and I make the alterations he has suggested. But I do not want to see these alterations appear in any copies of *The War of the Classes* which are to be sold in America. It would be damnable so far as I am concerned—the toning down of my original historically-correct statements.

And now, one other thing—and oh, by the way, now that the advance copy of *The Game* has come to me I want to tell you again how much I appreciate the way you have brought it out. The color-illustrations are excellent. It seems to me I have never seen anything to compare with them, while the running illustration of the text by Mr. Lawrence, including the Love and Death motives, are splendidly sympathetic in themselves, and also tremendously illuminative of the text. I must say that I like the get-up of this book more than any book that I have yet had published,—and that, in spite of the fact that I was not pleased with Mr. Hutt's *Metropolitan* illustrations. Said illustrations have certainly been transformed either by the color-process or by some other kind of doctoring.[3]

And now to the one other thing, broached at beginning of preceding paragraph: I'd like to get into my possession, for my own personal gratification and joy, and incidentally for the decoration of my own Den, a couple of the original drawings of Mr. Hutt's, namely, the one on page 159, where the two men are fighting with the referee in the Ring, and the one on page 57, of Genevieve, describing her remaining in the shop in a sort of waking trance. Also I want to know, if by any stroke of good luck, I can get hold of a few of the original drawings of Mr. Lawrence's.

Sincerely yours,
Jack London

P.S.–I am inclosing herewith a newspaper clipping which will show you the later doings of the flesh-and-blood prototype of my "impossible" Sea-Wolf, or Wolf Larsen.

MS: NN; 3 pp., tls.
    1. William Heinemann (1863–1920), English publisher and head of the firm bearing his name. He published *War of the Classes* in 1905.
    2. John D. Rockefeller (1839–1937), Standard Oil tycoon; Collis P. Huntington (1821–1900), Southern Pacific magnate. The unethical business practices of both men were favorite targets of the muckrakers, and JL criticized them in "The Scab."
    3. See JL to Brett, March 31 and May 26, 1905.

To George P. Brett

Glen Ellen, Calif.
Jun 27 1905

Dear Mr. Brett:
    Please find herewith my signed authorization for the cheap edition of *The Sea Wolf* in the Standard Library. I like this idea of yours very much, and if you succeed in reaching the great mass of at present non book-buying readers, you will have done a wonderful thing. And I imagine, if successful, it should pay as a large body of low-grade ore pays the modern mining engineer. It's a good idea.
    However, I am curious about two or three details of it. Is it to be paper-cover or cloth-cover? And is it to be sold through the present book-distributing channels, or have you in mind new and different channels. And have you an approximate idea of what the net profit per copy may amount to?
    As I understand it, you and I in this particular proposition of *The Sea Wolf* are going in together to speculate. We may make nothing out of it, and you are liable to lose something; and we may make something which we will divide between us. Have I got it straight?
    By the way, I notice some publisher in New York is getting out or has got out a cheap edition of *The Call of the Wild*.[1] I have a little natural curiosity to know how many copies of the book have been sold—a sort of

parental pride. And so I am wondering if you can give me any idea of how many copies are being sold by this New York publisher, and I'd like to know what the book is selling for.

I inclose you herewith a letter from Mr. F. J. de Giers. As you and I know, great profits are not to be expected from such a book as *The War of the Classes*, and I think under the circumstances that almost any kind of a fair arrangement of the German translation would be expedient and the right thing. I have told Mr. de Giers to write to you about this matter of translating, and to make any and all arrangements with you, and you have my authorization, of course, to go ahead and make them.[2]

Ground is broken to-day for the foundation of the barn. Also to-day I have completed the first thousand words of my *White-Fang* story—the companion-story to *The Call of the Wild*, which I mentioned to you some time ago.

Sincerely yours,
Jack London

MS: NN; 2 pp., tls.
    1. Possibly either the Regent Press or the Grosset & Dunlap edition of *The Call of the Wild*.
    2. Nothing came of this proposal.

To Cloudesley Johns

Glen Ellen, Calif.
Jun 27 1905

Dear Cloudesley—

How'd the lecture come off?[1] I'm anxious to hear. Did you read it, or did you shape up the line of argument & talk it? Tell me all about it.

But I'm not going ranching. The only cleared ground on the place will be used for growing hay for a couple of riding horses, a couple of farm horses, & a couple of cows. If there is any hay left over, of course I can sell it—and that would be like finding money.

No, no—only extravagance about it will be the hired man[2]—& he'll take care of the horses. By means of him & of the ranch I'll have no house-rent, no vegetable bills, fuel bills, milk bills, etc. etc.

Wolf.

MS: CSmH; 3 pp., als.
    1. See JL to Johns, April 6, 1905, n. 1.
    2. JL hired Werner Wiget as foreman of the ranch.

To Mr. Scott

[Glen Ellen]

Dear Mr. Scott:[1]   *Jun 27 1905*

If you will write to The Macmillan Company, New York City, you can get from them a copy of a pamphlet they have got out about me and my work.[2] From *The Editor*, published some two or three years ago, you will find an article by me descriptive of my early struggles to get into print.[3]

You should get a great deal of data from the foregoing articles. Now I will try to answer your questions. What first led me to take up writing?— I was hard up, couldn't get any work to do, had my name down in five employment agencies for any kind of work, and had put my last cent into ads for work in the daily papers (it was hard times), and then, not finding anything to do, and while waiting for something to do, I started in to write for the magazines. I was about twenty-three years old when I went at it then seriously.

My first story was accepted by *The Overland Monthly*.[4] It was entitled "To the Man on Trail." It was published in *The Overland Monthly* in January, 1899.

The foregoing was the first story I had accepted, but they were not accustomed to paying promptly, so the first money I received for a story was from the *Black Cat*, entitled "A Thousand Deaths."

How much time do I devote to writing a book?—anywhere from one month to six months. I wrote *The Call of the Wild* in one month. I wrote *The Sea Wolf* in six months. But when I work, I work.

As regards the conscious aim of my writing—as the public, as a general thing, and the reviewers as well, have quite ignored my motifs, I don't consider it as worth while to discuss my conscious aim. I am accredited generally with exploiting brutality for brutality's sake. This is the belief of the reviewers and the public, and it is hopeless to combat it. As for my really-and-truly conscious aim, it will be found woven into every bit of fiction I have written—the motif under the motif.

I am sending you herewith—separate cover—a photograph of myself, as you request. I haven't any pictures of myself in my study, so I cannot send you one.

Sincerely yours,
Jack London

MS: CU; 2 pp., tls.
    1. Scott was soliciting information for an article "The Newest Lights in American Literature," *Boston Herald Magazine*, August 13, 1905. Scott gave short biographical sketches of JL, Winston Churchill, Ellen Glasgow, David Graham Phillips, Booth Tarkington, and Edith Wharton, among others.
    2. See JL to Brett, December 22, 1904.

3. "Getting into Print," *Editor*, March 1903.
4. JL's first published story was actually "Two Gold Bricks"; see JL to Houghton, Mifflin, January 31, 1900, n. 12.

To George P. Brett

Glen Ellen, Calif.
Jul 3 1905

Dear Mr. Brett:

In reply to yours of June 27. I thoroughly realise the common-sense of publisher and author working together, and that is certainly both to the author's and the publisher's interest to have their relations long-standing. So, in reply to your request that I let you know how I feel about the renewal of our special agreement for monthly royalty advances, etc., and the publishing of books, I may say that I am quite pleased to go on with it. However, I am writing to ask you if it is not possible for me to get a slightly better royalty rate than I have been getting hitherto.

I haven't been down to Oakland (where all my contracts and business papers are), so I do not know just how this last contract stands between us. I do not know whether or not we are even, that is, whether or not I owe you a book to complete the contract.

I shall have for publication next year, *White-Fang*, which as you will remember is a companion-story to *The Call of the Wild*, and should, I am certain, become fairly popular. It might even equal the sales of *The Call of the Wild*. Then, sometime next year, of course, I shall have another volume of short stories ready for publication.[1] The foregoing is definite. I have three-quarters of the book of short stories already written, sold to the magazines, and awaiting publication. These stories will all be published by next year. I have 6,000 words completed on *White-Fang*, and expect to work uninterruptedly on it every day for the next several months.

In October I start East on this lecturing-trip, and during this lecturing-trip I have mapped out for myself to write a series of brief, nervous, strong, dramatic sketches, and, as I conceive them at the present moment, I think that not only will they be a departure from any kind of work I have done in the past, but I think that they will also constitute some of the best work I have done. This of course remains to be seen.

There you have my plans and work, up to the first part of next year. I expect to finish my lecturing-trip somewhere in New England, some time around January or February of next year, at which time I shall return to California and get ready for the building of the house on the ranch. (This summer I am contenting myself with putting up the barn, which is to be of stone and tile.) Of course, when I return to California the first part of next year, I shall go on steadily with my work, but just what it will be I do not yet know. I have lots of plans, lots of books I want to write, some of which I shall write, but I have always to sit down and think it over before I determine which it is that I shall immediately put my hand to.

I am sorry you expect to get out on the Coast in January, because at that time I shall be East; but I'll be out here and ready for you the year following, depend upon it. Only, I'd hate to see you come up to Glen Ellen just for a few hours. I'd like to take as much of your stay on the Coast as I possibly can. If you haven't forgotten riding in all these years, since last you rode in California, I can promise to have a good horse under you.

Sincerely yours,
Jack London

MS: NN; 2 pp., tls.
    1. *Moon-Face.*

To Frederick I. Bamford

[Glen Ellen]
Jul 6 1905

Dear Friend—

Checks received. It was all right. Half of it was all right—a quarter of it—none of it. If you bothered no more than I do about it, why, you would have forgotten to send the check—for in all truth I had quite forgotten the whole transaction.[1]

I am glad you are out of the Albany. I never liked to think of you there. It was not home at all.

I do not know what poem you [mean] by the "Bamford poem," which you ask to be returned.[2] But I have misgivings.

Don't forget—when I get my ranch going up here (which, alas! won't be until next year) that you must come up for week ends and also stop as long as you can any time. It is a thousand times finer (scenery) than Burke's.

Only I don't remember what I wrote in *People of the Abyss* to you.[3] You'll have to give me the words over again when I write in second copy.

Sincerely yours,
Jack London

MS: JL State Park; 5 pp., als. Pbd: *Mystery*, 190–91.
    1. See JL to Bamford, May 11, 1905.
    2. Possibly the poem Bamford sent JL the previous September. See JL to Bamford, September 16, 1904.
    3. JL inscribed: "Dear Comrade: Than whom there is no truer, nobler man fighting in the Cause."

To Cloudesley Johns

Glen Ellen, Calif.
Jul 6 1905

Dear Cloudesley—

I enjoyed your lecture.[1] It was *better* than I thought it would be; and I knew in advance it would be the right thing. My congratulations.

You have no idea how glad you're going into the fight has made me.

As regards the ranch—I figure the vegetables, firewood, milk, eggs, chickens, etc., procured by the hired man will come pretty close to paying the hired man's wages.

The 40 acres of cleared ground (hay) I can always have farmed on shares. The other fellow furnishes all the work, seed, & care while I furnish the land. He gets 2/3 of crop of hay. I get 1/3—about 25 or 30 tons for my share.

I'm going swimming. I take a book along, & read & swim, turn & turn about, until 6 P.M. It is now 1 P.M.

Wolf.

MS: CSmH; 4 pp., als.
   1. Johns had sent JL a copy of "No Compromise." See JL to Johns, April 6, 1905.

To Frederick I. Bamford

Glen Ellen, Calif.
Jul 12 1905

Dear Mr. Bamford:

Thank you very much for your kind invitation to join you and Mrs. Gilman[1] out in the Piedmont Hills. I am sorry I can't come. You see, I'm busy putting up a barn just now and can't get away from Glen Ellen very well.

As regards contributing money for the Mrs. Gilman lecture at the Alhambra, I really don't feel that it is up to me. I am sending off a contribution to the Party paper in Oakland, and now and again I take a hand in other similar things here and in the East (I recently sent $10.00 to *The Socialist*, Toledo, Ohio, which was in rather hard straits because of Titus' illness), etc.; and I always feel that the money is better spent on Socialist newspapers than on the lectures. And besides, I understand that Mrs. Gilman is to lecture more upon Woman Suffrage, or something of that order. It's just a matter of business expediency with me. I feel that there are better ways of spending the money.

I am inclosing to you the address of the Japanese Socialists to the Russian Socialists. Please be sure to return it when you are finished with it.

Mr. Taft I do not consider a statesman nor an intellectual (I interviewed him once, you know).² The best and the worst I can say of Mr. Taft, and all that I can say of Mr. Taft, is that he is a politician.

One of the inclosed excerpts from Nietzsche may possibly explain to you the "long sickness" through which I have passed, and from which I have recently emerged.³

Affectionately yours,
Jack London

MS: JL State Park; 1 p., tls. Pbd: *Mystery*, 191–92.

1. Charlotte Perkins Gilman (1860–1935), who delivered "America's Place To-Day" at the Alhambra Theatre in San Francisco on July 16.

2. William Howard Taft (1857–1930), Secretary of War in Theodore Roosevelt's administration from 1904 until 1909, when he succeeded Roosevelt as President. For JL's interview of Taft, see JL to Strunsky, January 22, 1902, n. 2.

3. "O my brethren, when I enjoined you to break up the good, and the tables of the good, then only did I embark man on his high seas. And now only cometh unto him the great terror, the great outlook, the great sickness, the great nausea, the great sickness," *Thus Spake Zarathustra*, section 56, part 29. JL had begun reading Nietzsche extensively in 1904. For the influence of Nietzsche on JL, see Patrick Bridgewater, *Nietzsche in Anglosaxony: A Study of Nietzsche's Impact on English and American Literature* (Leicester, England, 1972), pp. 163–70.

To George P. Brett

Glen Ellen, Calif.
Jul 18 1905

Dear Mr. Brett:

I have just sent the following letter off to Mr. Alf. Hayman, concerning his getting the dramatic rights of *The Game* for Charles Frohman.¹ This is in reply to a letter which he has just sent me directly, on top of having written to you about the matter. As you kindly suggested that you would accept an offer for me from Mr. Hayman, I have taken the liberty of referring Mr. Hayman back to you, as you will see in my letter to him which I now quote:

"In reply to yours of July 11. I have written to Mr. Geo. P. Brett, President of The Macmillan Company, who had already conveyed to me your letter to him upon the proposition of getting the dramatic rights of my novel *The Game* for Mr. Charles Frohman,—I have written to Mr. Brett asking him to make what arrangements he sees best with you in the matter. He has my full authorization to make such arrangements.

"You see, Mr. Brett is the publisher of most of my books, and of all my books of recent years, and is besides a very good friend of mine. And as he is in New York in the same city with you, it seems to me more expedient for the two of you to get together than for you and me to attempt to get together with the Continent between us—delays, misunderstandings and all the rest, you understand."

As you know, in the story of *The Game* itself there is no play whatever. A play could be based upon the story, but new characters would have to be created, new scenes, and totally new treatment would be necessary. In fact, as I see it, *The Game* would contribute little or nothing to such a play beyond the shadowiest foundation. So I would consider, under the circumstances that it would be well to accept almost any offer, so long as it is not really too moderate. I should prefer, of course, royalties to selling outright; but I guess you know more about such things than I do. And as said in my letter to Mr. Hayman, you have my authorization to conclude any and all arrangements in the matter of accepting an offer from Mr. Hayman for the dramatic rights of *The Game*.

Very truly yours,
Jack London

MS: NN; 2 pp., tls.
   1. Alfred Hayman (1865–1921), general manager of Charles Frohman, Inc.; Charles Frohman (1860–1915), "the Napoleon of the drama," New York theater owner and impresario, known as a maker of theatrical stars and successful playwrights. *The Game* was not dramatized.

To Frederick I. Bamford

Glen Ellen, Calif.
Jul 20 1905

Dear Mr. Bamford:
   All my scrap-books are down in Oakland, so I cannot very well find the date of that *Independent* article.[1]
   I am glad the lecture passed off so well (Gilman lecture), and I am now quite convinced, from all the reports of the lecture I have received, that I was quite right in contributing money to the Socialist papers rather than to this particular lecture. Not that I have anything against Mrs. Gilman, but from the standpoint of sheer utility.
   I think, as I have now left Oakland for good, that it would be best to accept my resignation as a regular member of the Ruskin Club, and to instate me as a visiting member or whatever other kind of special membership that will be peculiarly applicable to my Glen Ellen residence. Also, if the Treasurer of the Ruskin Club could send me my dues account up to date, so that I may straighten that up at the same time that I resign, it would simplify matters. So I guess that this paragraph should serve for my resignation. You see, it's not like a regular resignation. It's merely a change in status in the Club, brought about by change of residence.

Affectionately yours,
Jack London

MS: JL State Park; 1 p., tls. Pbd: *Mystery*, 192–93.
   1. Probably JL's "The Class Struggle," published on November 5, 1903.

To Joseph M. Chapple

Glen Ellen, Calif.
Jul 22 1905

Dear Mr. Chapple:

I am writing to you to place before you a little tale of woe.

You remember, years ago, the small sums the *National* could afford to pay for matter. I, as a writer, had discovered that. On July 13, 1899, I mailed you a little story of mine entitled "A Lesson in Heraldry." It was 3,500 words long. This was published in your March number of 1900, and for it you paid me $5.00.

Later on, I had occasion to send you another story, entitled "The One Thousand Dozen." I knew the situation thoroughly,—that it was a case of mutual help between the *National Magazine* and the author, that the *National Magazine* would profit by getting a story for a small sum, from a writer who could not otherwise dispose of it, and that the writer would profit by disposing of an otherwise undisposable story to the *National Magazine*. This story I sent to you on October 11, 1902. It was promptly accepted by Mr. Putnam. I promptly replied, in letter of November 15, 1902, asking Mr. Putnam to hold back the publication of the story. In reply to that I have Mr. Putnam's letter of November 22, 1902, from which I quote the following: "I have your letter of November 15, concerning your story entitled 'The One Thousand Dozen' and am sorry that there is any doubt about the *National* getting this story."

You will see that Mr. Putnam, by his own words, thoroughly understood that I had a string on the story. The situation is an understandable one—an author and a magazine, both possessed of the slimmest finances, and both struggling to keep heads above the water.

Also, I wrote a letter on March 9, 1903, asking return of Manuscript, because I had found a chance to get $200 worth of railroad transportation for it from the *Sunset Magazine*.[1] But alas, the story had already been published in the *National*, and a check for $20.00 been sent me. This check I returned.

Then, on March 29, 1903, Mr. Putnam sent me back the check, and offered to get me the transportation, which I had explained to him I needed in order to send my mother and nephew East.

In the meantime, I have forgotten to state, while I still kept my string on the story with the *National*, I had explained to Mr. Putnam the necessity I labored under of obtaining simultaneous serial publication in England and the United States, in order to protect my future book-rights in England. I had given Mr. Putnam the address of my English agents, Messrs. A. P. Watt & Son.

Nevertheless, and quite ignoring all these instructions, etc., Mr. Putnam went ahead and published the story.

I quote from a letter from Mr. Putnam of March 11, 1903, the following: "I notified our English agent that your story had already been sold in England."

So far as the losing of my English rights in the story by unexpected publication in the *National* is concerned, Mr. Putnam merely erred through ignorance. I quote from a letter from him dated March 23, 1903, written in reply to my reproach for his hasty publication of the story in the *National*: "My own experience in selling the *National* stories abroad has been that it (simultaneous publication) was not necessary." You see, Mr. Putnam was thoroughly ignorant of the question of copyright.

Now, to complete my story: London *Graphic* bought the English serial rights of the story, paying me, through Watt & Son, 21 pounds, 7 shillings.

All went well. I had lost my book rights in the story in England, and I had received but $20.00 cash (and no transportation) from the *National*; but I had yet managed to get something like $100 from the story in England. (In passing, I wish to mention that the story was 7,000 words long.)

Time passed, and a letter came from Watt & Son telling me that Mr. Shurmer Sibthorpe had sold the same story to the *Windsor Magazine* in England;[2] that the *Windsor Magazine* had published the story; that *The Graphic*, with the story in type (I had corrected the proof-sheets), was left in the lurch and wanted its money back.

I wrote to Mr. Shurmer Sibthorpe, and I quote to you the following from his letter: "My recollection of the matter is that your story, 'The One Thousand Dozen' appeared in the *National Magazine*, of Boston, Massachusetts, from whom I purchased the English serial rights, re-selling them to the *Windsor Magazine*."

And there you are. I am compelled to refund the $100 I received from the English serial rights of the story. I have received all-told from England and the United States, but $20.00, and I have lost the English book rights in the story—all this because of the errors of Mr. Putnam. This year, in the first part of this year, when the English *Graphic* came down upon me to refund the $100.00, I wrote a statement of the affair to Mr. Putnam, who disclaimed responsibility, but at the same time he said he saw a way in which he could make it square with me. This way he suggested was, namely, that I should write two articles on socialism for the *National*, and for them he would pay me $100.00. How this would reimburse me for the $100 he had lost me in England, I cannot see. When I explained to Mr. Putnam this matter, he became angry, called me several different kinds of names, chief among which I can remember is "hypocrite," and requested me to get off his doorstep and quit howling. Ergo, after six months of silence, I am now writing to you. I feel first, that I have been unjustly treated in this matter from a business standpoint, and that from a personal and social standpoint I have been shamefully treated, and I am now laying the details of the case before you, in order to see what can be done.

Very truly yours,
Jack London

MS: CSmH; 3 pp., cctl.

1. *Sunset*, a monthly magazine dealing with life in California and the Far West. It was founded in 1898 by the Southern Pacific Railroad, which published the magazine until 1931 when it was bought by the Lane family of Lane Publishing Company, Menlo Park, California.

2. *Windsor Magazine*, an illustrated monthly magazine published in London from 1895 until 1939.

To George P. Brett

Glen Ellen, Calif.
Aug 1 1905

Dear Mr. Brett:

In reply to yours of July 11. First of all, I want you to thoroughly understand my situation and point of view. You know I am pretty much of a hermit. I have never knocked around amongst writers nor publishers. About the ins and outs of the trade I know practically nothing. I have never received any information from anybody. I have simply staid out here in the West and butted around, by correspondence, finding out things for myself. I have never known, for instance, what were the best royalties paid to writers. In this case, you have told me, and if I hadn't butted around after increased royalties, I wouldn't have got this information from you. You see, I have to find out, and the only way I can find out is by letter.

Now, as regards royalties: You tell me that I am getting 20%. Yes, and no. I am getting 20% on all over 5,000 copies of any book, and 15% on the first 5,000. Now why can't we put it on a basis something like this— 15% on any book of mine (regular cloth-bound book) that sells less than 5,000; and 20% on every thousand of any book of mine that sells more than 5,000? You see what I am driving at is to avoid robbing you on a small-sale book of mine, one that sells less than 5,000, out of which sales the whole of the initial cost to you must come. But a book that sells more than 5,000, as I understand it, does not have a greater initial cost, and with a larger sale gives an increase of profit.

One thing must be considered in my favor, as regards advertising, and that is namely, that I am so peculiarly constituted that I manage to get a whole lot of advertising from sources other than my book-publishers, and which nevertheless conduces to the sale of my books. Just consider the amount of advertising I got out of the Hearst newspapers with their millions of circulation, in the course of the six months I was away in the Orient for them.

Going on the basis that *White Fang* is the long novel referred to in previous agreements, and that according to those agreements there is owing you in addition one book of short stories, then we shall have to consider that *The Game* is a book thrown in on the side. This is quite agreeable to me. Also, I thoroughly realize and appreciate your kindness to me in allowing me to be practically a year behind in fulfilling my agreements, and not saying anything about it. Anyway, as I understand the feeling that exists between you and me, these agreements are now more a matter of mere business form,—at least that's the way I feel about it, because I do not feel that there is any liability on my part of rushing away to some other publisher.

Now as to the new Agreement for the year beginning Dec. 1, 1905: I take all your suggestions as follows: I am to receive for that year $300.00 per month on account of general royalties; I am to give you for publication *White Fang* and a collection of short stories; you are to retain, in addition, book-rights for America in all other work completed by me during the year beginning Dec. 1, 1905.

As I say, all the foregoing suggestions from you for the new Agreement are perfectly satisfactory to me, and I now make one suggestion to you, about royalty, and that is, namely, 15% on any book of mine that sells less than 5,000, and 20% on every thousand of any book of mine that sells more than 5,000.

I have just read *A Publisher's Confession*[1] and found it interesting and instructive, and have learned a lot out of it that I did not know about the relations of publishers and writers.

According to my present lecture-itinerary, I should be in New York somewhere around next December.

Sincerely yours,
Jack London

P.S.—Oh, by the way, I've got another big project in view. After I have settled down and enjoyed my mountain ranch for about five years, it is my firm intention to build a boat about 40 feet long, and go off on a several years' cruise around the world. Now, don't think I am joking. I mean it. I never more ardently desired to do anything in my life. I don't care very much for ordinary travel anyway, and this certainly would be everything but ordinary. And Lord! Lord! think of the chance to write without interruption when I am between-ports. First rattle out of the box, 2100 miles sailing from San Francisco to Honolulu, and then the long stretch down into the South Seas, and some time ultimately, the stretch across the Atlantic to New York City![2]

MS: NN; 3 pp., tls. Pbd: *L*, 176–77.

1. Walter H. Page, *A Publisher's Confessions* (1905). Page, founder and editor of *The World's Work*, a monthly current events magazine, and a partner in the firm of Doubleday, Doran & Co., explained the process by which a manuscript is selected for publication, printed, advertised, and sold. He also discussed relations between authors and publishers.

2. See JL to Millard, February 18, 1906.

To the Editor, *Collier's Weekly*

[Glen Ellen]

Dear sir: *Aug 1 1905*

I am sending you herewith an article that may strike you as a regular firebrand; but I ask you to carry into the reading of it one idea, namely, that the whole article is a statement of *fact*. There is no theory about it. I state the facts and the figures of the revolution. I state how many revolutionists there are, why they are revolutionists, and their views—all of which are facts.[1]

It seems to me that this article would be especially apposite just now, following upon the wholesale exposures of graft and rottenness in the high places, which have of late filled all the magazines and newspapers. It is the other side of the shield. It is another way of looking at the question, and half a million of voters are looking at it in this way in the United States. And it might be interesting to the capitalists to see thus depicted this great antagonistic force which they, by their present graft and rottenness, are not doing anything to fend off. But rather are they encouraging the growth of this antagonistic force by their own culpable mismanagement of society.

Of course, should you find it in your way to publish this article, it would be very well to preface it with an editorial note to the effect that it is a statement of the situation by an avowed and militant socialist; and of course you would be quite welcome to criticize the whole article in any way you saw fit.

The rather disreputable appearance of the manuscript is due to the fact that Walker was going to publish it in *Cosmopolitan*, but that we disagreed about rates, and before we could settle said disagreement, the *Cosmopolitan* passed into the hands of Hearst.[2] And you can depend upon it that the article was too strong meat for any of Hearst's publications.

Sincerely yours,
Jack London

MS: CSmH; 1 p., cctl.

1. JL enclosed the manuscript of "Revolution." On August 30, 1905 (CSmH), Robert J. Collier replied: "I want to print your 'fire brand' as a piece of literature, even though a few hundred thousand of our capitalist readers *will* stop their subscriptions. . . . Don't penalize me too heavily for having the error to print it." *Collier's* set the essay in type, sending JL galley proofs on October 11, 1905, with a note from Managing Editor Albert Lee (ULA) requesting JL to trim the essay by thirty column inches. JL returned the proofs on October 20, according to his marginal comments on Lee's note, and he received payment of $500 on October 25. The essay never appeared in the magazine, however. See also JL to the Editor, *Atlantic Monthly*, May 6, 1905.

2. In 1905 John Brisben Walker sold *Cosmopolitan* for $400,000 to William Randolph Hearst (1863–1951), owner of the *San Francisco Examiner* and other newspapers; at this

time Hearst was a Congressman from New York City, an office he held from 1903 to 1907, though he also maintained residence in California.

To Frederick I. Bamford

Glen Ellen, Calif.
Aug 2 1905

Dear Mr. Bamford:

It's too bad the way the Taylor dinner misconnected.[1] Of course it threw a lot of extra and vexatious work upon you, and the futility of it could not have been anything but depressing.

I just wish you could get out of the city life for good and live in the country always; but then, I am afraid, as you once pointed out to me, that you are too much of a city creature to stick by the country for good; but oh, take my word, there is no place like the country.

Do you care much for Maeterlinck? I have some more beautiful excerpts from him, which I shall be sending you in a couple of days as soon as they are typed out.

Do you know the thing that startles and surprises and satisfies me these days? It is, that the big men of the world all agree as to how life should be lived, no matter how much they disagree about the meaning and essence of life. Take for instance, three divergent thinkers[2] such as Nietzsche, Maeterlinck and Schopenhauer. I have been reading a good deal of them recently, and they agree,—quite, quite agree.

Sincerely and affectionately yours,
Jack London

MS: JL State Park; 1 p., tls. Pbd: *Mystery*, 193–94.
  1. Possibly a dinner for Edward Robeson Taylor (1838–1923), poet, lawyer, physician, and, from 1907 to 1909, mayor of San Francisco.
  2. "Thinkers" was written twice.

To Minnie Maddern Fiske

Glen Ellen, Calif.
Aug 2 1905

My dear Mrs. Fiske:

Thank you for your kind criticism of my play.[1] I quite agree with you as regards the non-understanding of stage-managers.

I am afraid that in this, my first effort, I too bunglingly expressed my idea; what I did try to write was a play that departed frankly from stage-conventions, and cut itself off sharply from stage tradition. I didn't intend a hero in the play, nor did I intend stereotyped motives. The big motif was altruistic. This was the motive that actuated Freda and Mrs. Eppingwell.

Flossie was not the kind of a woman to *save* Floyd Vanderlip; she would simply mean hell for him after a while. But that had nothing to do with my motif anyway. Vanderlip was the last person in the world to be *saved*. Neither Freda nor Mrs. Eppingwell was trying to *save* Vanderlip. They were trying to save wishy-washy Flossie, about whom they knew nothing whatever, except that she was wishy-washy.

Pardon me for giving you the foregoing data. I have done so merely to show what I must have failed to show in the play; but then, you see, it was a first effort, and I hope to find clearer expression later on, and possibly some day to write a successful play which will not be very stereotyped nor traditional nor conventional. Big dramatic art, as I conceive it, on the part of the playwright, cannot very well rest on the stereotyped-traditional-conventional.

I am waiting for the play to arrive from New York, and when it does I shall let you know. Again thanking you for your kindness and trouble, I remain,

Sincerely yours,
Jack London

MS: DLC; 1 p., tls.
   1. *Scorn of Women.*

To Cloudesley Johns

Glen Ellen, Calif.
Aug 2 1905

Game reviews are interesting. One paper says classic—next say "Rotten, rotten, rotten." Most say disgustingly brutal, and then along comes *Life* and says it's a shame I've become a *candy-puller* in the literary kitchen when there are so few meat-cooks!

Only Julian[1] didn't write the *L.A. Examiner* review, even if his last name was affixed—more ethics of journalism.

The ankle's all right, & the stone barn's going up—even if they do have to rake the whole 130 acres for stone. There won't be enough stone left for a house—and this is no joke.

Wolf.

MS: CSfU; 2 pp., als.
   1. Probably Julian Hawthorne.

To Minnie Maddern Fiske

Glen Ellen, Calif.
Aug 4 1905

Dear Mrs. Fiske:
   I hardly know what to say in reply to your letter of Tuesday. That you do not understand me has certainly gone with the writing of said letter.

How possibly *could* you understand me? When I speak a language that is unintelligible to a certain group of people, and when my very thought-symbols are totally different from the thought-symbols of such a group of people, how possibly can such a group of people, having no understanding of me whatever, give *you* any understanding of me?

I should be quite happy to talk the matter over with you some time, if we ever chance to meet, but I am too dreadfully rushed for time just now to be able to take a day off in order to talk it over.

I remember the first case I ever saw tried in a court of law. At the conclusion of the hearing of the evidence pro and con, in my childish mind I could not for the life of me decide whether the man was innocent or guilty. Then the prosecuting attorney arose and addressed the Jury. As I listened, the whole thing seemed to become clear as print. The man was guilty. The man was an abominable wretch. The man deserved the extreme penalty of the law. No punishment could be severe enough for such a man. He was a contemptible scoundrel, etc., etc. So I concluded while talked the attorney for the prosecution. The attorney for the defence arose and addressed the Jury. I underwent a reversal of feeling while I listened to him. This poor, innocent man; this muchly-wronged and maligned individual; this man who had been so vilely treated, so unjustly treated—why, no jury under the sun could convict such a man. I flamed with indignation, and thought of all the injustice he had suffered. All this while talked the attorney for the defence. Then arose again the attorney for the prosecution, who made his final address to the Jury. As he talked, I began to reconsider; possibly I was mistaken after all. The man did not seem so innocent as he had seemed when his own attorney was talking. Here certainly he was guilty, and there certainly he was guilty. And the attorney for the prosecution talked on. I began to grow indignant on the other side of the case. The man certainly merited the utmost punishment that could be given him. He was deserving of no mercy whatever. He was as contemptible and vile as I had thought him when the prosecuting attorney first talked. . . . And then I went home. And when I cooled down, I considered what a fool had been made of me. And from this little affair I drew one conclusion which lasted me through all my life, namely, that very little reliance can be placed in special pleaders. Later I learned that every individual, when he pleaded for himself, made an unusually excellent special pleader.

A final word, in an effort to give you a clew to my character: What acts I have performed in this world have been directly in line with my highest conceptions of right conduct.

Sincerely yours,
Jack London

MS: DLC; 2 pp., tls.

To Frederick I. Bamford

Glen Ellen, Calif.
Aug 8 1905

My dear Comrade:

Check received all right. Please don't worry about it. I have told you repeatedly to take your time, and please do believe that I am truthful in the matter.[1]

No indeed, I don't care in the least if a lady copies the inscription from one of my books to you. That inscription is not mine, it's yours; I gave it to you along with the book.

As regards the excerpts I send you from time to time, in the main of course I agree with them. There may be minor qualifications; but as I say, in the main the agreement exists.

Good for you, for introducing Maeterlinck to the Oakland reading public.

It's warm, nay, hot. I am dripping sweat. Charmian, who is hammering the typewriter, says she is DRIBBLING sweat! (I didn't either, Mr. Bamford!!! C. K.) And we're going swimming; and after that, when it gets cooler, to drive an unruly cow up to the ranch.

With love from both of us,
Jack London

MS: JL State Park; 1 p., tls. Pbd: *Mystery*, 194.
1. See JL to Bamford, July 6, 1905.

To Anna Strunsky

Glen Ellen, Calif.
Aug 13 1905

Dear Anna:

First of all, if you ever write on the inside of your envelopes again, I shall immediately apply for admission to an insane asylum.

In reply to yours of August 10. Please let me know if the Macmillan Company has paid you directly your half of the royalties on the American edition of our book.[1] I labor under the impression that they have done so, and am asking you, in order to save myself the trouble of looking it up.

Now, concerning the English sales of our book. When I was in Manchuria, I received word that our English publishers, Isbister & Company, had failed, and that they were liquidating at a few pence on the pound. Then I learned, afterward, that Isaac Pitman Company was going to take over the books of Isbister Co., and would pay the authors in full for whatever they had lost with Isbisters.

Then, every little while, a small check would come from the Isbisters, and at the same time a larger check would come from the Pitman Co.

These checks have kept dribbling along until about three months ago, when my account with Isbisters, up to the time of the transfer to Pitmans, was paid up in full.

In the meantime I had forgotten you entirely. Forgive me. I have just now looked the matter up in my letter-files, and am forwarding you inclosed letter and account rendered from Mr. Brown of Isbister Co. You will see there that up to the time of transfer, the sales of our books amounted altogether to £15.11/11. This I have turned into American money, and amounts to something like $76.40. This, divided by two, brings $38.20, our respective shares in the English sales. And I am sending you herewith check for $38.20, and at the same time I am asking you to pardon my carelessness.

Please return, at your early convenience, the letter of Isbister & Co.

It's too bad about Count Lochwitzky. I met him, I believe, last winter some time. He was over to my house, and we had quite a talk together, in the midst of a crowd. Then I went away right afterwards.

So you have met Mr. Marshall Bond. It's a long time since I have seen him. I wonder if he has grown the least bit radical in the meantime, and I wonder what you think of him. If you see him again, give him my regards.

If there is anything in this Isbister-Pitman account that you cannot make out, please let me know, and I shall try to explain more fully.

This is a business-letter, and I can't get off the business tone of it to save my life. So I am going to say

Respectfully yours,
Jack London

MS: CSmH; 2 pp., cctl.
  1. *The Kempton-Wace Letters.*

To Anna Strunsky

Glen Ellen, Calif.
Aug 15 1905

Dear Anna—
Pardon my negligence in not sending lecture bureau addresses.

J. B. Pond Lyceum Bureau,
Everett House,
New York City.

The Slayton Lyceum Bureau,
Steinway Hall,
Chicago, Ill.

The last one will be the more satisfactory bureau I am confident.[1]

I liked Judge Bond[2] very much, and am glad you have come to know him. But how did you happen to meet Marshall Bond?

The sales of a book practically cease after the first few months. So, neither from Macmillans nor from Pitmans can we expect to receive much more for our book.

I can never forgive Wilshire[3] for "squealing" the way he did about that $500. He did it of his own initiative, to commence with, and he should never have opened his mouth.

Are you going direct to Russia in October?[4] I go East in October, but do not expect to be in New York until first part of December.

Am hard at work writing *White Fang*, a companion story to *Call of the Wild*.

Jack.

MS: CSmH; 5 pp., als.
    1. The Slayton Lyceum Bureau arranged JL's lecture tour.
    2. Hiram G. Bond.
    3. Gaylord Wilshire.
    4. Strunsky was going to St. Petersburg with the twin goals of reporting for a news syndicate and spreading revolutionary propaganda.

To the Editor, *New York Saturday Times*

Glen Ellen, Calif.
Aug 18 1905

Editor of *The New York Saturday Times*;

As one interested in the play of life, and in the mental processes of his fellow-creatures, I have been somewhat amused by a certain feature of the criticisms of my prize-fighting story, *The Game*.[1] This feature is the impeachment of my realism, the challenging of the facts of life as put down by me in that story. It is rather hard on a poor devil of a writer, when he has written what he has seen with his own eyes, or experienced in his own body, to have it charged that said sights and experiences are unreal and impossible.

But this is no new experience, after all. I remember a review of *The Sea Wolf* by an Atlantic Coast critic who seemed very familiar with the sea. Said critic laughed hugely at me because I sent one of my characters aloft to shift over a gaff-topsail. The critic said that no one ever went aloft to shift over a gaff-topsail, and that he knew what he was talking about because he had seen many gaff-topsails shifted over from the deck. Yet I, on a seven-months cruise in a topmast schooner, had gone aloft, I suppose, a hundred times, and with my own hands shifted tacks and sheets of gaff-topsails.

Now to come back to *The Game*. As reviewed in *The New York Saturday Times*, fault was found with my realism. I doubt if this reviewer has had as much experience in such matters as I have. I doubt if he knows what it is to be knocked out, or to knock out another man. I have had these experiences, and it was out of these experiences, plus a fairly intimate knowledge of prize-fighting in general, that I wrote *The Game*.

I quote from the critic in *The Saturday Times*: "Still more one gently doubts in this particular case, that a blow delivered by Ponta on the point of Fleming's chin could throw the latter upon the padded canvas floor of the ring with enough force to smash in the whole back of his skull, as Mr. London describes."

All I can say in reply is, that a young fighter in the very club described in my book, had his head smashed in this manner. Incidentally, this young fighter worked in a sail-loft and took remarkably good care of his mother, brother and sisters.

And—oh, one word more. I have just received a letter from Jimmy Britt, light-weight champion of the world, in which he tells me that he particularly enjoyed *The Game*, "on account of its trueness to life."[2]

Very truly yours,
Jack London

MS: CSmH; 2 pp., cctl. Pbd: "The Author of *The Game* Writes from Personal Knowledge Based on Experience," *New York Times Book Review*, September 2, 1905.

1. *The Game* had been reviewed anonymously in "The Prize Ring," *New York Times Saturday Review of Books*, August 12, 1905.

2. Jimmy Britt (1879–1940), lightweight champion in 1902. For Britt's comments, see "Jimmy Britt Reviews *The Game*, Jack London's Story of the Ring," *San Francisco Examiner*, August 27, 1905.

To Gustav A. Behrnd

Glen Ellen, Calif.
Aug 25 1905

Dear Mr. Behrnd:[1]

I am now waiting for the Lumber to arrive. I have all arrangements made for hauling the lumber up, and have engaged the carpenters—six carpenters altogether, two at $[3].00 a day and four at $2.50 a day. They will be ready as soon as the lumber is hauled up, to go to cutting, so the construction can start immediately after Pasquini's work is finished.[2]

Now, there are a lot of things the Foreman wants to know right away. In the first place, you have not indicated the dimensions of the timbers.

What distance apart are the floor joists?

Are there to be any wall-plates on top of cement, or embedded in cement, for the lower-floor where the doors occur—the big outside doors. The Foreman says that the uprights that are to rest on the concrete where the big doors are—the Foreman says these uprights are small, and that if they rest directly upon the concrete, the distribution of weight will be over so small a surface that the concrete is liable to give way, or that the uprights are liable to wear into the concrete. What is your judgment in this matter. Should there, or should there not be wall-plates? By wall-plates the Foreman means a piece of wood or board resting on cement, upon which in turn would rest the upright.

Now, how about *ladders?* You specify two (2) ladders to go up on out-side of barn. Do you mean that there is to be a 3-foot platform outside of barn at BOTH ends, with a ladder going up to each platform? In this case there would be two (2) ladders on the outside of barn. But I do not see any need of a platform on the *rear* end of the barn. In which case, with but one platform, at the front end of the barn, there is only place for one ladder to go up to it on the outside. The rest of the space is taken up by doors. As I see it, there will be the 3-foot platform at front end of the barn, with one outside ladder leading up to it. Please let me know about this.

Again concerning *ladders*. I look over the length of that barn, and I see that a man to feed the horses, after putting the horses into their stalls, would have to walk practically the length of the barn to the outside ladder or to the stairway, and then would have to walk the length of the barn back again, across the hay-loft in order to throw feed down to the horses, and then would have to walk the length of the barn again in order to get down to the ground—a distance altogether of a hundred and odd feet of walking. Now, since we have already put a stairway into the barn on the inside, so far as objection to fires is concerned, no objection can be urged against putting a ladder inside the barn, to go from where the horses are, up the inside partition-wall, near center where door-way is, to loft above.

According to the specifications, the concrete in the whole main portion of the barn, that is, in the carriage-room, is to be four (4) inches thick. Now, on each side of the carriage-room, where the three sliding-doors are, I am telling Pasquini to make the concrete thicker than four inches, because this edge of concrete will not only have to sustain the uprights based upon it, but will have to meet the brunt, being on the edge, of in-coming wagons and carriages.

Mr. Small,[3] the carpenter-foreman, tells me that he is likely to call upon you at your San Francisco office next Monday or Tuesday. But on the chance that he does not call, or on the chance that you are not there, I think it would be expedient to send me answers to all the questions pro-pounded in foregoing part of this letter.

I am sending this letter in triplicate, to your various addresses.

Affectionately yours,
Jack London

MS: CSmH; 2 pp., tls.

1. Gustav A. Behrnd, the San Francisco architect who designed JL's barn. He had a home near Lakeport, California, where JL had visited him on July 8, 1905.

2. Martin Pasquini, of Glen Ellen, the contractor for all the stone and concrete work on JL's barn. The walls Pasquini built were found to be defective the following spring, when the San Francisco earthquake shook them down.

3. "Judge" Small.

To the Central Labor Council, Alameda County

Glen Ellen, Calif.
Aug. 25, 1905

To the Central Labor Council, Alameda County:

I cannot express to you how deeply I regret my inability to be with you this day. But, believe me, I am with you in the brotherhood of the spirit, as all you boys, in a similar brotherhood of the spirit, are with our laundry girls in Troy, New York.

Is this not a spectacle for gods and men?—the workmen of Alameda County sending a share of their hard-earned wages three thousand miles across the continent to help the need of a lot of striking laundry girls in Troy!

And right here I wish to point out something that you all know, but something that is so great that it cannot be pointed out too often, and that grows only greater every time it is pointed out,—*and that is, that strength of organized labor lies in its brotherhood.* There is no brotherhood in unorganized labor, no standing together shoulder to shoulder, and as a result unorganized labor is weak as water.

And not only does brotherhood give organized labor more fighting strength, but it gives it, as well, the strength of righteousness. The holiest reason that men can find for drawing together into any kind of an organization is *brotherhood.* And in the end nothing can triumph against such an organization. Let the church tell you that servants should obey their masters. This is what the church told the striking laundry girls of Troy. Stronger than this mandate is brotherhood, as the girls of Troy found out when the boys of California shared their wages with them. (Ah, these girls of Troy! Twenty weeks on strike and not a single desertion from their ranks! And ah, these boys of California, stretching out to them, across a continent, the helping hand of brotherhood!)

And so I say, against such spirit of brotherhood, all machinations of the men-of-graft-and-grab-and-the-dollar are futile. Strength lies in comradeship and brotherhood, not in a throat-cutting struggle where every man's hand is against every man. This comradeship and brotherhood is yours. I cannot wish you good luck and hope that your strength will grow in the future, because brotherhood and the comrade world are bound to grow. The growth cannot be stopped. So I can only congratulate you boys upon the fact that this is so.

Yours in the brotherhood of man,

Jack London

SOURCE: *L*, 179; also pbd: *BJL*, II, 238–39.

To an Unnamed Correspondent

Glen Ellen, Calif.
Aug 30 1905

Dear friend:

I cannot tell you how deeply I appreciate your kind letter. Such a thing, straight out from the heart of a man, means more to me than a thousand of the best reviews in the world. When a man who has "read fights, seen fights, and been in fights," likes my description of a fight, I am praised indeed.

Who knows, we may run into each other yet. I for one will be glad of the meeting. In a few months I am setting to work to build a 40-foot yawl. And a year from the coming January, I set sail around the world in her, going first to Australia and then on, and if, when I fetch up in England, you are not there, the chances are that I'll run into you somewhere along the course. I am inclosing you herewith a couple of photographs, not up to much, but you'll recognize me by them if you ever see me.

Faithfully yours,
Jack London

P.S.—Oh, as regards earlier books than *The Call of the Wild*. Of said earlier books I have had published in England by Isbister & Company (now deceased, but whose business is now in the hands of Isaac Pitman & Sons), *The Son of the Wolf*, *The God of His Fathers*, *The Children of the Frost*, *A Daughter of the Snows*, *The Kempton-Wace Letters*, and *The People of the Abyss*.

MS: InU; 1 p., tls.

To Cloudesley Johns

Glen Ellen, Calif.
Sep 4 1905

Dear Cloudesley—

So you're going to begin writing for money! Forgive me for rubbing it in. You've changed since several years ago when you placed *ART* first and dollars afterward.[1] You didn't quite sympathize with me in those days.

After all, there's nothing like life; and I, for one, have always stood, and shall always stand, for the exalting of the life that is in me over Art, or any other extraneous things.

Wolf.

MS: CSmH; 2 pp., als.

1. See JL to Johns, September 26, 1899, January 30 and February 10, 1900. "Art" was underlined twice.

To Anna Strunsky

Glen Ellen, Calif.
Sep 4 1905

Dear Anna—

Austin Lewis quarreled with you over your revolutionary article because he doesn't believe much in the immediate success of the Russian Revolution.[1] It was *good* newspaper stuff. Why didn't you take longer to write it, and make it literature as well?

Great Interrogation—amusing. I was never more surprised in my life than to see it taken seriously—though I daren't say so publicly out of loyalty to the collaborator(?).[2]

But ye Gods! You ought to go and see the *Sea Wolf.*—Noel's, not mine.[3] Comedy! Farce! You'll have the time of your life.

My "Revolution" lecture has been accepted by *Collier's Weekly.*[4] Wouldn't that startle one! It's bound to do some good for the Cause.

*　　　*　　　*

Good for Morris![5]

Have I told you that I am going to build a sail-boat. You remember the *Spray* in which you sailed with me one day? Well this new boat will be six or seven feet longer than the *Spray*, and I am going to sail her around the world, writing as I go. Expect to be gone on trip four or five years— around the Horn, Cape of Good Hope, Europe, Asia, Africa, South America, Australia, and everywhere else. Expect to start in from 15 to 16 months. Wish me luck.

Jack.

MS: CSmH; 5 pp. fragment of 7 pp., als.

1. The Russian Revolution of 1905 had begun in January, when troops in St. Petersburg fired on a peaceful crowd of workers seeking to petition Czar Nicholas II. Widespread discontent with the czar's autocratic government, combined with the unexpected setbacks of the Russo-Japanese War, led to strikes, riots, assassinations, and naval mutinies in the succeeding months. Although in October the czar agreed to the granting of civil liberties and the establishment of a representative assembly (Duma), the reforms were largely nominal, and the revolutionary movement was ruthlessly suppressed.

2. See JL to Bascom, April 27, 1905.

3. Joseph Noel (*d.* 1946), Philadelphia-born journalist and playwright; staff writer for the *Oakland Herald, San Francisco Bulletin*, and *San Francisco Examiner*. In 1901 Noel interviewed JL for the *San Francisco Advance*, and he subsequently became a member of the Crowd. His dramatization of *The Sea-Wolf* opened on September 4, 1905, at Ye Liberty Playhouse in Oakland. According to Noel, JL allowed him to dramatize the novel because he had given JL the idea for Wolf Larsen; see Joseph Noel, *Footloose in Arcadia* (New York, 1940), pp. 233–34.

4. See JL to the Editor, *Collier's Weekly*, August 1, 1905, n. 1.

5. Morris Strunsky, one of Anna's brothers.

To Ida Winship

Glen Ellen, Calif.
Sep 4 1905

My dear Ida—

You can possibly make a stab at guessing why I don't answer some of your questions. Besides, I'm not stuck on my own judgement of people when said judgement is a snap-judgement. It takes me some time to decide.

Tell Ed I consider it a shame the fighting didn't go on into September. Also, I forget how much the bet was, & to please let me know.[1] I made a similar bet with a lot of other people and have got 'em all mixed up.

Nay, haven't seen the set of Oscar Wilde at Robertson.[2] I've been trying to get hold of his complete work for some time.

Oh, my rip-snorter "Revolution" lecture is sold to *Collier's*.

You didn't miss anything by not going to see *Great Interrogation*.

Jack London

MS: Bernatovech; 3 pp., als.

1. JL probably bet Ed Winship on the date of the termination of fighting in the Russo-Japanese War. On August 29, at a peace conference mediated by Theodore Roosevelt in Portland, New Hampshire, Count Sergei Y. Witte, the Russian plenipotentiary, accepted the Japanese terms for peace. JL wrote Ed Winship on September 14, 1905 (Bernatovech), acknowledging receipt of a dollar and saying: "I thought I owed you the dollar, but I see the fighting did continue after the first of September. You won in the spirit but not in the letter."
2. Robertson's Book Store, in San Francisco.

To Mabel Applegarth

Glen Ellen, Calif.
Sep 12 1905

Dear Mabel—

Every one of your whole family in my debt for letters—Ted, & your mother, and you. Then you write me a letter—not in payment, as it rightly should be,—charging me with being in debt a letter to you. Go to!

So you were not surprised at the announcement.[1] Why weren't you? Enlighten me. Charmian would thank you for congratulations, only she went to the city to-day, and I thank you for her, as well as myself.

No, I wasn't rattled—just was natural. You didn't miss anything by not being present.

Mrs. S. is still at 1068.[2]

She's coming to see me in camp Friday next.

I don't know whether I'll be able to finish *White Fang* before I start East, which is in early October.

And then, next winter (1906) I start around the world on a 5 years' cruise on a boat I shall build in the meantime. Said boat will be 7 1/2 feet longer than the *Spray* on which you sailed. How's that for a trip.

Have 130-acre mountain ranch up here. Am building stone barn with tile roof. Shall build house in similar fashion on return from around the world.

Do you ride horseback.

Must arrange for you to come up here on a visit next Spring or Early summer. I get back in February from East, and expect later, to go into King's river country.[3]

Sincerely yours,
Jack London

MS: CSt; 6 pp., als.

1. Although the divorce from Bessie London would not be final until November 18, JL had announced his engagement to CKL.

2. Eliza Shepard. Perhaps she had been anticipating her 1906 move to 1021 East 17th St., Oakland.

3. The Kings River originates in the Sierra Nevada and flows southwest for 125 miles before emptying into Tulare Lake in Kings County.

To an Unnamed Correspondent

Glen Ellen, Calif.
Sep 14 1905

Dear Comrade:

I am returning you herewith your manuscript. What can I say? It would be impossible for me to sit down and give you an extended criticism of the story. You see, I receive scores and scores of manuscripts of plays, stories, novels, essays, and every other thing under the sun, from people who want me to criticize same. If I did, it would take all my waking hours, and I'd have to sit up late at night as well. In fact, I have been compelled to have a stereotyped letter made, which I return with manuscripts, giving no personal word whatever. But as you are a comrade, I make this exception, as I have made it for all comrades.

Now to the story, briefly: The opening part on, as a character-study, is splendidly done. I like it immensely; but, and here I think I put my finger upon the weak point, the story peters out toward the end. The reason for this is, I think, that you have hung too fine a character-study upon too flimsy a motif. Think this over.

Yours for the Revolution,
Jack London

MS: MWalB; 1 p., als.

To Caroline Sterling

Glen Ellen,
Sonoma County, California,
September-15-05.

Dear Carrie:—

I have been a long while getting around to your letter. It caught me just before I went down to see the fight,[1] and ever since I came back from the fight I have been catching up with back work.

I wish you were here opposite me where I could talk to you, and where you could ask me a thousand-and-one questions which would naturally crop up and demand answers in the course of such conversation. However, here goes to do my best by letter in a limited space of time:

As regards Charmian's deliberately breaking up my family, I am upon known ground. I know the ground myself, pretty close to every inch of it. And I am going to try to tell you what I know.

During the time I lived in the Bungalow, Charmian was often at the house. There was not the least iota even of flirtation between us. During that time I was tangled up with Anna Strunsky—in fact, during that time (and Bessie kept me informed of it), Charmian was very solicitous on Bessie's behalf. I never gave Charmian the first thought, much less a second thought. During all the time that I was away in England, Charmian was a great deal with Bessie, cheering her up and bolstering her up, and telling her that everything would come out all right regarding the Strunsky affair.

Now, I come to the year 1903, the year of my separation. Somewhere in the latter part of June, 1903, Bessie and the children came up to Glen Ellen, camping. I was shortly to follow them. Up to this time there had never been a word exchanged between Charmian and me, nor a look. Just a short time previous to this, several weeks at the outside, one Sunday at your house, in the midst of the Crowd, I felt my first impulse toward Charmian. (This, of course, I have since told her about.) But this she knew nothing about at the time. I gave no sign of it, and as I say, it was my first impulse toward her. My first feeling about her in a sexual way. I, myself, gave no immediate further thought to it.

Bessie came up, as I have said, camping at Glen Ellen the latter part of June, to be followed by me later on.[2] In the meantime, I was going to take the *Spray* out on a cruise. Up to the time of Bessie's departure from the Bungalow on this camping-trip, I repeat, nothing had passed between Charmian and me,—not a word nor a look.

About this time I was not in a very happy state. You will remember, yourself, the black moods that used to come upon me at that time, and the black philosophy that I worked out at that time, and afterwards put into Wolf Larsen's mouth. My marriage was eminently unsatisfactory. I was preparing to go to pieces. Said going to pieces to culminate in my separation from Bessie. While she had started on her camping-trip up here, I was going out on the *Spray* to have a hell of a time, with any woman I could get hold of. I had my eyes on a dozen women—not alone in connection with the *Spray* cruise, but in any way that I could get hold of these women. It was then that my thoughts turned to Charmian amongst the rest. I was not in love with her, had never flirted with her, but I decided that she was a warm enough proposition to suit me in an illicit way. (By "warm proposition" I don't mean to say the easy proposition that a woman of loose career would mean, but by warm proposition I mean just a good warm human woman, as you are, for instance.) As I say, my thoughts turned to Charmian as one of the dozen likelihoods. On the other hand, she was not a likelihood sufficiently impelling for me to go out after her then.

Now, here's the situation: Bessie is camping at Glen Ellen, and I go out to your camp in the hills from Saturday night to Monday morning. I have not seen Charmian nor had a word with her nor a look with her. On Monday morning I get into the rig and drive into town with the rest of the Crowd coming in. My plan is to set about at once with the outfitting of the *Spray*, and to sail in a couple of days. No woman picked out yet. That was part of the outfitting! Coming in in the rig on Monday morning, the fifth-wheel carried away, I lost a few inches of skin, had seven different bandages upon my carcass, and a stiff knee. I had had stiff knees before, and I knew that the last place in the world for a stiff knee was on a rolling and plunging boat. So I decided to go up to Glen Ellen until I could get myself in shape for the cruise.

This was on Monday morning. That evening Charmian telephoned to find out if I was coming up to Glen Ellen, because Bessie had commissioned her to get some things for her to send up by me whenever I went up. These things Charmian said she had all ready for me to take. I told her I was packing that night and would start early next morning. She said she would come out right away with them. My knee was stiff, I was sick and miserable. All the places where the skin was off had stiffened up so that it was a grievous pain for me to move my arms or legs. I was looking on, directing, and Atherton[3] was packing my trunks for me, when Charmian arrived. She lent him a hand, packing in the things also that she had brought.

Here was my chance,—one of the likelihoods happened opportunely to hand. But I was too darned sick and miserable to go after it very hard. I wanted to get to bed,—alone. For possibly twenty minutes or half an hour, on the porch as Charmian was leaving, we talked. We talked philosophically, and at the same time personally. I believe I was busy telling Charmian some of the things in her that I didn't like. That was all. At the end of the talk, which was unsatisfactory as I had not succeeded in explaining to her what the things were that I didn't like, as Charmian was going, I took hold of her and kissed her; and that was all, absolutely all. The conversation had no connection whatever with the kiss. It was the conversation that relieved my own miserable feelings caused by the accidents of that day. The kiss was my sole effort to go after this one likehood in a dozen.

I went up to Glen Ellen. I dropped a line to Charmian, rather a letter, a propos of the conversation we had had.

(You see, Carrie, what I'm trying to do? I am trying to give you, just as it actually was, the working-up of my relation with Charmian from its very first inception, when I decided that she was one of a dozen likelihoods.)

Now, don't forget the basis of my life at that time. I had made up my mind to go to pieces,—to deliberately and intentionally go to pieces. Before my first trip down to town from Glen Ellen, I wrote a letter to Charmian asking to see her when I came down. Incidentally I came down. I saw her. I began to grow pretty desirous for her. At the same time that I was down, I met a girl, another man's wife, whom I had not seen for some years. I made a date with her. She was to start in a few days for Stockton and Sacramento, for a week or ten days' vacation, ostensibly to visit friends. We made it up to go together,—to go up on one of the river steamboats. Charmian and I came out to your camp on a Saturday afternoon. We returned on a Sunday afternoon. You will remember Charmian's and my conduct together at the camp-fire at your camp that Saturday night. We were just beginning to come together good and hard. On Sunday afternoon when we went in, I did my best to get Charmian to go out to Haywards with me that night. She said if I wanted to see her, I had to come to her house. And out to her house I came that evening in Berkeley. It was during this period, Saturday night and Sunday, that I was proceeding to fall in love with her, only I did not yet know it. I simply thought that I was growing more desirous of her, and more desirous for her to be my mistress.

I went back to Glen Ellen. Bessie was jealous and suspicious at that time. She feared every woman. She was jealous of the nurse-girl, a little scabby-faced maid. Jealous of everybody. Going through my wastepaper basket constantly, and piecing torn shreds of letters together, etc., etc. And I not caring a whoop to hell about anything she did in that way. For instance, the girl I was going up to Stockton and Sacramento with, wrote me several times (incidentally, I wasn't bothering about this girl, because I was falling in love with Charmian and didn't know it; and that took up all my interest). I did not reply to this girl's letters. Finally, came a telegram,—my last chance before she started, to let her know that I would accompany her on the trip. I received the telegram while I was eating supper. Bessie came around and wanted to see the telegram. I told her that it was for me and that I didn't think it would be good for her to see it. I had not yet read the telegram, but was tearing open the envelope. Bessie said she thought it was from her folks. I told her I thought it wasn't, and that if it was, I'd let her know. She insisted on looking at it as I opened it. I turned myself sideways so as to prevent her reading it. She moved around behind me so that she still could read it. And then I quit,—and let her read it. The girl's name was not signed, but the whole trip was given away. (I am giving you this to show you my frame of mind, and to show you that I was getting ready for a separation from Bessie.)

I went down to Oakland on a second trip. I called Charmian up at Berkeley, I being at the Bungalow. Incidentally, Charmian told me that Bessie had gone through my waste-basket and pieced together several shreds of the letter she (Charmian) had written me in reply to my request to see her (Charmian), and in which Charmian had told me to come see her at Berkeley. As it was typewritten, Bessie did not know who the woman was, and had no suspicions of Charmian. All this information had come to Charmian through her aunt, as so much gossip, for to her aunt promptly had Bessie gone to relate the discovery she had made in my waste-paper-basket. (It was always Bessie's way to shout all things from the house-top.)

In this talk over the 'phone with Charmian, in which I made mention of the fact of trouble arising if Bessie discovered the identity of the person who had written the letter, Charmian said she would be "game" for her share of the trouble. And in that moment, it came to me, without warning, for the first time, that I loved Charmian. And in that moment, on the very instant, spontaneously, without even thinking, I answered, "Then you'll be game for *all* of it!" The thought I had in mind was, that I would marry Charmian.

Now, don't forget my basis. All during this period, from before the beginning of the camping in Glen Ellen, I had made up my mind to go to pieces and get a separation. This without being in love with anybody, but from sheer disgust in life, such as I was living it.

I came back to Glen Ellen. There was hell to pay. Bessie was suspicious of everybody. She broached the letter to me that she had got from my waste paper basket. She didn't know but what it was from the girl from whom I had received the telegram. I was careful to steer her clear of Charmian. I had intended to bring about the separation after the camping-trip was over, and when Bessie had returned to the Bungalow. But this letter which she had discovered in the waste-basket, plus the telegram, and her discussing the matter with me, precipitated the separation. She asked me if I loved somebody else. I told her that I did, though I refused to tell her that person's name. And I told her frankly that it was because of the trouble she would make for that person, if she learned that person's identity. So the separation was thus precipitated. The story is all told.

Now, the source of this story that Charmian broke up the London household, is due directly to Bessie. It is the gossip of Oakland at the present moment. You say in your letter to me, that from things Bessie had said, etc., etc., you made up your mind that Charmian had broken up the household.

Now, Carrie, I have never made a defence of my actions in this matter before to any one, nor explained the course of events as they really happened,—and all this in the face of a countless number of lies that have been circulated. I am making this explanation to you, and you are the first one to whom I have made an explanation. I don't think you have ever heard me breathe a word against Bessie, nor anybody else ever heard me breathe a word against Bessie. Nevertheless, I now tell you that Bessie is one of the most colossal and shameless liars I have ever encountered. I'll give you but one instance. At the present time and for many months past, it has been going the rounds of Oakland gossip that financially I have treated Bessie shamefully, so shamefully that she was compelled even to sell her furniture in order to feed her babies.

Let me give you the real facts of the foregoing lie: When I went away to Korea, Bessie received from my publishers, the first of every month, $65.00—maybe it was $75.00 a month, I don't remember. In addition, all extraordinary expenses, doctor bills, nurse bills, etc., etc., were charged to me and paid by me. In addition to this I made arrangements with my publishers before I left, that if Bessie wanted money at any time, all she had to do was to write them or telegraph them, whereupon they would send her the money. This Bessie understood, and this she utilized while I was away. Bessie decided to go to Los Angeles for a while. She stored some of her furniture, and she sold some of it. The reason she gave me for selling it, was that she didn't want it any more. She wanted better. She got better, and I paid for it.

Now, Carrie, very little reliance can be placed upon any person who would circulate so shameless a lie about her husband, as Bessie did in the foregoing.

Do you remember how Bessie dragged Anna Strunsky's name through the mire? Through all the newspapers and pink-tea councils at the time of my return from Korea?

Do you wonder that I wanted to shield Charmian from the moment I knew that I loved her and wanted to marry her? I believe I shielded Charmian fairly well. In order to save Charmian from Bessie's shameless and lying tongue, at the time of my separation I counseled Charmian not to break off entirely from Bessie, but to see her occasionally. This she did no oftener than was absolutely necessary, seeing Bessie in the six months between my separation and my departure for Korea, but four or five times.

The one person before the separation, during the separation, and after the separation, who was practically above suspicion in Bessie's mind, was Charmian. And Charmian was practically above suspicion, because Charmian's conduct in the London family had been most exemplary. Remember Bessie's eagle eyes; remember the eagle eyes of any married woman so far as her husband is concerned, with other women in the house. During all this time Bessie never suspected Charmian once—BECAUSE THERE WAS ABSOLUTELY NO REASON TO SUSPECT HER, WHILE THERE WERE MANY REASONS FOR NOT SUSPECTING HER. During the time in the Bungalow, Charmian had a love-affair of her own with somebody else. Hints of this were given by her at the time to Bessie and carried on from Bessie to me. I know the ins and outs of this love-affair, myself, now, and during the whole of the period that Charmian dropped in at the Bungalow, she was badly tangled up with somebody else.

So well did I shield Charmian, that at the time of my departure for Korea, Bessie did not have the slightest suspicion that she was the woman. My sister, who has been uniformly loyal to me, at that time slipped and played me false. My sister [4] said to Bessie, "I am going over to the steamer to see Jack off. And I know that I shall there discover who the woman is." She did, and she promptly came back and gave Bessie the news. This was the first inkling Bessie had as to who the woman was.

Now you've got it all in a nut-shell. With an eagle-eyed, jealous wife in the house, the woman doesn't live who can go into that house and cut out that eagle-eyed, jealous wife's husband from under her nose, without that eagle-eyed, jealous wife getting some suspicions. I say again, the woman doesn't live who could accomplish that feat, and you know it yourself, Carrie. Again, and in connection with this, let me point out to you the fact that Bessie did not have the slightest suspicion as to Charmian's being the woman, until six months after the separation, and then, the news was carried to her by my sister.

Carrie, I have given you in downright frankness my love-affair with Charmian, its beginning and its culmination when I first became conscious that I loved her; I have pointed out to you that the separation had already been decided upon by me before I knew that I was in love, and before I had ever had a single thought about Charmian. I have been frank, almost [5] too frank in the matter, and if I hadn't cared for you I wouldn't have been frank with you at all, nor told you a word of it.

In conclusion, I want to tell you this: that according to my code, I don't consider it a crime for any woman, no matter what the circumstances, to attempt to cut out a man from under the guns of another woman. All women are so made, all women do these things,—at least all women who have the temptation. And if a woman loves a man so circumstanded, it is a temptation.

It happens in this case however, that the conduct charged against Charmian by you is considered a most heinous crime of conventional society. And, it also happens, that in this case Charmian is absolutely Not Guilty. It merely happens so; but it makes your mistake the more egregious in-so-far as you have made that mistake public. And public you have made it, because already, and for weeks past, the gossip has been dribbling back that the Crowd dropped Charmian because Charmian broke up the London family.

You say in your letter that "as a man and as Charmian's possible sharer in whatever blame is connected with this affair, you are in honor bound to find excuses for her in the matter." Your reasoning is fairly good if you fit it to the average man. The average man is not as truthful as I am, and you know it. The average man is more of a chivalrous liar than I am. If you will take my last bunch of correspondence with you, you will find that I was not chivalrous enough to lie in order to save other women or any woman. My rule of conduct is for every man to stand on his own legs, and for every woman too. In this last big correspondence with you and the rest of the Crowd, I made Charmian stand on her own legs, and I made every other woman stand on her own legs. I said the time was past for any beating about the bush and we threshed it out without any chivalrous lying, everybody standing upon their own legs.

I know that this is a very inadequate way to give to you all the events and all the psychology of the time before, during and after my separation from Bessie and my love for Charmian; and so I am quite willing, and not only willing but anxious, to answer any questions from you which may throw additional light on the matter;—light that I have forgotten to shed myself.

Jack London

MS: ULA; 7 pp., fragment of tl.; completed from 10 pp., typs., CSmH. Pbd: *L*, 180–86.
    1. The Jimmy Britt–Battling Nelson lightweight championship fight in Colma, California, took place on September 9. See "Brain Beaten by Brute Force," *San Francisco Examiner*, September 10, 1905.
    2. See JL to Partington, June 12, 1903.
    3. Frank Atherton.
    4. Corrected to "another person" by CKL. She made additional marginal notations throughout the letter.
    5. The ULA letter ends here.

To Cloudesley Johns

Glen Ellen, Calif.
Sep 20 1905

Read *The Divine Fire*, by May Sinclair,[1] and then get down in the dust at her feet. She is a master.

No, I don't think the Greek receives his old salary—only a portion of it.[2] We went to the fight together.[3] Great fight.

What the hell will you do with a thousand per month?

Yep—got dollar from Winship.

Say—what was the nature of the bet I made with all the Crowd at Greek's that Sunday? Do you remember? I've forgotten, & don't [know] whether I have to pay or collect.

Wolf.

MS: CSmH; 3 pp., als.
  1. Published in 1904. The novel's protagonist, Cockney writer Keith Rickman, strives to overcome his lack of refinement so that he will be accepted in literary circles. After struggling as a poet and a journalist he achieves fame and success, but he never does overcome his coarseness. For the influence of this book on JL, see T. E. M. Boll, "*The Divine Fire* (1904) and *Martin Eden* (1909)," *English Literature in Transition* (*1880–1920*), 14 (1971), 115–17.
  2. Sterling had resigned from his uncle's real estate firm and moved to Carmel.
  3. The Britt-Nelson fight.

To Caroline Sterling

[Glen Ellen]
Sept. 29, 1905

Dear Carrie:

This is a long-delayed reply to your letter of Sept. 19. I have read your letter through carefully, and in order to show you that every statement of fact you have made in it coincides with what I wrote to you, I make the following quotations;

(1) "We all knew and felt sorry for her (Charmian) as we thought it hopeless."

(2) "When [George] ¹ charged her (Charmian) with it once, (loving me, Jack) she did not deny him."

(3) "When Charmian went East, we thought it was to forget her love for you. Even Isabelle and Mother Sterling,² at the time, spoke of C.'s infatuation for you, and how she used to, when up there, talk of no one but you—before you and Bessie separated."

(4) "The only time I (Carrie) ever saw anything which led me to believe there was aught between you, was one Saturday night and Sunday, in June, at our camp."

(5) "Again, the faithful friend who dallied enough with the husband to cause disgust to an old reprobate like Joaquin Miller."

(6) "Then the night of your accident, she (Charmian) told me that she felt so sorry for you that while on her horse she put her arms around you."

Now let me reply to the foregoing quotations from your letter:

(1) You did not any of you know, nor feel sorry for Charmian, until after the separation.

(2) George charged Charmian out at Dingee's, after the separation. Charmian told me about it at the time.

(3) Charmian went East many months after the separation. As regards

Isabelle and Mother Sterling's statements that Charmian talked of no one but me before Bessie and I separated, this may well be correct. I was a protégé of Charmian's family; her Aunt Netta[3] in particular, and the whole family was particularly enthusiastic over me.

(4) This reference I covered in my letter to you. It was at the very moment of separation, when I was trying to get Charmian to be my mistress, and before I knew I was in love with her.

(5) Same date as (4),—at the very moment of separation.

Still referring to (5): I wonder if you sincerely mean precisely what you said there as quoted. I remember that Sunday very well. I spent a great deal of time—practically all the time—while Joaquin was present getting drunk, in fooling with the girls. I washed Kate's[4] face with cherries and dirt, if you will remember, and it took some time, all that squabbling around with Kate. I poured a lot of water over Charmian; also, when Carlt[5] and Charmian got to fooling with the box of powder, Carlt threw the box of powder into the brush, and I spent a good while getting said box out of the brush. Said box had fallen down through the brush into a creek, a dry creek, and we were all a long time locating it. Then part of the time I listened to Joaquin Miller and Austin Lewis recite, and altogether Joaquin Miller wasn't there a couple of hours. For a few minutes only, Charmian and I had our heads in your lap, together. Then for a time we lay feet touching feet, and heads in opposite directions, so that our heads came pretty close to being nine and ten feet away from each other. We did not lie alongside of each other at all. I am not denying that Joaquin made this remark. But anent this remark of Joaquin's, I am putting it up to you. Go over that day in your memory, and find out if Charmian's and my conducted MERITED such a remark from Joaquin Miller or anybody else.

(6) This also was at the very moment of separation.

Now, concerning [all] the foregoing. All the facts that you have stated occur within the time stated by me in my letter to you,—at the very moment of separation, or subsequent to the separation.

Now, Carrie, you know yourself that you had no suspicions whatever against Charmian, and so you have stated, prior to the separation or at the time of the separation. Why did you fail to have these suspicions? Because Charmian's conduct and mine had never given you cause for such suspicions. And you can go over every member of the Crowd on this point, and find a similar concensus of opinion. It was not until after the separation that any of you began to suspect that Charmian cared for me.

You mention at the time Bessie went up to Glen Ellen, Charmian's coming with a tearful message that it was a shame the way I was treating Bessie. She told me about this message, before I went to Korea. Incidentally, no finer proof could be given that there was nothing between Charmian and me than this same message which you have instanced. As I had kept my mouth shut with all of you, concerning Bessie and my life with Bessie, so had I kept it shut with Charmian concerning Bessie and my life with Bessie. And while Charmian liked me for a certain comradeship that was mine, and for the work I was doing in my writing, etc., etc., she none the less listened to the lies Bessie told about me, and believed those lies. Hence the tearful message instanced by you. She believed it at the time.

Now, concerning this tearful message: It was caused by my not going down to the train to see Bessie off to Glen Ellen. Bessie had told this same tearful story at Glen Ellen, of my ill-treatment of her in not coming down to see her off, and it had been believed. And everybody at Glen Ellen was righteously indignant about my conduct. Now let me give you the facts: There were two babies to be taken to Glen Ellen, and a lot of luggage. The luggage I paid an express company to hand[le]. The two babies had, to carry them, Bessie and a stout nurse-girl, one baby to each, and one of the babies able to walk. Those are the facts of it, and said facts must be taken in conjunction with one other fact, namely, that if I had accompanied Bessie I would have lost my whole morning's work writing. And who in hell was to pay for the express-wagon, and the railroad tickets, and the nurse-girl, if I wasn't?

I now quote from your letter: "I know of three parties who left your house in disgust at three different times, because of the actions of you and Charmian before Bessie." Now, Carrie, let me give you straight talk and plain talk. Never, in my house, have I romped nor cut up in any way with any woman, girl or child whatsoever, to the extent that I have done all these things in your house with yourself, and about every woman who was ever in your house while I was present,—except Charmian. And I am sure, that in this cutting up with you, and girls in your house, nothing so very reprehensible was thought of my conduct. There's no use in naming all the girls, with all the hugs and all the kisses, and all the rest of it. You know, you absolutely know, and you know that I know that you know. Now, one of two things concerning these three people who left my house in disgust because of my conduct with Charmian. Either these people lie, or else they are damn finicky. Practically the only cutting up, at least that I can remember, that I had with Charmian, was boxing. Also, I boxed with Ida Brooks, Anna Strunsky, the servant-girls, Bessie, and anybody who would put the gloves on with me.

Still anent my disgraceful conduct with Charmian in my house: I want to ask you a couple of questions, Carrie, and I want you to please answer them. First, do you think that I made a practice of putting on company-manners when you were at my house, with the Crowd[?]; and Second, did you, yourself, ever see any conduct of mine with Charmian that disgusted you, or that was likely to disgust anybody worthy to enter your house or mine? And before you answer these two questions, let me make the statement that I never in my life in my house put on company manners for anybody, and pray God I never shall.

Concerning the talk of people of the sort that say they were disgusted at what they saw in my house, let me give you the following, which was brought to me shortly after my separation, and which went the rounds of Alameda gossip. Namely: That other visitors at my house, eye-witnesses, had seen me offer personal, physical violence to Bessie. And this was told by the eye-witnesses themselves at Alameda dinner-parties and pink-teas.

In conclusion. After reading your letter, your statements, and your objections, the case stands just as I stated it in my letter to you. And in addition let me again assure you that I know, personally and convincingly, of the fact that right up to within a short time of my separation, a very short time, Charmian had a deep and tragic love-affair with somebody else. I knew who this person is, though at the time I did not even guess. At the time, however, I did know that Charmian did have this affair with somebody, and that it was causing her all kinds of worry and trouble. Once again let me say, that I am as certain that Charmian had this love-affair, as I am that I am sitting on this chair,—that I am certain this love-affair extended up almost to the moment of my separation, and was settled but a short time before.

Now, a little information, Carrie. This affair of Charmian's with somebody else, tragic and full of worry and anxiety, as I have told you, extended through about a year's time. Finally, and during Charmian's vacation in the first part of June, up here in Glen Ellen, she thought it all over and made up her mind to quit. Then it was that the affair was *settled*. She was a free woman again, and ready for any sort of a joyful [reaction] that could come along. It was at this time, as Charmian was coming back from her vacation, and Bessie was going up to take her vacation at Glen Ellen, that I came along Charmian's way, looking for a mistress. As I say, Charmian was ready for any kind of a joyful reaction that could come along. I came along, and it was a case of speedy falling in love for both of us. I have told you all this in my preceding letter.

As I told you before, I am not only willing, but anxious, that you should thoroughly understand the situation, and not allow a false judgment to rest upon anybody. And so, I not only am anxious, but glad, to have you ask any questions, the answers of which may explain things that appear contradictory or obscure in your mind. Please, dear Carrie, ask these questions, and state any further objections that you may have to the explanation that I have given.

Sincerely yours,
Jack London

MS: ULA; 5 pp., cctl. Pbd: *L*, 186–89.
1. Added interlinearly in a second hand. The numbering of JL's list of replies has also been corrected, and changes indicated by brackets throughout this letter were made in the same hand.
2. Mary Isabella Sterling (1875–1947), George's sister; Mary Parker Havens Sterling, George's mother.
3. Ninetta Eames.

4. Kate Partington.
5. Carlton Bierce, Ambrose Bierce's nephew and a member of the Crowd.

To Frederick I. Bamford

Glen Ellen, Calif.
Oct 2 1905

Dear friend:

No, it will be absolutely impossible for me to make that trip to Stanford. I simply have to get this book[1] finished. I have agreed to review *The Long Day* for *The Examiner* (the writer is a socialist woman, and 'the book is about the working girls of New York).[2] I have agreed to write an article on the Intercollegiate Socialist Society,[3] for an international News Syndicate. I have agreed to write a 500-word article on Upton Sinclair's *The Jungle* for the Trust Edition of *The Appeal to Reason*; and an additional review of *The Jungle* for either the Hearst Newspapers or the New York *Independent*.[4] Yet none of the foregoing, which is all work for socialism, shall I be able to tackle until I start East, and then in the three days between Oakland and Chicago, I hope to get that work done. In addition I am burdened with correspondence from the Socialists all over the country, asking me to lecture, because they understand that I am going on this lecture-tour, and shall be passing through different parts of the country. Incidentally, I may mention that the lecture I am supposed to give, I have not yet prepared; I mean the lectures for the Slayton Lyceum Bureau. I shall be in Oakland from October 14 to Oct. 20. And you and I should see something of each other during that time.

Affectionately yours,
Jack London

MS: JL State Park; 1 p., tls.

1. *White Fang.*
2. Dorothy Richardson, *The Long Day* (1905). See "Jack London Reviews 'The Long Day,'" *San Francisco Examiner*, October 15, 1905; reprinted in part in the December 2, 1905, *The Appeal to Reason.*
3. JL was first president of the Intercollegiate Socialist Society (I.S.S.), which was initiated September 1, 1905, at a gathering of literary figures and prominent socialists in a New York restaurant. A formal call was issued on September 20 and was signed by JL, Upton Sinclair, Leonard Abbot, William English Walling, Clarence Darrow, and others. It began: "In the opinion of the undersigned the recent remarkable increase in the Socialist vote in America should serve as an indication to the educated men and women in the country, that Socialism is a thing concerning which it is no longer wise to be indifferent. The undersigned, regarding its aims and fundamental principles with sympathy, and believing that in them will ultimately be found the remedy for many far-reaching economic evils, propose organizing an association, to be known as the Intercollegiate Socialist Society, for the purpose of promoting an intelligent interest in Socialism among college men and women, graduate and undergraduate, through the formation of study clubs in the colleges and universities, and the encouraging of all legitimate endeavors to awaken an interest in Socialism." JL served as president until May 1907.

4. JL's review of Upton Sinclair's *The Jungle* (1906) appeared in the *New York Evening Journal*, August 8, 1906, and in *Wilshire's Magazine*, January 1907. *The Jungle* was published serially from February 25 to November 4, 1905, in *The Appeal to Reason*, a socialist weekly published in Girard, Kansas, by J. A. Wayland from 1895 to 1919. For JL's enthusiastic promotion of the book, see JL to "Dear Comrades," ? December 1905.

To Cloudesley Johns

Glen Ellen, Calif.
Oct 4 1905

Dear Cloudesley—

I'd like to have seen that trial.[1] Must have been great!

Now to business.

To buy the ranch and build barn, I had to get heavy advances from Macmillan. I had already overdrawn so heavily, that Macmillan's asked me, & in common decency I agreed, to pay interest on these new advances made.

At present moment my check book shows me $207.83 to my credit at bank.

It is the first of the month & I have no end of bills awaiting me, prominent among which are:

My mother	$55.00
Outfit of tools for ranch	57.60
Rent here at Glen Ellen	$24.00

The smaller bills will total $50.00.

Now, I have to pay my own expenses East. Lecture Bureau afterward reimburses me.[2] But immediately I must pay my way and Manyoungi's way to Chicago. Charmian follows me inside 24 hours. There are her expenses.[3]

I haven't a cent coming to me now from any source, & must borrow this money in Oakland.

Also, in November I must meet between seven & eight hundred dollars insurance.

My mother wants me to increase her monthly allowance. So does Bessie.

I have just paid hospital bills of over a $100.00 for one of my sisters.

Another member of the family (whom I cannot refuse) has warned me that as soon as I arrive in Oakland they want to make a proposition to me. I know what that means.

I have promised $30.00 to pay printing of appeal to Supreme Court of Joe King, a poor devil in Co. Jail with 50 yrs. sentence hanging over him and who is being railroaded.[4]

And so on, & so on, and so on— Oh, & a bill for over $45.00 to the hay press.

So you see that I am not only sailing close into the wind but that I am dead into it & my sails flapping.

Wolf.

MS: CSmH; 9 pp., als. Pbd: *L*, 189–90.
 1. Possibly JL refers to the lawsuit in which Gavin McNabb, a director of the Continental and Phoenix Building and Loan Associations, sued William Randolph Hearst and the *San Francisco Examiner*, JL's occasional employer. The case came to trial in Sacramento in late September. At the time, Johns was a reporter for the *Los Angeles Evening Express*.
 2. JL received $600 a week plus expenses for two from the Slayton Lyceum Bureau.
 3. CKL later added: "C. to stay with friend until her marriage to Jack." She left California for Iowa on October 20 and met JL in Ames on October 28, after his lecture in Lincoln, Nebraska. From there she went to Newton, Iowa, to stay with Lynette McMurray, arriving on November 1.
 4. See JL to Shepard, ? April 1915.

To George P. Brett

Glen Ellen, Calif.
Oct 11 1905

Dear Mr. Brett:
 I have sent you off today, by express, copy of *White Fang*.[1] Hope you will like it. You will find there is not much resemblance between it and *The Call of the Wild*, and I don't think anybody will dare to assert that I have humanized the dog. Copy of the *Fish Patrol Stories* came to hand, and I like very much the way in which you got it up.
 I am leaving Glen Ellen to-morrow, and several days later am starting East.

In great haste,
Sincerely yours,
Jack London

MS: NN; 1 p., tls.
 1. In a letter of the same date to Cloudesley Johns (ULA), JL noted that he had completed *White Fang* and was sending a duplicate copy for Johns's corrections.

To George P. Brett

Ames, Iowa.
October 29 '05

Dear Mr. Brett:–
 Yes, please hold all mail for me until I arrive in N.Y. I now give you additional dates of my lecture trip, which I have just received:–

Nov. 7—Oberlin, Ohio.[1]
 "   9—Mercersburg, Pa.
 "   10—Orange, N.J.
 "   11—Brooklyn Heights, N.Y.

       "   13—Oneonta, N.Y.
       "   14—York, Pa.

Nov. 15—Oxford, Ohio.
   "   16—Sandusky, Ohio
   "   17—New Kensington, Pa.
   "   20—Lake Geneva, Wis.
   "   21—Elwood, Indiana
   "   22—New Harmony, Ind.
   "   23—Champaign, Ill.
   "   24—Grinnell, Iowa

Dec.   7—Brunswick, Maine

                Sincerely yours,
                Jack London.

MS: CSmH; 2 pp., als. CKL.
   1. Earlier, JL lectured in Kansas City; Matoon, Kansas; Mt. Vernon, Iowa; Chicago; Lincoln; Ames, Iowa; Indianapolis; Evanston, Illinois; Toledo; and Madison.

To Charmian Kittredge

                      N.Y.C.
                      Nov 12 1905
My Mate—
   I have told *Outing* to forward my check to Newton. Keep track of it. It should be for $3,700—1/2 of what they are to pay for American serial rights.[1] No so bad, is it?—$7,400 plus what I get from English serial rights, plus book royalties (which are bound to be larger still) all for a couple of months work.
   Save *all* letters I send you. Some of them I want for my collection.
   If you have not forwarded foto to me already,[2] please forward it directly to

                Mr. Jack Barrett,[3]
                Editorial Rooms
                S.F. Examiner.
Seal & register the photograph, writing your name on back of fotograph.
   All mail that comes to you for me, hold until I get there.
   What does Aunt Netta mean by saying that "all her moments are given to the work Jack set" her?
   I don't understand. Forwarding mail—yes. Keeping mice out of my clothes—yes. But what else?
   Building house? But that's her business. Tell me if you can.
   Don't exactly appreciate the "luxury" of the washstand, seeing, accord-

ing to Aunt Netta's plans, that you & I are to be in the annex[4] only for meals.

First, Aunt Netta gives all the details of the "luxuries" she is preparing for our enjoyment. And then she gives all the details showing us that we shall not be able to use them. She's a corker!

We'll need bedding for the yacht anyway, so explain to Aunt Netta that I'll get necessary bedding.

Yep—the death lines in "All Gold Canyon" came from my experience with the "little death in life," "the drunken dark," "the sweet thick mystery," etc.

Pinker[5] has *White Fang* you know.

Portrait attachment—in pigeon holes in cottage.

I *love* your letters.

And I read them again and again, & love them over & over.
Expressed you four or five[6]
I read your writing like print.
Be sure & save the Des Moines clipping. It is rich![7]
My God! these Iowa people who look upon a cold bath in the morning as a hobby!
Dear, dear Wolf Mate., the 25th. is very near—and very dear. Dear Wife![8]

Wolf.

MS: CSmH; 8 pp., als. Pbd: *L*, 190–91.
1. To *White Fang*.
2. Probably the photograph CKL had taken in Salt Lake City on October 20 en route to Iowa.
3. John P. ("Jack") Barrett, news editor of the *San Francisco Examiner*.
4. The Wake-Robin Lodge annex.
5. James B. Pinker.
6. Apparently JL failed to finish this sentence.
7. In a front page story entitled "Noted Author in Pretty Romance," *Des Moines Daily News*, November 7, 1905, the reporter gave a gossip-filled account of JL's courtship of CKL. He claimed that their romance began with love at first sight and mentioned rumors of their forthcoming marriage.
8. Originally the Londons planned to marry on November 25 in Newton. When the divorce decree was issued on November 18, however, JL telegraphed CKL from Elyria, Ohio (where he had lectured at the People's Institute), asking her to meet him in Chicago on November 19 for the ceremony. She recorded the event in her diary: "Left Newton for Chicago morning train, three hours late. Mate & Manyoungi met me—cab to *Examiner* office, elevated to West Side, Justice [J. J.] Grant married us, with my mother's wedding-ring. Back to Hotel Victoria,—night made hideous by reporters!—Jack adorable—my perfect bridegroom & lover, at last." The newspaper office belonged not to the *Examiner* but to the *Chicago American*, a Hearst paper. There they enlisted the aid of Mr. Harstone, the paper's city editor and a witness at the wedding ceremony, to find someone to marry them that night; in

return, Harstone got the exclusive story of the wedding. Once word of the marriage was made public, many people were outraged, and some of JL's lectures were canceled.

To George P. Brett

Newton, Iowa.
Nov 26 1905

Dear Mr. Brett:—

In reply to your letters of Nov. 13th., 16th., and 20th.

As I only rushed right through New York, I made no announcement of my coming. I do not now expect to be in New York until the first part of January, when I shall stop for a week or two.

I am writing this mail to *Outing* & to my English agent to arrange printing with each serial installment notice of copyright by me—*White Fang*.

I am glad you like the story. I do not think it will be as popular as *The Call of the Wild*, but in some ways I think it the bigger book.

I don't think any illustrations have yet been made for *White Fang*.[1] You see, I sent you a copy at the very moment I finished the story.

As regards sending check each month to my first wife. Please send the same amount monthly check, but change the name from "Mrs. Jack London," to "Bessie M. London." This, I am sure, will be satisfactory all around.

I received the check for November enclosed in your letter of November 20th.

I have somewhat changed my plans—as regards forwarding mail. Please now have my mail forwarded to Newton, Iowa until December 1st.[2] Then forward my mail until December 6th, Care of Mrs. R. J. Ham, Brunswick, Maine.[3] After December 6th., please forward mail: Care of Mrs. Augusta Gilpatrick, Northeast Harbor, Maine.[4]

Did you notice illustrations of my story "Love of Life," in December *McClure's*?[5] I think they are magnificent.

Sincerely yours,
Jack London

MS: NN; 6 pp., als.

1. The novel was illustrated by Charles Livingston Bull, who had worked on *The Call of the Wild*.

2. Following their wedding in Chicago, the Londons returned to the lecture circuit on November 20; see JL to Brett, October 29, 1905. They reached Newton on November 25. By December 2 they were back on the road, and JL lectured in Des Moines that night.

3. Mrs. R. J. Ham may have arranged JL's December 7 lecture at Bowdoin College.

4. Mrs. Augusta Gilpatrick, a relative of CKL.

5. "Love of Life," published in *McClure's Magazine*, December 1905, was illustrated by Ernest L. Blumenschein, a German magazine illustrator and artist, who founded the Taos School of painting. This story was also included in *Love of Life*.

To Werner Wiget

[Newton, Iowa]
Nov 28 1905

Mr. Wiget:

Please find herewith check for $45.00 for November. Kindly acknowledge receipt in same manner as before.

Also, let me know how Belle is getting along. Is she showing signs of having a colt? Is she getting larger?[1]

And Brown[2]—did you *see* him make connection with the shepherd bitch?

Also, let me know if Ban's[3] lame leg is getting better.

Did you get rid of the turkeys yet, or are you holding them to sell for Christmas.

I suppose by this time that you have had rain in California.

I am going down to Cuba in January.[4] Shall be back in California in February.

Jack London.

If that horse I let that woman try is no good, kill it and feed it to the chickens, or *sell* it. There is no use feeding such a horse through the winter.

MS: CU; 3 pp., als.
1. On June 19, CKL had taken Belle to breed with a stallion named Moralita.
2. Brown Wolf.
3. Washoe Ban.
4. On December 27, the Londons and Manyoungi sailed from Boston to Port Antonio, Jamaica, on the United Fruit Co.'s SS *Admiral Farragut*. After four days in Jamaica, on January 5 they voyaged on the SS *Oteri* to Santiago Harbor, Cuba.

To Cloudesley Johns

Newton, Iowa,
Nov. 30 '05

Dear Cloudesley:—

I am booked by the Lecture-Bureau to lecture in Santa Ana on Feb. 16. I am offered at Venice on Feb. 17, and there may be, immediately following, or, for all I know, immediately preceding, a Los Angeles date. Now,— I'd like to have this Debate with B. Fay Mills arranged within the 10 days succeeding say Feb. 17.[1] Please see the Socialist Party about this for me.

Also, please tell the Socialist party that within those 10 days I am willing to give them "Revolution." Tell them all I shall charge them is several dollars for expenses.

I'd like to camp out at your place for part of my stay there—on one consideration, namely, that you let me pay expenses.

Please reply to me care Macmillan Co., 66 Fifth Avenue, New York City. Reply as soon as you can, letting me know what arrangements and dates have been determined upon.

For that matter, I don't like to do Owen out of *his* debate,[2] & I should be willing to debate with him after the Mills, if Owen & his crowd are willing to go on with it.

I am looking expectantly forward to receiving congratulations from you upon my marriage, and am wondering what form they will take this time!![3]

Jack London[4]

The reviewers said the Sea Wolf was an impossible creature. How about Peter Widermeier?

Wolf.[5]

MS: CSmH; al. CKL, s. JL.

   1. Reverend Benjamin Fay Mills (1857–1916), lecturer and evangelist. Mills was ordained a minister in the Congregational Church but withdrew from that denomination because of his liberal views. He subsequently became minister of the First Unitarian Church of Oakland, and in 1904 he founded and became first permanent minister of the Los Angeles Fellowship. The *Los Angeles Examiner*, on December 10, 1905, announced "Jack London is to lecture here on February 20" and went on to say that JL would be in Los Angeles for ten days, during which he was to give three lectures and hold two debates, including one with Mills at Simpson Auditorium. These lectures and debates were canceled; see JL to Johns, February 3, 1906.

   2. Probably William C. Owen, who in his Progressive Club address "Tolstoy, the Apostle of the Right" at Symphony Hall in Los Angeles on September 3, 1905, disagreed with JL's philosophy as expressed in "The Class Struggle."

   3. See JL to Johns, April 3, 1900, n. 3, and April 16, 1900, n. 1.

   4. This letter is in CKL's hand. She added a postscript: "Me, too, Cloudesley! (C)."

   5. Signature and postscript in JL's hand.

To George P. Brett

Newton, Iowa
Dec 2 1905

Dear Mr. Brett—

In reply to yours of Nov. 29th.

I have not enough Klondike stories to make a volume by themselves, & I don't care to mix them up with other stories. I shall complete the volume of Klondike stories[1] next summer.

I find that I can't write that set of "Created He Them"[2] sketches, while traveling around.

I have just glanced at the Preface of Henry George's book which you so kindly sent me, & I know that I shall enjoy reading it, agreeing with his destructive criticism while disagreeing with his constructive theorizing.[3]

Please hold the parcel marked glass & all express packages; but forward mail according to directions in my last letter.

Am going to run down to Jamaica last part of December, from Boston, & shall arrive back in New York the middle of January.

I suppose you have learned from the papers ere this, that I've got married. This time I cannot deny. I plead guilty. It's true. As my wife is here to see what I write, I am enabled to explain to you that I got married in order to have one more member in the crew for the trip around the world.

Sincerely yours,
Jack London.

MS: NN; 4 pp., als. Pbd: *L*, 192.
　1. *Love of Life.*
　2. "Created He Them," *Pacific Monthly*, April 1907, later included in *When God Laughs*.
　3. Henry George, *The Menace of Privilege: A Study of the Dangers to the Republic from the Existence of a Favored Class* (1905), published by Macmillan.

To Frederick I. Bamford

Mt. Desert, Me.
Dec 15 1905

Dear friend & Comrade:—

I am returning Anna's letter herewith. It is indeed literature. And from what she says, I know I am justified in joining with her congratulations to you.

The Revolution goes! It goes!

Yes, received your letter at Newton, Iowa. Charmian is writing a reply to it soon.

Collier's paid me $500.00 for "Revolution"; I do not know when they will publish it. They may never publish it. You see, they may have got frightened.[1] *McClure's* long ago bought and paid me for "The Question of the Maximum," the[n] grew frightened, & never published it.[2]

Next Thursday I give "Revolution" at Harvard University, and soon after I shall give it at Yale, Columbia, and Chicago Universities[3]—all this under auspices of Intercollegiate Socialist Society.

Then I shall lecture for the Socialist locals in the several large cities.

It goes! It goes!

Oh, I have some stories to tell you when I get back about my clashes with the masters of society.

With love,
Jack London

MS: JL State Park; 5 pp., als. Pbd: *Mystery*, 199.
　1. See JL to the Editor, *Collier's Weekly*, August 1, 1905, n. 1.
　2. See JL to Johns, November 11, 1899, n. 8.
　3. JL lectured at the Harvard Union on December 21, 1905, at Yale on January 26, 1906, and at the University of Chicago on January 29, 1906. He did not lecture at Columbia.

To George W. Galvin

Mt. Desert, Me.
Dec 15 1905

Dear Comrade Galvin:—[1]

In reply to yours of Dec. 13th. Now I've got the Harvard date straight. And am ready, any date, to speak for the socialists of Boston.[2] Subject of both lectures the same, "Revolution."

Now as regards my stay in Boston. I believe it has already been arranged that Mrs. London and I are to stay with friends in Newton. But I'd like very much to see with you some of the "sights"—not the *tourist* sights, but the *sociologist's* sights. I'd like to take Mrs. London along, and if you can see your way to it, don't forget that Mrs. London is a good comrade, a man's woman, and for whom the worst of every sort is not too evil for her to know and understand. She has no taste for expurgated editions.

I do not know whether I have already told you, but I make no charge for lectures for the socialists—only expenses, which, in Boston dates, will be a matter of no more than several dollars.

I'll call you up by telephone after I arrive.

Yours for the Revolution,
Jack London.

MS: CSmH; 4 pp., als.

1. George W. Galvin (1854–1928), Boston physician, socialist, and author of *Crimes Against Our Criminals and Insane* (1905). The Londons stayed at his home during their visit to Boston. According to "Jack London Arrives in Boston," *Hearst's Boston American,* December 17, 1905, JL, after reading Galvin's article "Our Legal Machinery and Its Victims," *Arena,* November 1904, had written Galvin to express his appreciation and to commend the truth of Galvin's observations to JL's own humiliations in prison during his tramping days.

2. JL spoke at Tremont Temple on December 19, and at Faneuil Hall on December 26, in addition to the December 21 lecture at Harvard.

To "Dear Comrades"

[New York]
[? December 1905]

Dear Comrades:—

Here it is at last! The book we have been waiting for these many years! The *Uncle Tom's Cabin* of wage slavery! Comrade Sinclair's book *The Jungle*! And what *Uncle Tom's Cabin* did for black slaves, *The Jungle* has a large chance to do for the wage slaves of to-day.

It is essentially a book of to-day. The beautiful theoretics of Bellamy's *Looking Backward* are all very good. They served a purpose and served it well. *Looking Backward* was a great book, but I dare to say that *The Jungle*, which has no beautiful theoretics, is even a greater book.

It is alive and warm. It is brutal with life. It is written of sweat and blood and groans and tears. It depicts, not what man ought to be, but what man is compelled to be in this our world in the twentieth century. It depicts, not what our country ought to be, or what it seems to be in the fancies of Fourth-of-July spell-binders, the home of liberty and equality, of opportunity—but it depicts what our country really is, the home of oppression and injustice, a nightmare of misery, an inferno of suffering, a human hell, a jungle of wild beasts.

And there you have the very essence of Upton Sinclair's book—*The Jungle*! And that is what he has named it. This book must go. And you, comrades, must make it go. It is a labor of love on the part of the man who wrote it. It must be a labor of love on your part to distribute it.

And take notice and remember, comrades, this book is straight proletarian. And straight proletarian it must be throughout. It is written by an intellectual proletarian. It is written for the proletariat. It is published by a proletarian publishing house. It is to be read by the proletariat. And depend upon it, if it is not circulated by the proletariat it will not be circulated at all. In short, it must be a supreme proletarian effort.

Remember, this book must go out in the face of the enemy. No capitalist publishing house would dare to publish it.[1] It will be laughed at—some; jeered at—some; abused—some; but most of all, worst of all, the most dangerous treatment it will receive is that of silence. For that is the way of capitalism.

Comrades, do not forget the conspiracy of silence. Silence is the deadliest danger this book has to face. The book stands on its own merits. You have read it and you know. All that it requires is a hearing. This hearing you must get for it. You must not permit this silence. You must shout out this book from the housetops, at all times, and at all places. You must talk about it, howl about it, do everything but keep quiet about it. Open your mouths and let out your lungs, raise such a clamor that those in the high places will wonder what all the row is about and perchance feel tottering under them the edifice of greed they have reared.

All you have to do is to give this book a start. You have read the book yourselves, and you will vouch for it. Once it gets its start it will run away from you. The printers will be worked to death getting out larger and larger editions. It will go out by the hundreds of thousands. It will be read by every workingman. It will open countless ears that have been deaf to Socialism. It will plough the soil for the seed of our propaganda. It will make thousands of converts to our cause. Comrades, it is up to you!

Send Sinclair that $1.20 to-day.

Yours for the Revolution,
Jack London.

SOURCE: "Jack London and 'The Jungle,'" *Wilshire's Magazine*, December 1905.

1. *The Jungle* was published by Doubleday, Page & Co. in 1906. See also JL to Bamford, October 2, 1905, n. 4.

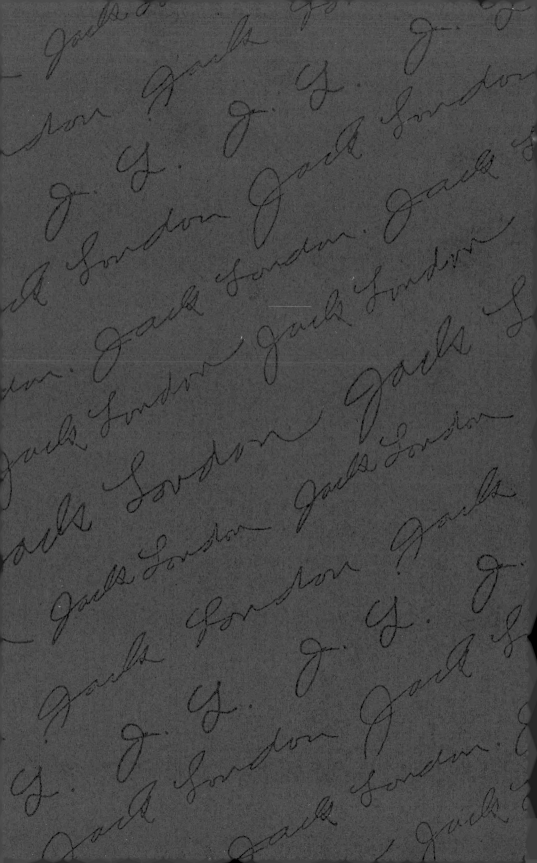